SCULPTURE AT VIJAYANAGARA
Iconography and Style

VIJAYANAGARA RESEARCH PROJECT MONOGRAPH SERIES

General Editors
JOHN M. FRITZ
GEORGE MICHELL
D.V. DEVARAJ

Vol. 1. *Pots and Palaces* by Carla M. Sinopoli

Vol. 2. *The Ramachandra Temple at Vijayanagara* by Anna L. Dallapiccola, John M. Fritz, George Michell and S. Rajasekhara

Vol. 3. *The Vijayanagara Courtly Style* by George Michell

Vol. 4. *Religious Traditions at Vijayanagara as Revealed through its Monuments* by Anila Verghese

Vol. 5. *The Irrigation and Water Supply Systems of Vijayanagara* by Dominic J. Davison-Jenkins

Vol. 6. *Sculpture at Vijayanagara: Iconography and Style* by Anna L. Dallapiccola and Anila Verghese

The General Editors of the Vijayanagara Research Project Monograph Series acknowledge the continuing encouragement of the American Institute of Indian Studies, especially its President, Professor Frederick Asher, and Director-General, Dr. Pradeep Mehendiratta.

We also extend our thank to Mr. Ramesh Jain and the staff of Manohar Publishers & Distributors for maintaining high standards while seeing this monograph through the press.

Jacket illustration: Bhadrakali, pillar-relief from the hundred-pillar hall of the Virupaksha temple at Vijayanagara (drawing by Tim Martin).

SCULPTURE AT VIJAYANAGARA
Iconography and Style

ANNA L. DALLAPICCOLA
ANILA VERGHESE

MANOHAR
AMERICAN INSTITUTE OF INDIAN STUDIES
NEW DELHI
1998

ISBN 81-7304-232-2

First published 1998

Published by Ajay Kumar Jain
Manohar Publishers & Distributors
2/6 Ansari Road, Daryaganj, New Delhi 110 002 for
American Institute of Indian Studies
D 31 Defence Colony, New Delhi 110 024

Laserset by AJ Software Publishing Co. Pvt. Ltd.
305 Durga Chambers, 1333 D.B. Gupta Road
Karol Bagh, New Delhi 110 005
and printed at Replika Press Pvt. Ltd.
Plot No. A-229, DSIDC Narela Indl. Park
Delhi 110040

Contents

List of Illustrations

Portfolio of Drawings

Figures

Plates

Preface

This book deals in detail with sculpture at Vijayanagara (present-day Hampi, Hospet taluka, Bellary district, Karnataka), the capital of the Vijayanagara kingdom from the mid-fourteenth century to 1565. The Vijayanagara kingdom, at its peak, extended over much of southern India. From Vijayanagara city ruled the monarchs of three dynasties: Sangama (1336-1485), Saluva (1485-1505), and Tuluva (1505-65).

The Vijayanagara rayas consciously promoted religion and culture. Hampi, which had been a Shaivite tirtha from pre-Vijayanagara times and which also had links with the *Ramayana*, was developed into a prosperous city. At Vijayanagara were incorporated many cults and religious traditions, not only Hindu, but also Jaina and Islamic. This explains the wealth of religious images found at the site. Alongside these are a variety of secular sculptural themes, including those depicting courtly and martial scenes. This rich intermixture of religious and secular topics is what makes Vijayanagara sculpture especially interesting and different from the earlier periods of southern Indian sculpture.

This volume is part of the Vijayanagara Research Monograph Series. Others in the series that deal, directly or indirectly, with Vijayanagara art and architecture are *The Vijayanagara Courtly Style* by George Michell, *The Ramachandra Temple at Vijayanagara* by A.L. Dallapiccola, J.M. Fritz, G. Michell and S. Rajasekhara, and *Religious Traditions at Vijayanagara* by Anila Verghese. The last two touch on some aspects of Vijayanagara sculpture. However, no study, either in this series or in the works of earlier art historians, has dealt in depth with Vijayanagara sculpture. The idea of this volume occurred to us as we keenly experienced the lacuna during fieldwork and research at the site. We felt the need to define what is the nature of Vijayanagara sculpture and to highlight the themes and iconography connected with it; to seek its roots in the diverse sculptural traditions of southern India, as also the new elements evident in it. We were also aware that what happened at the capital city not only influenced sculpture elsewhere in the kingdom, but also in its successor states, the Nayaka kingdoms.

During the course of extensive fieldwork, beginning in 1984, we have covered not only all the principal monuments and their sculptures within the core area of the city, but also in innumerable minor structures as well as those scattered on rocks and boulders all over the site. This monograph, however, deals only with the stone sculpture and stuccowork of the Vijayanagara period found at the site and in the Archaeological Museum located in Kamalapuram village. (Metal sculptures of the period are practically non-existent at Vijayanagara). Only the extant sculptures of the core area of the erstwhile capital city and of some of the principal monuments in the suburban centres have been included. Vijayanagara period sculpture within the wider area of the empire lies beyond the scope of this monograph.

This volume is written keeping in mind the needs of the specialist and the general reader. For the former, detailed references have been cited in the notes at the end of each chapter and in the Appendices. In these, fairly exhaustive lists of the sculptures and their exact locations have been provided. We believe that this work is of a pioneering nature as it is the first exhaustive attempt to evaluate Vijayanagara sculpture within the perspective of art in southern India since 1350.

Acknowledgements

We express our sincere gratitude to all those without whose help and encouragement this monograph would not have been completed. In particular, we are grateful to the Editors of the Vijayanagara Research Monograph Series, Dr. John M. Fritz, Dr. George Michell and Dr. D.V. Devaraj. We thank the Director of the Directorate of Archaeology and Museums, Karnataka State, and his staff, especially those in charge of the Excavation Camp of the Hampi Research Project for providing accomodation and assistance to us at the site. We thank Tim Martin and Graham Reed for the excellent drawings and maps. We acknowledge the help of all those who provided the photographs for reproduction in the volume, principally John Gollings. We are indebted to the authorities of the Hampi Archaeological Museum at Kamalapuram for permission to photograph some of the sculptures in their collection. We are grateful to Manohar Publishers & Distributors and the American Institute of Indian Studies for publishing this work.

Anna L. Dallapiccola
Anila Verghese

Note on Map Series

Throughout the text, the monuments and sculptures are listed according to the system followed in the Map Series, prepared by the Vijayanagara Research Project (see pp. 365-390). Map 1, includes the entire region around Vijayanagara, from Gangawati in the north-east, to Hospet in the south-west. This area, of about 25 square kilometres, is divided into 25 equal squares. Each square is designated by a capital letter from A to Z (omitting I). Thus square N is the area of the city proper. This square has again been divided into 25 squares (see map 2) and a second capital letter is used to denote each of these, e.g. NA, NB, NC, etc. Each of these has in turn been divided into 25 squares, each assigned a small letter, e.g. NHa, NHb, NHc, etc. Within this smaller square the individual structures are numbered 1, 2, 3, 4, etc. Thus, NFw/1 is the reference for the great Virupaksha temple and NHa/1 is that of the Vithala temple. Gateways have been usually designated only according to the square in which they fall, e.g. Gate NJs. The system provides an exact reference for each structure. Single sculptures, not part of any architectural scheme, have also been provided with a reference number.

PORTFOLIO OF DRAWINGS

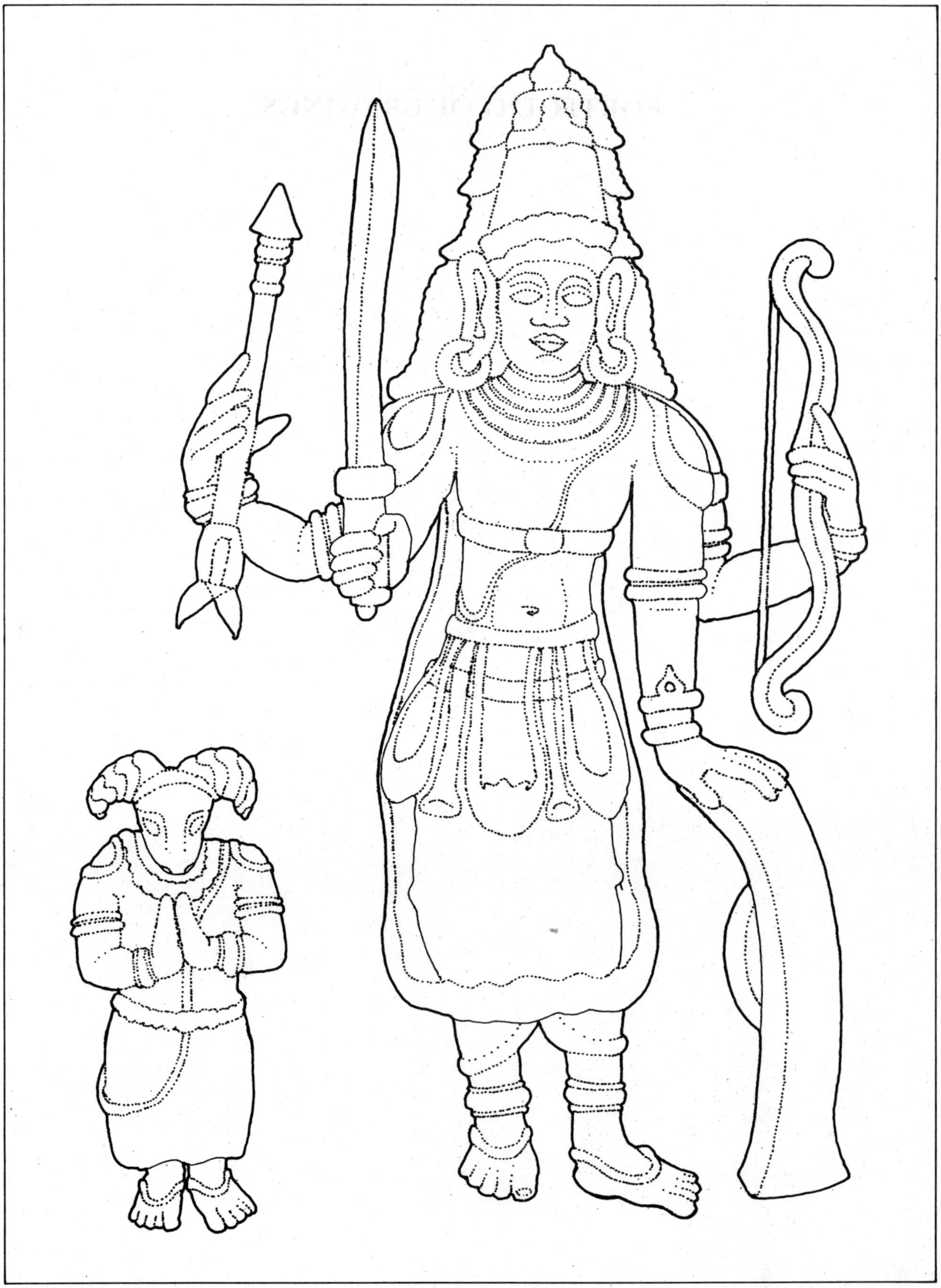

A. Virabadra.

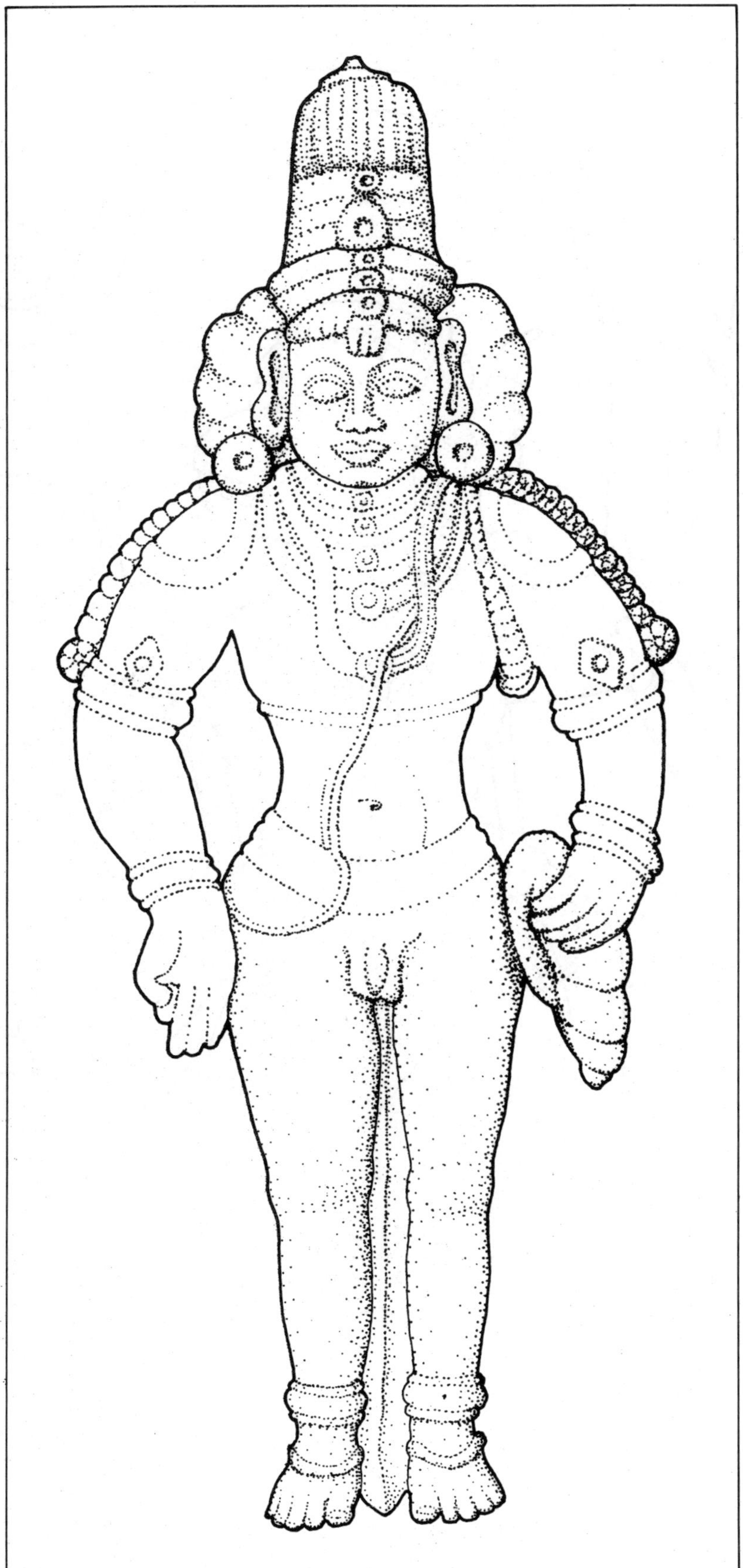

B. Vithala.

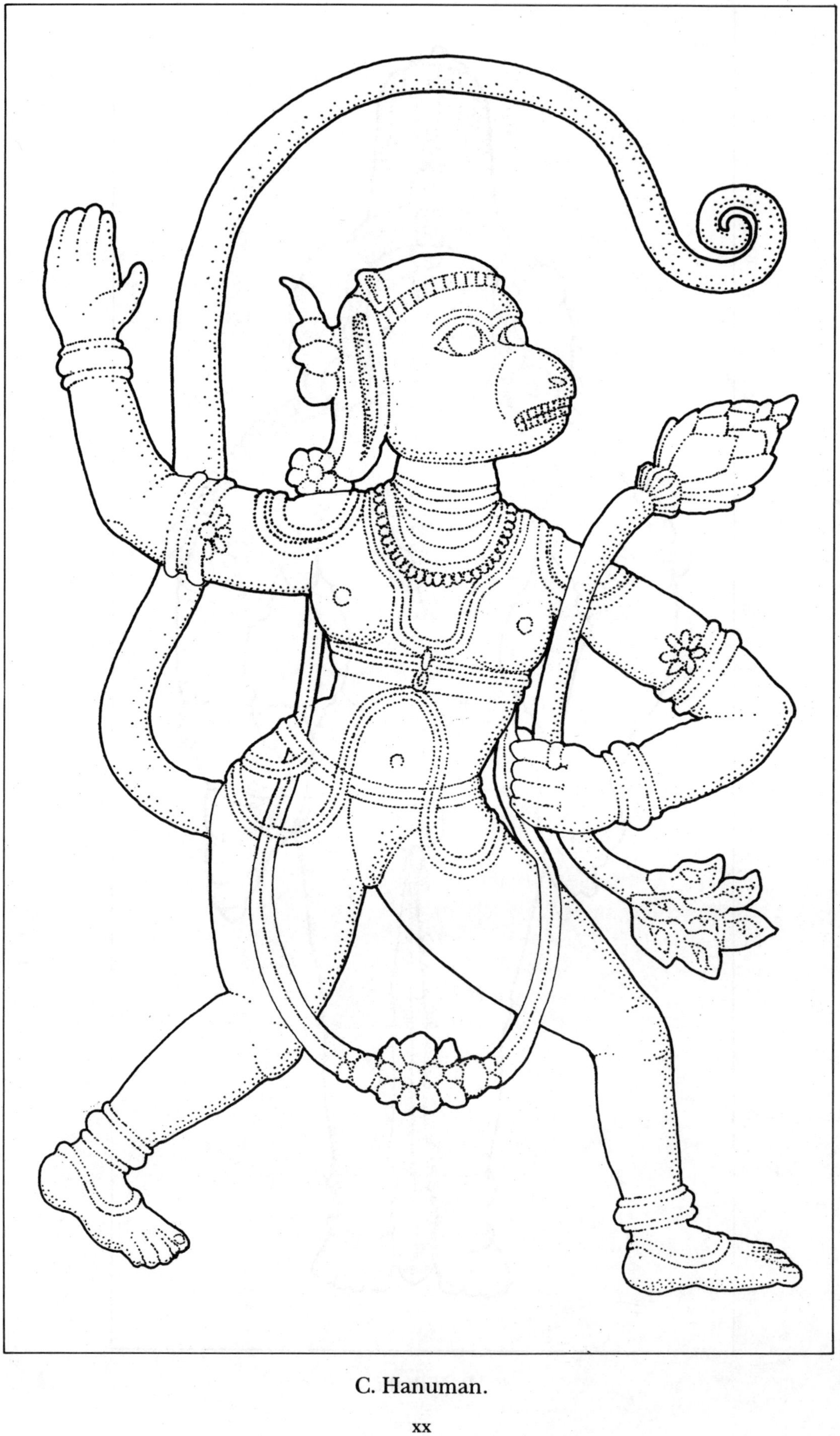

C. Hanuman.

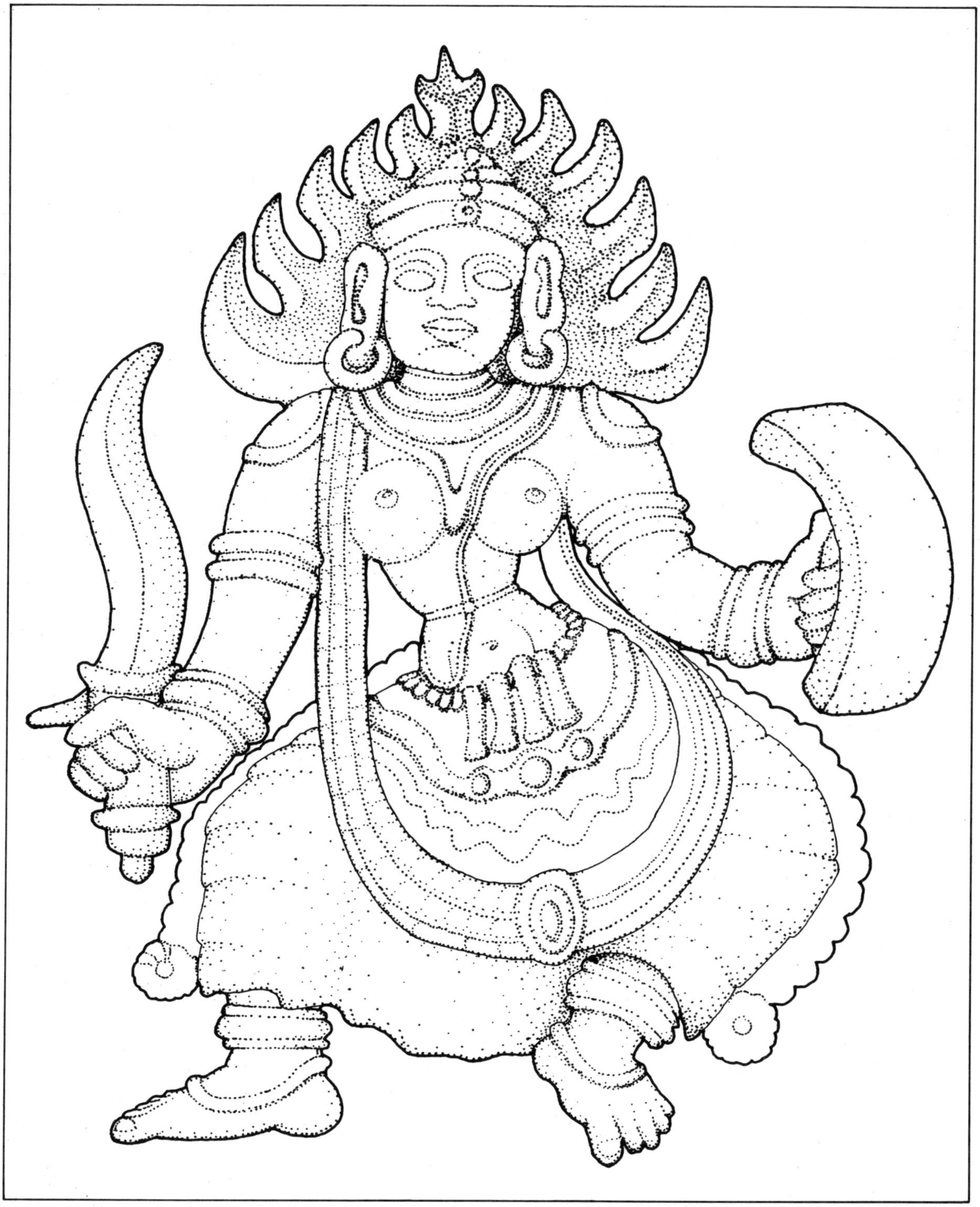

D. Bhadrakali.

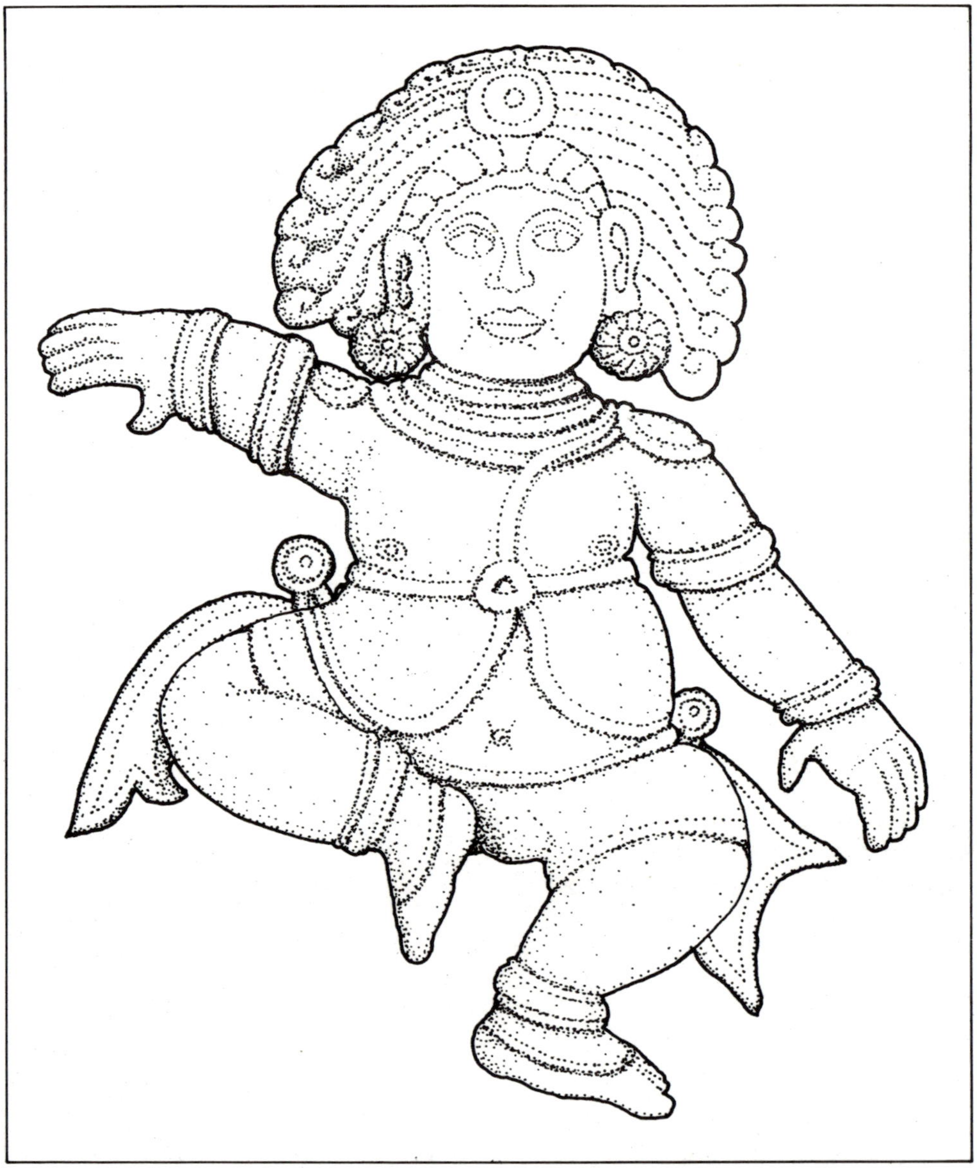

E. Dancing gana.

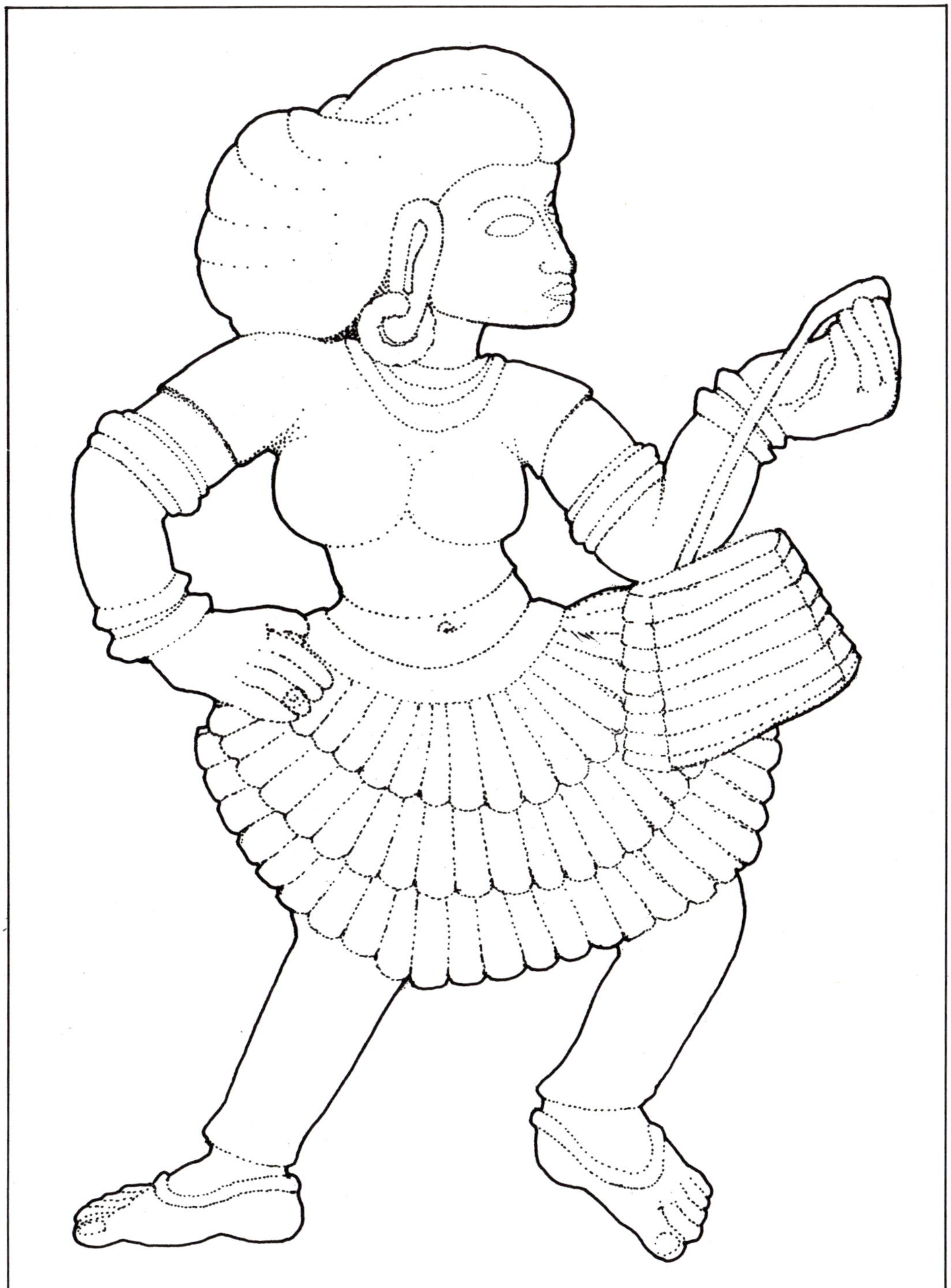

F. Lady with basket.

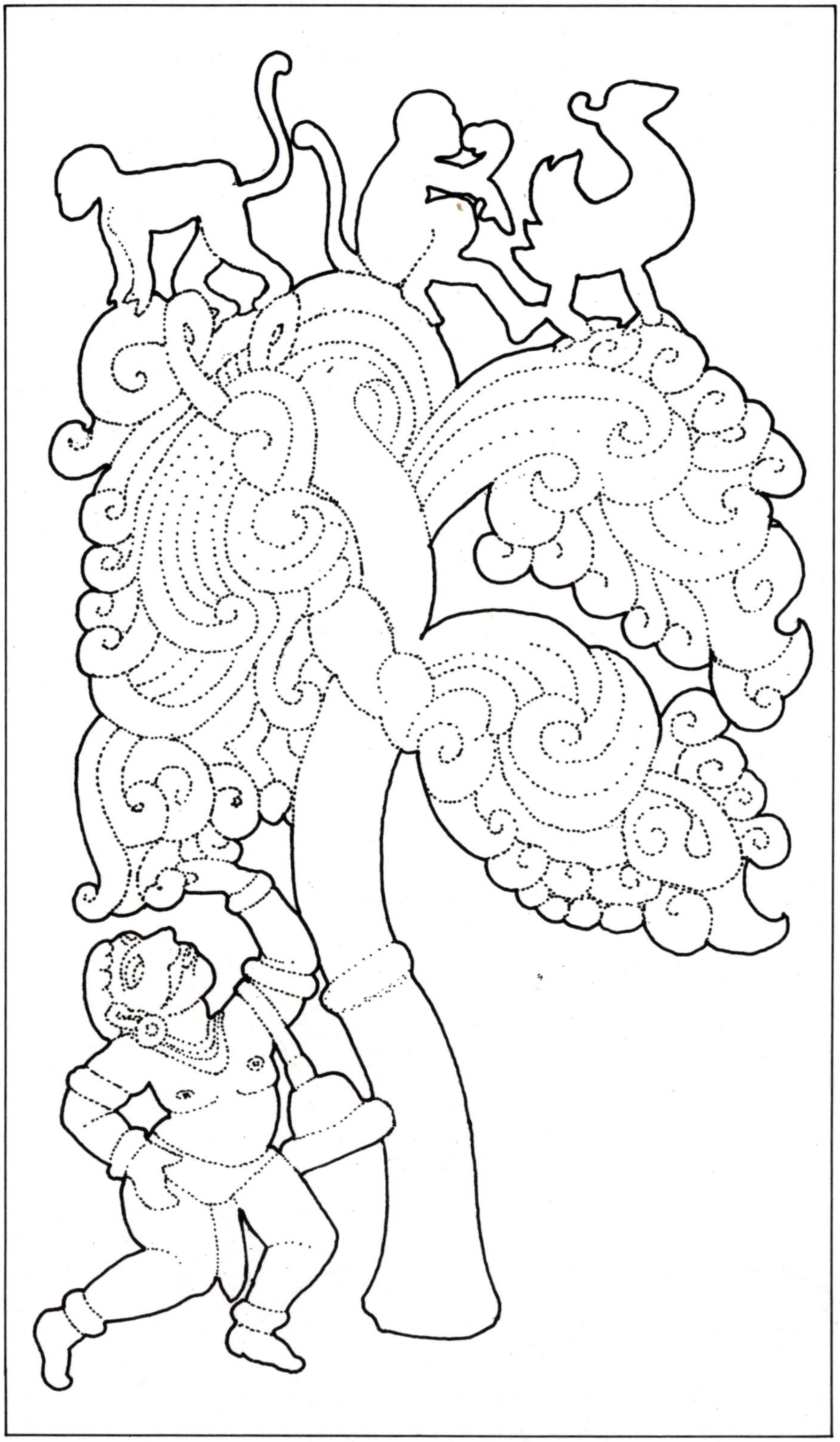

G. Hunter with monkeys.

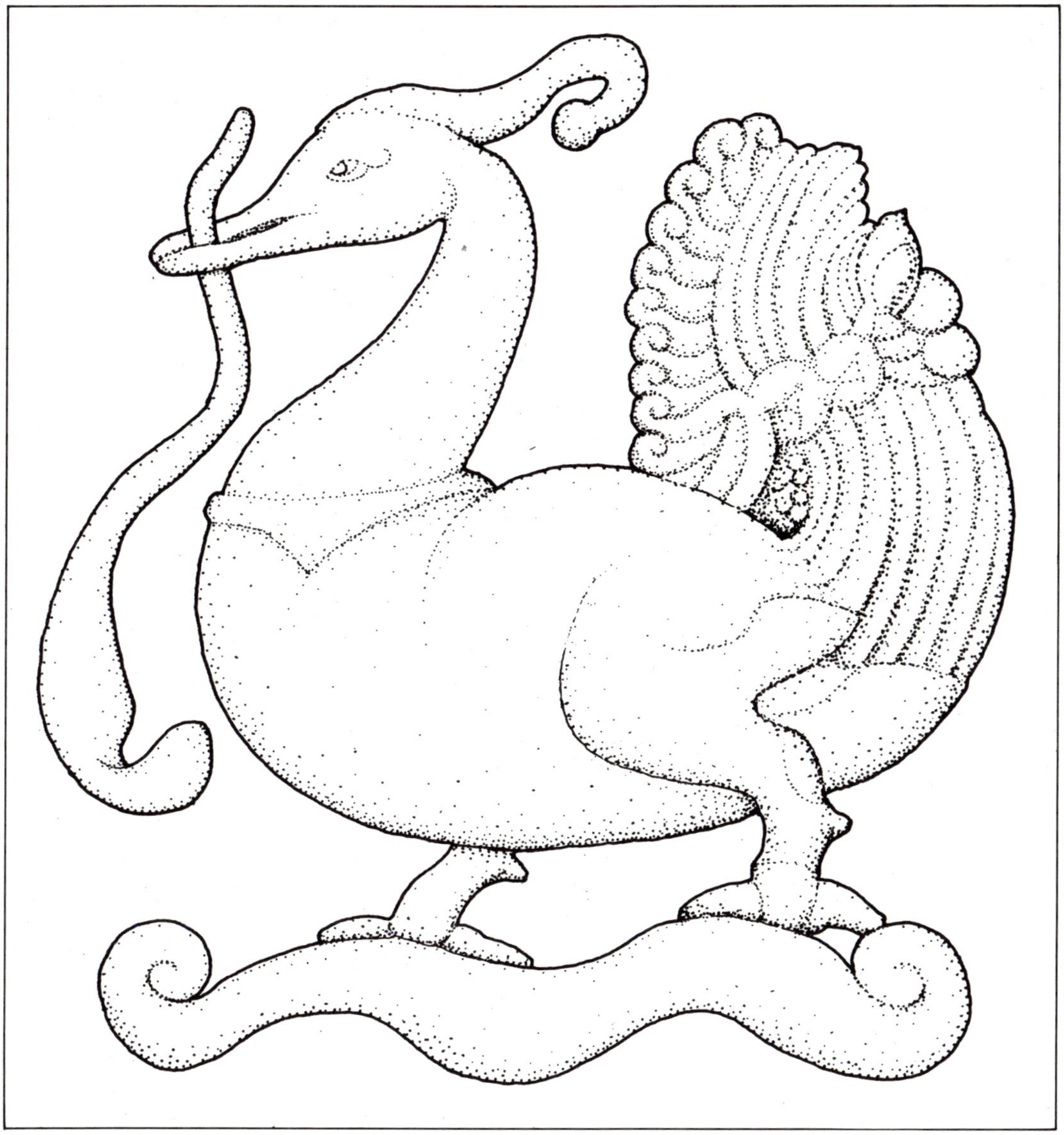

H. Bird.

CHAPTER 1

Appreciation of Vijayanagara Sculpture

Things occurred here [at Vijayanagara], not in human, but in fantastic, super-human dimensions. This is the place for heroic deeds. . . .[1]

Until the mid 1980s, art historians dealt with Vijayanagara art very superficially, mainly because of the comparatively late period in which it developed. A further cause was the relative inaccessibility of Vijayanagara until the end of the 1980s. Very few scholars were adventurous enough to risk the journey to obtain a first-hand experience of the site. Among them were, in the first half of this century, R.N. Saletore, Alice Boner, whose extraordinarily perceptive diary entries show how deeply impressed she was with the site and its monuments, and Herrman Goetz. Eventually, R.N. Saletore was the only one who espoused the cause of Vijayanagara art. He was the only one among over the thirty-odd contributors to the legendary *Vijayanagara Sexcentenary Commemoration Volume* of 1936 who visited the site repeatedly. In 1982, he published a substantial book *Vijayanagara Art,* based on the material of his much earlier doctoral dissertation. In this study he attempted to set Vijayanagara art in the context of south Indian artistic development.

Apart from visiting the site, the only other way scholars could familiarise themselves with Vijayanagara art was through its ubiquitous presence in southern India. This, however, was perhaps another cause for neglect. The majority of art historians felt that the Vijayanagara additions to pre-existing monuments were, in a certain sense, vandalism. They were confronted with a new style which they did not know in its entirety, and with which they could come to terms, only by comparison with the classic Chola style or the seventeenth-century Nayaka style. But Vijayanagara sculpture was more than a mere 'degradation of the later Cola style'.[2]

In order to re-assess Vijayanagara's place in the development of art in south India, it is necessary to begin with a brief review of what has been written on this subject in the leading books on Indian Art.

A. Early Opinions

In 1866 James Fergusson and P. Meadows Taylor published *Architecture in Dharwar and Mysore,* the first major work on the monuments of this area, in which Fergusson commented on some photographs depicting sacred and secular buildings at Vijayanagara. It is not known if Fergusson ever visited the site. The pictures, taken in the late 1850s and early 1860s made such an impact on him, that 'in all his subsequent major writings Vijayanagara was never omitted'.[3] Thus Vijayanagara was given a place in the history of Indian architecture.

Later, in his monumental *History of Indian and Eastern Architecture* (1876), Fergusson devoted a whole section of the chapter on the Dravidian Style to Vijayanagara, describing in detail the Vithala temple, which he dated to 1513:

> It is wholly in granite, and carved with a boldness and expression of power nowhere surpassed in the buildings of its class. As will be observed, it has all the peculiarities of the Dravidian style: the bold cornice of double flexure, the detached shafts, the Vyalis, the richly carved stylobate, etc. . . .[4]

He concluded that the stylistic innovations appearing for the first time in its architecture 'would inevitably have led in a short time to the new style of the Nâyyak dynasty'.[5] However, apart from mentioning the 'boldness and expression of power' of the carvings and the yalis, he did not comment further on sculpture. This is understandable as the available photographs were probably of architecture rather than of details of sculpture.

The date of the monument was given as 1513,

as there are no inscriptions in the Vithala temple complex prior to 1513. Recent scholarship, however, questions that date.[6]

Ananda K. Coomaraswamy, in his *History of Indian and Indonesian Art,* first published in 1927, briefly reviewed the major monuments at Vijayanagara. The first to be mentioned is the Vithala temple, followed by the Kadalekalu Ganesha, the Anantashayana temple near Hospet, and the Hazara Rama temple. The last of these, according to Coomaraswamy, 'probably Kṛṣṇa Deva Rāya's private chapel, is contemporary with and similar to the Viṭṭhalasvāmin, and equally typical of the period. The outer enclosure walls in both cases are covered with reliefs.'[7] The Mahanavami platform, called 'Dasara Dibba' is cursorily mentioned as being the best example of a basement decorated with friezes.[8] The chief characteristics of the style are summed up thus:

> . . . The full evolution of the pendent lotus bracket takes place; the monolithic columns unite to the main straight-sided shaft a number of slender cylindrical 'columnettes' with bulbous capitals . . . ; the roll cornice is doubly curved, the corners having upward pointing projections, the under side repeating the details of wooden construction.
>
> The pillar caryatides, whether rearing lions or *yālis* (*gaja-siṁhas*) are products of a wild phantasy; at the end of the sixteenth century rearing horses are also found, provided with fighting riders and groups of soldiers below . . . , but these are more specially a feature of the Madura style. Enclosing walls and basements are decorated with continuous reliefs representing epic and festival themes.[9]

Coomaraswamy's choice of religious monuments for discussion leads us to suspect that he may never have visited Vijayanagara, but worked from a very limited choice of photographs. Some of these were obviously mislabelled, as is evident from the mention of carvings on the enclosure wall around the Vithala temple, which is in fact plain. The date of the Vithala temple is given as 1513, as by Fergusson. In spite of inevitable inaccuracies, it is remarkable that the importance of Vijayanagara architecture and the salient features of its mature style were clearly recognized and highlighted in what is a broad survey of Asian art from India to the Far East and Indonesia.

A serious attempt at putting the architecture and art of the site in a wider context was made by Percy Brown. In his *Indian Architecture (Buddhist and Hindu)*, first published in 1942, he stated that:

> a change came over the spirit as well as the substance of architecture in southern India, when, after the somewhat temperate productions of the Pandyas, the country gradually became enriched with buildings in a style showing that the people had been aroused to a life of greater fulness, and one which moved them to express with marked freedom and fluency their aesthetic aspirations.[10]

This new impetus came from the Vijayanagara rulers, who were instrumental in inspiring this change in architecture as well as in sculpture. Brown commented:

> It is a record in stone of a range of ideals, sensations, emotions, prodigalities, abnormalities, of forms and formlessness, and even eccentricities, that only a super-imaginative mind could conceive, and only an inspired artist could reproduce.[11]

The obvious parallel in Western art was according to him Baroque art which 'is expressive in a degree of the same political and social conditions'.[12]

Brown had great admiration for the works of the mature and late Vijayanagara style. Characteristically, only two temples attracted his attention at Vijayanagara: the first was the Vithala as being the most lavishly ornamented, in a certain sense a forerunner of the full-fledged southern temple of the seventeenth century.[13]

The second was the Ramachandra (Hazara Rama) temple which Brown attributed to Krishnadevaraya, and, following Coomaraswamy, to 1513.[14] His attention was riveted on the exquisite stonework, on the careful elaboration of the walls in the typical Dravidian pattern of niche and pilaster, and he concluded that:

> There are not many buildings . . . of the period in which this very appropriate scheme of mural relief and decoration has been more skilfully applied and disposed than on the temple of Hazara Rama.[15]

Brown was obviously fascinated by the Dravidian element influencing the architecture and decoration of the Ramachandra temple, and by its subsequent elaboration and transformation which led to the 'mature' Vijayanagara style.

He did not, however, attempt to study other monuments at the capital, although he was aware of the peculiarity of the terrain on which the capital was built, and hypothesised the fascinating theory that the rugged landscape of the site might have had some influence on the style 'towards the invention of strange creatures such as chimera and other fabulous forms with which the style abounds'.[16]

The dramatic difference in workmanship between the carvings in granite and those in schist did not pass unnoticed, and led Brown to postulate the existence of two separate schools of sculpture. The first was 'graphically conceived but crudely and almost childishly fashioned' while the second was 'sharply cut and skilfully modelled . . .'.[17]

This discrepancy in the quality of the carvings is one of the most striking features of the sculpture of Vijayanagara. Brown comments both on carvings in schist and granite, but fails to describe the wide variations in the quality of the work executed in granite, unlike the carvings in schist which generally display a high standard of craftsmanship. However, the occasional fine piece in granite can be found among the ordinary or inferior work. As this totally different approach to sculpture could not pass unnoticed, scholars subsequently attempted to explain it in different ways.

In Benjamin Rowland's *The Art and Architecture of India*, first published in 1953, Vijayanagara is briefly mentioned.[18] The Vithala temple is the only monument discussed. The focus of the description, however, is not the temple complex, but rather the piers of the mahamandapa.

It appears that Rowland was not interested in assessing Vijayanagara architecture or sculpture in their own right, but saw them only as precursors of seventeenth century developments in Tamil Nadu. The Vithala temple was the ideal illustration of this point. Sculpture was mentioned only with respect to the piers and composite pillars which played a determinant role in the aesthetics of mature Vijayanagara and, more so, in later Nayaka monuments.

The situation changed dramatically in the early 1980s with the publications of the first specific articles on the site,[19] and, the book *Splendours of the Vijayanagara Empire, Hampi.* Now the subject of Vijayanagara could no longer be treated in vague terms, and in John and Susan Huntington's exhaustive *The Art of Ancient India*, 1985,[20] a full chapter is devoted to architecture, sculpture and painting at Vijayanagara. This too lacks discussion of the early monuments at the site: the focus is the Vithala temple, which is described in great detail. The Ramachandra temple with its sculptural friezes, the Ugra Narasimha (Lakshmi-Narasimha monolith) and the Kadalekalu Ganesha are briefly mentioned among the most notable works of sculpture. The Huntingtons concluded this chapter with the following statement:

> Recent excavations at Vijayanagar continue to reveal the impressiveness of Vijayanagar culture and promise to assure Vijayanagar period art its rightful place among the most impressive and dominant artistic traditions of south Asia.[21]

In 1986 James C. Harle published the next general survey of the art of India, *The Art and Architecture of the Indian Subcontinent.* Vijayanagara architecture is treated in detail and given its due as the origin of Nayaka architectural style:

> the Nayaka [style], however, is largely based upon the Vijayanagara style, whose emergence, spread, and eventual dominance during the fifteenth and sixteenth centuries in Tamilnadu and large areas of Karnataka, and instant recognizability of its most typical structure, the mandapa, is one of the most remarkable phenomena in the history of Indian art and architecture.[22]

Harle maintained that Vijayanagara art is:

> a Dravida style, which had persisted throughout the still largely Hindu south and, with a few unimportant exceptions, remained the style of all temples at the capital.[23]

There follows a discussion of the mandapa pillars, of the monolithic piers, of the rearing animals, a general evaluation of the Dravida style and of the Vijayanagara contribution to it. 'The Dravida style is extremely conservative, and Vijayanagara's contributions consist only of some degradation of the later Cola style and a few changes in detail. . .'.[24]

The last paragraphs of Harle's chapter are devoted to Vijayanagara and Nayaka sculpture, which according to him, 'show a tradition in decline, reliant on a rigid and uninspired translation of the prescriptions, including proportionate measurements, of the śāstras'.[25]

Three conclusions can be drawn from this brief survey: their authors were in general concerned with architecture; they restricted their considerations mainly to sixteenth-century monuments; and, with few exceptions, Vijayanagara art was evaluated less in its own right, than as an anticipation of the later Nayaka art. This explains the preoccupation of the majority of the writers with intricately carved piers and pillars, curved eaves and rearing animals. All these elements, further developed in Nayaka art, were invented in sixteenth-century Vijayanagara.

Very few of these scholars could have actually visited the site; they must perforce have worked from woodcuts or photographs, giving them a very limited spectrum of the actual monuments and sculptures. This would account for some of the rather biased views on Vijayanagara art.

There were, nevertheless, exceptions like Brown, who was one of the first to sense that something new had been created at the capital.[26] However it was not until several decades later that his insights were confirmed by the most recent study by George Michell, *Architecture and Art of Southern India, Vijayanagara and the Successor States* (1995). This survey directs scholars to a more balanced and comprehensive understanding of the seminal importance of the art of the capital, both in its local development and in its subsequent influence throughout the region.

B. The Vijayanagara Sculptural Style

Commenting on the difference in workmanship between the carvings in granite and those in schist, Brown postulated the existence of two separate 'schools'.[27] Subsequently, two famous scholars, both of whom were familiar with the site, tried to resolve the problem of style: Saletore and Goetz.

Saletore in his *Vijayanagara Art* is one of the few scholars who tackled the complicated problem of the sources of Vijayanagara sculpture.[28] He begins with a criticism of Goetz's:

> The indigenous sculpture of Vijayanagara developed from the style of the funeral *stelas* (*vīrakkal* and *satikkal*) and snake stones of western Chalukyan times. Their representation is naive, in flat stripes, without fore-shortening or perspective but immensely vital. Under Kṛṣṇa Deva Rāya it became an integral part of official art.[29]

According to Saletore, Goetz's theory that Vijayanagara sculpture has its roots in the carving on the memorial stones has no foundation, because, according to him, there is no sculpture worthy of the name on the *vīrakal* and the *satikal*; moreover there was no need for Vijayanagara artists to draw artistic inspiration 'from such poor specimens', as they had ample opportunity to follow the artistic standards set by the schools which preceded the establishment of Vijayanagara.[30] Saletore then proceeds to refute the theory of a possible origin of Vijayanagara sculptural art in the western Chalukya stela concluding that:

> As the Vijayanagara craftsmen had . . . acquired their ideas from various schools of art which had prevailed before them, there is no valid reason why they should in the execution of their sculpture, which formed but an element of their temple architecture, have depended or preferred western Chalukyan stela sculpture instead of any of the numerous styles often much better than that style.[31]

The attitude of Goetz regarding the naïve quality of the carvings, disposed in flat bands and devoid of foreshortening or perspective, is also criticised by Saletore on the grounds that panels by their very nature 'offered little scope for any foreshortening or perspective.[32]

Goetz's claim that 'under Kṛṣṇa Deva Rāya sculpture became integral to official art', is also refuted by Saletore for the simple reason that 'no distinction worth the same can be made of official and non-official art at any period of Indian art'.[33]

Unfortunately, Saletore does not develop his analysis of the nature of Vijayanagara sculpture, except to say that: 'The sculpture of the Vijayanagara school was new yet, like its architecture, composite'[34] and for the criticism of Goetz's statements.

As aptly noted by Saletore, many different aesthetic traditions coalesced in the formation of the 'Vijayanagara style': the Deccan, the Tamil and, most important of all, the local 'folk' responsible for the earliest sculptures at the site. While the influence from the Deccan, especially important for the architectural development, lost ground comparatively early, the Tamil tradition became dominant in the formation of the mature 'Vijayanagara style' architecture and sculpture.

The initial impact on scholars was the 'naïve quality' or 'crudeness' of the some of the works, qualities which they immediately connected with folk art; hence the style of Vijayanagara sculpture was defined as 'folkish'. It should be emphasized that, in spite of Saletore's criticism, Goetz's proposition that Vijayanagara sculpture 'developed from the style of the funeral *stelas*' cannot be completely dismissed as absurd.[35]

For example in spite of their limited iconographic repertory, the carvings on the memorial stones are of extreme importance for the reliefs on the older parts of the Mahanavami platform. Firstly, because of the material and carving technique: memorial stones are carved in granite, in an expressionistic but technically unsophisticated style. Second, it is men and not deities who are celebrated in the memorials. 'Both in style and purpose, these commemorative folk monuments are far removed from temple art.'[36]

The artists responsible for the royal carvings on the Mahanavami platform looked for inspiration to the heroic scenes on the memorials, developing the small-scale reliefs on the slabs into monumental art. However, this reference to folk tradition was not repeated in the schist carvings of the sixteenth century which follow the style of contemporary temple sculpture.

The royal theme, although ever-present in the sculpture at the capital, was never treated again so prominently as on the Mahanavami platform. This explains why the folk art element, generally reserved for the celebration of the heroic deeds of the warriors and the ruler, disappeared from the monuments at Vijayanagara. This change, which gradually took place in the first half of the fifteenth century, may be due to various reasons. By the mid-fifteenth century there is a substantial alteration in the rendering of the 'royal figure'. The strong influence of the Rama cult and the resulting homology between the king and the divine hero Rama causes the king to be no longer the 'folk' hero, but a god. The 'royal figure' is hence fashioned like a divine image in temple art.

Ideological and artistic changes notwithstanding, a number of memorial stones and images carved on boulders or on sheet rock continued to be sculpted in the traditional, forceful style typical of the 'folk' sculpture. The 'folk' style and sophisticated 'temple' style both co-existed at Vijayanagara, serving different purposes. The one celebrated heroes and godlings; the other gods and their attendants, human and divine. In conclusion, both Goetz and Saletore were absolutely correct in their observations.

Another possible reason why Vijayanagara sculpture was ignored by the scholarly world is that, unlike the work produced under preceding dynasties, which generally had a very high level of workmanship, sculpture at the capital never achieved such a high quality, except for individual pieces. This lack of excellence is due partly to the material. The locally quarried granite has a flaky texture, preventing the rendering of detail. Sculptors were perfectly capable of careful modelling and sensitive rendering of dress, jewellery, headgear and hairstyles, as is amply demonstrated in the vestiges of stuccowork on vimanas, parapets and gopuras, as well as by carvings in schist. Unfortunately, the bulk of sculpture at the capital is on granite slabs, not necessarily of high quality.

In spite of the rather poor quality granite with which the artists were working, there is an astonishing variety in scale. Monumental carvings like the Lakshmi-Narasimha monolith or the gigantic linga near the Krishna temple contrast with minute, delicate friezes, such as the ones depicting horsemen and traders on the plinth of the mahamandapa of the Vithala temple, or the Vasantotsava scenes beneath the wheels of the stone chariot in the same complex. Scale notwithstanding, Vijayanagara sculpture is always full of vigour and expression. These qualities have probably baffled art historians who were not prepared for such an expressionistic sculptural style, dubbing it as 'crude'. Yet, in such a dramatic natural setting where, in the words of Boner, 'the rebellious and the arrogant shape the landscape and architecture', sculpture had to be forceful.[37]

Although the workmanship may be 'crude', the imagination of the artists is unrivalled. New themes, patterns and iconographic formulas appeared here for the first time in Indian art; new icons were created and everyday life came to the fore. This artistic movement had a vital regenerating power, thereby creating a new aesthetic which determined the direction of subsequent artistic activity. Boner, the sculptress, was greatly moved: 'I have seen works of art in India, but nowhere monuments which are filled so intensively with such a spirit of the present.'[38]

There is yet another factor to be considered, namely the unusually large sculptural output in the relatively brief time in which Vijayanagara was capital of the empire. In little over two centuries over half a dozen major temples were built and refurbished, and new pillared halls and corridors added. There were, moreover, non-religious structures decorated with sculptures, such as numerous palaces and halls with elaborately carved basements. It should not be forgotten that the capital was, so to speak, an experimental ground for the artists. It was here that different artistic traditions were eventually mingled and transformed according to a newly created aesthetic, which emerged at the beginning of the sixteenth century. The mature 'Vijayanagara' sculptural style found its characteristic personality with flamboyant creations, especially the transformation of architectural piers in dramatic sculpted compositions out of which emerged human figures and mythical beasts. This new artistic idiom was in due course disseminated throughout the whole Vijayanagara empire and eventually developed into the Nayaka sculptural style of the seventeenth and eighteenth centuries.

NOTES

1. G. Boner, L. Soni, J. Soni, *Alice Boner Diaries—India 1934-67*, p. 262.
2. See note 24.
3. G. Michell, 'A never forgotten city', in *Vijayanagara City and Empire*, ed. by A.L. Dallapiccola in collaboration with S. Zingel-Avé Lallemant, Vol. I, p. 198.
4. J. Fergusson, *History of Indian and Eastern Architecture*, Vol. I, p. 401.
5. Ibid.
6. G. Michell, *Architecture and Art of Southern India, Vijayanagara and the Successor States*, p. 39.
7. A.K. Coomaraswamy, *History of Indian and Indonesian Art*, p. 123.
8. Ibid., p. 124.
9. Ibid.
10. P. Brown, *Indian Architecture (Buddhist and Hindu)*, p. 91.
11. Ibid.
12. Ibid.
13. Ibid., pp. 92-3.
14. Ibid., p. 93.
15. Ibid.
16. Ibid. p. 92.
17. Ibid.
18. B. Rowland, *The Art and Architecture of India*, pp. 180-1.
19. John M. Fritz and G. Michell, 'The Vijayanagara Documentation and Research Project: A Progress Report', in *South Asian Archaeology 1981*, ed. by B. Allchin, pp. 295-304.
20. J. Huntington and S. Huntington, *The Art of Ancient India*, pp. 573-86.
21. Ibid., p. 586.
22. J.C. Harle, *The Art and Architecture of the Indian Subcontinent*, p. 328.
23. Ibid., p. 329.
24. Ibid., pp. 333-5.
25. Ibid., p. 337.
26. See note 10.
27. P. Brown, op. cit., p. 92.
28. R. N. Saletore, *Vijayanagara Art*, pp. 130ff.
29. Saletore, op. cit., p. 130, quoting from H. Goetz, *India: 5000 Years of Indian Art*, p. 186.
30. Ibid., p. 131.
31. Ibid.
32. Ibid.
33. Ibid.
34. Ibid., p. 130.
35. Ibid.
36. G. Michell, 'Folk tradition in a Monumental Setting', in *Dimensions in Indian Art*, ed. by Lokesh Chandra and J. Jain, p. 289.
37. G. Boner, L. Soni, J. Soni, op. cit., p. 256.
38. Ibid., p. 261.

CHAPTER 2

Techniques, Styles and Forms

A. Background

From the second half of the fourteenth century the empire of Vijayanagara encompassed territories from the Arabian Sea to the Bay of Bengal, across the Deccan plateau and southern India. These regions had once seen the rule of the renowned dynasties of the Chalukyas, Cholas, Pandyas and Hoysalas, with different artistic traditions, each of which found its way into what was eventually to become 'Vijayanagara art'.

As far as sculpture is concerned, the developments are less obviously traceable than in architecture. On the one hand, there is strong attachment to long established forms, on the other, there is an undeniable fascination with newly popular forms. The local folk tradition, as seen for instance in memorial slabs commemorating the death of heroes, the self-immolation of widows, and numerous snake-stones, had a direct bearing on Vijayanagara aesthetics in the fourteenth-and part of the fifteenth centuries. This epoch is characterised by a preference for shallow relief carvings disposed in bands, depicting vigorous figures, preferably in movement: marching, running, and dancing. The Tamil influence that played such a determinant role in architecture was also instrumental in the development of sculpture. Shallow relief was abandoned in favour of a bolder and more elaborate technique. In the sixteenth-century Vijayanagara artists had evolved their own style which, when disseminated throughout the empire, was to be further elaborated by the successors of the Vijayanagara imperial power.

B. Materials and Techniques

Granite is the first medium to be considered as it was the material commonly used by the Vijayanagara artists. Imposing monolithic compositions were carved out of individual boulders. Reliefs on walls, pillars and columns of religious buildings were carved on granite quarried at the site itself. The particular texture of this material, however, makes it prone to flaking and surface alterations,[1] thus the comparative rarity of well-finished sculptures and the rendering of intricate details. The vast majority of the sculptures are roughly, sometimes even crudely, executed. This quality, however, was not important as the reliefs were covered with a thin layer of plaster, enabling artists to conceal the unevenness of the stone and improve on detail. Finally, they were painted in lively colours.

It is unfortunate that the granite of sculptures is no longer covered with the original plaster work and, therefore, the fine and sensitive modelling cannot now be appreciated. However, plaster work remaining on parapets and gopuras gives some indication of the high standard of workmanship that was achieved.

Extensive carvings and a small number of sculptures were made of schist, a material not found at the site, and probably imported from the Gadag region. Finely carved schist slabs were placed on the west face of the Mahanavami platform in the sixteenth century, covering up the original granite bas-reliefs. Grey-green schist is used for images of the Alvars and Acharyas found in the vicinity of the Vithala temple; since these were cult images they were executed in the round. This material enabled the artists to display their virtuosity in the rendering of details of dress, headgear and jewellery.

Stucco was extensively used in the fashioning of human figures, animals, birds and foliage motifs to decorate the parapets of mandapas, the superstructures of vimanas and the ascending storeys of gopuras. Most of this fragile plaster work has been eroded by the elements. Even so, it is clear from the remaining fragments that the artists had the opportunity to lavish great care and attention in the rendering of minute variations in costumes and other motifs.

Relief carving

There is an extensive use of shallow relief, as if the sculptors were seeking to achieve a two-dimensional, almost pictorial, effect in stone. This technique seems to have been used mostly in friezes, as seen in the shallow reliefs on the lower tiers on the south face of the Mahanavami platform, which is among the earliest building projects at the site, probably dating around the close of the fourteenth century and the beginning of the next. The carvings are disposed in flat bands without foreshortening or perspective. A more sophisticated version of the same style is exemplified in the friezes decorating the exterior and interior faces of the enclosure wall of the Ramachandra temple. Further examples are the aquatic motifs carved on the inner and outer faces of the enclosure wall of the Malyavanta Raghunatha temple.

A bolder relief was used in wall panels: for instance, in the narratives on the principal and the minor shrines in the Ramachandra temple complex, as well as in the four magnificent pillars of the rangamandapa in front of the principal sanctuary of the same complex. The figures stand out from the stone, and the decorative motifs surrounding them are carved in a shallow relief. This juxtaposition of bold and shallow relief is common in ceiling medallions where figural motifs are boldly carved in contrast with floral and vegetal motifs in low relief.

At the end of the fifteenth century and during the sixteenth century, the shallow relief technique is used sparingly. It occurs mainly in decorative patterns, as in the festoon and bead motifs on the pilasters on the external walls of the sacred buildings. While there continued to be narrow friezes on the basements of palaces and sacred buildings, monumental wall friezes and wall carvings ceased to be in fashion. Attention tended to centre on the embellishment of newly built pillared halls. Sculptors started experimenting with new techniques on pillars. Composite pillars, constituted by central shafts and clusters of subsidiary colonnettes and piers adorned with three-dimensional leaping animals, became the focus of their artistic and technical efforts. These leaping or rearing mythical beasts 'emerging' from the pillars were to become the hallmark of mature Vijayanagara art and a source of great inspiration for the art of the seventeenth-century Nayakas. Moreover, not only mythical beasts, but also divine and human figures started to free themselves from the supporting pillars, thereby giving the impression of free-standing statues. The striking group of Vaishnava images in the north hall of the mahamandapa of the Vithala temple (1554), is the first example of this new technique at the site. A few years later the capital was sacked, but the idea of an almost free-standing statue emerging from a pillar had already been invented at the site.

Apart from the monumental Lakshmi-Narasimha[2] and the Ganesha on the slopes of Hemakuta hill,[3] free-standing statues are no longer in situ. Beautifully finished schist images of the Alvars, courtly figures and sacred images both in granite and schist are now preserved in the local Archaeological Museum at Kamalapuram.

C. Spatial Organization

Processional friezes

The obvious choice for an extensive set of narrative carvings is either the wall of a temple or any other suitably large surface which can easily accommodate sculpted friezes. Thus the lowest tier of the Mahanavami platform and the outer face of the Ramachandra temple complex enclosure were chosen for the depiction of royal activities. These two monumental friezes are similar in character. In both, processions of men and animals are shown moving clockwise towards a point: the western face on the Mahanavami platform, the eastern gateway on the Ramachandra temple. This movement may not be altogether clear in the arrangement of the friezes on the lowest tier of the Mahanavami platform, as part of it was reassembled at the beginning of this century, but the direction of the procession is remarkably well expressed in the Ramachandra carvings.

The spatial organization of the sculpted masses

differs widely. While the friezes on the Mahanavami platform, especially those depicting soldiers, have the tendency to be overcrowded (the occasional overlapping of figures is a well-known artistic device to suggest a crowd), those on the enclosure wall of the Ramachandra temple are unusually well balanced. Sculpted and unsculpted spaces follow each other, imparting a unique rhythmic quality to the ensemble of this monumental frieze. Moreover, the Mahanavami carvings display a greater variety and inventiveness in the layout of the friezes. Although the thrust of the movement is towards the west face, there are some parts of the friezes in which the figures move towards the east, especially in the hunting scenes of the second frieze from the bottom, on the south face of the monument. The unconventional, meandering layout of this register is interesting, because it contrasts with the rest of the frieze in which all the figures are arranged in parade order. Here, men in the heat of hunting expeditions are shown marching through the forest, unleashing their dogs, chasing, wounding and eventually killing various animals. Sometimes the hunters are themselves chased by tigers and climb trees to seek refuge. The artists' virtuosity comes to the fore in the empathy in the rendering of animals, variety of movement, and organization of space. Fleeing animals generally follow a diagonal line; animals startled by the sudden appearance of a dog or a hunter are disposed in a circular pattern: their heads face the danger they have just sensed while their bodies turn the opposite way, ready to flee. Fierce fights between a hunter and a lion or a tiger are laid out in a triangle, the apex of which is constituted by their heads, the hunter in the act of thrusting his dagger in the gaping mouth of the animal.

A tendency to compartmentalization is observed on the upper tiers of the Mahanavami platform. While on the lowermost tier there is practically no halting of the narrative between one block and the other, the carvings on the second tier, constituted by smaller blocks of granite, tend to be self-enclosed units. This trend is perfected in the uppermost tier, where elephants and horses and the architectural and decorative motifs are carefully carved in an area delimited by pilasters to give a rhythmic quality to the whole frieze. Schist carvings of the sixteenth century continue this tradition, introducing the foliage scroll motif as a division between two scenes in the same panel.

There is yet another development: apart from framing the scene with trees, pillars, vegetal scrolls, etc., the tendency is to use smaller panels and miniature the friezes. This tendency towards minute, jewel-like work is especially visible in the schist carvings on the western face of the Mahanavami platform and the horse-traders' frieze on the basement of the mahamandapa of the Vithala temple.

Epic narratives

In the Ramachandra temple, the inner face of the enclosure wall and the walls of the rangamandapa of the principal shrine were selected by artists for the rendering of the two most renowned depictions of episodes from the *Ramayana* at the capital.

The set of carvings on the enclosure wall are due to the structure of the wall itself, executed on large slabs of granite about 80 cm wide and 3 m long, each slab depicting more than one incident. The narrative frequently overlaps the panels, flowing from one block to the next without being interrupted by the narrow frames around each block. This gives artists ample opportunity to express themselves freely and to develop narrative themes with richness of detail and humour. Each slab is connected to the preceding and following ones by the movement of the figures, often looking backwards or forwards to adjacent panels, propelling the story to its inevitable climax (see Appendix I, C). The technique, vigorous throughout, is endowed with the same energy and vitality as that on the lower tiers of the Mahanavami platform, and the processional frieze on the outer face of the wall of the Ramachandra complex, though without the courtly formality of the latter.

There is, however, a substantial difference between the carvings on the inner face of the enclosure wall and those on the principal shrine. While on the enclosure the narrative flows unhindered from one block to the next, the narrative on the shrine is constituted by 108 individual panels (see Appendix I, A). Here, too, there is a compartmentalisation of each carving. This consequent division of one scene from the next is partly due to the wall with its pilasters placed at regular intervals, and partly to a stylistic device in which most of the lower tier panels are framed by an arch. This framing device has been abandoned in the case of the panels on the upper tier, which incidentally, are somewhat smaller in size and not as elaborately finished as the bottom tier. In this case there is no connection between one scene and the next, each episode being treated as a tableau laid out around the main characters of the incident. The same phenomenon can be observed in the carvings on the adjacent minor shrine, dating probably from the last quarter of the fifteenth century (see Appendix I, B).

The *Ramayana* carvings on the gopura of the Ramanuja temple, probably of the early sixteenth century, come as a surprise.[4] The carvings, generally small in size, are laid out in a very intricate way around the building (see Appendix II). The style demonstrates that the artists were drawing inspiration from the great narrative sets of the Sangama epoch, as evident in the large carvings sculpted in the entryway of the gopura.

The reliefs of the Virupaksha and Krishna temples are the last examples of carvings on temple walls at the site: the former probably executed at the close of the fifteenth century, the latter in the second decade of the next.

Here, the pilasters, kumbha-panjaras and niches determining the rhythm of the wall have no bearing on the carvings. The scenes illustrated on these monuments are not drawn from a single narrative but are a collection of various Vaishnava or Shaiva topics connected to each other only by overall religious affiliation. In the Krishna temple, however, there is an exception. The sculptures on the outer wall of the sanctuary, visible from the circumambulation path inside the temple itself, are largely inspired by the Krishna-lila.

D. Depiction of Figures

Sculptors at the site generally followed the traditional guidelines for the representation of the divine personages. For the portrayal of human beings, however, they relied more on observation than on prescriptions of the texts, which generally read 'In the case of those born of woman, one should exercise one's own judgement. . . .'[5]

This apparent lack of 'reference material' compelled Vijayanagara sculptors to create a type of human figure which would satisfy the aesthetic ideals of their patrons. A source of inspiration for the creation of human figures in the early Sangama period were images carved on the hero stones. The figures on the early monuments display the same physical type as those on memorial stones. Both male and female figures are characterized by robust yet well-proportioned bodies, either shown in vigorous action, or as the case with many female figures on sati-stones, in dignified and majestic stillness. Physical power, expressivity and immediacy are perhaps the most typical characteristics of the early-Vijayanagara figures. These expressionistic qualities were probably those which baffled the early writers on Vijayanagara art.[6]

Influenced possibly by works of art from the Telugu and Tamil countries, a slightly more elongated and elegant type of figure gradually evolved during the fifteenth century. Sculptures on the walls of the two shrines of the Ramachandra complex exemplify this gradual change in taste. The new idiom, further refined, gained popularity in the sixteenth century. Examples are the schist carvings on the western face of the Mahanavami platform, the exquisite granite carvings of the avataras of Vishnu adorning the basement of the mahamandapa of the Vithala temple, and the stucco images fashioned with great delicacy and sensitivity on the gopuras of the Vithala and Malyavanta Raghunatha temples. This sixteenth-century type of figure, with a relatively elongated face and nimble body, was further developed by artists of the Nayaka period.

Changes in the aesthetic perception of the human figure through the Sangama, Saluva and Tuluva eras have been accentuated by changes in fashion, hairstyle and jewellery to be discussed below.

Profile and frontality

Since the early years of Vijayanagara sculpture, men and women have, in numerous carvings on the lower tiers of the Mahanavami platform, been shown in a variety of ways: in profile, three-quarter profile and frontally. The figures are agile, immensely vital and full of power. There is a great interest in the rendering of movement: apart from royal figures seated on thrones or platforms, everyone seems to be walking, jumping, running, dancing, hunting or wrestling, thus imparting an extraordinary liveliness to the monument.

Most of the figures carved on the older parts of the Mahanavami platform have faces in profile, with frontal torsos but legs again in profile. Among the reliefs here are many examples of figures carved frontally, as for instance the three male dancers on the lowermost tier, south face, fourth register. An impressive array of frontal male figures is carved on the rear wall of the eastern 'chamber' in the same platform. Here are gate-keepers, musicians and dancers, the majority of whom wears outlandish garb and headgear. Carved in bold relief, with great care as far as facial features and details of the costumes are concerned, these vigorous figures stand out among the carvings of the earliest phase of the platform. The general impression is one of movement and unrestrained vitality.

As noted elsewhere, the processional carvings on the exterior of the enclosure wall of the Ramachandra temple share much in theme, layout, general appearance and costumes with those of the earlier parts of the Mahanavami platform. In this case, however, these parading, wrestling and dancing figures have all a dignified, slightly remote air which contrasts with the vitality of the figures on the Mahanavami platform, and with the immediacy of the *Ramayana* narrative on the inner face of the same wall. The rhythmic quality of the layout of the processional friezes, the careful execution of the carvings, and the exquisite finish stifled spontaneity in favour of an unparalleled elegance. Most of the figures are shown in profile, although there is the occasional frontal depiction, such as that of the foreign horse trader on the second register, on the east side.

The characters animating the *Ramayana* narrative situated on the inner face of the enclosure wall of the Ramachandra temple complex derive from carvings on the Mahanavami platform. There are, however, some changes: the figures are no longer carved in shallow relief, but emerge boldly from the stone. The folkish air which pervades the carvings on the older part of the Mahanavami platform has been replaced by courtly sophistication. The artists are now status-conscious, rendering the most important characters in the story larger than the others. They are no longer gesticulating, and their demeanour is more restrained. This tendency toward a more subdued depiction of gestures and emotions is admirably exemplified in the *Ramayana* carvings on the main shrine of the same complex. Here the figures have lost the immediacy which was one of the characteristics of early Vijayanagara sculpture, in favour of a stifling formality. This is emphasized, as noted above, by the strict division of the narrative in panels. As in the previous instances, figures appear in profile. Especially impressive are courtly scenes, such as the putrakameshti yajna performed by the deer-headed sage Rishyashringa, or the arrival of the ascetic Vishvamitra in the hall where king Dasharatha is seated in the company of his sons. The size of the figures varies according to status, as in the first mentioned example where the sage Rishyashringa is the larger of the two figures. His importance is further enhanced by the fact that he is seated on a tall stool, while the king stands before him in obeisance. In the second example, the pivotal figure is the king who is larger than the others. There are many other instances of figures depicted frontally, as for example, Lakshmana, who stands resting his left hand on the bow and carrying an arrow in his right, in the panel representing the killing of the demoness Tataka. The demoness, with dishevelled hair and round eyes—physiognomical traits typical of the asuras—is shown in three-quarters profile, on the verge of collapse, pierced by Rama's arrow. Her uplifted arms convey her distress.

In the highly sophisticated sixteenth-century schist carvings on the western face of the Mahanavami platform there are occasional examples of figures in three-quarters view. This is observed in the numerous dancing scenes in which, for instance, dancers turn their heads to look at a person standing in the middle of the panel although their bodies are depicted frontally. Another example of figures in three-quarters profile is in the top row of carvings on the west face of the platform where a noble man gently lifts the chin of a lady.

Sacred images carved on boulders and pillars and in niches, are generally depicted frontally. This is true for the sets of carvings on the rock shelf at Koti-tirtha depicting the ten incarnations of Vishnu and the twenty-four aspects of the same deity,[7] the group of Shaiva deities and ascetics on the three boulders on the ridge to the north of the Royal Centre,[8] the images of Durga and Bhairava located on the pilasters in the eastern gateway of the Ramachandra temple complex, the ten incarnations of Vishnu in niches in the basement of mahamandapa of the Vithala temple. The frontal portrayal of the deities is hardly surprising because of the conviction that contact between deity and devotee is established through darshana.

Some deities are shown in profile. Particularly good examples are the striding Hanuman and striding Garuda, whose faces and legs are in profile while the torsos face the viewer.

In the case of religious images, Vijayanagara artists generally followed the long-established iconographic tradition prevalent in southern India which did not permit much improvisation. However, they introduced variations in the iconographic repertoire, and created new images such as the image of Madana-gopala, as on the Ramachandra temple, west wall of the vimana, or the already mentioned striding Garuda, derived from the striding Hanuman.

E. Costumes

Courtiers

Male attire is simple in the early Sangama period. The 'royal figure' depicted in numerous carvings on the Mahanavami platform and on the exterior of the enclosure wall of the Ramachandra temple is clad in a short dhoti or lungi ending above the knee. A conspicuous yajnopavita generally appears on his bare chest. He wears necklaces, earrings, armlets, bracelets and anklets. The hair is tied in a large bun resting on the nape of the neck. Noteworthy is the attire of the 'royal hunter' in a carving on the lowest tier, second row, on the south face of the Mahanavami platform. He wears the usual bun at the back of the head, sports a beard and a conspicuous moustache. The dhoti reaching to his knees forms a small fan in front. A dagger with an elaborate handle is stuck in the dhoti. Earrings, two necklaces, armlets and bracelets complete his dress.

Two major innovations in costumes are seen in the sculpted portraits of king Mallikarjuna and his chauri-bearer Shirangu that grace the entrance to the sanctuary of the so-called Anjaneya temple.[9] The long scarf thrown over one arm, forming a loop near the left shoulder, a sign of royalty, is worn here for the first time by Mallikarjuna. The most important change in costume, however, is the kulayi worn by the king and his chauri-bearer. Both Mallikarjuna and Shirangu wear a cloth or girdle tied around the waist over the lower garment which appears to be longer than in the earlier period. Both are apparently bare-foot and bare-chested.[10]

The most typical item of sixteenth-century courtly attire is the kulayi. There are, however, slight variations in size, denoting the status of the wearer, and in fashion. For example, two tassels or streamers enhance the kulayi worn by the 'royal figure' carved on the pillars in the subsidiary shrine of the Tiruvengalanatha temple. Sixteenth-century visitors to the city often mention the kulayi worn by royal figures. Domingo Paes describes Krishnadevaraya as wearing 'on his head a cap of brocade in fashion like a Galician helmet, covered with a piece of fine stuff all of fine silk'.[11] Fernao Nuniz writes: 'on the head they wear caps of brocade which they call culaes'.[12]

The high-necked, full-sleeved and close-fitting shirt or jacket is yet another important innovation in sixteenth-century fashion. It has no collar and is buttoned down the front. This item of dress, either waist length or full length, seems to have been popular among courtiers.[13]

The sixteenth century also brings a greater variety of lower garment fashions, from knee-length to ankle-length. The way this item is draped is similar to the lungi, although the more elaborate, dhoti-like style is also evident. Over the lower garment is wound usually a broad girdle or sash, 'very tightly in many folds'[14] sometimes covering not only the waist but the hips also.

Compared with the earliest phase of Vijayanagara costume, as illustrated in the carvings on the lowest tier, south face, of the Mahanavami platform and on the exterior of the enclosure wall of the Ramachandra temple, there is less evidence of jewellery. This is probably because shirts and jackets were fashionable. Large, usually round earrings were, however, worn by all.

Little knowledge of footwear is to be gleaned from the sculptures. According to Domingo Paes, to be barefooted seems to have been a court custom.[15]

The scarf, first noted on the portrait sculpture of Mallikarjuna, is now worn by kings, dignitaries and other eminent persons at the court. It appears to have been first wound around the waist and then over the arm. It was folded in such a way as to form a large loop held at the crook of the left elbow. It seems to have been either a symbol of dignity or sign of importance. According to Paes, such a scarf was given as a 'token of friendship and love'.[16]

Soldiers

Although soldiers occur in considerable number in the carvings, these have weathered and it is difficult to discern the different costumes of the Vijayanagara troops. In the Sangama period, some soldiers wear a short lower garment; they have bare arms and chests, their hair is tied in a large bun resting on the nape of the neck, and little jewellery is worn. Soldiers belonging to another corps, armed with round shields and curved swords, wear the same attire, but for their headgear.

Sixteenth-century accounts provide literary evidence of the splendid costumes of the officers and grandees of the army, the sculpted counterpart of which has not yet been discovered at the site. After describing the sumptuous trappings of elephants and horses, Paes proceeds to the attire of the commanders:

> Their head-pieces are in the manner of helmets with borders covering the neck and each has its piece to protect the face. . . . They wear on the neck gorgets (cofos) all gilded, others made of silk with plates of gold and silver, others of steel as bright as a mirror. At the waist they have swords and small battle axes and in their hands javelins with the shafts covered with gold and silver. All have their umbrellas of State made of embroidered velvet and damask, with coloured silk on the horse.[17]

Foreigners

Foreigners, generally identified as Arabs or Turks,[18] are clad in long coats reaching to their feet, with sleeves covering their hands. Almost invariably they have beard and moustache, and apparently a long headcloth with tassels(?) hanging from the back. The sixteenth-century friezes decorating the basement of the mahamandapa of the Vithala temple depict a group of Portuguese horse-traders wearing typical hats, jackets, trousers and boots.

Female dancers

The costume of the kolata dancers remains unchanged from the fourteenth to the early fifteenth centuries. They wear pleated skirts reaching the ankles, and long hair tied in large bun or plaited. The jewellery consists of the usual items, the most typical being large round earrings. In the sixteenth-century short skirts, barely to the knee, came into vogue both for kolata and temple dancers.

Depictions of temple dancers appear in sixteenth-century carvings on the Mahanavami platform. Beneath their short skirts the dancers wear close-fitting tights. An elaborate girdle consisting of a sash ending in an elegantly pleated fan completes their attire. The hair is tied into a large knot either on the crown or at the side of the head.

Male dancers

On south face of the Mahanavami platform, in the fourth row of the lower tier, the frieze is occasionally interrupted by spirited renderings of male dancers, some wearing a ribbed cap, some others bare-headed. All have a short triangular-shaped trimmed beard, and are dressed in a skirt-like undergarment and a full-sleeved jacket with large lapels or shoulder pieces. They seem to be the prototype for the so-called 'folk-dancer', one of the most typical figures in Vijayanagara art.

This character, as much dancer as jester, is shown wearing a tall cap, sometimes with as many as three peaks, a short jacket and a lower garment fashioned out of a piece of material cut to resemble a leaf skirt. The drooping moustache and pointed beard, as well as the typical flat tambourine or the chauris he holds in the hands, are characteristic.

Women

Apart from numerous representations of kolata dancers or tribal women clad in leaf attire, the Sangama epoch does not show a great variety of women's fashions.

Fashionable ladies in the sixteenth century wear a long sari tied below the waist. It is not clear, however, whether it is tied like a dhoti or a lungi, often with an elegant fan at the front. The girdle worn on the lower garment can be constituted by various strings, it can look like a pleated sash or it can imitate the bead-festoon motif seen on pillars; there is no end to the imaginativeness of the wearer. Hairstyles are also more diverse than in previous centuries: the bun is no longer tied at the nape of the neck but on the crown or at the side of the head. Long plaits and the low bun are still seen occasionally but are apparently out of fashion. Head ornaments are conspicuous: pins, studs, and chains. Various types of necklaces, armlets, bracelets and anklets are also in vogue. Details of jewellery can be gleaned from the accounts of foreign travellers who were overwhelmed by the riches that these women wore. Paes states that on the occasion of the Mahanavami festival, such was the weight of the golden bracelets and jewels carried by the women that they had to be supported by attendants.[19] This was not an exaggeration as confirmed by the account of Nuniz who visited the capital shortly afterwards: 'These women are so richly bedecked with gold and precious stones that they are hardly able to move.'[20]

The study of pillar carvings and memorial stones, however, reveals that ordinary women wore a simpler attire.

Ornaments

Sacred images generally wear the kirita-mukuta. This is 'slightly conical with a little flaring up of the coni-cylinder towards the top, where it has a bud-shaped tip on a bulbous cushion'.[21] A second type is the karanda-mukuta, a tiered crown reminiscent in its shape of a pile of pots.

There are various kinds of kundalas. The most frequent are the simpler shapes: patrakundalas, consisting of plain bands, and ratnakundalas, circular, set with gems. Neck ornaments are a solid flat kanthi worn at the base of the neck, and strings of bead or pearls, with or without pendants, falling on the chest.

An ornament peculiar to some male divine personages is the chhannavira. This is a circular flat medallion worn on the chest, kept in position by a string tied around the neck and then tied at the back of the waist. It is generally worn by Lakshmana, Krishna and Karttikeya.

Other ornaments worn on the chest are the udarabandha, generally rendered very simply, and finally the yajnopavita worn only by men.

Skandhamala are shown consisting of two strands: one encircling the shoulder at the top, the other hanging loose.

Various types of bracelets and armlets, as well as anklets complete the ensemble.

F. Representation of Nature and Architecture

Animals and birds

Animals are a great source of inspiration for Vijayanagara artists. The most spectacular example of animal sculpture occurs on the south side, lowest tier, of the Mahanavami platform where gazelles, bears, boars, tigers, lions and dogs have been rendered with an unique immediacy and empathy in forest scenes. Running, jumping, climbing on tree, mating and fighting with each other, fleeing from dogs and hunters, these animals have here the pride of place, the human figures being only accessory to the scenes. The freshness of approach, the distribution of animals in the panel, and the lively treatment of time and space sequences are unparalleled: no other animal carving at the capital can be compared with this early work.

Apart from hunting scenes, animals occur in various other contexts. Animals and mythical beasts were used as a decorative element in architecture on basement mouldings, balustrades, walls, pilasters, pillars and eaves. Thus elephants tend to appear on the walls of early Vijayanagara monuments, but in a later period on basement mouldings and balustrades.

Aquatic fauna are occasionally on the walls of temple precincts: the most outstanding example is on the interior of the enclosure wall of the Malyavanta Raghunatha temple. Fish are carved in the eastern gopura of the Krishna temple. A huge snake decorates the exterior of the enclosure wall of the Tiruvengalanatha temple, to the west of the southern door. Elegantly modelled plaster parrots grace the roofs of the vimanas while, in the interior of mandapas, parrots and other birds have been used as ornamental motif on ceiling medallions.

Numerous animals appear along with people, deities, plants and geometrical motifs and pillar blocks, one of the most popular being the squatting lion.

The most typical creations of the Vijayanagara artists are the yalis, mythical beasts, which occur as a decorative element in sixteenth-century temple pillars and balustrades.

Landscape

Rocks, mountains, rivers, ponds and seas occur rarely. Artists generally limited themselves to mountains and seas. Mountains are suggested by a pyramidal pile of semi-circular shapes, as for instance in the carving of the death of Kumbhakarna in the main shrine of the Ramachandra temple complex.[22] The impressive seascapes, waters teeming with fish, turtles, crabs and all sorts of fabulous aquatic creatures, appear in the famous *Ramayana* episode relating Hanuman's tremendous leap from India to Sri Lanka. The scene appears in all major *Ramayana* narrative sequences at the site, as on the main shrine of Ramachandra complex.[23] It is found in the narrative sequence on the inner face of the enclosure wall of the same temple complex. Here, however, the panel is partly obliterated by the later wall of the north-east mandapa. Another lively rendering of the ocean is seen in the *Ramayana* narrative on the gopura of the Ramanuja temple.[24]

If trees are not important to a narrative, they occur comparatively rarely. An exception is the tree on which Hanuman is perched when, peeping down from its crown, he discovers Rama and Lakshmana resting beneath it.[25]

The inclusion of a tree is generally intended to suggest that an incident took place outdoors. Trees and shrubs are used with great inventiveness both as decorative motifs and in narrative cycles, where a tree or a creeper is placed to subdivide panel for successive episodes.[26]

An exceptional treatment of landscape, however, is found the lowest tier of the Mahanavami platform, especially on the southern face, where panels, showing forest and hunt scenes are located. The artists here were obviously keen observers of nature, taking great pride in illustrating various species of trees. They occasionally delight in showing birds and men perched on trees, safe from wild animals below.[27] Another popular theme on the same monument is elephants encircling or uprooting trees with their trunks.

Buildings

Architectural features, separating scenes and leading the eye onwards, are equally significant in the organisation of successive episodes within a single panel. Even when reduced to merely conventional elements, architecture serves to frame figures, indicating their place or urban settings by the simplest means.[28]

Rendering of palaces or simple dwellings are found in the three *Ramayana* narrative cycles, in the processional friezes on the exterior walls of the Ramachandra temple, as well as in the group of family portraits of Rayasta Ramachandra Dikshita in the mandapa of the large temple at Koti-tirtha.[29] The structures shown here are elevated on finely moulded plinths; there is no suggestion of walls as the curved eaves of the roof are supported by slender pillars.

A more sophisticated rendering of architectural structure is found on the schist carvings on the western face of the Mahanavami platform. The intention of the artists to reproduce miniature models of extant buildings is clearly conveyed, although most of these projecting aedicules have been savagely vandalised. Each aedicule has its own miniature basement in which each moulding renders with great precision, pilasters, overhanging eaves, parapets and surmounting roofs. The aedicules incorporate small animals and birds as well as depictions of court scenes. Architecture and sculpture have fused in a work of outstanding sensitivity and fineness of detail.

NOTES

1. P. Filliozat, 'Techniques of Chronolgy and Construction in the temple of Vithala at Hampi', in *Vijayanagara, City and Empire*, ed. by A. L. Dallapiccola in collaboration with S. Zingel-Ave Lallemant, Vol. I, p. 296.
2. NLm/1.
3. NLg/2.
4. A.L. Dallapiccola and Anila Verghese, 'Ramayana Panels on the Gopura of the "Old Shiva" temple at Vitthalapura', in *Vijayanagara Progress of Research 1987-88*, pp. 143-53.
5. Goswamy, B.N. and A.L. Dahmen-Dallapiccola, *An Early Document of Indian Art, The Citralaksana of Nagnajit*, p. 107.
6. R.N. Saletore in *Vijayanagara Art*, p. 52, quotes the opinions of A. Rea and V.A. Smith on the Vijayanagara style.
7. NGn/6.
8. NMx/2.
9. NVo/1.
10. Anila Verghese, 'Court Attire at Vijayanagara', in *The Quarterly Journal of the Mythic Society*, Vol. LXXXII, Nos. 1-2, p. 52.
11. R. Sewell, *A Forgotten Empire*, p. 252.
12. R. Sewell, op. cit., p. 383.
13. Anila Verghese, op. cit., p. 56.
14. Duarte Barrbosa, quoted in Anila Verghese, op. cit., p. 56.
15. Anila Verghese, op. cit., p. 56.
16. R. Sewell, op. cit., p. 252.
17. R. Sewell, op. cit., pp. 276-7.
18. H. Goetz, 'Muslims in Vijayanagara: The Record of the Monuments', in *Studies in Indian Culture, Dr. Ghulam Yazdani Commemoration Volume*, pp. 66-70.
19. R. Sewell, op. cit., p. 274.
20. R. Sewell, op. cit., p. 378.
21. C. Sivaramamurti, *South Indian Bronzes*, p. 26.
22. Main shrine, south entrance, west side, top register.
23. Main shrine, north entrance, east side, top register.
24. NCw/3. West side of the gopura, inside the prakara, third register.
25. Vithala temple, main shrine, north porch, north-east pillar.
26. A.L. Dallapiccola, 'Sculpture', in A.L. Dallapiccola, J.M. Fritz, G. Michell and S. Rajasekhara, *The Ramachandra Temple at Vijayanagara*, p. 86.
27. For instance, the tree near the cross-shaped tank. Mahanavami platform, lower tier, south face, second register.
28. A.L. Dallapiccola, J.M. Fritz, G. Michell and S. Rajasekhara, op. cit., p. 86.
29. NGm/2.

CHAPTER 3

Settings

A. Natural Settings

One of the important features of Vijayanagara sculpture is its occurrence on boulders, monoliths and slabs.

Boulders

Artists could take maximum advantage of the numerous boulders which dot the terrain on which the capital was built. At Vijayanagara innumerable images, mostly sacred, were carved on boulders, sometimes in inaccessible locations. Frequent among such carvings are images of Hanuman, purposefully striding ahead, a tree resting on his left shoulder and his right hand raised, ready to strike a potential enemy;[1] four-armed Bhairava standing, accompanied by his dog;[2] and Ganesha, comfortably seated, his trunk dipping into bowl of sweets he carries in his left hand, keeping an eye on the path below.[3]

One important cluster of sacred images is disposed on three boulders close to each other on the ridge north of the Royal Centre.[4] Images of Ganesha, Lakshmi, Durga, Mahishasuramardini are carved on the first boulder; on the second boulder are Karttikeya and a panel consisting of five figures, possibly Shiva, Vishnu and ascetics; the third boulder, the most interesting, has images of Brahma and Kali on one side, and on the other Bhairavi, Kali (beneath whom is carved a pot flanked by two human heads) and Bhadrakali. Further sculptures occur on nearby rocks and shelters. The most conspicuous is a standing Bhairava flanked by a large scorpion and a snake.[5]

Koti-tirtha, on the bank of the Tungabhadra, has innumerable lingas carved on the sheet rock. Two groups merit attention. One has a large linga at the centre, surrounded by smaller ones; the other has 108 lingas arranged in regular formation around a larger central one.[6]

There is also a group of very striking Vaishnava images at the same site. On an almost inaccessible rock shelf are reliefs of the ten avataras of Vishnu and the twenty-four aspects of the same god. Close by, in an equally inaccessible place, is a superb small carving of Lakshmi-Narasimha, Narasimha holding the bow and arrow in one of his hands.[7] The image of Anantapadmanabha is carved on a boulder near the shrine among the rocks at Koti-tirtha. Another significant group of Vaishnava images, consisting of the ten incarnations and the story of Narasimha, occurs in a rock shelter east of the Elephant Stables.[8] An image of Rama shooting the bow is carved on a boulder on the ridge north-east of the Tiruvengalanatha temple.[9] Numerous other groups of individual images are tucked away among the rocks or concealed by vegetation.

There is yet another category of carvings on boulders around which a temple has been constructed. The most notable example is on Malyavanta hill. The Rama-Sita-Lakshmana-Hanuman group here is carved on a boulder enshrined in the sanctuary of the structural vimana. In the sanctuary of the Kodandarama temple is a large rock with a relief of standing Rama, Sita and Lakshmana, with Sugriva making obeisance to one side.[10] Rudimentary thatch and foliage shelters were erected to protect such carvings on boulders, as indicated by holes on the boulders into which a wooden frame was fixed to support the thatched roof. One such shelter stood above the carving of the ten-armed Athikayiamma south of the Tiruvengalanatha temple.[11]

Monoliths

The obsession with carving images on boulders extended to monolithic sculptures hewn out of boulders. Two monoliths depicting Ganesha are situated on the rocky ridge above Hampi; the seated four-armed god has his trunk plunging into the bowl of sweets which he carries in the left hand. A large monolithic Nandi, his head unfortunately damaged, is carved out of a boulder at the end of the Virupaksha chariot street.

The most spectacular monolith at the site, the 6.7 m high Lakshmi-Narasimha, was commissioned at the orders of Krishnadevaraya in 1528.[12] Even in its mutilated and recently restored condition, the image conveys ferocity through bulging eyes and open mouth. A snake expands its hoods above Narasimha's head. The image of the goddess Lakshmi seated on the left thigh of the god is badly damaged. Nearby, a simple structure encloses a gigantic monolithic linga, about 3 m high, whose pitha is nowadays constantly under water because of the rising of the water-table.[13]

Slabs

Sculpted slabs served a similar purpose to monoliths. They were set up in temple sanctuaries or in the open-air. Among these are naga-stones placed either in temple compounds or under trees in fields or near tanks, and sati- and hero-stones, or memorial stones such as the one commemorating a family at Talarighat. Sculpted slabs depicting striding Hanuman, Bhairava and Virabhadra were placed for protection at crossroads and spots of lurking danger.

B. Architectural Settings

Balustrades

A feature common to temples and palaces are the balustrades flanking the stone steps leading from one level to the next. Balustrades display various motifs. One common design is the surul-yali, firmly planted on the ground and looking backwards with bulging eyes. There are, however, variations on this theme: the surul-yali is often shown walking, with one paw raised and the others resting on the ground. From the mouth issue curved, multi-faceted mouldings terminating in a roll and diminutive lotus bud. Artists usually took great care with the details of the manes and tails.[14]

A further elaboration of this animal theme is seen on the south staircase of the Mahanavami platform. An elephant accompanied by a groom lifts a tree; above this group, a lion fights against a makara(?). Elephants occur repeatedly as balustrade designs in palaces[15] and temples.[16] The animals usually stride forward, carrying lotuses in their trunks. An exceptional balustrade design, a horse drawing a chariot, is seen on the temple near the gateway on the north side of Hemakuta hill.[17]

Another unusual motif is found on the staircases on the north side of the hundred-pillar hall and on one of the palace complexes. The balustrades display full lotus medallions flanked by single pilasters with miniature curved brackets.[18]

Walls

Major changes are seen in the disposition of sculptures on temple walls. These are rhythmically divided by pairs of pilasters into alternating projections and recesses. Deep niches for sculptures occur on the projections, framed by shorter pairs of pilasters. As there are practically no sculptures or other identifiable remains in the niches, we might assume that they were decorative, or else that sculpted slabs, now lost, were once inserted in them. Examples of niche sculptures are seen in the main shrine of the Virupaksha complex where crudely cut slabs were later placed in the wall niches.

Wall recesses are embellished by the typical kumbha-panjara motif. Isolated, highly decorated pilasters stand in pots, with sprouting foliage occasionally emerging from the mouth of a makara, with bands and tassels.

The walls of some temples, such as the principal shrine in the Ramachandra complex, are particularly rich in carvings; while the walls of the rangamandapa are occupied by *Ramayana* carvings disposed in three ascending rows of panels, the walls of the vimana display numerous Vaishnava images in spaces between the niches and kumbha-panjaras.

The layout of the walls in the minor shrine of the same complex is similar, although here the *Uttara-Ramayana* carvings are placed exclusively on the projections of the wall, while kumbha-panjaras occupy the recesses, thus breaking the continuity of the narrative. As far as the basement mouldings are concerned, the vertical element between the beaded part-octagonal moulding and the overhanging cornice is wider and is occupied by a set of mainly mythological carvings divided by vertical foliage-scroll bands. A petal frieze surmounted by a bracket-like motif supports overhanging cornices with a sumptuous decoration of miniature roofs embellished by kudus.

Columns and piers

Sixteenth-century sculptors were evidently no longer greatly interested in the embellishment of temple walls; indeed, this century marks the decline of narrative carvings. From now on attention is focused more on mandapas. With the introduction of large pillared halls, pavilions for ritual purposes and colonnades for visitors to relax, pillars, piers and other supporting elements offered ample scope for decoration.

The artists accepted the challenge and developed a series of variations on the simple triple-block shaft with single or double capital. The outer piers of these halls became elaborate sculptural compositions, surrounded by clusters of cut-out colonnettes carved from a single block and supported by crouching yalis. Full scale leaping yalis often carrying diminutive riders are reserved for piers in the middle of each side. Yali piers are also used to define open inner spaces; the earliest example is the maharanga-mandapa of the Virupaksha temple.

Ceilings

Ceilings were generally ornamented with simple medallions with a central lotus pattern. This is surrounded by musicians in the temple possibly dedicated to Nammalvar south of the Vithala[19] or, more frequently, by a frieze of dancing girls, geese or foliage motifs. A medallion with representations of the Vasantotsava festivities decorates the ceiling of one of the bays of the south-east mandapa in the Vithala complex.

One of the most elaborate ceilings at the site, however, is in the 1554 mahamandapa of the main Vithala temple. The hall is subdivided into a nave and two side-aisles, of which only the ceilings of the north and south aisles are extant. In the variety of decorative patterns displayed here the lotus medallion is the main motif. This simple ornamental element is shown inscribed into complex geometrical patterns or surrounded by divine images, generally aspects of Vishnu, undergoing permutations in each of the squares into which the ceilings are divided.

The ceiling of the central open space of the mahamandapa of the Ramanuja temple is noteworthy. Raised on high corbels and wide recessed beams, it displays a wealth of decorative motifs such as parrots facing each other in the corners of the central square, a flat octagonal band with creeper design, a vertical octagonal band with dancers, a circle of scroll designs, a circle of birds and a large lotus with a pendant bud in the centre. Images of the Alvars and the Acharyas, flanked by deities and devotees, are carved on the recessed beams on which the ceiling rests.[20]

Parapets and towers

Even in their dilapidated state, the vimanas and gopuras preserve vestiges of sixteenth-century stucco gods, semi-divine beings, courtly figures, animals, mythical beasts and, above all, decorative motifs. Especially impressive even in the their present fragmentary condition, are the remains of stucco-work on the gopuras of the Krishna, Vithala and Malyavanta Raghunatha temple. On the inner side of the eastern gopura of the Krishna temple there is a particularly interesting scene. A battle episode on the lower storey with armed warriors, horsemen, foot soldiers and chariots may commemorate the famous Udayagiri campaign which marked Krishnadevaraya's victory over the Gajapati king of Orissa in 1513-14.

Stucco images of Rama, Sita, Lakshmana, Durga Mahishasuramardini and Krishna, are still in pristine condition on the eastern gopura of the Vithala temple. The best preserved images at the site are on the gopuras of the Malyavanta Raghunatha temple. Here deities stand in niches, flanked by attendant figures, devotees, heavenly beauties and courtly and guardian figures.

In course of time, the ends of the barrel vaulted shalas were transformed into huge yali heads, with bulging eyes and open mouths. They were placed over curved frames decorated with rows of miniature warriors, geese with foliated tails, occasionally parrots, and vegetal motifs such as creepers with sumptuous leaves and foliated tufts.

Stucco-work is also visible on the porch extension of the main shrine in the Ramachandra temple complex. Guardians, devotees and courtly figures are interspersed among niches containing major deities, such as Rama and Sita, Venugopala and Narasimha. In the Virupaksha temple stucco figures are on the parapet surmounting the maharangamandapa, as well as the parapets over the north and south pillared corridor in the inner courtyard. These sculptures are undoubtedly of the post-Vijayanagara era. Stucco embellishments were evidently not only the prerogative of sacred buildings; small sacred images, mainly of Nandi, are seen on fragments of parapets in some houses of the Hampi bazaar street.

NOTES

1. Outside NRb/2.
2. NRh/2.
3. Near gate NRb.
4. NMx/2.
5. NMz/2.
6. NGm and n. See Chapter on Shaiva Images, p. 31.
7. Near NGn/3.
8. NSa/2.
9. Near NMe/1.
10. NGw/1.
11. NMh/2.
12. NLm/1.
13. NLm/2.
14. For illustrations see J. Fritz, G. Michell, M.S. Nagaraja Rao, *The Royal Centre at Vijayanagara, Preliminary Report*, p. 120, Fig. 6.21.
15. Nobleman's palace 2.
16. E.g. Tiruvengalanatha, Krishna and Pattabhirama temples (see Chapter 13, section on elephants pp. 100-2).
17. See Chapter 13, section on horses, pp. 102-3.
18. For illustrations see J. Fritz, G. Michell, M.S. Nagaraja Rao, *The Royal Centre at Vijayanagara, Preliminary Report*, p. 120, Fig. 6.21, structure XXVI/1.
19. NHa/10.
20. A.L. Dallapiccola and Anila Verghese, 'The so-called "Old Siva" temple in Vithalapura', in *Vijayanagara Progress of Research* (in press).

CHAPTER 4

Narratives

An important aspect of sculpture at Vijayanagara is the development of narrative art. Series of panels assembled in friezes depict the epics, puranic myths and local legends. In spite of the marked preference for sacred subjects, however, the earliest series of 'narrative carvings' found at the site—those on the Mahanavami platform—are devoted not to the celebration of a deity, but of the king.

A. *Ramayana*

Vaishnava narrative carvings form a unique and important group within Vijayanagara sculpture. The *Ramayana* narratives, in particular, are of immense interest.

The ubiquitous presence of the icons of Anjaneya is a reminder of the *Ramayana* association with the site. For centuries, thousands of pilgrims have paid homage at a number of locations in and around Hampi, believed to be sanctified by Rama's presence and valorous deeds. The origin of this tradition dates back to pre-Vijayanagara times, developing greatly at the beginning of the fifteenth century. Pilgrims continue to visit these places in large numbers today.

The *Ramayana* incidents connected with the Vijayanagara area centre on Rama's meeting with Hanuman and his alliance with Sugriva. After Sita's abduction, Rama and Lakshmana went in search of her. While wandering through the Dandaka forest, they met the rakshasa Kabandha, who advised them to go to the Pampa lake and Rishyamukha hill. Rama and Lakshmana eventually reached the shore of Pampa lake where they visited the hermitage of the old ascetic woman Shabari. At the same time, the exiled prince Sugriva, accompanied by Hanuman and a few other companions, was living at Rishyamukha. Sugriva had seen Sita being carried away by Ravana and had gathered up the garment and ornaments she had dropped. When Rama and Lakshmana approached the hill, Hanuman was sent by Sugriva to ascertain who the strangers were; then a treaty of friendship was concluded between the two brothers and Sugriva.

Thereafter Rama and Sugriva went to Kishkindha, where, after Rama had killed Vali the reigning king, Sugriva was consecrated as monarch. In the meantime, the rainy season had begun and all activities had to be suspended for four months during which Rama and Lakshmana took shelter on mount Malyavanta. At the end of the monsoon, after Lakshmana had reminded Sugriva of his obligations to Rama, the latter sent his vassals in all directions in search of Sita. Hanuman, travelling southwards, discovered Sita captive in Lanka. On his return to Kishkindha, Hanuman and his companions celebrated their success by alighting at Madhuvana, the park of the monkey king, where they indulged in unrestrained revelry. When Hanuman had revealed to Rama the whereabouts of Sita, the hero accompanied by Sugriva's army moved towards Lanka.

Ramayana sites

All the places referred to above are believed to be in or around Hampi. Kishkindha is said to be located in the hills surrounding Anegondi. To the north-west of Anegondi is Anjandari hill, the birthplace of Hanuman. Lake Pampa is situated at the foot of this hill. Near the lake, a small cavern is pointed out as Shabari's hermitage. On a large island in the Tungabhadra is Rishyamukha hill. A small cave amid boulders on the south bank of the river, known as Sugriva's cave, is deemed to be the place where Sugriva hid Sita's garment and jewellery. At Chintamani, in Anegondi, Rama is said to have given Sugriva the garland to wear in order to distinguish him from his brother Vali in their duel. The combat between Sugriva and Vali is stated to have taken place on a rocky island in the Tungabhadra. The remains of Vali, a huge mound of ash, are pointed out at Nimbapuram, a village on the south bank. The Kodandarama temple is declared to be the spot where Sugriva was consecrated king. During the monsoon Rama and Lakshmana waited on Malyavanta hill. The Madhuvana grove is claimed to be situated on the Hospet-Kamalapuram-Kampili road.

In spite of all the mythological associations of this site, the Rama cult at Vijayanagara is not very ancient. It only received official patronage from the fifteenth century onwards. Subsequently, themes from the *Ramayana* grew in popularity and were frequently carved on temple columns, basements and mouldings, as well as on stray boulders. For example, there are a number of pillar reliefs on the columns of the colonnade of the early Shiva temple on the south bank.[1] But the Vijayanagara patrons were obviously not satisfied with these occasional depictions of *Ramayana* incidents. Their interest in Rama as the ideal hero and king, led them to extend their patronage to three extensive sets of sculptures displaying the whole *Ramayana*.

Ramachandra complex, principal shrine (see Appendix I, A) (Plates 2-6)

The Ramachandra temple is situated in the heart of the Royal Centre in the middle of the royal enclosures. From the small size of the complex and the outstanding quality of its architecture and sculpture it is assumed that this was a royal chapel. A careful analysis of the inscriptional evidence suggests Devaraya I as the probable patron.[2]

The Ramachandra temple is axially and visually aligned with the hills to the north and the north-east mentioned in the epic. If extended, the north-south axis of this temple, passes through the Kodandarama temple, skirts the Rishyamukha hill and passes through Anjandari hill. The north-east axis points to the Malyavanta hill. The 'route of Rama' starting at the Rishyamukha hill to the north, the Malyavanta hill to the north-east and lastly the departure for Lanka to the south, form a half circle around this temple.[3]

This temple is justly renowned for its sculptures. There are two sets of panels illustrating the complete *Ramayana*, the first around the rangamandapa of the principal shrine, the second on the inner face of the enclosure wall between the northern and the eastern gateways. The Uttarakanda has also been illustrated on the walls of the minor shrine north-west of the principal shrine.[4]

The series on the principal shrine is presented in clockwise order in three ascending rows around the exterior of the rangamandapa. It is noteworthy that the sculpted narrative starts on the north side of the west wall, and is thus aligned with the beginning of the 'route of Rama', and ends on the south side of the same wall, the very direction the hero and his allies took when setting off for Lanka. Three circumambulations of the structure are required to view the entire narrative.

The panels are placed with precision: the main sections of the story begin and end at the three doorways on the east, south, and north sides. Crucial events are significantly positioned at cardinal points, corners and doorways.[5] The sculptures are presented in highly articulated manner. Most panels in the bottom row are framed by a pair of pilasters supporting makara-toranas with kirti-mukhas at the apexes.

One hundred and eight panels are devoted to some forty incidents from the *Ramayana*. The first panel, as the prologue of the story, depicts a conversation between a king and a sage. The king is Dasharatha and the sage is probably Vasishtha. The narrative is divided into six parts; these correspond to the books within the original epic. The Balakanda which relates Rama's childhood and adolescence, and the marriage of the hero and his brothers, occupies the bottom row of panels in the north, east and south sides, ending at the doorway in the middle of the south side. This part of the narrative gave great scope to the artists, conscious of the milieu in which they lived and worked, to mirror the splendour of their patrons and the court.

The Ayodhyakanda, which is concerned with the intrigues at court that lead to Rama's banishment, completes the bottom row at the south-west corner of the hall. Here again splendid processions and ceremonies for welcoming the newly wed couples and sumptuous palaces have pride of place. Less varied, however, is the way in which life in the forest (Aranyakanda) is depicted in the middle row, which is also completed at the south doorway.

The events of the Kishkindhakanda introduce the monkey characters of the story. These appear in the panels that complete the middle row, and continue around the building in the top row in the north until the doorway on that side is reached. The preparations for the Lanka war, dealt with in the Sundarakanda, are represented in panels of the top row that proceeds around the north, east and south sides of the building, once again terminating at the south doorway. In both these sections the sculptors focused on Hanuman's personality and exploits. The final battle scene, somewhat unimaginatively portrayed, and the ultimate enthronement of Rama and Sita, related in the Yuddhakanda, occupy panels in the remainder of the top row and are completed in the south-west corner of the building.

Ramachandra complex, enclosure wall (see Appendix I, C) (Plates 7-9)

The *Ramayana* series on the inner face of the enclosure wall is arranged in five rows beginning on the inner east face of the north gateway and then running eastwards to the east gateway, the main entrance to the complex. The story opens with the episode of Shravanakumara, which serves as a prologue. Omitted in the sculpted series on the principal shrine, this episode is prominently developed to occupy all of the *Ramayana* panels on the north gateway. The narrative then proceeds in a clockwise direction from bottom to top. The fifth and topmost row, however, proceeds in the reverse (anti-clockwise) direction, ending at the north gateway, above where the story first began. This curious device of reversing the direction of the topmost row brings the viewer back to the north gateway above the point where the narrative started and ensures that the final image of the series, depicting Vishnu on the serpent Ananta, appears precisely above the scene showing the invitation of Rishyashringa to Ayodhya in the bottom row. The cycle of events initiated by the sacrifice performed by Rishyashringa on behalf of king Dasharatha is thus concluded and the transition is made from the earthly realm of Rama to the celestial realm of Vishnu.

The panels are simply framed by an uncarved band on four sides. Although the abutment of the north-east mandapa and some modern masonry props obscure portions of the panels, the narrative flow is hardly interrupted.

The *Ramayana* illustrated on the enclosure wall is based probably on the Telugu version of the poem;[6] in contrast, the principal shrine closely follows Valmiki's narrative. For example, on the third row, the involved story of Jambukumara introduces the Shurpanakha incident. Following the Telugu tradition, Jambukumara, who is accidentally killed by Lakshmana, is the son of Shurpanakha; in order to avenge his death Shurpanakha appears on the scene. Again, in the depiction of Ravana's death on the fourth row, following the Telugu story, Rama is shown aiming at Ravana's navel where the nectar of immortality was contained.

The overall impression of the *Ramayana* panels on the enclosure wall is of immense vitality. The flow of narration, unconstrained by architectural elements as in the principal shrine, runs smoothly along each row, progressing upwards. Separated from one another only by thin frames, the carved areas of the panels connect easily. Their generous size encouraged the artists to express themselves freely; the narrative themes are sculpted with richness of detail. Characteristic of this series, in contrast to the stiffness of the sculptures on the principal shrine, is the sense of movement. The figures are rarely still; the majority are shown walking, running, jumping and fighting. Even when seated, they lean forward or turn their heads, always involved in the dynamic of the plot. Liveliness and spontaneity are the dominant qualities of the narrative style.

Ramanuja temple (see Appendix II) (Plates 10, 11)

The third complete *Ramayana* series at the site is sculpted on the walls of the south gopura, the main entrance of the Ramanuja temple. The 131 panels are set in four rows all around the gopura and its entrance chambers. One panel on the north wall is missing. As was the case with the previous example, the narrative sequence here is based on the Telugu version of the *Ramayana*. It starts at the lowermost tier on the east side of the gopura outside the prakara and proceeds in an intriguing pattern around the whole of the gopura and its porches on the southern side.[7]

In contrast to the two Ramachandra temple series, which employ a prologue or an introductory scene, the Ramanuja temple narration begins abruptly with the sacrifice of Rishyashringa. While the series on the principal shrine of the Ramachandra temple concluded with Rama's coronation and the series on the enclosure wall with Vishnu on Ananta, here the story ends with the battle between Rama and Ravana. Since the lintels of the inner and outer door frames of the gopuras are missing, it is possible that the scenes depicting Ravana's death and Rama's pattabhisheka might have been carved there: alternatively, they may have appeared on the brick and mortar superstructure that no longer exists.

Each of the three sets under review shows obvious preferences in the distribution of the panels and in the choice of episodes. The Balakanda is well represented in all three examples. By the very nature of its subject matter—the birth of an heir to a king, his upbringing, his heroic deeds and finally his winning the hand of a beautiful princess—the Balakanda is popular and attractive. The Kishkindhakanda comes second. This is also an obvious choice as its episodes are believed to have taken place in the immediate environs of Vijayanagara. There is much divergence, however, in the representations of the Yuddhakanda. It is elaborated upon at great length on the gopura, but is not given much importance in the two other series. This gopura reflects a change of focus on the part of the sculptors. The decisive battles, Rama against Kumbhakarna, Lakshmana against Indrajit, and Rama against Ravana, have pride of place since they have been carved on the interior wall of the gopura. Moreover, beneath the scene depicting Rama and Ravana fighting with magical weapons there is a significant episode from the Balakanda: Rama and Lakshmana subduing the demons Subahu and Maricha in order to protect the yajna of the sages. Of exquisite workmanship and extraordinary inventiveness, these panels demonstrate the expressive power of Vijayanagara sculpture of the sixteenth century at its best.

Selected episodes (see Appendix III, A and IV)

In addition to these three complete series of *Ramayana* carvings, there are two partial series. In both, the Kishkindha and Yuddha sections, in which Hanuman and his monkey companions play a prominent role, are emphasized. The first set is on the two pillars, with 12 panels on each, on the north porch of the Vithala temple rangamandapa. The series begins with the incident of the golden deer that results in Sita's abduction and ends with the Lanka campaign. An unusual relief, not found in any other series, is of Kumbhakarna so deep in sleep that he is undisturbed by cattle walking all over him. The second is on the east gopura of the Tiruvengalanatha temple. The *Ramayana* panels are sculpted on the west side of the granite base of this gateway, on both sides of the entryway. These 13 panels, of stray incidents of the epic, begin with Hanuman encountering Rama and Lakshmana at Rishyamukha and end with the combat between Rama and Ravana in Lanka. There are also 12 *Ramayana* panels on the inner north gopura of the Tiruvengalanatha temple.

Uttarakanda carvings (see Appendix I, B, and III, B) (Plate 12)

There are also two series of the Uttarakanda, the seventh 'book' of the epic. The more complete series is on the vimana of the minor shrine of the Ramachandra complex. The main episodes of the Uttarakanda are arranged in two tiers of small panels: Sita being sent away to the ashrama of Valmiki, the birth of the two young princes Lava and Kusha, the capture of the horse for the ashvamedha by the twins, their combat with each of their uncles in turn when they attempt to retrieve the sacrificial horse, the meeting of Rama with Sita and his sons, Sita's descent into mother earth and the final epiphany of Rama, Sita and Lakshmana as Vishnu, Anantashesha and Bhudevi respectively. The panels, though small, are expressive.

The second, less complete series is found in

the mahamandapa of the Vithala temple on the recessed beams above the pillars in the open area on the north side of this hall. The story unfolds in continuous narration on long panels, separated form each other by a narrow frame, along the eastern, southern and part of the western sides: the ceremonial release of the horse designated for the ashvamedha sacrifice by Rama, seated with the golden statue of Sita beside him, the capture of the horse by Lava and Kusha, their taking it to the hermitage of Valmiki, and the encounter of Rama with Sita and her twins sons in the ashrama.

These narrative sculptures of the *Ramayana* form a unique and significant contribution by the Vijayanagara sculptors and their patrons.

B. *Mahabharata* (Figure 1, Plates 13, 14)

In contrast to the overriding importance given to the *Ramayana*, the *Mahabharata* seldom features in Vijayanagara sculpture. There are no narrative reliefs of this work, though there do exist a few stray sculptures.

The best example is on the 'Bhima's gate',[8] where there are two vividly carved panels showing the hero Bhima killing Duhshasana by tearing him open. In fulfilment of the vow made when Duhshasana had publicly humiliated her, Draupadi is seen tying up her hair after dipping it in her tormentor's blood. Also within this gate is a large relief on a stone slab of Bhima, in the pratyalidha pose, holding his characteristic weapon, the gada, in one hand and a flower or plant in the other. On a boulder just outside another large gate in the north-west end of the Urban Core is rock-carving of the same hero. Evidently Bhima is invoked as a protective divinity, as he is found in or near two gates into the city. Apart from these two large carvings, there are very few pillar reliefs of Bhima in the entire site.

Only two other *Mahabharata* panels have been discovered at the site. One is a representation of the shami-tree episode, carved on the fragments of a huge granite basin lying on the ground in the vicinity of the gateway to the east of the Elephant Stables, the so-called Singharada Hebbagilu.[9] The other is a relief on the vimana of the Virupaksha temple that may represent the Kiratarjuniya incident.

Among the post-Vijayanagara ceiling paintings in the Virupaksha temple is a depiction of the Draupadi-svayamvara, of Arjuna winning Draupadi by his skill in archery.[10]

C. *Bhagavata Purana* (see Appendix III, C) (Plate 15)

The *Bhagavata Purana* is the only Purana whose myths are found in the Vijayanagara sculptural repertory. Its popularity arose from the wide following Krishna enjoyed in the city. There are numerous reliefs at Vijayanagara of Krishna's exploits as related in the *Bhagavata Purana.* But apart from these isolated carvings, there are some narrative reliefs of the *Bhagavata.*

The most extensive series is found in the mahamandapa of the Vithala temple, on the narrow recessed beams above the pillars, around the open space in the south wing of this hall. The story unfolds continuously along the north, east and south sides: the child Krishna destroying the various demons sent to kill him, his mischievous deeds such as stealing butter and teasing the gopis, Krishna as Venugopala, his miraculous feat of lifting mount Govardhana and finally the scenes at Kamsa's court leading to the destruction of Kamsa and the enthronement of Ugrasena. The panels are filled with action and though they are separated by vertical bands there is no interruption in the flow of the narrative.

In the Ramanuja temple mahamandapa, one pillar in the north-west corner has five reliefs of *Bhagavata* themes: Krishna overcoming the fire demon, Keshi, Aghasura, and Bakasura, and also of Krishna combating a wrestler sent by Kamsa. The Keshi-vadha episode appears nowhere else in the entire site. There are also some incidents of the *Bhagavata Purana* carved on the recessed beams above the pillars of the partially collapsed mandapa in the Madhava temple within the Royal Centre[11] as well as on the walls of the sanctuary in the Krishna temple.

D. Narasimha Narratives (Figures 2, 3, Plate 16)

Other than the *Ramayana*, the *Mahabharata* and the *Bhagavata*-inspired series, Vijayanagara sculptors also narrated the legend of Narasimha repeatedly.

Probably the oldest sets are the ones on the wall of the steps on the south face of the Mahanavami platform depicting the life and exploits of Narasimha among the hunters culminating in his marriage with the Chenchu girl.[12] The sequence depicts the Narasimha story in detail on the backdrop of the sylvan landscape inhabited by the Chenchus. The main episode, which is depicted twice, is that of the huntress leaning against a tall bow while a small figure is extracting a thorn from her foot. This theme is very popular in Vijayanagara iconography and is frequently found carved on pillar blocks. The fact that two very similar depictions of this theme appear at a short distance from each other on the same monument is an indication of how relevant it was for the Vijayanagara rulers, stressing their connections with the Narasimha temple at Ahobalam and with the Chenchu tribe.

The more popular story of Narasimha killing the tyrant Hiranyakashipu is carved in great detail and with exquisite finish on the east wall of the minor shrine in the Ramachandra complex.[13] The sequence of the narrative starts with Prahlada worshipping Lakshmi-Narasimha, proceeds with the attempted murder of Prahlada—an elephant should trample to death the youth, but refuses to obey the mahout—and continues with Hiranyakashipu chiding Prahlada for worshipping Vishnu, culminating in the emergence of Narasimha from the pillar. The last scene shows the eight-armed Narasimha wrestling with Hiranyakashipu.

E. Story of Gajendra (Plate 56)

The story of Vishnu as Varadaraja,[14] rescuing Gajendra, from the crocodile, has also been treated by artists as a narrative sequence. The most important rendering of this myth is in the southern aisle of the mahamandapa of the Vithala temple. The carvings are located on three sides on the top of one of the pillars. The narrative sequence commences on the south face with the carving of the elephant in distress. Vishnu on Garuda appears on the eastern face and the god is shown blessing the elephant on the northern one.

Less elaborate versions of the same three phases of the legend are found on pillars. The best examples are on the south pillar of the east porch of the Ramanuja temple. Here, however, the sequence ends with a panel depicting Varadaraja.

F. Secular Narratives

As noted above, the oldest 'narrative friezes' at the site are those on the Mahanavami platform depicting life at court, with the king in all his might and splendour.

The Mahanavami-Vijaya-Dashami was undoubtedly the most important festival, which celebrated the victory of the goddess Durga over Mahishasura. According to one tradition, Rama started his expedition against Ravana on the auspicious Vijaya-Dashami day. Another tradition, however, associates this day with the Mahabharata war and the victory of the Pandavas over the Kauravas. Irrespective of which tradition was followed, Vijaya-Dashami was essentially a Kshatriya festival and it was usual for the rulers to review their armies on this meaningful day and to have them ready for military action. This was the best time of the year for embarking on military ventures because by the month of Ashvin, corresponding to October-November, the rains were over, the roads dry, the rivers easily fordable and there was plenty of water for the army.[15]

The spectacular annual celebration of the Mahanavami or Navaratri festival made a deep impression on foreign visitors to Vijayanagara. The most detailed accounts of the festival are those of Paes[16] and Nuniz.[17] Abdur Razzak has also left a description of a courtly festival that fits only partially with those of the Mahanavami. He speaks only of a three-day celebration and a different date.[18]

Primarily a religious festival, the Mahanavami at Vijayanagara was a sumptuous public ritual that had political as well as social, economic and military overtones. The importance of this occasion was such that after the fall of the Vijayanagara empire, the celebration of Navaratri was introduced in states which were created from its ruins, such as Mysore and even minor states such as Ramnad.[19]

The Mahanavami platform

Although there is only one inscriptional reference to Mahanavami-Vijaya-Dashami, namely, on the Vithala temple,[20] there is ample architectural and sculptural evidence of this festival at the site. In the Royal Centre there are a number of platforms, the most magnificent of which is the so-called Mahanavami Dibba, constructed in at least three phases. The earliest phase is contemporary with the early history of the city; the third and last, the 'schist phase', dates from the sixteenth century.[21]

The account of Paes refers to the king who watched the Mahanavami celebrations from the summit of a platform 'served by a kind of staircase of stone beautifully wrought' with 'two platforms one above the other, beautifully sculptured, with their sides well made and worked'.[22] This platform dominates the Royal Centre from its location on a rocky outcrop, the highest point in the area, and by its imposing architecture. Undoubtedly this is a royal monument and place of public display which 'provided a setting for royal rituals of greatest importance'.[23] This monument was, very probably, used for the court celebrations of the Mahanavami festival. As far as it is ascertainable today, it is one of the rare examples of a Hindu monument on which there is not a single divine image.

The carvings on the lowermost tier of the Mahanavami platform represent various royal pursuits. To begin with are processions of animals: elephants, horses, generally with grooms, and camels carrying the occasional kettledrum-players. There are scenes depicting military parades: soldiers with long spikes ushering some nobleman on a horse, or marching soldiers. Especially conspicuous are the processional scenes on the south face of the monument, from the west corner to the steps leading to the second tier. A few processional scenes, possibly the continuations of those found on the southern face of the platform, are carved on the lowermost tier on the western face of the building as far as the south of the stairs. The eastern and the northern faces of the platform have comparatively few weathered carvings. These, however, seem to depict individual scenes rather than trying to achieve the effect of an ensemble as in the other parts of the lowermost tier.

Since the platform has been reassembled in modern times, it is difficult to ascertain whether in the course of the conservation the stone blocks were repositioned in their correct place. Although at first sight there does not seem to be a coherent iconographic programme determining the layout of the carvings, this possibility cannot be ruled out. Comparing the processional friezes of the Mahanavami platform with those of the exterior enclosure wall of the Ramachandra temple, there are marked affinities which suggest a link, perhaps, merely ideological, between both sets of sculptures. The message contained in these sculptures is undeniably the might of the ruler.

The Ramachandra complex, enclosure wall (Plate 1)

This message is conveyed, not so much by the carvings of the Mahanavami platform, but by the superbly organized and clearly discernible iconographic programme of the friezes decorating the enclosure wall of the Ramachandra temple. The carvings are here more controlled, exquisitely finished, and less lively than those on the Mahanavami platform. The first (lowermost) register shows elephants, some with mahouts; the second register, the horses accompanied by their grooms; and the third, parading soldiers. The depiction of rulers or noblemen witnessing the procession are repeated at given intervals interrupting the flow of the movement. The fourth register depicts musicians and dancers. Finally the fifth (topmost) row is entirely devoted to the rendering of the celebration of the Vasantotsava, one of the important festivities at the capital, known also as Smaramahotsava, the festival of the god of love. All these figures move in the clockwise motion around the monument from the south-western corner to the eastern gateway. As noted before, the lower four registers have as a last vignette a ruler seated in a structure, to which all these animals, men and women come to pay homage.

The first four registers of the frieze correspond precisely to the description of the Mahanavami procession given by Paes. It has been suggested that these processional friezes are a sculptural account of this important event.[24] Moreover, since Paes' account dates from the sixteenth century and the carvings were executed roughly some hundred years earlier, it is possible to infer that there must have been a remarkable continuity in the performance of the Mahanavami rituals.[25]

The rigorous division of the iconographic programme in five themes is in itself striking. As demonstrated elsewhere,[26] these four lower registers exemplify kingly powers such as military force, wealth and statecraft symbolically represented by the presence of various queens and concubines, possibly an allusion to marital alliances with neighbouring rulers. These topics were of importance here since they enabled the king to uphold the dharmic order. There is a marked shift of mood between the lower four friezes and the uppermost. While the Mahanavami rituals were a splendid solemn occasion in which the king appeared as a dignified ritualist, the depiction of the Vasantotsava festival suggests a world of pleasure, aesthetic enjoyment and fecundity.

The Vasantotsava (Plates 17, 18)

The Vasantotsava celebrations occur at prominent places in the carvings of the Mahanavami platform and of the Ramachandra temple.

Though somewhat similar to the modern Holi, Vasantotsava is not identical with it. It occurs on the full moon of the month of Chaitra (March-April), exactly one month after Holi (full moon day of Phalguna). While there are no epigraphical references to Holi, literary and archaeological data on the Vasantotsava celebrations at Vijayanagara are available (see below). The festival focuses on the worship of the god of love, Kama, who had been reduced to ashes by the wrath of Shiva. Through the intercession of Kama's wife, Rati, Shiva relented and agreed that on one day in the year, Kama would reassume his bodily form. On this day the Vasantotsava celebrations take place.

The spring festival connected with the god of love was popular from at least the third to the twelfth centuries,[27] while Holi was celebrated only after the fourteenth century.[28] Vasantotsava, however, continued to be popular up to the end of the sixteenth century. At a certain point, however, the festival merged with Holi.[29]

Vasantotsava at the capital coincided with the celebration of the chariot festival of Virupaksha. The festival is described in Ahobala's *Virupaksha Vasantotsava Champu*. According to this work, dating from the sixteenth century, images of Kama and his retinue were placed in the front row on the Virupaksha chariot and people threw saffron coloured water at each other.[30] During this boisterous festival common people and nobility mixed freely in unrestrained merry-making.

The earliest carvings of the Vasantotsava celebrations are probably those found on the steps on the southern face of the Mahanavami platform. Here the fifth register (from the bottom) on both the south and east face of the staircase is entirely devoted to the representation of scenes of music, dance and water-squirting. On the south side, women in dancing pose holding watersquirts or sticks celebrate the beginning of the spring. The women all wear the typical long pleated skirt with their hair in a bun at the nape of the neck. There are huge vessels containing the coloured water which they throw at each other. An embracing couple is flanked by female musicians playing the mridangam and blowing a pipe and by women busily dipping out coloured water from the vessels. On the east side there are more scenes of dance and music.

That Kama and Rati are connected with the spring festival celebrations is proven by the uppermost frieze on the exterior wall of the Ramachandra temple. On the north section of the frieze, a man and some women throw coloured water at each other. The water squirts are clearly discernible in the hands of some of the women. On the east side, among the ladies squirting coloured water at each other, there are dancers, musicians and merrymakers; in the proximity of a stepped tank a couple embraces in the presence of Kama and Rati. The deities, both armed with bows, aim flowery arrows at each other while riding on chariots drawn by parrots; they are accompanied by their revelling retinue. Kama and Rati are among the few sacred images in the iconographic programme. Mythological episodes from the Krishna-lila also make an occasional appearance on this register. Krishna tied to the mortar is seen on the north and east walls, and Krishna stealing the clothes of the gopis hiding in the crown of a tree appears on the east and the west walls.[31]

Sixteenth-century representations of the festival occur on the west face of the Mahanavami platform. On the second tier, north of the stairs, is a possible depiction of Vasantotsava. In one panel there is male figure wearing a tall kulayi with two women. The next panel is entirely occupied by three women. The scene is dominated by a big container out of which they ladle water into pots they carry in their hands.

The most detailed representations of the Vasantotsava festivities are in the Vishnu temple within the Royal Centre, near the Singharada Hebbagilu.[32] The central part of the enclosed rangamandapa is slightly elevated on horizontal slabs which rest on pillars. On these slabs are carved eight panels depicting the spring festival. Women, occasionally with a man in their midst, are engaged in squirting water at each other. A woman carries a water-squirt, while others are busy scooping water out of a huge container, either with small cups or with their cupped hands. A male figure seated in a crescent-shaped tub(?) appears in two reliefs. The presence of a male musician, female dancer and hunchback clown holding a water-squirt renders the light-hearted fun typical of this festival.

There is yet another fine representation of the Vasantotsava on the plinth of the maha-mandapa of the Vithala temple. Here on the east side are friezes of kolata-dancers and water-squirting scenes. Also in the same complex on the basement of the north-east mandapa and on the south side of the stone chariot are spirited scenes depicting dancing, watersquirting and Kama on his chariot.

NOTES

1. NGt/3.
2. Anila Verghese, *Religious Traditions at Vijayanagara: as Revealed Through its Monuments,* p. 47.
3. J.M. Fritz, G. Michell and M.S. Nagaraja Rao, *The Royal Centre at Vijayanagara, Preliminary Report,* pp. 149-50.
4. For a detailed discussion of the sculptural programme of this temple see: A.L. Dallapiccola, 'Sculpture', in A.L. Dallapiccola J.M. Fritz. G. Michell, and S. Rajasekhara, *The Ramachanda Temple at Vijayanagara,* pp. 81-130.
5. A.L. Dallapiccola, ibid., pp. 91-7.
6. C.R. Sarma, *The Ramayana in Telugu and Tamil: A Comparative Study,* pp. 29-49.
7. A.L. Dallapiccola and A. Verghese, 'Ramayana Panels on the Gopura of the "Old Shiva" Temple at Vitthalapura', in *Vijayanagara: Progress of Research 1987-88,* pp. 143-53.
8. NXo.
9. NSg.
10. A.L. Dallapiccola, 'Ceiling paintings in the Virupaksha temple, Hampi'. *South Asian Studies 13,* 1997.
11. NRt/2
12. South side staircase, bottom register on the south and the east face.
13. A.L. Dallapiccola, 'Sculpture', in A.L. Dallapiccola, J.M. Fritz, G. Michell and S. Rajasekhara, op. cit., p. 100.
14. See Chapter 6, Varadaraja.
15. K. Sarojini Devi, *Religion in Vijayangara Empire,* p. 275.
16. R. Sewell, *A Forgotten Empire,* pp. 262-5.
17. R. Sewell, op. cit., pp. 376-9.
18. R.H. Major (Ed.), *India in the Fifteenth Century,* pp. 35-8.
19. Anila Verghese, op. cit., p. 105.
20. *South Indian Inscriptions* IX, Pt. II, No. 668.
21. See Appendix VI.
22. R. Sewell, op. cit., p. 264.
23. G. Michell, 'The "Royal Centre" and the great Platform at Vijayanagara', in *Rupa Pratirupa, Alice Boner Commemoration Volume,* ed. by B. Baümer, p. 113.
24. Anila Verghese, op. cit., p. 106.
25. Ibid.
26. A.L. Dallapiccola, 'Sculpture', in A.L. Dallapiccola, J. M. Fritz, G. Michell, and S. Rajasekhara, op. cit., p. 129.
27. N.K. Basu, 'The Spring Festival in India', in *Man in India,* VII, p. 145.
28. S.S. Mehta, 'Holika Celebrations', in *Journal of the Anthropological Society of Bombay,* X, p. 31.
29. N. K. Basu, loc. cit.
30. Anila Verghese, op. cit., p. 52, no 31 and p. 106.
31. A.L. Dallapiccola, 'Sculpture', in A.L. Dallapiccola, J. M. Fritz, G. Michell, and S. Rajasekhara, op. cit., p. 85.
32. NS1/1.

CHAPTER 5

Shaiva Images

Hampi was traditionally associated with Shiva long before the founding of the Vijayanagara empire. The Virupaksha temple was and remains the principal temple at the site. The Vijayanagara rulers placed themselves under the protection of Virupaksha and adopted the motto 'Shri Virupaksha' as their sign-manual. The numerous Shaiva shrines and temples, especially in the vicinity of the Virupaksha temple and on Hemakuta hill, many of them dating back to pre-Vijayanagara and early-Vijayanagara times, highlight the importance of the site as a Shaiva-kshetra.

Yet, surprisingly, when compared to Vaishnava themes found at this site, Shaiva sculptures are far fewer in number and in variety. This can be attributed to the fact that these Shaiva structures are mainly of the pre- and early-Vijayanagara periods, when temples were rather small, with minimal decorative elements. It was only in the sixteenth century when temples were developed into large religious complexes that they were elaborately sculpted. With the shift in court patronage during the first half of the sixteenth century, Vaishnavism surpassed Shaivism in importance at the site. The only dated sixteenth-century Shaiva structures of significance are the additions to the great Virupaksha temple and the construction of the Mudu Viranna (now locally known as the Uddhana Virabhadra) temple in 1545.

Alongside the fairly limited range of Shaiva sculptural subjects, is the predominance of a few and specific Shaiva iconic themes. Thus, on the one hand, forms of Shiva such as Lingodhbava, Nataraja, Gangadhara, Chandrashekhara, Somaskanda, Vishnuanugrahamurti, Ravanaugrahamurti, Dakshinamurti, Gajantakamurti, and Tripurantaka are either found occasionally or not all in the sculptural repertoire of the Vijayanagara period. On the other hand, the linga continued to be widely represented, although with little variation in its depiction. In addition to the linga, the most frequently sculpted Shaiva deities were Bhairava and Virabhadra, both destructive aspects of Shiva, as well as Ganesha and Nandi.

A. Lingas

Numerous lingas are found at the site. There are lingas in the round on the yoni-pitha, the mulamurtis in extant and a few deserted Shaiva shrines. There are also small lingas cut into sheet rock, reliefs of lingas carved on boulders, wall surfaces and gateways, and small examples on temple pillars.

Lingas in the round (Plates 19-21)

There is nothing exceptional about lingas in the round. They are of the ordinary, simple variety set in yoni-pithas. There are no examples of mukha-linga or sahasra-linga.

In the Virupaksha temple, besides the Virupaksha linga in the sanctuary, there are a few more lingas in the sub-shrines. Other lingas are found in the Mula-Virupaksha temple and the Gayatri-pitha, both on Hemakuta hill, in the Mudu Viranna temple and in a number of shrines.[1] As many of these are still in worship, it is impossible to determine if they are of the Vijayanagara period. There are also a number of lingas in the Archaeological Museum at Kamalapuram.

Only three lingas are of any artistic significance. The first stands about 3 m high in a small shrine next to the colossal Lakshmi-Narasimha monolith.[2] The base of this linga is now permanently under water due to a rise in the local water-table. The second example is in the Archaeological Museum collection.[3] It is a pancha-linga, with five small lingas set in the circle on the yoni-pitha. On the side of the pitha is a relief of Hanuman seated in yoga-mudra. The third and most interesting example is the 'sarvanga-linga', in the antechamber of the Mudu Viranna temple. It is a triangular prism of black basalt, about 60 cm. in height, excluding the pedestal, each face having a width of 40 cm. All three faces terminate smoothly into a convex top which is covered by 36 bubble-shaped protuberances. Each of the three faces displays three diagrammatic carvings, thus totalling nine diagrams. A linga on a pedestal is the feature common to all nine diagrams, but the circumscribing frame designs vary. It is argued that this prismatic linga is an iconic representation of the Virashaiva philosophical concept known as shatsthala-siddhanta.[4] Whether this linga is of the Vijayanagara period cannot definitively be determined. It has been tentatively ascribed to the latter half of the sixteenth century or later.[5] An unusual carving depicting a linga superimposed by another linga is found on the shaft of the dipa-stambha placed in front of the Uddhana Virabhadra temple. This very rare image has been recently discussed by C.T.M. Kotraiah in an article in *Vijayanagara: Progress of Research 1988-91.*

Monolithic lingas (Plates 22, 23)

Lingas cut into the rock surface occur frequently, especially along the south bank of the Tungabhadra river. Others are in the groups of three, four or more, forming a mandala. Often reliefs of Nandi or even of prostrating devotees are carved nearby.

At the Chakra-tirtha, the most holy bathing ghat at the site, there is a linga encircled by twelve pairs of footprints carved in low relief. Another linga nearby is flanked by two shallow reliefs, each showing a prostrating couple.

West of the Malyavanta Raghunatha temple complex is a deep rock crevice which serves as a natural cistern. On both sides are lingas set in small square depressions with channels leading into the crevice. Adjacent to the row of lingas is a row of Nandis carved in relief. There are 20 lingas on the south side, nine on the north and two on the east.

The most interesting examples of this variety of lingas are two clusters at the holy Koti-tirtha on the south bank of the river, about halfway between the Virupaksha and Vithala temples. One cluster comprises a large linga surrounded by innumerable smaller ones forming a square, the other a large linga and 108 smaller ones.[6]

Reliefs of lingas (Figures 4-8)

Lingas carved in relief occur frequently. Some are accompanied by reliefs of Nandi, devotees or of other Shaiva deities.[7] They are engraved occasionally on the walls of structures, including gateways, but more commonly on boulders.

The linga in relief, with sun and moon above on either side, is also carved on top of many inscriptions, and on many boundary stones. Such demarcation stone-slabs are referred to in epigraphs as 'linga-mudre kallu'. The linga, together with Nandi, the sun and crescent moon, can be seen on most of the sati- and hero-stones.

The linga is the most widely represented theme on Shaiva temple pillars. It even occurs in a number of Vaishnava temples at Vijayanagara.

There are carvings of the linga by itself, the linga set under a tree, the linga being worshipped by human devotees, and the linga venerated by animals. Some of these representations refer to stories drawn from the sthalapuranas of famous Shaiva temples. Among these pillar reliefs are a few rare examples of mukha-lingas, for example in the Kannappa relief in the maharanga-mandapa of the Virupaksha temple.

Thus the relief of Devi embracing the linga illustrates the popular story from Kanchipuram: the goddess Kamakshi fashioned a sand linga and protected it from the floods sent by Shiva to test her devotion, by embracing it. In doing so she left the imprint of her breasts and bracelets on it.

The occasional relief of a boy or a man enfolding the linga with his arms could be a representation of the story of the blind Shamanidhi from the *Sri Pampa Mahatme*, the local sthalapurana. Shamanidhi always carried a personal linga. One day he stumbled and fell into the Tungabhadra and was swept away by the current. Although he managed to save himself, his personal linga was lost. The pious Shamanidhi refused to eat without first worshipping his linga. Seeing him waste away, a young hermit took pity on him and gave him a mango claiming that it was the lost linga. As the weak Shamanidhi began to perform the prescribed rituals, the mango fell from his palm and stuck to the ground in the form of a large immovable linga. The young devotee refused to depart from the spot without his linga. He clung to it, meditated and fasted for a whole month. Pleased with his devotion, Shiva appeared to Shamanidhi and blessed him with the gift of sight.[8]

Animal devotees worshipping the linga are the cow pouring its own milk over one or licking it with its tongue, the elephant washing a linga with water brought in its trunk, the snake protecting it from the elements with its hood, and the lizard. The story of the cow devotee is associated with a number of Shaiva sites, particularly the Mallikarjuna temple at Srisailam.[9] The occurrence of a lizard devotee near the linga is rather unusual. It could refer to a lesser known episode from a sthalapurana of some southern temple. The tradition from Kalahasti recounts the story of spider, snake and elephant, worshipping Shiva in the best way they could: the spider by spinning a web above the linga, the snake by spreading its hood over it and the elephant by bathing it with water.[10] A similar story of a spider and an elephant worshipping the linga is linked with the Jambukeshvara temple near Srirangam.[11] The spider devotee does not appear among the Hampi sculptures.

B. Aspects of Shiva

Standing forms (Plate 24)

These are extremely rare at the site. There is only one such image of any significance. It is in the larger shrine set among the rock at Koti-tirtha on the south bank, on the rock wall alongside the approach to the actual temple. It is a fairly fine relief of Shiva as Chandrashekhara. The god stands in *samabhanga.* He holds an axe and an antelope in the back right and left hands respectively. The front right is in abhaya-mudra; the left hand hangs down. Chandrashekhara is flanked by two diminutive female attendants, each holding a lotus. The sun and crescent moon appear on either side of Chandra-shekhara's head. The figure is framed in a makara-torana culminating in a kirti-mukha. This image has all the attributes of Chandra-shekhara, even though the moon is not actually visible on his mukuta.

Pillar reliefs of standing Shiva are also infrequent. The only temple with a few standing Shiva pillar reliefs is the Harihara temple.[12] On one pillar there are a number of Shaiva figures, including three images of Shiva standing. In the first, Shiva is shown with four arms standing in samabhanga. In the upper hands he holds the trishula and damaru while the lower hands are in abhaya- and varada-mudras. The second carving shows the god in a similar pose: in the upper right and left hands he holds an ankusha and an antelope. The lower hands carry indistinct objects. The third image shows the four-armed Shiva holding a trishula diagonally across his shoulder. The remaining attributes are not clear.

Seated forms (Figure 9, Plate 40)

Sculptures of Shiva seated alone occur rarely. There are two carved on boulders. The first example is a small relief of the four-armed Shiva, who is seated cross-legged.[13] His hair is tied in a big turban-like topknot. He holds the trishula and the damaru in the upper right and left hands respectively. The attributes in his lower hands are not distinguishable. The second example, a very interesting and well-executed relief, is found among a group of sculptures carved on three boulders.[14] Shiva is seated cross-legged wearing elaborate jewellery including sarpa-kundalas. His hair flows in luxurious jatas; over his head is a serpent hood. The expression on the deity's face is benign and meditative. He holds the trishula and the damaru in his upper hands, the akshamala and bowl in the lower.

A fine sculpture in the Archaeological Museum depicts Shiva seated cross-legged with his hair arranged in the jatabhara fashion.[15] His upper left hand holds the crescent moon, his upper right the tail of a large snake whose multi-hooded head appears below him. In the lower right and left hands he carries the akshamala and a small linga.

Pillar reliefs of Shiva seated by himself are very uncommon. The best of these is to be found in the maharangamandapa of the Virupaksha temple. The seated Shiva has four hands; the ankusha and antelope are held in the upper ones, the lower ones are in abhaya- and varada-mudras.

Dakshinamurti (Figure 9)

Dakshinamurti at Vijayanagara appears in the yoga and vinadhara forms. An exceptionally fine relief of Yoga Dakshinamurti is found in the larger shrine among the rocks at Koti-tirtha. Here Shiva is depicted as the supreme teacher. He is seated on a hillock, under a tree with his left leg crossed over his right leg which rests on the prostrate form of Apasmara. A yogapatta is worn around the knees. Shiva holds an akshamala in the lower right hand which is in chin-mudra, a snake is in the upper right hand, fire in the upper left and the lower left rests on the knee. Shiva wears a short dhoti, bracelets, armlets, shoulder ornaments, anklets, sarpa- and chakra-kundalas, and a decorative band on the forehead. His hair is arranged in exuberant jatas. The goddess Ganga appears in his locks. Crouching Nandi is shown below Shiva. Dakshinamurti is flanked by a rishi standing with hands folded in anjali-mudra. On the tree behind Shiva are depicted two monkeys and a bird.

Another carving representing Dakshinamurti is in the Archaeological Museum.[16] As in the example discussed above, this too holds the snake and fire in the upper hands. The lower pair is broken.

A pillar relief of Dakshinamurti is found in a temple within the Royal Centre in the north-east valley.[17] Two images are also found in the Virupaksha temple complex.

While there are no large carvings depicting Vinadhara-Dakshinamurti, some pillar reliefs show this theme, one of which is in the Prasanna Virupaksha temple, now locally known as the Underground temple. In these, Shiva is represented playing the vina with two hands, while in the remaining two he holds the fire and the snake or akshamala.

Forms with Devi

Uma-Maheshvaramurti rarely appears at this site. In the Tarakeshvarasvami shrine, within the Virupaksha temple, there is a fine Uma-Maheshvara statue. On stylistic grounds, however, it is clear that this piece predates the Vijayanagara period, and there is no other stone statue of it at the site. There are, however, two pillar reliefs depicting this theme: one in the Virupaksha temple complex, the other in an early-Vijayanagara Shaiva temple on the Tungabhadra.[18] A unique representation of this form of Shiva is on the lintel of the door of a small Shaiva temple to the east of the Ramachandra temple complex.[19]

The depiction of Shiva and Parvati standing together is also uncommon. In the Virupaksha temple, some crude stucco images of this theme appear to be of the post-Vijayanagara period. Similarly, among the paintings on the ceiling of the maharangamandapa, probably datable in the post-Vijayanagara period, there is a fine representation of Uma-Maheshvaramurti.[20] In the Harihara temple is a pillar relief with Shiva and Parvati standing together.

For an account of the reliefs showing Shiva and Parvati seated on Nandi see below.

Riding forms (Plate 26)

Shiva is often depicted either riding on Nandi or standing leaning on the animal—these images are called Vrishabharudha and Vrishavahana forms. Only one pillar relief in the Virupaksha complex depicts Shiva leaning on Nandi. Similarly, as with Uma-Maheshvaramurti, there are some post-Vijayanagara stucco figures of this form of Shiva.

In the few surviving representations of Shiva seated on Nandi, the god is accompanied by his consort. On a rock on the ridge north of the Royal Centre is a small carving of Shiva and Parvati seated on Nandi, together with a male attendant, perhaps a soldier carrying a weapon, and a divine pair on horseback.[21] Shiva is depicted with two arms: in one hand he carries the trishula while the object held in the other hand is unclear. The goddess carries a lotus in one hand.

The Archaeological Museum possesses a hero-stone depicting a hero fighting an elephant. He receives blessings from Shiva and Parvati on Nandi.[22]

Another interesting representation of Vrishabharudha is carved on the exterior wall, north side, of the Virupaksha temple vimana. One panel shows Shiva and Parvati on Nandi and a man with a bow standing with his hands in anjali-mudra facing the divine couple. Shiva has only two hands. One holds a weapon which looks like a staff or a sword; the other is raised in benediction. Devi holds the usual lotus in one hand: possibly a rendering of the scene from the Kiratarjuniya, in which Shiva bestows on Arjuna the Pashupata weapon. The latter had performed severe penances to secure this weapon from Shiva. To test the hero, Shiva appeared in the guise of a forest hunter and provoked a quarrel over a prey that both claimed to have killed. Failing to vanquish his adversary in combat, Arjuna recognized him as Shiva and offered him his adoration. Shiva then assumed his divine form, blessed Arjuna and bestowed the Pashupata weapon upon him. This panel perhaps represents Shiva revealing his divine nature and blessing Arjuna. There is also a pillar relief of the same scene in a four-pillared structure within the outer courtyard of the Virupaksha temple.

Dancing forms (Figure 10)

In Vijayanagara sculpture, no independent sculptures or large reliefs of dancing Shiva exist. Only three pillar reliefs appear to depict the dancing form.

Within the Virupaksha temple complex, in the multi-pillared hall in the south-west corner of the outer courtyard, is one of the two reliefs showing Shiva as Nataraja, so popular throughout southern India.[23] In this dance pose, Shiva has the front left hand thrown across the body in the gaja-hasta-mudra, the back left hand carried the fire, the front right hand is in abhaya-mudra, while the back right hand carries the damaru. The right leg is slightly bent and is placed on the back of the Apasmara. The left leg is lifted up and held across the body. Nataraja is framed within a prabhavali. The other column relief of Nataraja is found on a pillar in the mandapa of the mid-fifteenth-century temple of Saumya-Someshvara on the south bank of the river, east of Talarighat.

In the sixteenth-century Tiruvengalanatha temple complex, an interesting relief of Shiva in the urdhvatandava pose occurs on a pillar in the hall in the north-west corner of the outer courtyard.[24] The dancing Shiva is shown with six arms. His right leg is lifted above his head, while his slightly bent left leg rests on the ground. In the top right and left hands Shiva holds the damaru and touches the raised foot respectively. In the middle right and left hands he carries a kapala turned downwards, and a trishula. In the lowest pair of hands he is holding and playing on a drum. A dog accompanies the dancing Shiva. The story of Shiva performing the urdhva-tandava originates at Chidambaram.

Bhikshatanamurti (Figure 11)

Vijayanagara has some pillar reliefs of Bhikshatana shown nude, his expression pleasant and gracious. He carries a long trishula placed diagonally across his shoulders; in another hand he holds a damaru. Bhikshatana is often accompanied by a gana, who carries a bowl on his head, and by an antelope.

Kalyanasundaramurti

The core of the *Sri Pampa Mahatme* focuses on the story of the austerities performed by Devi, locally known as Pampa, to win the favour of Virupaksha. The main festivals at the Virupaksha temple are the celebrations of the betrothal and marriage of the god and the goddess.

In spite of the great importance of the marriage myth, not a single stone sculpture or pillar relief of Kalyanasundaramurti is to be found at the site. However, a depiction of the marriage scene is among the post-Vijayanagara paintings on the ceiling of the maharanga-mandapa of the Virupaksha temple. In the same temple complex there is an elaborate stucco representation of the marriage scene, but this work is also post-Vijayanagara in date. In spite of the local myth, this was not a significant theme in Vijayanagara stone sculpture.

Samharamurtis (Figure 12)

Shiva is often depicted in sculpture and painting in his fearsome manifestation as destroyer of evil forces. At Vijayanagara the Samharamurtis are few.

One Sangama narrative relief of Shiva's victory over Yama is inserted into a buttress on the outer wall of the east gopura of the Virupaksha temple.

The episode unfolds from right to left. First comes Yama, who has thrown his noose around the young Markandeya, and his attendant. The centre of the panel is occupied by Markandeya embracing the linga in a Shiva shrine, praying to Shiva to save him from the clutches of death. To the left stands multi-armed and majestic Shiva, piercing Yama with his trident and placing his foot on the prostrated god. Yama surrenders, his hands joined in anjali-mudra.

In the pillared hall in the outer courtyard of the same complex is a single relief of Shiva piercing Yama with his trident.[25] The Harihara temple has one pillar with many Shaiva reliefs. On two facets of this pillar are seen a man praying before a linga, and Shiva emerging from it and blessing his devotee: these possibly depict the story of Markandeya.

Shiva as Gajantakamurti is traditionally presented as dancing on the head of the vanquished elephant-demon whose skin he holds up as a backdrop. There is a fine relief of Gajantaka on the exterior south wall of the central vimana of the early-Vijayanagara, triple-shrine Gayatri-pitha on Hemakuta hill.[26] Here the four-armed Shiva is prancing on the head of his defeated foe. With his hands Shiva spreads out the skin of Gajasura. Shiva has flowing jatas and his third eye is prominently rendered.

One relief of Gajantakamurti appears in the Virupaksha temple complex on a pillar along the inner courtyard's cloister.[27]

Shiva as Tripurantaka and Kamantaka does not feature in the sculptures at the site. There are, however, superb post-Vijayanagara pictorial renderings of these episodes on the ceiling of the maharangamandapa of the Virupaksha temple.

Composite forms (Figure 13, Plate 25)

We might expect that Harihara would be a favoured theme with Vijayanagara artists, since this deity was widely worshipped in the Deccan; moreover, two Vijayanagara kings bore this name. Yet, in the entire site there are only two reliefs of Harihara.

On a rock in the Royal Centre is a sculpture of Harihara.[28] He stands in samabhanga, wearing an elegant kirita. His left side is Vishnu and his right Shiva. Harihara has four hands. The upper and lower left hands hold the Vaishnava emblems, chakra and shankha respectively. In the upper hand he holds the trishula and lower right hand is shown in abhaya-mudra. This carving is framed by a relief shrine surmounted by a triangular canopy.

The second relief of this composite deity is found in the pillared hall in the northwest corner of the outer courtyard of the Tiruvengalanatha temple.[29] Harihara is depicted in samabhanga. As usual, the right half is Shiva and the left Vishnu. A line runs down the middle as if to stress this division. The right side of the head has the jatamukuta and the left, the kiritamukuta. Harihara holds the antelope and shankha in the upper right and left hands, the lower hands being in abhaya- and varada-mudra respectively.

It should be noted that in general the sculptural representations of Shiva in those iconographic forms popular in south India (standing, seated or dancing forms, Shiva with his consort, Shiva in his benign and destructive manifestations and in the composite aspects) are scarce at Vijayanagara.

Folk forms

Mailara or Khandoba is a Shaiva folk deity worshipped in Karnataka, Maharashtra and parts of Andhra Pradesh.[30] A late fourteenth-century inscription[31] and an early fifteenth-century inscription[32] at Vijayanagara refer to Mailara-deva and Mailara-shankara respectively; hence Mailara must have a god who was worshipped at Vijayanagara. On the north ridge is a rock carving of a male and female deity on horseback, along with Shiva and Parvati on Nandi.[33] The god on the horse holds a sword or staff in his right hand and a trishula in the left. Between the two groups of deities is a male attendant or soldier. There is also slab with a relief of a god and goddess on horseback.[34] They hold the traditional attributes of Mailara such as the sword, trishula, damaru and kapala. In the Archaeological Museum are two slabs on which are carved a male and a female deity on a horse. In one of these the god carries a sword and the goddess a lotus.[35] All these figures on horseback are divinities and not human beings, as they wear the crown, and carry attributes, and in the first sculpture an umbrella is held over them. Moreover, though there are Vijayanagara sculptures of men riding on horseback, there is none of a man and a woman riding together. In addition to Mailara, other deities who may be represented on horseback are Kubera, the god of wealth, and Revanta, the son of Surya. However, we believe that these sculptures at the site are of Mailara and not of either of the two other divinities. This is because of the presence of the consort. Sculptures of Mailara elsewhere show the god riding on a horse with his wife Mhalsa seated behind him, and they are accompanied by a soldier.[36] In all these depictions the god is shown holding one or more of the attributes of Mailara. In the first sculpture, the deities on the bull, Shiva and Parvati, and those on the horse form a group. There is no connection between Revanta or Kubera and Shiva, while Mailara is a Shaiva deity. Furthermore, in one of the slabs in the Archaeological Museum the divinities appear to be blessing a hero who fights an elephant; a linga is carved above the group.[37] Yet another slab similar to this one exists in which Shiva and Parvati bless a hero attacking an elephant.[38] Thus the Shaiva nature of the male god on horseback is clear: it is Mailara. In all these sculptures but one, Mailara is two-armed.

C. Destructive Manifestations of Shiva

Bhairava (Plate 67)

Bhairava is one of the most frequently sculpted Shaiva forms at Vijayanagara as he was the favourite deity of the Kapalikas and the Kalamukhas. The latter Shaiva sect had a large following in the Deccan in the pre-Vijayanagara and early-Vijayanagara periods. Gradually, the Kalamukhas were absorbed into reforming Virashaiva sect and Bhairava's popularity continued with the Virashaivas.[39]

Bhairava is nude: He wears a garland of skulls, at times he wears earrings and armlets of snakes and a serpent wound around his head. His dishevelled hair forms a large jatabhara. In Vijayanagara sculpture, the usual attributes held by Bhairava are the trishula and the damaru in the two upper hands, and the khadga and the kapala in the lower hands. At times a severed head, supposedly the fifth head of Brahma cut off by Shiva, is attached to the hand holding the kapala. Bhairava often wears very distinctive high sandals.

The dog, considered an unclean animal, is the vahana of this gruesome deity, thus emphasizing his unorthodox character. In Vijayanagara sculptures, Bhairava is usually accompanied by the dog, shown either behind him or his side, or leaping up to lick the blood that drips from the severed head of Brahma. Bhairava is also flanked by a snake. To further stress the terrifying nature of this deity a scorpion is sometimes carved either below or beside the Bhairava image.

There are a number of very fine Bhairava sculptures at the site, some in the round, others in relief on slabs or on boulders. In addition there are pillar reliefs and other small reliefs of this god.

Four-armed standing Bhairava:[40] (Figures 14-16, Plates 29-31) In this image the god holds the damaru and trishula in his upper hands. These are held interchangeably and the khadga and kapala in the lower. The khadga is held upright. In some rare example the khadga is held downwards, touching the ground.[41] These are the four usual attributes but there are some uncommon Bhairava figures with different weapons. In the Archaeological Museum there is a Bhairava sculpture in which the god is depicted in samabhanga with the dog behind him.[42] Bhairava holds the damaru, pasha, trishula and kapala in the upper right, upper left, lower right and lower left hands respectively.

One of the finest Bhairava reliefs among this four-armed standing variety is found on the north ridge in a small rock shelter formed by an overhanging rock.[43] Bhairava stands in dvibhanga within a makara-torana. He wears elaborate jewellery. To his left is a dog that licks the blood dripping from the severed head; to his right is a small snake. On either side of this group is a large scorpion and a seven-hooded serpent.

Two-armed standing Bhairava: There are two such reliefs. One is in a small shrine, within the Royal Centre, built against a rock on which there is a relief of Bhairava in pratyalidha with outstretched arms.[44] In the right hand he carries a trishula and in the left a kapala. The other example, in the Archaeological Museum, is of two-armed Bhairava in a makara-torana,[45] holding the same two attributes as the former image.

Seated Bhairava: (Figure 17, Plate 32) These images are four-armed and the ayudhas held in the their hands are the same as those already described. The best example of this variety is on a boulder near Malyavanta hill.[46] Bhairava is seated cross-legged within an arch. His countenance is fierce; he has a moustache. He wears a yajnopavita of skulls. He wears also necklaces, an udarabandha, bracelets and round earrings. A scorpion is depicted below him.[47]

Bhairava with consort: Bhairavi has the same attributes as her husband. In the Royal Centre is a well executed relief of the god and goddess both seated cross-legged.[48] Bhairava has a prominent vertical third eye and a moustache; his countenance is fierce. He holds the damaru and trishula in the upper hands and the khadga and kapala in the lower ones. Bhairava is adorned with snakes: earrings, necklace, armlets, bracelets and waistband. Bhairavi is also bejewelled. She wears a mukuta and holds the same weapons as Bhairava, and is draped in a sari from the waist downwards. To the right of Bhairavi is a female attendant waving a scarf. On the north ridge is an unfinished sculpture of standing Bhairava and Bhairavi.[49] Among a group of Shaiva sculptures carved on four boulders on the north ridge are two reliefs showing Bhairava and Bhairavi seated.[50]

In addition to these sculptures, there are a number of pillar reliefs, mainly in Shaiva temples. The one Vaishnava monument of importance having some fine Bhairava reliefs is the Ramachandra temple, where he is depicted seven times. The finest of these is the carving on an engaged pillar in the east gateway. Besides the pillar reliefs, he appears as a guardian deity on one of the door-jambs of the entrance to the sanctuary in a small Shaiva temple in the Royal Centre.[51]

Virabhadra (Figure A)

Virabhadra was a very popular deity in Vijayanagara, particularly among the Virashaivas.[52] This explains the numerous Virabhadra sculptures at the site.[53]

Virabhadra's usual weapons are arrow and bow, sword and shield. He often has a third eye on the forehead. He wears a kirita, on which a linga is carved at times. This is evidently on account of Virashaiva influence. Virabhadra is heavily bejewelled with earrings, necklaces, armlets, bracelets and anklets. In some cases he wears a yajnopavita and a waistband, with a dagger tied to the waist. The diminutive figure of Daksha with a ram's head is present at the side of Virabhadra, usually to the right; his hands are joined in anjali-mudra. Some of the Virabhadra sculptures are framed by a makara-torana culminating in a kirti-mukha.

Virabhadra images are carved in the round as well as in shallow relief of varying size. The latter are found on boulders or slabs. A number of pillar reliefs and a few stucco figures depict this deity.

General type:[54] (Plate 33) Sculptures of this category are found frequently all over the city. Virabhadra is usually standing in tribhanga. He has four hands holds the arrow in the upper right, the bow in the upper left, the sword in the lower right and the shield, usually resting on the ground, in the lower left. One of the most interesting examples of this type is the 3.6 m high image in the Mudu Viranna temple. Another fine example is found on the wall of the passageway to the larger shrine among the rocks at Koti-tirtha. To Virabhadra's right are Daksha as well as Bhadrakali who carries the same weapons as the god, with Nandi crouching to his left. In the Archaeological Museum are some large and well-executed sculptures in the round of this type of Virabhadra. One of the these in nearly 2 m high. Virabhadra stands under a makara-torana wearing all the usual ornaments.[55]

Virabhadra holding the shield at shoulder level: There is only one sculpture of this type. It is carved on the rock face of a natural water cistern on the north ridge.[56] Virabhadra stands in samabhanga with the usual attributes. The only difference is that the shield is held at shoulder level.

Virabhadra in movement: In these sculptures Virabhadra is in the pratyalidha.[57] There are five examples of this type, in three of which he is shown pulling out the arrow from the quiver tied to his back.

Virabhadra kneeling: The only example is in a shrine to the east of Matanga hill where the deity is shown kneeling with the usual attributes.[58] The shield is held at waist level.

Virabhadra with two hands: In such sculptures, of which there are four in the Archaeological Museum, Virabhadra holds only the sword and the shield.[59] In some examples the shield is held at the waist or at shoulder level, while in the others it is held down with the left hand resting on it.

Virabhadra with multiple hands: This unique type is in the Archaeological Museum.[60] Virabhadra has ten hands; besides the usual weapons he also holds the ankusha, trishula, damaru, dagger and pasha.

Besides the Virabhadra pillar reliefs at Hampi, some interesting carvings are found at the Jambukeshvara temple on Jambunatha hill south-east of Hospet. Among the many pillar reliefs of Virabhadra here are the unusual ones of the god in sitting posture and of him with numerous arms.

D. Ganesha (Figure 18, Plates 34, 35, 67)

Ganesha is one of the most popular Shaiva deities at the site. His statues and reliefs are found in temples and shrines, also carved on boulders and rocks or placed near strategic places such as the intersection of roads, gateways, ferry landings, wells and cisterns.[61]

The typical Vijayanagara icon shows Ganesha seated with one leg folded and resting flat on the seat, the other bent at the knee with the foot placed on the seat. The pot belly also rests on the seat. Ganesha is four-armed. He usually holds the ankusha and pasha in the upper right and left hands, the danta and a laddu or modaka in the lower right and left hands respectively. The tip of Ganesha's trunk is always shown nuzzling the laddu. Occasionally in place of the ankusha the deity holds a parashu. In a few rare examples, the ankusha takes the place of the pasha in the left upper hand. There are a few pillar reliefs of dancing Ganesha in which the snake replaces the pasha. Ganesha generally wears the karanda-mukuta and much jewellery. The mouse, the vahana of the deity, is at times carved on the base of the image.

One image of Ganesha is different to this type. This is a broken schist statue located near a Shaiva shrine.[62] Here Ganesha is six-armed and holds a Devi by his side. The stone used and the style of the sculpture indicate that it is probably pre-Vijayanagara. Another damaged image of Shakti-Ganesha is available in the Archaeological Museum.[63] It is difficult to determine whether or not it is of the Vijayanagara period. Thus there are no clearly identifiable Vijayanagara period sculptures of Ganesha with consort, and none that is not four-armed.

One of the finest Ganeshas among the Vijayanagara sculptures, is the 2.4 m high monolithic statue in the round, in a small pillared pavilion on the southern slope of Hemakuta hill, popularly known as the Sasivekalu or 'mustard-seed' Ganesha.[64] It is very well executed. Ganesha wears intricately carved amulets, bracelets, anklets, rings, necklaces, shoulder ornaments, yajnopavita and udarabandha. A snake is tied like a belt around his full belly. The trunk and lower left hand of the statue are broken. A damaged sculpture of a mouse faces the god.

Not far from this sculpture is the largest Ganesha image at the site, a 4.5 m high mutilated Ganesha in a temple locally called Kadalekalu—the 'gram' Ganesha.[65] He carries all the traditional attributes and wears the usual jewellery items. Though its size makes it more imposing then the Sasivekalu Ganesha, the sculpture is not as well executed as its smaller neighbour.

There are also reliefs of Ganesha, either alone or with other deities, on boulders, walls and gateways.[66] Ganesha even appears on the lintels of some Shaiva temples.[67]

Although no sculptures or large reliefs of the standing or dancing Ganesha are extant at Vijayanagara, these varieties are frequent on pillar reliefs in addition to the usual images of Ganesha seated. So great was the popularity of this deity that his images occur not only in Shaiva temples, but also in all major Vaishnava ones.

Pillar reliefs depicting the standing god differ little from those showing him seated. The dancing form shows him balancing on one leg while the other leg is uplifted. Some of the best examples are in the Ramachandra temple. In a pillar relief in the south porch, the dancing Ganesha holds the parashu and snake in the upper hands, the usual attributes in the lower hands. In the east porch is another dancing Ganesha holding the snake instead of the pasha. In an early-Vijayanagara triple-shrine Shaiva temple, on Hemakuta hill, a relief of the dancing Ganesha is found on the south end of the lintel over the door leading from the verandah into the mandapa.[68] On the north end of the slab is a dancing Devi and in the centre is an unusual form of Gajalakshmi, with a full-blown lotus replacing the figure of the goddess.

E. Karttikeya (Figure 19)

This god appears to have had little following at Vijayanagara. There is no evidence of any independent Karttikeya temple, and images of this god are not particularly common.

Among the sculptures of Karttikeya extant at the site there are two at the Archaeological Museum,[69] and a beautiful statue which was discovered during the excavations of the Archaeological Survey of India in the 1980s in a small Shiva temple within the Royal Centre.[70] There are three statues of this deity in the Virupaksha complex and a few reliefs carved on rocks or on stone slabs, either alone or with other deities.[71] One of the sub-shrines, south of the main temple, in the Krishna complex has a number of stucco figures, now damaged, on its superstructure, showing this deity riding on a peacock.

A study of the statues and reliefs reveals that Karttikeya at Vijayanagara is almost always shown seated on his bird vahana; sometimes the peacock has a snake in its beak. These riding forms of the god can be classified into three groups. The first and common form depicts Karttikeya with one head and four arms. The second variety is the god with three heads and either six or twelve arms. Only three of the six heads are shown, three being supposedly at the back. The third form is Karttikeya with five heads and twelve arms. In this case also, the sixth head, not visible in the sculpture, is meant to be either at the top or at the rear of the others. Many of these examples are not of a high quality, and the weapons held by the god cannot be differentiated.

In the relief showing the five-headed, twelve-armed Karttikeya, found among the sculptures on three boulders on the north ridge, the following attributes can be identified: sword, arrow, spear, damaru, trishula, noose, bow and shield. The remaining two hands are in the abhaya- and varada-mudras.[72] This sculpture is aesthetically of a poor quality.

A fine example of twelve-armed Karttikeya is in the Shri Kumarasvami shrine within the Virupaksha complex. Stylistically it appears to be of the Vijayanagara period, but cannot be definitively identified as such. In this sculpture Karttikeya is seated in lalitasana on a peacock with a snake in its beak. The sculpture is enclosed within a makara-torana. Karttikeya has five visible heads and twelve arms. In his right are (from top to bottom): ankusha, parashu, sword, arrow, tanka and abhaya-mudra. In the left hands are: lotus, trident, shield, bow, thunderbolt and varada-mudra. The deity wears a kirita-mukuta, shoulder ornaments, bracelets, chhannavira, udarabandha, waistband, and anklets.

Apart from the riding forms, the god is also depicted seated or standing, with or without his vahana. The only seated image of Karttikeya at the site is a small four-armed sculpture in a niche on the south side of the rangamandapa of the Virupaksha temple. The deity is seated in lalitasana. In his upper hands he holds what appear to be the tanka and the kukkuta. The lower hands are in abhaya- and varada-mudras. This may or may not be a Vijayanagara period image. No sculptures or large reliefs of the standing Karttikeya have been discovered at the site.

Pillar reliefs of Karttikeya are found occasionally in Shaiva temples. In the Vaishnava temples, however, these are not common except in the Ramachandra temple. In these examples the god is sometimes depicted standing together with the peacock, but generally he is shown seated on the bird. Reliefs of Karttikeya are found on two gopuras. On the outer east gopura of the Virupaksha temple complex there is a fairly large Sangama relief, of the four-armed god seated on his vahana, carved on a block inserted on the west wall of the granite base. On the east gopura of the Krishna temple complex, on the east side of the granite base, is another relief of this divinity. Here too, he is seated on his peacock. He holds the vajra and tanka in the two upper hands, while the lower ones are in abhaya- and varada-mudras.

F. Nandi (Plates 36-39)

Only the zoomorphic form of Nandi is found in Vijayanagara period sculpture. Nandi was an extremely popular minor divinity and there are innumerable depictions of him in stone sculpture, relief and stucco-work.[73] Generally Nandi is depicted in sculptures as a crouching bull, although on rare occasions he is shown standing. A number of Nandi statues are found all over the site and also in the Archaeological Museum.[74] Among these, the only one that is different is a triple-headed Nandi located in the outer courtyard of the Virupaksha temple, inside the east gopura. It is difficult to determine whether or not this is a Vijayanagara-period sculpture. Nandi is also found sculpted on the pitha of the main image in a few Shaiva shrines[75] and there is a rare example on the lintel of a door to a Shaiva temple.[76] Stucco figures of Nandi occur on the superstructure of certain small monuments,[77] as well as in the Virupaksha complex; the latter, however, may belong to the post-Vijayanagara period. Reliefs of Nandi facing a linga or accompanying Shaiva deities are found frequently on boulders, gateway walls, etc.[78] Pillar reliefs of Nandi are common not only in Shaiva but also some Vaishnava temples.

G. Shaiva Attendants and Devotees

Chandikeshvara (Figure 20)

In the Virupaksha temple complex there is a tiny Chandikeshvara shrine north of the principal vimana. Inside is a small stone statue of Chandikeshvara seated in lalitasana with the axe in his right hand. On account of the poor condition of the image it is difficult to ascertain its date.

Two damaged reliefs appear to represent Chandikeshvara. In both he is seated in lalitasana and holds an axe in his right hand. One relief is on the north wall of the larger shrine among the rocks at Koti-tirtha; the second is in a dilapidated mandapa.[79]

Vyaghrapada and Patanjali (Figures 21, 22)

Vyaghrapada is frequently represented at Vijayanagara, mainly on temple pillars. He generally holds a bell in one hand and an arati-dish in the other. He is sometimes seen worshipping the linga and often shown bearded and wearing a mukuta. Apart from pillar reliefs, the figure of this saint is found on the south side outer wall of an early-Vijayanagara temple on Hemakuta hill,[80] and again near the entrance to the larger shrine among the rocks at Koti-tirtha.

Patanjali appears rarely in Vijayanagara sculpture. There are only two reliefs, the first on the exterior south wall of the Virupaksha temple vimana, the second on a pillar in the hundred-pillared hall in the Vithala temple complex.[81]

Bhringi

The three-legged skeletal Bhringi does not appear in Vijayanagara sculpture, except in two reliefs on column blocks in the Ramachandra temple. Here Bhringi, seated with a drum, is shown to the right of Bhairava.

Shaiva dvarapalas (Figure 23)

The Shaiva door-keepers feature in all Shiva temples of the Vijayanagara period, primarily in relief on door-jambs, although there are also a few statues in the round, as for instance those at the east entrance of the rangamandapa of the Virupaksha shrine.

The dvarapalas are invariably four-armed. In the upper hands they hold the trishula and damaru. The lower hand nearest the door is placed on the gada resting on the ground, while the other is generally held in abhaya-mudra. The representation of the Shaiva dvarapalas came to be standardized in the Vijayanagara period. The only exception to this standardized type are the dvarapalas on the south side door into an early-Vijayanagara temple on Hemakuta.[82] Here, one dvarapala holds a trishula and snake and the other a gada and damaru. These are unique at the site.

Animal devotees (Figures 5-8)

Apart from Nandi other animals are also associated with Shiva. These include the cow, elephant, snake and lizard already mentioned in the section on the linga. Generally these animals occur together with the linga only on pillar reliefs. The one exception is a large carving on the south wall of the double shrine temple on Hemakuta hill in which two elephants are performing the linga-abhisheka.[83]

Shiva is Nageshvara, serpents adorn his person. The only independent carving of Shiva's snake devotee is found in the Harihara temple, on the eastern flank of Hemakuta hill, where on one wall of the mandapa are Hanuman and Nandi and on the other Garuda and a large coiled snake. Animal devotees connected with both Shiva and Vishnu find their place here.

NOTES

1. E.g. NLm/2, NLc/3, NQq/1, NQg/1.
2. NLm/2,
3. No. 527.
4. C.T.M. Kotraiah, 'A Cave Linga at Hampi', in *Journal of the Andhra Historical Research Society*, 32, pp. 121-5.
5. Ibid., p. 125.
6. Noteworthy examples of lingas cut in the basal rock: NDy/8; NFr/1; west of NGh/1 a few lingas in a cluster of 3 and 5 lingas; two groups of lingas of Koti-tirtha (NGm and n); NGn/5; a few small lingas at Sita-kunda (NGo/2); at Chakra-tirtha (NGr)—four small lingas, one with a circle of footprints around it; another with a couple prostrating on either side of it; near NLb/17—three separate lingas; north-east of NLb/21—a group of five lingas and another of three; NMg/4—a linga in a cave on Matanga hill; near NMz/2; NNv/2; NTc/1; in the colonnade around NTd/4; NTd/7—lingas and Nandis on either side of the crevice on Malyavanta hill; NUh/1; NYf/1 near NYf/2.
7. Noteworthy reliefs depicting lingas: on the exterior south wall of temple NFw/5 on Hemakuta hill—two reliefs: one of Vyaghrapada and one of a man both worshipping a linga; NFw/5—on the south wall of the north side mandapa of this double-shrine temple is a large relief; two elephants performing linga abhisheka; NLh/5—rock carving: a linga, Nandi and a male devotee; NMm/1—relief of a linga and Nandi flanked by Virabhadra and Ganesha with a male devotee below; NM/2—rock carvings of a linga, flanked by Ganesha and Virabhadra; in front of NQj/2 relief on a boulder of a linga and standing Nandi. On another boulder is a rough outline of a linga and Nandi; NRj/2, the sanctum of this shrine abuts a rock on which are carved a linga and two nagas; NSa/3—a linga and Nandi are carved on the south wall of the cistern; near NSo/1—reliefs of a linga, sun and moon on a boulder; NTk/3—relief of a linga and Nandi; east of NTk/3—a boulder on which are carved a linga and Nandi; west of NTk/4—carving of miniature linga and Nandi; near NTk/5—a broken stone on which are carved a linga an Nandi; on the wall of NVo—relief of a linga, Nandi and a male devotee; on the wall of NYx—relief of a linga, Nandi and male devotee
8. *Sri Pampa Mahatme*, First Part, chapter 66.
9. M. Rama Rao, *The Temples of Srisailam*, p. 7.
10. N. Ramesan, *Temples and Legends of Andhra Pradesh*, pp. 74-5.
11. T.A. Gopinatha Rao, *Elements of Hindu Iconography*, Vol, 2, Pt. II, pp. 407-8.
12. NLc/3.
13. NMr/5.
14. NMx/2.
15. No. 1102.
16. No. 339.
17. NSl/2
18. NGt/3.
19. NRy/1.
20. For a discussion of the date of the Virupaksha temple paintings, see A.L. Dallapiccola 'Ceiling paintings in the Virupaksha temple, Hampi' *South Asian Studies 13*, 1997.
21. Near temple NNx/5.
22. No. 278.
23. Nataraja: In the Virupaksha temple, carving in the hundred-pillar hall in the south-west corner of the outer courtyard: first pillar from the east, first detached pillar from the south, north face, middle square.
24. Urdhvatandava: In the Tiruvengalanatha temple, carving in the pillared hall in the north-west corner of the outer courtyard: slightly raised section of the hall, second pillar from the north, sixth from the east, east face, middle square.
25. Yamantakamurti (Kalarimurti): In the Virupaksha temple, carving in the hundred-pillar hall in the south-west corner of the outer courtyard: seventh pillar from the east, fourth from the south, south face, middle square.
26. NLb/1.
27. Gajantakamurti: In the Virupaksha temple, carving in the inner courtyard cloister, first pillar on the south side, south face, middle square.
28. NQu/4.
29. Harihara: In the Tiruvengalanatha temple, carving in the pillared hall in the north-west corner of the outer courtyard: slightly raised section of the hall, fifth pillar from the east, second from the north, north face, lower square.
30. G.H. Khare, *Mahārāshtrācī cār daivete*, summary in English.
31. *Vijayanagara: Progress of Research 1983-84*, no. 105, pp. 49-50.
32. *South Indian Inscriptions*, Vol. IX, Pt. II, no. 436.
33. Near NNx/5.
34. NTp/1.
35. No. 124.
36. G.H. Khare, op. cit., p. 159.
37. No. 834.

38. No. 278.
39. Anila Verghese, *Religious Traditions at Vijayanagara: as Revealed Through its Monuments*, p. 22.
40. Noteworthy images of four-armed standing Bhairava sculptures: In the north gopura of the Virupaksha temple and just outside it (NFw/1); near NGm/1; NGm/2; at Chakra-tirtha (NGr); in front of NGs/3; NLh/6; in the courtyard of NLw/3; NMm/3; NMr/3; NMx/2—among the Shaiva and Shakta sculptures on three boulders; NMz/2; NNv/1; north of NSz/1; NUg/1; on NVk; Archaeological Museum: Nos. 83, 217, 244, 305, 668, 676, 706, 748, 754, 1623, 1698, 2221, 2146.
41. E.g. No. 518, Archaeological Museum.
42. No. 671.
43. NMz/2.
44. NRh/2.
45. No. 347.
46. NUf/6.
47. For another example of seated Bhairava: Archaeological Museum, No. 7142.
48. NQo/2.
49. NMy/2.
50. NSu/6.
51. NRx/1
52. Anila Verghese, op. cit., pp. 23-4.
53. Balasubramanya, 'Vīrabhada Sculptures in Hampi', in *Vijayanagara Progress of Research 1983-84*, pp. 133-5.
54. Noteworthy images of Virabhadra of the general type: On a slab built into gate NFw/8 on Hemakuta hill; NGm/2; NGn/5; NLh/5; two in the Virabhadra temple (NMg/1) on top of Matanga hill; NMs/2; NQd/2; NQj/4, NQu/1; NSs/1; NXk/1; Archaeological Museum: e.g. Nos. 261, 419, 509, 1614, 02114.
55. No. 631.
56. NSa/3.
57. Noteworthy images of Virabhadra in movement: NMy/3; NTk/3; NTz/4 (in these examples Virabhadra is taking an arrow out of the quiver); NNv/4; NPs/1.
58. In NNa/1.
59. Nos. 87, 684, 749, 750
60. No. 0628.
61. Noteworthy examples of Ganesha statues, carvings on slabs, murtis in temples: NDu/1; shrine at NFv/1; a number in the Virupaksha temple complex (NFw/1)—some of which may be post-Vijayanagara; Ngw/2; NLw/3; NNm/2; NPx/1; NRd/1; NRg/3; NXh; shrine in NXo; near NYf/2; NYm/3; Archaeological Museum: e.g. Nos. 209, 233, 380, 405, 484, 624, 646, 667, 697, 702, 723, 725, 1000, 1005, 1062, 1100, 1721, 1722, 1731.
62. NVj/1
63. No. 179.
64. NLg/2.
65. NLc/2.
66. Reliefs of Ganesha on boulders, etc., either alone or with other deities: NDy/8; two near NGm/1; NGn/5; below NGy/1; near NLh/4; two at NMh/2; NMm/1; NMs/2; NMx/2; NMy/3; near NNh/1; NNt/4; NNz/1; NQd/1; NQj/3; NQq/2; near NRb; NRh/3; NRo/1; on the wall of cistern NSa/3; NSg; near NWb/1; near gate NYe; NYm/3; NYx.
67. Examples of Ganesha images on the lintels of temple doors: NFw/5; NMd/1; NNx/3; NNy/3.
68. NFw/6.
69. No. 4 and No. 1738.
70. NRp/2.
71. Noteworthy Karttikeya sculptures: Three statues in the Virupaksha temple complex (NFw/1)—it is not clear whether or not these belong to the Vijayanagara period; near NGm/1—in a panel along with Parvati and Ganesha; NGn/5—in a relief along with the linga and other Shaiva deities; NMx/2 among the Shaiva and Shakta reliefs; NMy/3—on a panel carved on a low slab, on which feature also Ganesha, Mahishasuramardini and Bhairava.
72. *Vijayanagara: Progress of Research 1983-84*, p. 136.
73. For a discussion of the Nandi cult, see A. Verghese, op. cit., pp. 29-30.
74. Some monolithic Nandi images: NDy/8; Near NFr/1—about three statues; In the Virupaksha temple there are a number of Nandi statues, some of the these, however, may be post-Vijayanagara; in NFw/5; in NFw/6; in NGm/1; in NJx/1; in NJx/2; in NJx/3; near NLb/20; in NLc/3; in NLh/7; in NLw/3; in NMb/1—this is the large Nandi monolith at the end of the Virupaksha car-street; in NMf/3; in NMg/1; in NMg/4; in NMh/3; in NMj/1; in NMs/1; in NNc/1; in NNh/1; in NNn/1; in NNr/1; Near NNy/2; in NOc/1; in NPo/1; in NPr/2; NPs/1; outside NQs/2; in NQy/1; in NSz/2; in NTc/1; near NUs/1.
75. E.g. NNx/3.
76. NMs/1.
77. E.g. NGp/1, NLb/2, and NMa/1.
78. Some reliefs of Nandi: Near NFr/1—a large relief on a rock in the river; in NGm/2—in a relief along with Virabhadra, Bhadrakali and Daksha; on the inner south wall of the mandapa of temple NLc/3; NLh/5; near entrance of NMg/4; NMm/1; in NMs/2; in NQj/2; NQq/2; at NSa/3; on the wall of the gate NSg; NTd/7; near NTk/3; to the east of NTk/3; NTk/4; NTk/5; on the wall of the gate NVk; on the wall of gate NVo; on the wall of gate NVx.
79. NMs/2.
80. NFw/5.
81. Vithala temple, hundred-pillar hall: raised middle section, third pillar from north, second from east, north face, middle square.
82. NFw/5.
83. NFw/5.

CHAPTER 6

Vaishnava Images

In number, variety and quality, Vaishnava sculptures comprise the most outstanding group of Vijayanagara stone sculptures. There are statues in the round, large reliefs, narrative sculptures, pillar reliefs and other small carvings. Some of the largest and best sculptures in the city illustrate Vaishnava themes. Although the site was originally a Shaiva kshetra, it also has pre-Vijayanagara links with Vishnu, especially with his avatara as Rama. As already noted in Chapter 4 certain episodes of the *Ramayana* are believed to have taken place in and around Hampi. Yet the Vaishnava association with the city only gained significance in the Vijayanagara period. In the fourteenth and early-fifteenth centuries, Shaivism was the dominant sect in the capital, but by the end of the fifteenth and the early-sixteenth centuries, Vaishnavism had usurped this position. In this phase, temple building was undertaken on a massive and elaborately decorative scale, accounting for the larger number of Vaishnava than Shaiva sculptures. With the exception of the Ramachandra temple, which dates back to the early fifteenth century, the other great Vaishnava temples (Vithala, Malyavanta Raghunatha, Krishna, Tiruvengalanatha, Pattabhirama and Anantashayana near Hospet) were entirely or mostly built during the sixteenth century.

The two important Vaishnava sects at Vijayanagara were Shri-Vaishnavism and Madhvaism. Both had their impact on Vijayanagara sculpture, in which there appear certain variations or new forms: the Madanagopala image, Krishna within a prabhavali, the four-armed Rama icon, Rama seated like a king, and Sthauna-Narasimha reliefs resembling the Shaiva Lingodbhavamurti.

Standing, seated and recumbent images of Vishnu as the primordial being are comparatively rare in the city. There are two groups of the Chaturvimshatimurtis, but few of these twenty-four appear individually. The dashavataras are very popular and appear as a group or individually. Some incarnations were greatly favoured and are frequently represented, especially Narasimha, Rama and Krishna. Aspects of Vishnu related to local legends and special places in peninsular India are common, such as Venkateshvara of Tirumalai, Ranganatha of Srirangam, Vithala of Pandharpur and, to a lesser extent, Varadaraja of Kanchipuram. Minor aspects of Vishnu, such as Mohini, occur occasionally. Vishnu's attendants are prominent, especially Garuda and Hanuman, who are the most popular of all. Adishesha, the Vaishnava dvarapalas, Vishvaksena and Vishnu's personified chakra, Sudarshana, also appear. The two main emblems of Vishnu, chakra and shankha, gain in importance during this period and are separately carved. The namam appears in art during Vijayanagara times.

A. Vishnu as Primordial Being

Standing images (Plate 41)

Sthanaka images of Vishnu include pillar reliefs of the deity in samabhanga, with the chakra and shankha in the upper right and left hands, and the lower right and left in abhaya- and varada-mudras, respectively. In the Archaeological Museum is a sculpture of the standing Vishnu of the bhoga variety.[1] The deity stands erect in samabhanga, flanked by his two consorts. The upper hands hold the chakra and shankha, and the lower right the gada, while the lower left, which is in the blessing mudra, also carries an akshamala.

The most significant standing image of Vishnu is a relief on a slab that once served as an image for worship, now kept in the west-facing shrine within the Lokapavana tank-complex to the rear of the Virupaksha temple. The god is in the unusual form of ashtabhuja. Two hands are broken, but the others hold the chakra and shankha, bow and arrow, sword and shield. A diminutive devi is carved to the right. Vishnu wears necklaces, earrings, kirita-mukuta, tulsi-mala, shoulder ornaments, girdle and bracelets as well as an elaborately draped dhoti. He stands under an arch culminating in a kirti-mukha. The many arms of the figure and the variety of weapons held indicate that his may be an image of Vishnu in the Vishvarupa form. However, he has only one face and not four as is usual in Vishvarupa images.

Seated images (Plate 40)

Among the asana forms, there is on the south-west pillar in the rangamandapa of the Ramachandra temple a rare pillar relief of Adi-murti. Here Vishnu is seated on the coils of Adishesha, the serpent's hoods overshadowing his head. Vishnu holds the chakra and the shankha in his upper hands, while the lower ones rest down. He is flanked by his two consorts, who are also seated, encased by a finely carved arch. There are also a number of pillar reliefs of Vishnu seated in lalitasana, with chakra and shankha in his upper hands and the lower ones in abhaya- and varada-mudras. Apart from these column reliefs, seated images of this deity are rare. There is one example among the group of Shaiva and Shakta sculptures on three boulders on the north ridge, with one panel of five figures: standing rishi, seated rishi, Matsyendranatha, seated Shiva, and seated Vishnu. The last is in padmasana, the upper hands with chakra and shankha and the lower in abhaya- and varada-mudras. Vishnu wears a kirita-mukuta and makara-kundalas. In the Archaeological Museum there is a sculpture of Vishnu in lalitasana with the upper hands holding chakra and shankha, the lower right in abhaya-mudra, and the left with gada.[2]

Reclining images (Figure 46, Plates 57, 58)

The images of the reclining form of Vishnu with or without consorts, mainly of the yoga and vira varieties, will be discussed in detail below.

Vishnu with consort (Figure 24)

In the Lakshmi-Narayana icon the god is normally seated in lalitasana his right leg hanging down. He has four arms and carries a shankha and chakra in his upper hands, while the lower right is in abhaya-mudra and the lower left encircles the goddess' waist. The goddess, generally seated on the left knee of Vishnu, has a flower in her left hand and embraces Vishnu with her right. Besides the pillar reliefs of Lakshmi-Narayana, only one sculpture of this aspect remains at the site, now in the Archaeological Museum: it is about one metre in height and is well carved and decorated.[3]

Vishnu on Garuda

Vishnu is also depicted riding on Garuda, sometimes but not always in the narrative reliefs of the Varadaraja episode. In the minor shrine of the Ramachandra temple there is a pillar relief of the ashtabhuja Vishnu seated on Garuda, holding the sword, mace, arrow and varada in his right hands, and the bow, shield, discus and conch in the left.

B. Special Forms of Vishnu

Chaturvimshatimurtis (Plate 42)

The Chaturvimshatimurtis were not greatly favoured by the Vijayanagara sculptors. Only two sets of the entire group are to be found and there are few extant examples of individual icons. There is clear evidence of only one temple dedicated to one of the Chaturvimshatimurtis, the Madhava shrine (now called the Ranga temple) east of the Ramachandra temple complex.[4]

In the city the entire group of Chaturvimshatimurtis is sculpted twice. The first series is in the rock-shelter near Koti-tirtha, with carvings on the north, east and south boulders of this west-facing rock-cut shelter.[5] On the north is a long narrow panel depicting the incarnations of Vishnu, on the east a very long frieze of the Chaturvimshatimurtis, and on the south Vithoba, Venkateshvara and Narasimha. Each of the twenty-four forms stands in samabhanga and is labelled with an inscription in Kannada on the top, an incised kneeling Garuda is shown below.

At the beginning of the series, another Garuda turns towards the panel.[6]

The second series occurs on the four highly polished granite pillars in the rangamandapa of the Ramachandra temple. Here each of the twenty-four figures appears seated in lalitasana, carrying the four attributes and flanked by the seated consort goddesses, Shri and Bhu, under an elaborate makara-torana. The only difference between one panel and another is the manner in which the ayudhas are distributed. These reliefs are partly damaged which makes the identification of some icons difficult. The figures are generally carved on the top and middle blocks of the columns. This group of the Chaturvimshatimurtis is iconographically unusual as the figures of the god are seated together with the consort goddesses.

As already noted, statues of the individual Chaturvimshatimurtis are extremely rare at the site. In the rangamandapa of the Mukti-Narasimha temple at Anegondi[7] there are some sculptures including one of Keshava, with the shankha and chakra in the upper right and left hands and the padma and gada in the lower right and left hands respectively. This is possibly the only Vijayanagara period example here of a vyuha. In the Gulagunji Madhavasvami shrine in the Virupaksha temple complex is a pre-Vijayanagara icon that could also be of one of the twenty-four forms. There are also a few sporadic pillar reliefs,[8] but no large carvings of the Chaturvimshatimurtis.

C. Dashavataras (Plate 43)

The dashavataras as a group were a popular subject on rock surfaces, basements, pillars and beams. Both varieties of the dashavataras, the one including Buddha and the other Balarama, are to be found. The set with Buddha is more common, especially among column reliefs of the dashavataras. An interesting Vijayanagara variation is that the Buddha is generally replaced by the nude figure of Jina.

On a rectangular niche recessed into the boulder in a rock-shelter dedicated to Vaishnava deities to the north-east of the Elephant Stables, is a well carved representation of the ten incarnations.[9] The first four avataras are shown in the half-human and half-animal (therioanthropomorphic) form. While Matsya and Kurma are shown with human top, their lower half is that of the fish and a tortoise respectively. Varaha and Narasimha have a human body standing in samabhanga, but with the heads of the boar and the lion respectively. All four wear kirita-mukutas and carry chakras and shankhas in the upper hands, with the lower hands in abhaya- and varada-mudras. Vamana is shown as a standing dwarf holding a kamandalu and umbrella. Parashurama, Ramachandra, and Balarama are in samabhanga and have two hands each. Parashurama carries the parashu and bow, Rama a bow and arrow, and Balarama a hala in his right hand while the left is in varada-mudra. The ninth incarnation is of the Jina who is in the kayotsarga posture. Kalki appears in samabhanga, with the horse's head and a human body; his hands are in the same mudras and bear the same attributes as the first four figures. Krishna, surprisingly, is left out of this series, but both Balarama and the Jina are present.

In the Koti-tirtha rock-shelter are nine avataras on the north boulder and two unfinished avataras on the east boulder.[10] On the north side appear, Matsya, Kurma, Varaha and Narasimha, all in the same manner as in the above panel. Vamana, holding kamandalu and umbrella, stands in dvibhanga. Parashurama, wielding axe and bow, appears in tribhanga. Rama with bow and arrow and Balarama with hala are also in dvibhanga. Next Krishna stands in samabhanga, holding chakra and shankha in his upper hands and the lower ones in abhaya- and varada-mudras. The two unfinished forms on the east are the standing Jina and the therioanthopomorphic Kalki, both in samabhanga. In this group are both Balarama and the Jina, making a total of eleven instead of the traditional ten.

The clearest representations of the dashavataras is on the basement of the mahamandapa of the Vithala temple, in magnificently sculpted niches set into the three open sides of the plinth. Balarama is absent, while the nude Jina in kayotsarga is evident. The exquisitely carved figures are iconographically similar to those of the previous group, except that Krishna has only two hands (in one he holds a ball of butter).

A carved panel of the avataras occurs in the mahamandapa of the same temple, on a recessed beam above the pillars in the central open part of the hall. Only the first five avataras are now visible, the remainder are covered by a modern conservation masonry prop.

Pillar reliefs of the dashavatara group[11] occur in many of the principal Vaishnava temples in the city, the Ramachandra, Vithala, Krishna and Pattabhirama. They also occur in the Harihara temple, in a Vaishnava temple along the chariot street of Vithala temple,[12] and the mandapa at the end of this street.[13]

In all except one dashavatara pillar reliefs at Vijayanagara, Matsya and Kurma appear in the four-armed therioanthropomorphic form. However, in one group on the Ramachandra temple, on the two pillars flanking the entrance to the first antarala, they take the zoomorphic form. The Buddha appears once in the group in the Vaishnava temple along the Vithala chariot street, and the Jina in the Harihara temple group. Balarama is also present in the former.

Vamana, Parashurama, Rama and Balarama, appear in the standard manner, two-armed, standing, holding their respective attributes, but Varaha, Narasimha, Krishna and Kalki are seen in various poses. Varaha is always in the therioanthropomorphic form, but may be standing, seated in lalitasana or accompanied by his consort Bhu in the Bhu-Varaha image. Narasimha is carved standing, seated in lalitasana, or with his consort Lakshmi, or in yogic pose. Krishna is seen dancing, seated holding a pot, carrying a ball of butter, or as Kaliyamardana. Kalki is shown both in his therioanthropomorphic manifestation and in the form of a rider on a horse. In the former he is standing or seated. As a man on horseback, he is shown either two-armed or four-armed.

Individual sculptures of each of the major avataras are also to be found, some being highly popular, others much less so or not at all. Narasimha, Rama and Krishna appear more frequently in Vijayanagara sculpture than any other form of Vishnu himself. Because of the special relevance of the cults of Narasimha, Rama and Krishna, these aspects are treated separately below.

Matsya (Figure 25)

The image of Matsya, as already noted, may be that of an ordinary fish, or a half-man and a half-fish with four arms. The upper (human) half is decorated with ornaments usually worn by Vishnu, including the kirita-mukuta. At the site there are innumerable pillar reliefs of Matsya, both in the zoomorphic as well as in the therioanthropomorphic form. The latter, besides featuring in the dashavatara series, also appears individually on column reliefs, but nowhere else.[14]

Kurma (Figure 26)

Like Matsyavatara, Kurma too is seen in both zoomorphic and therioanthropomorphic forms. In the latter case, the lower part is that of tortoise, while the four-armed upper part of the deity is arranged similarly to that of the half-human, half-fish Matsya. In both his forms, Kurma occurs frequently on Vijayanagara temple pillars. Independent reliefs of the zoomorphic Kurma are not common, though occasionally they are seen on the walls of shrines, for example on the exterior south wall of the verandah of the Mukti-Narasimha temple at Anegondi and on the inner wall of the mandapa of a Ranganatha temple.[15] A few independent stone and stucco sculptures of therioanthropomorphic Kurma have been found. There is a fine rock-carving of Kurma, flanked by the adoring Hanuman and Garuda, in front of a shrine in the western end of the Royal Centre.[16] There is also a sculpture in the mandapa of the Mukti-Narasimha temple. Stucco images of this avatara are among those on the brick and mortar superstructures of the east and north gopuras of the Vithala temple.

Varaha (Figure 27, Plate 44)

At Vijayanagara there are a few pillar reliefs and other small carvings of the boar by itself, but it is not clear whether or not these represent Vishnu's avatara. Varaha in therioanthropomorphic form is found only in the dashavatara groups.

Besides the occasional pillar reliefs, there is one fine Varaha statue, a little under one metre in height, made of schist, now in the Archaeological Museum.[17] This piece was brought in from the great sixteenth-century temple of Anantashayana. The lord is seated cross-legged on a pedestal. With four hands, he holds in the upper hands the chakra and shankha (now damaged); the lower hands are in abhaya- and varada-mudras respectively. The top part of the statue, including the kirita, is mutilated. The ornaments consist of a pearl necklace, chhannavira, udarabandha, armlets, wristlets and anklets. The deity is seated erect, the boar head facing straight ahead. The details of the snout and tusks are clearly visible. Two locks of hair are shown behind the ears. On the shoulders he wears a skandhamala of pearls.

This sculpture is carved in schist, whose texture is finer than the rough textured granite generally used by Vijayanagara sculptors, thereby providing greater scope for the stone carver's ability and craftsmanship. Yet the mass of stone between the hands and the body has not been completely removed, as is the case even in granite statues. It is the only Varaha image almost in the round at the site.[18]

Vamana (Figures 29, 30, Plate 43)

In this avatara, Vishnu is depicted as Vamana and also as Trivikrama. Reliefs of the former, apart from the dashavatara group sculptures, are infrequent. Vamana is portrayed as a small youth, carrying a kamandalu and parasol. He wears a loincloth and his hair is twisted into a knot.

Trivikrama is shown with four or more arms, his left leg raised as if pacing with one step the distance from earth to heaven. There are a few pillar reliefs of Trivikrama. One is of the four-armed god on a pillar in the outer mandapa of the Ramachandra temple. At his feet is seen king Bali with hands folded respectfully. There is an extremely fine example on a composite pillar facing the north side open space in the mahamandapa of the Vithala temple. A pillar relief in the mandapa at the end of the Vithala chariot street presents a ten-armed Trivikrama with cosmic water pouring down onto his raised foot.[19]

There are few narrative reliefs of the Vamana-Trivikrama story. The finest is found on a pillar in the south side of the Vithala mahamandapa. The reliefs appear on top of the pillar, on four facets below the capital. On the east side is seated Bali with Vamana before him as a suppliant; the gods appear in the clouds above. On the north side is Bali pouring a libation of water into Vamana's hand as proof of the gift made to him. In the third panel, also on the north side, is ten-armed Trivikrama with the left leg raised to the sky. Above his foot the triple-headed Brahma appears. Trivikrama holds two indistinct objects, the chakra and shankha, arrow and bow, sword and round shield, and has hands in abhaya- and varada-mudras. In the fourth panel, on the south side, is eight-armed Trivikrama with his foot pressing Bali down to patala; the god has in his hands chakra and shankha, bow and arrow, sword and shield, abhaya- and varada-mudras.

In the rock-shelter north-east of the Elephant Stables,[20] apart from the dashavatara frieze, the Narasimha story and depictions of Vaishnava saints, are also found reliefs of the Vamana legend: Vamana before Bali, Bali giving something to Vamana, and Trivikrama with raised leg.

Parashurama (Figure 31, Plate 43)

Parashurama appears only in the dashavatara group, where he is shown standing, two-armed, with a parashu in one hand and bow in the other. Parashurama also appears in the appropriate place in the *Ramayana* narratives, where he meets Ramachandra, is forced to acknowledge the latter's superiority, and retires after handing him Vishnu's bow.

Balarama (Plate 43)

Balarama is sometimes included among the ten principal avataras and is depicted in some of the dashavatara groups. Apart from these there are only a handful of pillar reliefs of this god. He can be identified by the hala that he carries. In the Ramachandra temple there are two column reliefs of Balarama. In one he appears alone, in the other he is accompanied by his consort Revati.

Buddha (Figures 34, 111)

There is only one independent relief of Buddha and possibly another of a Jina: both are on the exterior wall of the vimana of the Ramachandra temple. Buddha is seated in padmasana, hands in dhyana-mudra, wearing an ushnisha and prominent Vaishnava tilaka on his forehead. The Jina is depicted like Buddha, except that he had no ushnisha and no tilaka.

Kalki (Figure 35, Plate 43)

Kalki is usually found only in the dashavatara series; however, there are a few pillar reliefs. In therioanthropomorphic form he has a horse's head and a human body and is shown with four arms. When depicted as a four-armed rider on a horse, he carries the chakra and shankha in his upper hands, the sword and shield in his lower hands. He is shown as a rider without attributes in the dashavatara group sculpted on the two engaged pillars flanking the entrance to the outer antechamber of the Ramachandra temple.

D. Narasimha (Plates 43, 45, 46)

Narasimha is depicted in a variety of forms, Kevala, Sthauna and Ugra, and with his consort. The most common form of the solitary Narasimha image is of Yoga-Narasimha seated in utkutikasana or yogasana, with the yogapatta around his knees. This image may have either two or four arms, in the latter case the upper right and left hands carry the chakra and shankha respectively, while the lower hands generally rest on the knees. In Sthauna-Narasimha images the god emerges from the pillar to fight the demon Hiranyakashipu, while Ugra-Narasimha is in the terrifying act of killing the demon. In Lakshmi-Narasimha images the deity is accompanied by his consort: he is usually seated in lalitasana, the right led hanging down and the left on the seat, holding chakra and shankha in the upper hands, with the lower right in abhaya-mudra and the lower left around the waist of the Devi, seated on his left knee.

Narasimha is probably the earliest Vaishnava deity to be formally worshipped in Vijayanagara city, having been a favoured deity in southern India including Hampi well before the founding of the Vijayanagara empire. The cult continued to be popular and to enjoy much patronage throughout the empire.[21] Both Madhvas and Shri-Vaishnavas have a great reverence for Narasimha, and the rulers of the Saluva and the Tuluva dynasties were deeply devoted to the man-lion incarnation. They lavishly patronised the centres of Narasimha worship in the empire, especially the Narasimha temple at Ahobalam in present-day Andhra Pradesh.

There are a large number of Narasimha sculptures at the capital, some of superb quality. These include narrative reliefs, large sculptures, smaller statues, rock carvings, stucco figures and innumerable pillar reliefs.

The coalescing of two streams of religious traditions is reflected in the Narasimha sculptures at Vijayanagara: the 'greater' tradition of canonical Hinduism with its source in the Puranas and other Sanskrit texts, and the 'lesser' tradition of folk and tribal religion whose origins lay in the exuberant religiosity of the masses who worshipped a lion divinity, gradually identified as Narasimha, the man-lion.[22]

Canonical forms of Narasimha (Figures 28, 36)

There are some excellent narrative reliefs of the Puranic stories of Narasimha. The best are carved in the minor shrine of the Ramachandra temple: four panels on the west wall of the mandapa, one on the side wall of the entrance into the outer antechamber, and one on the north exterior wall of the structure. The story unfolds as follows. The seated Hiranyakashipu orders an attendant to kill Prahlada and a mounted elephant is sent to kill the boy, but the beast, though prodded by a standing man, refuses to harm Vishnu's devotee. Hiranyakashipu in rage taunts his son and kicks the pillar from which the awesome, multi-armed Narasimha emerges. Narasimha grabs Hiranyakashipu who is attempting to flee; the eight-armed man-lion god kills the demon lying on his lap. Finally, on the exterior wall, Lakshmi-Narasimha seated in divine splendour appear with Prahlada in adoration before them.

In the rock-shelter north-east of the Elephant Stables,[23] the narrative of Prahlada immediately follows the dashavatara reliefs. First, the diminutive Prahlada is seen standing with his hands in anjali-mudra. In front of him is a circular pillar, split open, from which issues Narasimha. He has four hands, in two of which he holds a shankha and a chakra, while with the other two he catches the demon and delivers him a blow. Hiranyakashipu is shown kicking the pillar with his left leg, while holding a sword in his right hand and a curved, rectangular shield in the left. The fight then gains momentum; Hiranyakashipu retreats, but Narasimha grabs him by the hair and the waist, the chakra and shankha are visible in the two other hands of the god. The demon, in panic, hits at the left thigh of Narasimha with a short sword held in his right hand while still holding the shield in his left. The final scene is of Ugra-Narasimha, seated in lalitasana with the demon king lying on his lap. The god has eight hands, with two he rips the demon open and removes his intestines. The top two hands are lifted above the head as though Narasimha is garlanding himself with the intestines of his adversary. The last two hands hold the chakra and shankha. Throughout the narrative is expressive, showing power, movement and ferociousness.[24]

In the Madhava temple,[25] on a recessed slab above the pillars of a small mandapa in front of the sub-shrine, is a panel with carvings of Sthauna-Narasimha, Ugra-Narasimha and Lakshmi-Narasimha. Elsewhere two or more scenes of the story are found together. Thus in the Royal Centre there are some reliefs on a boulder, including two extremely fine examples of Ugra-Narasimha and Yoga-Narasimha.[26] On the south boulder in the rock-shelter at Koti-tirtha,[27] standing Narasimha is shown with a nine-hooded serpent head over him; to his left is his consort; then is the ferocious Ugra-Narasimha and Prahlada to his right offer obeisance at the god's feet.

A number of statues of Narasimha have been found at the site. In the Mukti-Narasimha temple at Anegondi is a well-executed image of the standing four-armed Kevala-Narasimha in the rangamandapa. In the sanctuary is an image of Lakshmi-Narasimha seated on a pitha in lalitasana, with the goddess on his left knee; she holds a lotus in one hand. Narasimha carries chakra and shankha in his upper hands, his lower right is in abhaya-mudra, and the lower left is around Lakshmi: he wears a kirita-mukuta, skandhamala, chhannavira, yajnopavita, kundalas, bracelets and anklets. The goddess, too, has a kirita and other jewellery. The couple are framed by a torana surmounted by a kirti-mukha.

There are a few other statues, including a number in the Archaeological Museum, some intact, others damaged. These include two of Lakshmi-Narasimha,[28] one of Kevala-Narasimha seated cross-legged,[29] and another of Narasimha standing in samabhanga with Prahlada to one side.[30]

The best Narasimha statue and one of the finest pieces of the Vijayanagara sculptor's art is the remarkable, gigantic Lakshmi-Narasimha monolith, 6.7 m high, executed on the orders of Krishnadevaraya in 1528.[31] Despite its sadly mutilated and poorly restored condition, this monolith remains one of the most impressive sights in the city. Narasimha is under a large makara-torana that rests on two pillars. He is seated in utkutikasana on the three coils of the cosmic serpent which spreads its seven hoods over his head. The deity wears a kirita-mukuta, his forehead is adorned with the namam; armlets, anklets, a waist-band and skandhamalas decorate his body. The four hand and the legs are broken and so is the figure of Lakshmi once seated on his knee; but the pieces found in the debris near and around the statue indicate that Narasimha had a yogapatta around his knees, and held a chakra in his upper right hand and a dhanus and bana in the upper left hand, while the lower ones were in abhaya- and varada-mudras. Iconographically, this statue is unusual. Although the *Skanda Purana* describes Lakshmi-Narasimha as holding a discus and bow,[32] this type of image in which the god has a bow and arrow in one hand is exceptional. It is possible that the sculptors of this monolith were following the *Skanda Purana*, but more likely they were influenced by the folk tradition of Narasimha as a hunter, wandering with his Chenchu consort in the Nallamalai forest. If so, there was blending of 'lesser' with 'greater' traditions in the making of this icon.

Stucco figures of Narasimha are also extant: for example, that of the seated god on the superstructure of the north gopura of the Vithala temple.

Many rock-carvings of Narasimha have been recorded at the site. Some are carved on exposed boulders, or in rock-shelters or caves; yet others are on rock against which shrines have been built. These examples vary greatly in the quality and type: Kevala-Narasimha seated or standing, Lakshmi-Narasimha and Ugra-Narasimha.[33] A very fine rock carving of Lakshmi-Narasimha at

Kòti-tirtha[34] seems to be a relief miniature of the colossal monolith dated 1528. The sanctuary of the Vaishnava temple north of the Krishna temple complex is built against a rock-carving of standing four-armed Narasimha in samabhanga, with the chakra and shankha in the upper hands, the gada in the lower left, and the lower right in abhaya-mudra.[35] This sculpture is set within an elaborate makara-torana; the god is flanked by Hanuman with a male devotee to his right, and Garuda and a female devotee to his left.

Pillar reliefs of Narasimha are found abundantly not only in Vaishnava temples, but also in many Shaiva monuments. They include four-armed standing Narasimha in samabhanga, four-armed seated Narasimha in yogasana, lalitasana or cross-legged, Lakshmi-Narasimha, two-armed seated Narasimha, Sthauna-Narasimha, and Ugra-Narasimha grabbing the demon. In some Sthauna-Narasimha reliefs, the man-lion deity emerging from the pillar is shown almost in the same manner as Shiva in the Lingodbhava episode, manifesting himself within the giant linga. An exceptional group of pillar reliefs is found in the mahamandapa of the Vithala temple, on the composite pillars facing the open space on the north side. Carved in high and medium relief, they include four-armed Sthauna-Narasimha, six-armed Ugra-Narasimha, two of Lakshmi-Narasimha (in one the god is in utkutikasana, in the other he is in almost a standing pose, embracing the goddess and with Prahlada to one side), and two-armed standing Narasimha with Garuda near his feet. In this last mentioned example, the god has no kirita or ayudhas.

Non-canonical forms of Narasimha (Figures 37-39, Plate 47)

There are narrative reliefs, statues, and numerous pillar and other small reliefs of the folk varieties of this god, but no rock-carvings.[36]

The best example of the folk variety of the Narasimha statue is now located in the Narasimhasvami shrine within the Virupaksha temple complex. The god is portrayed with a lion head and human body, squatting in maharajalilasana. There are no ayudhas in his two hands, which rest lightly on his knees. The deity wears armlets, wristlets, anklets and shoulder ornaments. The small kirita is the only indication of his divine status.

Among pillar reliefs and other small carvings, the non-canonical forms are very popular especially the scenes of Narasimha removing the thorn from the foot of Chenchu-Lakshmi and of the tribal goddess leaning on her tall bow. Representations of the former are found on temple pillars throughout the site, dating from the early Vijayanagara period to the mid-sixteenth century. They occur in Vaishnava temples and also Shaiva temples. Besides pillar reliefs, this theme is found on plinths and gopuras. For example, there is a stucco figure of this motif on the east gopura of the Vithala temple.

Other folk forms of Narasimha are two-armed standing, dancing or seated Narasimha, holding no attribute, shown with or without a kirita. There are also two-armed standing or dancing figures of the man-lion holding a snake in one hand. One of the most unusual representations is a small relief on the south gopura of the Vithala temple, on the south basement east of the entrance passageway. Here Narasimha is seated in utkutikasana; he has four hands, the lower two resting against his knees, the upper two each hold a pot. Except that he is four-armed, this figure displays no distinguishing features of divinity.

E. Ramachandra (Figure 32, Plates 48, 49)

At Vijayanagara Rama is generally portrayed standing, with his body in dvibhanga or tribhanga, wearing the kirita-mukuta and other ornaments. He has two hands in which he carries a bow and an arrow. He is often accompanied by his wife Sita (who holds a lotus flower in one hand), his faithful brother Lakshmana (who resembles Rama and carries a bow, his hands are normally in anjali-mudra), and his devotee Hanuman. Rama's two other brothers, Bharata and Shatrughna, rarely appear with him except in the pattabhishekha scene where Rama and Sita are usually seated surrounded by standing figures.[37]

In Vijayanagara art there are many pillar reliefs and small carvings of Rama, who is often depicted alone, two-armed, holding a bow and arrow. The arrow may have either a pointed or a crescent-shaped tip. There are reliefs of Hanuman before Rama, who is generally seated. An unusual form of Rama, found normally only in pillar reliefs, show the god seated on a throne-like seat, leaning against a cushion or bolster, with one leg crossed over the other, with one hand in tarjani-mudra. He often has a shawl draped over one arm and is portrayed like the Vijayanagara rulers who are similarly depicted in many sculptural panels. Occasionally in such reliefs Rama is accompanied by Lakshmana or Hanuman, either in the same panel or in the adjacent one. The only distinguishing mark of divinity on Rama in these reliefs is the kirita-mukuta. This icon does not conform to the canonical rules. It is a Vijayanagara variation, in which, as noted already, a deliberate parallel seems to have been made by sculptors between the divine king Rama and the earthly ruler of the capital city.

Another innovation of the Vijayanagara period is the four-armed Rama,[38] the god holding a chakra and shankha in the two upper hands and bow and arrow in the lower ones. Such reliefs, though rare in the city, do exist. For example, there is one pillar relief in the south-east corner pavilion in the Vithala temple and another on the exterior wall of the Ramachandra temple vimana. A variant of the four-armed type is found on a pillar in the mahamandapa of the Ramanuja temple, north-east of the Vithala temple. Rama is seated with one leg crossed over the other. He holds the chakra and shankha in his upper hands, while the lower right hand is in abhaya-mudra and the lower left rests against his leg. On one side is a small figure of Bhakta-Anjaneya.

Among the larger sculptures of this god are those still worshipped in temples. These are all carved on boulders. Detached images are no longer in situ in any of the Rama temples at the site, but the presence of a Rama sculpture in the Archaeological Museum indicates that they once existed.

The sanctuary of the Malyavanta Raghunatha temple is built around a large rock almost completely incorporated into the temple, only protruding above the roof. Carved onto the rock face are the Rama-Sita-Lakshmana-Hanuman group in high relief. Rama is in the centre, seated cross-legged with his right hand in jnana-mudra, while the left hangs downwards. To Rama's right stands Lakshmana with a bow and his hands joined in adoration. Sita is seated cross-legged to Rama's left, carrying a lotus in her left hand and the right hand in varada-mudra. Above the three figures is a makara-torana. Hanuman kneels to the right of Rama.

The Kodandarama temple, on the banks of the Tungabhadra, has in its sanctuary a large, rather crudely cut relief of the standing Rama-Sita-Lakshmana group, with Sugriva in obeisance to one side. Rama, the central figure of the panel, has a naga hood over his head.

Within the Urban Core is a double-shrine temple, one sanctuary dedicated to Virabhadra and the other to Rama.[39] In the Rama temple sanctuary is a rare carving of Rama, seated in lalitasana within an arch, his left hand resting on his lap, his raised right hand broken at the tip. The chakra and shankha are carved on either side of his head. Sita is seated in lalitasana to Rama's left. She holds a lotus flower in the right hand, the left is in lolahasta. Rama and Sita are flanked by three standing males, hands in anjali-mudra; two of them also holding bows: these are Lakshmana, Bharata and Shatrughna. The presence of all four brothers reveals that this rock carving represents the pattabhisheka of Rama in Ayodhya, after his victorious return from Lanka.

In the Yantroddharaka Anjaneya temple, on the bank of the Tungabhadra, there is another relief carved on a side boulder.[40] Rama is seated in lalitasana with Sita on his left knee. His right hand is in jnana-mudra, the left embraces the goddess. They are framed within an arch. To their right is standing Lakshmana, hands joined in anjali-mudra, with a bow slung on his left shoulder and a quiver of arrows on his back.

Apart from these Rama sculptures, there are other large reliefs of Rama, some carved on rocks, others in religious structures.[41] For example, at the southern end of Hemakuta is the only Vaishnava rock-carving within the walled area of this hill.[42] Hanuman at the centre is flanked by the standing Rama-Lakshmana-Sita group to his left and a male and two female devotees to his right. In a mandapa near the river is a large, finely carved relief of the Rama-Sita-Lakshmana group.[43] Rama and Sita are seated, Lakshmana is standing; at either side are male chauri-bearers, both standing with hands joined. Near a dilapidated temple in the rocks above the Tiruvengalanatha chariot street is a magnificent relief on a boulder of the standing Rama and Lakshmana.[44] The former is in the act of shooting an arrow from his bow.

F. Krishna (Figures 33, 40-43, Plates 50, 51)

Though there was only one great temple dedicated to Krishna at Vijayanagara, namely the monument built by Krishnadevaraya in 1515 in commemoration of his conquest of Udayagiri fort from the Gajapati ruler of Orissa,[45] there are innumerable sculptures of the god, all comparatively small in size. There are no large sculptures or rock carvings of this god. The Madhvas and to a lesser degree the Shri-Vaishnavas are great adorers of Krishna and Vithala. The Madhvas worship Krishna as a child; Vithala is considered to be another form of Krishna. The centre of Madhvacharya's religion is bhakti to Krishna as taught in the *Bhagavata Purana*—Radha having no place in it.[46] As the Madhvas were an influential group in the capital city, Krishna sculptures were highly popular. It is probably due to their influence that the vast majority of Krishna sculptures at Vijayanagara depict him as a baby or as a child. Only in Venugopala sculptures, some Govardhanadhara reliefs, and one panel of Parthasarathi, does Krishna appear as an adult. As a child, Krishna is generally portrayed as nude chubby boy. His hair is either tied in a knot on top of his head or is arrayed in wild curls around his face. Sometimes he is so plump and pot-bellied that he resembles a gana. It was probably also due to Madhva influence that the stories of the *Bhagavata Purana* inspired individual reliefs as well as narrative panels.

Of all the themes found in Vijayanagara sculpture, among the most recurrent are the diverse feats of Balakrishna. The Krishna-lila scenes are found in Vaishnava and Shaiva structures alike. His sculptures appear in pre-early- and late-Vijayanagara period structures.

The Vijayanagara variations in the Krishna sculptures are: Madanagopala, eight-armed Krishna playing on the flute attracting the cows and cowherds, multi-legged Venugopala within a circle, and Krishna encased in prabhavali. The first is the most important and entered the southern sculptural repertory in Vijayanagara times.

Carvings on lintel slabs: Krishna is the only Vaishnava deity who occasionally adorns lintel slabs. The earliest example is the pre-Vijayanagara door into the cave-like sanctuary of the Gavi Ranganatha temple in Anegondi, where he appears as a dancing child; in the Krishna temple in the early-Vijayanagara style within the Urban Core, a side door is adorned with the figure of the crawling Balakrishna in the centre of its lintel.[47] In the mid-fifteenth-century temple of king Mallikarjuna's reign, set within one of the gates of the wall around the Urban Core, is a lintel figure of Damodara Krishna, holding a ball of butter in one hand.[48]

Reliefs on temple plinths: Sometimes the basements of the temples have carvings on the recessed flat mouldings and also in the kudus that decorate the top of the upana course. These plinth sculptures generally include many scenes of the child Krishna's exploits. The only representation of Krishna as Vatapatrashayi is found in a kudu in the south-eastern corner of the top moulding of the plinth of the mahamandapa of the Vithala temple. This shows baby Krishna lying on a banyan leaf on the waves of the cosmic ocean. Balakrishna is shown lying flat on his back, sucking the big toe of his left foot.

Reliefs on brindavanas: (Figure 98) Brindavanas of nine Madhva saints are seen at Nava-brindavan near Anegondi. The most imposing example is that of the great sage Vyasaraya. On each of its four faces are reliefs of Vaishnava gods, including one of Damodara Krishna flanked by a female attendant and an ascetic, and another of Vithala. On the brindavana of Raghunandana, on the south bank of the Tungabhadra, again there are four reliefs.[49] Here Krishna appears as Venugopala; Vithala is also represented.

Pillar reliefs: The figure of Krishna, in various poses and activities, was carved repeatedly on temple pillars. Some of the favourite themes are: crawling Balakrishna, who at times is seen holding a ball of butter in one hand; Navanita Krishna stealing butter, or Navanitanrittamurti dancing with joy at having secured a ball of butter to eat; Balakrishna holding his ears in penitence; the Yamalarjuna-bhanga episode (or Damodara Krishna) showing naughty Balakrishna tied with a rope to a mortar trying to pass through the Yamala and Arjuna trees, uprooting them in the process; Krishna as Kaliyamardana and Kaliya-Krishna subjugating the serpent Kaliya; Krishna as Gopikavastraharana; and Venugopala delighting the gopas, gopis and cows with his enchanting flute music. The last is shown in a unique pillar relief in the mahamandapa of the Krishna temple. Four-armed Venugopala has one torso and head with many pairs of legs, carved in a circle around his body, which perhaps is to denote movement. An exceptional relief of Kaliyamardana Krishna, dancing on the head of the serpent Kaliya, with a ball in one hand and the serpent's tail in the other, is found on a column in the south-west corner of the Vithala mahamandapa, facing outwards; the figure is carved in high relief. In addition to the above-mentioned themes which occur constantly, there are a few pillar reliefs of other stories from the *Bhagavata Purana*: Krishna lifting mount Govardhana, vanquishing the demons Putana, Bakasura and Aghasura, subduing the elephant Kuvalayapida, wrestling with Chanura and Mushtika and killing Kamsa. It may be noted that the child Krishna within the prabhavali, typical of the Nataraja image, is a Vijayanagara iconographic innovation.[50] It occurs in column reliefs.

Reliefs on walls: Krishna-lila scenes appear frequently on exterior and interior walls of shrines, on stone basements of gopuras and on enclosure walls. There are a number of reliefs on the exterior wall of the triple-shrine temple on Hemakuta hill, locally called Gayatri Pitha.[51] These include Venugopala flanked by two devis on the west wall, a relief of Balakrishna stealing curds from hanging pots on the north wall, and Balakrishna eating butter on the south wall. In the last panel, standing Yashoda is engrossed in her task of churning; the pot and the churning stick are vividly rendered. Balakrishna is seated in front of her, one hand in the pot and the other taking a pat of butter.

Krishna playing the flute appears on the exterior wall of the Ramachandra temple vimana: one carving of two-armed Venugopala, two of the four-armed variety, and one of eight-armed Madanagopala, flanked by two devis and two cows. The deity holds in his eight hands the chakra, shankha, bana and dhanus, two indistinct objects, and the flute. The graceful Madanagopala is adorned with exquisite jewellery and an elaborate dhoti. On the outer face of the enclosure wall, on the top-most frieze, are a number of Krishna-lila scenes, including Gopikavastraharana and Yamalarjuna-bhanga.

The exterior walls of the vimana and rangamandapa of the Krishna temple have many Krishna reliefs; those carved on the inner wall of the vimana can only be seen from the enclosed pradakshina. An unusual relief is that of Krishna overturning a cart to destroy the demon who had alighted on it.

Carvings on stone slabs: There are a few such sculptures of Krishna at the site and in the Archaeological Museum.[52] Several deserve special mention. In the Archaeological Museum there is carved on a stone slab, the only extant Vijayanagara depiction of Krishna as Parthasarathi.[53] Krishna is seen driving the chariot in which Arjuna stands shooting an arrow from his bow; two male attendants are behind him on the chariot. A small figure of flying Hanuman appears on top. In the same Museum is a long slab with relief carvings, in the centre of which is four-armed Venugopala with seven standing women, each holding a lotus, to his right, and Shiva and Parvati on Nandi, Brahma on his swan and standing Virabhadra on his left.[54] Another slab portrays Venugopala and seven gopis.[55]

Statues in the round: (Plate 50) The most significant Krishna statue discovered at Vijayanagara is the one unearthed from the sanctuary in the Krishna temple during clearance work in the 1910s. It is a mutilated stone image of seated Balakrishna. The deity is represented as a chubby boy sitting on a pitha with his right foot resting on a lotus flower, which serves as a footstool. The arms are broken, but the left hand evidently rested on the left thigh, for a part of the hand remains there. Krishna has a top-knot and wears the usual jewellery. This statue, including the pedestal, is about one metre in height. It is now in the Government Museum, Madras. There is some dispute as to whether or not it is a Vijayanagara sculpture. According to one authority, it was brought back as a war-trophy from Udayagiri by Krishnadevaraya.[56] However, another scholar asserts that it is Vijayanagara icon.[57]

Stucco figures: On the east gopura of the Vithala temple, there is a beautiful Gopikavastraharana scene on the east face. On the superstructure over the sanctuary of the so-called Sarasvati temple is a damaged figure of Damodara Krishna.[58] A number of stucco images have survived in the temple at the end of the Tiruvengalanatha temple chariot street.[59] On the superstructure of this temple is a Navanita Krishna, while on a recessed beam above the pillars within its mandapa are a number of Krishna-lila scenes, including one of the Gopikavastraharana episode.

G. Minor Forms of Vishnu
(Figure 44, Plates 59, 60)

In addition to the ten principal incarnations, Vishnu is also believed to have assumed a number of minor avataras. In Vijayanagara sculpture only the Mohini avatara is commonly found.

Mohini appears only on pillars, either alone or with rishis at her feet. She is represented in relief as a beautiful youthful woman with a narrow waist, full breasts and ample hips. She is nude expect for a strip of cloth loosely wrapped around her legs and thrown over one arm.

At Vijayanagara there are two pillar reliefs of Annamurti, a minor form of Vishnu, both in the Ramachandra temple. One is on the south-east corner pillar of the rangamandapa, the other on a pillar in the east porch. In both, the god appears as an elegant, youthful two-armed male figure sitting cross-legged with a halo behind his head. He wears a kirita and other ornaments. In both reliefs the pot of payasam is clearly visible in the left hand. The ball of rice is evident in one relief and partly damaged in the other.

H. Other Aspects of Vishnu

Certain manifestations of Vishnu, associated with famous pilgrimage spots outside the Vijayanagara capital, were incorporated into the religious life of the city. It seems to have been the deliberate policy of the Vijayanagara rayas to patronise all the important religious centres within their boundaries and at the same time instal these deities in newly built temples in the capital city.[60] The Vaishnava deities who were thus introduced included Vithala, Venkateshvara, Varadaraja, and Ranganatha or Anantapadmanabha.

Vithala (Figure B, Plate 55)

Vithala appears on pillar reliefs, mainly in Vaishnava temples from the fifteenth century onwards. There are no carvings of this deity in the pre- and the early-Vijayanagara monuments. There are also independent sculptures of this god.[61]

In the reliefs and sculptures in Vijayanagara Vithala is sometimes shown nude, but usually clothed. He wears typical ornaments of Vishnu like the tall cylindrical crown. He stands in samabhanga, with the feet together, arms akimbo. The Vithoba image at Pandharpur, possibly a post-Vijayanagara icon, stands on a brick, holds a shankha in his left hand and a lotus with a stalk in the right. Vithala is sometimes shown holding a conch-shell, but never a lotus, and the brick is not often shown. At times the god has one or both hands placed near the hips, in varada-mudra . He is often depicted holding by the collar a pot-shaped bag, in one hand or in both. (Vithala as Balakrishna is said to hold a bag containing round nuts used by children as marbles for playing.[62]) Vithala is usually alone, but sometimes flanked by consorts; but occasionally he is accompanied by only one consort.

One of the finest Vithala images at the site is found in a niche on the outer wall beside the small south entrance of the Ramachandra temple. He is nude, wearing the kirita-mukuta and elaborate jewellery. The conch is held in one hand, the other is in varada-mudra. In an exquisitely sculpted niche on the north face of the south gopura of the Vithala temple is another fine image of this god. Here he is in his more usual clothed form. Both hands are on the hips and in one he holds a small bag.

Venkateshvara (Figure 45)

For a number of Vijayanagara rulers, including the great Krishnadevaraya, Tiruvengalanatha of Tirumalai was their personal patron deity. The unparalleled importance of Venkateshvara from the mid-fifteenth century onwards is reflected at the capital city in the construction of temples and in the fashioning of sculptures of this god.

Venkateshvara is traditionally depicted in samabhanga with the chakra and shankha in his upper right and left hands respectively, the lower right in varada-mudra, and the lower left in katyavalambita. At Vijayanagara, Venkateshvara is occasionally shown with the lower right hand in abhaya-mudra and sometimes flanked by two consorts.

Sculptures of Venkateshvara are found on Vaishnava temple pillars from the early fifteenth century onwards but they do not occur as often as those of Krishna, the *Ramayana* and Narasimha. Venkateshvara is somewhat stiff and stylised iconographically, and does not offer as much opportunity for the sculptor's virtuosity as some other Vaishnava themes. Besides column reliefs, Venkateshvara appears in the sanctuaries of some shrines, on boulders against which structures are built, in rock-shelters, on gopuras, and on basements. There are also rock-carvings and statues of the deity.[63] Among the finest representation is one on a boulder in the Royal Centre where, alongside two reliefs of Narasimha, there is a well-executed relief of Venkateshvara with two consorts.[64] A relief of him alone appears on a rock near Chakra-tirtha.[65] None of the sculptures of this god found at the site are very large.

Varadaraja (Plate 56)

Varadaraja is seen on a rock-carving as well in reliefs occurring sporadically on temple walls, recessed beams and pillars.[66] Although the static form of this god is not common at the site, narrative reliefs of the Gajendramoksha story appear on pillars in many Vaishnava temples. In most of these instances, there are three panels: the elephant in distress, Vishnu appearing on Garuda, the god blessing the elephant. In the south pillar in the east porch of the Ramanuja temple a fourth panel of Varadaraja in samabhanga is also included.

The most vivid depiction of the Gajendramoksha story is found on three sides on the upper part of a pillar in the southern wing of the mahamandapa of the Vithala temple. On the south facet the elephant is in distress because the fierce reptile has caught its leg in its jaws. On the east facet appears Vishnu on Garuda. On the north facet we see Vishnu as Karivarada. At the god's feet is a prostrate adoring figure which is the crocodile transformed into its original form of a gandharva: the touch of Vishnu had released him from the curse that had metamorphosed him into a reptile. From the elephant emerges a human form, with two hands in anjali-mudra and carrying the chakra and shankha in two additional hands. This is the devotee of Vishnu whom a curse had transformed into an elephant, and who now reverts to his original nature. To emphasize his devotion to Vishnu, the devotee is made to carry the main emblems of his god.[67]

Ranganatha and Anantapadmanabha (Figure 46, Plates 57, 58)

Ranganatha was represented more or less the same as Anantashayana of pre-Vijayanagara days, but the style is different. Shesha's seven hoods forming a canopy over Vishnu's head are shown in profile, and the god lying on his right side on the coiled body of the snake. His head rests on his lower right palm and his left arm is stretched along his upper side. In the pre-Vijayanagara example at Anegondi, the hood-canopy of Ananta is shown frontally, the lower right of the deity is in yoga mudra and his attributes are by his side.[68] If four-armed, Ranganatha is shown holding a shankha and a chakra in his upper hands.

Unlike other popular deities, Ranganatha rarely appears on temple columns, probably because it was difficult to carve such an image in the limited space available on pillars. However, he is found on boulders, in the sanctuaries of temples, on exposed rocks, and occasionally on wall surfaces and gopuras. He is also seen once on the lintel of a temple entrance. As well as these reliefs, there are also some statues of Ranganatha.[69]

The finest carving of Ranganatha, and an outstanding example of the Vijayanagara sculptor's art is located on a natural rock by the river, at Koti-tirtha.[70] This four-armed image is of the vira variety, with the two consorts at the god's feet. He wears rich and intricately decorated jewellery and a dhoti to his ankles.

Another fine relief, also of the vira variety, is in the sanctuary of the Ranganatha temple near the Tungabhadra.[71] The fish appearing in the waters below the cosmic serpent adds a touch of naturalness to the scene.

Ranganatha images are not as numerous as those of other forms of Vishnu. Yet what is lacking in number is made up in quality; most of these sculptures are well finished, and provided with a wealth of detail.

I. Garuda and Hanuman

Garuda (Figures 48, 49, Plate 61)

In Vijayanagara sculpture Garuda is depicted as a crowned young male figure with wings and a sharp, beak-like nose. At times, the wings are only lightly carved and are barely visible.

Garuda appears in four different iconographic forms: striding, holding a snake in one hand with the other raised (strongly reminiscent of the popular Vira-Anjaneya icon); standing with hands folded in anjali-mudra (a stance inspired by the image of Bhakta-Anjaneya); kneeling or flying with hands in anjali-mudra; and carrying Vishnu.

Garuda is frequently depicted on column reliefs in all the above-mentioned poses. He is also found in the adoring and heroic postures on pithas within the sanctuaries of Vaishnava temples, flanking the entrances to Vaishnava structures, on walls and gopuras, in the vahana shrines of a few Vaishnava temples (for example in the stone chariot of the Vithala complex), and on independent stone slabs.[72] Sculpturally none of these Garuda images are of outstanding interest.

Hanuman (Figures C, 50-58, Plates 62, 63)

Sculptures of Hanuman, known popularly as Anjaneya, are ubiquitous at Vijayanagara. There are a number of reasons for this. First, as already noted in Chapter 4, Anjanadri hill on the north bank of the river is reputed to be Hanuman's birth place, and many spots in and around Hampi are associated with him. Second, Anjaneya is worshipped by votaries of Vishnu, Shiva and Shakti.[73] It is believed that he was fathered by the gods to assist Vishnu in his incarnation as Rama. Third, the Madhvas, who were influential in the city, have a particular reverence for Hanuman because they believe that he is one of the three incarnations of the wind god, Vayu (the other two being Bhima, of the *Mahabharata*, and their own great preceptor, Madhvacharya).[74] The Madhva sage Vyasaraya widely popularised Hanuman worship in the city. It is even claimed that he installed 732 Hanuman idols.[75] As the popularity of Hanuman is a particularly Vijayanagara period phenomenon,[76] there are few sculptural representations of pre- and early-Vijayanagara period in Hampi.

The earliest representations are a pillar relief on an early-Vijayanagara, double-storeyed gateway on the northern slope of Hemakuta hill,[77] and the reliefs that flank the entrances to two early Narasimha temples, one in Anegondi[78] and the other on the Tungabhadra.[79] During the fifteenth and sixteenth centuries Hanuman rose to great heights of popularity, enjoying a wide following from all sections of society as is seen in he innumerable little Hanuman shines, many still in worship, and sculptures that are found all over the site.

In addition to Hanuman images in shrines, either sculpted on slabs or on boulders against which the sanctuaries have been built, there are numerous reliefs of this god carved on boulders and rock surfaces. There are also many stone slabs, varying from about 1 m to 3.5 m in height, with reliefs of Anjaneya. Many are no longer in situ. Hanuman is also found on pillars, walls gateways, and entrances to Vaishnava temples, on sides of tanks, and rock-shelters.[80] That this god was considered a powerful protection is revealed by the location of Hanuman images at gateways and crossroads.[81] Hanuman is portrayed with a human body and monkey face and tail. He is simply clad, almost invariably without a crown, his miraculous tail being his foremost characteristic.

There are two popular iconographic forms of Hanuman. The first, in the vira posture, striding majestically in order to protect Rama, his devotees and his city from evil. Vira-Anjaneya is shown in profile, his right hand lifted, and left near his waist, often holding a stemmed lotus or an uprooted tree. The long tail rises over his head. Often a demon is shown between the striding legs of the god. The second form is that of Anjaneya as devotee, his hands joined in the adoration of Rama. Generally Bhakta-Anjaneya appears in profile, only rarely frontally. Only few of the Vira-Anjaneya and Bhakta-Anjaneya sculptures are finely sculpted.

Two exceptional reliefs of this deity are of special significance for the Madhvas. The first, in the Yantroddharaka Anjaneya temple, shows Hanuman carved on a rock. The god is seated in padmasana, wearing a kirita and other ornaments. His right hand, which is in jnana-mudra, holds a rosary, the left is in dhyana-mudra. Hanuman sits in the centre of two intersecting equilateral triangles which form a star. Around this is a circle with lotus petals, on which is string of twelve leaping monkeys, each holding the tail of the one in front. In the spaces between the circle and the star are inscribed letters in Grantha and Kannada characters, only faintly visible.[82] This relief is a yantra of great sanctity.

The second relief is on a rock facing the Brindavana of the Madhva saint Raghunanda.[83] A shrine has been built against this rock on which an unusual image of the Chaturbhuja Hanuman is carved. It shows Hanuman in striding posture with a demon beneath his feet. His two upper hands hold the chakra and shankha, the lower ones a palm-leaf book (symbol of Madhvacharya) and the gada (symbol of Bhima). Thus it is a composite image representing the three incarnations of Vayu.

As well as larger sculptures, Hanuman appears repeatedly on temple pillars. After the Vira and Bhakta forms, the other themes most favoured by temple sculptors are: Hanuman jumping through the air carrying rocks in either hand (in some rare example there are rocks even on both his feet), flying from the Himalayas bearing the Sanjivini mountain on which the miraculous healing herb grows; Hanuman before Rama, or giving Rama's signet ring to Sita, or seated on his tail before Ravana conversing as an equal with the demon king. Interesting and unusual pillar reliefs of Anjaneya show him variously: with his tail coiled around a linga tying to uproot it; leaping with a linga in each hand; posed as a seated singing devotee holding a vina and clappers; meditating in padmasana with his hands in jnana- and dhyana-mudras; jumping across the sea to Lanka; escaping from the mouth of the sea-monster Surasa. Hanuman and his varied adventures evidently offered temple sculptors much scope to exhibit their skills.

J. Vaishnava Attendants and Devotees

Adishesha

As we have already seen, Adishesha appears with Vishnu in his seated form as Adimurti, and in his reclining form as Ranganatha. In Vijayanagara sculpture he is always represented as a multi-hooded serpent. Shesha never appears on pillars or in reliefs or sculptures by himself. Besides his depictions as the couch of Vishnu, there is only one other relief at the site in which he appears. Here, on a rock-carving in the Royal Centre are reliefs of Harihara in an arch, and another of the seated Rama and Sita and standing Lakshmana.[84] Below the latter group is a rather crudely cut portrayal of the three principal attendants of Vishnu, Garuda, Hanuman and Adishesha. Shesha with his multiple hoods unfurled is in the centre, with Anjaneya and Garuda on either side, facing each other and holding onto the serpent's body. Independent chakra and shankha are carved on either side of this group.

Vishvaksena (Figure 47)

Vishvaksena, or Senai Mudaliyar, is portrayed seated in lalitasana with the right leg pendant, the left folded and resting on the seat. He holds the chakra and shankha in the upper right and left hands, while the lower left hand holds the gada, or is in varada-mudra and the lower right is in abhaya-mudra. Images of Vishvaksena can be differentiated from those of seated Vishnu by the absence of the yajnopavita and shrivatsa mark.[85]

Although Vishvaksena is not one of the minor Vaishnava divinities commonly found at Vijayanagara, several examples are known. During clearance work in the Krishna temple in the 1980s a schist statue of Vishvaksena was unearthed. There is a relief of this god on the side wall of the antechamber of the Ranganatha temple on the Tungabhadra. He appears also in a panel, along with Ramanuja and some Alvars, in a rock-shelter.[86] There are some scattered pillar reliefs of Senai Mudaliyar.[87] His statues and reliefs are fairly well executed, but are in no way exceptional.

Vaishnava dvarapalas

Vishnu's door-keepers, Jaya and Vijaya, appear in Vaishnava temples at the site throughout the period of occupation. They are invariably standing, four-armed male figures, beautifully ornamented. In the upper right and left hands they carry a chakra and a shankha respectively; in one lower hand the gada, the other in abhaya-mudra. Usually the dvarapalas are in tribhanga, with one leg crossed over the other; occasionally they are found in dvibhanga with the legs placed side by side. They appear at the bottom of the door-jambs; sometimes they are seen on pillars, always in the lowest square and generally as a pair flanking a passage. Besides these reliefs, only one pair of large dvarapala sculptures in the round is available: badly mutilated, larger than life-size Vaishnava dvarapalas are seen in the mahamandapa of Tiruvengalanatha temple.

K. Vaishnava Emblems (Figures 59-61, Plate 64)

Apart from appearing on Vishnu images, Vaishnava emblems and symbols are found by themselves in Vijayanagara sculpture. These include the Vaishnava sectarian mark, called variously urdhvapundra, tirunamam or namam, and the two most characteristic ayudhas of Vishnu, the chakra and shankha. These three emblems are found independently and also together. There are also sculptures of the personified discus of Vishnu, the Sudarshana-chakra.

The namam begins to appear in the Shri-Vaishnava temples from Vijayanagara times onwards.[88] It appears in the mid-fifteenth-century temple of king Mallikarjuna's reign,[89] and thenceforth is a common feature. It has been claimed that only the Tengalai namam occurs in Hampi monuments,[90] but a detailed survey reveals that, although the Tengalai namam is more common, and the Tengalai influences were, therefore, greater in the city, the Vadagalai namam is also occasionally present. The unusual feature is the presence of both Tengalai and Vadagalai sectarian marks in many temples in Vijayanagara, but in these, the Tengalai namams outnumber the Vadagalai. There are a number of temples in which only the Tengalai mark is seen, but only one, namely the Kodandarama temple, in which the Vadagalai occurs on its own. The differences between the two sub-sects were apparently not so great at this time.[91] The chakra and shankha are sculpted on temple pillars, walls, gopuras, basements and elsewhere. The chakra is depicted with flames issuing from its cardinal points; it often has a scarf around it, with its ends hanging from both sides. Vishnu's wheel is represented at times with eight spikes, symbolising the eight points of the compass; at other times, it has two concentric circles with a full-blown flower in the centre.

The shankha developed from a simple conch-shell to the stylised variety with flames. It is generally represented vertically with flames issuing from its tips and usually with a scarf tied around its widest part. Occasionally, as on pillar reliefs, it is represented horizontally. In such cases, it is normally shown as a simple conch-shell with no fiery tips.

The namam, flanked by the chakra on the left and the shankha on the right, sporadically also with sun and crescent moon above, occurs widely at Vijayanagara. In such a group the Tengalai namam is usually depicted. These three Vaishnava emblems appear frequently together on the top of Vaishnava stone inscriptions, occasionally also on temple pillars, bases of temple lamp-staffs or flag-staffs, the plinths of gopuras, stone troughs or containers, lintels of door frames, as well as various rock-carvings.

There are two statues of Sudarshana-chakra; one is located near the Tungabhadra and the other in Anegondi. Both are now wrongly termed as Suryanarayana icons. The first example is in an inconspicuous modern shrine at Chakra-tirtha. According to local tradition, it was at Chakra-tirtha that Vishnu propitiated Shiva and received the gift of the fiery wheel from him. Having used the chakra to kill innumerable demons, Vishnu returned to his celestial abode after establishing Sudarshana at Chakra-tirtha.[92] This legend accounts for the presence here of the image of the personified discus.

The image of Sudarshana-chakra stylistically appears to be of the Vijayanagara period and has been tentatively assigned to the fifteenth or sixteenth century.[93] The image is sixteen-armed, and is shown frontally in samabhanga.[94] The deity is depicted as a youthful male figure. The attributes held by him do not strictly conform to the iconographic rules for the sixteen-armed Sudarshana-chakras.[95] It is not possible to identify all the weapons held in the hands as these are carved close to each other, radiating like spokes of a wheel from a single elbow on each side, with the weapons almost merging one into each other. Moreover, as this image is still being worshipped, the image is encrusted an blackened due to ritual anointing. It is nevertheless possible to make out the following ayudhas or mudras: varada-mudra and abhaya-mudra, chakra and shankha, bana and dhanus, parashu and an indistinct object, an unclear object and pasha, khadga and an indistinct weapon, ankusha and hala, gada and an unclear ayudha. A circular disc, with a kirti-mukha on top, forms the backdrop for this ornate and beautifully sculpted image, recessed into the surface of the stone slab. The rim of the wheel is decorated with eight marginal flames of equal size and sixteen small floral medallions on its facing. The deity wears a tall kirita-mukuta which partially obstructs the flames rising from behind the head. The flames symbolise the fiery nature of this ayudha. The god is heavily bejewelled. His intricately draped garment extends from the waist to the ankles; the trailing ends of the wide scarf hang from the waist in a graceful pattern. Although the image is placid, the pointed teeth protruding from the mouth indicate the fierce quality of the deity.

The second image is within a Vijayanagara period shrine on a small island off Anegondi. This is finely carved sixteen-armed image, framed by a circular disc with sixteen lotus flowers on it and flames on the outside. Small lozenges are carved in the spaces between the flowers. The attributes in the eight pairs of hands are from top to bottom the anjali-mudra, shankha and chakra, bow and arrow, noose and parashu, mace and trident, full-blown lotus and mace, shield and sword, ankusha and dagger.[96]

NOTES

1. No.1612.
2. No.682.
3. No. 665.
4. *South Indian Inscriptions*, IV, no. 248.
5. NGn/6.
6. For details see, *Vijayanagara, Progress of Research 1983-84,* pp. 138-9 and plates LXXXVII-LXXXIX.
7. NEm/1.
8. Noteworthy reliefs of individual Chaturvimshatimurtis: Mudal-alvar temple (NCw/2), two reliefs on a pillar in the mandapa; on the brindavana of Raghunadansvami (NGn/1), on the north face; Vaishnava temple (NGt/1), relief on a pillar in the mandapa: first from the east, second from the north, west face, lower block; Vithala temple (NHa/1) rangamandapa, three reliefs on one pillar: first from the south, second from the east, on the middle and top blocks of the north face and the top block of the south face; Hanuman temple (NJs/2), a relief on a pillar in the mandapa; in the temple complex of Anantashayana, in the south-east corner pavilion, there are six pillar reliefs of the standing Chaturvimshatimurtis and one seated in lalitasana.
9. NSa/1.
10. NGn/1.
11. Pillar reliefs of the dashavatara group: Vithala temple (NHa/1), south-east corner pavilion, on the pillar to the north of the steps on the western side; Vaishnava temple (NHj/1), on the second pillar from the east and the first from the north—in this group Buddha as well as Balarama are present, but there is no Krishna; mandapa NJg/1, on the pillar to the left of the steps—Varaha is missing from this group; Harihara temple (NLc/3), on the pillar in the mandapa, to the north of the steps; Krishna temple (NLm/4) in the rangamandapa, on the south-east corner pillar; Ramachandra temple (NRw/1), on the two engaged pillars flanking the entrance to the outer antechamber; Pattabhirama temple, pillared hall in the prakara, on the sixth pillar from the north, third from the west.
12. NHj/1
13. NJg/1.
14. The fish motif is often carved on the walls of temples and even gateways. For example there are a number of reliefs depicting fish on the enclosure wall of the Malyavanta Raghunatha temple (NTd/1) and the Domed Gate (NYx). It is unlikely that these frequently depicted reliefs of fish are symbolic of Matsyavatara.
15. NGs/2.
16. NQt/3.
17. No. 1078.
18. D.K. Sinha, 'A Rare Varaha Image of Hampi', in *Journal of Indian History*, Vol. 53, pp. 356-9.
19. NJg/1.
20. NSa/1.
21. Anila Verghese, *Religious Traditions at Vijayanagara: as Revealed Through its Monuments*, p. 34.

22. For a discussion of the relevance of the Narasimha cult, see Anila Verghese, op. cit., pp. 34-42.
23. NSa/1
24. *Vijayanagara: Progress of Research 1979-83*, p. 38.
25. NRt/2.
26. Near NRk/1 and 2.
27. NGn/6.
28. Nos. 659 and 1707.
29. No. 1079.
30. No. 399.
31. *Epigraphia Indica*, Vol. I, pp. 398-402.
32. K. Desai, *Iconography of Viṣṇu*, p. 94.
33. Important rock-carvings of Narasimha: Kevala Narasimha (standing or seated in the yoga pose): In mandapa NGn/5; sanctuary of temple NLh/1; near NRk/1 and 2.
    Lakshmi-Narasimha: Two at Koti-tirtha, one in rock-shelter NSa/1.
34. Near NGn/3.
35. NLh/1.
36. For a discussion of the origin and development of the non-canonical forms of Narasimha, see Anila Verghese, op. cit., p. 39.
37. R. Champakalakshmi, *Vaiṣṇava Inconography in the Tamil Country*, p. 125.
38. Ibid., p. 124.
39. NTz/5.
40. NGw/3.
41. Important large reliefs of Rama: In mandapa NGn/5; Yantroddharaka Anjaneya temple (NGw/3); near NLb/14 on the wall of the porch of temple NQn/1; NQu/4; rock-shelter NSa/1; in one shrine of the double-shrine temple NTz/5.
42. Near temple NLb/14.
43. NGn/5.
44. NMe/1.
45. *South Indian Inscriptions* IV, nos. 254 and 255.
46. K.A. Nilakantha Sastri, *A History of South India: from Pre-historic times to the Fall of Vijayanagara*, p. 420.
47. NNz/2.
48. NVo/1.
49. NGn/1.
50. An example of this motif is carved on a pillar in the porch of the Tiruvengalanatha temple, locally known as Chandikeshvara temple, (NLw/6) on the Hampi-Kamalapuram road.
51. NLb/1
52. In the Archaeological Museum there is a large, unfinished Venugopala statue, No. 610.
53. No. 1641.
54. No. 798.
55. No. 243.
56. *Annual Report of the Archaeological Department, Southern Circle*, Madras, 1916-17, pp. 28-30.
57. V. Filliozat, 'Iconography: Religious and Civil Monuments', in *Vijayanagara City and Empire*, ed. by A.L. Dallapiccola in collaboration with S. Zingel-Avé Lallemant, Vol. I, p. 312.
58. NLs/1.
59. NGx/1.
60. Anila Verghese, op. cit., p. 67.
61. Important sculptures of Vithala: rock-shelter NGn/6; on the unfinished gopura NHa/6; rock-shelter NSa/1; on the wall of the Mint Enclosue.
62. K. Sarojini Devi, 'The Cult of Vithoba in Vijayanagara', in *Dr. N. Venkataramanayya Commemoration Volume*, ed. by R. Subrahmanya and V.V. Krishna, p. 97.
63. Noteworthy sculptures of Venkateshvara: In rock-shelter NGn/6; on a rock behind NGw/3; the central shrine of the triple-shrine temple NGx/1; NMr/2; NQm/1; near NRk/1 and 2; Archaeological Museum: nos. 48, 65, 144, 535, 612, 1772.
64. Near NRk/1 and 2.
65. Behind and slightly above temple NGw/3.
66. Images of Varadaraja: NMz/3—rock carving of Varadaraja flanked by two consorts; reliefs on the vimana exterior south wall of the Ramachandra temple (NRw/1); relief of Kari-Varada on the enclosure wall of the Mint Enclosure.
67. V. Filliozat, op. cit., p. 311.
68. A. Sundara, 'New Light on Religious Trends in Anegondi Region during the Vijayanagara Period', *Quarterly Journal of the Mythic Society*, Vol. LXVIII, pp. 12-13.
69. Ranganatha images: Outside NGo/1—rock-carving; sanctuary of temple NGs/2—rock carvings; NGw/5—a statue; superstructure of NGx/1—a stucco figure; south-east of NGx/1—rock-carving; shrine NLh/9—rock-carving; opposite MMr/2—small rock-carving; porch of temple NQn/1; NTz/5—a small rock-carving: enclosure wall of the Mint Enclosure: Archaeological Museum: nos. 329 and 1611.
70. Near temple NGm/1.
71. NGs/2.
72. Large images of Garuda: In front of the Kodandarama temple (NGw/1); outside NGw/2; Krishna temple (NLm/4); mandapa of temple NNx/5; Archaeological Museum: e.g. nos. 185, 609, 640.
73. K.C. Aryan and S. Aryan, *Hanuman in Art and Mythology*, p. 19.
74. A.P. Karmarkar, *The Religions of India, Vol. I: The Vratya or Dravidian Systems*, p. 187.
75. B. Venkoba Rao, Introduction to *Sri Vyasayogicaritam*, pp. xiv-xv.
76. S.V. Padigar, *Visnu Cult in Karnataka*, p. 108.
77. NFw/3.
78. NEm/1.
79. NGt/4.
80. Large sculptures of Vira-Anjaneya: slabs with relief carvings of Vira-Anjaneya now in shrines or temple (some of these are not in their original places): NDy/2; NDy/4; NDy/6; a shrine within the Virupaksha complex (NFw/1); NLb/16; sub-shrine in NLh/1; NNs/2; NNy/1; NOj/4; NOw/1; NQe/1; NQn/1; NQy/2; outside NQz/1; NRg/2; NRg/3; NRo/1; *mandapa* of temple NRt/2; NSb/1; NSd/1; NSy/2; NTj/1; NTo/4; NTq/2; NVo/1; NXq/1; NYe/1; NYj/1; NCv/2 (this was recently moved within the Vithala complex); NJs/2.
    Rock carvings of Vira-Anjaneya within shrines: NGp/3; NMb/8; NQm/1; NRq/2; NSo/1; NSp/4; subshrine of NSz/3; NTd/6; NTo/2; NTw/1; in one shrine of double-shrine temple NXk/1; NJx/2.

Rock-carvings of Vira-Anjaneya on exposed boulders: Near NDy/5; south-west of NLb/14: Vira-Anjaneya flanked by Rama-Sita-Lakshmana on one side and devotees on the other; in front of NGw/5; NMz/4; in front of NNx/4; north-west of NNz/1; north of NNz/2; NPx/2; NQu/2; in front of NRe/4; NSo/2; NSp/6.
Vira-Anjaneya carved on slabs (some are not in their original places): In front of temple NGk/2; in front of NGw/1; Chakra-tirtha (NGr); in the antarala of NGw/5; in front of NLw/3; one in the a modern shrine, one exposed slab; NPt/1; outside NRb/2; behind NRw/1; in front of NRw/1; outside NYj/; NYm/1; Nym/5; NYx.
Vira-Anjaneya carved on walls etc.: on the wall of NVk; on the wall of the Mint-Enclosure; on the wall of NYx.
Bhakta-Anjaneya, slabs with reliefs:
Outside temple NGw/2; colonnade of the Prasanna Virupaksha temple; NYm/2.
Bhakta-Anjaneya, rock carvings: Rock-Shelter NSa/1; NUg/2. Carved on walls etc. On the wall of the Mint-Enclosure; side of well NHf/5.
Anjaneya (in the vira as well as bhakta poses) is often found carved flanking entrances of shrines and temples—usually on the other side in Garuda: e.g. in NGn/1, NGt/4, NGw/1, NLc/3, NLh/4, unfinished gopura NHa/6.

81. Gates NVk, NYx, see also note 80.
82. These have not as yet been satisfactorily interpreted.
83. NGn/1.
84. NQu/4.
85. R. Champakalakshmi, op. cit., p. 236.
86. NSa/1.
87. For examples of pillar reliefs of Vishvaksena see Appendix VIII.
88. K.V. Raman, *Srī Varadarājaswāmi temple—Kāñchi*, p. 87.
89. NVo/1.
90. K.V. Raman, loc. cit.
91. The Vadagalai-Tengalai schism in medieval Shri-Vaishnavism was as yet only a scholastic controversy. It became a full-fledged battle for temple control only during the late sixteenth, seventeenth and eighteenth centuries. See also A. Appadurai, *Worship and Conflict under Colonial Rule: A South Indian Case Study*, p. 154.
92. *Sri Pampa Mahatme*, First Part, Chapter 76.
93. W.E. Begley, *Viṣṇu's Flaming Wheel: The Iconography of Sudarśana-Cakra*, p. 72, footnote 311.
94. Generally images of sixteenth-armed Sudarshana-chakra, show the deity in striding posture. The image discussed here is an exception being in samabhanga.
95. W.E. Begley, op. cit., pp. 73-4; and T.A. Gopinatha Rao, *Elements of Hindu Iconography*, Vol. 1, Pt. I, pp. 291-2.
96. Sugandha, *History and Archaeology of Anegondi*, pp. 228-9.

CHAPTER 7

Devi Images

In Vijayanagara art there are a great variety of goddesses, the benign or auspicious manifestations of Devi, as well as the terrible, awesome and destructive types. The river goddess Ganga also occurs. The peaceful manifestations of Devi are the spouses of the triad gods, Brahma, Vishnu and Shiva, namely Sarasvati, Lakshmi and Parvati. There are other minor peaceful goddesses. In her wrathful forms, Devi is directly or indirectly associated with Shiva. It is mainly in her fierce aspect that she is worshipped at Vijayanagara, where she appears as the terrifying Durga or Mahishasuramardini, Kali, Bhairavi and Bhadrakali.

The original principal deity of the site is the eponymous goddess Pampa, from whom the name Hampi is derived. This local goddess is married to the form of Shiva called Virupaksha, the principal deity of Hampi. Pampadevi, though mentioned in Vijayanagara literary and epigraphical sources, does not reveal herself prominently in Vijayanagara art. As a consort of Shiva, she appears in the manner typical of consort goddesses. Other goddesses venerated at the site are Yellamma and the fertility goddess Lajja-Gauri.

A. Benign Aspects of Devi

Parvati and other goddesses associated with Shiva (Figures 62, 63)

This goddess is commonly portrayed standing in dvibhanga. She has two hands, the right holding a lotus flower (in some rare examples she carries the lotus in the left) and the left resting lightly by her side in lolahasta. There are a number of rock carvings and other reliefs of such a goddess as well as pillar reliefs of the same.[1] Most of these carvings are of Parvati, since they are found along with other Shaiva deities or in Shaiva structures, but a few are of Lakshmi or her incarnations. For example, the goddess in a niche on the south gopura of the Vithala temple, on the north wall of the base, is evidently Vishnu's consort, for in another niche on the same is found Vithala and the two are clearly a pair.

Of all images of Shiva's consort in her peaceful manifestations, the best is found in the smaller shrine among the rocks, by the Tungabhadra, where the goddess is carved on the wall encased in an arch culminating in a kirti-mukha. The posture of the Devi is graceful, the expression is gracious and she wears elaborate jewellery and fine clothing.

Besides this standard form of the goddess there are some other interesting reliefs. A beautiful figure is found on the ridge north of the Royal Centre, south-west of the Virabhadra and Bhadrakali temples.[2] The four-armed Devi stands in samabhanga. A seven-hooded naga coils upwards behind her and shelters her under its hoods. A small linga is carved on the goddess's kirita-mukuta. She holds lotuses (now broken) in her two upper hands, while the lower hands are in vyakhyana- and varada-mudras. This fine relief is set within an arch formed by two split pilasters on which rests a makara-torana. Not far from the above is another relief, rather crudely cut, of a similar goddess.[3] There is a rearing naga head over this four-armed Devi. The attributes in the upper hands are not distinguishable; the lower ones are in abhaya- and varada-mudras.

The two consort shrines in the Virupaksha temple complex are dedicated to Pampadevi and Bhuvaneshvari. The Pampadevi image is in the standardised form of the peaceful goddess, standing in dvibhanga with a lotus in one hand. However, this seems to be a modern icon and there is no image of this goddess which can be dated to the empire period. The image of

Bhuvaneshvari, seated in lalitasana, with her traditional attributes, the ankusha and pasha, in her two upper hands and the two lower ones in abhaya- and varada-mudras, appears to be modern. Bhuvaneshvari is associated with some of the foundations myths of the city. According to certain traditions, this goddess revealed herself to the sage Vidyaranya and blessed him with the wealth to build the city.[4] Given this legend, she might be expected to play an important role in Vijayanagara art; like Pampa, however, Bhuvaneshvari too is surprisingly rare at the site. In the Archaeological Museum there is an unfinished statue of a seated Devi, holding the ankusha and pasha in her upper hands, and with her lower hands in abhaya- and varada-mudras.[5] Evidently this is Bhuvaneshvari. This Vijayanagara period sculpture of Bhuvaneshvari is the only example at the site.

The Sapta-matrikas are also linked with Shiva. In the city, however, there is no Sapta-matrika panel. In the Virupaksha temple complex, in the so-called Navadurga shrine, is a group of female deities. Though worshipped as the Navadurgas, these are in realtiy the seven divine mothers flanked by Virabhadra and Ganesha. This schist panel is assigned to the twelfth century.[6] There are no identifiable sculptures of these goddesses, apart from one in the Archaeological Museum, labelled as Vaishnavi.[7]

There are many more depictions of terrible forms of the Shaiva goddesses at the site than of auspicious ones. This is understandable as Shiva's consort is more popularly worshipped under her diverse wrathful manifestations.

Lakshmi and other goddesses associated with Vishnu (Figures 65, 66)

In Vijayanagara sculpture Lakshmi appears alone as well as with Vishnu. As seen in Chapter 6, Vishnu is accompanied by one or two consorts in a number of sculptures. If two Devis flank him, Lakshmi is the one to the right. In some of the Ranganatha image the two goddesses are seen behind the reclining god. When two wives are present, Lakshmi is differentiated from Bhudevi by the kuchabandha she wears. When Vishnu has one consort, it is always Lakshmi.

When the goddess is shown on her own, she is seated cross-legged, sometimes on a lotus flower. She generally has four hands, the upper two holding lotus flowers and the lower ones in abhaya- and varada-mudras. Rare examples of the two-armed seated Lakshmi show her carrying lotuses in both hands. Pillar reliefs of her are common. There are also a few larger reliefs and sculptures.[8] The finest is in a gate on the route to Matanga hill from the Royal Centre, where a boulder has reliefs of the squatting Ganesha, seated Lakshmi and a standing ascetic.[9] The goddess of fortune was of great importance at the site, as can be seen from the reliefs present in temples from early-Vijayanagara times until the last phase of the city.

Lakshmi is believed to reside in the doorways or entrances to houses, palaces and at the gates of cities. This idea led to her images being carved on door lintels, where she usually appears in the form of Gajalakshmi.[10] She is depicted on a lotus throne, four-armed as in other Lakshmi images, but here flanked by elephants who shower her with water from two pitchers held in their trunks. Gajalakshmi is considered to be singularly auspicious. The icon is sculpted on the lintel of temple doors, both Shaiva and Vaishnava, all over the site throughout the Vijayanagara period, occasionally also in pre-Vijayanagara temples, as on the door into the antechamber of the Mula Virupaksha temple.[11] An interesting variation of the Gajalakshmi theme is on the main door leading into the early-Vijayanagara triple-shrine temple on Hemakuta, where the goddess is symbolised by the full-blown lotus on to which one elephant is pouring water, while the other elephant carries a flower in its trunk.[12] A similiar motif appears on the early-Vijayanagara gateway on Hemakuta.[13] Thus, the lotus itself is taken to be the goddess Lakshmi.

Bhudevi is represented as a standing or seated woman, holding lotuses or nilotpala flowers in one or both hands. At Vijayanagara, Bhudevi does not appear alone but is found in some of the Vishnu sculptures in which the god is flanked by two consorts. She is also seen on occasional pillar reliefs of Vishnu in the Varaha avatara, when he is represented as Bhu-Varaha, with Bhudevi seated on his knee or carried in his arms. In all these reliefs Bhudevi is shown as a two-armed goddess, usually holding a lotus in the hand.

Sita too appears in Vijayanagara sculpture, in large independent reliefs or sculptures of the Rama-Sita-Lakshmana group, or in *Ramayana* episodes. In the former she is shown in the standardised manner of the benign Devi, standing or seated with a lotus in one hand. In the latter, she is presented in her human form in diverse episodes of the epic.

Sarasvati

Extant Brahma sculptures only depict the god seated alone; there is no Vijayanagara sculpture or relief that can be definitely identified as Sarasvati, his consort. Among the sculptures on three boulders on the north ridge is a relief of Brahma and, on a slightly different level, that of an eight-armed Devi.[14] Her proximity to Brahma would indicate the possibility of this goddess being his consort. She sits cross-legged within an unfinished arch. In her right hands are the damaru, an indistinct object and an arrow, with the lowest in the vyakhyana-mudra, possibly holding an akshamala. The left hands hold the trishula, mace, bow(?) and a small palm-leaf book(?). Some of these attributes are those of Sarasvati, but the damaru and trishula are not. It is therefore difficult to make a definite identification of this goddess. There is another problematic goddess relief within a small shelter in the Irrigated Valley near the Mudu Viranna temple.[15] This two-armed Devi has been identified by one scholar as Sarasvati holding a palm-leaf book.[16] However, on closer examination it would appear that the goddess carries a ball of rice in one hand and a ladle held horizontally in the other. She is therefore not Sarasvati, but probably Annapurna, the goddess of food, who is said to hold a vessel of honey and a spoon containing delicious rice.[17] If so, this is the only portrayal of Annapurnadevi at the site.

The image of Sarasvati in the Sharadadevi shrine of the Virupaksha complex is clearly modern. Thus there seems to be no Vijayanagara period sculpture of the goddess of learning in Vijayanagara city.

B. Fierce Aspects of Devi

Devi reveals herself in a number of terrible forms. In these she is usually considered to be the shakti of Shiva, although she is also believed to be an independent divinity, not necessarily linked to any male god. In her destructive forms she is famous as Durga, Kali and Bhairavi.

Durga/Mahishasuramardini (Figures 64, 67)

Three varieties of this goddess are found at the site: seated on her lion, killing Mahisha, and standing on the decapitated head of Mahisha. Of these, the second is the most important and frequent.

The unique pillar relief of Durga seated on her vahana, the lion, is in the south side mandapa of the early-Vijayanagara, double-shrine Shaiva temple on Hemakuta hill.[18] Of the goddess standing on the severed head of the buffalo asura, there are only a few exceptional pillar reliefs in the Ramachandra temple, in the Prasanna Virupaksha temple, and in a temple within the Royal Centre.[19] In these examples the goddess is in samabhanga with four arms. The upper two hold the chakra and shankha, while the lower two are in abhaya- and varada-mudras in three examples, and in the fourth example the lower hand rests on the goddess' hip while the other is broken. The chakra and shankha are among the weapons most commonly associated with the goddess. They reveal the affinity between this Devi and Vishnu, for in southern India she is believed to be the latter's sister.

There are a few pillar reliefs of the goddess in the act of killing Mahishasura. But these are of little interest compared with the extensive number of sculptures and large reliefs of this form.[20] Mahishasuramardini even serves as a guardian deity, for she is found occasionally on gateways and doors: the relief on a gateway leading into the Hemakuta hill enclosure,[21] the magnificent carving on a pillar in the east gate of the Ramachandra temple, and the relief on the door-jamb of the sanctuary of the Shaiva temple, east of the Ramachandra temple.[22] In all these sculptures the goddess is eight-armed. The weapons generally held are the chakra and shankha, bow and arrow, sword and shield and trishula, grasped in two hands, with which the Devi is killing the demon. Usually, the human form of the asura is seen emerging from the body of the buffalo.

One of the finest Mahishasuramardini sculptures at Vijayanagara is in the large shrine among the rocks by the river, where she appears in a relief on one wall.[23] The goddess is gracefully carved showing the natural contours of the body and limbs. She holds a sword, elephant goad, chakra, trishula, shankha, noose and shield. She stands on the supine buffalo, pressing it to the ground, with its body pierced by the trishula, and her lion vehicle attacking it from the rear. The human form of Mahisha emerging from the buffalo's body and holding a sword and shield is prevented from escaping by the goddess' firm grasp of his hair. The sculpture is framed by an unfinished arch.

Another fine relief is among the Shaiva and Shakta sculptures on three boulders on the north ridge. On one rock is a panel with Ganesha, Lakshmi, Mahishasuramardini (centre), Bhairavi and Bhairava. Mahishasuramardini stands in an arch and over her head is a seven-hooded serpent. She has eight arms and carries the shankha, chakra, bow, arrow, sword, shield and trident, the last of which is thrust into the buffalo-demon. She also pierces her sword into the back of her adversary. From the animal emerges the demon in human form holding a sword and a shield. The Devi's lion also joins in combat against Mahishasura.

Kali (Plates 66, 68)

There is a magnificent sculpture of Kali striding to battle carved on a rock south of the Tiruvengalanatha temple.[24] Her sharp fangs and garland of heads denote her terrifying nature. The goddess holds an assortment of weapons in her ten hands. In the right hands, she has a straight sword, axe, arrow, snake and a curved sword, while in her left hands she bears a rectangular shield, noose, bow, possibly a kapala and a round shield. This image is enclosed within an arch. The image is still worshipped and is heavily encrusted with bright paint, which is annually renewed. She is locally known as Shri Athikayamma, this is probably a corruption of Hathu-kayi-amma or Goddess with Ten Hands.

A second interesting image is found among the Shakta sculptures on three boulders on the north ridge. On one rock there is a panel of three Devis set within arches. In the centre is four-armed Kali, seated cross-legged, wearing exquisite jewellery. She bears a sword and a trident in her two upper hands; the lower right is in abhaya-mudra and the lower left holds a kapala. Kali is flanked by standing figures of Bhairavi and Bhadrakali. Below Kali is a pot flanked by two severed heads. These represent the severed heads of Chanda and Munda. The pot may symbolise collection of the blood of Raktabija to prevent it from spilling on the ground.

There are no pillar reliefs of Kali.

Bhairavi (Plates 67, 68)

The consort of Bhairava is the fierce goddess Bhairavi. She is often shown in Vijayanagara sculpture either seated or standing alone, accompanying her spouse or with other goddesses.[25] She holds the same attributes as her husband: the damaru and trishula, sword and kapala. There are two Bhairavi reliefs among the Shaiva and Shakta carvings on three boulders on the north ridge, and many elsewhere.

Bhadrakali (Figure D, Plate 68)

Bhadrakali, consort goddess of Virabhadra, shares the same attributes as her husband, the bow and arrow, sword and shield. Generally she is four-armed, but there are also some six-armed images of her at the site. In such cases, the goddess also holds the damaru and trishula. Occasionally flames encircle her head.

There are some fine Bhadrakali sculptures.[26] Although usually appearing alone, there are some exceptions. In the exquisitely carved panel in the passageway leading to the larger of the two shrines at Koti-tirtha, is a magnificent Virabhadra, an elegant Bhadrakali to his right and Nandi to his left. Bhadrakali is also enshrined in a temple of her own on the north ridge,[27] south of the temple dedicated to Virabhadra. In her shrine, the goddess is carved on the boulder against which the sanctuary is built. Six-armed Bhadrakali stands in samabhanga, holding sword, shield, bow, arrow, trishula and damaru. The sculpture is set within an unfinished arch. The lower portion of this image is now buried.

An interesting pillar relief, the only one of this goddess, is found in the hundred-pillar hall in the outer enclosure of the Virupaksha temple. Here the goddess is in a pose that suggests dance. She holds a curved sword and a shield in her two hands. Flames encircling her head highlight her destructive nature.

C. Other Forms of Devi

There are a few reliefs of dancing Devis. In the mahamandapa of the Krishna temple are two pillar reliefs of a four-armed dancing Devi, wearing a mukuta, surrounded by a circle of flames.[28] In both cases, the lower hands of the goddess are in lolahasta with the upper arms raised. One goddess holds a trishula in one upper hand and possibly a kapala in the other. The Shaiva affiliation is clear from these attributes. She may be a dancing Bhairavi. The other goddess grasps a shankha in one upper hand, but has no other ayudhas. Since Durga is shown carrying a shankha, this may be the dancing Durga.

A large and more interesting relief of a dancing sixteen-armed goddess is carved on a block inserted in the main east gopura of the Virupaksha temple. The carving, probably of the Sangama period, is on the west side of the granite base, north of the entrance passageway. The objects held in the hands of this figure are unfortunately indistinct. The deity is flanked by two standing males. Perhaps this is a sculpture of the dancing Kali, for in the Shaiva tradition, there is legend from Chidambaram about Kali challenging Shiva to a dance context.

Another small relief of a four-armed dancing goddess is found on the lintel of the door into the mandapa of the early-Vijayanagara triple-shrine temple on Hemakuta hill.[29] At one end of the lintel is dancing Ganesha and at the other end, dancing Devi.

D. River Goddesses (Figure 68)

Ganga is noticeably absent on temple doorways in pre- and early-Vijayanagara monuments at the site. Perhaps the first important example of Ganga sculpture at Vijayanagara is seen on the fifteenth-century gopura of the so-called Varaha temple, located at the end of the Tiruvengalanatha temple chariot street.[30] Ganga appears in the gopura, on both the door frames of the gateway, flanking the entrance passageway. On one side the goddess stands on the makara, while on the other side the makara is missing. Compared with sixteenth-century examples, these reliefs of Ganga are in a rather archaic style. The goddesses on doorways with or without attributes and vahanas, are intended to be Ganga and Yamuna.[31]

In the sixteenth-century temples of the city, especially the Krishna, Malyavanta Raghunatha, Vithala, Tiruvengalanatha and Pattabhirama temples, Ganga is prominently displayed in the gopuras, being placed either side on the inner faces of the jambs at the bottom of the two door frames. The current and ripples of the flowing water are captured in her swaying stance. She holds a creeper issuing from the mouth of her makara, or from below her if the vahana is not carved: The creeper meanders to form circles that sometimes frame panels which enclose miniature deities or other figures. The creepers climb upward along the inner surface of the jambs, meeting the lintel to form a continuous scroll-like pattern from one side to the other.

It is evident from the presence of Ganga on the jambs of an unfinished sixteenth-century gopura in Vithalapura, south-west of the Vithala temple,[32] that the carving of Ganga became a standard feature in gopura architecture at the city. While Ganga is prominent on sixteenth-century gopuras, she is not quite so common on the doorways of vimanas and mandapas. In some cases, she is seen on the doors into the rangmandapa of a temple, but rarely on the doors of the antechamber, and never on the door leading into the sanctuary. This highlights the fact that the function of the goddess is that of purifying the devotee. Once regeneration occurs at the crossing of the threshold of the gopura in which Ganga is prominently placed, there is little necessity for a further transmutation on entering the temple itself. Besides, the devotee may only enter the outer precincts of the god's abode, the sanctuary itself is out of bounds of all except the priests.

It is also significant that apart from temple gateways and doors, there are no other sculptures of Ganga or any other river goddesses extant at the site, neither pillar reliefs nor large carvings or statues. Alone of all the river deities Ganga was revered in Vijayanagara. But she had a specific and restricted role and was not the main deity in any shrine.

E. Local and Folk Goddesses

Alongside the numerous forms of Devi belonging to the Sanskritic tradition there are also present at the site certain female divinities of the non-Sanskritic tradition. These include the local goddess Yellamma, and a folk fertility deity, Lajja-Gauri.

Yellamma

While the major divinities are housed in large temples, the gramadevatas are placed in small shrines, or in no shrine at all.[33]

In the Royal Centre is the temple of Yellamma,[34] the guardian deity of this area, locally known as Pattanada Yellamma, Yellamma of the City. The goddess worshipped in this temple is four-armed and seated, about one metre high, a damaru and a khadga are held in her right hands and the trishula and kapala in the left ones. She wears a skull-garland. The sculpturing of the stone idol is in the archaic manner and the temple is now below ground level.[35] As worship still continues in this shrine and the idol is covered with clothing and decorations, it is difficult to determine whether or not it is a Vijayanagara-period image. Domingo Paes has referred to a temple near the king's palace where many sheep were killed daily.[36] Possibly this is the temple of Pattanada Yellamma, as the village godlings were almost universally worshipped with animal sacrifices.

Apart from the Pattanada Yellamma temple, there is a Yellamma temple of the Vijayanagara period in Anegondi. The object of veneration here is a large boulder considered to be an aniconic representation of this folk goddess. Besides these two depictions of Yellamma, there are no others of the empire period, of Yellamma or any other gramadevata in the city.

Lajja-Gauri (Figures 69, 70, Plates 69, 70)

There are no statues or large reliefs of Lajja-Gauri at Vijayanagara, this not being one of the principal local goddesses. However, there are a number of pillar reliefs of her and she also occurs occasionally on temple plinth mouldings. There are even some rough etchings of Lajja-Gauri found on the sheet-rock and there is one stucco figure.[37] All this proves that this goddess was well-known in Vijayanagara and was of interest to the sculptors. Yet there is no evidence that she was enshrined or received formal worship. In Vijayanagara sculpture, Lajja-Gauri is shown with a head, she is nude and from the waist downwards her body is in the typical birth-giving pose. But the arms are held in varied positions: with her arms bent at the elbows and raised;[38] with the left hand in the usual raised position, and with the right hand resting on the right knee; with both hands either resting downwards against her knees, or stretching horizontally sideways; with one hand resting on her genitals and the other resting downwards; and, finally, with both hands on her genitals, emphasizing thus the generative aspect. In addition, she is also shown with a pot. There are several variations of this type: she holds a pot in one hand, while the other rests against her knee: she holds a pot aloft in one hand, while the other points to or touches her genitals; or, she touches a pot with one hand and her genitals with the other.

The presence of the pot reinforces the nature and the function of the goddess, for the kalasha is a symbol of fertility, filled as it is with the fecund waters of life.[39] The pot is also a symbol of the womb.[40]

Most Lajja-Gauri sculptures at the site are small, crudely carved and hidden away in obscure corners of temples. Thus Lajja-Gauri is not of much sculptural significance in Vijayanagara art; but from the iconographic viewpoint, on account of the great variety of her images, she is of much interest. There are variations of Lajja-Gauri found at Vijayanagara not seen in earlier versions.

NOTES

1. Sculptures of the standing goddess holding a lotus in one hand: NGn/5—along with Virabhadra, Ganesha and Karttikeya; NGm/1; near NGm/1—flanked by Ganesha and Karttikeya; Vithala temple (NHa/1), south gopura, in a niche on the north wall of the basement; NLc/3—flanking the entrance to the sanctuary; NLh/5—in a panel with three sections, in the first is Devi; in the second a linga, Nandi and devotee, in the third Virabhadra; NMs/2—along with Bhadrakali; Archaeological Museum: nos. 539 and 758.
2. NMy/3.
3. NMr/4.
4. Local tradition.
5. No. 2145.
6. S. Rajasekhara, *Masterpieces of Vijayanagara Art*, p. 22.
7. No. 529.
8. Sculptures of Lakshmi: Slab in front of NGw/1; relief in the NMx/2 group of sculptures; gate NRb: Archaeological Museum: no. 1874.
9. Gate NRb.
10. R. Champakalakshmi, *Vaiṣṇava Iconography in the Tamil Country*, p. 46.
11. NLb/13.
12. NFw/6.
13. NFw/3.
14. NMx/2.
15. NLs/2.
16. D. Devakunjari, *Hampi*, p. 48.
17. T.A. Gopinatha Rao, *Elements of Hindu Iconography*, Vol. 1, Pt. II, 370.
18. NFw/5.
19. NSl/3.
20. Sculptures and large reliefs of Mahishasuramardini: NFv/1—in the antechamber of the east-facing shrine; three reliefs on slabs in and near the Virupaksha temple (NFw/1) and the image of the Durga-devi temple north of this temple, some of the these may be modern; NFw/8; near NGm/1; NGm/2; east gopura of Vithala temple (NHa/1)—a stucco figure; NMr/1; among the sculptures at NMx/2; NMy/3—on a slab on which are also carved Karttikeya, Ganesha and Bhairava; Archaeological Museum: no. 755 (this is a four-armed image).
21. NFw/8.
22. NRx/1.
23. NGm/2.
24. NMh/2.
25. Reliefs and sculptures of Bhairavi: One in the Virupaksha temple (NFw/1); NGm/2; NMm/2—with Bhadrakali; two reliefs among the sculptures at NMx/2; NSy/2; gate NXo; along with Bhairava, e.g. NMy/2, NQo/2 and two in NSu/6.
26. Sculptures of Bhadrakali: NGm/2; NMm/2—along with Bhairavi; NMy/3 —in the central sanctuary of the Bhadrakali temple; among the sculptures at NMx/2; Archaeological Museum: no. 08.
27. NMy/3.
28. Reliefs of a dancing goddess in the mahamandapa of the Krishna temple include: Devi holding a trishula and a kapala(?): first pillar from the east, first pillar from the north, south face, lower block; Devi holding a shankha: second pillar from the east, third from the north, west face, lower block.
29. NFw/6.
30. NGs/1.
31. S. Kramrisch, *The Hindu Temple*, Vol. II, p. 316.
32. NHa/6.
33. H. Whitehead, *The Village Gods of South India*, pp. 16-18; and D. Kinsley, *Hindu Goddesses: Visions of the Divine Feminine in the Hindu Religious Tradition*, pp. 197-8.
34. NRy/4.
35. D. Devakunjari, op. cit., p. 39.
36. R. Sewell, *A Forgotten Empire*, pp. 254-5.
37. Depictions of Lajja-Gauri: In the traditional pose: on the plinth of the east gateway of the Ramchandra temple (NRw/1), north side.
Lajja-Gauri with one hand raised and the other resting against the knee: Vithala temple (NHa/1) east gopura, on the brick and mortar superstructure there is a stucco Lajja-Gauri in the south-west corner; Vithala temple (NHa/1) hundred-pillar hall middle section: fifth pillar from the east, second pillar from the north, north face, top block; pillar relief in mandapa NHb/6: first pillar from the north, third pillar from the east, east face, top block; Tiruvengalanatha temple (NMh/1), pillared hall in the outer enclosure, mid-section: third pillar from the east, second from the south, south face middle block.
Lajja-Gauri with both hands resting downwards or stretched horizontally: pillar relief in temple NGt/1: third pillar from the north, first from the west, west face, lower block; Vithala temple (NHa/1), hundred-pillar hall, mid-section: fourth pillar from the east, fourth from the north, lower block; Vithala temple (NHa/1), plinth of the mahamandapa, in a kudu arch on top of the moulding, north-west corner; pillar relief in a temple in gate NSg; NSz/4—an etching on the sheet rock.
Lajja-Gauri with one hand on her genitals: Tiruvengalanatha temple (NMh/1), pavilion in the south-east corner of the inner enclosure: third pillar from the east, third from the north, east face, top block; Tiruvengalanatha temple (NMh/1), cloister around the inner enclosure, south side: third pillar from the west, front row of pillars, east face, top block; Pattabhirama temple, pillared hall: fourth row from the north, fifth from the east, north face, middle block.
Lajja-Gauri with both her hands on her genitals: Virupaksha temple (NFw/1), hundred-pillar hall in the outer prakara, mid-sections: last pillar from the east, third pillar from the north, west face, middle block.
Lajja-Gauri with a pot: Vithala temple (NHa/1), plinth of the cloister around the enclosure wall, south-east corner; Krishna temple (NLm/4), on the

exterior wall of outer enclosure, north side; Tiruvengalanatha temple (NMh/1), mahamandapa: first pillar from the north, second from the east, south face, middle block; Tiruvengalanatha temple, maha-mandapa: third pillar from the north, third from the east, south face, middle block; Tiruvengalanatha temple, cloister around the inner enclosure wall, west side, front row: fourth pillar from north, west face, top block.

38. There is an example on the east gateway of the Ramachandra temple, which is possibly the earliest representation of the goddess in the city, as it follows the traditional pattern.
39. P.K. Agrawala, *Pūrṇa Kalāśa: Or the Vase of Plenty*, p. 8.
40. A number of excavations at proto-historic sites in the Deccan have unearthed pot burials, symbolising the idea of the dead going back to the womb of the earth. See R.C. Dhere, *Lajja Gauri*, p. 105.

CHAPTER 8

Minor Divinities

Besides the sculptures of the principal Hindu deities, Shiva, Vishnu and Devi, there are also those of Brahma and the minor divinities which include astral deities such as Surya, Chandra and the Ashtadikpalas, Kama and his consort Rati, and various heavenly beings such as Narada, the gandharvas, kinnaras, kinnaris, nidhis and ganas. Sculptures of popularly worshipped nagas are ubiquitous; indeed among all these minor divinities at Vijayanagara, only nagas appear to have enjoyed a widespread following, with innumerable nagakals erected in their honour. Probably none of the other divinities in this category received formal worship. Neither were shrines constructed in their honour, nor are there statues or large independent sculptures of most of them. While they are seen in reliefs, occasionally by themselves, they occur more frequently on temple pillars as part of the decorative motifs.

A. Brahma (Figure 71, Plate 71)

Iconographically Brahma is found in representations of the Trimurti; he is shown by himself and occasionally he is present in renderings of mythical incidents involving Vishnu or Shiva. Thus in the Tripurantaka episode, he drives Shiva's chariot. In the Lingodbhava form of Shiva, Brahma is depicted as a swan attempting to reach the top of the flaming linga, while Vishnu, as a boar, delves down to plumb its depths. Eventually both have to accept defeat and acknowledge the superiority of Shiva. In Vaishnava iconography, in the Ranganatha image, Brahma, seated on the lotus flower, issues from the navel of Vishnu, who is afloat on the cosmic ocean. At Vijayanagara there are no sculptural representations of the Tripurantaka and Lingodbhava stories but, Brahma is present in many of the Ranganatha sculptures and reliefs.

The only sculptural depiction of the Trimurti is on a pillar in the enclosed cloister around the early-Vijayanagara Shaiva shrine on the Tungabhadra.[1] On one face of this pillar are seated Uma-Maheshvara in the upmost panel, Lakshmi-Narayana in the middle, and Brahma in the lowest. The three-headed Brahma seated in padmasana, holds in his top right and left hands the akshamala and kamandalu, while the lower right and left hands are in abhaya-mudra and rest on his knee, respectively. Post-Vijayanagara paintings of the Trimurti appear on the ceiling of the maharangamandapa of the Virupaksha temple, as noted earlier.

No statues or sculptures in the round of Brahma are extant at the site. The only independent relief of this god is located among the group of Shaiva and Shakta sculptures carved on three boulders on the north ridge.[2] Here, on a boulder facing north-west, set within an arched niche, is a relief of triple-headed Brahma seated in padmasana. A lotus flower is carved in the rock below the god, giving the impression that he is seated on it. Instead of the conventional jata-mukuta, Brahma wears the kirita-mukuta on each head. Other pieces of jewellery are also evident. He holds a lotus(?) and a sruva in his two upper hands, while in the lower ones are akshamala and kamandalu. A seated Devi is carved on the same boulder to the left of Brahma, at a different level.

There are also a few smaller carvings of this god on pillar reliefs and some on the central kudus of the superstructures of the early fourteenth-century (pre-Vijayanagara) triple-shrine temple on Hemakuta hill.[3] Among the pillar reliefs, the finest one of Brahma is located in the detached mandapa in the Prasanna Virupaksha temple. The god is squatting cross-legged under a makara-torana surmounted by a kirti-mukha. His lower hands are in dhyana-mudra, while the upper ones hold the rosary and kamandalu. Kirita-mukutas adorn the three heads. Brahma wears heavy jewellery. Apart from this carving, there are no other pillar reliefs of Brahma in any major temple in Hampi proper. In the temple of Anantashayana are two pillar reliefs of this deity, one in the mahamandapa and the other in a pavilion in the south-east corner of the enclosure.

B. Astral Divinities

Surya (Figures 72, 74)

Evidently Surya was important in Hampi in pre-Vijayanagara times. For in the two triple-shrine temples on Hemakuta hill[4] that date immediately prior to the founding of the empire, Surya appears in some of the kudus in the centre of each tier of the vimana superstructures.

The finest pre-Vijayanagara period Surya at the site is now located in the Surya-Narayanasvami shrine in the Virupaksha complex. This sculpture is about 1.5 m in height. The well ornamented god stands in samabhanga, holding the customary lotuses. There is a small Devi on either side, each holding a lotus. Above the goddesses appear Usha and Pratyusha, driving away darkness with their bows and arrows. The use of schist as the medium and the nature of the carving indicate a Hoysala period date.

In the Vijayanagara period images of Surya at the site, Surya is never accompanied by goddesses or other attendant beings. He has a large circular halo behind his head. His two lotuses are either half open or in the form of buds, with the hands held either at the elbow or at shoulder levels. Surya often appears on pillar reliefs. There are also a number of larger reliefs of this god, some flanking the entrances to shrines. One independent sculpture of the composite form of this god is carved on a stone slab.

Surya in a chariot: (Figure 73) The best example of this variety is found in the larger shrine among the rocks by the Tungabhadra.[5] Surya is carved on the east wall of the enclosed hall of this cave-like structure. Holding two lotuses, crowned with a high kirita-mukuta and adorned with jewellery, Surya stands in samabhanga on a chariot drawn by seven horses. The charioteer, Aruna holds the reins of the horses in his left hand and whip in the right. To one side of the chariot is a pillar representing the mythical mountain Meru.

Among the boulders close to this temple, in the area known as Koti-tirtha, is another fine relief set within an arch. It shows Surya standing in a chariot drawn by horses, with Aruna guiding the vehicle.

Surya in his chariot is carved above the dvarapala on one side of the doorway leading into the sanctuary of the Ranganatha temple. This shrine is on the path between the Virupaksha and Vithala temple.[6]

Surya standing in samabhanga: This is the most common type of Surya image. The god holds the traditional lotuses and his head is framed by a prabhamandala. The best example of this variety, most of which are pillar reliefs, is found in a niche in the basement of the south gopura of the Vithala temple, west of the south entrance to the passageway. The deity wears intricate jewellery and appears calm and dignified. In the Harihara temple,[7] to the north of the doorway is a relief of the standing Surya.

Surya in alidhasana: A variation found at Vijayanagara, which does not conform to the iconographic norms, is that of flying Surya, holding two lotuses, riding on a cloud in alidhasana. These examples appear only on a few pillar reliefs, Here Surya is differentiated from the gandharvas by the presence of the full solar disc forming a halo behind his head.

Seated Surya: This variety is rare. On a pillar relief in the columned hall in the south-west corner of the outer enclosure of the Virupaksha temple, Surya is seated in lalitasana. He has four hands: the upper two hold a lotus each, while the lower two are in the abhaya- and varada- mudras. A small rather crudely carved statue of this god is found in a niche on the vimana wall of the Virupaksha temple. Surya is seated cross-legged, holding a lotus in each of his upper hands, and the lower ones are in abhaya- and varada-mudras. On the pedestal of the image is a relief depicting the seven horses and Aruna. Since this image is covered with oil and grime, it is difficult to determine whether it belongs to the Vijayanagara period.

Composite form: There is one unique sculpture of this variety, now placed in the antechamber of a small west-facing shrine near the Lokapavana tank complex south-west of the Virupaksha temple. It is a relief carved on a stone slab; apparently it once served as an image used in worship. The male deity stands in samabhanga. Above his head is an arch, culminating in a kirtimukha. There is no prabhamandala. The four-armed figure holds the shankha and chakra in the two rear hands and two closed lotus flowers in the two front hands. This combination of attributes reveals that this is an image of Surya-Narayana. The high kirita-mukuta and elaborate jewellery adorning the figure highlight his importance.

Except for this example, no other extant images of Surya could have served as the principal icon in a shrine or temple. In spite of the popularity of Surya and the many representations of this god at Vijayanagara, there is no evidence of any shrines dedicated exclusively to his worship. Most Surya images at Vijayanagara conform to the iconographic rules, but four-armed forms and those of Surya in alidhasana are Vijayanagara variations.

Chandra (Figure 75)

Apart from pillar reliefs, there is only one extant sculpture of Chandra at Vijayanagara. This is in a niche on the granite base of the Vithala temple's south gopura, east of the south entrance to the passageway. Being the counterpart of the Surya image in the niche opposite (already noted), the moon and sun gods are very similar. Like Surya, Chandra too stands in samabhanga and has a lotus flower in each of this two hands. The only iconographic difference is that Chandra has the crescent moon behind his head.

Pillar reliefs of Chandra usually depict him on a cloud, either in alidhasana or standing. He holds a lotus in one or both hands. He can be differentiated from the gandharvas and Surya only by his crescent moon.[8]

Ashtadikpalas (Figures 76-83)

There are one pre-Vijayanagara and one post-Vijayanagara depiction of the ashtadikpala group. In the Bhuvaneshvari shrine within the Virupaksha temple complex the ashtadikpalas form part of the intricate ceiling composition of the mandapa in front of the sanctuary. They are placed in the correct direction and are sculpted according to the iconographic rules. This beautiful schist ceiling, as well as the pillars and other architectural elements of the shrine, are in the Hoysala style. On the ceiling of the maharangamandapa of the Virupaksha temple is a long post-Vijayanagara painted panel of the dikpaplas.

There is only one ashtadikpala group of the Vijayanagara period. This is rough carving in the Vithala temple complex on a recessed band of the plinth of the square platform east of the stone chariot. Some of the figures carry no attributes but others hold indistinct objects. The only ones clearly discernible are Kubera's sword, Yama's danda, Varuna's staff and Vayu's staff or sword. The dikpalas are mounted on their respective vahanas. The kirita-mukuta worn by each, besides the ayudhas and the vahanas, indicate that they are divinities. At present, four ashtadikpalas are wrongly situated: Indra and Agni appear on the north and northeast respectively, while Kubera and Ishana are on the east and south-east. If these two sets were interchanged then the positioning of all eight would be correct. It is likely that the misplacement of the four reliefs was the result of conservation work conducted in recent times.

Individual sculptures or reliefs of the dikpalas are uncommon. There are two pillar reliefs of Varuna on the makara. He also appears occasionally on temple gateways or doors at the base of the scroll design that frames these entrances. In all these reliefs he holds a staff or a flower or has no ayudha. The sculptors were evidently not following the strict rules of iconography when carving these figures.

A man holding a staff riding on an elephant appears in two column reliefs in the Ramachandra temple.[9] However, as the typical ayudhas of the Indra are not present in either of these, it is difficult to determine whether or not these represent him.

In one sculpture in the Archaeological Museum conventional attributes are not found, but it is identified as Kubera.[10] Thus, from the paucity of sculptures of the ashtadikpalas either as a group or individually, it can be concluded that they were unimportant in Vijayanagara art.

C. Other Divinities

Kama and Rati (Plate 72)

Pillar reliefs and other carvings or friezes, and one independent sculpture occur of Kamadeva. In the pillar reliefs, Kama appears either by himself or with Rati. One of the finest carvings of Kama on pillars is in the Shiva temple of the early Vijayanagara period on the Tungabhadra.[11] The god is in alidhasana, riding on a chariot drawn by two parrots. Kama's banner is planted on the chariot. The bejewelled youthful god holds aloft his bow, apparently having just released his flowered arrow. In the Vithala temple there are a number of pillar reliefs of Kamadeva. In the rangamandapa is an interesting example in which Manmatha, standing in a parrot-drawn chariot, shoots an arrow with his bow. Behind Kama is a woman who holds an umbrella over him; in front is another woman so overcome with desire that her lower garment slips off her body. In the south-east corner mandapa in this complex is a column with three superimposed panels of the god of love. In the topmost panel Kama is in his traditional chariot, shooting an arrow from his sugarcane bow. In the middle panel standing Manmatha and Rati appear; in the lowest panel, they are depicted embracing. In the south-west mandapa in the Ramachandra temple complex is a pillar relief of the youthful standing god of love, armed with a bow and five arrows.

Other carvings of this deity are more dramatic than the pillar reliefs. Thus, in the Ramachandra temple, on the north side basement of the minor shrine, Kama is shown shooting an arrow at two women. On the outer enclosure wall of the same temple (topmost row, north-east corner), Kama appears along with his wife Rati, both in their respective chariots drawn by a parrot, flanked by female attendants, shooting arrows at each other. The Vithala temple has some of the finest friezes of Kama's exploits. On the south-facing plinth of the north-east corner pavilion is a magnificent panel of Manmatha in his chariot together with consorts. Provided with a quiver full of arrows on his back, Manmatha is in vigorous action with his bow. The three goddesses, each holding a sugarcane, are seated on their bird vahanas, two on a parrot, one on a hamsa. Another frieze of Kama in his chariot, surrounded by a host of beautiful women and parrots, is seen on the plinth of the stone chariot.

In the Archaeological Museum is a sculpture of standing Manmatha and Rati, each holding a flower.[12] Manmatha lightly embraces Rati, who playfully puts her right hand under her husband's chin.

In all these reliefs and sculptures, Kama appears as a handsome youth. He usually wears a mukuta and exquisite jewellery which enhance his charm.

Narada and Tumburu (Figures 84, 85)

The mythical seer Narada is often present on temple pillar reliefs at Vijayanagara. He is depicted as a rather plump elderly man, with a flowing beard, his hair tied in a topknot, wearing a garland of rudraksha beads, and carrying the vina on his shoulders. One of his hands is slightly raised as if he were singing. His celestial nature is denoted by the cloud on which he stands.

Tumburu rarely occurs in Vijayanagara art. There are a few pillar reliefs of him on a cloud, holding a musical instrument. His horse face distinguishes him from the other gandharvas, of whom Narada is the chief.

Gandharvas (Figure 86)

In Vijayanagara art, the gandharvas are generally shown in alidhasana on a cloud, carrying either a lotus or vina in one or both hands, though sometimes they appear empty-handed. The gandharvas are young, handsome males who wear the kirita-mukuta, sacred threads and jewellery that include necklaces, earrings and bracelets. Pillar reliefs of gandharvas are common in both Shaiva and Vaishnava temples all over the site. They are generally seen on the top or middle panels of columns. Stucco figures of these heavenly beings also appear on the tiers of the superstructures of shrines.

Kinnaras and kinnaris (Figures 87, 88)

These are always depicted as half-human and half-bird, with elaborate feathery tails. Generally the kinnaras and kinnaris carry a vina in their hands. They occur on pillar reliefs in almost all the major temples in the city from early-Vijayanagara times onwards. Because of their celestial association, they are usually placed on the topmost panels of the columns. At times they form part of the decorative programme on doorways, especially on the lower portion of door-jambs.

Nidhis (Figures 89, 90)

Shankhanidhi and Padmanidhi occur only among temple sculptures at Vijayanagara. They have ample chests, slightly obese bodies and peaceful countenances; they wear heavy jewellery including the kirita-mukuta. They are generally seated, Padmanidhi holding a lotus in one hand and Shankhanidhi carrying or blowing a conch. There are no independent reliefs or statues of these nidhis. Their presence, as well as that of their leader Kubera, is auspicious for the temple, the patrons, and the community. These two nidhis consistently appear on the bottom panel of temple columns of all sects. They may also be carved on door-jambs or in the immediate proximity of the entrances to sacred spaces.

Ganas (Figures E, 91)

In Vijayanagara temples the ganas serve almost exclusively as decorative elements. Ganas commonly appear in both Shaiva and Vaishnava temples. A favourite motif of sculptors, they are seen on pillar reliefs or in other parts of the building, on the base of composite pillars, below architectural elements such as beams, or on the superstructures of shrines.

Dancing gana: This type is extremely common among pillar reliefs. The fat and dwarfish gana in dancing pose looks quite comical.

Gana playing a musical instrument: This type also appears on pillar reliefs. The instruments held include the trumpet, horn, flute, conch, tambourine, clappers and drum.

Gana carrying a load such as a heavy parcel or jackfruit: In some temples, rows of ganas are carved under architectural elements, creating the impression that they are carrying the weight of the structure on their hands, backs, or heads.

Nagas (Plates 73-76)

In Vijayanagara times as well as today, the installation of snake-stones is linked with the desire for progeny. This is indicated by an unusual nagakal now in the Archaeological Museum.[13] On this slab is carved a three-headed serpent and another with a single hood. A small cradle guarded by a cat is seen on one side.

The placing of snake-stones under trees is a common practice at Vijayanagara, as can be seen for instance in the nagakals grouped beneath a neem tree in front of the Yellama temple.[14] It is always a cobra that is carved on the nagakal. Only the cobra raised to the status of a divine being.[15] Sometimes is this is a realistic effigy of an actual cobra; more often, presumably to emphasize its divinity, the cobra is multi-headed or given a hybrid half-human, half-snake, form. The naga is invariably shown standing on the tip of its tail and curling upward with expanded hood.

Snake-stones show a variety of patterns:

Nagakals with a single cobra: This is the most common type. In the simplest form, the cobra has only one hood; in others, the serpent is depicted with three, five, seven (always an uneven number) heads forming the hood.

Nagakals with two intertwined cobras: In this type the two snakes, each rearing up on the tip of its tail are intertwined as though in the act of copulation. Usually both are single-headed, although there are examples, in which one is single-headed and the other multi-headed. In the nagakals of this type found at Hampi the two cobras generally face each other with hoods seen in profile. However, there are some, usually of the post-Vijayanagara period, in which the heads are full face.

Nagakals with a hybrid naga: This is the most elaborate type of snake-stone. In it the serpent deity has the upper half in human form and the lower in serpentine form. The hood rises over the crowned human head. Almost all the nagakals of this group are female, representing the serpent goddess Mudarna. Her hands are joined in anjali-mudra. In the crook of each elbow she holds a baby snake. Over her head she wears the usual hood of one, three, five or seven heads. There are some rare examples of this variety in which the naga has a male torso.

The nagakals at Vijayanagara, of which hundreds are still extant, vary in size from a few centimetres to almost 2 m in height. On some the carving is very crude, while others are finely sculpted. The vast majority belong to the Vijayanagara period.

Besides the stone slabs on which are carved the naga divinity, there are some rock carvings of nagas. For example, the sanctuary of a shrine on the north ridge abuts a rock on which are carved two nagas.[16] One is a hybrid with a male torso, a multi-headed hood over his head, and hands in anjali-mudra. The second is of a multi-headed snake. Nagas are carved or etched on a few rock surfaces, either the single cobra or intertwined pair, or the hybrid variety.[17]

Pillar reliefs of snakes are to be found carved on temple columns, but these are usually ordinary serpents and not the naga divinity.

NOTES

1. NGt/3.
2. NMx/2.
3. NFw/9.
4. NFw/9 and NLb/3.
5. NGm/2.
6. NGs/2.
7. NLc/3.
8. It may be of interest that though Surya and Chandra appear individually, no images of the Navagrahas have been found at Vijayanagara.
9. A.L. Dallapiccola, 'Sculpture', in A.L. Dallapiccola, J.M Fritz, G. Michell, and S. Rajasekhara, *The Ramachandra Temple at Vijayanagara*, p. 121.
10. No. 1648.
11. NGt/3.
12. No. 732.
13. No. 147.
14. NRy/4.
15. J. Ph. Vogel, *Indian Serpent Lore or the Nagas in Hindu Legend and Art*, p. 27.
16. NRj/2.
17. Noteworthy snake-stones found at the site: NFw/1—three: in front of temple NFw/27—about 34 small snake stones; in and around NFw/29—about 90 stones; front of NGw/1—four stones, some are modern; in front of NGw/3—about 24, some are modern; front of NGw/5—several; NLw/3—about ten, some may be modern; NMg/1—one; NMs/1 one; NMs/2—two; near NNh/1—three; near NNs/1—six large snake-stones; near NNs/3—five; near NNx/5—about eight; near NNz/1—about 60 small snake-stones; near NQd/1—several small ones; NQe/1—one; NQq/1—one; near NQt/3—one; NQu/1—two; in and near NQu/3—two; NQy/2—two, may be modern; NRe/3—ten; in and near NRe/5—three; NRj/1—about seven; NRj/2—the sanctuary of this shrine is built against a boulder on which are carved two nagas in relief; in front of NRy/4 -two; NSd/1—two; NSh/1—one: NTp/1—several; NTv/2—about ten; NVc/2—three; near NXq/1—three; NYe/1—several; NYx—four: NZg/1—one; Archaeological Museum: e.g. nos. 54, 55, 160, 161, 224, 277, 307, 378, 655, 656, 689, 816, 981, 983, 984, 985, 1036, 1060, 1061, 1068, 1070, 1672, 1673, 1675, 1676, 1679, 1681, 1682, 1686.

CHAPTER 9

Saints and Ascetics

Numerous saints of the Shaiva and Vaishnava sects who had been raised to semi-divine status and accorded worship are found among the Vijayanagara sculptures. They include the Shaiva Nayanmars, who were responsible for the revival of Shaivism in southern India. Yet the Vaishnava Alvars and Acharyas are more common, whose images came to the installed and venerated in many of the Vaishnava temples of the city. The Nathas, especially Matsyendranatha, also appear in the Vijayanagara sculptural repertory.

In addition to these semi-divinized saints are the ascetics of various Shaiva and Vaishnava sects who were, presumably, based in the city in large numbers. Some preceptors are famous in Vijayanagara history. The most renowned is Vidyaranya, of the Smarta school, who is associated with the origin stories of both the city and the empire. The Shaiva teachers of the Kalamukha sect, with the title Kriyashakti, served as the family gurus of the first rulers of the Vijayanagara empire. Virashaivism was dominant in the capital city in the mid-fifteenth century, enjoying a wide following. Virashaiva ascetics were located there from pre-Vijayanagara to post-Vijayanagara times. In the sixteenth-century Vaishnavism replaced Shaivism in popularity and patronage at the court and capital. A number of Vaishnava sages feature prominently in the sixteenth-century history of the city. Ascetics of the sect founded by Madhvacharya were present at the site from pre- to post-Vijayanagara times. Of all of these the most famous was Vyasaraya, the leading spiritual light during the reigns of Krishnadevaraya and his successors. Within the Madhva sect were the poet-saints, the Haridasas, who preached intense devotion to Vishnu. The greatest of these, Purandaradasa, lived in Vijayanagara for many years before his death in 1564. The Shri-Vaishnavas received the maximum court patronage in the decades preceding the city's destruction. A number of Shri-Vaishnava gurus are named in the inscriptions and literature relating to the city.[1]

Although numerous ascetics lived in the city, some of whom enjoyed great fame and immense prestige, there is no Vijayanagara sculpture that can be identified with any particular teacher or ascetic of the Vijayanagara period. Out of the large number and variety of reliefs of ascetics, none are portrait sculptures. They are depicted in a standardized manner and therefore difficult to group according to definite sects or sub-sects. Yet because of their diversity these sculptures are of great interest.

A. Saints

Nayanmars (Figure 92, Plate 77)

Only one of the 63 Nayanmars is clearly identifiable in Vijayanagara sculpture: Kannappa, the hunter, associated with the great Shiva temple at Kalahasti. Even Kannappa appears only in temple pillar reliefs. There are no statues or large reliefs of this figure. From the rarity of the Nayanmar statues and reliefs it may be presumed that the cult of the Nayanmars was not very popular in Vijayanagara.[2] Yet the Nayanmars were also revered by the Virashaivas, an important group in the city, who refer to them as Puratanas.

The pillar reliefs of Kannappa date from early Vijayanagara times onwards; for example, he is seen in one of the temples on Hemakuta hill.[3] These reliefs are found mainly in Shaiva temples and only rarely in Vaishnava temples.

Kannappa is usually shown as a hunting figure. The large bow indicates his profession. The standing or kneeling Kannappa has one foot resting on the linga to mark the spot of Shiva's eye. With his arrow the hunter gouges out one of his own eyes. These reliefs capture the moment of supreme sacrifice, depicting movement and emotion.

Alvars and Acharyas (Figures 93, 94, Plate 78)

During the Vijayanagara period these deified saints grew greatly in popularity, with separate shrines being built for them in and near the great Shri-Vaishnava temples of the captial.[4] The veneration of the Alvars and Acharyas became an important feature of Shri-Vaishnavism.

In Vijayanagara, the sculptures and reliefs of the Alvars and Acharyas do not appear before the mid-fifteenth century. Neither in the temples on Hemakuta hill dating from the pre-Vijayanagara or early-Vijayanagara times nor in the early fifteenth-century parts of the Ramachandra temple complex, are there any representations of these figures. However, in a dated mid-fifteenth-century temple,[5] the Alvars and Ramanuja appear in pillar reliefs. From this time onwards they are found frequently on temple columns, in both Vaishnava and Shaiva temples.[6] In the sixteenth century, when Shri-Vaishnavism became the dominant sect in the city, their statues were installed for worship in many temples. For example, an inscription from the Vithala temple dated 1534 states that the 13 Alvars, including Tirukachinambi (an Acharya who was a contemporary of Ramanuja), were installed in a specially constructed shrine within the temple complex.[7] Unfortunately, none of these images are now in situ. A record from the Ramachandra temple mentions the installation of the Alvars there,[8] in the sixteenth century.[9] Numerous mutilated statues of the Alvars and Ramanuja discovered during the excavations carried out at the site in the 1970s and 1980s indicate that the Alvar-Acharya images were consecrated in almost all of the Shri-Vaishnava temples in the city.

Separate shrines were also built for them in the area around the Vithala temple. Epigraphical and archaeological evidence reveals the existence of the shrines of the Mudal-Alvars (the first three Alvars), Tirumangai, Nammalvar, Tirumalishai, and Ramanuja.[10]

Images of the greatest of the Acharyas, Ramanuja, occur frequently at Vijayanagara. He is generally shown in the seated posture of meditation, hands in anjali-mudra, with a flag in crook of his arm; this is the kashayadanda, the mark of a sannyasi, who symbolically carries a cloth for straining water tied to the end of his staff. Ramanuja has either completely shaven head or wears the topknot. Occasionally Ramanuja is observed with the right hand in vyakhyana-mudra and the left holding a palm-leaf manuscript.[11]

The Alvars were a popular theme in Vijayanagara sculpture. They are commonly portrayed seated cross-legged with hands joined in anjali-mudra. Although they usually have shaven heads, they are sometimes shown either with a topknot or tuft of hair. They wear the tulsimala and possibly bracelets and armlets of tulsi beads. The Vaishnava namam may adorn their foreheads. Since they are depicted in a standardized manner, it is difficult to differentiate one Alvar from another. However, Nammalvar is shown with his hands in traditional dhyana- and vyakhyana-mudras. There are some reliefs of Tirumangai holding a sword and shield and a few rare instance of Tondaradippodi and at least one of Tiruppan. There is no sculpture that can be definitely identified with Andal, the woman saint. Even in the extant groups of the Alvars, Andal is noticeably absent. Besides Ramanuja, none of the other Acharyas can be recognized. Some standardized Alvar 'type' figures may represent Acharyas; from the 1534 epigraph it is known that Acharya Tirukachinambi was installed along with the Alvars in the Vithala complex. It is therefore likely that other Acharyas, besides Ramanuja, were consecrated in Vijayanagara temples.

Pillar reliefs: Alvar-Acharya pillar reliefs are common in Vaishnava and some Shaiva temples from the mid-fifteenth century onwards. However, as the Alvars and Ramanuja are portrayed in a stereotyped manner, these column reliefs are not of much interest. Of all the Alvars, the only ones who can be recognized are Nammalvar and occasionally Tondaradippodi. Tirumangai appears once, facing the sanctuary in the temple dedicated to him located north-west of the Vithala temple.[12] The pillar on which he appears has on the four facets of the middle block reliefs of Ramanuja, Nammalvar and a seated Alvar, besides that of Tirumangai standing with a sword and shield in his hands.[13]

Other reliefs: Apart from the column carvings, Alvar-Acharya figures are seen in reliefs elsewhere. On a rocky outcrop directly north-west of the Elephant Stables is a rock-shelter dedicated to Vaishnava deities carved on the vertical face of the rock 16 m above grouped level.[14] Here are found the dashavatara panel, episodes of the Narasimha story and at either side carvings of the Alvars and Ramanuja. Below this group are seen Ramanuja and an Alvar wearing a kirita, seated cross-legged with hands in anjali-mudra and with a staff resting against his left shoulder. The kirita suggests that this could be Kulashekhara. Next to him, is Tondaradippodi, seated with his right and left hands in the jnana- and dhyana-mudras respectively.

In the small Ranganatha temple, on the way to the Vithala temple from the Virupaksha complex, on the north-east side wall of the antechamber, is a relief of the seated figures of Ramanuja and Nammalvar.[15] Both have the namam carved on their foreheads. Nammalvar has his hair piled into a topknot.

In the temple possibly dedicated to Nammalvar, facing the south gopura of the Vithala complex, appear reliefs of the standing Tirumangai and Tiruppan Alvars, flanking the east entrance into the rangamandapa.[16] Tirumangai on the south side holds a sword in the right hand and a shield resting on the ground in his left. He wears a kirita-mukuta and elaborate jewellery. Tiruppan on the north side is simply clad in a dhoti and wearing a tulsimala. The vina held in his left hand and the upraised right hand depict him as a minstrel, singing the praises of Vishnu. Reliefs of Alvars including Nammalvar are also found on the exterior wall of this temple.

In the mandapa at the end of the original Vithala chariot-street,[17] the central part of the ceiling is raised on four recessed slabs. Each slab is carved with a deity in the centre, flanked by an Alvar on Ramanuja.[18] The most unusual of the reliefs of these saints appear in the temple north-east of the Vithala complex, recently identified as the Ramanuja temple.[19] Here the central part of the ceiling of the maharangamandapa is raised on recessed slabs. On each of the four sides are three Alvars or Acharyas, 12 in all, flanked by deities or devotees.[20]

Sculptures in the round: A few statues of Alvars and Ramanuja exist which were either installed in sub-shrines within Shri-Vaishnava temples dedicated to the manifestations of Vishnu or as murtis in Alvar-Acharya shrines. Most were recovered during the excavations and clearance work carried out at the site in the 1970s and 1980s, although others are still among the debris in and around temples. None of these images are in their original positions.[21]

The Alvar-Acharya statues are usually made of greenish coloured schist and not locally available granite.

Being badly mutilated, most of these statues are not of much interest, but there are some of iconographic significance. The finest, and one of the best pieces of Vijayanagara sculpture is the statue recovered from a mandapa south-east of the Vithala temple. It has since been placed in the sanctuary of the temple south of the Vithala complex and is now locally known as the image of Purandaradasa.[22] This identification is obviously incorrect as Purandaradasa died in 1564, while the city was sacked and worship discontinued in and around the Vithala temple in 1565. Hence, it is not possible that he could have been deified and his image installed for worship before the desertion of the city. This exquisite statue depicts Tondaradippodi Alvar, as can be confirmed from a similar bronze of this saint now in the Government Museum, Madras.[23] The only difference is that, in the latter, he is in the standing pose. In both examples a small flower-basket hangs on the left arm of the saint. The Vijayanagara image is made of a highly polished black stone. The Alvar is seated in ardhapadmasana on a pitha, with his hands in anjali-mudra. A small tuft of hair appears at the top of the otherwise shaven head. A garland and bracelets of tulsi beads, the sacred thread and the namam on the forehead are his only ornamentations. The face is calm and radiant. A broken, well polished granite statue, also found during recent excavations, now in the north-east corner outside the enclosure wall of the Ramanuja temple, is probably also of the same saint. In this image he is also seated cross-legged on a pedestal, but his hands are in jnana- and dhyana-mudras. He wears a long tulsimala and bracelets.

Stucco figures: Very few stucco figures of the Alvars now exist. There are none of Ramanuja or any other Acharya. On the roof of the mandapa at the end of the Vithala temple car-street are seen a few mutilated ones.[24] Two fairly well preserved groups of Alvars are on the superstructure of the Vaishnava shrine at the end of the Tiruvengalanatha temple street.[25] In all these stucco images, the Alvars appear in the standardized manner, seated cross-legged with hands in anjali.[26]

The innumerable Alvar-Acharya reliefs and statues distributed all over the site demonstrate the immense popularity of these saints at Vijayanagara. However there are no pre- or early-Vijayanagara images. Apparently the Alvar-Acharya cult only became popular from the mid-fifteenth century onwards and achieved great importance in the following century. The Alvars and Ramanuja formed one of the favoured themes of the Vijayanagara sculptors.

Other saints (Figures 95-97)

Unlike the Vaishnava Alvars and Acharyas, who received formal worship and even had some separate temples built to enshrine them, the Shaiva saints, who by the Vijayanagara period had been elevated to a superhuman status, did not seem to enjoy the same status. There are no clearly identifiable extant statues or large independent reliefs of either the Nayanmars or the Nathas.

There appear among the Vijayanagara sculptures, mainly on pillar reliefs, curious ascetic figures seated on an assortment of fantastic creatures. The most common is the sage squatting on a fish in both Shaiva and Vaishnava monuments, from the early Vijayanagara times till the last phase of temple architecture in the city. The others, of which at the site there are a single example of each, are those of an ascetic on a scorpion, kurma and makara. In the Hosuramma temple, in Hosur village near Hospet is a Vijayanagara period column relief of an ascetic seated on a bull. From the extraordinary nature of the vahanas, it is obvious that these sculptures could not portray living ascetics. The rudraksha beads and dishevelled hair, that adorn some of these strange yogis and the trident found with some of them, reveal the Shaiva nature of these ascetics.

These reliefs may be depictions of the Nathas or Siddhas, of the sect known as the Natha, Kanphata or Yogi Sampradaya. Either Gorakhanatha or Matsyendranatha, also known as Minanatha, can be considered the founders of this sect.[27]

The Natha sampradaya was prevalent in the Vijayanagara empire, particularly in the South Kanara district, with Kadire being an important centre,[28] as well as in Andhra, especially at Srisailam.[29]

The yogis, beside being characterized by their split ears and big earrings, have other appurtenances such as a wallet, bowl, staff or trident.[30] In many of these carvings, the ascetics on the fabulous creatures have noticeable earrings and carry a staff or trident. One pillar relief in an early-Vijayanagara temple on Hemakuta hill shows the ascetic on the fish with the typical slit ears and sizeable earrings, with a waterpot nearby and a bowl(?) hanging from one shoulder.[31]

The most popular of these Nathas in Vijayanagara sculpture, and the only one identifiable, is Matsyendranatha seated on a fish. In addition to the innumerable pillar reliefs there are also some carvings. Thus, on the north ridge, among the Shaiva and Shakta carvings on three boulders on the north ridge, is a panel of five figures of whom the central one is Matsyendranatha.[32] He also appears occasionally on temple door-jambs. The most interesting are those of a shrine within the Royal Centre, hidden among high boulders and built against a crevice in the rocks.[33] One door-jamb has the relief of this sage on his fish, while the second has that of a yogi, seated cross-legged on a makara, with his hands resting on a staff, his ears elongated with the weight of his circular earrings.

In the Tiruvengalanatha temple complex, in the pillared hall in the north-west corner of the outer enclosure, is a pillar relief of a yogi seated on an enormous scorpion, with his trident beside him. He has a pipe-like object in his mouth. He may be smoking some narcotic, such practices being associated with the tantric nature of the cult. In the same hall there is another pillar relief, rather-damaged, of an ascetic seated on a kurma. In the Virupaksha temple complex there is a pillar relief of a yogi seated on a strange animal, a cross between a boar and a mouse.[34]

The reliefs of these Nathas, Siddhas or Yogis of the Kanpatha sect form an interesting group among the Vijayanagara stone sculptures. But they served mainly as decorative motifs.

B. Ascetics (Figures 99-106, Plates 40, 79)

Numerous ascetics and mathas of different sects were present in Vijayanagara.[35] The ascetics belonged to the Smarta sect and to various Shaiva and Vaishnava schools. Of the Shaivas alone the *Sri Pampa Mahatme* mentions the Pashupatas, Kalamukhas, Kapalikas and Jangamas.[36]

Among the ascetics who found their way to Vijayanagara the most famous was Vidyaranya of the Smarta sect who followed the Advaita system of philosophy. He was the head of the famous Advaita monastery at Shringeri, reputedly founded by the great Shankaracharya. Though Vidyaranya is reputed to have been actively involved in the foundation of both the city and the empire, not a single extant sculpture or painting of him of the Vijayanagara period survives. A modern image, it is true, can be seen today in the shrine of Vidyaranya, west of the Virupaksha temple. Vidyaranya is seated cross-legged, holding a palm-leaf book in his left hand and his right hand in jnana-mudra.

The Kalamukha gurus with the honorific title of Kriyashakti, were also influential in the initial years of the Vijayanagara empire. Again, as in the case of Vidyaranya, there are no identifiable images of any of these Kriyashaktis. Virashaivas have been present at Hampi from the Vijayanagara period to modern times. In the fifteenth century, Virashaivism was a very popular sect in the city and there must have many of its influential teachers in the capital. However there are no portrait sculptures of any of them.

In the sixteenth century Vaishnavism became the dominant religion of the court and capital. Among the Vaishnava sects, Madhvaism was prevalent in the city from the pre- to the post-Vijayanagara times, with a number of Madhva gurus making Vijayanagara their home. The most famous of these was Vyasaraya who became the guardian saint of the empire and who made the capital his base from 1498 till his death in 1539.[37] There was a matha belonging to this saint in the capital city, besides others elsewhere in the empire. However, there is not a single sculpture of Vyasaraya. A number of the Haridasa poet-saints of the Madhva sect were also located at Vijayanagara. The most famous of these was Purandaradasa. Although, in the Purandaradasa Mandapa at Hampi there is a modern relief of the saint, there is no statue or carving of him belonging to the Vijayanagara period. The only sculptural remains of the Madhva ascetics are the brindavanas of some of them. These are the memorials set up to mark the final resting place of some of the Madhva sages who died at the site. There are eleven such brindavanas. Nine form a cluster on an island on the Tungabhadra, near the village of Anegondi. Among the nine, is the one of Vyasaraya. In Hampi itself there is the brindavana of Raghunandana-svami[38] and also that of Narahari Tirtha[39] on an island on the river, north of the Vithala temple. These brindavanas are cubical platforms, often decorated with fine Vaishnava reliefs.

Of the Vaishnava gurus of the Shri-Vaishnava sect, of whom many made their home in the city, we have no evidence of particular preceptors as far as sculptures are concerned. No doubt there are some reliefs that could be of ascetics of this sect since they are found on Shri-Vaishnava temples. On the vimana wall of the temple to the south of Vithala[40] there are a few reliefs of Vaishnava ascetics, who sport the Vaishnava namam on their foreheads: one holds a flower garland, two carry a kamandalu in one hand and another has his hands raised in adoration.

An unusual mendicant figure occurs frequently among Vijayanagara reliefs. It is of a shepherd or cowherd. His head and body are covered with a hood or a cape and he usually holds a staff in his hand and leans on it. Hoods made of rough woollen blankets were used by shepherds or cowherds for protection against the rain and the cold. Besides appearing on temple pillars at Vijayanagara, such figures are prominently displayed near entrances. For example, they are found on either side of the Garuda shrine of the Tiruvengalanatha temple. They probably represent the Golla-dasas, usually Vaishnava, belonging to the Golla or cowherd community.[41] Some may be Goravas, mendicant devotees of Mailara, who also wear a woollen blanket.[42]

Among the reliefs on pillars and elsewhere, are ascetics in strange garb. The garment is a slip-over that covers the body including the arms from the neck down to below the knees or to the ankles. It has been suggested that these reliefs might be representations of Virashaiva jangamas, itinerant preachers of the sect.[43]

Although there are no portrait sculptures of ascetics, there are a host of carvings, largely pillar reliefs, of the most varied groups of ascetics and yogis. The majority of these appear to be Shaiva. The *Sri Pampa Mahatme* describes some of the types of Shaiva ascetics at the site. Some ascetics are doing penance standing on one leg, others have both their hands raised, while others stand on their toes or on their heads with their feet pointed to the sky. Some sit in penance with bowed heads; others are seated naked amid five fires performing severe austerities. Many are covered with sacred ash, while others have it applied only on their foreheads. As for their hair styles: there are sages with one, three, five or many braids of hair; a number have their hair tied to form a great knot or twisted into a crown; a few have left their half untied and free, tossed by the wind.[44]

A study of the carvings of the ascetics reveals the varieties mentioned in the *Sri Pampa Mahatme* as well as many other types. Regarding clothing, some appear dressed in a dhoti, others are almost naked and wear only a brief loin-cloth. Some have shaven heads, but the majority display elaborate hairdoes: matted flowing locks, hair gathered up to form a large crown on the top of the head or tied into a big bow-like knot, and short dishevelled hair that frames the face in the jatabhara fashion. They appear in a variety of postures: seated cross-legged or in the yogic pose, squatting in relaxed manner, standing, walking, or with their bodies contorted in elaborate yogic poses. Their hand are joined in adoration, lifted above their head in penance, in the meditation or teaching mudras, or raised in supplication. At times they hold diverse objects: a rosary, staff, trident, kamandalu, umbrella or musical instruments. The pillar reliefs of ascetics portray on extensive variety of such figures.[45] Carvings of sages are found not only on pillar reliefs but also on boulders, gateways and wall surfaces. For example, among the Shaiva and Shakta reliefs, on three boulders on the north ridge,[46] there is one panel of five figures, of whom the first is a standing sage with his flowing locks arranged in a fantastic jatamandala and the second is of a seated ascetic holding his ears which are adorned with large earrings. On a boulder, on which are also carved Ganesha and Lakshmi, is a fine relief of an ascetic.[47] He is stands holding a staff in his right hand and a kamandalu in the left. He only wears a loin-cloth; his hair is arranged in the shape of a large bow and he carries a bundle on his shoulder.

NOTES

1. Anila Verghese, *Religious Traditions at Vijayanagara: as Revealed Through its Monuments*, pp. 111-15.
2. There is a marked contrast between the limited presence of the images of the Nayanmars compared with those of the Alvars, who enjoyed great popularity at Vijayanagara. It appears that in the city the Tamil influence was greater in the Vaishnava religion and iconography than in the Shaiva.
3. NFw/13.
4. In the area around the Vithala temple there are the Mudal-alvar (NCw/2), Nammalvar (NHa/10), Tirumalishai Alvar (NHj/1), Tirumangai Alvar (NCv/3) and Ramanuja (NCw/3) temples.
5. NVo/1.
6. See Appendix VII: Pillar reliefs in the principal temples.
7. *South Indian Inscriptions*, IX, Pt. II, No. 566.
8. *Vijayanagara: Progress of Research 1983-84*, no. 67, p. 49.
9. Anila Verghese, op. cit., p. 79.
10. Ibid.
11. For details about the Alvars and the Acharyas see: R. Champakalakshmi, *Vaiṣṇava Iconography in the Tamil Country*, pp. 238-44; T.A. Gopinatha Rao, *Sri Subrahmanya Ayyar Lectures on the History of the Śri Vaiṣṇavas*, pp. 2-40; J.S.M. Hooper, *Hymns of the Alvars*, pp. 9-21.
12. NCv/3.
13. Important Alvar-Acharya pillar reliefs on the middle block, south-east corner pillar in the rangamandapa of the Tirumangai Alvar temple (NCv/3): east face—Ramanuja, he wears a tulsimala and has a namam on

his forehead; south face—Nammalvar, he has namam on his forehead; west face—standing Tirumangai, with a sword and a shield in his right and left hands respectively; north face—seated Alvar.

14. NSa/1.
15. NGs/2.
16. NHa/10.
17. NJg/1.
18. Important Alvar-Acharya reliefs on recessed ceiling slabs. Raised central ceiling of mandapa NJg/1—east facing slab: Krishna holding a ball of butter flanked by Nammalvar and an Alvar; south facing slab—Vithala flanked by two Alvars; west facing slab—Venkatesha flanked by two Alvar; north facing slab—Krishna in penitent attitude flanked by Ramanuja and an Alvar.
19. A.L. Dallapiccola and Anila Verghese, 'The so-called Old Śiva Temple at Vithalapura', in *Vijayanagara: Progress of Research* (in press).
20. Raised central ceiling of the maharangamandapa of the Ramanuja temple (NCw/3):
    East side (north to south):
        Alvar flanked by two devotees.
        Alvar flanked by Rama and Lakshmana.
        Alvar flanked by two devotees.
    South side (east to west):
        Alvar flanked by Krishna and Hanuman.
        Ramanuja flanked by Rama and Surya.
        Alvar flanked by two devotees.
    West side (south to north):
        Ramanuja flanked by two devotees.
        Alvar (? the relief is hidden by a modern conservation masonry prop) flanked by two Vaishnava dvarapalas.
        Alvar flanked by Vithala and a devotee.
    North side (west to east):
        Tirumangai flanked by two devotees.
        Nammalvar flanked by Varadaraja and Vithala.
        Alvar flanked by two devotees.
21. Noteworthy Alvar-Acharya statues found during recent excavations. In and around the Vithala temple complex: The fine, intact black stone statue of Tondaradippodi, a mutilated statue of Tondaradippodi, an unfinished Alvar murti, some broken Alvar images.
    In the Krishna temple complex: three broken statues of seated alvars, a broken image of Tirumangai, possibly a mutilated statue of a standing Alvar.
    In the Royal Enclosure: a broken statue of Ramanuja.
    In the Vaishnava temple NSl/1: a statue of Nammalvar.
    In and near the Vaishnava temple NS1/3: a broken image of Ramanuja and a broken Alvar.
    In temple NRq/3: a small image of Nammalvar.
    Lying amidst ruins: a broken Alvar statue, in the debris to the west of the Ramachandra temple.
    Other examples in the Archaeological Museum, seated Alvar images: nos. 188, 297; two unnumbered ones; a standing Alvar statue, a statue of Ramanuja. Nammalvar statues: nos. 1193 and un unnumbered broken statue.
22. NHa/10.
23. Hooper, op. cit., plate opposite p. 15.
24. NJg/1.
25. NGx/1.
26. Noteworthy stucco figures of the Alvars: mandapa NJg/1: on the roof of this mandapa is a stucco parapet with niches on all four sides. The niches are now empty, except for the north side on which are found three headless stucco Alvar figures, each seated cross-legged with the hands in anjali-mudra. On the superstructure over the porch of temple NGx/1: Along the circular griva of the brick and mortar superstructure there are stucco images of eight Alvars. Below the superstructure, on a recessed slab there is a stucco image of Ranganatha. On the pitha on which Ranganatha is reclining are 12 stucco figures of the Alvars.
27. For details on the Natha sect see: G.W. Briggs, *Gorakhnāth and the Kanphaṭa Yogīs*.
28. K.V. Ramesh, *A History of South Kanara*, pp. 294-9; K.G. Vasantha Madhava, *Religions in Coastal Karnataka 1500-1763*, pp. 55-6.
29. H.K. Sherwani and P.M. Joshi (Eds), *History of Medieval Deccan 1294-1724*, Vol. I, p. 210.
30. A.P. Karmarkar, *The Religions of India, Vol. I: The Vratya or Dravidian Systems*, p. 246.
31. NFw/5.
32. NMx/2.
33. NQt/3.
34. Noteworthy reliefs of Nathas/Yogis in the pillared hall in the outer enclosure of the Tiruvengalanatha temple: Yogi seated on a scorpion: in the front portion of the hall; second row from the east, fourth pillar from the north, north face, central block.
    Yogi seated on a tortoise: in the rear raised portion of the hall: first row from the east, fifth pillar from the north, south face, top block.
35. Anila Verghese, op. cit., pp. 115-17.
36. *Sri Pampa Mahatme*, Middle Part, Chapters 2 and 19.
37. B. Venkoba Rao, Introduction to *Sri Vyasayogicaritam*, p. xiii, and p. cxviii.
38. NGn/1.
39. NCm/3.
40. NHa/10.
41. S.U. Kamath (Ed.), *Karnataka State Gazetteer*, Part I, p. 470.
42. V. Sri Ramachandra Murthy, 'Mailara cult in Andhra'. in *Quarterly Journal of the Mythic Society*, Vol. LXXIV, p. 352.
43. Y. Nirmala Kumari, *Social Life as Reflected in Sculptures and Paintings of laterr Vijayanagara Period*, p. 32.
44. *Sri Pampa Mahatme*, Middle Part, Chapter 2.
45. See Appendix VII: Pillar reliefs in the principal temples.
46. See footnote 32.
47. Gateway NRb.

CHAPTER 10

Satis and Heroes

Those who died heroically were greatly venerated and memorial stones were erected in their honour. Some such stones, mainly slabs with relief carvings, are found in Vijayanagara city. There are also some forty examples in the Anegondi area, many of the post-Vijayanagara period, as this village has been continually inhabited until the present-day.[1] A number of memorial stones are displayed in the Archaeological Museum.

There are three main types of memorial stones: sati-stones, satikals or mastikals; sati-and-hero stones, called sati-virakals; and hero-stones or virakals.

Satikals commemorate the brave wife who perished, usually by fire, at the death of her husband. The sati-virakals are composite slabs celebrating the heroic death of a man and the sati performed by his wife or wives. Virakals keep alive the memory of a dead hero who may be considered as a divinity, but a sati is invariably raised to the status of minor goddess.[2] Whether the dead hero is deified or not, the virakal is perceived as the abode of the sacred presence.[3] The sun and crescent moon which often appear at the top of these memorial slabs indicate the lasting glory of the sati or hero. In a few monuments there is a label inscription giving the name of the person honoured.

A. Satikals (Figures 107-109, Plates 80-84)

The custom of sati was widely prevalent in pre-Vijayanagara and Vijayanagara times. At Vijayanagara the common method of performing sahagamana was through immolation by fire. However, among the Virashaivas sati by burial was also practised.[4] Foreign travellers to Vijayanagara have left detailed descriptions of the sati ritual.[5] These travel accounts reveal that the practice was highly revered, but not obligatory. Differences recorded by these visitors may reflect variations in the customs of diverse social groups or changes with the passage of time.

The raised arm of the sati, bent at the elbow, with the palm facing forward in abhaya-mudra and with bangles adorning the wrists, is the essential feature in all satikals. Usually the women who committed sati are fully shown, accompanied by the husband, who has hands in anjali-mudra. In a few satikals, only the right bejewelled arm of the sati is carved as if emerging from a pillar, emphasizing the importance of the arm raised in blessing. The sati blessed the people with her right hand before entering the fire, and she continues to bless her devotees.[6] The left hand of the sati in all the mastikals at the site is extended downwards. A lemon or a pot, is sometimes grasped in this hand. In a sati- and-hero stone, at Anegondi, the sati holds a mirror as well as a lemon.[7] The custom of the woman about to commit sati carrying a mirror has been highlighted by both Nuniz[8] and Caesar Frederick.[9] Both also refer to pot of oil used in the sati ceremony.

Nuniz mentions a ritual performed by the mother or some other relative of the widow about to commit sahagamana. She placed a pot of water on her head and walked three times around the fire pit, at each round making a hole in the pot. On completing the three rounds she broke the pot. Then the sati herself put a pot of oil on her head and cast herself into the fire. According to Frederick, the sati was anointed by another woman with the oil from the pot. The sati with the pot then stepped into the flames. It is likely that the pot held by the sati in some Vijayanagara satikals is a container of either water or, more probably, oil. The exact explanation for the lemon seen in the hands of some satis is not known. However, lime has a variety of ritual significances, one of them being fertility.[10] Lime is also associated with sacrifice, for there are known instances of offerings of lime being presented as substitutes for human sacrifice.[11]

Only a few satikals are still standing at the site. In the Mudu Viranna temple lies one stone within the courtyard and one practically buried just outside.[12] A fine sati-stone is seen on the Tungabhadra, along the path to the Vithala temple.[13] It is divided into two panels. In the lower one are carved two satis and their husband with an elephant and diminutive attendant in front. The presence of the elephant suggests the elevated social status of the family. In the top panel the man and his two sati wives stand with joined hands in the abode of Vishnu, represented by the chakra and shankha, flanked by Garuda and Hanuman. This is the only Vaishnava memorial stone in the entire city. In all others, sectarian symbols are always Shaiva, usually the linga and Nandi.

One of the finest satikals at Vijayanagara is found within the Urban Core of the city.[14] In the lower register are depicted the man with his sati wife. Both have their hair tied in a large knot to one side. Their finely draped costumes and jewellery are carefully rendered. The top portion of the slab shows the couple in svarga, adoring the Shiva-linga. Before it is the crouching Nandi and an imposing pujari waving an arati lamp and ringing a bell.

Among the other satikals on the site is that of a sati by herself, west of Hemakuta hill.[15] The woman is shown beautifully dressed, with well draped sari, elaborate coiffure and heavy jewellery. Another sati-stone, on which is sculpted a sati holding a lemon in her left hand and accompanied by her husband, is located in the corner of a tank.[16] Near Bhima's gate is a small shrine beside which is a broken satikal;[17] here the woman carries a pot and is alongside her husband. On a rock at Koti-tirtha is carved a group of two men, two women and a small boy. One woman has her right hand in the typical sati-mudra.

North-west of the Virupaksha complex is another satikal. An inscription gives the name of the widow portrayed as Virayamma, daughter of Viranna. She holds a pitcher in her left hand.[18]

To the east of the car-street of the Tiruvengalanatha temple there is a group of four satikals, two carved on a boulder and two on stone slabs.[19] One of those on the boulder is particularly striking: in it the sati is represented in the form of a pillar from which emerges the hand raised in benediction. To the north-east of the Narasimha temple on the south bank there is a narrow stab depicting a sati.

There are a little over forty satikals at the site, including those in the Archaeological Museum. This is not a large number for such a vast city that served as the capital of a mighty empire for more than 200 years. It can therefore be concluded that, although the practice of sahagamana was encouraged and the satis were honoured and worshipped, the custom of sati was not so widespread as reports of foreign travellers would indicate. For them, this practice was so bizarre that they possibly exaggerated its popularity in their travelogues.[20] On the other hand, it is probable that not every act of sahagamana was commemorated by a memorial stone. A study of these satikals also proves that not all co-wives committed sati at the death of their husband. In one satikal in the Archaeological Museum three women are shown, only one of whom has her hand in the typical sati-mudra.[21] In another slab in the Museum only one of two wives is a sati.[22]

The satikals follow a general pattern, the slabs being divided into two panels. In the lower panel are seen the woman or women, never more than four, generally with the husband. In the upper panel they are shown in svarga. Sometimes only the man is seen in svarga. Thus, not only was the woman committing sati liberated, but also her family and in particular her dead husband. The linga, occasionally flanked by Nandi and/or a pujari, are depicted in the top panel of a few examples.

Satikals can be classified into a number of types. In rare instances the woman appears alone. Many satikals depict a man and his sati-wife, while others have a man and two sati-wives or a man and three satis. In a few examples, a man and two or three wives are seen, of whom only one is a sati. Finally, there are those mastikals in which the sati is represented only by the raised right hand attached to a pillar.[23]

B. Sati-Virakals

In mastikals the husband is portrayed either standing or seated, with hand joined in anjali-mudra. He may or may not have died in the course of a gallant action. In sati-virakals the man is presented in a heroic pose, while the sati or satis stand with raised right hand.

A large number of sati-virakals were erected at Vijayanagara. Most of them have been removed to the Archaeological Museum. In Anegondi the majority of existing memorial stones commemorate heroes and their satis. A unique example has a relief of a man killing a tiger with his dagger in the company of his sati-wife holding a mirror and a lemon.[24]

The simplest type of sati-virakal consists of a single panel on which are sculpted the hero and his consort. The more elaborate are divided into two or three panels. All these varieties are displayed in the Archaeological Museum.

Of the one-panelled type is a stone slab in which a warrior is depicted bending his bow: at his side is his sati.[25]

In a two-panelled sati-virakal, the hero rides a horse, brandishing a dagger.[26] An umbrella held over him denotes his importance or the respect due to him; to his right is his sati. The top register shows a linga flanked by sun and moon. Another slab at the Archaeological Museum shows on the lower panel a man carrying a dagger flanked by his sati, and on the upper the couple seated in svarga.[27]

In one example of the three-panel variety, the lowermost register shows two fighting men armed with daggers.[28] One figure is followed by an attendant, also armed with sword and shield. In the central section, the dead hero, with his hands in anjali-mudra, is accompanied by his wife, who has committed sahagamana. A tiny figure holds an umbrella over them. The sun and moon are carved in the top of the slab.

A fine sati-virakal shows two men fighting on horseback; the middle panel is occupied by the hero and his four satis.[29] In the top panel the hero is in Kailasha, represented by a linga and Nandi. As usual, the sun and moon also appear.

In a notable sati-virakal, the lowermost panel depicts two riders engaged in combat.[30] The central panel shows the hero and his wife seated with hands in anjali-mudra before a Shiva-linga. The woman is depicted near a sati pillar, indicating that she has committed sati. Sun, moon and a linga are carved on the top panel.

C. Virakals (Plate 85)

Virakals commemorate an act of valour that, usually ended in the hero's death: chivalrous service in war, retrieving cattle from raiders, protecting the honour of women, defending a city or village, resisting bandits, killing wild animals, etc. Virakals have one or two panels, while the more elaborate variety have three. The bottom panel shows the heroic deed resulting in the death of the hero; in the central panel, the deceased is journeying to svarga, and in the top panel he worships a linga.

Besides the memorial stones found in Anegondi, there are very few virakals still in situ. Two stand in the Mudu Viranna temple.[31] One depicts a man shooting an arrow with his bow. The second shows in the lower panel a duel between two men; in the top panel is the dead hero, seated with his hands in anjali-mudra beneath an arch culminating in a kirti-mukha. He has reached Kailasha where he faces the linga, Nandi, sun and moon.

On the southern slope of Hemakuta hill is a small shrine built against a boulder on which is a relief showing a man defending himself from an enraged elephant.[32] One hand firmly holds the trunk and tusk while kicking the prancing animal. Behind him is a woman carrying a pot on her head, followed by a smaller tame elephant. This may be a commemorative stone recording some historical event. If so, it is the only extant temple in the city dedicated to a hero. The same scene occurs, in a smaller scale, among Shaiva reliefs, in a tiny rock-shelter to the south-west of the Vitthala temple complex.[33]

The same theme is found on two virakals in the Archaeological Museum. In the first example a man fighting an elephant is the centre of the composition.[34] Behind him are two women, one carrying a pot on her head, and in front Shiva and Parvati on Nandi bless him. A standing male figure concludes the panel.

The second virakal shows a mad elephant in one corner.[35] The hero subdues the animal by grabbing its tusk with one hand, stabbing it with his sword, and kicking the beast. At the other end of the slab are Mailara and consort on horseback blessing this act of bravery. In the centre, a man stands with his hands in anjali-mudra.

Three rock-carvings depict the same incident. One is carved on a boulder within a natural rock-shelter.[36] At one end of this panel is a elephant with a rider holding a spike or a spear. In the centre the hero is attacking the elephant. As usual, he grabs the animal's tusk and trunk with his hands and administers a kick. On the ground is a ring-shaped object, which could represent a pot laying on its side with its rim facing the viewer. Behind the hero is a male figure on horseback armed with a staff or sword, wearing a kirita-mukuta on his head. He may be identified as Mailara. Behind Mailara stands yet another elephant with upraised trunk.

The second rock-carving depicts the same theme.[37] In the centre of the panel the hero is fights the enraged beast. He seizes its trunk and tusk and kicks it. An overturned pot with its distinctly visible rim lies on the ground between the hero and the animal. Behind the hero is a man on horseback holding a staff-like weapon. A second elephant raises its trunk over the rider.

In the third rock-carving, similar to the one in the shrine the hero grabs the elephant by its trunk and tusk and kicks it. Behind him is a woman with a pot on her head; a smaller elephant stands behind her.[38]

All of these representations at the site show the hero wearing a cap and in most he carries what appears to be a back-pack. In four sculptures the woman with the pot is present, in two the overturned pot, in five a second elephant, and a deity blessing the hero possibly in three.

It would appear that these hero-stones relate the same historical or mythical incident as the fight between the man and the elephant is the same in all examples. It is probable that the hero was a traveller, as indicated by his back-pack, and that he saved one or more women from the fury of the mad elephant.

The identity of this hero is unknown. No doubt, there are stories of Shaiva saints who grappled with elephants.[39] These include that of Madivalu Machayya who took the bundle of washing off his back and placed it in the sky before confronting the enraged elephant. However, these stories do not have all the elements found in these Vijayanagara virakals.[40]

There are yet other virakals of the single-panel type. In one example, now in the Archaeological Museum the hero on a galloping horse holds a spear aloft.[41] Two male attendants follow him, one of whom bears an umbrella. In another the hero on horseback carries a spear; he is flanked by male retainers, the one at the rear holding the ceremonial umbrella over the hero's head.[42]

In other virakals the hero is depicted shooting an arrow from his bow.[43] A small slab shows a man carrying a dagger, with linga, sun and moon above.[44]

There are two virakals of the three-panel type. In one,[45] the bottom panel depicts a sword fight between a man on a horse and another on foot. In the central panel the fallen hero is carried to svarga by two apsaras. In the top panel the hero is in Kailasha, where he is shown in the company of a woman and two rishis. All worship the Shiva-linga, their hands joined in anjali-mudra. Above are carved the sun and moon.

In a similar virakal, the bottom panel shows a fight between a rider and a man on foot. In the central section, two apsaras, bearing fly-whisks, escort the hero to svarga. In the top panel, he is shown squatting with hands in anjali-mudra before the Shiva-linga and Nandi.[46]

D. Memorials (Plates 86-88)

Another category of virakal is the memorial stone honouring the memory of a person who deliberately sacrificed his life as a religious act. Here death is not the unfortunate result of a brave action, but self-inflicted and glorified.

Acts of self-immolation were perhaps undertaken in fulfilment of a vow to a deity or as an expression of gratitude for bestowing some great favour. This practice was particularly common among the Shaivas and Shaktas. In pre-Vijayanagara times, shrines dedicated to Bhairava, Virabhadra and Kali, were sometimes intended to be used by devotees wishing to sacrifice their own lives, usually by severing their heads.[47]

Self-immolation by throwing oneself under

the wheels of a moving temple chariot is mentioned by Nicolo Conti.[48] Foreign visitors record another custom at Vijayanagara, self-torture by hook-swinging as a thanksgiving to a deity for a prayer that had been fulfilled.[49] There do not appear to be any extant sculptural representations of either of these practices, but some memorial stones depict other forms of self-immolation.

The most impressive example is a magnificently carved stone-slab in the Urban Core of the city.[50] It is divided into three registers. The bottom depicts a courageous man unflinchingly preparing to decapitate himself. His head is tied to a mechanical contraption for this purpose. He has pulled the lever down with his left hand while holding a sword in his right. When he releases the left hand, the lever would fly upwards and the weapon would sever his head, leaving it hanging on the lever. An attendant is at one end working the mechanism. The hero is flanked by two consorts who have already committed sati. The man and his wives are well clothed and bejewelled. The middle register shows the three flying towards svarga, cross-legged with their hands joined in anjali-mudra. In the top register is a Shiva-linga on a high pitha faced by Nandi. A bearded Shaiva priest with a heavy topknot performs puja. The sun and moon are prominently carved at the top of the slab. This is a self-immolation memorial of the sati-virakal category.

There is a memorial stone in the Archaeological Museum in the form of a multi-faceted, tapering pillar with a square base, on two faces of which is a relief of a man in the process of decapitating himself with his sword. The other two faces show a standing woman who has committed sati.[51]

On a third self-immolation stone in the Archaeological Museum, the hero appears to be in the act of disemboweling himself.[52] The slab is divided into three panels. The bottom shows the hero impaled on a pointed instrument. In one hand he holds aloft a dagger or a sword, while an attendant holds an umbrella over him. On either side two musicians celebrate this meritorious act by playing on drums, flute and tambourine. The central panel is occupied by four apsaras who carry the hero to svarga in a palanquin. In the top panel he is seated along with many others in svarga adoring a Shiva-linga while a priest with flowing jatas performs puja. Two other stone slabs in the Museum commemorate heroes who have decapitated themselves.[53]

E. Slabs Depicting Feet (Figure 110)

Flat slabs on which are sculpted a pair of feet, often encircled by a serpent, may be included here, although the depictions are of a different nature from the memorials—they do not commemorate heroic deeds. Sometimes such feet are carved on the sheet-rock.

Feet may be symbolic representations of revered deities, saints or great persons. South of the Sasivekalu Ganesha temple is a small sanctuary enshrining a pair of feet, with a naga around it, carved on the sheet-rock.[54] This is now known as Vishnu-pada.[55] A brief record on a boulder in the Tungabhadra engraved around a carve pair of feet, identifies it as the feet of Virupaksha.[56] However, this does not mean that all such carvings necessarily represent the feet of Vishnu or another deity. That such feet could also represent heroes or other persons worthy of veneration is indicated by the presence of such stones in front of two rock carvings of a hero grappling with a furious elephant.[57] In the first case, the feet encircled by a serpent are carved on a flat rock in front of the rock-shelter. In the second case, the pair of feet appear without the snake on a horizontal rock surface in front of the hero-stone.

The most elaborate example of such a carving is located to the south-west of the Vithala temple complex. Here, in a natural depression in the sheet-rock near the river, is carved a large pair of foot-prints, placed side by side with the feet facing in opposite directions, encircled by a naga. This sculpture is set within a rectangular frame along which are reliefs of the shankha, chakra, trishula, sun, crescent moon and other motifs, as well of as the Shiva sectarian marks.[58]

NOTES

1. Sugandha, *History and Archaeology of Anegondi*, p. 282.
2. M. Chidanandamurti, 'Two Masti Temples in Karnataka', in *Memorial Stones*, ed. by S. Settar and G.D. Sontheimer, p. 129.
3. D.D. Shulman, *The King and the Clown in South Indian Myth and Poetry*, p. 351.
4. Duarte Barbosa, *The Book of Duarte Barbosa*, ed. by M. Longworth Dames, pp. 217-18; and Nuniz, in *A Forrgotten Empire*, p. 393.
5. Such as Caesar Frederick, see note 9; and Nicolo Conti, see note 48.
6. M. Chidanandamurti, loc. cit.
7. Sugandha, op. cit., pp. 282-3.
8. Nuniz, op. cit., p. 392.
9. Caesar Frederick, in *Purchas His Pilgrimages*, by Samuel Purchas, Vol. X, p. 95.
10. E. Masilamani-Meyer, 'The Changing Face of Kattavarayan', in *Criminal Gods and Demon Devotees*, ed. by A. Hiltebeitel, p. 101, fn. 23.
11. E. C. Visuvalingam, 'Bhairava's Royal Brahminicide: The Problem of the Mahabrahmana', in *Criminal Gods and Demon Devotees*, ed. by A. Hiltebeitel, p. 206.
12. NLw/3.
13. NGo/3.
14. NPq/1.
15. NLf/2.
16. NNm/3.
17. NXo/1.
18. *Vijayanagara: Progress of Research, 1984-1987*, No. 7, p. 29.
19. NGy/2.
20. Anila Verghese, *Religious Traditions at Vijayanagara: as Revealed Through its Monuments*, p. 94.
21. No. 212.
22. No. 733.
23. Noteworthy examples of satikals:
    Satikals depicting the sati alone: NLf/3; Archaeological Museum, no. 407.
    Satikals depicting one sati and husband: Outside NLw/3; NNm/3; NPq/1; Outside NXo//1; Archaeological Museum, nos. 168, 203, 213, 257, 261, 384, 402, 404, 409, 421, 438, 513, 606, 739, 747, 833, 1063.
    Satikals depicting two satis and husband: NGo/3; Archaeological Museum, nos. 41, 335, 382.
    Satikals depicting three satis and husband: In NLw/3; Archaeological Museum, no. 608.
    Satikals in which one out of three women is a sati: One at Koti-tirtha: Archaeological Museum, nos. 212, 733.
    Satikals in which the sati is represented by a sati-pillar: Archaeological Museum, no. 835.
    Satikals in which the sati/satis hold a lemon in the left hand: In NNm/3, Archaeological Museum, no. 168, 212, 438, 608, 739, 833, 835.
    Satikals in which the sati holds a pot in hand: outside NXo/1: Archaeological Museum, nos. 257, 261, 606, 835.
24. Sugandha, loc. cit.
25. No. 406.
26. No. 250.
27. No. 463.
28. No. 832.
29. No. 830.
30. No. 831.
31. See note 12.
32. NLg/3.
33. NHf/6.
34. No. 278.
35. No. 834.
36. NOx/3.
37. NPv/1.
38. NN1/1.
39. Velcheru Narayana Rao (Trsl.), *Śiva's Warriors*, pp. 133-7.
40. The *Sri Pampa Mahatme* does not throw any light as to who this hero could be.
41. No. 744.
42. No. 820.
43. Nos. 35, 742, 836.
44. No. 1700.
45. No. 256.
46. No. 165.
47. M.S. Sarma, *History of the Reddi Kingdom: Circa 1325 to circa 1448 AD*, p. 342.
48. Nicolo Conti, 'The Travels of Nicolo Conti in the East in the Early Part of the Fifteenth Century', in *India in the Fifteenth Century*, ed. by R.H. Major, p. 28.
49. Nicolo Conti, loc. cit.; and Duarte Barbosa, op. cit., pp. 220-2.
50. North of temple NNz/2.
51. No. 219.
52. No. 251.
53. Nos. 524 and 525.
54. NLg/1.
55. D. Devakunjari, *Hampi*, p. 50.
56. NFr. See also, *Vijayanagara: Progress of Research, 1984-87*, No. 20, p. 31.
57. NOx/3 and NPv/1.
58. NGk/7.

CHAPTER 11

Jaina Images

Jaina sculptures at Vijayanagara are both limited in number and in variety. The only Jaina themes present are Tirthankaras in static poses on the lintels of temple entrances, on stone slabs, memorial carvings and on the wall of one temple; a Jaina saint in one sculpture; few Jaina holy men and devotees in the memorial sculptures; and a few yakshas and yakshis, minor divinities who appear in Jaina iconography. None of the Jaina sculptures are of monumental size or remarkable in iconographic style or sculptural virtuosity.

With six temples within the Urban Core and one in Anegondi,[1] the Jainas were an influential community in Vijayanagara city, especially in the fourteenth and fifteenth centuries.[2] One of the earliest dated Vijayanagara-period temples at the site is the Jaina shrine built by Irugappa in 1385 for Kunthu Jinanatha, now locally called the Ganigitti temple.[3] In addition, two other Jaina monuments also have foundation inscriptions, namely the Parshavanatha temple built in 1426 by Devaraya II,[4] and the temple in Anegondi of 1402.[5] However, in spite of the prominent Jaina presence in the city, there are only a few sculptures of Jaina themes.

A. Reliefs (Figures 111, 112)

In general, Jaina temples are austere, with little or no ornamentation. The only carving is on door frames decorated with bands of foliation and a relief of a seated Tirthankara in the centre of the lintel. The lintel icons are stereotyped: the Tirthankara is nude, seated in padmasana, with hands in dhyana-mudra. A triple umbrella is sometimes carved over the head.

In addition to these reliefs, two elephants are carved on the walls of the Jaina temple at Anegondi. The larger of two Jaina temples within the east valley of the Urban Core has pillar reliefs of birds, squatting lions and animal and floral motifs in its outer mandapa.[6] This temple has also two striking reliefs of yakshas on the south wall of the outer mandapa, flanking the entrance into the inner mandapa. On either side of the doorway is a relief of a rider on an elephant. Each figure is four-armed and wears a kirita. The lower two hands of each yaksha are joined in anjali-mudra while the upper two hold round objects, possibly pots, that rest on the kirita.

B. Stone Slabs and Boulders

The finest examples of this category are the six well-executed Tirthankara images carved on stone slabs about one metre in height, recovered during the excavations in and around the Parshvanatha temple. All six figures are depicted in the nude, standing in kayotsarga with triple umbrellas over the heads. Each Tirthankara is flanked by a small relief of a yaksha and a yakshi. One of these sculptures depicts Parshvanatha, recognized by the five-headed naga hood over his head. This elegantly sculpted image was probably originally enshrined in the sanctuary.

There are two Jaina sculptures in the Archaeological Museum, one of Gommateshvara (Bahubali)[7] and the second, a stone slab with four Tirthankaras in relief.[8]

A series of fourteenth-century Jaina memorials are carved on a rock below the Gavi Ranganatha in Anegondi.[9] Each consists of a sculpture of a Tirthankara standing in kayotsarga. On either side are figures of a preceptor reciting from a manuscript on a stand, and a deceased devotee seated with hands in anjali-mudra. An inscription below each group lists the names of the preceptors, their lineages and the names of their deceased devotees.[10] Apart from these memorial reliefs in Anegondi there are two other Jaina sculptures: one of the group of Jaina images on a platform,[11] the other a row of Tirthankara images.[12]

C. Hindu Monuments

Jaina images occasionally appear in Hindu temples and sculptural groups, although never on temple pillar reliefs. There is , however, one example of a Jina image on the vimana wall in the Ramachandra temple. The small relief of a seated Tirthankara is in padmasana and dhyana-mudra.[13]

As mentioned earlier in Chapter 6, a Jina replaces Buddha in certain dashavatara groups at Vijayanagara. The best example of the Jina images among the avataras of Vishnu is on the plinth of the mahamandapa of the Vithala temple.

NOTES

1. NRp/1, NSq/1 (Parshavanatha temple), NSt/2, NSu/3, NSu/5, NXn/1 (Kunthu Jinanatha temple).
2. Anila Verghese, *Religious Traditions at Vijayanagara: as Revealed Through its Monuments*, pp. 121-5.
3. *South Indian Inscriptions*, I, No. 152.
4. Ibid, No. 153.
5. Anila Verghese, op. cit., p. 124.
6. NSt/2.
7. No. 766.
8. No. 1424.
9. HYa/2
10. *Vijayanagara: Progress of Research 1984-87*, Nos. 170, 171, 172, 174, pp. 67-8.
11. JQh/4.
12. JQm/1.
13. On the same wall is a Buddha image, merely differentiated from the one of the Tirthankara by the ushnisha on its head.

CHAPTER 12

Non-Religious Themes

R.N. Saletore was perhaps the first scholar to mention the vast repertory of non-religious themes in the carvings at Vijayanagara.[1] It is not only the world of the gods and of epic heroes which holds the stage; there is keen interest in the everyday life of the ruler and of his subjects.

A. Courtly and Martial Themes

The royal figure (Figures 113, 114, Plates 90-92)

The artists of Sangama epoch created a distinctive male type which may be termed royal. This figure is generally shown seated, accompanied by one or more standing chauri-bearers. Until the mid-fifteenth century the distinctive features of the 'royal figure' are the hair tied in a bun on the nape of the neck; the seated posture on the low throne, one leg is crossed over the other; and occasionally the right hand raised in tarjani-mudra.[2] The attire is a simple short dhoti or lungi and the usual jewellery.

The standard royal figure evolves over time. The two portrait sculptures placed on either side of the sanctuary doorway of the Anjaneya temple depicting king Mallikarjuna and his chauri-bearer Shirangu are a case in point.[3] This is one of the few examples of portrait sculptures at the site in which the donors are clearly identified by inscriptions. Both Mallikarjuna and Shirangu have their hands in anjali-mudra, thus stressing that they are both devotees of the enshrined deity. Here, for the first time, the king wears the long scarf thrown over one arm, a device which is to become a sign of royalty in the sixteenth century. The most important change in the courtly attire is, however, the kulayi worn by both figures.

The most popular carvings of the royal figure at worship are those on the porch-like projection of the open mandapa of Krishna temple. On one of the four pillars is the carving of a noble, or possibly a royal personage, engaged in the worship of Balakrishna. On another pillar, a similar figure is paying homage to a linga, possibly representing Virupaksha. Local tradition claims these royal figures to be portraits of Krishnadevaraya but there is no way of ascertaining their identity.

A small image, also reputed to be a portrait of Krishnadevaraya, shows a royal figure standing with hands joined in anjali-mudra, holding a sword in the crook of his arm. This carving is located in the Virupaksha complex, on the west wall of the north gopura leading to the Manmatha tank. The two-line inscription near the carving read: *shri raya naraja*.[4]

One more portrait sculpture is locally identified as Krishnadevaraya and his two queens: a royal figure accompanied by two ladies, all standing with hands in anjali-mudra, is carved at the base of the 'King's Balance' near the Vithala temple.

Four interesting portrait sculptures represent noblemen and royal personages on columns in the subsidiary shrine in the Tiruvengalanatha complex. Two show a nobleman wearing a tall cap standing in attitude of reverence with his hands in anjali-mudra. Of the remaining two, one is of a high dignitary or maybe even a king, as he wears the scarf on his left shoulder, addressing a minister or court officer. The size of the two figures conveys their difference in status. Both wear kulayis, the royal personage being the taller. The minister carries a stick in his left hand. In the last relief, another royal figure, with scarf and kulayi, is giving a gift to a young Brahmin. Local tradition claims that these carvings are portraits of Achyutaraya after whom the temple is generally named. But there is no way of ascertaining the identity of figures.

Apart from the portraits of king Mallikarjuna

and Shirangu, therefore, no royal image can be definitely identified as an actual portrait.

Other examples of sixteenth-century courtly images not necessarily related to a particular ruler are seen in the schist carvings on the west face of the Mahanavami platform. One shows a standing royal or noble figure with courtiers before him. Another shows a seated figure, possibly a king accompanied by a female retinue, greeted by courtiers.

Granting audience (Plate 96)

This is one of the most frequently depicted royal pursuits. One of the earlier depictions of this theme is carved on the lower tier of the Mahanavami platform, south face, first panel from the west. A royal personage seated on a low throne receives two foreigners. Behind him stands a young attendant waving a long scarf. The same scene, with slight variations, occurs repeatedly in the iconographic programme of the oldest part of the platform.

On the east side of the enclosure wall of the Ramachandra temple, second register, the head of a caravan of foreign horse-traders is paying homage to the ruler seated on a throne beneath a structure. In the course of time these foreign horse-traders disappear from the courtly milieu and are replaced by elegantly dressed noblemen, who are shown in the act of paying homage to the ruler, as for instance in the schist carvings of the Mahanavami platform, south of the west side stairs.

Parades and sports (Plates 93-96)

Another royal pastime was military parades and martial sports, especially fencing, wrestling and boxing. Military parades are frequently carved on the lower tier of the Mahanavami platform. Rows of footmen carrying long spears, noblemen riding horses, soldiers armed with swords and shields parade before seated courtly figures. On the exterior of the enclosure wall of the Ramachandra temple (third frieze from the bottom), the ruler and his attendants review troops and martial exercises. Scenes depicting fencing with long spears and wrestling are carved on the western and northern walls, thus interrupting the series of footmen, archers and spearmen parading, as it were, around the monument. The kingly figure, which in the other registers is seated at the point where the eastern wall abuts the main gateway, appears three additional times in this tier: at the juncture of the western and the northern walls; on the northern wall, near the north gateway; at the eastern end of the north wall.

A lively wrestling match in the presence of a ruler, two noblemen and various attendants is carved on the south face, bottom register of the Mahanavami platform. What appears to be the referee, majestically resting his hands on a long staff, watches the progress of the match. A similar scene is on the otherwise plain wall of the Zenana-Enclosure near the Elephant Stables.

Music and dance (Plates 96, 104)

Numerous scenes show musicians and dancers entertaining the ruler. Suffice it to mention that the complete fourth register on the exterior of the enclosure wall of the Ramachandra temple is devoted to the rendering of a musical performance of music and dance. The ruler is seated as usual on a throne beneath a structure at one end.

In a more private setting, on the east face of the staircase on the south side of the Mahanavami platform, on the last but one register, a ruler or nobleman watches the performance of a young girl acrobat, who walks on her hands, and some female dancers. Standing behind the courtly figure are two ladies, one of whom is waving a scarf or a chauri.

Hunting (Figures G, 115, 116, Plate 96)

This was a popular royal activity. The appearance of animals running in the forest, or standing paralysed with fear, or mating, bear testimony to the unparalleled familiarity with animal forms and exquisite sense of observation of the early sculptors. There are comparatively few carvings depicting a royal or noble hunter. One exceptionally interesting composition is on the south face of the Mahanavami platform, on the second register where it abuts the steps. The scene is doubtless among the most artistically ambitious of this phase. It involves a great number of landscape elements, especially animals and trees.

To the left is the royal hunter, armed with bow and arrow, escorted by a diminutive attendant and accompanied by two hounds.

As stated earlier, among the most noteworthy carvings on the Mahanavami platform are those depicting forest scenes where hunters, whether kings, noblemen or tribals, chase various animals, or in turn are chased by them. The forest renderings are an outstanding testimony to the ability of the Vijayanagara artists to deal imaginatively with spatial arrangements and complex temporal sequences of a given narrative. A particularly dramatic scene is carved on the second tier, second row of carvings, on the south side of the monument. Here a hunter perched on a tree tries to kill a tiger with his sword while the surroundings are filled with wild animals. A similar scene on the lower tier of the monument shows a bowman and attendant chasing wild animals. The attendant wounds a lion; the same two men are then shown escaping from the attacks of a lion in the crown of a tree in the proximity of cross-shaped tank.

Soldiers and warfare (Plate 1)

Soldiers occur in considerable numbers on the Mahanavami platform and on the processional friezes on the enclosure wall of the Ramachandra temple. From literary sources it is known that the Vijayanagara rulers had a vast army comprising several divisions. In the reliefs, however, only infantry, cavalry and the elephant-corps are clearly discernible.[5]

Archers, swordsmen and spearmen appear repeatedly in the reliefs. Among these, the archers were the most closely observed by the foreign guests at the capital. In his account Paes describes with great precision the archers' and swordsmen's apparel:

> . . . they have bows plated with gold and silver, and others have them polished, and their arrows very neat, and so feathered that they could not be better; daggers at their waists and battle axes, with shafts and ends of the gold and silver.

On occasion of the annual review the sword-bearers stood there

> with their shields, with many flowers of gold and silver on them, . . . others all covered with silver leaf-work beautifully wrought, others with painted colours, others black and (so polished that) you can see into them as into a mirror, and their swords so richly ornamented that they could not possibly be more so.[6]

Archers can be seen on the third register of the processional frieze. They carry bows in the left hands and arrows in the right. Like most male figures of the period, they wear their hair tied in a bun at the back of the head; their chest and arms are bare, except for occasional jewellery items, and they have a short dhoti tied at the waist by a cloth or a girdle arranged like a small fan at front.

Swordsmen are to be seen repeatedly, on the lowermost tier, south side, of the Mahanavami platform and on the outer wall of the Ramachandra temple, third register, especially in proximity of the northern gate to the complex. They have small round shields held up against their chests in their left hands, and swords slightly curved towards the ends in their right, which rest on the shoulders. They wear the same attire as the archers and headgear which looks like a turban. In Mahanavami platform carvings the soldiers wear conspicuous daggers stuck in their girdles. Some figures seem to have closely cropped hair or tight-fitting caps, instead of turban-like headgear.

Spearmen engaged in martial exercises, in similar costume to the archers, appear on the third register of the processional frieze of the Ramachandra temple. Parading spearmen, on the westernmost block on the southern side of the Mahanavami platform, lower tier, proudly carry tall spears which protrude into the second row of panels.

According to Paes, the cavalry were mounted on fully caparisoned horses. The details of trappings and costumes, painstakingly described by this and other eye-witnesses, are difficult to trace in the weathered sculptures. The umbrella of state, however, held by a groom or a lesser noble over the head of some important personage on horseback, frequently appears, as on the processional frieze of the Ramachandra temple, third register, western side.

Mounted swordsmen are seen in many of the Mahanavami platform carvings. In fact, no two figures are the same; each has been depicted in a different attire and posture.

Foreign visitors were greatly impressed by the

elephants of the Vijayanagara rulers. The Russian traveller, Athanasius Nikitin, who visited the capital in 1474, wrote:

> Elephants are greatly used in battle, large scythes are attached to the trunk and tusks of the elephants and the animals are clad in ornamental plates of steel. They carry a citadel and in the citadel twelve men in armour with guns and arrows.[7]

War-elephants do not seem to occur in the carvings at the capital. However, parading elephants with beautifully embroidered trappings with or without riders, are frequently on monuments, especially in the processional friezes on the Mahanavami platform and on the walls of the Ramachandra temple.

An interesting, unfortunately much damaged, scene of a battle between armies is depicted on the western face of the Mahanavami platform, south of the stairs. This sixteenth-century scene, carved on a schist slab, bears a strong resemblance to a stucco rendering of a battle on the inner face of the eastern gopura of the Krishna temple. This could be a depiction of the celebrated conquest of the Udayagiri fort. It may be assumed that Krishnadevaraya was very proud of this victory.

B. Donors and Devotees
(Figure 117, Plates 99-101)

The ruler and the royal household were among the main sponsors of building activity at the capital. Yet they were not the exclusive patrons of the arts; other benefactors were also involved in giving financial support to the establishment of religious institutions. This can be clearly seen by the donor and devotee figures which are relatively common in the sculptures at Vijayanagara. The donor figures are easily recognized by their location, facing or flanking the temple image. They stand with their hands folded in anjali-mudra, often accompanied by their spouses, sometimes also by attendants or children.

The most finely finished portraits of donors at Vijayanagara are those of the family of Rayasta Ramachandra Dikshita in the mandapa of the larger temple at Koti-tirtha on the Tungabhadra.[8] Three groups of portrait sculptures are carved on the interior walls of the temple. The sculptured figures on the northern wall stand within a mandapa: three of the six people represented are identified by labels in Kannada as being the family of Nagappa, son of Rayasta Ramachandra Dikshita.[9] Between the three large figures are three smaller ones. All stand with hands in anjali-mudra. The same group is repeated with some variations on the western wall. The third group consisting of six people is seen once more on the same wall. Here the main figure is Rayasta Ramachandra Dikshita with his wife and four sons. The figures, identified again by a Kannada inscription, are proportional: the tallest is that of Rayasta Ramachandra Dikshita and the smallest that of this youngest son. The men wear lower garments to the ankles, full-sleeved shirts and cloth bands around the waist. Their hair, as usual, is tied in a bun on the crown of the head.

A further group of donor or devotee sculptures in the same area seems to be a memorial for two families.[10] There are five figures: one group consists of a man, a woman and a male child all standing with the hands in anjali-mudra. The man has a beard and moustache. His dhoti reaches to the ankles, he has a full sleeved shirt and a waist band. His son is similarly dressed but has no beard or moustache. The hair of the two men are tied in a bun. Another group depicts a man and a woman. The man, without beard or moustache, is dressed in a similar manner to the men described earlier. His wife wears her sari in the usual style. Interestingly, she raises her hand in the typical sati pose. This indicates that she has committed sati after the death of her husband.[11]

Two donor or devotee couples are sculpted to the left of the goddess Athikayamma, carved on a boulder south of the Tiruvengalanatha temple.[12]

In the twin temples dedicated to Anjaneya and Virabhadra there is a relief of a donor or devotee couple carved on the boulder on which Virabhadra is sculpted.[13] Both stand with their hands in anjali-mudra. The man has a beard, his hair is tied in a bun on the side of the head. His dhoti reaches his ankles. The woman has a sari tied below the waist and her hair is also tied into a large bun. Both husband and wife wear the customary jewellery.

In the Harihara temple an inscribed group of donor portraits is carved on the north and south walls of the mandapa.[14] The male figure in both groups wears a dhoti and a small turban or a small cap. He is flanked by two women.

Male donors or devotee figures are sometimes shown in panels depicting the linga and Nandi. Thus, for instance on the Domed Gate, or on the wall of the gateway south-west of the Royal Centre.[15]

Another category of devotee images is constituted by the ubiquitous figures prostrating themselves before a deity, their hands raised above their heads. They are carved in shallow relief or etched on flat horizontal surfaces, on stairs to sacred buildings, in courtyards, at thresholds, and on pavements leading to sanctuaries.

On the sheet rock at Chakra-tirtha, a male and a female devotee are depicted prostrating towards the north, to where the Tungabhadra makes a bend. Some carvings of prone devotees, their hands joined above their heads, are seen on the floor at the door of the sanctuary of the Kodandarama temple. South of the King's Balance[16] four adults and one child are shown prostrating themselves towards the Vithala temple. There is a brief inscription above their heads.

On the floor of the eastern gopura of the Vithala complex, either end of the passageway, there are carvings of prone devotees, with hands above their heads.

C. Entertainers

Musicians and dancers
(Figures 118-123, Plates 102-104)

Displays of music and dancing were much developed in the Vijayanagara period. As far as dance is concerned, a study of the sculptures on the monuments reveals two types of dance: temple and folk dance. So, for instance, among the schist carvings on the western side of the Mahanavami platform there are many carvings of dancers in costumes and poses typical of the temple style. The popularity of the folk-style is exemplified by the ubiquitous rows of graceful dancing girls performing the kolata, in which each performer carries a stick in her hand. Depictions of this theme are found in the carvings of the Mahanavami platform, on the south stairs and on both the south and the eastern sides. Kolata dancers occupy the entire fourth register on the exterior wall of the Ramachandra temple, and they are seen on the fifth register, among the celebrations of the Vasantotsava.

The kolata inspired the Vijayanagara artists to dispose the figures rhythmically, so that the compositions flow uninterrupted in a meandering line from one dancer to the other. In addition, this motif is found on ceiling medallions, as in the Ramanuja temple,[17] and in a temple (of Nammalvar?) south of the Vithala complex.[18]

The kolata dancers appear as a decorative motif also on the plinths of various monuments: for instance, on the mouldings of the pillared hall of the outer prakara of the Virupaksha temple complex, in the kantha frieze on the plinth of the mahamandapa of the Vithala temple, and on the broad kantha band of the plinth of the north-eastern pavilion in the same complex.

Individual dancers appear in various wall panels and on pillar blocks. Among individual panels, mention may be made of two Sangama carvings inserted in the granite base on the east gopura of the Virupaksha temple: on the west face a female dancer performs before a seated, probably royal, figure. She is accompanied by two male musicians. On the same face three male musicians accompany a dancer. Pillar reliefs of female kolata dancers are frequent, as on two pillars in the so-called Gayatri-pitha on Hemakuta hill.[19]

Among male dancers, there is one which is typical of the Vijayanagara style. This is the already discussed 'folk-dancer'. As noted,[20] the prototype for this figure is to be found in a group of energetic male dancers on the southern face of the Mahanavami platform, near the staircase. Three dancers and tambourine player stamp vigorously on the ground with their feet. Two dancers wear pointed ribbed caps, long jackets or overcoats and handle long scarves. The tambourine player wears a similar costume and sports a conspicuous moustache and pointed beard.

An early example of the 'folk-dancer' is seen in the Shaiva temple of 1386, where this motif is repeated three times on the pillar blocks.[21] A much later example of the same motif is to be found in the Ramanuja temple, on the west wall of the vimana, within the inner circumambulation corridor.[22]

Male dancers occur frequently as a decorative motif on pillars. For instance a number of male dancing figures is seen in the double-shrine temple on Hemakuta hill.[23] One, in the interior of the south mandapa, carries a vina. In the same mandapa, there are pillar reliefs with various musicians: one panel shows a flute player and a trumpeter; on another pillar is a carving of a man playing the mridangam. A mridangam player is repeated in the same temple, in the north mandapa.

Almost life-size musicians are seen at the east end of the mahamandapa of the Vithala temple. Here are two sets of pillars with high-relief carvings of musicians. Two of these play the mridangam, one has a pair of cymbals, another a large damaru. In the passageway of the unfinished gopura to the west of the Vithala temple are reliefs depicting male and female musicians.[24] Three of the four male musicians carry the same instruments as described earlier: the damaru, large cymbals and a mridangam. The woman carries a vina.

Musicians appear as ceiling decoration in the already mentioned temple south of the Vithala complex. Here a circle of male musicians playing the mridangam and of female musicians playing large drums are carved on the ceiling of the rangamandapa.

Female musicians appear frequently in the friezes on the Mahanavami platform as well as on the exterior wall of the Ramachandra temple. On the southern stairs of the Mahanavami platform they provide the musical accompaniment to the Vasantotsava and to the performance of the young female acrobat walking on her hands before a seated ruler. They play on large drums placed on the ground, seen commonly on the Vasantotsava friezes. Female musicians are also a popular motif on pillar blocks, as in the double-shrine temple on Hemakuta hill. In the south mandapa a standing woman, playing a tambourine, appears on a pillar carving; in the north mandapa a female musician is shown playing a damaru.

Acrobats, jesters and wrestlers (Figures 124, 125)

Representations of acrobats are relatively rare at Vijayanagara. The only wall relief is the already mentioned female acrobat on the Mahanavami platform. More frequent is the decorative motif of two acrobats forming a circle with their bodies on pillar reliefs. Two such motifs are seen in the double-shrine temple on Hemakuta hill.

Clowns of various descriptions occur frequently as a decorative motif on pillars. One of these is the knock-kneed clown sometimes wearing a peaked cap or other conspicuous headgear, a short lower garment, and a full-sleeved shirt. On some occasions this clown, slightly on the portly side, is carrying chauris or a scarf. His smiling and jolly countenance and his crooked stance because of his knees make him a jovial figure. An example can be seen on a mandapa pillar in the Gayatri-pitha on Hemakuta hill.[25]

A hunch-back clown holding a water-squirt has been noted in the description of the Vasantotsava festivities in the Vaishnava temple in the Royal Centre.[26] Another hunch-back clown, carrying a child dressed as a clown on his back, is carved on a pillar in the rangamandapa of the Tirumangai-Alvar temple, north-west of the Vithala complex.[27]

During the Mahanavami festival a whole day was devoted to dancing and wrestling. According to Nuniz:

> The king has a thousand wrestlers for these feasts who wrestle before the king, but not in our manner, for they strike and wound each other with two circlets with points which they carry in their hands to strike with, and the one most wounded goes and takes his reward in the shape of a silk cloth, such as the king gives to these wrestlers. They have a captain over them, and they do not perform any other service in the kingdom.[28]

Wrestlers occur repeatedly on the Mahanavami platform south face, on the first and second tiers. A wrestling match before a ruler or nobleman and his entourage is seen on the bottom frieze of the lower tier; two wrestlers, practise on the second tier, third register. Wrestlers are also shown in the third register on the western exterior wall of the Ramachandra temple. Wrestling matches occurs on isolated carvings: one, already mentioned, on the exterior wall of the Zenana-Enclosure and one on the wall of the gateway to the west of the Royal Centre on the Kamalapuram-Hampi road.[29] They are all powerfully built figures, with closely cropped hair.

D. Tribal Hunters

Tribal hunters or Chenchus play a conspicuous role in the iconographic traditions of Vijayanagara. They are clad in typical leafy costumes wearing small caps made out of foliage. Their characteristic weapon is the bow, indicating that roaming in the forest hunting wild animals was their main occupation.[30]

The important sets of carvings of tribal hunters are shown on the lowermost level on the south and east faces of the south staircase of the Mahanavami platform. The same theme with some minor variations is repeated on the lowermost register on the eastern side of the staircase. The hunter-milieu and the jungle setting enlivened by a wealth of trees and wild animals running, jumping and mating are the backdrop to the story of Narasimha among the Chenchus. As previously noted (see Chapter 6), this incident, reduced to the scene of Narasimha extracting the thorn from the foot of Chenchu-Lakshmi, is often found on pillar blocks. Narrative sequences involving tribal life, however, become increasingly rare after the end of the fourteenth century.

There are further depictions of Chenchus, which are to be found on the plinth of the main gateway to the Ramachandra temple complex. Here, on the north side of the entrance passageway there are some interesting variations on this theme. The leaf-skirted huntress is shown leaning on a bow, shooting an arrow at a deer or at a boar, holding a bow while touching the sole of her foot with an arrow, as if to remove a thorn. The huntress is also shown hunting with a male companion. On another occasion, she is seen leaning on a bow, while a male figure carries a dead deer on his head; a tree and deer between them suggest a forest setting.

In the so-called Chandrashekhara temple there are two reliefs showing a Chenchu man wearing a leaf skirt pointing a bow and an arrow above his head.[31]

E. Women (Figures F, 127, 128)

The women appearing in the oldest carvings at Vijayanagara represent two opposing worlds. The first is the courtly, urbane world of the capital exemplified in the most sensitive and exquisite depictions of men and women in elegant attire, engaged in refined pursuits. The second is the forest, exemplified by Chenchus clad in short skirts and wearing headdresses made of forest leaves, armed with a huge bow and arrow, following husbands on their hunting expeditions. Sixteenth-century carvings focus almost exclusively on the courtly milieu.

Along with these depictions of contemporary life, there are others, which look back to traditional motifs in Indian art. One of these is the representation of the young woman squeezing the water from her hair into the beak of a hamsa. This motif occurs in the early temples on Hemakuta hill, such as on a pillar in the double-shrine temple. Shalabhanjikas or latasundaris, holding the branch of a tree or a creeper, appear along with the river goddess Ganga on doorways. So, for instance, in the passageway of the gopura of the Varaha temple there is Ganga on one side, and a latasundari leaning on a creeper on the other.[32] In the gopura entryway of the Ramanuja temple, either side of the inner jambs south side of the door frame, there is a latasundari. Ganga and a latasundari are on the north side. Occasionally the lastasundari appears as decorative motif on pillars, for example on the porch of the main shrine of the Ramachandra temple.

Individual women are also to be found in carvings on pillars. The most common motifs are a dancer, a woman carrying a flower or a chauri, a woman with a tray of offerings or carrying a plate with arati lamps, a woman carrying a basket or a pitcher, a woman applying a tilaka to her forehead or looking at herself in a mirror, a woman carrying a child on her hip or holding a child by the hand, and a woman with a parrot perched either on her wrist or shoulder. An exceptional figure in the hundred-pillar hall of the Vithala temple, shows a pregnant woman. This is the only representation of this theme at the site.

Beneath the neem tree in front of the Pattanada Yellamma temple are a number of slabs still in worship. Among these is one representing a nude woman. Details of the carving cannot be properly studied in view of the poor condition of the slab.[33]

F. Erotic Carvings (Figure 129)

Erotic carvings are comparatively rare at the site. They are inconspicuous, most of them belong to a late period. The most substantial group is in the hundred-pillar hall in the north-west corner of the outer courtyard of the Tiruvengalanatha temple.[34] The theme of the carvings varies from an amorous couple, to group-sex involving two men and a woman, to a human being copulating with a horse.

Erotic carvings in the Ramachandra temple are found in the later additions to the complex. There is, for instance, an amorous couple on a pillar block of the south-west mandapa. Another such pair is depicted on a basement panel on the minor shrine, at the corner of the south and west walls.

In the Vithala temple there is an embracing couple on a pillar in the southern aisle of the mahamandapa. A few erotic carvings, in a rather poor state of conservation, can be seen on an unfinished gopura north of the Vithala complex.[35]

A rare early example of an amorous couple decorates a pillar of a mandapa, in a shrine on the Hemakuta hill.[36]

G. Composite Figures (Figure 130)

In another popular theme, Vijayanagara artists playfully combined human forms to create novel and interesting composite beings.

On the balustrade of the south steps of the Mahanavami platform is a relief of three clowns with only four legs. This carving was found near the platform during the excavations of the mid-1970s; it is not certain, however, whether or not it has been correctly positioned. In the north mandapa of the double-shrine temple on Hemakuta hill is the similar relief of three men with only four legs.[37]

In the Vishnu temple in the Royal Centre is a pillar relief showing a three-headed figure wearing clown-caps, with four legs, four arms and only one body.[38] A further variation of this is carved on a pillar in the north-west mandapa in the outer courtyard of the Tiruvengalanatha temple: a three-headed figure wearing clown-caps, with six arms and six legs and a single torso.

H. Foreigners (Figures 131, 132, Plate 105)

Considering the number of foreign visitors to Vijayanagara it is not surprising that depictions of these figures, easily recognizable by their exotic dress, appear in the wall carvings and friezes.[39]

Arab or Turkish horse-traders occur repeatedly in the lowest tier of the Mahanavami platform and in the processional frieze on the exterior wall of the Ramachandra complex. In both monuments, the foreigners are depicted parading their animals. On the second register on the east side of the enclosure wall of the Ramachandra temple, the head of the delegation, dressed in a characteristic long coat whose sleeves conceal his hands, is shown paying homage to the ruler seated on a throne in a pavilion.

A few representations of foreigners are seen in the monuments on Hemakuta hill. On the south gateway is a carving showing two foreigners, one performing a jumping dance step, the other playing on a tambourine.[40] This relief is on the east wall of the building, to the south of the entrance passageway. The other carving, depicting two foreigners wearing skirt-like garments, is seen on a porch pillar relief in a temple on the same hill.[41]

Portuguese horse-traders are found on friezes. The examples on the Vithala temple, on the jagati moulding of the mahamandapa plinth, show a detailed rendering of a procession of horse-dealers with animals. Occasionally the frieze is interrupted by a seated royal figure. A similar frieze is found on the plinth of the unfinished gopura south-west of the Vithala temple.[42] Their boots, trousers, coats, hats, triangular beards and upward-turned moustaches are keenly observed and precisely rendered. Moreover, the artists observed that Europeans carry their bodies differently from Indians. This has been precisely documented in these friezes.

I. Other Figures (Plate 106)

Three further examples of human figures should not be omitted. One of these, on a pillar relief in the Shiva temple on Hemakuta hill, depicts a man in a dancing pose holding a heavy ring in his hands.[43] This could perhaps be a discus thrower.

An elongated male figure wearing a tall cap and holding a dagger is carved on the inner enclosure wall of the Mint Enclosure.[44]

Two carvings depicting boatmen with oars are placed near the gateway on the river bank at Anegondi.

NOTES

1. R.N. Saletore, 'Some Aspects of Art during the Reign of Krishnadevaraya, the Great', in *Vijayanagara Sexcentenary Commemoration Volume*, p. 202.
2. Anila Verghese, 'Court Attire of Vijayanagara (From a Study of Monuments)', in *The Quarterly Journal of the Mythic Society*, LXXXII. 1991, nos. 1-2, pp. 49-50.
3. NVo/1.
4. *Vijayanagara: Progess of Research 1983-84*, p. 41, Pl. LV.
5. D. Sridhara Babu, *Kingship, State and Religion in South India According to South Indian Historical Biographies of Kings*, 1975, pp. 100-101.
6. R. Sewell, *A Forgotten Empire*, p. 277.
7. Major, R.H., (ed.), *India in the Fifteenth Century*, p. 12.
8. NGm/2.
9. *Vijayanagara: Progress of Research 1983-84*, pp. 140-1, pls. XCIa, XCIb, XCIIa.
10. West of NGh/1 and north-east of NGm/1.
11. *Vijayanagara: Progress of Research 1983-84*, p. 143, pl. XCVIb.
12. NMh/2.
13. NYk/1.
14. NLc/3.
15. NYx (domed gate) and NVo.
16. NHa/7.
17. NCw/3.
18. NHa/10.
19. NLb/1.
20. See Chapter 2, p. 13.
21. NGt/3.
22. See note 17.
23. NFw/5.
24. NHa/6.
25. See note 19.
26. NSl/1.
27. NCv/3.
28. R. Sewell, op. cit., p. 359.
29. Gate NQh.
30. The Chenchus live in Andhra, in the area which extends from Srisailam to the Amarabad plateau in Mahbubnagar district and to Ahobalam. They are equally connected, therefore, to the Shaiva shrine at Srisailam as well as to the Vaishnava one at Ahobalam. One of their functions was to act as guides for the pilgrims to both of these shrines, which are located in remote and densely forested hilly areas. As the temples of Srisailam and Ahobalam were connected with the Vijayanagara rulers since the very beginning of their history, it is not surprising to find the Chenchus carved on the monuments at the capital. See. D. Rabinandan Pratap, *Tribes of Andhra Pradesh*, p. 39.
31. NX1/1.
32. NGs/1.
33. NRy/4.
34. These sculptures have been already noted by Klaus Fischer, 'Iconology of devatā and devadāsī, tapasvin and Mohinī, Sṛṅgāraṇavidhi and mithuna on some maṇḍapa pillars from the Vijayanagara period onward?', in *Vijayanagara City and Empire*, ed. by A.L. Dallapiccola in collaboration with S. Zingel-Avé Lallemant, Vol. I, pp. 317-25.
35. NCv/5.
36. NGw/13.
37. See note 23.
38. See note 26.
39. Muslim ambassadors came from the Deccan Muslim States and also from abroad: the most renowned among the latter, was the envoy of the ruler of the Herat, Abdur Razzak, who visited the capital at the time of Devaraya II and wrote an often quoted account. Apart from the occasional European visitior like Nikitin who visited the capital around 1474, and Varthema about thirty years later, both of whom wrote eloquently about its riches, regular contacts with Europeans were only established in the sixteenth century. The Portuguese were involved in the horse-trade and, because horses were among the most prized possession of the court and the nobility, this link was established. Among the Portuguese vistitors were the two chroniclers, Domingo Paes and Fernao Nuniz.
40. NLq/4.
41. NFw/13.
42. NHa/6.
43. NLh/4.
44. Near NWb/1.

CHAPTER 13

Animals, Birds and Mythical Beasts

A. Lions (Figures 133-135)

The Vijayanagara lion, shown pacing, rearing, sitting or, most often, squatting, is perhaps the most conspicuous of all animal motifs on pillars, basement mouldings and balustrades.

Squatting lions at Vijayanagara generally have a decorative function, although groups of seated lions may act as supports for colonnettes surrounding a pier, as in the maharanga-mandapa of the Virupakasha temple. The physiognomy of these animals is more in the nature of a mythological or heraldic beast than a naturalistic lion. They have bulging eyes, bared fangs and pointed ears emerging from a wavy mane with a curly edge which surrounds the face of the animals like a ruffle. The lion's body, when depicted in profile, is often decorated by a foliated motif extending from its hind quarters to its shoulders.[1] The tail, at times bent in fanciful loops, ends in a spear-like shape. The animal is shown with a conspicuous mane and pronounced mouth. It is mostly ithyphallic and occasionally engaged in masturbatory practices. Such squatting lions are almost exclusively positioned at the base of columns.

Noteworthy among the lion depictions is a pillar carving of a seated lion, his front paw raised as if in teaching attitude, in the minor shrine of the Ramachandra complex. What seems to be a pacing lion is seen on the lowermost block of a pillar in the mandapa of the Mudal-Alvar temple.[2] Two seated lions facing each other are carved on a mandapa pillar of the Gayatri- pitha,[3] and a medallion with lions and foliage motif is sculpted on a porch pillar of a temple on Hemakuta hill.[4]

B. Elephants (Plate 107)

Elephants formed a unit of the Viyajanagara army; according to the reports of the visitors, they were treated with great reverence. Abdur Razzak records that there were more than a thousand elephants in the capital. The king owned a white elephant of great size which was speckled with grey spots and was considered sacred. Abdur Razzak notes that every morning this animal was paraded before the monarch and 'the sight of it seems to have acted as a happy omen'.[5]

Elephants splendidly caparisoned in richly embroidered cloth, decked with ornaments and bells, their head-plates studded with metal, and their trunks and eyes painted in special patterns were noted by visitors to the Mahanavami parade.

Parading elephants

Two impressive friezes of parading elephants are seen on the walls of the Mahanavami platform and on the enclosure wall of the Ramachandra complex. In both cases, no two animals are alike as far as movement or details of trappings are concerned.

Most of the upper row on the southern face of the Mahanavami platform, lower tier, is devoted to elephants. The frieze is partly damaged, the details being lost.

Friezes of elephants, with the occasional groom leading the animals, are on the uppermost level of the staircase on the south of the Mahanavami platform, on both the south and east faces. The same motif is repeated on a smaller scale on the upper tier of the platform, top row, south side. Here, however, each elephant is separated not by a tree as previously, but by a pillar which is more or less elaborately finished: on some slabs the pillars with their capitals and their base moulding are precisely rendered.

A large slab depicting a huge elephant, with its groom holding it by a chain, is placed at the base of the staircase on the south side of the platform. The various chains on the body of the elephant are clearly visible.

Elephant processions of the smaller scale appear on both the first and the second tiers in the schist carvings on the Mahanavami platform, north and south of the stairs. Since schist is softer than granite, the artists had greater scope to render fine details such as the embroidered edges of the elephants' cloths or the beads of the chains.

As already mentioned, an elephant parade occupies the bottom register of the processional friezes on the enclosure wall of the Ramachandra temple. Elegantly caparisoned elephants with their mahouts comfortably seated on their necks, move towards a seated ruler, who is in a small pavilion at the end of the frieze. As in the case of the parading elephants on the lower tier of the Mahanavami platform, diminutive trees occasionally separate one animal from the next. Most elephant carry a bunch of leaves in their trunks and are adorned with thick chains of large beads which hang slightly in front. Other chains are wound around the stomachs and beneath the tails. Rings are placed round their legs. Only one or two persons are shown riding on the elephants. According to the Italian traveller Varthema, up to seven persons could ride on an animal.[6]

In course of time, elephant friezes were shifted from the walls of building to the lower parts of structures. Elephant parades are a common motif on plinths. In the Vithala complex there are three major structures in which a frieze of elephants occurs on the plinth: the north-east corner mandapa, the hundred-pillar hall, and the surounding colonnade. Here too richly caparisoned elephants are shown uprooting foliage or carrying branches, if not entire trees, in their trunks. The occasional mahout also appears.

Elephants, riders, and mahouts

A related motif is the elephant being pulled by its mahout, as in the lively relief on a boulder opposite the Venkateshvara shrine on the south side of the Turutta canal.[7]

Elephants and riders are shown on the jambs of the doorway of the Narasimhaswami shrine in the Virupaksha temple complex. The riders, possibly courtly personages, have their hands folded in anjali-mudra and are each accompanied by an attendant.

Elephants at work

Elephants are often shown uprooting trees or carrying branches and foliage in their trunks, as on the reliefs of the Mahanavami platform. This motif also appears on the exterior of the Jaina temple in Anegondi, on either side of the west door, and on the north and the south sides of the exterior wall of the rangamandapa.[8] Generally, early temples often seem to have elephant images carved on their exterior walls.[9]

Enraged elephants (Figure 136)

The elephants uprooting a tree in rage appears twice in the pillar reliefs of the Tirumangai-Alvar temple.[10] Enraged elephants attacking their grooms are also common. The most impressive rendering of this theme is perhaps that on the western face of the Mahanavami platform, on the granite portion north of the steps. Here a man is being torn apart by an elephant. While the animal tears his left leg with its trunk, it crushes the other with its right. Five men armed with forked sticks or spears attempt to curb the enraged elephant. Among the schist reliefs north of the stairs, is a simplified version of this motif. A man is trampled to death by an elephant, while two men try in vain to restrain the animal.

An elephant trampling a man to death is occasionally illustrated on walls, pillars and basement mouldings. Referring to this mode of capital punishment, Nuniz observes that it was one of the 'more fanciful of their punishments, for when the king so desires, he commands a man to be thrown to the elephants and they tear him in pieces'.[11] Examples of this motif are to be found on a pillar in the mandapa of the Gayatri-pitha.[12] On a pillar in the colonnade of the small Shiva temple of 1386 on the Tungabhadra, an elephant is shown trampling a man and turning another over.[13]

Scenes of capital punishment are carved at various places. On the kantha moulding of the plinth of the hundred-pillar hall in the Virupaksha temple complex, two elephants are depicted in the process of tearing a man apart.

Fights with other animals (Plate 108)

A fight between an elephant and a lion or a tiger are depicted on the western face of the Mahanavami platform. Placed above the elephant frieze on the north side of the stairs is the scene of a fight between a lion or a tiger and an elephant. Such animal fights, as shown here, may have been a form of entertainment. A courtly personage seated on a horse, over whom an umbrella is held, accompanied by a retinue of footmen armed with swords and shields, goads the animals on. The schist panel is notable for its liveliness and the fineness of its detail.

Elephant-devotees (Figure 6)

Elephants paying homage to a linga appear on the double-shrine temple on Hemakuta hill.[14] On the south wall of the structure is a large relief showing two elephants performing linga abhisheka. The same theme is illustrated on the south wall of the main shrine in the Virupaksha complex. The elephant performing the linga abhisheka is a frequent motif on pillar reliefs.

Elephants as decorative elements (Plate 109)

Elephant carvings are used frequently as embellishment. Elephant balustrades decorate the steps of various buildings in temple complexes. In the Tiruvengalanatha temple, the steps to the mahamandapa on either side of the vahana mandapa have elephant balustrades. The same applies to the balustrades of the south side steps to the mahamandapa of the Krishna temple, to the east side steps of the Vithala temple, and to the entrance to the mandapa of the subsidiary shrine of the Pattabhirama temple.

In the Malyavanta Raghunatha complex, the east side steps of the mahamandapa are flanked by balustrades in the shape of elephants picking up lotuses with their trunks. That this type of decoration was not reserved for sacred buildings is shown by the elephant balustrades found in the Noblemen's quarters.[15]

The two elephant statues in front of the stone ratha in the Vithala temple have been positioned there at a later point of time.

C. Horses (Figure 137, Plates 110, 111)

Along with the elephant, the horse is perhaps the only other animal that has been carved with true freedom, gusto and empathy. The Vijayanagara artists show horses cantering, rising up on their haunches, trotting and galloping. The animals are gracefully attired with saddles and reins, generally proudly parading, led by grooms.

At Vijayanagara, the horse was not only a status symbol, being a rare and costly animal, but was also held in great reverence. In the course of the Mahanavami festival, a sumptuously decorated horse with two state umbrellas was paraded before the king. According to Paes:

> Now you must know that this horse which is conducted with all this state is a horse that the king keeps on which they . . . are sworn and received as kings and on it must be sworn all those that shall come after them; and in case such horse dies, they put another in its place.[16]

As in the case of elephants, the most impressive and numerous renderings of horses are found on the Mahanavami platform and on the outer wall of the Ramachandra temple complex, second register.

On the lower tier on the south face of the Mahanavami platform, the third row is devoted almost exclusively to depictions of horses. Some animals are pacing, others are galloping. Some are led by a groom, most of them carry armed riders. There is a great variety in the way the animals appear. Small details, such as the bend of the neck, the posture of the head, the gait, the saddle and the bridles, have all been carefully studied by the artists. At the western end of the frieze, there are two foreigners, possibly Arabs or Turks, paying homage to a ruler (or nobleman) seated on a high platform. The foreign visitors could be horse-traders, as they are followed by a groom leading an unsaddled horse by the bridle. Another groom behind the seated noblemen also leads a horse.

On the bottom row on the same side of the monument there are more carvings of armed horsemen. Some are in full armour, others are only armed with swords and spears. This seems to be a military parade in which the cavalry and infantry were reviewed by a seated ruler, who is at the western end of the register. In this case also, the ruler is granting audience to two foreign guests, similar in attire and stance to those mentioned above.

A similar scene occurs on the south face of the Mahanavami platform, second tier, bottom row: three foreign horse-traders display a horse before a seated ruler.

Apart from these parade scenes on the second tier on the south side, there is one carving of a state horse with a parasol which recalls the description given by Paes. This horse, however, has only one umbrella of state, and not two as stated by Paes.

Additional processional scenes with a royal or noble figure inspecting horses are found on the west face of the monument, lower tier, north of the stairs.

The horse frieze which occupies the second row on the exterior of the enclosure wall of the Ramachandra temple is better organised and more coherent as far as the proportions between animals, human beings and structures are concerned. A caravan of horse-traders is carved on the east and north walls: all of the second register is devoted to horses, grooms and horsemen. Foreign traders, leading horses towards a kingly or noble figure seated within a structure, are conspicuously rendered on the east wall. They are accompanied by grooms, some foreign, leading horses by the bridle. The western wall is devoted to parading horsemen, some armed with swords and spears. Among them is a nobleman accompanied by an attendant holding an umbrella, and preceded by a group of three men, two of whom carry long swords.

As in the elephant parades, horse processions were also moved from the main walls of the buildings to plinth mouldings. An extremely fine carving of horse procession led by Portuguese fidalgos is seen on a moulding on the plinth of the mahamandapa of the Vithala temple. A similar frieze in the same position is carved on the unfinished gopura west of the Vithala temple.[17]

Single horses are rarely found. Two renderings are on blocks inserted in the granite basement of the east gopura of the Virupaksha complex: The most notable is the horse and attendant carved on the granite basement of the east gopura of the Virupaksha temple complex. On the opposite side is a horse led by an Arab trader. Both carvings are of the Sangama period. Another relief of a horse is found on the wall of a gateway south-west of the Royal Centre.[18]

Horses as decorative motifs on balustrades are only known on the temple near the north gateway end of Hemakuta hill.[19] A horse drawing a chariot is here sculpted on the balustrade of the steps leading to the mandapa. Rearing horses, instead of rearing yalis, appear at the entrance of the Vithala temple tank.[20]

Horse-riding warriors engaged in battles or duels have already been noted on hero-stones (see Chapter 10).

D. Cows, Calfs and Bulls (Plate 116)

At Vijayanagara cows and calves often appear on pillars. The cow is shown licking its hind leg, giving birth to a calf, suckling it, or performing linga-abhisheka. Of these motifs, the most interesting is the cow performing a linga-abhisheka with its own milk, a frequent motif in local sthalapuranas.[21]

At Vijayanagara, this theme is vividly depicted on an inscribed stone slab, possibly the memorial of a family, located near Talarighat.[22] Three people, two adults and possibly a child, stand with their hands in anjali-mudra, with chauris resting on their shoulders. The top of the slab is occupied by a fine carving of the cow with a calf performing linga-abhisheka. Shiva's trishula and damaru and the sun and moon flank the group. A fully sculpted crouching Nandi crowns the slab.

The only example of a cow giving birth to a calf is depicted in the Tirumangai-Alvar temple: on the top block of an engaged pillar in the eastern wall of rangamandapa, north of the door.[23]

Carvings of ordinary bulls are not common, as it is Nandi who is generally represented. Shiva's mount is easily recognized by the crouching posture and ornaments. However, a relief showing a bull eating is found on a pillar in the colonnade of the Shiva temple of 1386, near the Tungabhadra.[24]

E. Other Animals

Camels

A frieze of camels occupies the penultimate register on the lower tier on the south face of the Mahanavami platform. The animals are led by grooms, some of whom are foreigners, possibly Arabs. The frieze is interrupted occasionally by spirited renderings of male dancers, some holding a long scarf behind their shoulders, others playing on a tambourine. A kettle-drum player majestically seated on a camel, followed by three musicians playing mridangam, cymbals, and trumpet conclude the western end of the frieze. In the upper tier, on the south face, second row, more camels are rendered. It is not clear if there was a camel corps in the Vijayangara army. According to Varthema, at the time of Vira Narasimha there were dromedaries in the army which ran with speed.[25] This force continued to serve in the reigns of Krishnadevaraya and Achyutaraya.[26]

Apart from those on the Mahanavami platform, camels occur only rarely. One example, however, is in the Ramanuja temple on the western wall of the vimana, visible from the inner pradakshina-patha.[27]

Monkeys (Figure G)

In addition to their appearance in the extensive *Ramayana* narratives, monkeys are frequently found on pillar reliefs as in the double-shrine temple on Hemakuta hill, and the colonnade of the Shiva temple of 1386 near the Tungabhadra, where one of the two carvings of monkeys shows two animals eating fruit.[28]

Antelopes

Antelopes occur in numerous hunting scenes on the Mahanavami platform and in the passageway of the eastern gateway of the Ramachandra complex. They are seldom used as a decorative motif. An exception is the antelope standing near a tree, carved on a pillar in a Shiva temple near the Krishna temple complex.[29]

Lizards (Figure 138)

Lizards occasionally appear on temple reliefs. The lizard on the south wall of the main shrine in the Virupaksha complex is shown worshipping the linga. On a few other carvings the lizard is engaged in the worship of the linga. There are also some in which it is merely a decorative motif: in the mahamandapa of the Chandikeshvara temple,[30] on the exterior south wall of the Tirumangai-Alvar temple,[31] and in the Ramanuja temple on the western wall of the vimana, visible from the inner pradakshina-patha.[32]

Scorpions

Scorpions are generally associated with Bhairava icons. In the Shiva temple near the Krishna temple complex, already mentioned, a scorpion is carved on one of the pillars. An impressive example of a scorpion is found in a small rock shelter on the north ridge, flanking the Bhairava image.[33]

Snakes (Figure 139)

The snake is a frequent decorative motif on pillars: intertwined snakes and 'eternal knots' constituted by snakes are found at various places: in the south aisle in the inner prakara of the Virupaksha complex, and on the curved eaves of the roof of the north colonnade near the northern gopura. A nagapasha occurs on a rocky outcrop north-east of the Elephant Stables near the dashavatara reliefs.[34]

In the Ramanuja temple a snake about to swallow a frog is the theme of an elegant carving on the west wall of the vimana, visible from the inner pradakshina-patha.

The snake and the hare in the moon occur occasionally together as a decorative motif, which is probably connected to the motif of Rahu swallowing the sun or the moon. Examples of this motif are carved on the ceiling in the hundred-pillar hall in the outer courtyard of the Virupaksha complex, also in the entrance gateway of the Varaha temple.[35]

Snake-stones have already been discussed in Chapter 8.

Domestic animals (Plate 117)

Dogs occur frequently in forest and hunting scenes on the Mahanavami platform, although there are few individual dogs. An exceptional carving of a man holding a dog on the leash is seen on the outer wall of the gateway west of the Royal Centre on the Kamalapuram-Hampi road.[36]

Cats seldom appear: a carving on a pillar in the porch of the Ramachandra temple shows a seated cat watching Balakrishna dancing. An unusual snake-stone in the Archaeological Museum shows two nagas and a cat guarding a cradle.[37]

F. Birds

Geese and peacocks (Figure H)

On the lower tier, southern face, of the Mahanavami platform, a frieze of hamsas appears twice on both sides of the staircase and again on the upper tier of the monument. These examples are elegantly carved, each bird being enclosed in a circle formed by the lotus creeper, which it holds in its beak. In the sixteenth century the same hamsa in a creeper frieze appears decoratively on the curved eaves of the roof of the mahamandapa of the Vithala temle.

Elongated necks and foliated tails of birds were the focus of artistic attention: in course of time, geese and peacocks became indistinguishable. Consider for instance the hamsa/mayura design on pillars where two birds are shown with intertwined necks. Examples are seen in the Ramachandra temple, on an engaged pillar in the rangamandapa, in the double-shrine temple on Hemakuta hill,[38] and in the so-called Varaha temple.[39] In the Tirumangai-Alvar temple three interlaced hamsas are carved on the engaged pillar against the wall of the antarala.[40]

Among the numerous hamsa/mayura representations in the south mandapa of the double-shrine temple on Hemakuta hill, there are four birds shown with one head and four bodies. Two birds face each other on a pillar relief in the Gayatri-pitha.[41]

Peacocks with or without snakes in their beak make an occasional appearance on the Mahanavami platform, lower tier south face, in the various forest scenes and among the camels in the penultimate frieze. These birds are sometimes shown on basement panels, as on the Ramachandra temple, east gate, passageway, but are comparatively rare as pillar decoration.

Parrots

The parrot is seldom used in the decoration of pillars. In a rare example, two parrots back-to-back look over their shoulders at each other. This is carved on an engaged pillar on the west wall in the rangamandapa of the Tirumangai-Alvar temple. More frequently parrots are incorporated into ceiling designs or are found on the stucco-work embellishing vimana towers.

The role of parrots as household pets sometimes inspires artists, as, for instance, the parrot perching on the wrist of seated girl in one of the basement panels south of the passage in the east gateway of the Ramachandra complex.

G. Mythical Beasts

Yalis (Plates 112-115)

The yali is the most conspicuous composite animal on the piers of sixteenth-century temples. It has the body of a lion and either a head of a lion with its ruffle-like mane, or that of an elephant with a long trunk, also with bushy eyebrows, round bulging eyes and sometimes horns. Yalis invariably stand on their hind paws, on either an elephant or a makara judging from the foliage motif connecting the two animals. Foliage enhances the hind quarters and shoulders of the yali. Small tusks appear on each side of the long trunk and wavy mane, neatly curled at the ends, generally in two rows.

The function of yalis is to define open spaces. They are thus found flanking the central aisle of the mahamandapa of the Virupaksha temple. They are positioned at the main entrances of the mandapas, almost always on the east, but occasionally on the north and the south, as in the Virupaksha temple complex main shrine, Vithala temple mahamandapa; and the Pattabhirama temple mahamandapa.

A more subdued form of yali, the surul-yali, is a decorative motif on balustrades flanking the entrance steps to a mandapa or palace.[42] In this case the yali is not rearing on its hind quarters but is firmly planted on earth. Pacing towards the building, with its bulgings eyes it looks back over its shoulder. From its open mouth with redoutable fangs, the yali spits out the scalloped edge of the balustrade. As in the case of the rearing yalis, the surul-yali too has foliage motifs on its hind quarters and shoulders. Its tail, ending in a spear-like shape, is wound in a decorative loop surmounting its back. Noteworthy is the elegant shape of the lithe, lion-like body, echoing the profile of the balustrade. Examples of yali balustrades are those flanking the north side steps of the mahamandapa of the Krishna temple, the east side steps to the maharangamandapa of the Virupaksha temple, and the north and south entrances to the mahamandapa of the Vithala temple.

Makaras

The makara is a common sight in the decoration of sanctuary doorways at Vijayanagara. Popular variations are the makara holding its tail in its trunk, the makara and foliage motif, and the makara out of whose mouth issues a creeper. The first and second types are frequenlty found carved in the form of medallions on pillars, while the third type is generally used in the decoration of door-jambs, door frames and entryways of gopuras.

The foliated tail of the makara inspired artists to develop a further design: the medallion of foliage, constituted solely by the tail of the animal, revealing the actual makara at its centre. Examples are known on a pillar in the minor shrine of the Ramachandra temple complex and in the Varaha temple.[43]

A fabulous creature with a makara head and bird tail is carved on a pillar in the south mandapa of the double-shrine temple on Hemakuta hill.[44] On a pillar in the north mandapa of the same temple, a circle is formed by three makara-like creatures.

H. Composite Animals (Figure 140)

Examples of the bull and elephant with a common head are in the mandapa of the Gayatri-pitha,[45] in the Ramachandra temple on the plinth of the passageway of the east entrance, and along the kantha moulding of the plinth of the south-east corner pavilion in the Vithala temple complex.

Other composite creatures in pillar decoration falls into no specific category.

A deer with two heads appears as a pillar relief in the Gayatri-pitha. A bird with a lion's head as in the minor shrine in the Ramchandra temple complex, is also seen among the reliefs in the rangamandapa of the Ramanuja temple where also the carvings of a half-lion and half-deer creature can be found.

A creature looking like a combination of a boar and mouse is carved on one of the pillars in the northern colonnade of the inner prakara of the Virupaksha complex.

Among the elephants on the upper row of the lower tier, on the southern side of the mahanavami platform, a composite lion with an elephant head is of interest.

NOTES

1. E.g. Tiruvengalantha temple, north-west corner mandapa, external pier to the south-east.
2. NCw/2.
3. NLb/1.
4. NFw/13.
5. R.H. Major (ed.), *India in the Fifteenth Century*, p. 22. This probably relates to the notion that white elephants symbolise clouds, hence are capable of attracting rain and bringing fertility.
6. R.N. Saletore, *Vijayanagara Art*, p. 178.
7. NMr/2.
8. HZv/1.
9. NFw/5 and NGt/4.
10. NCv/3.
11. R. Sewell, *A Forgotten Empire*, p. 384.
12. See note 3.
13. NGt/3.
14. NFw/5.
15. *Vijayanagara: Progress of Research, 1983-84*, Nobleman's Palace 2, Fig. 5.
16. R. Sewell, op. cit., p. 272.
17. NHa/6.
18. NVo.
19. NHd/1.
20. NFw/12
21. The Ramalingeshvara temple at Tadapatri, Anantapur district, Andhra Pradesh, is connected with the story of the svayambhu linga which was covered by earth and anthills. It was found because a cow used to come everyday to the spot and give its milk as an offering to the linga. N. Ramesan, *Temple Legends of Andhra Pradesh*, p. 47. As already noted, a similar story is told about the Mallikarjuna temple at Srisailam.
22. NDy/10
23. NCv/3.
24. NGt/e.
25. R.N. Saletore, op. cit., p. 165.
26. Ibid.
27. NCv/3.

28. See note 24.
29. NLh/4.
30. NLw/6.
31. See note 23.
32. NCw/3.
33. MNz/2.
34. NSa/1a.
35. NGs/1.
36. NQh.
37. No. 147.
38. NFw/5.
39. See note 35.
40. See note 23.
41. See note 3.
42. *Vijayanagara: Progress of Research, 1983-84*, Nobleman's Palace 2, Fig. 5.
43. See note 35.
44. See note 38.
45. See note 3.

CHAPTER 14

Decorative Motifs

A. Floral and Vegetal Themes

Lotus flowers (Figure 141)

At Vijayanagara, the lotus appears variously as a full flower, petal, or bud. As a flower, the lotus occurs with four, eight, twelve or twenty-four petals.

These four varieties can be further classified according as they are inscribed in a circle, in a square, in a eight-pointed rotating square or surrounded by nagas.

Lotus flowers or lotus-derived designs are ubiquitous. In the case of the lotus flower being used in the decoration of a pillar, it will usually be carved on the upper or middle block of the column, exceptionally on the bottom. The lowermost block is traditionally reserved for vegetal scrolls or, in the case of mythological figures, for shalabhanjikas/latasundaris, Shankhanidhi or Padmanidhi (see Chapter 8).

Many lotus rosettes and medallions are carved on the central panel of the mandapa ceilings. Sometimes the central lotus motif is surrounded by rows of musicians and dancers, birds or creeper motifs.

Stylised lotus petals appear on basement mouldings, forming the padma, a scalloped moulding on the plinth of temples, mandapas and statues, which may perhaps convey the notion that the sacred building or image rests on a lotus. The same motif has also been widely used for embellishing door frames.

Bud-like pendants on brackets are typical of the Vijayanagara architectural style.

Creepers

The creeper design has been widely used for decorative bands of differing width and thickness, horizontally or vertically, on various parts of basement mouldings, pilasters, pillars and doorways. Creepers perform a specific function as a divisional element between different scenes in a narrative sequence, or between one panel and another in a frieze. In the Mahanavami platform carvings, especially of the later phase, and on the basement of buildings like the Ramachandra temple minor shrine, this device appears consistently.

The creeper with scrolls of thick winding stalks and foliage is commonly used as the doorway decoration of temples. It issues generally from the mouth of a makara placed at the door-jamb and winds its way up to the door lintel ending either in a dedicatory plaque containing the image of a deity, or in an emblem.

In the case of gopuras, the creeper, originating again from the mouth of a makara, serves as a support for the elegantly poised river goddesses or latasundaris (see Chapter 7). It then proceeds up the jambs to the undersides of the lintels where it generally ends in a sumptuous floral medallion. The numerous foliated circles of the creeper sometimes contain mythological scenes such as the dashavataras, also ganas, loving couples, musicians and dancers.

A wide range of linear patterns are developed on the basis of the intertwined creeper. The foliage scroll is also used as a decorative device on pillars and for framing niches.

Foliage

Foliage tufts are shown issuing from the mouth of makaras, yalis and kirti-mukhas. Kudus are sometimes shown as foliage issuing from the mouth of the kirti-mukha, as on the basement of the mahamandapa in the Vithala temple. From the mouth of kirti-mukha topping a prabhavali, issue garlands of foliage and flowers. Lush foliage sprouts from the flanks of the kumbha-panjara, a popular decorative motif in Vijayanagara architecture. Sometimes the foliage decorating the sides of the pitcher issues from a diminutive kirti-mukha mask.

A decorative pipal leaf enhances the centre and corners of the eaves of sixteenth-century temples. Notable examples are the pipal leaves on the eaves of the mahamandapa of the Vithala temple. The same theme occurs occasionally as a decoration on pillar blocks.

A great variety of trees and shrubs appears on the oldest carvings on the Mahanavami platform. In the course of time, representations of trees became comparatively rare.

Beads and beaded strings

Beads are used in several ways. Bands of large and small beads forming a decorative pattern are usually placed at the edges of doors. Multiple strings of beads hang like festoons on pillars and pilasters. Such strings can also be seen bordering a band of lotus petals. This motif occurs in architecture in the kumuda-valaya moulding on the temple plinth where the beads are rendered as rows of high-relief circlets.

B. Geometric Motifs

These shapes, generally based on the circle or on the rotating square, are frequently found as pillar decorations. Occasionally a lotus or lotus medallion enlivens the centre of the design.

Concentric circles appear in the decoration of the pillars of the hundred-pillar hall in the south-west corner of the outer courtyard of the Virupaksha temple.

Among the most sophisticated examples of geometric designs based on the rotating square are those carved on the porch pillars of the east gate of the Ramachandra complex.

C. Sun and Moon

The crescent moon appears occasionally on pillars, in the Ramanuja temple,[1] and in a Vaishnava temple on the Tungabhadra.[2]

The crescent moon and sun together have so far been discovered only on a pillar in the south-west mandapa of the Mallikarjuna temple in Malpannagudi.[3] They often occur on inscription slabs above the writing and on top of satikals and virakals.[4]

D. Pots

The spouted pitcher, the typical attribute of Brahma, also used by ascetics, appears as a decorative motif on a pillar in the Vaishnava temple near the gateway west of the Royal Centre on the Kamalapuram-Hampi road.[5]

Auspicious pots are found carved on the doorways of early monuments, such as the Ganigitti temple and the Jaina temple in Anegondi.[6]

E. Vijayanagara Emblem (Figure 142)

The Vijayanagara rulers adopted the boar crest as their royal emblem, showing the boar with a sword in front and the sun and moon above. Thus this emblem was distinguished from its Chalukyan antecedents by the additions of a sword.[7] The varaha was the most important denomination of gold coins of the empire. Incidentally it is unlikely that this crest had any connection with Vishnu's incarnation as Varaha.

This dynastic emblem occurs on pillars, for instance, in the hundred-pillar hall in the north-west corner of the outer courtyard of the Tiruvengalanatha temple, and in the north-east corner mandapa in the outer courtyard of the Ranganatha temple in Anegondi.[8]

Frequently it occurs on outer frames, as for example on the south side entrance to the north gopura of the Vithala temple, where on either side of the door, the Vijayanagara emblem is placed along the edge of the granite basement. On the north side entrance, on the outer door frame, in line with the kapota moulding of the plinth, the emblem appears again, reduced to a boar and sword.

In the Varaha temple the emblem is depicted twice on each wall of the entrance, between the scrollwork and the door frame.[9] The top carvings show two varahas facing each other, with a sword in between.

Other examples of this emblem appear in the Virupaksha temple complex, facing the passage-way on the inner side of the outer east gopura, and on the Domed Gate.[10]

NOTES

1. NCw/3.
2. NGt/1.
3. On the Hospet-Kamalapuram road, ca. 5 km north of Hospet.
4. See Chapter 10, p. 83.
5. NQs/1.
6. NXn/1 and MZv/1.
7. R.N. Saletore, *Vijayanagara Art*, p. 184.
8. MZw/12.
9. NGs/1.
10. NYx.

APPENDIX I

Ramayana Panels on the Ramachandra Temple

A. Principal Shrine

Bottom Row: West Wall (north side)

1. Seated royal figure with a sage
2. Dasharatha and Vasishtha

Bottom Row: North Wall

3. Dasharatha and Rishyashringa: performance of the putrakameshti yajna
4. Dasharatha divides the payasam among his three queens
5. Dasharatha and his four sons
6. Vishvamitra with Rama and Lakshmana. Rama kills Tataka.

7 & 10. Lady with lamp tray

8-9. Two sages

11. Release of Ahalya
12. Rama and Lakshmana fighting demons
13. King Janaka welcomes Rama, Lakshmana and Vishvamitra
14. Rama strings Shiva's bow

Bottom Row: East Wall

15. Janaka and the four princesses
16. Rama, Lakshmana and Vishvamitra

17-20. Marriage scenes

21-22. Marriage processions

Bottom Row: South Wall

23. Rama and Parashurama: Rama strings Vishnu's bow
24. Rama shoots the arrow
25. Marriage procession
26. Lady with lamp tray and marriage procession
27. Lady with child
28. Couples inside the palace (end of the Balakanda)
29. Dasharatha and his queens
30. Lady with a lamp tray
31. Kaushalya and Sumitra
32. Kaikeyi and Manthara
33. Kaikeyi with Dasharatha: Kaikeyi persuades Dasharatha, against his will, to banish Rama
34. Bharata worships Rama's sandals, indicating that he is willing to rule only in the name of Rama, the legitimate heir

Bottom Row: West Wall (south side)

35. Rama and his parents
36. Rama taking leave of Kaushalya (end of the Ayodhyakanda)

Middle Row: West Wall (north side)

1-2. Forest scene: Rama, Sita and Lakshmana are welcomed by sages

Middle Row: North Wall

3. Rama kills Viradha(?)
4. Rama and dying Viradha(?)
5. The three exiles welcomed by Sharabhanga(?)
6. The three exiles welcomed by other sages

7 & 10. Lady with chauri

8. Rama with Agastya
9. The exiles
11. Lakshmana and Shurpanakha
12. Lakshmana with Rama and Sita
13. Rama and Dushana
14. Rakshasas

Middle Row: East Wall

15. Rama and Trishiras
16. Rama and Khara
17. The golden deer
18. Rama departs to capture the golden deer
19. Rama and the golden deer
20. Rama shoots the deer

21. Lakshmana before Rama
22. Sita and Ravana

Middle Row: South Wall

23. Abduction of Sita by Ravana
24. Jatayu and Ravana
25. Dying Jatayu
26. Rama kills Kabandha (end of the Aranyakanda)

27 & 30. Lady with chauri

28. Rama and Lakshmana meet Hanuman
29. Rama with Sugriva
31. Rama and Lakshmana
32. Rama shoots through seven trees that are supported on Shesha's body
33. Death of Vali
34. Sugriva before Rama

Middle Row: West Wall (south side)

35-36. Coronation of Sugriva

Top Row: West Wall (north side)

1. Seated Sugriva
2. Monkeys

Top Row: North Wall

3. Sugriva and Tara
4. Sugriva and Lakshmana
5. Jambavan and Angada

6-7.. Defaced

8. Hanuman and monkeys (end of the Kishkindhakanda)
9. Hanuman jumps over the waters and arrives in Lanka
10. Defaced

11 & 12. Hanuman in Lanka

13. Hanuman fighting against the rakshasas
14. Hanuman and Sita

Top Row: East Wall

15 & 16. Hanuman and rakshasas

17. Hanuman captured by Indrajit
18. Hanuman seated on his coiled tail before Ravana
19. Hanuman returns to Rama
20. Monkey and bear(?)

21 & 22. Monkeys carrying Rama and Lakshmana

Top Row: South Wall

23 & 24. Monkeys

25. Defaced
26. Rama and Lakshmana (end of the Sundarakanda)
27. Defaced
28. Building the bridge to Lanka
29. Death of Kumbhakarna(?)
30. Death of Ravana
31. Hanuman
32. Ravana's wives
33. Consecration of Vibhishana

Top Row: West Wall (south side)

34. Hanuman (panel partly damaged)
35. Coronation of Rama
36. Sugriva and Jambavan (end of Yuddhakanda)

B. Minor Shrine

(Uttarakanda)

Lower Row: South Wall

1. Lakshmana escorts Sita
2. Sita arrives at Valmiki's hermitage

Lower Row: West Wall

3. Sita at the hermitage with her two sons, Kusha and Lava, at the feet of Valmiki
4. Valmiki with Lava and Kusha

Lower Row: North Wall

5. Rama(?) and sage

Lower Row: West Wall

6. Sacrificial horse

Lower Row: North Wall

7. One of Rama's sons fighting against Shatrughna
8. Lava and Kusha fighting against Bharata

Lower Row: East Wall

9. Rama enthroned, flanked by Sita as Bhudevi and Lakshmana holding Shesha. In this panel the main actors of the epic reveal their divine nature: Vishnu enthroned, together with Ananta and Bhudevi

Upper Row: South Wall

10. Lava and Kusha fighting Lakshmana, Hanuman and Jambavan

Upper Row: West Wall
11. Sita, Lava and Kusha stand before Valmiki, who instructs them to leave for Ayodhya
12. Rama and Sita
13. Rama, Lava and Kusha
14. Sita engulfed by Mother Earth

Upper Row: North Wall
15. Rama enthroned: Lakshmana leaves his earthly form and assumes his original form as Adishesha
16. Worship of Lakshmi-Narayana by a sage; Rama driving in a chariot towards Narayana, to merge into his original form
17. Vishnu on Ananta, with Lakshmi at his feet

C. Enclosure Wall

North gateway (east side from bottom to top)
1. Shravanakumara carries his parents
2. Shravanakumara collects water, is shot by an arrow by Dasharatha who mistakes him for an animal
3. Dasharatha conversing with the dying boy
4. Dasharatha begs forgiveness from Shravanakumara's parents
5. Dasharatha and attendant

First (bottom) Row, North Wall (eastwards from the north gateway)
1. Rishyashringa with dancer
2. Rishyashringa in Ayodhya: the putrakameshti yajna; Dasharatha with his four sons
3. Vishvamitra, Rama and Lakshmana
4. Tataka is killed by Rama
5. Rama and Lakshmana before Janaka
6. Rama strings the huge bow of Shiva
7. Journey to Mithila of Dasharatha and his three queens

First (bottom) Row, East Wall (southwards from north-east corner)
8. Religious ceremonies
9. Blessing of Rama and Sita
10 & 11. Blessing of the married couples
12, 13 & 13A. (below 13) Return to Ayodhya

Second Row, North Wall (eastwards from north gateway)
14. The meeting of Rama and Parashurama
15. The journey to Ayodhya is resumed
16. Procession
17. Procession
18. Rituals
19. Welcoming ceremonies
20. Welcoming ceremonies
21. Dasharatha and Kaikeyi

Second Row, East Wall (southwards from the north-east corner)
22. Departure for the forest
23. Rama, Lakshmana and Sita crossing the river
24. The exiles welcomed in the forest
25. Five rishis
26. Agastya presents Rama with miraculous weapons

Third Row, North Wall (eastwards from north gateway)
27. The game of chess: Rama and Sita playing chess, Lakshmana stands in attendance. To the right, Lakshmana is shown killing Jambukumara: Shurpanakha appears to take revenge
28. Lakshmana cuts off Shurpanakha's nose and ears
29. Lakshmana and Shurpanakha
30. Sita's abduction
31. Rama kills the golden deer
32. Meeting between Rama and Sugriva
33. Monkey
34. Rama received by monkeys

Third Row, East Wall (southwards from north-east corner)
35. Exploits of Rama to prove to Sugriva his superhuman strength: kicking the carcass of Dundubhi and shooting through seven palmyra trees
36. A jackfruit tree
37. Fight between Vali and Sugriva
38. Vali is slain
39. Standing male figure
40. Sugriva's coronation
40A. Rama and monkeys
41. A tree
42. Rama in conference

Fourth Row, North Wall (eastwards from north gateway)

43. Monkeys in search of Sita
44. Monkeys meet Sampati
45. Hanuman leaps to Lanka
46. Hanuman and Sita
47. Hanuman fights Indrajit
48. Hanuman before Ravana
49. Hanuman escapes
50. Hanuman returns to Rama

Fourth Row, East Wall (southwards from north-east corner)

51. Rama and Sagara
52. Building the bridge to Lanka
53. Battle scene
54. Wounded Lakshmana
55. Battle scene
56. Rama and Ravana
57. Death of Ravana

Fifth (top) Row, East Wall (northwards from east gateway)

58. After the battle: Ravana's wives mourn his death
59. Vibhishana, Lakshmana, Rama, Sita and Hanuman
60. Largely obscured panel, only a monkey is seen
61. Sages engaged in ritual
62. Vibhishana's consecration (?)
63. Rama
64. Monkeys
65. City gateway
66. Monkeys
67. Monkeys
68. Female figure

69-71. Monkeys and bears in procession

Fifth (top) Row, North Wall (westwards from north-east corner)

72-74. Monkeys

75. Damaged panel
76. Procession
77. Rama enthroned
78. Panel obliterated
79. Sages
80. Sita's ordeal (?)
81. Procession
82. Panel defaced by a modern column
83. Sita and Hanuman (Sita is in a chariot)
84. Rama and attendants in a chariot
85. Monkeys
87. Palace scene
88. Panel obliterated by the wall of the mandapa

89-91. Rama being honoured

92-93. Coronation of Rama in Ayodhya

95-96. Rishis pay homage to Vishnu who reclines on Ananta

APPENDIX II

Ramayana Panels on the gopura of the Ramanuja Temple

The narrative is divided into five sections: three on the walls of the gopura outside the prakara and two on the walls within the prakara. Section A of the narrative is on the eastern side and section B on the western side of gopura, outside the prakara. Sections C and D are on the western and eastern sides of the gopura within the prakara. Section E is , once again, outside the prakara on the east and west walls of the porches of the gopura.

A. Outside the prakara, east of the entrance passageway. [East side of the gopura; along the outer wall of the east side, outer south wall and inner south wall, i.e. inside the porch, and one panel on the inner east wall, i.e. on the side (inside) of the porch on the west-facing wall.] Balakanda and Ayodhyakanda from the putrakameshti yajna to the exile of Rama.

East side of the gopura, exterior (from north to south)
Lowermost tier:
1. Female attendant
2. King Dasharatha, the sage Rishyashringa and a female attendant
3. Two chamaradharinis
4. Putrakameshti yajna
5. The sage Rishyashringa gives the payasa to Dasharatha and Kaushalya

South side of the gopura, exterior (from east to west)
Lowermost tier:
6. Sumitra and Kaikeyi
7. Chamaradharini

South side of the gopura, interior (inner wall of the porch) west corner
Lowermost tier:
8. Rama, Lakshmana, Bharata and Shatrughna practising archery

South side of the gopura, interior (inner wall of the porch) (from west to east)
Second tier from the bottom:
9. The sage Vishvamitra asks Dasharatha to send Rama and Lakshmana to destroy the demons polluting the yajna
10. Rama and Lakshmana walking
11. Two rishis

East side of the gopura, interior (east wall of the porch, west-facing wall)
Lowermost tier:
12. Rama and Lakshmana fighting against Subahu and Maricha

South side of the gopura, exterior (from south to north)
Second tier from the bottom:
13. Rama and Lakshmana
14. Rama, Lakshmana with the sage Vishvamitra on a boat crossing the river Sona

East side of the gopura, exterior (from south to north)
Second tier from the bottom:
15. Rama releases Ahalya
16. Rama breaks Shiva's bow, the king Janaka stands before him
17. Man striding
    (Nos. 18-24. Marriage procession)
18. Two women in a palanquin
19. Dasharatha and his three queens in a palanquin
20. A man leading a horse
21. An elephant with a rider
22. Two men standing

East side of the gopura, exterior (from north to south)
Third tier from the bottom:
23. Man riding on a camel

24. Man riding on a camel
25. Chamaradharini
26. King Janaka welcomes king Dasharatha and his entourage
27. Two couples: Rama-Sita: Lakshmana-Urmila
28. Two couples: Bharata-Mandaviya: Shatrughna-Srutakirti
29. Two women in a palanquin

South side of the gopura, exterior (from east to west)
Third tier from the bottom:
30. The meeting of Rama and Parashurama
31. Man riding a horse

South side of the gopura, interior (inner wall of the porch from east to west)
Third tier from the bottom:
32. Chowkidar at a palace gate in Ayodhya
33. Two ladies in a palace in Ayodhya
34. Two ladies in a palace in Ayodhaya
35. One lady in a palace in Ahodhya

South side of the gopura, interior, (inner wall of the porch) west corner
Fourth tier from the bottom:
36. Dasharatha swooning hearing Kaikeyi's wish to send Rama in exile.

South side of the gopura, exterior (from south to north)
Fourth tier from the bottom:
37. Rama takes leave of Dasharatha

East side of the gopura, exterior (from south to north)
Fourth tier from the bottom:
38. Rama, Sita and Lakshmana walking
39. Two sages under a tree, one sage under a tree.
40. Rama, Sita and Lakshmana crossing the Ganga
41. Rama and Sita in Chitrakuta
42. Lakshmana standing
43. One rishi with Kamandalu

B. Outside the prakara, west of the entrance passageway. [West side of the gopura: along the inner south wall, i.e. inside the porch, the outer south wall and the outer west wall.] Aranyakanda and a part of the Kishkindhakanda: the exile, the abduction of Sita, the meeting with Hanuman and Sugriva.

South side of the gopura, interior (inner wall of the porch)
Lowest tier, east corner:
44. Rama and Lakshmana fighting with Viradha

South side of the gopura, interior (from east to west)
Second tier from the bottom:
45. Rama, Sita and Lakshmana walking
46. The sage Agastya welcomes the exiles
47. Rama, Sita and Lakshmana in Panchavati

South side of the gopura, interior (west to east)
Third tier from the bottom:
48. Rama seated
49. Shurpanakha tries to tempt Rama
50. Lakshmana cuts Shurpanakha's nose; Shurpanakha retreats

South side of the gopura, interior
Fourth tier from the bottom:
51. Rama and Sita seated in a hut

South side of the gopura, exterior (from east to west)
Lowest tier:
52. Rama and Sita seated in a hut
53. The golden deer

West side of the gopura (exterior from south to north)
Lowest tier:
54. Rama pursues the golden deer
55. Rama kills the golden deer
56. Rama carries the golden deer on his shoulders
57. Ravana abducting Sita (they are both in the aerial chariot) and the fight with the vulture Jatayu
58. Cremation of Jatayu

West side of the gopura, exterior (from north to south)
Second tier from the bottom:
59. Lakshmana standing

60. Rama and Shabari
61. Three rishis
62. Rama and Lakshmana
63. Two rishis
64. Rama resting under a tree on Rishyamukha hill
65. Rama and Lakshmana meet Hanuman

South side of the gopura, exterior (from west to east)
Second tier from the bottom:
66. Sugriva and Hanuman bowing
67. Rama and Lakshmana

South side of gopura, exterior (from east to west)
Third tier from the bottom:
68. Lakshmana and Hanuman
69. Rama holding Sugriva's hand in friendship

West side of the gopura, exterior (from south to north)
Third tier from the bottom:
70. Two monkeys standing with hands folded in anjali mudra
71. One monkey
72. Rama, Lakshmana and Hanuman walking
73. Two monkeys
74. Sugriva, Rama and Lakshmana
75. One monkey
76. One monkey

West side of the gopura, exterior (from north to south)
Fourth tier from the bottom:
77. Two monkeys
78. Rama and Lakshmana
79. Sugriva
80. Rama and Lakshmana

South side of the gopura, exterior
Fourth tier:
81. Two monkeys

C. Inside the prakara, west of the entrance passageway. [Along the west and north walls—there is no porch on the inner side of the gopura, so these are the exterior walls.] Kishkindhakanda completed, the whole of the Sundarakanda and the beginning of the Yuddhakanda (from Rama proving his prowess to Sugriva and the subsequent killing of Vali, to the arrival of Vibhishana).

West side of the gopura, exterior (from south to north)
Lowest tier:
82. Rama and Sugriva
83. Rama shooting an arrow through the shala trees

North side of the gopura, exterior (from west to east)
Lowest tier:
84. The fight between Vali and Sugriva. Rama shoots Vali, Lakshmana looks at the scene
85. Rama and Lakshmana before the dying Vali

North side of the gopura, exterior (from east to west)
Second tier from the bottom:
86. Sugriva's coronation
87. Sugriva and a rishi
88. Rama and Lakshmana
89. Sugriva prostrates before Rama

West side of the gopura, exterior (from north to south)
Second tier from the bottom:
90. Three monkeys and one monkey
91. Three monkeys armed with swords and shields standing on rocks
92. Three monkeys armed with swords and shields standing
93. Angry Lakshmana reminds Sugriva of his promise to help in the search for Sita

West side of the gopura, exterior (from south to north)
Third tier from the bottom:
94. Three monkeys with swords and shields standing on rocks. The monkey-army in search of Sita
95. One monkey with sword and shield
96. The ocean
97. Hanuman meets Sita in the ashoka grove

North side of the gopura, exterior (from west to east)
Third tier from the bottom:
98. Hanuman seated on his coiled tail before Ravana

99. Two monkeys
100. Hanuman returns from Lanka and reports to Rama
101. Vibhishana arrives and prostrates before Rama

North side of the gopura, exterior west corner (one panel is missing from the east corner)
Fourth tier from bottom:
102. Three monkeys

West side of the gopura, exterior (south corner)
Fourth tier from the bottom:
103. One monkey

D. Inside the prakara, east of the entrance passageway. [East side of the gopura, along the north and east walls. Since there is no porch on this side of the prakara these are the exterior walls.] Yuddhakanda continued.

East side of the gopura (from south to north)
Lowermost tier:
104. A man standing
105. A monkey (Hanuman?) emerging from a sea monster (makara? Surasa episode?)
106. Standing youth

East side of the gopura (from north to south)
Second tier from the bottom:
107. A monkey catching a rakshasa by the hair—Shuka, Ravana's messenger to Sugriva being mishandled?
108. Hanuman and a monkey standing
109. Two rishis on a cloud
110. Narada on a cloud

East side of the gopura (from south to north)
Third tier from the bottom:
111. Rakshasa with sword and shield
112. Ravana and attendant
113. Two rakshasas with swords and shields
114. Angada's embassy to Ravana

East side of the gopura (north corner)
Fourth tier, from the bottom:
115. A fight between a rakshasa and a monkey

North side of the gopura (from east to west)
Lowermost tier:
116. Three monkeys
117. Hanuman and the rakshasa Kalanemi in the guise of an ascetic

North side of the gopura (from west to east)
Second tier from the bottom:
118. Hanuman revives Lakshmana by bringing the aushadha parvata
119. Hanuman carries two aushadha parvatas
120. Hanuman, Rama, Lakshmana
121. A striding monkey. A monkey fighting

North side of the gopura (from east to west)
Third tier from the bottom:
122. Ravana and attendants
123. Two monkeys
124. Two monkeys
125. Rama, Lakshmana and two monkeys

North side of the gopura (from west to east)
Fourth tier from the bottom:
126. A rakshasa and a monkey fighting
127. A battle scene

E. Outside the prakara, inside the porches along the side walls. Yuddhakanda continued.

West side of the entrance passageway
Bottom panel:
128. Fight with Kumbhakarna. Rama decapitates Kumbhakarna whose head remains stuck on the wall of Lanka
Top panel:
129. Lakshmana kills Indrajit; Ravana is depicted in one corner shooting a terrible weapon

East side of the entrance passageway
Second panel from the bottom:
130. Rama and Ravana fight using powerful weapons
Top panel:
131. Fight between Rama and Ravana continued

The death of Ravana and the coronation of Rama are missing.

APPENDIX III

Partial *Ramayana* and *Bhagavata* series on the Vithala Temple

A. *Ramayana* on the Pillars of the North Porch of Rangamandapa

	Lower Square	Middle Square	Top Square
East Pillar			
W.	Sita asks for the golden deer	Four monkeys	Monkey king and queen
S.	Rama pursues the golden deer	Hanuman encounters Rama and Lakshmana at Rishyamukha	Rama and dying Vali
E.	Rama shoots the golden deer	Rama bends a bow to show his prowess	Vali and Sugriva fighting
N.	Rama and Lakshmana	Rama, Lakshmana and Sugriva	Rama shoots an arrow through the seven trees
West Pillar			
W.	Rama, Lakshmana and Hanuman	Kumbhakarna fights two monkeys	Rama, Sita and Lakshmana
S.	Hanuman in Lanka	Sleeping Kumbhakarna	Fight between Lakshmana and Indrajit
E	Hanuman in the ashokavana	Hanuman before Rama	Hanuman carries boulders
N.	Building the bridge to Lanka	Rama and Hanuman	Rama and Hanuman

B. The Uttarakanda on the Beams of the Mahamandapa *(North hall)*

East side (from the north-east corner southwards)

1. Rama seated with the golden statue of Sita beside him; Lakshmana before Rama; the sacrificial horse and an attendant.
2. Rama ties the letter of instruction to the horse's head; Bharata and Shatrughna lead the horse.
3. Lakshmana and Sugriva(?) take the horse to the forest and let it loose.

South side (from the south-east corner westwards)

4. Hanuman reports back to Rama; the horse is seen walking away.
5. Lava and Kusha capture the horse and fight Rama's allies.
6. Lava and Kusha before Sita and Valmiki.

West Side (from the south-west corner northwards)

7. Sita, Kusha and Lava are escorted to Rama's presence by Valmiki.
   (The rest of the panels are not of the *Uttara-Ramayana*)

C. *Bhagavata Purana* Panels of the Beams of the Mahamandapa *(South hall)*

North side (from the north-west corner eastwards)

1. Standing Krishna flanked by two male devotees
2. Standing male figure
3. Putanavadha
4. Bakasuravadha
5. Kaliyamardana
6. Aghasuravadha
7. Shakatabhanga
8. Standing male figure
9. Krishna kicking a tree(?)
10. Krishna stealing curds

East side (from the north-east corner southwards)

11. Standing figure
12. Venugopala
13. Standing Krishna and gopi who carries a pot on her head
14. Venugopala
15. Krishna eating butter
16. Krishna and Balarama(?) eating butter

South side (south-east corner westwards)

17. Govardhanadhara; on either side of this panel is one of standing Krishna
18. Kamsa in his court, surrounded by sages, suppliants, etc.; in one corner is the elephant Kuvalayapida
19. Krishna wrestling with either Chanura or Mushtika
20. Kuvalayapidavadha
21. Unclear panel
22. Fight between Krishna and Kamsa
23. Kamsavadha
24. Enthronement of Ugrasena
    (The rest of the panels are not of the *Bhagavata Purana*)

APPENDIX IV

Partial *Ramayana* Series on the Tiruvengalanatha Temple

A. East Gopura

On the west side, on the granite base, carved on either side of the entryway

South of the entryway (from the bottom to the top)

1. Hanuman encounters Rama and Lakshmana at Rishyamukha
2. Hanuman talking to a rishi
3. Hanuman before Sita in the ashokavana
4. Hanuman damaging the ashokavana
5. Hanuman seated on his tail before seated Ravana
6. Hanuman handing over Sita's chudamani to Rama

North of the entryway (from the bottom to the top)

1. Rama shooting an arrow
2. Rama and Lakshmana with monkeys
3. Building the bridge to Lanka
4. Rama examining a weapon
5. Rama on a war chariot
6. Rama on foot fights Ravana on a chariot
7. Rama and Ravana, both in chariots, fighting

B. North Gopura (of inner courtyard)

On the north side, on the granite base, carved on either side of the entryway

West of the entryway (from bottom to top)

1. Hanuman before a seated person
2. A standing male and a seated rishi
3. Rama hunting the golden deer
4. Lakshmana goes to help Rama; Sita in front of her hut
5. Lakshmana meets Rama
6. Rama seated with Hanuman in front of him

East of entryway (from bottom to top)

1. Rama handing ring to Hanuman
2. Hanuman standing on the head of a seated sage
3. Hanuman before Sita in the Ashokavana
4. Hanuman climbing on the rooftops of Lanka
5. Hanuman taken captive by Indrajit
6. Hanuman seated on his tail before Ravana

APPENDIX V

Unusual Sculptures Difficult to Identity

In several cases it has not been possible to identify the sculpted images. For instance, a hero wielding a club, a hero grappling with the elephant, noted in Chapter 10, and a dancing goddess, who appears several times as noted in Chapter 7.

There are four temples in which such difficulties of identification arise.

Ramachandra Temple

In the mahamandapa, on the west face of the top block of the second pillar from the east, and second from the south, is seen a four-armed Vaishnava deity, human from head to waist and the lower half a recumbent animal (lion, bull?). The deity holds the chakra, shankha, and gada(?), with one hand in abhaya-mudra.

In the east porch, on the north face of the top block of the second pillar from the north, a four-armed deity reclines on a tree or a lotus flower. Two hands hold indistinct weapons; one hand rests along his side, while the other supports his head.

In the rangamandapa, on the east face of the lower block of the north-east pillar, a man stands holding on to a pillar upon which a circular object (a mirror?) rests.

Prasanna Virupaksha Temple

In the south-west corner mandapa, on the north face of the top block of the first detached pillar from the south, third from the east, a man before a Shiva-linga is shown in a striding pose with a raised hand holding a gada.

Vithala Temple

In the south-east corner mandapa, on the south face of the top block of the second pillar from the north, second from the west, against a background of fire, two men ride in a chariot with one at the rear grasping the other by the hair and kicking him.

In the mandapa of the shrine in the west side of the gallery along the enclosure wall, on the south face of the lower block of the first row from the east, fourth from the north, a four-armed Vaishnava deity runs, his upper two hands holds the chakra and shankha while the two lower hands are in lolahasta.

Pattabhirama temple

In the rangamandapa, on the north face of the lower slab of the first detached pillar from the east, the first detached pillar from the south, a standing male figure wearing a kirita holds a padma in his right hand and a gada in his left.

Others

There is one Bhairava-like image. This figure, in striding pose, wears a short dhoti and a crown of leaves. He holds a curved sword in one hand and a kapala in the other. A dagger is stuck in his waistband. He is accompanied by a diminutive woman holding two infants. Two examples of this image are in the collection of the site office of the Directorate of Archaeology and Museums, Karnataka state, and one in the museum.

APPENDIX VI

Chronology of Monuments

Pre-Vijayanagara Period

Some of the temples and gateways on Hemakuta hill date from the first decades of the fourteenth century immediately prior to the foundation of the capital. Among the most noteworthy buildings of this period are the two almost identical triple-shrine temples.[1]

Sangama Period

In spite of the considerable building activity which characterized the Sangama period, few monuments can be dated with certainty.

Some monuments, such as the Virupaksha temple (of AD 1398, on Hemakuta)[2] the Gayatri-pitha,[3] and the double-shrine temple[4] on the slopes of Hemakuta hill are possibly among the earliest Sangama projects.

Located in the Royal Centre, the Prasanna Virupaksha temple begun in the mid-fourteenth century, replicates the Virupaksha temple at Hampi.[5]

On the Tungabhadra a short distance east of Hampi are three important temples close to each other. The oldest is the Narasimha temple, whose construction pre-dates 1379.[6] In its proximity are the Shiva temple of 1386,[7] and near Chakra-tirtha, the Prata Vithala,[8] which on stylistic grounds can also be dated to the late fourteenth century.

In 1385 Irugappa, a minister of Harihara II, constructed near Kamalapuram a temple dedicated to Kunthu Jinanatha, known locally as Ganigitti temple.[9]

Among the achievements of the early Sangama period is the lower tier of the Mahanavami platform, probably dating from the second half of the fourteenth century.

The most significant architectural project of the Sangama dynasty is the Ramachandra temple, a royal foundation ascribable to Devaraya I. Much of the sculpture on it, but not all, dates from the first quarter of the fifteenth century.[10] The name of Devaraya II is mentioned in an inscription on a Jaina temple in the eastern part of the Royal Centre.[11]

A small temple to the south-west of the Royal Centre was built during the reign of Mallikarjuna. This monument, as already noted, is important for the portraits of Mallikarjuna and his chauri-bearer Shirangu.[12]

Some monuments were constantly enlarged during the Sangama period. In the Sacred Centre, an important addition to the Virupaksha temple was the north gopura. In the Royal Centre, the last tier was built on the Mahanavami platform.

Saluva and Tuluva Periods

Though no monuments at Vijayanagara have been positively identified as Saluva, it is possible that the core of the Vithala temple complex may belong to this period.[13]

The climax of the architectural development coincided with the zenith of power and extent of the empire under the Tuluvas.

At Vijayanagara, older temples were refurbished and enlarged. Krishnadevaraya built the maharangamandapa of the Virupaksha temple in 1509-10.[14] His queens, Chinnadevi and Tirumaladevi added gopuras to the Vithala temple complex in 1513.[15] After the victorious Orissa campaign, Krishnadevaraya refurbished the Mahanavami platform, its west face was covered with sculpted chlorite slabs.

New temples were built, in 1515 the large Krishna complex,[16] and in 1524 the Ananta-shayana temple, near Hospet.[17]

Achyutaraya did not commission any temple at the capital. However, the Tiruvengalanatha temple was built in 1534 by Hiriya Tirumalaraja, the brother-in-law of Achyutaraya.[18] The Pattabhirama—near Kamalapuram—was also erected during his reign.

The Tiruvengalanatha temple, known as Chandikeshvara, and the Mudu Viranna temple,[19] both on the Kamalapuram-Hampi road were built in 1545 by General Jangamaya.[20]

Sadashivaraya and Ramaraya, too, did not venture on temple building. However, influential members of the court and officials patronised extensive work undertaken within the Vithala temple complex, particular mentions must be made of the mahamandapa of 1554, built by Udayagiri Timmaraju.[21]

The Aravidu chief, Aubalaraju built in 1556 the Tirumangai-Alvar temple near the Vithala complex.[22]

The names of the patrons responsible for the sculptures are not often known. Numerous epigraphical records, however, commemorate the consecration of several images. Most of these images no longer exist.

The Lakshmi-Narasimha monolith was erected on the orders of Krishnadevaraya in 1528 by Arya Krishna Bhatta, who appears to have been his chaplain.[23]

In 1534 Gandhada Tippisetti made provision for setting up the statues of the thirteen Alvars, including Tirukachinambi, in the Vithala temple.[24] These, however, are no longer in situ.

The Mudu Viranna image, if the present image is the original, was consecrated by Jangamaya in 1545.[25]

Post-Vijayanagara Period

In the early nineteenth century work was undertaken at the site. The Virupaksha temple was extensively renovated. The eastern gopura, a new structure incorporating old slabs, the present paintings on the ceiling of the maharangamandapa,[26] and the numerous stucco statues embellishing the parapets of the buildings in the inner prakara date from this period. Between 1987 and 1989, new sacred images and a new navagraha-shrine were donated to the temple.

NOTES

1. NFw/9 and NLb/3.
2. NLb1/19. *Annual Report on South Indian Epigraphy of 1934-35,* Nos. 351-2.
3. NLb/1.
4. NFw/5.
5. NQy/1.
6. NGt/4. See Anila Verghese, *Religious Traditions at Vijayanagara: as Revealed through its Monuments,* p. 35.
7. NGt/3. *Vijayanagara: Progress of Research 1983-1984,* No. 2.
8. NGw/5.
9. NXn/1. *South Indian Inscription,* I, No. 152.
10. NRw/1. *South Indian Inscriptions,* IV, No. 252; Anila Verghese, op. cit., p. 47.
11. NSt/1. *South Indian Inscriptions,* I, No. 153.
12. NVo/1. *Annual Report on Indian Epigraphy of 1957-58,* Nos. 104 and 205.
13. NHa/1. G. Michell, *Architecture and Art of Southern India,* p. 39.
14. *Epigraphia Indica,* I, pp. 360-71; *South Indian Inscriptions,* IV, No. 258.
15. *South Indian Inscriptions,* IV, Nos. 273 and 278.
16. NLm/4. *South Indian Inscriptions,* IV, Nos. 254 and 255.
17. *Annual Report on South Indian Epigraphy of 1922,* No. 683.
18. NMh/1. *South Indian Inscriptions,* IX, Part II, No. 564.
19. NLw/3 and NLw/6. *South Indian Inscriptions,* IV, Nos. 265, 266.
20. *South Indian Inscriptions,* IV, Nos. 265 and 266.
21. *South Indian Inscriptions,* IX, Part II, No. 653.
22. NCv/3. *South Indian Inscriptions,* IV, No. 280.
23. NLm/1. *Epigraphia Indica,* I, pp. 398-402.
24. *South Indian Inscriptions,* IX, Part II, No. 566.
25. *South Indian Inscriptions,* IV, No. 266.
26. Dallapiccola, A.L., 'Ceiling paintings in the Virupaksha temple, Hampi *South Asian Studies 13,* 1997.

APPENDIX VII

Pillar Reliefs in the Principal Temples

	Virupaksha				Prasanna Virupaksha	Kadalekalu Ganesha (NLc/2)	Vithala				Pattabhirama			Malyavanta Raguunatha			Krishna			Tiruvengalanatha (Achyutaraya)				Ramachandra					
	Hundred-pillar Hall	Maharangamandapa	Rangamandapa	Cloister of inner courtyard	South-west corner pavilion	Mandapa	Rangamandapa	South-east pavilion	North-east pavilion	Hundred-pillar Hall	Mahamandapa	Rangamandapa	Hundred-pillar Hall	Hundred-pillar Hall	Mahamandapa	Rangamandapa	Mahamandapa	Rangamandapa	Mandapa of subsidiary shrine	Mahamandapa	Rangamandapa	Mandapa of sub-shrine	Hundred-pillar Hall	Mahamandapa	Rangamandapa	East porch	North porch	South porch	South-west corner pavilion
SHAIVA THEMES																													
Linga	24	2		18	9	5				2			1										2						
Linga with cow doing abhisheka	5	5	1	3	2	3				3	8			1									1						
Linga with snake's hood over	5	3		9	6	7																							
Elephant doing abhisheka to linga		1		2	2																								
Linga with lizard		2		2	1	2																							
Linga with man doing abhisheka	1	1		3																									
Linga and Nandi	1																												
Linga under a tree	1	1		2							1																		
Devi embracing linga	2	1		2	1	1																							
Devi seated before linga				1																									
Man clinging to linga		2		1						1																			
Linga and standing man in anjali-mudra	1																												
Man with a bow doing					1																								

	Virupaksha				Prasanna Virupaksha	Kadalekalu Ganesha (NLc/2)	Vithala				Pattabhirama			Malyavanta Raguunatha			Krishna			Tiruvengalanatha (Achyutaraya)				Ramachandra					
	Hundred-pillar Hall	Maharangamandapa	Rangamandapa	Cloister of inner courtyard	South-west corner pavilion	Mandapa	Rangamandapa	South-east pavilion	North-east pavilion	Hundred-pillar Hall	Mahamandapa	Rangamandapa	Hundred-pillar Hall	Hundred-pillar Hall	Mahamandapa	Rangamandapa	Mahamandapa	Rangamandapa	Mandapa of subsidiary shrine	Mahamandapa	Rangamandapa	Mandapa of sub-shrine	Hundred-pillar Hall	Mahamandapa	Rangamandapa	East porch	North porch	South porch	South-west corner pavilion
abhisheka to linga																													
Linga with a man holding aloft a gada					1																								
Standing Shiva with Devi				1																									
Standing Shiva						1																							
Dakshinamurti		1		1																									
Vinadhara Dakshinamurti			1		1																								
Seated Shiva	1	3		2	1								1																
Standing Shiva, leaning against Nandi	1																												
Shiva as Nataraja	1																												
Urdhva-tandava Shiva																							1						
Umamaheshvaramurti				1																									
Bhikshatanamurti	3	3		1						2	1																		
Gajantakamurti				1																									
Yamantaka	1																												
Harihara																							1						
Four-armed standing Bhairava	3	1		1	1																		4			1		1	
Two-armed standing Bhairava		2				1																							
Four-armed Bhairava in a striding pose				1																									
Four-armed standing Virabhadra	5	3		2	1	2											1												
Seated Ganesha	12	3	1	5	2	2				2	2		3	1	3		2						4		1	1		1	1
Standing Ganesha	1	1		2	1										1														
Dancing Ganesha	3	4				3	1										3									1		1	
Ganesha on his vahana	1																												
Karttikeya		1			2											1										2	2		

	Virupaksha				Prasanna Virupaksha	Kadalekalu Ganesha (NLc/2)	Vithala				Pattabhirama			Malyavanta Raguunatha			Krishna			Tiruvengalanatha (Achyutaraya)				Ramachandra					
	Hundred-pillar Hall	Maharangamandapa	Rangamandapa	Cloister of inner courtyard	South-west corner pavilion	Mandapa	Rangamandapa	South-east pavilion	North-east pavilion	Hundred-pillar Hall	Mahamandapa	Rangamandapa	Hundred-pillar Hall	Hundred-pillar Hall	Mahamandapa	Rangamandapa	Mahamandapa	Rangamandapa	Mandapa of subsidiary shrine	Mahamandapa	Rangamandapa	Mandapa of sub-shrine	Hundred-pillar Hall	Mahamandapa	Rangamandapa	East porch	North porch	South porch	South-west corner pavilion
Nandi					5	1				1					1														
Vyaghrapada	3			1	1	3		1	1	1	1	1								2			1						
Patanjali										1																			
Shaiva dvarapala		3	1	1	4	1																							
VAISHNAVA THEMES																													
Standing Vishnu								1	1	1				4									3						
Seated Vishnu				1	1					2	3		2					5	1				2	1	1				1
Lakshmi-Narayana	1			1			1	2					1					1						1					
Vishnu on Garuda									1				2		1			1				1	1						
Lakshmi-Narayana on Garuda								1																					
Kari-Varada								1					1									1							
Individual reliefs of Chaturvimshati-murtis							3																		24				
Zoomorphic Matsya	2										1									2									
Therioanthropomorphic Matsya				1				2			2		6	5	2			1	1				1	1					
Therioanthropo-morphic Kurma					1			6					2	5	2				1				2						
Zoomorphic Kurma	6			1					1	5	2		9		7	3			1	3			12						
Zoomporphic Varaha				1						2																			
Therioanthropomorphic Varaha													1	1	1				1					1	1				
Bhu-Varaha		1		1				1																	1				
Lakshmi-Narasimha		1					1	1			1												1						
Four-armed standing Narasimha								2						6						2									
Two-armed standing Narasimha holding a snake								1					1	2	3					1									

	Virupaksha				Prasanna Virupaksha	Kadalekalu Ganesha (NLc/2)	Vithala				Pattabhirama			Malyavanta Raguunatha			Krishna			Tiruvengalanatha (Achyutaraya)				Ramachandra					
	Hundred-pillar Hall	Maharangamandapa	Rangamandapa	Cloister of inner courtyard	South-west corner pavilion	Mandapa	Rangamandapa	South-east pavilion	North-east pavilion	Hundred-pillar Hall	Mahamandapa	Rangamandapa	Hundred-pillar Hall	Hundred-pillar Hall	Mahamandapa	Rangamandapa	Mahamandapa	Rangamandapa	Mandapa of subsidiary shrine	Mahamandapa	Rangamandapa	Mandapa of sub-shrine	Hundred-pillar Hall	Mahamandapa	Rangamandapa	East porch	North porch	South porch	South-west corner pavilion
Narasimha in lalitasana						2	1		1	1	4	1						1						1					
Two-armed standing Narasimha in a dancing pose	6			2					1	1	1																		
Two-armed standing Narasimha with Prahlada								2						1															2
Two-armed Yoga-Narasimha											2	1	1		1					1	1								
Narasimha in padmasana																	1												
Four-armed Yoga-Narasimha	2		1	1	2			2	1	4	3	2	3	1			5	3						2					1
Two-armed seated Narasimha						2	1		1	1	4	1																	2
Sthauna-Narasimha								3											1										
Narasimha catching Hiranyakashipu		1		1			1	2									1												1
Ugra-Narasimha							1	2		1	1						1												
Four-armed standing Narasimha within a prabhavali										1	2						1												
Narasimha removing a thorn from foot of Chenchu-Lakshmi	1	2	1	1		3	1	2				1											1	1					1
Chenchu-Lakshmi leaning on/holding a bow	1	1				2	1			2		1	1	1						1			1						
Vamana								1			1		1	5					1										
Trivikarama																								1					
Parashurama								1											1										
Parashurama and Rama standing side by side								1																					
Four-armed standing Rama								1																					
Standing Rama, holding bow and arrow	10	1	1	2	3	4		5	7	12	17	9	10	4	6		7	1	1	5	1	1	9						1

	Virupaksha				Prasanna Virupaksha	Kadalekalu Ganesha (NLc/2)	Vithala				Pattabhirama			Malyavanta Raguunatha			Krishna			Tiruvengalanatha (Achyutaraya)				Ramachandra					
	Hundred-pillar Hall	Maharangamandapa	Rangamandapa	Cloister of inner courtyard	South-west corner pavilion	Mandapa	Rangamandapa	South-east pavilion	North-east pavilion	Hundred-pillar Hall	Mahamandapa	Rangamandapa	Hundred-pillar Hall	Hundred-pillar Hall	Mahamandapa	Rangamandapa	Mahamandapa	Rangamandapa	Mandapa of subsidiary shrine	Mahamandapa	Rangamandapa	Mandapa of sub-shrine	Hundred-pillar Hall	Mahamandapa	Rangamandapa	East porch	North porch	South porch	South-west corner pavilion
Rama bending bow							1				1						1												
Seated Rama						4	1		3		2	3		2			2			2			2	3					
Seated Rama with Hanuman							1	1		1				3	1			1		1									
Seated Rama and standing Lakshmana							1	1									2												
Rama and Sita seated, Lakshmana standing							1	1							1														
Rama, Sita and Lakshmana standing								1																	1				
Hanuman before Rama and Lakshmana								1							1														
Hanuman before Sita in ashokavana															1														
Seated Rama, giving signet ring to Hanuman							1																						1
Standing Lakshmana		2		1		1		3			3	4		19										1					2
Rama and Sita seated Lakshmana, Bharata and Shatrughna standing								1																					
Standing Sugriva						1					2	1		15										1	1				
Jambavan												2	1																
Rama shooting the golden deer								1																					
Monkey in devotion								1							3														
Rama shooting Vali, during fight between Vali and Sugriva														1															
Hanuman giving Rama's ring to Sita in ashokavana							1																						

	Virupaksha				Prasanna Virupaksha	Kadalekalu Ganesha (NLc/2)	Vithala				Pattabhirama			Malyavanta Raguunatha			Krishna			Tiruvengalanatha (Achyutaraya)				Ramachandra					
	Hundred-pillar Hall	Maharangamandapa	Rangamandapa	Cloister of inner courtyard	South-west corner pavilion	Mandapa	Rangamandapa	South-east pavilion	North-east pavilion	Hundred-pillar Hall	Mahamandapa	Rangamandapa	Hundred-pillar Hall	Hundred-pillar Hall	Mahamandapa	Rangamandapa	Mahamandapa	Rangamandapa	Mandapa of subsidiary shrine	Mahamandapa	Rangamandapa	Mandapa of sub-shrine	Hundred-pillar Hall	Mahamandapa	Rangamandapa	East porch	North porch	South porch	South-west corner pavilion
Vali and Sugriva fighting								1	1						2		2											1	
Hanuman seated on his tail before Ravana								1																					
Standing Rama, Sita and Hanuman							1																						
Standing Hanuman before standing Rama															1														
Hanuman carrying Rama																						1							
Lakshmana reminding Sugriva of his promise to help Rama															1														
Lakshmana cutting off the nose of Shurpanakha								1																					
Hanuman fighting 3 demons								1																					
Standing Hanuman offering rocks to Rama																		1											
Hanuman before seated Rama and Lakshmana							1																						
Standing Lakshmana and Sugriva							1																						
Dancing Krishna	5	5		6	2	1	2	6	5	9	6	3	5	27	6	1	10	3		2		1	3	2		2			5
Krishna eating butter	3	1		2	1	1		2	1	1	6	1	6	18	6	1	2			2		1	8	1			1		3
Crawling Krishna	5	1		1			2				4	3	1	1						3			5						
Seated Krishna											1		1	5															
Krishna holding ears	2			1	2	1	1	1	5		3		2	25	1		4		1			1	1	1			1	1	1
Crawling Krishna holding a butter ball														1	1	1						1							
Kaliya-mardana Krishna	8	5		5	1	5	2	13	4	8	9	5	5	13	3	1	7	2		2	1	2	9	3		1	1	1	

	Virupaksha				Prasanna Virupaksha	Kadalekalu Ganesha (NLc/2)	Vithala				Pattabhirama			Malyavanta Raguunatha			Krishna			Tiruvengalanatha (Achyutaraya)				Ramachandra					
	Hundred-pillar Hall	Maharangamandapa	Rangamandapa	Cloister of inner courtyard	South-west corner pavilion	Mandapa	Rangamandapa	South-east pavilion	North-east pavilion	Hundred-pillar Hall	Mahamandapa	Rangamandapa	Hundred-pillar Hall	Hundred-pillar Hall	Mahamandapa	Rangamandapa	Mahamandapa	Rangamandapa	Mandapa of subsidiary shrine	Mahamandapa	Rangamandapa	Mandapa of sub-shrine	Hundred-pillar Hall	Mahamandapa	Rangamandapa	East porch	North porch	South porch	South-west corner pavilion
Krishna stealing butter as Yashoda churns							1	2																					
Kaliya-Krishna	6			4		3		5	2	3	3	1	2	15	1		3		1	2			8	2					
Krishna and another lad stealing from a pot																											1		
Yamalarjuna-bhanga	1			3			5	2	2	2	7	3	2	10	4	2	9			2		1	1	4			1	1	2
Gopikavastraharana		1				1		3	1		2		2	2									5						
Four-armed Venugopala with consorts																									1				
Standing Venugopala	2	2		1			3	5		2	1	1	1	8	1		1*					1	2			2			
Seated Venugopala		1		1																									1
Venugopala within a chakra																	1												
Krishna killing Bakasura							1	2						1	1		1							1					
Krishna killing Aghasura								3						1	4														
Krishna killing Putana							1	2																					
Krishna wrestling with Chanura and Mushtika								1																					
Govardhana-dhara Krishna							2			1				6			1									1			
Krishna killing Kuvalayapida							1	1									1												
Krishna killing Kamsa																	1												
Seated Krishna holding a ball of butter														1															
Standing Krishna holding a ball of butter								3	2					9															
Standing Krishna														7			1												1
Krishna and a gopi								1																					
Krishna and Balarama		1																											
Balarama								1			2		1	10					1						1				
Therioanthropomorphic Kalki													1					1							1				

	Virupaksha				Prasanna Virupaksha	Kadalekalu Ganesha (NLc/2)	Vithala				Pattabhirama			Malyavanta Raguunatha			Krishna			Tiruvengalanatha (Achyutaraya)				Ramachandra					
	Hundred-pillar Hall	Maharangamandapa	Rangamandapa	Cloister of inner courtyard	South-west corner pavilion	Mandapa	Rangamandapa	South-east pavilion	North-east pavilion	Hundred-pillar Hall	Mahamandapa	Rangamandapa	Hundred-pillar Hall	Hundred-pillar Hall	Mahamandapa	Rangamandapa	Mahamandapa	Rangamandapa	Mandapa of subsidiary shrine	Mahamandapa	Rangamandapa	Mandapa of sub-shrine	Hundred-pillar Hall	Mahamandapa	Rangamandapa	East porch	North porch	South porch	South-west corner pavilion
Kalki on horseback								1																					
Mohini						2							3	1			1						2						
Annamurti																									1	1			
Venkateshvara	8						1	18	2	3	6		5	10	6		8	3		2		3	7	1					2
Varadaraja						1				1				3												1			
Vithala						5	1	10	9		8	4	9	39	1		1			5	1		10			1	1	1	1
Vishvaksena								5	1			2					4												
Bhakta-Garuda						3	1	5		4	14	4	4	20	1	1	18	2	1	4	1		2			1			5
Garuda holding a snake		1				1		7			3		7	17	4	1	1					1	1	1					1
Garuda and Hanuman, face to face							1																						
Vira-Ajaneya	16	3		6		4	1	7	5	12	9	6	20	30	11	3	17		2	12	1	3	12	4					3
Bhakta-Anjaneya	4		1	1		1	1	6	5	4	8	4	4	29	3		4	1	2	5			3	1		1			1
Flying Hanuman				1					1			1	1				1												
Flying Hanuman carrying rock(s)	2					1		9		1	6	1	6	11	5		1			3			5						2
Hanuman seated on tail								1	1		1	1	1	3						2									
Hanuman holding a ring											1	1																	
Seated Hanuman	1	1				1			1			1		3			2												
Hanuman with tail coiled around a linga		1																											
Hanuman with a linga in each hand					1					1																			
Vaishnava dvarapala								4						3				2					5		2		2	2	2
Namam	1								8	11	16	4	20	10	2	5			5	5	1		41						3
Chakra	1			2	2			1	9	21	11	12	37	35	6	5			14	10	2	1	36	2					4
Shankha	4			1	2				10	38	26	15	35	19	5	4			8	17	3	2	36	1					3
DEVI THEMES																													
Lakshmi seated		1				1	1	3		4		1		4				3		2			1	1		2	2		

	Virupaksha				Prasanna Virupaksha	Kadalekalu Ganesha (NLc/2)	Vithala				Pattabhirama			Malyavanta Raguunatha			Krishna			Tiruvengalanatha (Achyutaraya)				Ramachandra					
	Hundred-pillar Hall	Maharangamandapa	Rangamandapa	Cloister of inner courtyard	South-west corner pavilion	Mandapa	Rangamandapa	South-east pavilion	North-east pavilion	Hundred-pillar Hall	Mahamandapa	Rangamandapa	Hundred-pillar Hall	Hundred-pillar Hall	Mahamandapa	Rangamandapa	Mahamandapa	Rangamandapa	Mandapa of subsidiary shrine	Mahamandapa	Rangamandapa	Mandapa of sub-shrine	Hundred-pillar Hall	Mahamandapa	Rangamandapa	East porch	North porch	South porch	South-west corner pavilion
Lakshmi standing	1																												
Devi in a dancing pose	1																2												
Standing Devi, holding a lotus	4	1			1	1		1		2	2			14			2						4						
Seated Devi with a lotus		1			1									2										1					1
Devi seated on Nandi, holding a lotus				1																									
Mahishasuramardini	1	1					1																						
Durga standing on the buffalo's severed head					1																				1		1		
Lajja-Gauri	4									3			1							2			1						
MINOR DIVINITIES																													
Brahma					1																								
Surya in a chariot								1																					
Standing Surya in samabhanga			1	1	1	1		7	3		6	1	7	14	1		1			1	1	2	5			2			
Surya on a cloud		1			1			1										1						1					
Seated Surya	1																												
Chandra on a cloud	1			1					1		1			3															
Varuna on a makara						1																							
Kama on a chariot		1					1	1																					
Kama standing				1																									
Kama and Rati							1	2																					
Narada		8		1	4	1		1			4	2					1	1											
Tumburu																									1				
Gandharva	8	17	2	18	4	5		7	4	5	20	3	13	16	7		10	2	1	?	1	2	4						3
Gandharva with musical instrument		2				1		1			2	1	2																1

	Virupaksha				Prasanna Virupaksha	Kadalekalu Ganesha (NLc/2)	Vithala				Pattabhirama			Malyavanta Raguunatha			Krishna			Tiruvengalanatha (Achyutaraya)				Ramachandra					
	Hundred-pillar Hall	Maharangamandapa	Rangamandapa	Cloister of inner courtyard	South-west corner pavilion	Mandapa	Rangamandapa	South-east pavilion	North-east pavilion	Hundred-pillar Hall	Mahamandapa	Rangamandapa	Hundred-pillar Hall	Hundred-pillar Hall	Mahamandapa	Rangamandapa	Mahamandapa	Rangamandapa	Mandapa of subsidiary shrine	Mahamandapa	Rangamandapa	Mandapa of sub-shrine	Hundred-pillar Hall	Mahamandapa	Rangamandapa	East porch	North porch	South porch	South-west corner pavilion
Kinnara	2		2	2					1	2	3	1		5			2			2		1	3						
Kinnari		9	2		2	1	1	2	1		1		1	1			1			1			1						2
Shankhanidhi	3	2	1	8	5	1	1	1	1	6	4	3	5	2	5	1	5						5	3	2				
Padmanidhi	8	11	5	15	9	5		2	1	14	19	5	9	2	8	1	16	3	1	9	1		3	3					1
Standing Gana	17	1		17	2	2		3			14	7	1	2			11			12	1		10						1
Seated Gana	7										1	2	5				4		1										
Dancing Gana	21	2	1	3		2				33	15	3	19				16												
Gana holding a snake		1		6	1	5		1	1	1	7	4	11	3	4		7	1	1										
Gana blowing a conch	4			2		2			1		7	1		6			2												
Gana with hands in anjali																	2												
Gana with musical instrument	11	3	2	5	1		1	1	1		3	3					1												1
Gana carrying a load	5			1		1					1																		
Gana with a jackfruit		1						1				1	1																
SAINTS AND ASCETICS																													
Kannappa Nayanar	1		1	1	2										1														
Seated alvar in anjali-mudra	1		1			4		2	7	8	8	4	17	19	21		3	4		10	2	3	20	1					4
Seated alvar in dhyana-mudra	1										2		1	1	4		1												
Nammalvar												1		7					1					1					2
Tondaradippodi-Alvar																													1
Ramanuja		1						2	5	2	3	1	3	14	2		2			3		1	1	2		2			2
Matsyendranatha	11	3		6	2	7				3	12	2	6	1	2		1			4			6	1					
Natha(?) on a scorpion																							1						
Natha(?) on a kurma																							1						
Natha(?) on a boar(?)				1																									
Ascetic wearing a hood/cape	1			1	3	1		1		3	4	2	12	8	2		1			3			5						1

	Virupaksha				Prasanna Virupaksha	Kadalekalu Ganesha (NLc/2)	Vithala				Pattabhirama			Malyavanta Raguunatha			Krishna			Tiruvengalanatha (Achyutaraya)				Ramachandra					
	Hundred-pillar Hall	Maharangamandapa	Rangamandapa	Cloister of inner courtyard	South-west corner pavilion	Mandapa	Rangamandapa	South-east pavilion	North-east pavilion	Hundred-pillar Hall	Mahamandapa	Rangamandapa	Hundred-pillar Hall	Hundred-pillar Hall	Mahamandapa	Rangamandapa	Mahamandapa	Rangamandapa	Mandapa of subsidiary shrine	Mahamandapa	Rangamandapa	Mandapa of sub-shrine	Hundred-pillar Hall	Mahamandapa	Rangamandapa	East porch	North porch	South porch	South-west corner pavilion
Ascetic (jangama?) wearing slip-over	3	1		1	2					2	1		2		1					1			7						
Ascetic in a yogic pose	2			2	1																		2						
Seated ascetic with hands in anjali over his head					1	2	1				3		3	1	2		1			1			1						
Seated ascetic	23	12	2	19	6	11	1		3	6	26	8	18	8	6	1	3		1	3			9						
Standing ascetic with hands in anjali over his head	1					2											1												
Standing ascetic with umbrella and kamandalu	2									1																			
Standing ascetic holding a kamandalu	1			4	1	2					2						2						1						
Standing ascetic holding an umbrella	1	1		3	1	1				1	3	2	1	4	4							1	1						
Standing ascetic holding a musical instrument	2	1		4							2																		
Seated ascetic with an ascetic stick	1	1									1																		
Standing ascetic with a staff	2	6		1						7	3						2			1				1					
Standing ascetic holding a mala										1																			
Seated ascetic holding a mala	1			2	1																								
Standing ascetic	5			2	1		1	1			3		1				1												
Ascetic performing a fire ritual	1			1																									

	Virupaksha				Prasanna Virupaksha	Kadalekalu Ganesha (NLc/2)	Vithala				Pattabhirama			Malyavanta Raguunatha			Krishna			Tiruvengalanatha (Achyutaraya)				Ramachandra					
	Hundred-pillar Hall	Maharangamandapa	Rangamandapa	Cloister of inner courtyard	South-west corner pavilion	Mandapa	Rangamandapa	South-east pavilion	North-east pavilion	Hundred-pillar Hall	Mahamandapa	Rangamandapa	Hundred-pillar Hall	Hundred-pillar Hall	Mahamandapa	Rangamandapa	Mahamandapa	Rangamandapa	Mandapa of subsidiary shrine	Mahamandapa	Rangamandapa	Mandapa of sub-shrine	Hundred-pillar Hall	Mahamandapa	Rangamandapa	East porch	North porch	South porch	South-west corner pavilion
Seated ascetic holding a book											2																		
Two ascetics, one with a stick, other with a vina							1																						
NON-RELIGIOUS THEMES																													
Seated royal/courtly male figure	3	5	1	5	2	2	1				3	1	3	2	1							1							
Standing royal/courtly male figure				1		7					4	1	5	31	1		17		2			2	5						
Standing courtly male with consort											2			1	1														
Hunter										1		1		1									1						
Huntress	2	1		4								2											1	1					
Soldier with sword and shield	2	1												1			1						2						
Man holding a sword	1									2		1	2																
Man shooting an arrow	1			1																									
Standing male devotee	13			3	1			1		22	1			1			1	2	3								1		
Female devotee								1																					
Male musician	7	4		6		3	3	3		8	1	1	2	7	2		4				1		9	1					2
A male musician and a female musician							1																						
Male folk dancer	4																												
Male folk dancer with chauris	8	5		5	3	7				6	15	2	15	11	7	1	2		1	10			8	4					1
Male folk dancer with tambourine	15	8	2	11		6					8	3	5				4		1	7				2					
Male folk dancer with mridangam																								1					

	Virupaksha				Prasanna Virupaksha	Kadalekalu Ganesha (NLc/2)	Vithala				Pattabhirama			Malyavanta Raguunatha			Krishna			Tiruvengalanatha (Achyutaraya)				Ramachandra					
	Hundred-pillar Hall	Maharangamandapa	Rangamandapa	Cloister of inner courtyard	South-west corner pavilion	Mandapa	Rangamandapa	South-east pavilion	North-east pavilion	Hundred-pillar Hall	Mahamandapa	Rangamandapa	Hundred-pillar Hall	Hundred-pillar Hall	Mahamandapa	Rangamandapa	Mahamandapa	Rangamandapa	Mandapa of subsidiary shrine	Mahamandapa	Rangamandapa	Mandapa of sub-shrine	Hundred-pillar Hall	Mahamandapa	Rangamandapa	East porch	North porch	South porch	South-west corner pavilion
Male folk dancer with tambourine and chauri	1													4	3	1													
Two male folk dancers							2																						
Male dancer	17			2				1			5	1					3						4						
Two male dancers	1																												
Female dancer	12	5	2	6		3				16	2		1	2	1		10			2			3			2		1	1
Two female kolata dancers							2																						
A female dancer and a male dancer		3																											
Female dancer and male musician(s)							2																			1			
Acrobat	2								1						2					3			2						
Two acrobats	1			2							1									1									
Clown	6	1		2	3	1	1	1	1	4				2	1		1			1			5						2
Wrestlers				1		1	1							1	2									2					1
Seated man	3				1			1				2			1														
Standing man	7	1									2	1																	
Man in a running pose	2	1																											
Reclining man	1																												
Man carrying something		1								2			1	1	1		1												
Snake-charmer															1														
Man fighting an animal							1																						
Man with a staff or mace										2							2												
Bhishti (man carrying a water-bag)								1	1				1																
A man on a hamsa										1									2	2									
A man on an elephant																											1		
A man and a woman							2	1		1										1									

	Virupaksha				Prasanna Virupaksha	Kadalekalu Ganesha (NLc/2)	Vithala				Pattabhirama			Malyavanta Raguunatha			Krishna			Tiruvengalanatha (Achyutaraya)				Ramachandra					
	Hundred-pillar Hall	Maharangamandapa	Rangamandapa	Cloister of inner courtyard	South-west corner pavilion	Mandapa	Rangamandapa	South-east pavilion	North-east pavilion	Hundred-pillar Hall	Mahamandapa	Rangamandapa	Hundred-pillar Hall	Hundred-pillar Hall	Mahamandapa	Rangamandapa	Mahamandapa	Rangamandapa	Mandapa of subsidiary shrine	Mahamandapa	Rangamandapa	Mandapa of sub-shrine	Hundred-pillar Hall	Mahamandapa	Rangamandapa	East porch	North porch	South porch	South-west corner pavilion
Male chauri-bearer											1	1											1						
Female chauri-bearer	1	1						1		1			1	1															3
Female musician		1		1																					1				
Seated woman										5					1		1						1						1
Standing woman	6	1	1	1	1			1	3								4												1
Woman and child	1													2									1						
Woman holding a parrot				1		1				4																			
Latasundari	5	3		1	2	1	3	1			1	1		1			1		1				3	1		2	1		
Nude woman	4					1		2		2	1			1			2		1				2						
Woman whose lower garment is slipping down										1																			
Woman carrying a tray						1																							
Seated woman with a mirror		1									1											1							
Woman churning													1				1												
Woman in a running pose					1																								
Erotic sculpture														1	1								3						1
Composite figure															1								1						
ANIMALS, BIRDS AND MYTHICAL BEASTS																													
Squatting lion	101	23	2	67	17	23	6		16	96	46	19	62	25	26	11	25		18	27	6	2	45	15					3
Lion	7	1		4	1	3					5	4	2		5	3	5		3			2	7						2
Two lions, head to head														1	1				2										
Two prancing lions						1																							
Elephant	6			7	1	1	4		1		2		3		1	1							6						
Enraged elephant													1																
Elephant trampling a man		1				1																							

	Virupaksha				Prasanna Virupaksha	Kadalekalu Ganesha (NLc/2)	Vithala				Pattabhirama			Malyavanta Raguunatha			Krishna			Tiruvengalanatha (Achyutaraya)				Ramachandra					
	Hundred-pillar Hall	Maharangamandapa	Rangamandapa	Cloister of inner courtyard	South-west corner pavilion	Mandapa	Rangamandapa	South-east pavilion	North-east pavilion	Hundred-pillar Hall	Mahamandapa	Rangamandapa	Hundred-pillar Hall	Hundred-pillar Hall	Mahamandapa	Rangamandapa	Mahamandapa	Rangamandapa	Mandapa of subsidiary shrine	Mahamandapa	Rangamandapa	Mandapa of sub-shrine	Hundred-pillar Hall	Mahamandapa	Rangamandapa	East porch	North porch	South porch	South-west corner pavilion
Cow	4			2		1					2	2	4	2			1			5	1		8						2
Cow and calf															1														
Buffalo	1																												
Standing bull						2																							
Monkey	7	1		2		4	1		2		6	2	4	6	3				1		2		4						
Monkey holding a snake						1						1	3																1
Two monkeys															1														
Snake		1														1							4						
Naga-pasha						1							1																
Two snakes intertwined				1																									
Two snakes face to face				1																									
Hamsa	16	6		7		14			5		11	5	37	25	12	6	2		5	11	2		33	1					2
Two hamsas, necks intertwined						1																							
Tiger killing an animal/human being														1									5						
Lizard																							2						
Deer																							3						
Two deer with one head																							1						
Makara/mythical creature							1				4	2	1	13	2				2				1	1					
Two birds																			1										
FLORAL, VEGETAL AND OTHER DECORATIVE MOTIFS																													
Lotus medallion,	207	1		159	12	18	76	13	16	80	45	31	85	44	24	4	5		111	12	4	3	76	1					6

	Virupaksha				Prasanna Virupaksha	Kadalekalu Ganesha (NLc/2)	Vithala				Pattabhirama			Malyavanta Raguunatha			Krishna			Tiruvengalanatha (Achyutaraya)				Ramachandra					
	Hundred-pillar Hall	Maharangamandapa	Rangamandapa	Cloister of inner courtyard	South-west corner pavilion	Mandapa	Rangamandapa	South-east pavilion	North-east pavilion	Hundred-pillar Hall	Mahamandapa	Rangamandapa	Hundred-pillar Hall	Hundred-pillar Hall	Mahamandapa	Rangamandapa	Mahamandapa	Rangamandapa	Mandapa of subsidiary shrine	Mahamandapa	Rangamandapa	Mandapa of sub-shrine	Hundred-pillar Hall	Mahamandapa	Rangamandapa	East porch	North porch	South porch	South-west corner pavilion
vegetal motifs and geometric designs																													
Tree						1					12	2	8										13						
Purna-kumbha													1						4				3						
Sun																							4						
Crescent moon															3				2	1			3						
Vijayanagara royal emblem																							1						

NOTE:
Given the large number of pillar reliefs in all these temples, it is possible that there may be certain minor discrepancies in the numbering or even the classification of themes. For those themes that occur frequently, the number given here have to be taken as approximate numbers and not as exact numbers. In the case of the Malyavanta Raghunatha temple, parts of its hundred-pillared hall are dark or the pillars are covered with soot; the mahamandapa and rangamandapa of this temple have been whitewashed. Due to these reasons, some of the pillars reliefs in this temple could not be examined or identified.

Glossary

Abhaya-mudra, gesture of protection. The palm and fingers of the right hand are held upwards and facing outwards.

Abhicharika, enchanting, exorcising. A class of Vaishnava images of which there are four varieties. A terrifying aspect of particular deities venerated by those who wish to harm their enemies by magic. See also *Bhoga, Vira, Yoga.*

Abhisheka, consecration (by sprinkling water), ritual bathing of an image.

Acharya, teacher, spiritual guide. The Acharyas flourished from the 10th/11th century onwards, the greatest of them, Ramanuja, established Shri-Vaishnavism on a solid philosophical foundation. Many of the Acharyas are considered to be partial incarnations of Vishnu and his various attributes and subsequently raised to the status of minor deities. The deification of the Acharyas followed that of the Alvars. See *Alvar.*

Adimurti, the primeval personification, aspect of Vishnu.

Adi Shesha, primeval Shesha. King of the serpents on which Vishnu sleeps. See *Ananta.*

Advaita, non-dualist philosophy preached by Shankara.

Agastya, Mover-of-the Mountains(?). A rishi revered in southern India.

Aghasura, bad, dangerous, sinful, impure. Name of a demon who assumed the form of a gigantic python and was eventually defeated by Krishna.

Agni, fire, flame (a) god of the sacrificial fire mediating between men and gods; (b) symbol of annihilation/destruction. Agni is one of the regents of space, he is the lord of the south-east. His vehicle is a ram. He is often shown with two heads adorned with flames. His attributes include the oblation spoon, the spear, the fan and the fire.

Ahalya, wife of the rishi Gautama cursed by him to become a stone because of her infidelity. Rama restored her to her pristine form and reconciled her with Gautama.

Akshamala, string of beads. General designation for all kinds of rosaries. Held in the hands by various deities.

Alidhasana, jumping position. Kneeling pose in which the right knee is thrown to the front with the leg retracted, and the left leg is diagonally stretched behind.

Alvar(s), drowning, immersed, lost in God. South Indian Vaishnava poet-saints, traditionally 10 or 12 in number. Their dates are still controversial but they may be roughly placed between the sixth and the ninth centuries AD. Their devotional songs, consisting of four thousand verses in classical Tamil are collected in the Divyaprabandham, compiled by Nathamuni (*c.* tenth century), the first of the Vaishnava Acharyas. In Shri-Vaishnavism, the Alvars are distinguished from the Acharyas, scholars or philosophers. The Alvars are considered partial incarnations of Vishnu and his various attributes and are thus regarded as minor deities. The worship of the Alvars was probably current by the eleventh/twelfth centuries AD. See also *Andal, Bhutam, Kulashekhara, Madhurakavi, Nammalvar, Periyalvar, Pey, Poygai, Tirumalishai, Tirumangai, Tiruppan, Tondaradippodi.*

Amsha, part, share. Partial incarnation of a deity (especially of Vishnu).

Ananta, Endless, one of the names of Adi Shesha. Ananta the chief of the Nagas is the great world serpent lying in the sea and encircling the earth. Between the periodic annihilations and recreations of the world, Vishnu is believed to recline on the coils of Ananta in the cosmic ocean. Occasionally Vishnu sits on the coils of Ananta.

Anantapadmanabha, see *Padmanabha.*

Andal, also known as Goda or Sudikkodutta-nacchiyar, Andal the only woman among the Alvars, was the adopted daughter of Periyalvar. As a rule she is represented standing, holding a lotus in one hand. She is reputed to be the incarnation of Bhudevi.

Antarala, vestibule fronting the shrine in a temple.

Anantashayana, Anantashayin, Sheshashayin, name of Vishnu when laying on the coils of the cosmic snake Ananta.

Angada, son of the monkey-king Vali and of Tara. Heir apparent to the kingdom of Kishkindha.

Anjali-mudra, gesture of devotion/respect. Both hands are held together, close to the chest, palms touching.

Anjaneya, son of Anjana. Name of Hanuman. See also *Hanuman.*

Ankusha, elephant-goad. Attribute of various gods, especially of Ganesha, consisting of a sharp metal hook attached to a wooden handle.

Annamurti, minor aspect of Vishnu as the presiding deity of the kitchen.

Apasmara(purusha), forgetfulness. The demon of oblivion. Represented as a prostrated dwarfish figure under the feet of Shiva Nataraja.

Appar, one of the four principal Shaiva poet-saints. He is generally shown holding a spud. He took it with him on his wanderings, using it to remove such grass as had grown between the stones in the pavement of the Shaiva temple he visited. See also *Nayanmar(s)*.

Apsaras, going into the waters. Heavenly nymphs who came forth from the churning of the milky sea and inhabit the sky. Regarded as the wives of the gandharvas, they are generally represented dancing and playing music.

Arati, ceremony performed in adoration of a god by moving circularly around the head of the idol a platter containing a burning lamp.

Ardhanarishvara, the Lord being half woman. Shiva and Shakti as one person. Androgynous form of Shiva. Usually the right side of the image is represented as male, the left as female.

Ardhapadmasana, half lotus sitting attitude. Cross-legged sitting position.

Arjuna, white. The chief hero of the Pandavas, regarded as son of Indra. The story of the rivalry between the Pandavas and their cousins the Kauravas is narrated in the *Mahabharata*. See also *Mahabharata, Pandava(s)*.

Asana, seat, throne, seated position; generally with reference to deities or religious practitioners.

Ashokavana, grove of ashoka-trees in Ravana's palace, where Sita was held captive.

Ashrama, hermitage, abode of ascetics.

Ashtabhuja, eight-armed.

Ashtadikpala(s), the eight regents or guardians of the regions or quarters of the sky. In sculpture the Ashtadikpalas often appear as a group, each placed in the appropriate direction. See *Agni, Indra, Ishana, Kubera; Nirruti, Varuna, Vayu, Yama*.

Ashvamedha, sacrifice of a horse. The greatest sacrificial festival in Vedic age.

Asura(s), anti-god.

Aushadha-parvata, the mountain in the Himalayas, on which medicinal herbs were growing. It was uprooted by Hanuman in the course of the Rama-Ravana war, in order to restore to life the fallen heroes.

Avatara(s), descent of a god, in order to save the world from a peril and to restore the balance between good and evil. The term avatara generally refers to the incarnations of Vishnu. See also *Dashavatara*.

Ayodhya, invincible. Capital of Rama's kingdom.

Ayudha, weapon. Name given to the different weapons and attributes which the gods hold in the hands.

Bahubali, strong in arms. See *Gommata*.

Baka (asura), crane or heron (demon). A demon vanquished by Krishna.

Balakrishna, child Krishna. Krishna depicted as dancing, or as a chubby child crawling on all fours.

Balarama, Rama the strong. The elder brother of Krishna. According to tradition Balarama is the incarnation of Vishnu's great serpent, Ananta.

Bali, an asura king, who had gained dominion over all the worlds and the gods by his valour and asceticism. He was, however, outwitted by Vishnu in his Vamana aspect. See *Vamana*.

Bana, arrow.

Bhagavata Purana, the ancient story of the Blessed One. A chronicle of Vishnu and his avataras. Especially important are the portions of the narrative dealing with the life of Krishna as a child and of his youthful exploits with the gopis. This Purana constitutes the base of the Krishnaite devotion.

Bhadrakali, the auspicious Kali. She emerged from Uma's wrath when her husband Shiva was insulted by Daksha who had omitted to invite him to attend his sacrifice. Bhadrakali is the consort of Virabhadra.

Bhairava, terrible. Name of one of the fierce aspects of Shiva. He is also described as Kala-Bhairava, for, according to the Puranas, even Kala or Yama, the god of death is afraid of him. In the classical myth, after severing one of the heads of Brahma, Shiva is forced to wander about begging for his livelihood to atone for the sin of brahminicide. See *Bhikshatana*. In another version, however, this sin is transferred to Bhairava, an aspect of himself created by Shiva on that occasion.

Bhairavi, terrible. Name of a form of Durga.

Bharata, one of the brothers of Rama, son of Kaikeyi.

Bhikshatana(murti), wandering about for alms. A representation of Shiva as a wandering mendicant. Bhikshatana is wandering about to atone for the sin of having severed one of Brahma's heads. This representations is very much like that of Shiva as Kankalamurti. See also *Kankalanatha*.

Bhima, terrible. Name of a Pandava prince. Brother of Arjuna, he is regarded as the son of the wind god Vayu. Renowned for his formidable strength.

Bhoga, enjoyment, wealth. A class of Vaishnava images of which there are four varieties. The bhoga aspect of Vishnu is worshipped to attain worldly enjoyment, wealth and pleasure. See also *Abhicharika, Vira, Yoga*.

Bhringi(n) wanderer. The three-legged, skeletal great devotee of Shiva. Sometimes he is represented standing, playing the cymbals, at the side of Shiva Nataraja or of Uma-Maheshavara.

Bhu, Bhudevi, goddess personifying the earth. She is the consort of Vishnu, since she was rescued by him in his aspect as Varaha. She is usually represented standing (sitting) to the left of Vishnu when he is accompanied by two consorts. Her breasts are bare and she wears a chhannavira.

Bhu-Varaha, the earth and the boar. Depiction of Vishnu in his incarnation as Varaha accompanied by Bhudevi.

Bhutam, one of the first three Alvars with Pey and Poyagi, Bhutam is believed to be a partial incarnation of Vishnu's mace.

Brahma, the creator of the orthodox Brahmanical triad. Brahma represents the equilibrium between the two opposing principles Vishnu (centripetal) and Shiva (centrifugal). Unlike the other two members of the Trimurti, he is not of great importance. There is no Brahma cult and temples dedicated to him are extremely rare. Although, in practice, Brahma has been relegated to the status of minor god, yet he does receive puja. The niche on the northern wall of the central shrine of a Vishnu or Shiva temple should, in theory, contain an image of Brahma. The four faces of Brahma are symbolic of the four Vedas. According to the myth there were originally five heads, but Shiva cut one off. The four heads face the four quarters, hence in the representation of Brahma, only three heads are visible as the fourth is presumed to be at the back. Brahma's attributes include the rosary, the water-pot, the sruk and the sruva—two kinds of oblation spoons used for pouring libations in the sacrificial fire—and the palm-leaf book.

Brindavana, memorial erected in the memory of a Madhva (Vaishnava) saint.

Buddha, enlightened. The title of the founder of Buddhism. The great success of Buddha as a religious teacher resulted in his being sometimes regarded as an avatara of Vishnu.

Chakra, discus, wheel: a weapon. One of the attributes of Vishnu. See also *Sudarshana.*

Chakra-kundala, circular earring.

Chamara, fly whisk made of yak hair. Symbol of royalty. The *chamara* is associated with a number of deities .

Chamaradharini, female attendant carrying a fly-whisk.

Chamunda, another name of the goddess Kali. The name is said to originate from a contraction of the names Chanda and Munda, demons which were killed by Kali. Chamunda symbolises universal destruction and death as well as delusion.

Chandesha, Chandikeshvara, is said to have been a young Brahmin cowherd and great devotee of Shiva. In his devotion to Shiva he set up lingas of sand, and worshipped them by pouring over them the overflow of the cow's milk. His father, angered by what seemed to him a waste of milk, kicked one of the lingas. The youth then with his axe cut off his father's foot.

Chanda, fierce, violent. Name of a demon killed by Chamunda. See also *Munda.*

Chandra, the moon-god. His head is ornamented by a crescent. In each of his hands he carries a water-lily. Can be represented seated or standing.

Chandrashekhara, moon-crested. Aspect of Shiva having the crescent moon as head ornament.

Chanura, one of Kamsa's wrestlers defeated by Krishna. See also *Mushtika.*

Chattra, umbrella, parasol. An insignia of royalty.

Chaturbhuja, four-armed.

Chaturvimshatimurti, twenty-four forms (or aspects) of Vishnu. These images are represented generally standing, wearing the usual ornaments and crown, each holding the four principal attributes of Vishnu: chakra, shankha, gada and padma. All these images are identical but for the order in which the attributes are positioned in their four hands, the number of permutations being exactly twenty-four.

Chauri, see *Chamara.*

Chenchu-Lakshmi, one of the forms of Lakshmi. The Chenchu girl with whom Narasimha fell in love.

Chhannavira, ornament constituted by two chain-like elements worn crosswise on the torso. A flat disc is placed on their junction near the centre of the chest.

Chin-mudra, reflection-, realization-handpose. Teaching gesture. See *Vyakhyana-mudra.*

Chitrakuta, having a bright crest. Name of a mountain. It was on Chitrakuta that Rama, Sita and Lakshmana spent some time in the course of their exile.

Chudamani, a jewel worn on the top of the head.

Dakshinamurti, the southern image. A peaceful form of Shiva as the supreme teacher of Yoga (Yogadakshinamurti), of knowledge (Jnanadakshinamurti) of music (Vinadhara-dakshinamurti) and of the scriptures (Vyakhyanadakshina-murti). Dakshinamurti is generally found on the southern wall of temples.

Damaru, small drum, shaped like an hour-glass. Attribute of Shiva and of various other deities.

Damodara, having a rope around the waist. Epithet of Balakrishna depicted as tied with a rope to a mortar.

Danda, staff, rod, club. Attribute of various deities.

Dandaka, a forest where Rama, Sita and Lakshmana lived during their exile.

Danta, tooth, fang, elephant's tusk. Generally danta refers to the tusk carried in the hand by Ganesha.

Darshana, seeing, auspicious sight. The central act of Hindu worship of seeing and being seen by the image of the deity enshrined in the sanctuary.

Dasharatha, king of Ayodhya, father of Rama.

Dashavatara(s), ten incarnations (lit: descents) of Vishnu. According to Vaishnava mythology, whenever virtue and righteousness are jeopardised and vice and unrighteousness raise their head in this world, Vishnu appears to redress the balance between good and evil and firmly establish dharma. Vishnu is unique as being the only one among the Hindu deities to be credited with avataras. He is believed to have assumed several forms in his role as protector, a fact explained by the recurring Puranic motif of the unceasing conflict between the gods and their antagonists, the asuras. Vishnu's major incarnations are usually considered to be ten: Matsya, Kurma, Varaha, Narasimha, Vamana

(Trivikrama), Parashurama, Ramachandra, Krishna, either Buddha or Balarama, Kalki. Some, however, do not consider Buddha to be an incarnation of Vishnu. The Shri-Vaishnavas regard Balarama as the eighth avatara and Krishna and Kalki as the ninth and the tenth respectively. The Madhvas exclude Balarama from the list of the dashavataras and include Buddha. There are, moreover, numerous minor avataras.

Deva, god.

Devata, tutelary deity of a particular place or locality. They are called devata to differentiate them from the major gods of orthodox Hinduism known as deva. See also *Gramadevata*.

Devi, goddess. Although there is a host of goddesses in Hindu mythology, there is a tendency in many texts, myths and rituals to subsume them all under one great female being called Devi or Mahadevi, the great goddess. One characteristic feature of Devi mythology is the fact that she assumes both benign and terrifying forms, being both auspicious and bloodthirsty.

Dhanus, bow. This weapon belongs to the insignias of royalty. As an attribute dhanus has often a proper name: Shiva's is called Pinaka, Vishnu's Sharanga, Arjuna's Gandiva.

Dharma, moral and religious duty; law; custom.

Dhoti, men's attire consisting of a cloth worn around the waist, passing between the legs and tucked in behind.

Dhvaja, flag.

Dhyana-mudra, meditation handpose, also called yoga-mudra. The palm of the right hand is placed in that of the left, and together they rest in the lap of the seated person.

Dikpala, regent or guardian of a quarter of the sky, regent of (a) direction. There are eight Dikpalas. See *Ashtadikpala(s)*.

Draupadi, the common wife of the five Pandava-princes in the *Mahabharata*.

Duhshasana, name of Kaurava-prince in the *Mahabharata*.

Dundubhi, drum. Name of a demon.

Durga, inaccessible. Wife and aspect of the shakti of Shiva. A composite goddess who embodies a number of local deities and female demons. Associated with elemental forces. One of the primary mythological functions of Durga is to combat the demons who threaten the stability of the cosmos, the most famous of them being the buffalo-demon Mahisha. Unlike the normal female, Durga does not lend her power to a male consort, but takes power from male gods in order to perform her own valorous exploits. Later, however, Durga became linked with Shiva. See also *Mahishasuramardini* and *Shakti*.

Dvarapala(s), door guardians placed at the entrances of Vaishnava and Shaiva temples. They carry the attributes of the enshrined deity.

Dvibhanga, twofold bend. Posture with two flexions in the body.

Gada, mace, club. Symbol of power. Attribute of Vishnu. The name of Vishnu's mace is Kaumodaki.

Gaja-hasta-mudra, elephant-arm-handpose. Gesture in which one arm is thrown in front of the breast—across the chest—in imitation of the elephant's trunk.

Gaja-Lakshmi, elephant-Lakshmi. Form of the goddess Lakshmi generally four armed, in which two elephant sprinkle water on her.

Gajantaka(murti), destroyer of the elephant-demon. Aspect of Shiva.

Gajendra, elephant-king. Name of a king changed into an elephant. While bathing he was seized by a crocodile and prayed fervently to Vishnu for help. The god rushed to the spot on his vahana, the eagle Garuda, and rescued his devotee. Hence Gajendra is also the name of Vishnu in his aspect as rescuer of the king of the elephants. See also *Karivarada* and *Varadaraja*.

Gana (Ganadevatas), flock, body of attendants or followers. Specifically the ganas are the host of goblins who make up the entourage of Shiva. Their chief is Ganesha. The term is also loosely applied to any figure displaying the same physiognomic features of goblins such as dishevelled hair, round or fiery eyes, protruding fangs or other grotesque characteristics. They are represented as obese dwarfs. The ganas though originally associated with Shiva, were incorporated as decorative motifs in buildings unrelated to Shaivism.

Gandharva(s), semi-divine beings living in the sky. The chief function of the gandharvas is to serve the major deities by their songs, music, and offerings of flowers and fruits. In Indian art, whether Buddhist, Hindu or Jaina, gandharvas are depicted in flight through the sky, carrying offerings or musical instruments in their hands, to do service to the deity on whom they attend.

Ganesha, lord of the ganas. The elephant-headed son of Shiva and Parvati. He is regarded as the remover of the obstacles and as the god of wisdom. He is the first to be worshipped or invoked in Hindu rituals. He stands at the doorway of temples and shrines and allows the devotee access to other deities and to whatever blessing may flow from them. Ganesha is known by many different names, the most popular of which are Ganapati, Vighneshvara and Vinayaka.

Ganga, the Ganges. River goddess, Shiva's second wife. The Ganga is the most sacred among the rivers of India. The many myths concerning the descent of the Ganga to earth emphasise this point; they stress the rivers's heavenly origin, and her association with the great male deities Brahma, Vishnu and Shiva. Although all rivers are revered as removers of pollution, the Ganga is preeminent as a purifying power. The personified image of the Ganga riding on the makara is placed at the doorways of temples in force of her purificatory powers. See also *Yamuna*.

Gangadhara, the bearer of the Ganga. Aspect of Shiva carrying the Ganga in his locks.

Garbhagriha, womb-house. The sanctuary of a temple.

Garuda, devourer(?). The mythical eagle, the vehicle of Vishnu. Represented as half-eagle, half-man. He is said to be one of the two sons of Vinata, wife of Kashyapa. In order to free his mother from bondage to her co-wife Kadru, Garuda had to secure the pot of ambrosia of the latter's snake sons. The snakes are hence enemies of Garuda. Though Garuda is said to be a bird, he generally appears in art in winged human form, with rounded eyes and a beak-like nose.

Gommata, Gommateshvara, name of a Jaina saint, regarded by the Digambara-Jainas as a prophet. Other name: Bahubali.

Golla-dasas, class of mendicants, usually Vaishnava, belonging to the Golla or cowherd community.

Gopa, cowherd.

Gopi(s), cowherdess. The milkmaids who were the companions of Krishna.

Gopikavastraharana (Gopivastraharana), theft of the milkmaids' clothes (by Krishna). An episode of the Krishna story.

Gopura. Ornamented, pyramidal entrance gateway to a temple or temple complex.

Gorava(s), mendicant devotees of Mailara.

Govardhanadhara, the act of supporting the mount Govardhana. Episode of the Krishna story in which Krishna lifts up Govardhana on the little finger of his right hand.

Gramadevata, village deity. Tutelary deity of a particular place or locality. Such local divinities are not restricted to villages, but are also found in towns and cities. They have a strictly local jurisdiction.

Hala, plough. Symbol of agriculture. Characteristic attribute of Balarama.

Hamsa, (wild) goose. The hamsa, symbol of supreme spiritual achievement, is the vehicle of Brahma.

Hamsa-mayura, hamsa and peacock. Decorative motif in sculpture, in which the characteristics of the two birds are intermingled.

Hanuman, heavy-, large-jawed. The monkey-chief, son of Vayu (the Wind-god) and Anjana. Hanuman helped Rama to rescue Sita and recover his kingdom. He is portrayed as human being, with a monkey's head and a long, powerful tail.

Hara, (a) remover, seizer, destroyer. A name of Shiva. (b) garland of pearls, necklace.

Hari, yellow, greenish. A name of Vishnu.

Harihara, composite deity half Shiva and half Vishnu.

Hasta(s), particular position of the hand and of the arms, each endowed with a specific meaning. See also *Mudra(s)*.

Hiranyakashipu, golden-robed. A daitya king, father of Prahlada. He was slain by Vishnu in his form as Narasimha. See *Narasimha*.

Hiranyaksha, golden-eyed. A daitya, brother of Hiranyakashipu. Hiranyaksha threw the earth into the ocean and for this act he was killed by Vishnu in his boar-incarnation. See *Varaha*.

Holi, spring festival with obvious fertility connotations. It is celebrated in the month of Phalguna (February-March).

Indra, name of a Vedic god connected with valour, strength, courage and leadership. He gradually declined in importance and became the leader of the Dikpalas and the lord of the eastern direction. He rides on the elephant Airavata. His attributes include the thunderbolt and the elephant goad.

Indrajit, conqueror of Indra. Name of Meghanada, one of the sons of Ravana.

Ishana, ruler, master, lord. Aspects of Shiva. Name of one of the eight Dikpalas, the regent of the north-eastern direction. Ishana rides a bull and his attributes are those of Shiva.

Jagati, basement moulding.

Jambavan or *Jambavat*, king of the Bears, who helped Rama in his fight against Ravana.

Jambukumara, son of Shurpanakha accidentally killed by Lakshmana.

Janaka, king of Mithila, father of Sita.

Jangama, moving, movable. Itinerant preacher especially of the Virashaiva sect.

Jata, knot of matted hair. Thick piled up matted hair, characteristic of Shiva.

Jata-mukuta, crown of matted hair. An elaborate hairstyle where the matted locks are built up to resemble a crown. Characteristic of Shiva and other deities.

Jatabhara, mass of braided hair. An elaborate method of braiding or tying the hair to resemble a crown. The jatabhara is characteristic of Shiva.

Jatamandala, circle of matted hair. Characteristic of Bhairava, Kali and other deities. The hair is dressed like a halo around the head.

Jatayu or *Jatayus*, the gallant chief of the vultures who fought against Ravana.

Jnana, knowledge.

Jnana-mudra, gesture of knowledge. The tips of the thumb and index finger touch to form a circle, and the hand is held against the heart. This mudra is sometimes identified with the dhyana-mudra.

Kabandha, a rakshasa with his face where his stomach should be, and with an enormous eye protruding from the centre of the chest.

Kaikeyi, the youngest queen of Dasharatha, mother of Bharata.

Kailasha, the abode of Shiva located on a mythical mountain allegedly in the Himalaya range.

Kala Bhairava, death (or time) Bhairava. One of the forms of Bhairava.

Kalanemi, a rakshasa deputed by Ravana to obstruct the path of Hanuman when the latter started for the Himalayas to search for the aushadha parvata.

Kalasha, water-pot, pitcher, jar, vase.

Kali, power-of-Time, destroyer-of-Time, black. Name of the shakti of Shiva symbolising the natural force of destruction, but also the Supreme Power. Kali is usually shown naked, with long dishevelled hair, lolling tongue, wearing a garland of severed heads and a girdle of freshly cut arms. Many texts treat Kali as an independent deity, unassociated with any male god. However, when she is linked to a male deity, it is generally Shiva.

Kaliya, five-headed serpent demon who was tamed by Krishna.

Kaliyadamana or (*-mardana*), taming or crushing the serpent Kaliya. Form of Krishna.

Kalki or *Kalkin*, having a white horse. Name of the tenth and future incarnation of Vishnu who will appear at the end of the present age. He will be seated on a white horse, with drawn sword. blazing like a comet, for the final destruction of the wicked and the renovation of creation. Kalki is generally depicted as a warrior on a white horse.

Kalyana-mandapa, wedding-hall. A special pavilion or hall in a temple, in which the ceremonial wedding of the god and the goddess is celebrated annually.

Kalyanasundara(murti), representation of the wedding of the Charming One. The depiction shows Shiva's marriage with Devi. In this form the two stand side by side with their hands joined together for the marriage-ceremony. Kalyanasundara is worshipped especially in southern India.

Kalamukha, black-face. Name of a Shaiva sect. Its members wear a characteristic black streak across the forehead.

Kama(deva), love, desire especially sexual love. Kama is the presiding deity of love, the god of beauty and youth. He is pictured with either two, four or eight arms, as a proud adolescent, riding a parrot. He holds a bow made of sugarcane; the bowstring is a line of bees; his five arrows, symbolising the five senses, are made of five fragrant flowers which arouse desire. On his banner is a makara. His wife is Rati, or delight. She rides a hamsa or a parrot. His second consort is Priti, or love. Other name: Manmatha.

Kamandalu, vessel, water-jar, especially the water-jar of an ascetic. It denotes the mendicant's life. The kamandalu is an attribute of various deities, Brahma, Sarasvati, and Shiva.

Kamsa, tyrant of Mathura. He was son of Ugrasena and cousin of Devaki, the mother of Krishna. Kamsa was killed by Krishna.

Kankala, skeleton, necklace of skeletons.

Kankala(murti), representation together with a skeleton. A fearful aspect of Shiva who killed Vishvaksena, the door-keeper of Vishnu, because of Vishvaksena's having refused him permission to enter into the presence of Vishnu. Kankalamurti is depicted carrying a staff or a trishula on the point of which hangs the skeleton of his victim.

Kannappa, he who gave his eye to the god. His real name was Tinnappa. He was one of the sixty-three Nayanmars, a hunter by caste who offered his eye to Shiva. One day, to test his sincerity, Shiva made it appear as if water was dropping from the eye of the linga the hunter was worshipping. Believing that the eye had been damaged, Tinnappa removed one of his eyes and replaced the injured eye with it. After some time, Tinnappa noticed that the other eye of the linga was also affected. He began to pluck out his second eye. As the removal of both eyes would have blinded him and he would not have been able to locate the Lord's eye, he placed his foot on the linga at the exact spot of the apparently injured eye. Pleased with his devotion, Shiva manifested himself, restored the hunter's eyesight and gave him the name 'Kannappa', 'the one who gave his eyes'. He is especially worshipped at Kalahasti in Andhra where his image is placed near the linga and puja is offered to him before Shiva.

Kantha, basement moulding.

Kanthi, necklace.

Kapala, cup, dish, alms-bowl of beggar, skull. The kapala was fashioned from the top half of a human skull. Attribute of Shiva's and Parvati's terrific forms (e.g. Bhairavi, Kali, Durga).

Kapalika, skull-carrier. Name of a Shaiva sect, the members of which drank out of a kapala.

Karanda-mukuta, a small crown resembling an inverted bowl or basket. It indicates subordinate status.

Karivarada, conferring a boon on the elephant. Representation of Vishnu showing him rescuing Gajendra, the king of the elephants, from the fangs of the crocodile. See *Gajendra*.

Karttikeya, related to the Krittikas (the Pleiads). Karttikeya, who incorporates a number of local deities, is reputed to be the second son of Shiva, commander-in-chief of the divine armies. In southern India Karttikeya is worshipped under the name of Subrahmanya or his Tamil name Murugan. A peacock, symbol of immortality, is his vahana. According to the southern tradition his two consorts are Devasena and Vali (or Mahavalli). His favourite weapon is the shakti, the spear or javelin: his banner bears the emblem of a cock, symbolising the solar energy, and occasionally he carries one. His other names include Kumara, Kumarasvami, Skanda and Shanmukha.

Kashayadanda, staff to which a saffron cloth is tied. The Kashayadanda is carried by ascetics.

Katibandha or *Katisutra*, an elaborate waistband worn round the hips to support a loincloth.

Katyavalambita-mudra, position of ease in which an arm hangs down with the hand resting gracefully on the hip.

Kaumodaki, name of Vishnu's gada.

Kaupina, loin-cloth.

Kaurava(s), the hundred sons of Dhritharashtra. The story of their rivalry with their cousins the Pandavas is narrated in the *Mahabharata*. See also *Pandava(s)*.

Kaushalya, the eldest queen of Dasharatha, mother of Rama.

Kaustubha, a jewel worn by Vishnu.

Kayotsarga, loosening, setting free, suspending of the body. A pose generally described as standing on even feet.

Keshi(n), name of a horse-demon killed by Krishna.

Kevala Narasimha, Narasimha standing or seated alone.

Khandoba, see *Mailara*.

Kinnara(s), Kinnari(s), what sort of a man? A kind of semi-divine being. They have human faces and birds' bodies with a conspicuous foliated tail. The kinnaras like the gandharvas, minister to the gods' needs. While the gandharvas serve the gods by their songs and offerings of flowers and fruit, the kinnaras please them by playing on their musical instruments.

Kirata(murti). Aspect of Shiva. The god assumed the guise of a Kirata hunter, when he fought with Arjuna over a boar, which each claimed to have killed.

Kirita-mukuta, diadem, crest, jewelled crown. Type of crown which consists of a conical cap sometimes ending in a central pointed knob. The kirita-mukuta is typical of Vishnu.

Kirti-mukha, face of glory. A face of terrific shape, or a lion's face which is seen on top of a prabhatorana or prabhavali, and which is also found on doorways and niches of temples. See also *prabhavali*.

Kishkindha, name of an ancient monkey-kingdom in south India.

Kolata, folk dance, in which performers carry sticks.

Koti-linga or *Koti-tirtha*, one crore (ten million) lingas. Place on the bank of the Tungabhadra. The name refers to the numerous lingas carved in that locality.

Krishna, black, dark blue. The eighth and one of the most popular incarnations of Vishnu. The latter took birth as Krishna in order to destroy the tyrant of Mathura, king Kamsa.

Krishna-lila, Krishna's sport. The account of Krishna's life and exploits.

Kshetra, field or region.

Kubera, the god of riches and treasure and of the power of productivity. He is one of the ashtadikpalas, the lord of the north. Kubera is mounted on a horse, bearing in his hands sword and shield, or the club.

Kuchabandha, breast-band. Flat band used to keep the breasts in position.

Kudu, bird's cage, bird's nest. Name of horse-shoe-shaped decorative element on the facade of monument.

Kukkuta, cock. One of the attributes of Karttikeya. The cock, symbol of solar energy, is found as an emblem on the god's banner, and occasionally Karttikeya is depicted with the kukkuta in his hand.

Kulayi, tall conical cap worn by Vijayanagara kings and courtiers.

Kulashekhara, one of the Alvars, Kulasekhara is reputed to be the incarnation of Vishnu's kaustubha jewel. Having been a king, Kulasekhara was well attired and ornamented.

Kumara, Kumarasvami, son, adolescent, youth. A form of Karttikeya.

Kumbha, vase, jar, pot.

Kumbhakarna, pot-eared. A rakshasa, brother of Ravana. He was defeated by Rama.

Kumbha-panjara, vase-cage. A niche adorned with a vase and foliage. This motif is typical of the architecture of the Vijayanagara period.

Kumuda-valaya, moulding found on the temple plinth. The patterns on it imitate jewellery designs.

Kundala, ear-ring, ornament of the ear.

Kunthu-Jinanatha, the seventeenth Tirthankara.

Kurma, tortoise. The second incarnation of Vishnu. Vishnu manifested himself as Kurma when the gods and the demons churned the sea of milk. Kurma placed itself at the bottom of the sea, its back providing the base for the mountain Mandara, which served as the churning rod. The great serpent Vasuki was coiled around it as churning rope, its head and tail being pulled by the two parties. Many precious objects emerged from the sea, among these were the goddess Lakshmi, Vishnu's bow Sharanga, the apsaras and Indra's elephant, Airavata.

Kusha, son of Rama.

Kushadhvaja, brother of Janaka, father of Mandaviya and Shrutakirti.

Kuta, name of a temple square in plan.

Kuvalayapida, the mad elephant of king Kamsa killed by Krishna.

Laddu, a kind of sweetmeat made from pulses or cornflour mixed with sugar and spices and fried in ghee or oil. A characteristic attribute of Ganesha.

Lajja-Gauri. A folk, fertility goddess which has been revered since ancient times. In cave 21 (Rameshvara) at Ellora (*c.* eighth century AD), there is a goddess with a female attendant on either side. She is seated with thighs apart, prominently showing the genital region. However, since this sculpture is damaged, it is not certain whether the figure was originally nude. If it was, then it would appear that Lajja-Gauri had been accepted into the Rashtrakuta pantheon and transformed into a regular goddess with attendants. Such figures of the naked, squatting goddess continued to be made until fairly recent times. This goddess is especially invoked for progeny, and butter and vermilion are applied on the vagina and breasts of the image. She was also the goddess of vegetative fertility and hence of special importance in the Deccan which is prone to droughts and famine.

Lakshmana, endowed with aupicious marks. A younger brother of Rama, and the embodiment of loyalty. Lakshmana is regarded as incarnation of Ananta.

Lakshmi, mark, sign, a good or bad sign. Lakshmi, she of the hundred-thousands. Consort of Vishnu, goddess of fortune and prosperity. Originally Lakshmi was a mother and fertility goddess. The lotus is her main attribute, hence she is also called Padma or Kamala. When the cosmic ocean was churned by the gods and anti-gods, Lakshmi sprang up from the waters and is therefore known as the one born of water, Jaladhija. Later she became associated with beauty, fame, good luck, and riches and is then known as Shri. She appears with Vishnu in each one of his avataras. Thus, as the consort of Rama, she emerged from a furrow made by a plough in the earth and she was called Sita, or furrow, and when Vishnu took the form of Krishna, Lakshmi became Rukmini.

Lakshmi-Narasimha, the representation of Vishnu as Narasimha together with Lakshmi, who is seated on his left thigh.

Lakshmi-Narayana, the representation of Vishnu (Narayana) seated, with Lakshmi on his left thigh.

Lalitasana, posture of relaxation, in which one leg, usually the left, rests upon the seat while the right dangles down along it.

Lanka, the modern Shri Lanka. The mythical kingdom of Ravana.

Lata, creeper. Attribute held in one hand. Characteristic of the latasundari(s), the creeper beauties.

Lava, one of the sons of Rama, brother of Kusha.

Linga(m), sign, the sign of gender or sex. Phallus, a symbol of the male principle. The linga is worshipped as a symbol of Shiva. Among the numerous types of sculpted lingas some of the most important are: Mukha-linga or face-linga (on the outside of which one or more faces, representing different aspects of Shiva, are carved). Pancha-linga or five lingas. (five small lingas all on the same pitha). Sahasra-linga or thousand lingas. (A linga on whose shaft are carved a thousand small lingas.) Sarvasama-linga or all equal-linga (where all the three parts constituting the linga are of equal length).

Lingodbhava(murti), aspect of Shiva emerging from the linga.

Lolahasta, a mudra in which one arm hangs like the tail of a cow by the side of the body.

Madanagopala, herdsman of love, a name of Krishna. In this aspect Krishna is shown with eight arms.

Madivalu-Machayya, a Shaiva saint, washerman by profession.

Madhurakavi, one of the Alvars. Madurakavi was a disciple of Nammalvar. He is reputed to be the incarnation of Garuda and is generally shown as a seated figure with hands joined in anjali-mudra.

Madhva (1238-1317), a devotee of Vishnu and a Vedantic philosopher, who preached dvaita, or dualism.

Madhva(s), the followers of Madhva and his philosophy.

Mala, wreath, garland, string of beads.

Mahabharata, the great (war of the descendants of) Bharata. Epic poem narrating the war between the Pandavas and their cousins the Kauravas.

Mahamandapa, *Maharangamandapa*, great mandapa. Frontal pillared hall of the entrance of a temple.

Mahavira, *Jina*, the great hero. Epithet of the founder of Jainism, Vardhamana, (540?-477 BC).

Maharajalilasana, see *Sukhasana*.

Mahishasuramardini, slayer of the buffalo demon. One of the principal aspects of Durga, under which she subdued the asura Mahisha. Mahisha by heroic austerities has received the boon that he would be invincible to all opponents except a woman. After having been defeated, the gods combined their fiery energies to create a splendid woman, to whom each of them gave a weapon. With the lion as her vehicle, the goddess Durga successfully fought Mahisha. On the battlefield she created helpers from herself, the most famous being the goddess Kali and the Matrikas. See also *Saptamatrikas*.

Makara, mythological sea monster, often described as a crocodile (or a dolphin), with an elephant trunk and a foliated tail. It symbolises the life-force of the waters.

Makara-kundala, ear-ring in the shape of a makara. Ornaments made of thin leaves of metal, ivory or wood, in the shape of a crocodile. Especially a man's ornament.

Makara-torana, portal adorned with makara motifs. Name of a decorative motif constituted by a garland issuing from the mouth of two makaras placed on the top of two columns which forms an arched festoon above an image.

Mailara, a folk form of Shiva worshipped in Karnataka, Maharashtra and parts of Andhra. He is a combination of Shiva, Bhairava and Surya. He is worshipped as a formless stone, as a linga or as an image. The horse and the bull are his vahanas. His attributes include the sword, trishula, damaru and kapala. He is depicted standing, riding on a horse or seated. Generally accompanied by two consorts. Also known as Khandoba.

Mandapa, open or closed pillared hall.

Mandara, the mountain that was used as a churn-staff at the churning of the ocean of milk.

Manikkavachakar, he whose utterances are rubies. One of the most eminent of the sixty-three Nayanmars, who lived in the ninth century. He was a prime minister at the Pandya court. He left the worldly life in order to devote himself to the worship of Shiva. He composed the Tiruvachakam, 'Sacred Utterances'. poems in honour of Shiva.

Manmatha, the churner of the heart. Name of Kama.

Manthara, the hunch-back servant of Kaikeyi.

Manu, Vaivasvata Manu, man, mankind. Name of mythological progenitor of mankind.

Maricha, the uncle of Ravana, who took the form of a golden deer.

Mastikal, sati-stone.

Matha, cloister, college. Monastery.

Matrikas, mothers. Collective name of the Divine mothers. See *Saptamatrikas*.

Matsya, fish. The first avatara of Vishnu. The myth of the Matsya avatara appropriates to Vishnu the legend of the deluge. The details of the story vary slightly in the different Puranas. The object of this incarnation was to save Vaivasvata Manu, the progenitor of the human race, from destruction in a mighty flood.

Mayura, peacock. Vehicle of various deities, e.g. Karttikeya, Sarasvati, etc. Used frequently as a decorative motif.

Meru, mythical mountain reputed to be at the centre of the universe.

Mithila, the capital of king Janaka, father of Sita.

Mithuna, loving pair.

Modaka, see *Laddu*.

Mohini, the illusive or illusion. Name of a female aspect of Vishnu. According to one tradition Shiva requested Vishnu's help to curb the pride of the sages of the Daruka forest. The two gods went to the forest, Vishnu as Mohini (i.e. the Enchantress) and Shiva as beautiful naked beggar (Bhikshatana). While the former seduced the rishis and made them lose control of their sense, the latter ravished the hearts of their wives. According to another tradition, at the time of the churning of the ocean of milk by the devas and the asuras to obtain the nectar conferring immortality, the asuras seized the jar of nectar by force. Then Vishnu appeared as Mohini, lured the asuras and deceived them into giving him the jar of nectar for distribution to the gods.

Moksha, final liberation. Realisation or perfection.

Mridanga, large barrel-shaped drum.

Mudama, serpent-goddess especially worshipped in southern India.

Mudra, seal, sign, token. Symbolic arm and hand poses which are used to express facts, feelings, emotions, etc.

Mukuta, crown, diadem, tiara.

Munda, one of the demons defeated by Kali. See *Chanda*.

Murti, manifestation, form, likeness, image, statue. Icons of the god. Mula-murti, fixed image, not used in processions.

Mushtika, name of one of Kamsa's wrestlers who was defeated by Krishna.

Naga, snake. Symbol of fertility and water. Attribute of various deities. Snakes were and are worshipped in the belief that they are able to confer a number of blessings, including the birth of a child, good health and immunity from disease, especially leprosy and skin diseases.

Nagabandha, frieze of nagas. Decorative motif in architecture.

Nagakal, snake-stone.

Nagapasha, decorative motif, similar to the eternal knot, constituted by snakes.

Nageshvara, lord of the snakes. Aspect of Shiva.

Nagini, snake goddess. Represented with a human body and a serpentine tail.

Namam, mark. Term designing the mark on the forehead. See also *Shri-Vaishnava(s)* and *Tilaka*.

Nammalvar, our Alvar. The greatest of the Vaishnava poet-saints. He was a Shudra and is also known as Maran, Shathagopa or Parankusha. Nammalvar is reputed to be the avatara of Vishvaksena and is usually represented seated with his left hand in dhyana-mudra on the lap, or with a palm-leaf book, and his right hand in vyakhyana-mudra.

Nandaka, joy. Name of Vishnu's sword.

Nandi, rejoicing, gladdening. Name of the white bull of Shiva. Usually Nandi is represented as a bull. Occasionally he is found in the therioanthropomorphic form, (Nandikeshvara) with a bull's head and a human body. There are also rare images of him in fully anthropomorphic form, holding Shaiva attributes. In this form he is called Adhikaranandi. The only detail that differentiates Adhikaranandi from Shiva are the lower hands held in anjali-mudra.

Narada, one of the five Devarishis said to be inventor of the vina and the author of treatises on musical theory. The chief of the gandharvas. See also *Tumburu*.

Narasimha, man-lion. Name of the fourth avatara of Vishnu. The demon Hiranyakashipu had received the boon from Brahma that he would not meet death at the hands of men, beasts, gods or demons; that he would not die inside or outside the house, by day or by night, nor by any weapon. In his extreme arrogance Hiranyakashipu forbade the worship of Vishnu in his kingdom. However, his own son Prahlada, an ardent devotee of the god, defied the royal order. Finally, promoted by Hiranyakashipu's mocking query to his son whether the deity resided in a pillar of the hall, Vishnu as man-lion burst out of the pillar, grabbed the demon king and killed him at dusk by tearing open his abdomen with his claws.

Narayana, the abode of man, or moving in the waters. A name of one of the twenty-four aspects of Vishnu.

Natha, name of a sect also known as Kanphata or Yogi sampradaya. Its votaries worship the nine Nathas, the most important of which are Gorakhnatha and Matsyendranatha who lived between the tenth and twelfth centuries and are considered to be the founders of this sect. The second name, Kanphata, meaning split-eared, originates from their unique practice of having the cartilage of their ear slit for the insertion of large earrings. The third name refers to their traditional practice of Hatha Yoga. The followers of the Natha school were votaries of the Shiva and Shakti, with a strong bias towards the Shakta tradition.

Navagrahas, nine planets. The navagrahas are worshipped as minor gods especially in south Indian Shaiva temples. They are placed on a platform, no two of them being made to face each other. The navagrahas traditionally are Surya (Sun), Chandra (Moon), Mangala (Mars), Budha (Mercury), Brihaspati (Jupiter), Sukra (Venus), Shani (Saturn), Rahu and Ketu (the ascending and descending nodes of the moon). The Sun is the chief of the navagrahas.

Navanitanritta-Krishna, butter-dance Krishna. Name of a representation of Krishna as dancing child.

Nayanmar(s), leader. The Shaiva counterpart of the Alvars were the sixty-three Nayanmars who flourished in southern India for about seven centuries from the second to the ninth. They belonged to different castes, the hunter Kannappa (see *Kannappa*) and the outcaste Nanda, being as much entitled to sanctity as the Brahmins among the Nayanmars. Their lives are described in the Periya-Puranam, compiled in the twelfth century by Sekkilar. The devotional poems of the Nayanmars, which brought a great upsurge of Shaivism, are divided into 11 collections, all written in Tamil. These, together with the Periya-Purana, form the Tamil Shaiva canon. The four most famous of the Nayanmars were Appar, Manikkavachakar, Sundaramurti, and Tirujnanasambandhar.

Nidhi, treasure. Kubera, the god of wealth, is said to have eight (or nine) treasures or nidhis. These treasures represent the different aspects of material wealth and prosperity. Of these Padma- and Shankha-nidhi are the most popular. They are frequently represented in personified form as attendants of Kubera. See *Padmanidhi*, *Shankhanidhi*.

Nilotpala, blue lotus.

Nirruti, one of the eight regents of the directions, Nirruti presides over the south-west. He is mounted on the shoulders of a giant. In his hands he carries club, sword and shield.

Pada, see *Paduka*.

Padma, lotus flower. Scalloped moulding on the basement of buildings and images.

Padma-pitha, lotus pedestal.

Padmanabha or *Anantapadmanabha*, lotus-navel. A name of the recumbent form of Vishnu from whose navel emerged the cosmic lotus, signifying the beginning of a new creation. One of the most important centres of worship of this particular form of Vishnu is the Anantapadmanabha temple in Tiruvananthapuram, Kerala.

Padmanidhi, lotus-treasure. As a personification Padmanidhi is an attendant of Kubera. Padmanidhi stands for wealth consisting of gold, silver, copper and other metals. Padmanidhi makes the wordly enjoyment possible. See also *Nidhi*.

Padmasana, lotus sitting attitude; lotus seat. Sitting posture in which the legs are crossed and both feet rest on the opposite thighs.

Paduka, foot-mark, -print; shoes, slippers. Used as a symbol of a god (e.g. Vishnu) or royalty (e.g. Rama's sandals put on the throne as a symbol of his ruling power during his absence).

Pampa, local goddess of the Hampi area.

Pancharatra, name of the Vaishnava sect following the doctrine of the sacred text called Pancharatra. Traditionally the Pancharatra doctrines were first systematized about AD 100 by Sandilya, who emphasized the duty of devotion to Vishnu as the supreme deity.

Panchavati, a sacred place on the southern bank of the Godavari, where Rama, Sita and Lakshmana lived during their exile. The name Panchavati derives from five banyan trees standing there in a circle.

Pandava(s), sons of Pandu. They were: Yudhishthira, Bhima, Arjuna, Nakula and Sahadeva. Their wife was Draupadi. The story of their rivalry with their cousins, the Kauravas, is narrated in the *Mahabharata*. See also *Kaurava(s)*.

Parashu, axe, hatchet. Characteristic attribute of various deities, especially of Shiva and Skanda in various forms.

Parashurama, Rama with the battle-axe. The sixth avatara of Vishnu. Parashurama, son of Jamadagni, saved the world from the tyranny of the warriors.

Parshvanatha, the 23rd Tirthankara. Possibly an historic person living between the 8th and the 7th centuries BC and the true founder of Jainism. Represented with a many-headed snake hood growing from his shoulder.

Parthasarathi, the charioteer of Partha (i.e. Arjuna). Name of a form of Krishna who acted as Arjuna's charioteer in the Mahabharata war.

Parvati, daughter of the Mountain. Daughter of Parvata, the personification of the Himalaya, and sister of Ganga. Parvati is the gracious, friendly aspect of Shiva's Shakti. She is generally looked upon as a fertility and mother deity.

Pasha, noose, fetter. A cord-snare carried in one hand. Attribute of various divinities (e.g. Shiva, Ganesha, Yama).

Patala, lowest of the seven regions under the earth, whose lord is the snake Ananta.

Patanjali, a devotee of Nataraja of Chidambaram. According to the myth, as Patanjali did not wish to crush insects with his feet while gathering the offerings for Nataraja, he received from Shiva the benefit of a snake's tail instead of legs. He is generally depicted as a rishi with a snake's tail.

Pattabhisheka, coronation.

Pattrakundala, plain earring.

Payasa(m), sweet prepared of milk and rice.

Pey, one of the first three Alvars with Bhutam and Poygai, Pey is reputed to be the incarnation of Vishnu's sword, Nandaka.

Periyalvar, also known as Vishnuchitta. One of the Alvars, he is reputed to be an incarnation of Garuda, like Madhurakavi. Periyalvar is usually represented standing or seated, with hands in anjali-mudra. His adopted daughter, Andal, is of particular interest, as she is the only woman among the Alvars.

Pitha, bench, seat, throne. Pedestal of an image.

Poygai, one of the first three Alvars with Pey and Bhutam, Poygai is reputed to be the incarnation of Vishnu's conch.

Prabha, halo, ray.

Prabhamandala, circle of rays. Designations for the circle of flames which surrounds Shiva-Nataraja and other deities.

Prabhavali, glory, halo. A large ornamental circular oval halo (pabhatorana), sometimes with projecting flames which surround the whole figure of a deity.

Pradakshina, moving to the right. Name given to clockwise movement round a person or a cult object as a sign of honour or reverence. Pradakshina-patha, circumambulatory path.

Prahlada, joyful excitement, happiness. Name of the son of Hiranyakashipu, who was an ardent worshipper of Vishnu against the will of his father. Vishnu as Narasimha helped him and killed Hiranyakashipu.

Prakara, courtyard.

Prasada, favour. This term signifies also the food presented to an idol, or the remnants of food left by a spiritual teacher, which anyone may freely take.

Pratyusha, daybreak. One of Surya's attendants.

Pratyalidha, striding posture in which the left foot is advanced and the right drawn back.

Puja, honour, worship, adoration of the gods.

Pujari, priest who performs the puja.

Purana(s), group of Sanskrit texts dealing mainly with mythology. There are 18 maha- (i.e. major) and 18 upa- (i.e. minor) Puranas.

Puratana(s) elders. Name under which the Virashaivas refer to the Nayanmars.

Purnaghata, full pitcher. A symbol of abundance.

Pustaka, book.

Putana, putrid. Demoness sent by Kamsa to destroy Krishna. Putana went to Krishna's house disguised as a cowherdess and fed him on her poisoned breasts. But the child extracted her life with the milk. Putana then assume her real form and died.

Putrakameshti yajna, great sacrifice celebrated by king Dasharatha of Ayodhya in order to beget male progeny.

Rakshasa(s), Rakshasi(s), demon, demoness. Chief of the rakshasas was Ravana.

Raktabija, name of an asura who fought Chamunda. Each drop of blood from his wounds became a powerful warrior like himself until Chamunda drank the blood as it fell and finally defeated him.

Rama(chandra), Rama the moon. The hero of the *Ramayana*. The seventh avatara of Vishnu. Son of Dasharatha, king of Ayodhya, Rama, the embodiment of righteousness, was born for the purpose of destroying Ravana.

Ramanuja (1017-1137?). A devotee of Vishnu, founder of the vishistadvaita (qualified monism) philosophical system and of Shri-Vaishnavism. The main seat of his activity was Srirangam, near Tiruchirapalli.

Ramayana, Rama's career. An epic poem in seven books dealing with the adventures of Rama and containing many other stories deriving from folk beliefs of pre-Buddhist India. Its alleged author was the poet Valmiki.

Rangamandapa, enclosed pillared hall with four openings, usually having four pillars in the centre and twelve or more on the periphery.

Ranganatha, lord of the assembly hall, of the temple. One of the reclining forms of Vishnu. The great temple at Srirangam, in Tamil Nadu, one of the most important pilgrimage places in southern India, is dedicated to this aspect of the deity.

Rati, delight, desire, sexual lust or union. Name of one of the wives of Kamadeva. She is depicted riding on a parrot or a swan.

Ratna-kundala, circular earring set with gems.

Ravana, roaring, causing to cry. The ten-headed chief of the rakshasas or demons, who ruled over Shri Lanka. He has three incarnations: the first is an Hiranyakashipu; in his second incarnation he is one of the chief characters of the *Ramayana*, and finally he is subdued by Rama; his third incarnation is as Shishupala.

Ravananugraha(murti), aspect of Shiva conferring a boon to Ravana.

Raya, king.

Revati, rich. One of the wives of Balarama.

Rishi, inspired poet or sage.

Rishyashringa, deer-horned. Hermit with magical powers, who officiated at the successful sacrifice instituted by Dasharatha to ensure the birth of a son.

Rudraksha (mala), Rudra-eyed (garland). Name of the dark berries used to make Shaiva rosaries (mala), or necklaces.

The berries have five divisions signifying Shiva's five faces. The rudraksha is an attribute of various deities like Shiva, Brahma and Sarasvati.

Sagara, the ocean.

Sahagamana, the act of going with. Especially of a woman burning herself together with the body of her husband. See also *Sati.*

Sakata (asura), cart (demon). Kamsa deputed the asura Sakata to kill Krishna. He approached the sleeping Krishna in the form of a cart and raised a great noise. Krishna awoke and kicked the cart into hundred of pieces. This episode is also known as Shakata-bhanga.

Samabhanga, holding the feet even. Name of a posture in which the idol stands symmetrically with straight legs.

Samharamurti(s), terrific, destructive manifestation (of a deity), especially of Shiva. The most popular samharamurtis are: Kalarimurti, the vanquisher of the god of death Kala or Yama; Gajantakamurti, the one who defeated the elephant demon; Tripurantakamurti the triumpher over the demons or the three cities; Kamantakamurti or the destroyer of Kama: Andhakasuravadhamurti or the destroyer of the demon Andhaka, the demon of the darkness. Of all these Kalarimurti, also known as Yamantaka (destroyer of Yama) or Markandeya-moksha (liberation of Markandeya), Gajantaka and Tripurantaka are particularly popular in southern India.

Sampati, name of a vulture, brother of Jatayus.

Sampradaya, sect or order.

Saptamatrika(s), seven mother goddesses. The saptamatrikas are linked not only with Mahishasuramardini, but also with Shiva. According to mythology, when Shiva was fighting Andhakasura, the principal gods sent their shaktis to his aid. The Saptamatrikas are Brahmani, Maheshvari, Kaumari, Vaishnavi, Varahi, Indrani and Chamunda. Sometimes Yogeshvari is added to their number. Each of the matrikas is armed with the same weapons and rides the same vahana as the corresponding god.

Sangita-mandapa, hall of musical performances.

Sannyasi, renouncer.

Saranga see *Sharanga.*

Sarasvati, the Flowing-One. Originally Sarasvati was the name of a holy river, which in the course of time disappeared. Sarasvati was later identified with the goddess of speech, and regarded as a manifestation of knowledge, learning and speech, and also of poetry and music. She is usually mentioned as the wife—sometimes the daughter—of Brahma. She is generally shown with four arms and carries a vina, a palm-leaf book, a rosary and a water-pot.

Sarpa-kundala, serpent earring. Earring in the shape of a snake.

Sati, good, faithful wife. The wife who immolates herself on the funeral pyre of her husband, thereby winning merit for her family as well as expiating all its sins. See also *Sahagamana.*

Satikal and *Satikkal,* sati-stone. In general a memorial slab erected at the place where a faithful wife committed sati.

Sati-virakal, sati- and hero-stone in one. Slab commemorating the death of a hero and the subsequent immolation of his wife.

Shakata-bhanga, see *Sakata(asura).*

Shakti, (a) Energy of a god personified in his female counterpart. In a restricted sense shakti refers to the personification of the energy of Shiva in his different aspects, and she is therefore the chief deity of the Shakta cult. (b) Weapon: spear, lance.

Shala, shrine with a barrel-vault roof.

Shalabhanjika, breaking a branch of a shala-tree. Posture of a woman standing close to a tree and gathering flowers from its branches. Also tree-nymph.

Shankara (781-820). The founder of the advaita (non-dualistic) system of Vedantic philosophy.

Shankha, conch, conch-shell. Attribute characteristic of Vishnu and other deities. Vishnu's conch is called Panchajanya.

Shankhanidhi, conch-treasure. Attendant of Kubera. Shankhanidhi favours self-realization and eternal bliss. See also *Padmanidhi.*

Shanmukha, six-headed. A twelve-armed form of Karttikeya.

Sharabhanga, a rishi who lived in the Dandaka forest. Rama visited his ashrama in the course of his wanderings.

Sharanga, made of horn(?). Name of Vishnu's bow, which came forth at the churning of the ocean. Hence Vishnu is known as Sharangapani, the wielder of the Sharanga bow.

Shatsthala-Siddhanta, Virashaiva doctrine of the sixfold stages which lead to spiritual progress and perfection.

Shatrughna, son of Sumitra and brother of Rama. He was married to Shrutakirti.

Shayana(asana or *murti),* lying posture. Representation of a god in a recumbent posture. Characteristic attitude of Vishnu.

Shesha(naga), remainder. Epithet of the snake Ananta.

Shiva, auspicious. Shiva is usually included in the Hindu triad as the 'Destroyer'. There are five main types of Shiva images the destructive, the boon-granting, dancing, yogic and philosophical and musical.

Shravanakumara, name of young ascetic killed by mistake by Dasharatha.

Shri, Shridevi, prosperity, welfare, wealth, beauty personified. Shri was early combined with Lakshmi, who is also name Shri-Lakshmi. She is the consort of Vishnu.

Shri-Vaishnava(s), Vaishnava Brahmins of southern India, followers of Ramanuja's philosophy, who worship Vishnu and Shri. The most important temples of this sect are the Varadaraja temple at Kanchipuram, the Ranganatha temple at Srirangam, and the Venkateshvara temple at Tirumalai.

Prior to the establishment of the Vijayanagara empire, the Shri-Vaishnavas had split into two sub-sects, the Vadagalai (or northern, Sanskritik) school and the Tengalai (southern or Tamil). The Vadagalai namam is shaped like a 'U', the Tengalai one is somewhat like a 'Y' with a distinct projection at the bottom.

Shrivatsa, beloved-of-fortune. A triangular mark, symbol of Shri, on Vishnu's chest.

Shrutakirti, name of the daughter of Kushadhvaja and wife of Shatrughna.

Shurpanakha, having fingernails like winnowing fans. Name of Ravana's sister who fell in love with Rama.

Sita, furrow. Daughter of Janaka and wife of Rama. Sita was abducted by Ravana and held captive in Lanka.

Skanda, one who jumps or hops. Name of Karttikeya, the son of Shiva.

Skandhamala, shoulder tassels.

Smarta(s), followers of Shankara's philosophical system.

Somaskanda, aspect of Shiva with Uma and Skanda.

Sruk, a kind of large wooden ladle used for ritual purpose.

Sruva, small sacrificial wooden ladle used for pouring clarified butter into the sruk.

Sthalapurana, foundation legends relating to a particular place.

Sthanaka(murti), representation of a standing deity.

Sthauna-Narasimha, Narasimha emerging from the pillar.

Subahu, a demon killed by Rama.

Sudarshana(chakra), of good appearances. Name of Vishnu's chakra. Sudarshana is the name of the chakra as an independent cult emblem.

Sugriva, king of the monkeys, who after having been dethroned by his brother Vali, was later reinstated by Rama at Kishkindha.

Sukhasana, comfortable sitting posture. One leg, generally the left one, rests flat on the seat while the right knee is raised upward from it and the right arm is stretched out on the raised knee.

Sumitra, wife of Dasharatha, mother of Lakshmana and Shatrughna.

Sundaramurti, Sundarar, also known as 'Tambiran Tolan', i.e. 'Friend of the Lord'. One of the four principal Nayanmars, who lived in the eighth century. Born in a Brahmin family, he was a great friend of the Chera ruler. Cheraman Perumal. His poems left an everlasting impression on the literary works of the following centuries. He was the first to codify the list of the great devotees of Shiva.

Surasa, demoness who obstructed Hanuman's passage to Lanka in order to test whether he possessed power enough for searching Ravana's palace and finding Sita. Hanuman eventually outwitted her by reducing his size: he entered her mouth and came out from her ear.

Surul-yali, see *Yali*.

Surya, Sun-god, chief of the navagrahas. In southern India figures of Surya usually have their hands lifted as high as their shoulders, holding half open lotuses. The feet and torso are bare.

Surya-Narayana, composite image of half Surya, half Narayana.

Svarga, world of light. The abode of the gods.

Tambura. A stringed instrument.

Tanka, hatchet, stone chisel, axe. When held by Shiva it usually resembles an axe, and the blade faces away from the deity. Characteristic attribute of various deities, especially of Skanda.

Tara, wife of Vali and later of Sugriva.

Tarjani-mudra, threatening finger. A hand pose in which the index is raised in a menacing attitude and the other fingers are locked up in the fist.

Tataka, demoness killed by Rama.

Tilaka, mark on the forehead made with coloured earth of unguents. See also *Namam, Shri-Vaishnava(s)*

Tirtha, bathing place, stairs for landing and descent in a river, passage. A shrine, or sacred bathing place, or place of pilgrimage.

Tirthankara(s), ford-finder. Name of the 24 Jaina teachers.

Tirujnanasambandar, Sambandar, one of the four principal Nayanmars. He lived probably in the seventh or the eighth century and wandered from one sacred Shaiva site to the next singing the praise of his Lord. The legend tells that Sambandar as a child was fed by Parvati's own milk. Most of the images of this saint depict him as a young boy, carrying a cup, symbolising Parvati's milk, in the left hand.

Tirumalishai, one of the Alvars. He is reputed to be the incarnation of Vishnu's chakra. Tirumalishai is generally shown seated in the mediation posture, or standing with hands holding cymbals, or joined in adoration.

Tirumangai, one of the Alvars. Having been a petty chieftain turned highwayman, he is usually depicted with sword and shield.

Tiruppan, one of the Alvars, reputed to be the incarnation of Vishnu's shrivatsa. He was a low caste minstrel and he is depicted with a vina resting on his shoulder.

Tiruvengalanatha, name of Vishnu. See Venkateshvara.

Tondaradippodi, one of the Alvars. He is reputed to be the incarnation of Vishnu's garland.

Torana, arch, arched doorway, portal. Also an arch erected during a festivity. Torana also refers to the circle of flames in which Shiva-Nataraja dances.

Tribhanga, three bends. A common stance of many figures

in which the body shows three lateral bends from feet to hip, from hip to shoulder, and from shoulder to crown.

Trimurti, triple representation. The triad constituted by the principal Hindu gods Brahma, Vishnu and Shiva.

Tripurantaka(murti). Aspects of Shiva as destroyer of the three cities of the asuras.

Trishiras, three-headed. Name of a rakshasa killed by Rama.

Trishula or *Shula*, trident one of the most important attributes in Indian iconography. Emblem characteristic of Shiva denoting his function as creator, preserver and destroyer.

Trivikrama, taking the three steps; he who strode over the three worlds: conqueror of the three worlds. Epithet of Vishnu in the Vamana avatara.

Tulasi, Tulsi, holy basil. Name of a small shrub, which is sacred to Vishnu.

Tulasimala, Tulsimala, garland of basil beads.

Tumburu, name of a gandharva, leader of the celestial musicians generally associated with Narada. Tumburu besides being proficient on the vina, is probably associated with another variety of stringed instrument from which the present tambura is derived. Tumburu is easily recognizable by his horse face. See also *Narada*.

Udarabandha, band, girdle around the belly. Waist-band.

Ugrasena, king of Mathura, father of the tyrant Kamsa. Kamsa usurped the throne and threw Ugrasena in prison. After killing Kamsa, Krishna reinstated Ugrasena.

Uma, epithet or form of Parvati, especially as the daughter of Daksha.

Uma-Maheshvara, representation of Shiva and Uma seated. The goddess is depicted sitting on the left thigh of the god.

Upana, bottom moulding of a basement, characterized by a rounded shoulder.

Urdhvapundra, upright mark on the forehead. Vaishnava sectarian mark. See *Namam*.

Urdhvatandava, the erect tandava-dance. Dance pose in which one foot is thrust upwards. According to tradition, Kali challenged Shiva to a dance contest. Whatever dance pose Shiva adopted, Kali imitated him. Finally Shiva performed the urdhavatandava with one foot thrust into the sky. Modesty prevented Kali from emulating this pose. She was thus forced to acknowledge defeat.

Urmila, daughter of Janaka, wife of Lakshmana.

Usha, dawn. One of the attendants of Surya. See also Pratyusha.

Ushnisha, top-knot like protuberance on the head.

Utkutikasana, name of the yogic posture where one sits with heels kept close to the bottom, with the back slightly curved and the forearms resting on the knees. A yogapatta supports the raised knees. See *Yogapatta*.

Utsava-mandapa, festival pavilion. Temple pavilion in which special festivities are celebrated.

Uyyale-mandapa, swing pavilion. Temple pavilion in which the ceremonial swing is suspended.

Vahana, vehicle, mount of a deity. The animal on which the deity rides. The vahana represents the energy and the character of the deity.

Vaikuntha, the abode of Vishnu.

Vajra, thunderbolt. Attribute of various deities , especially of Indra.

Vali, monkey-king, son of Indra and brother of Sugriva. He was killed by Rama.

Valmiki, ant-hill. Name of the poet who composed the *Ramayana*.

Vamana, dwarf. The fifth avatara of Vishnu. The god assumed this form to curb the pride of king Bali. According to the legend, king Bali had, by his devotions and austerities, acquired control over the three worlds. The gods felt threatened and in order to redress the situation, Vishnu was born as Vamana. He appeared before Bali and begged as much land as he could step over in three paces. The generous monarch complied with the request. Vamana immediately assumed the giant form of Trivikama and with two strides covered the earth and the heavens; with the third, placed on the demon king's head, he pushed Bali down to the nether world, leaving that to his dominion. Vamana is also the name of one of the twenty-four forms of Vishnu.

Valaya, armlet, ring worn on the wrist by men and women.

Vanamala, forest-garland. A long garland of flowers either worn on the body or carried in one hand. One of the typical attributes of Vishnu.

Varada-mudra, gesture of granting wishes. A gesture indicating the giving of boons in which the left hand is held out palm uppermost with fingers pointing downwards.

Varadaraja, king among boon-bestowers. The image of this aspect of Vishnu enshrined at the Varadaraja temple in Kanchipuram—one of the three main Shri-Vaishnava shrines in southern India—shows the deity standing in samabhanga, carrying the chakra and the shankha in the upper right and left hands; the lower right is in abhaya-mudra and the lower left carries the gada. He is flanked by a consort on each side. See *Gajendramoksha* and *Karivarada*.

Varaha, boar. The third avatara of Vishnu. The god assumed this form to rescue the earth which had been dragged to the bottom of the sea by a demon, Hiranyaksha. Vishnu defeated the demon and raised up the earth, Bhudevi. Varaha can be depicted in animal form or as half-human and half-animal.

Varuna, one of the eight regents of the directions, Varuna presides over the west. He is the lord of water and seas and has the makara as conveyance. He carries the noose, the water-pot, or a snake.

Vasantotsava, spring festival. Other name: Smaramahotsava.

Vasishtha, a hermit, son of Brahma. Vasishtha was the spiritual guide of king Dasharatha of Ayodhya.

Vatapattrashayi(n), lying on a fig-leaf. Name of Krishna in the form of a baby, sometimes sucking his toe, lying on his back on a fig-leaf. It symbolises the god resting, floating upon the world ocean after destroying the cosmos at the end of a cosmic period.

Vayu, one of the eight regents of the directions, Vayu presides over the north-west. He is the lord of the air and wind. His conveyence is a gazelle, or a deer. He carries a flag and a staff.

Venkateshvara, Lord of Venkata (a sacred hill). Name of a form of Vishnu worshipped at Tirumalai, Andhra Pradesh, one of the three most important Shri-Vaishnava shrines in the south. The god is known by a number of other names, Shrinivasa, Venkataramana, Tirumaladeva, Tiruvengala-natha. North Indians address him as Balaji.

Venugopala, the cowherd with the flute. A form of Krishna represented playing the flute.

Vibhishana, terrifying. Brother of Ravana. He joined Rama and after Ravana's defeat he was consecrated king of Lanka.

Vimana, chariot of the gods. In southern temples, the term refers to the main shrine and its superstructure.

Vina, lute, staff-zither. A popular musical instrument, supposed to have been invented by Narada.

Vinadhara, holding the vina. Epithet of Shiva.

Vira, hero. A class of Vaishnava images of which there are four varieties. The vira aspect is worshipped by warriors and kings to attain military success and power. See also *Abhicharika, Bhoga* and *Yoga.*

Vira-Anjaneya, Anjaneya as a hero. A form of Hanuman in which he is shown striding, with the upraised right arm and carrying an uprooted tree or a flower in the left.

Virakal or *Virakkal,* hero-stone. Slab commemorating the heroic death of a person.

Virabhadra, distinguished hero. An emanation of Shiva. Who was created in order to destroy Daksha's yajna. A popular deity in Karnataka and Maharashtra.

Viradha, a rakshasa who was killed by Rama and Lakshmana in the Dandaka forest.

Virashaiva, Shaiva sect founded by Basava in the thirteenth century.

Virupaksha, of-misformed-eyes. A form of Shiva. One of the most important deities worshipped in the Vijayanagara period.

Vishnu, all-pervading. The preserver of the universe, a member of the Hindu triad consisting of Brahma, the creator, and Shiva, the destroyer. His attributes are the shankha called Panchajanya; the chakra called Sudarshana; the gada termed Kaumodaki; the bow, Sharanga and the sword, Nandaka. The first two are favourite attribute of the god. He also sometimes holds a lotus. His principal wife is Shri or Lakshmi, and Bhudevi is the secondary consort. Shri is said to reside on the breast of Vishnu, so on the right side of his chest is the shrivatsa mark. Vishnu wears a conical tiara, the kirita-mukuta and the shining kaustubha gem. The garland, vanamala, and a string of basil (tulsi) beads complete his attire.

Vishnu-anugraha(murti), aspect of Shiva conferring a boon on Vishnu.

Vishvaksena, minor Vaishnava deity, also known as Senai Mudaliyar. He is the commander-in-chief of Vishnu's forces, door-keeper of Vaikuntha, custodian of the personal effects of Vishnu and controller of his finances.

Vishvamitra, universal friend. Name of the most eminent of the Vedic rishis, who represents the power of dharma which hold society together.

Vishvarupa, having all forms. Cosmic aspect of Vishnu.

Vithoba, Vithala, a form of Vishnu especially worshipped at Pandharpur (Maharashtra). Vithoba is usually depicted standing on a brick, with his hands resting on his hips. The main centre of Vithoba worship is Pandharpur.

Vrishabharudha, epithet of the Shiva when seated on his bull.

Vrishavahana, epithet of Shiva when standing by his bull.

Vyaghrapada, having tiger-feet. Name of a sage, devotee of Nataraja of Chidambaram. According to tradition Vyaghrapada was a young *rishi,* whose duty was to pick flowers for Nataraja. In order to prevent the thorns from hurting him while engaged in this task, Shiva bestowed tiger's feet on him. This also enabled him to climb on the trees and gather the blossoms before the bees could defile them. This devotee is generally depicted as half human with the feet of a tiger.

Vyakhyana-mudra, gesture of explanation. Gesture in which the tips of the index finger and thumb are pressed together, thus forming a circle. The palm faces the spectator, the tips of the fingers upwards.

Vyala see *Yali.*

Vyuha, manifestation, appearance. An emanatory form of Vishnu, There are 24 vyuhas.

Yajna, sacrifice, oblation, offering.

Yajnopavita, investiture with the sacred thread. This thread is worn only by men of the three upper castes, over the left shoulder and hanging down under the right arm.

Yaksha(s), Yakshi(s), ghost. Designation for mysterious godlings who haunt field, forest and jungle, and who play in important role in Indian folklore.

Yali, horned lion. Mythical composite beast generally depicted rearing. Surul-yali: a composite beast, represented standing on all fours.

Yama, one of the eight regents of the space, Yama presides over the south. He is the god of death and of the nether world and rides a buffalo. He carries the sword, the shield, the noose and the staff.

Yamantaka(murti). Aspect of Shiva as destroyer of Yama.

Yamuna, name of the river Jumna, one of the tributaries of the Ganges. It is personified as a goddess, and is mythically identified with Yami, sister of Yama. The personified image of the Yamuna is placed along with that of the Ganga at the doorways of temples. Yamuna carries a water-pot, a fly-whisk and a blue lotus. A tortoise is her conveyance, probably because the Jumna teems with tortoises. See also *Ganga.*

Yantra, tool. Mystic diagram; two-dimensional object of worship, relating circle, square and central point.

Yashoda, wife of the cowherd Nanda, foster-mother of Krishna.

Yellamma, a folk goddess, whose main centre of pilgrimage is Saundatti in Belgaum district, Karnataka. There are two traditions regarding the origin of the goddess Yellamma. According to one she is Renuka, the mother of Parashurama, Vishnu's avatara, who was ordered by is father Jamadagni to cut off his mother's head for her unchaste thoughts. To seek comfort, Renuka embraced an outcaste woman and Parashurama cut off both their heads. For his obedience, Jamadagni told his son to ask a favour. The latter wanted his mother's life restored. In his haste Parashurama stuck the wrong heads on the two bodies. The woman with the Brahmin body and the outcaste's head became Yellamma, while the other is worshipped as the gramadevata Mariyamman. According to the other myth, Yellamma is the virgin mother born from the earth.

Yoga, yoking, joining, union. Set of psycho-physiological techniques. Types of Vaishnava image venerated especially by ascetics for spiritual realisation.

Yoga-Narasimha, aspect of Narasimha. He is portrayed seated in utkutikasana with a band to hold one or both knees in position.

Yogasana, see *Utkutikasana.*

Yogapatta, cloth or band round the knees encircling the hips.

Yogi, a person adept at yoga.

Yoni, female sexual organ, vulva. Name of the female principle.

Bibliography

A. Primary Sources

I. ARCHAEOLOGICAL SOURCES

Annual Reports of the Archaeological Department, Southern Circle, Madras, Madras: Government Press, 1902-3 onwards.

Annual Reports on South Indian Epigraphy, Madras/Calcutta: Government Press, 1887 onwards.

Epigraphia Indica, Calcutta/New Delhi: Archaeological Survey of India, 1892 onwards.

Hultzsch, E. *et al.* (eds.), *South Indian Inscriptions,* 23 Volumes, Madras: Government Press (Vols. 1-13); New Delhi: Archaeological Survey of India (Vols. 14-23), 1890-1979.

Rice, Lewis B. *et al.* (eds.), *Epigraphia Carnatica.* 16 Volumes, Madras/Bangalore/Mysore: Government Press, 1886-1958.

II. LITERARY SOURCES (INDIAN)

Somanatha, *Sri Vyasayogicaritam: The Life of Sri Vyasaraja, A Champu Kavya in Sanskrit,* with an historical introduction in English by B. Venkoba Rao, Bangalore: Murti, no date.

Sri Pampa Mahatme or the Holy Eminence of the Pampa: as described in the travelogue of the seven sages which is part of the Hemakuta chapter of the Skanda Purana, by Sri Guru Omsiddhalingeshvara Swamiji, Holagundi: Sri Guru Vrishabhashrama, 1983 (translated from the Kannada into English by G.S. Kalburgi). This Kannada work is based on the Sanskrit text in Telugu characters entitled *Sri Pampa Mahatme: describing the travelogue of the seven sages which is part of the chapter on Mt. Hemakoota in the Skanda Purana,* ed. by Vedanta Vidvashiromani Koratamaddi Venkataramasastri, No. 3 in the Shankarananda Book Series, 1933.

III. TRAVELLERS' ACCOUNTS

Abd-er Razzak, 'Narrative of the Journey of Abd-er Razzak', in *India in the Fifteenth Century being a Collection of Narratives of Voyages to India,* ed. by R.H. Major (rpt), Delhi: Deep Publications, 1974.

Barbosa, Duarte, *The Book of Duarte Barbosa. An Account of the Countries Bordering on the Indian Ocean and their Inhabitants, written by Durate Barbosa and completed about the year 1518 AD.* Translated, edited and annotated by M. Longworth Dames, 2 Volumes, London: Hakluyt Society, 1918.

Conti, Nicolo, 'The Travels of Nicolo Conti, in the East, in the Early Part of the Fifteenth Century', in *India in the Fifteenth Century being a Collection of Narratives of Voyages to India,* ed. by R.H. Major (rpt), Delhi: Deep Publications, 1974.

Frederick, Caesar, in *Hakluyutus Posthumus or Purchas His Pilgrimes: Containing a History of the World in Sea Voyages and Lands Travels by Englishmen and Others,* by Samuel Purchas, Vol. X, Glasgow: James MacLehose and Sons, 1905, pp. 88-143.

Nuniz, Fernão, 'Chronicle of Fernão Nuniz', in *A Forgotten Empire,* by R. Sewell (rpt), New Delhi: Asian Educational Services, 1984, pp. 291-395.

Paes, Domingo, 'Narrative of Domingo Paes', in *A Forgotten Empire,* by R. Sewell (rpt), New Delhi: Asian Educational Services, 1984, pp. 236-90.

B. Secondary Sources

I. BOOKS, MONOGRAPHS AND THESES

Agrawala, P.K., *Pūrṇa Kalaśa: or the Vase of Plenty,* Varanasi: Prithvi Prakashan, 1965.
Appadurai, A., *Worship and Conflict under Colonial Rule: A South Indian Case,* Cambridge: Cambridge University Press, 1981.
Aryan, K.C. and S. Aryan, *Hanuman in Art and Mythology,* Delhi: Rekha Prakashan, no date.
Ayyar, P.V.J., *South Indian Festivities,* Madras: Higginbotham Ltd., 1921.
Banerjea, J.N., *Development of Hindu Iconography,* Calcutta: University of Calcutta, 1941.
Begley, W.E., *Viṣṇu's Flaming Wheel: The Iconography of the Sudarśana-Cakra,* New York: New York University Press, 1973.
Boner, G., L. Soni and J. Soni, *Alice Boner Diaries—India 1934-67,* Delhi: Motilal Banarsidass, 1993.
Briggs, G.W., *Goraknāth and the Kānphata Yogīs,* Calcutta: Y.M.C.A. Publishing House, 1938.
Brown, P., *Indian Architecture (Buddhist and Hindu),* Bombay: Taraporevala, 5th edn, 1965.
Champakalakshmi, R., *Vaiṣṇava Iconography in the Tamil Country,* New Delhi: Orient Longman, 1981.
Coomaraswamy, A.K. *History of Indian and Indonesian Art,* New York: Dover, 2nd edn, 1965.
Courtright, P.B., *Gaṇeśa: Lord of Obstacles, Lord of Beginnings,* New York: Oxford University Press, 1985.
Dallapiccola, A.L. in collaboration with S. Zingel-Avé Lallemant, (eds.), *Vijayanagara—City and Empire: New Currents of Research,* 2 Volumes, Stuttgart/Wiesbaden: Franz Steiner Verlag, 1985.
Dallapiccola, A.L., J.M. Fritz, G. Michell and S. Rajasekhara, *The Ramachandra Temple at Vijayanagara,* New Delhi: Manohar Publications and American Institute of Indian Studies, 1992.
Daniélou, A., *Hindu Polytheism,* Bollingen Series, no. 73. Pantheon Books: London/New York, 1974.
Deleury, G.A., *The Cult of Viṭhobā,* Poona: Deccan College, 1960.
Desai, K., *Iconography of Viṣṇu,* New Delhi: Abhinav Publications, 1973.
Devakunjari, D., *Hampi,* New Delhi: Archaeological Survey of India, 2nd edn, 1983.
Devaraj, D.V. and C.S. Patil (eds.), *Vijayanagara: Progress of Research 1984-87,* Mysore: Directorate of Archaeology and Museums, 1991.
———, *Vijayanagara: Progress of Research 1987-88,* Mysore: Directorate of Archaeology and Museums, 1991.
———, *Vijayanagara: Progress of Research 1988-91,* Mysore: Directorate of Archaeology and Museums, 1996.
Dhere, R.C., *Lajja-Gauri,* Pune: D.D. Kulkarni, Sri-Vidya Publisher, 1978 (in Marathi).
Fergusson, J., *History of Indian and Eastern Architecture,* 2 Volumes, New Delhi: Munshiram Manoharlal, 2nd Indian edn, January 1972.
Fergusson, J. and P. Meadows Taylor, *Architecture in Dharwar and Mysore,* London: John Murray, 1866.
Fritz, J.M., G. Michell and M.S. Nagaraja Rao, *The Royal Centre at Vijayanagara Preliminary Report,* Melbourne: Department of Architecture and Building, University of Melbourne, 1984.
Goetz, H., *Five Thousand Years of Indian Art,* London: Methuen, 1959.
Gollings, J., J.M. Fritz, and G. Michell, *City of Victory: Vijayanagara—The Medieval Hindu Capital of Southern India,* New York: Aperture, 1991.
Gopinatha Rao, T.A., *Elements of Hindu Iconograhy,* 2 Volumes, Madras: Law Printing House, 1914-16.
———, *Sri Subrahmanya Ayyar Lectures on the History of Sri Vaiṣṇavas,* University of Madras, 1923.
Goswamy, B.N. and A.L. Dahmen-Dallapiccola, *An Early Document of Indian Art, The Citralaksana of Nagnajit,* New Delhi: Manohar, 1976.
Gururaja Bhatt, P., *Studies in Tuḷuva History and Culture (from pre-historic times up to the Modern),* Manipal: P. Gururaja Bhatt, 1975.
Hari Rao, V.N., *The Śrīrangam Temple: Art and Architecture,* Tirupati: The Sri Venkateswara University, 1967.
Harle, J.C., *The Art and Architecture of the Indian Subcontinent,* Harmondsworth: Penguin Books, 2nd edn, 1987.

Hiltebeitel, A. (ed.), *Criminal Gods and Demon Devotees, Essays on the Guardians of Popular Hinduism.* Albany: State University of New York Press, 1989.

Hooper, J.S.M., *Hymns of the Āḷvārs,* Calcutta: Oxford University Press, 1929.

Huntington, S.L. and J.C. Huntington, *The Art of Ancient India: Buddhist, Hindu, Jain,* New York: Wealtherhill, 1985.

Jouveau-Dubreuil, G., *Iconography of Southern India* (Translated from the Fench by A.C. Martin), Varanasi: Bharat-Bharati, 1978.

Kamath, S.U. (ed.), *Karnataka State Gazetteer,* Parts I and II, Bangalore: Government of Karnataka, 1982, 1983.

Karmarkar, A.P., *The Religions of India, Vol. I: The Vrātya or Dravidian Systems,* Lonavla: Mira Publishing House, 1950.

Khan, Md. Abdul Waheed, *An Early Sculpture of Narasimha (Man-Lion Incarnation of Vishnu with Pañcha Vīras),* Hyderabad: The Government of Andhra Pradesh (Andhra Pradesh Archaeological Series No. 16), 1964.

Khare, G.H., *Mahārāshtrācī cār daivete,* Pune: G.H. Khare, 1958, (in Marathi).

Kinsley, D.R., *Hindu Goddesses: Visions of the Divine Feminine in the Hindu Religious Traditions,* New Delhi: Archives Publications, 1987.

Karmrisch, S., *The Hindu Temple,* 2 Volumes, Delhi: Motilal Banarsidass, reprint, 1980.

Krishnaswami Aiyangar, S., *A History of Tirupati,* 2 Volumes, Madras: Tirumala-Tirupati Devasthanam, 1940-1.

Liebert, G., *Iconographic Dictionary of the Indian Religions. Hinduism-Buddhism-Jainism,* Leiden: E.J. Brill, 1976.

Longhurst, A.H., *Hampi Ruins: Described and Illustrated,* New Delhi: Asian Educational Services (rpt) 1982.

Major, R.H. (ed.), *India in the Fifteenth Century,* London: Haklyut Society, 1857.

Michell, G., and V. Filliozat (eds.), *Splendours of the Vijayanagara Empire, Hampi:* Bombay: Marg Publications, 1981.

Michell, G., *Vijayanagara, Architectural Inventory of the Urban Core,* 2 Volumes, Mysore: Directorate of Archaeology and Museums, 1990.

————, *The Vijayanagara Courtly Style,* New Delhi: Manohar Publications and American Institute of Indian Studies, 1991.

————, *The New Cambridge History of India I.6 Architecture and Art of Southern India, Vijayanagara and the Successor States,* Cambridge: Cambridge University Press, 1995.

Nagaraja Rao, M.S. (ed.), *Vijayanagara: Progress of Research 1979-1983,* Mysore: Directorate of Archaeology and Museums, 1983.

————, *Vijayanagara: Progress of Research 1983-1984,* Mysore: Directorate of Archaeology and Museums, 1985.

Narayana Rao, V. (trsl.), *Śiva's Warriors, the Basava Purana of Palkuriki Somanatha,* Princeton: University Press, 1990.

Nilakanta Sastri, K.A., *A History of South India: from Prehistoric Times to the Fall of Vijayanagara,* Madras: Oxford University Press, 2nd edn, 1958.

Nirmala Kumari, Y., *Social Life as Reflected in the Sculptures and Paintings of the Later Vijayanagara Period (AD 1500-1650) (with special reference to Andhra),* Madras: T.R. Publications, 1995.

O'Malley, L.S.S., *Popular Hinduism: The Religion of the Masses,* London: Cambridge University Press, 1935.

Padigar, S.V., *Visnu Cult in Karnataka,* Mysore: Directorate of Archaeology and Museums, 1996.

Panchamukhi, R.S., *Gandharvas and Kinnaras in Indian Iconography,* Dharwar: Kannada Research Institute, 1951.

Rabinandan Pratap, D., *Tribes of Andhra Pradesh,* Hyderabad: World Telugu Conference Office, 1975.

Rajasekhara, S., *Masterpieces of Vijayanagara Art,* Bombay: D.B. Taraporevala Sons and Co., 1983.

Raman, K.V., *Srī Varadarājaswāmi Temple—Kāñchi: A Study of its History, Art and Architecture,* New Delhi: Abhinav Publications, 1975.

Rama Rao, M., *The Temples of Srisailam,* Hyderabad: Government of Andhra Pradesh (Andhra Pradesh Government Archaeological Series No. 29), 1969.

Ramesan, N., *Temples and Legends of Andhra Pradesh,* Bombay: Bharatiaya Vidya Bhavan, 1962.

Ramesh, K.V., *A History of South Kanara (from the earliest times to the fall of Vijayanagara)*, Dharwar: Karnatak University, 1970.

Rowland, B., *The Art and Architecture of India,* Harmondsworth: Penguin Books, 2nd revd edn, 1959.

Saletore, R.N., *Vijayanagara Art,* Delhi: Sundeep Prakashan, 1982.

Sarma, C.R., *The Ramayana in Telugu and Tamil. A Comparative Study,* Madras: Amra Press, 1973.

Sarma, M.S., *History of the Reddi Kingdoms: Circa 1325 AD to circa 1448 AD,* Waltair: Andhra University, 1948.

Sarojini Devi, K., *Religion in Vijayanagara Empire,* New Delhi: Sterling Publishers, 1990.

Sewell, R., *A Forgotten Empire,* New Delhi: Asian Educational Services, rpt, 1984.

Sherwani, H.K. and P.M. Joshi (eds.), *History of Medieval Deccan (1295-1724),* 2 Volumes, Hyderabad: the Government of Andhra Pradesh, 1973, 1974.

Shulman, D.D., *Tamil Temple Myths: Sacrifice and Divine Marriage in the South Indian Śaiva Tradition,* Princeton: Princeton University Press, 1980.

————, *The King and the Clown in South Indian Myth and Poetry,* Princeton: Princeton University Press, 1985.

Sivaramamurti, C., *Royal Conquests and Cultural Migrations in South India and the Deccan,* Calcutta: Indian Museum, 1964.

————, *Rishis in Indian Art and Literature,* New Delhi: Kanak Publications, 1981.

————, *South Indian Bronzes,* New Delhi: National Museum, 1983.

Sridhara Babu, D., *Kingship: State and Religion in South India according to South Indian Historical Biographies of Kings (Madhurāvijaya, Acyutarāyābhyudya and Vemabhūpālacarita),* Ph.D thesis, University of Göttingen, 1975.

Soundara Rajan, K.V., *The Art of South India: Tamil Nadu and Kerala,* Delhi: Sundeep Prakashan, 1978.

Stutley, M., *The Illustrated Dictionary of Hindu Iconography,* London: Routledge & Kegan Paul, 1985.

Stutley, M. and J. Stutley, *A Dictionary of Hinduism,* London: Routledge & Kegan Paul, 1977.

Sugandha, *History and Archaeology of Anegondi,* Ph.D. thesis, Poona University, 1986.

Vasantha Madhava, K.G., *Religions in Coastal Karnataka 1500-1763,* New Delhi: Inter-India Publication, 1985.

Verghese, Anila, *Religious Traditions at Vijayanagara: As Revealed through its Monuments,* New Delhi: Manohar Publications and American Institute of Indian Studies, 1995.

Vijayanagara Empire Sexcentenary Association and Karnatak Historical Research Society (eds.), *Vijayanagara Sexcentenary Commemoration Volume,* Dharwar: Vijayanagara Empire Sexcentenary Association, 1936.

Vogel, J. Ph., *Indian Serpent-Lore or the Nāgas in the Hindu Legend and Art,* London: Arthur Probsthain, 1926.

Whitehead, H., *The Village Gods of South India,* Calcutta: Oxford University Press, 2nd edn, 1921.

II. Articles

Balasubramanya, 'Vīrabhadra Sculptures in Hampi', in *Vijayanagara: Progress of Research 1983-84,* ed. by M.S. Nagaraja Rao, Mysore, Directorate of Archaeology and Museums, 1985, pp. 133-5.

Basu, N.K., 'The Spring Festival in India', in *Man in India,* VII, 1927, pp. 112-85.

Chidanandamurti, 'Two Masti Temples in Karnataka', in *Memorial Stones: A Study of their Origins, Significance and Variety,* ed. by S. Settar and G.D. Sontheimer, Dharwad/New Delhi: Karnatak University and South Asia Institute of University of Heidelberg, 1982, pp. 117-31.

Dallapiccola, A.L., 'The City of Vijayanagara: Kishkindha, the Monkey-Kingdom', in *The Legend of Rama: Artistic Visions,* ed. by Vidya Dehejia, Bombay: Marg, 1994, pp. 61-72.

Dallapiccola, A.L., 'Ceiling Paintings in the Virupaksha temple, Hampi', in *South Asian Studies 13,* 1997.

Dallapiccola, A.L. and Verghese Anila, 'Ramayana Panels on the Gopura of the "Old Shiva" Temple, Vitthalapura', in *Vijayanagara: Progress of Research 1987-1988,* ed. by D.V. Devaraj and C.S. Patil, Mysore: Directorate of Archaeology and Museums, 1991, pp. 143-53.

———, 'The Old Śiva Temple at Vithalapura' in *Vijayanagara: Progress of Research,* ed. by D.V. Devaraj and C.S. Patil, Mysore: Directorate of Archaeology and Museums, (in press).

Devanthachariar, K., 'Sri Vaisnavism and its Caste-Marks', in *The Quarterly Journal of the Mythic Society,* V, 1915, pp. 125-39.

Filliozat, P.S., 'Techniques of Chronology of Construction in the Temple of Vithala at Hampi', in *Vijayanagara City and Empire—New Currents of Research,* ed. by A.L. Dallapiccola in collaboration with S. Zingel-Avé Lallemant, Stuttgart/Wiesbaden: Fanz Steiner Verlag, 1985, Vol. 1, pp. 296-307.

Filliozat, V., 'Iconography', in *Splendours of the Vijayanagara Empire: Hampi,* ed. by G. Michell and V. Filliozat, Bombay: Marg Publications, 1981, pp. 127-32.

———, 'Iconogaphy: Religious and Civil Monuments', in *Vijayanagara City and Empire—New Currents of Research,* ed. by A.L. Dallapiccola in collaboration with S. Zingel-Avé Lallemant, Stuttgart/ Wiesbaden: Franz Steiner Verlag, 1985, Vol. 1, pp. 308-16.

Fischer, K., 'Iconology of Devatā and Devadāsī, Tapasvin and Mohinī, Sṛṅgaraṇavidhi and Mithuna on some Maṇḍapa Pillars from the Vijayanagara Period onward?', in *Vijayanagara City and Empire—New Currents of Research,* ed. by A.L. Dallapiccola, in collaboration with S. Zingel-Avé Lallemant, Stuttgart/Wiesbanden: Franz Steiner Verlag, 1985, Vol. 1, pp. 317-25.

Fritz, J.M., 'Was Vijayanagara a "Cosmic City"?', in *Vijayanagara City and Empire—New Currents of Research,* ed. by A.L. Dallapiccola in collaboration with S. Zingel-Avé Lallemant, Stuttgart/ Wiesbaden: Franz Steiner Verlag, 1985, Vol. 1, pp. 257-73.

Fritz, J.M. and G. Michell, 'The Vijayanagara Documentation and Research Project: A Progress Report', in *South Asian Archaeology 1981,* ed. by Allchin, Cambridge and London: Cambridge University Press, pp. 295-304.

Goetz, H., 'Muslims in Vijayanagara: The Record of the Monuments', in *Studies in Indian Culture, Dr Ghulam Yazdani Commemoration Volume,* ed. by H.K. Sherwani, Hyderabad: Maulana Abdul Kalam Azad Oriental Research, 1966, pp. 66-70.

Kalidos, R., 'Iconography of Mahisasuramardini: A Probe into Stylistic Evolution', in *Acta Orientalia,* Vol. 50, 1989, pp. 7-48.

Kotraiah, C.T.M., 'A Cave Linga of Hampi', in *Journal of the Andhra Historical Research Society,* 32, 1971-2, pp. 121-5.

Kotraiah, C.T.M., 'Linga superimposed by another Linga at Hampi', in *Vijayanagara: Progress of Research 1988-91,* ed. by DV Devaraj and CS Patil, Mysore: Directorate of Archaeology and Museums, 1996, pp. 135-40.

Kramrisch, S., 'An Image of Aditi-Uttānapad', in *Exploring India's Sacred Art,* edited with a biographical essay by B.S. Miller. Philadelphia: University of Pennsylvania Press, 1983, pp. 148-58.

Hegde, R., 'Decorative Motifs in the Vijayanagara Sculpture', Paper presented at the Congress of Asian and North African Studies, Hong Kong, 22-8 August 1993 (Typescript).

Löschhorn, E., 'Vijayanagara as seen by European Visitors', in *Vijayanagara City and Empire—New Currents of Research,* ed. by A.L. Dallapiccola in collaboration with S. Zingel-Avé Lallemant, Stuttgart/Wiesbaden: Franz Steiner Verlag, 1985, Vol. 1, pp. 344-53.

Masilamani-Meyer, E., 'The Changing Face of Kattavarayan', in *Criminal Gods and Demon and Devotees,* ed. by A. Hiltebeitel, Albany, N.Y.: State University of New York Press, 1989, pp. 69-103.

Mehta, S.S., 'Holika Celebrations', in *Journal of the Anthropological Society of Bombay,* X, 1913, pp. 131-7.

Michell, G., 'The "Royal Centre" and the Great Platform at Vijayanagara', in *Rupa Pratirupa, Alice Boner Commemoration Volume,* ed. by B. Bäumer, New Delhi: Biblia Impex, 1982, pp. 109-17.

————, 'A Never Forgotten City', in *Vijayanagara City and Empire—New Currents of Research.* ed. by A.L. Dallapiccola in collaboration with S. Zingel-Avé Lallemant, Stuttgart/Wiesbaden: Franz Steiner Verlag, 1985, Vol. 1, pp. 196-297.

————, 'Folk Tradition in a Monumental Setting: Sculptures on the Great Platform at Vijayanagara', in *Dimensions in Indian Art,* ed. by Lokesh Chandra and Jyotindra Jain, Delhi: Agam Kala Prakashan, 1986, pp. 287-90.

————, 'Royal Architecture and Imperial Style at Vijayanagara', in *The Powers of Art, Patronage in Indian Culture,* ed. by B.S. Miller, Delhi: Oxford: Oxford University Press, 1992.

Murty, M.L.K., 'Ethnoarchaeology of the Kurnool Cave Areas', in *World Archaeology,* 17, 1985, pp. 192-205.

Nagaraja Rao, M.S. and C.S. Patil, 'Epigrahical References to City Gates and Watchtowers of Vijayangara', in *Vijayanagara: Progress of Research 1983-84,* pp. 96-100.

Patil, C.S., 'Sculptures at Kotilinga', in *Vijayanagara: Progress of Research 1983-84,* Mysore: Directorate of Archaeology and Museums, 1985, pp. 138-143.

Ramachandra Murthy, V. Sri, 'Mailara Cult in Andhra', in *The Quarterly Journal of the Mythic Society,* LXXIV, no. 4, 1983, pp. 351-4.

Saletore, R.N., 'Some Aspects of Art during the Reign of Krishnadevaraya, The Great', in *Vijayanagara Sexcentenary Commemoration Volume,* Dharwar: Vijayanagara Empire Sexcentenary Association and Karnatak Historical Reseach Society, 1936, pp. 198-205.

Sankalia, H.D., 'The Nude Goddess or "Shameless Woman" in Western Asia, India and South-Eastern Asia', in *Artibus Asiae,* XXIII, 1960, pp. 111-23.

Sarojini Devi, K., 'The Cult of Vithoba in Vijayanagara', in *Dr. N. Venkataramanayya Commemoration Volume: Journal of the Andhra Historical Research Society, Vol. XXXVIII,* ed. by R. Subrahmanyam and V.V. Krishna Sastry, Hyderabad: The Government of Andhra Pradesh, 1987, pp. 93-9.

Sinha, D.K., 'A Rare Varāha Image of Archaeological Museum Hampi', in *Journal of Indian History,* LIII, 1975, pp. 353-9.

Sontheimer G.D., 'Folk Deities in the Vijayanagara Empire: Narasimha and Mallanna/Mailar', in *Vijayanagara City and Empire—New Currents of Rsearch,* ed. by A.L. Dallapiccola in collaboration with S. Zingel-Avé Lallemant, Stuttgart/Wiesbaden: Franz Steiner Verlag, 1985, Vol. 1, pp. 144-58.

Soundara Rajan, K.V., 'The Typology of the Anantaśayī Icon', in *Artibus Asiae,* XXIX, 1967, pp. 67-84.

Stein, B., 'Devi Shrines and Folk Hinduism in Medieval Tamilnad', in *Studies in the Language and Culture of South Asia,* ed. by E. Gerow and M.D. Lang, Seattle and London: University of Washington Press, 1793, pp. 75-90.

Sundara, A., 'Narasiṁha Sculptures from Hosa Mahākuṭa and Kuppaṭūru: Some Types and Significance', in *Karnatak Historical Review,* XIII, 1977, pp. 9-12.

————, 'New Lights on Religious trends in Anegondi Region during Vijayanagara Period', in *The Quarterly Journal of the Mythic Society,* LXVIII, 1977, pp. 9-18.

Venkatasubba Ayyar, V., 'Kalahasti and Its Inscriptions', in *The Quarterly Journal of the Mythic Society,* XVI, 1925-6, Parts 1 and 3, pp. 20-4.

Verghese, Anila, 'Court Attire of Vijayanagara (from a Study of Monuments)', in *The Quarterly Journal of the Mythic Society,* LXXXII, 1991, nos. 1-2, pp. 43-61.

————, 'Archaeology as a Tool in Historical Research: A Case Study of Vijayanagara', in *The Quarterly Journal of the Mythic Society,* LXXXIII, 1992, no. 2, p. 169-97.

————, 'Vaishnavism in Vijayangara', in *Indica,* Vol. 32, 1995, no. 2, pp. 95-112.

————, 'A Rare Image of Sudarśana-Chakra at Hampi', in *Śrī Nāgābhinandanam: Dr M.S. Nagaraja Rao Festschrift,* ed. by L.K. Srinivasan and S. Nagaraju, Bangalore: Dr M.S. Nagaraja Rao Felicitation Committee, 1995, pp. 407-14.

Visuvalingam E-C., 'Bhairava's Royal Brahminicide: The Problem of the Mahabrahmana', in *Criminal Gods and Demon Devotees,* ed. by A. Hiltebeitel, Albany, N.Y.: State University of New York Press, 1989, pp. 157-229.

Iconographic Index

FIGURES, PLATES AND MAPS

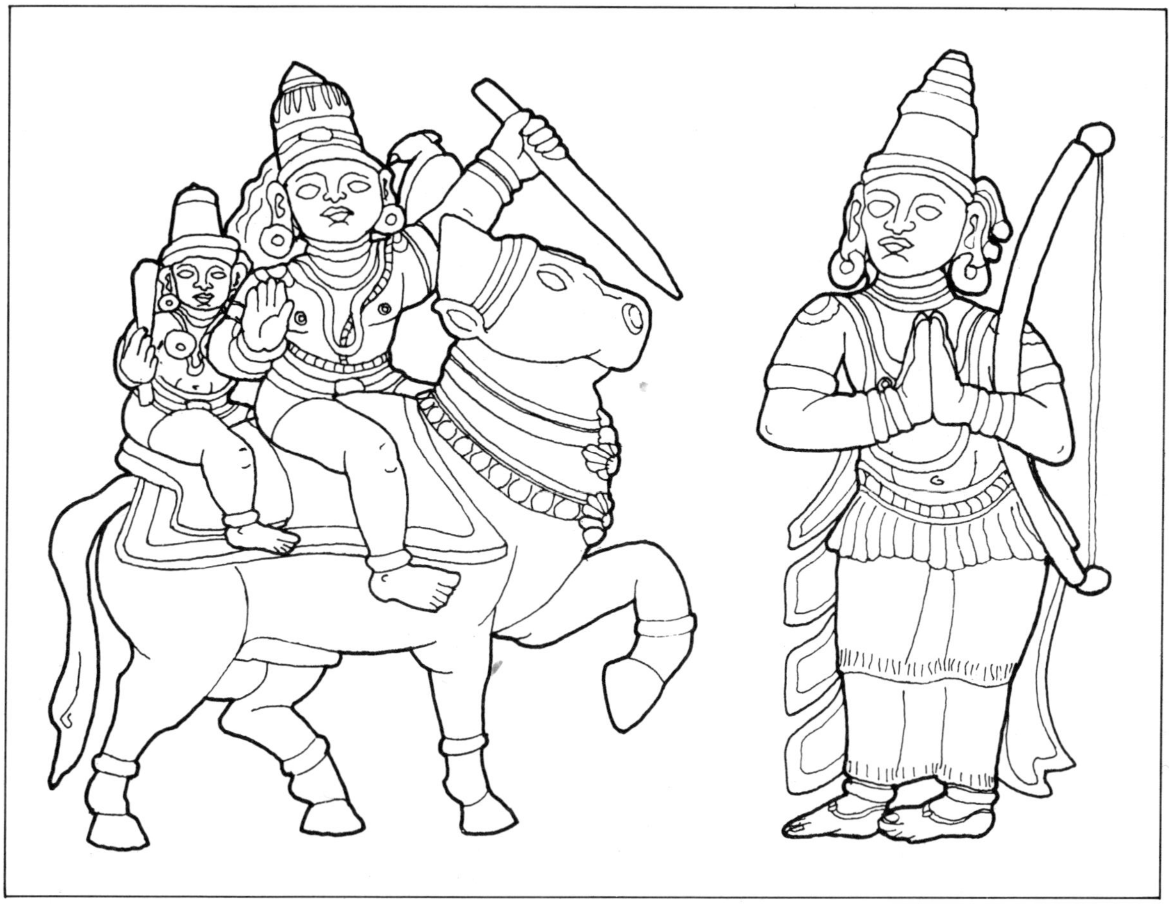

1. Kiratarjuniya episode.

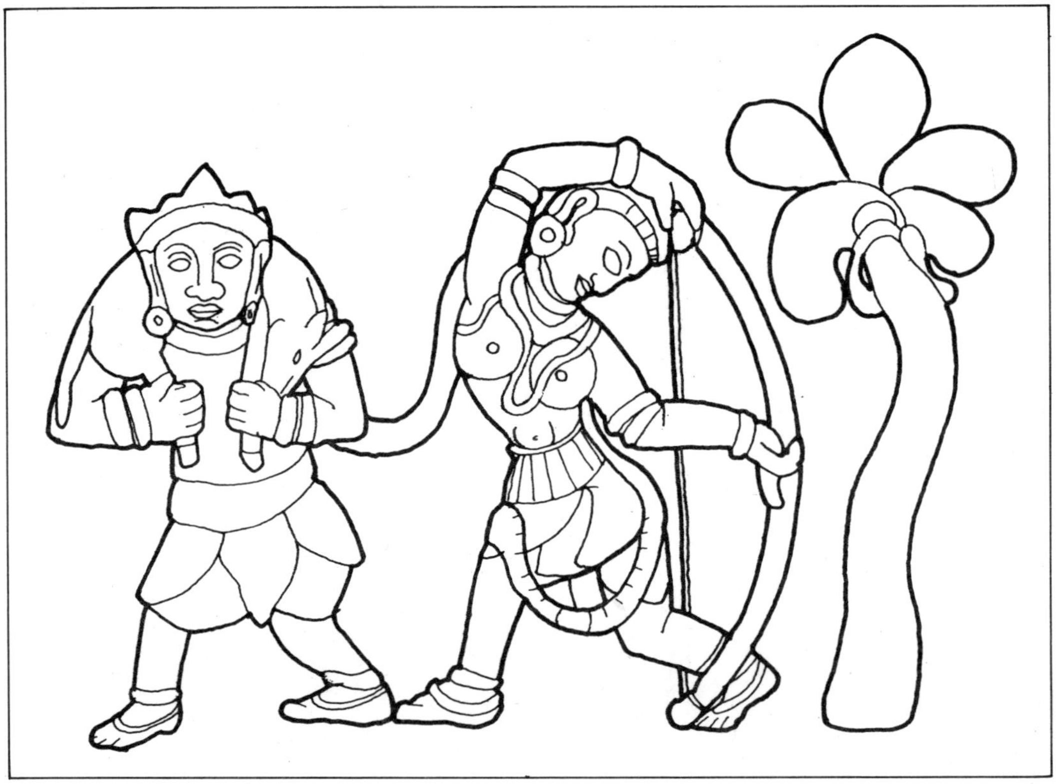

2. Narasimha and Chenchu-Lakshmi.

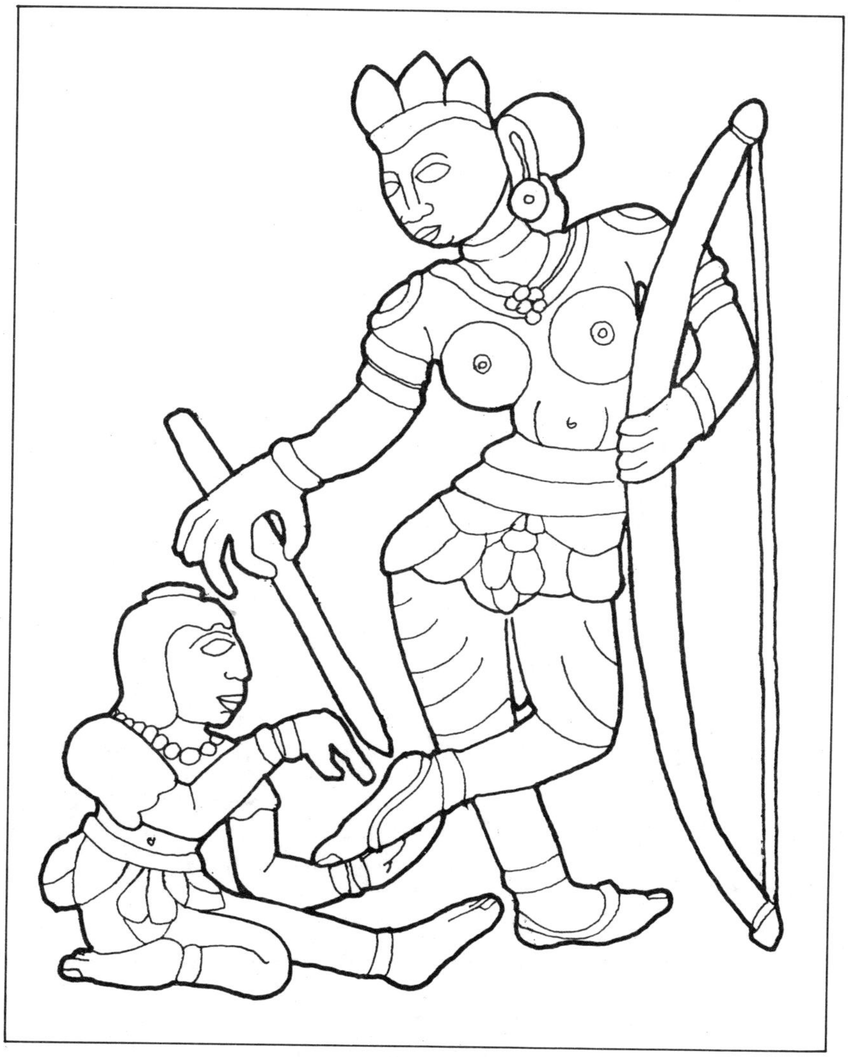

3. Narasimha extracting a thorn from the foot of Chenchu-Lakshmi.

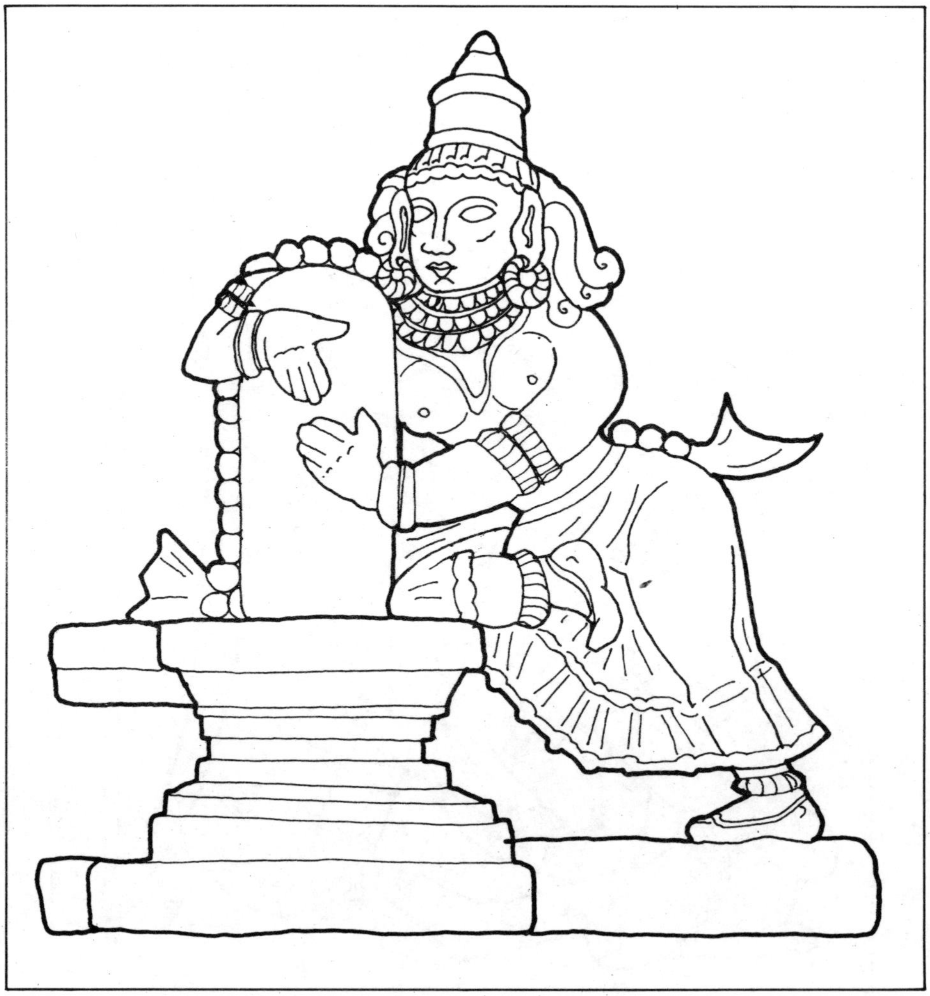

4. Devi embracing the linga.

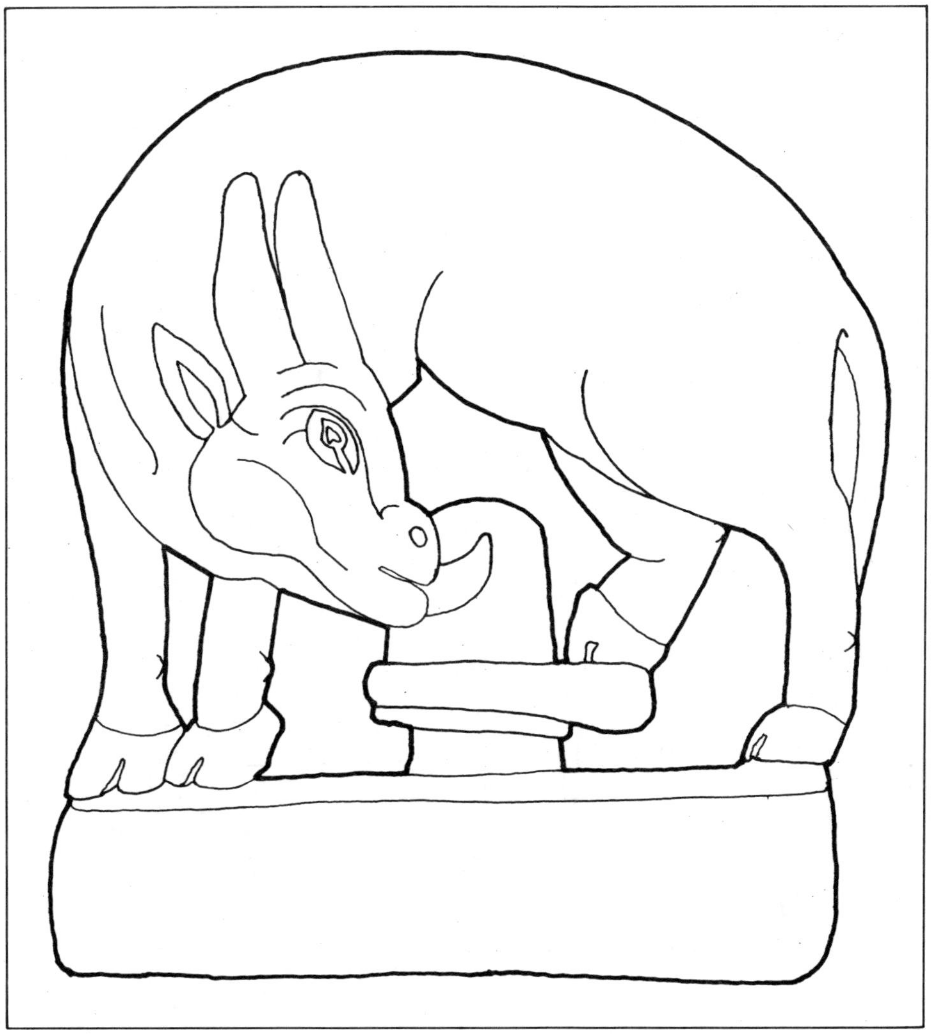

5. Cow worshipping the linga.

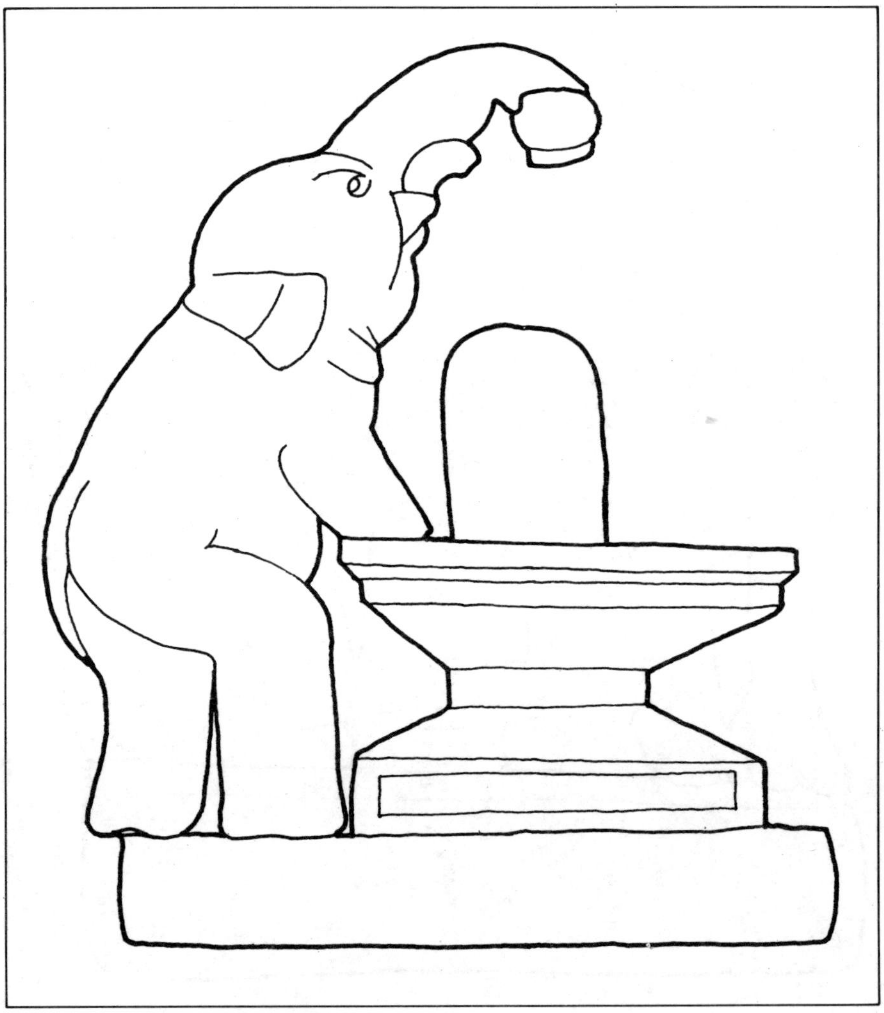

6. Elephant worshipping the linga.

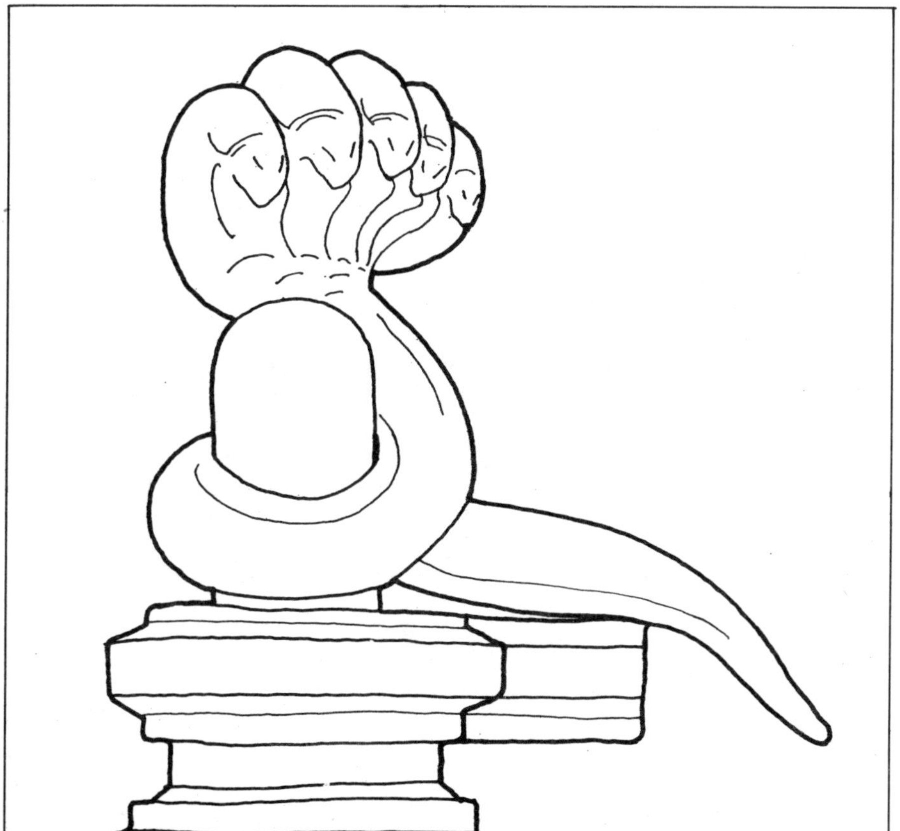

7. Snake protecting the linga with its hood.

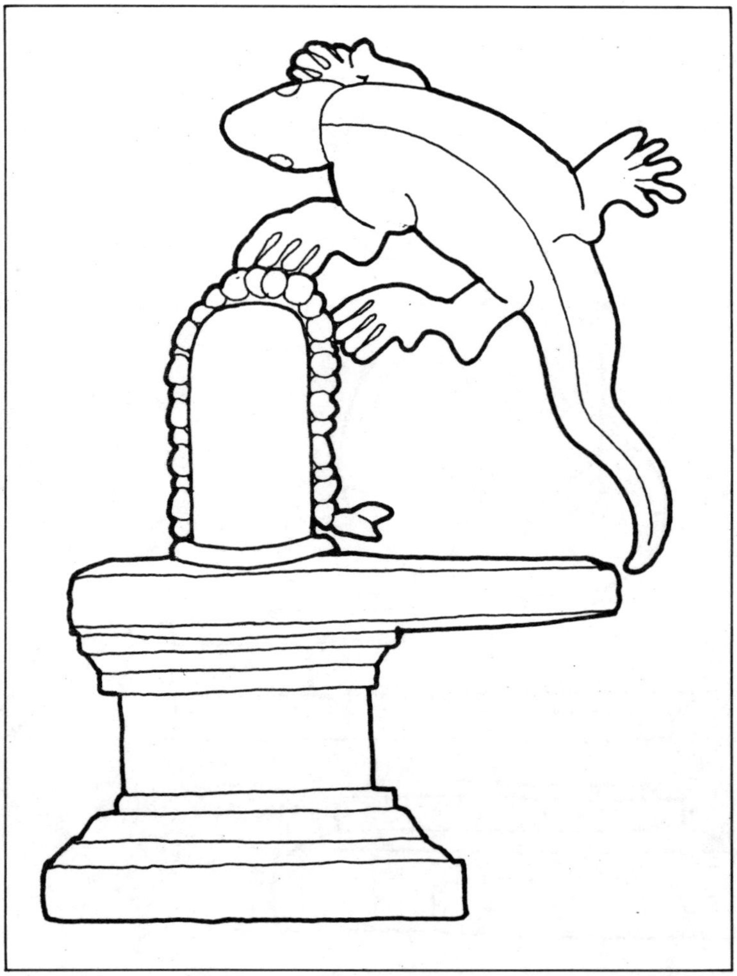

8. Lizard worshipping the linga.

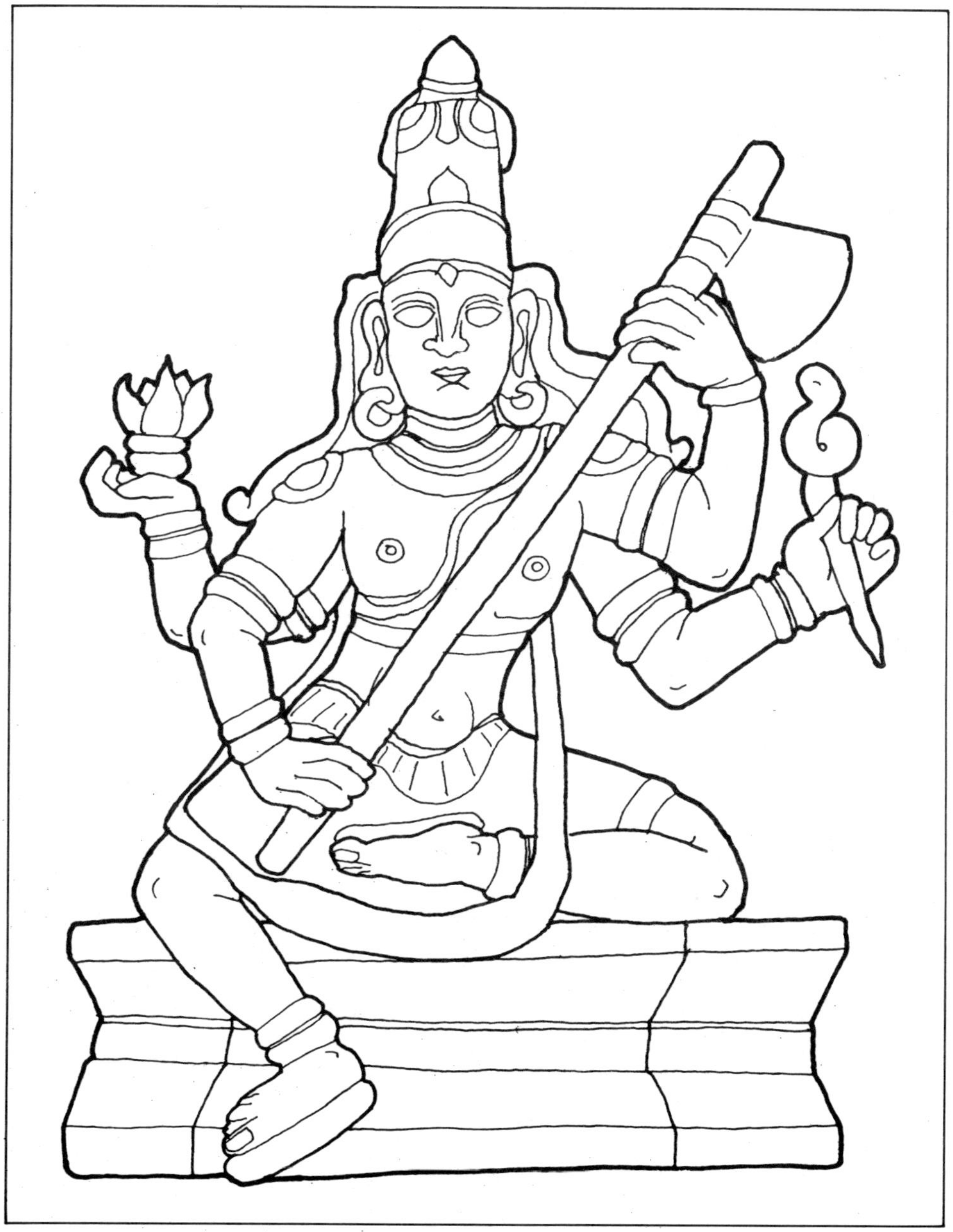

9. Vinadhara Dakshinamurti.

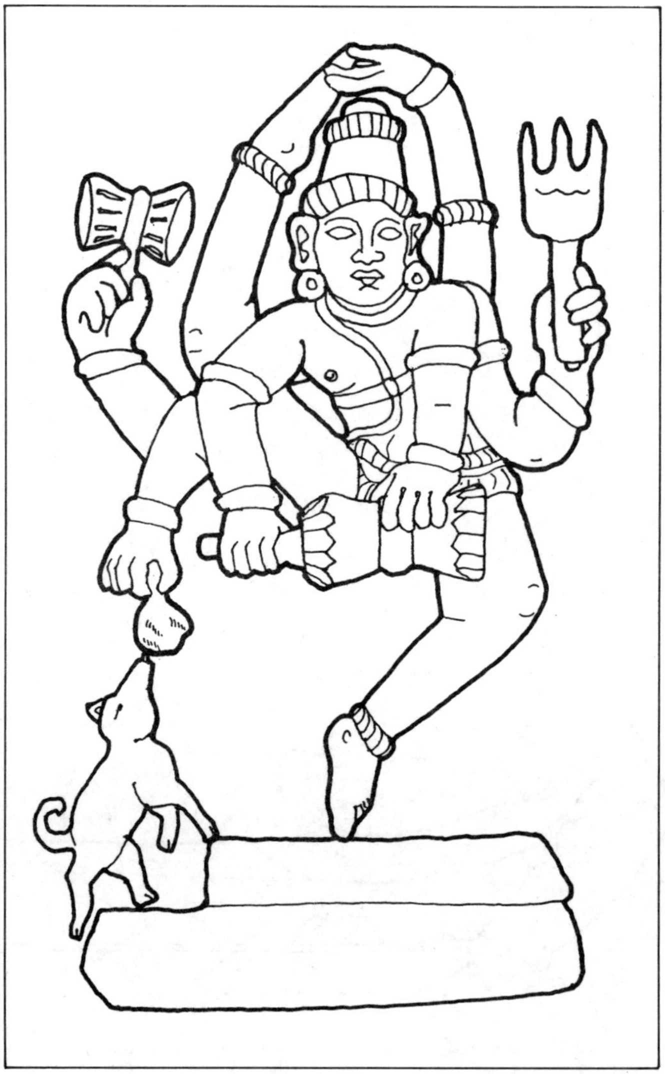

10. Shiva in urdhvatandava pose.

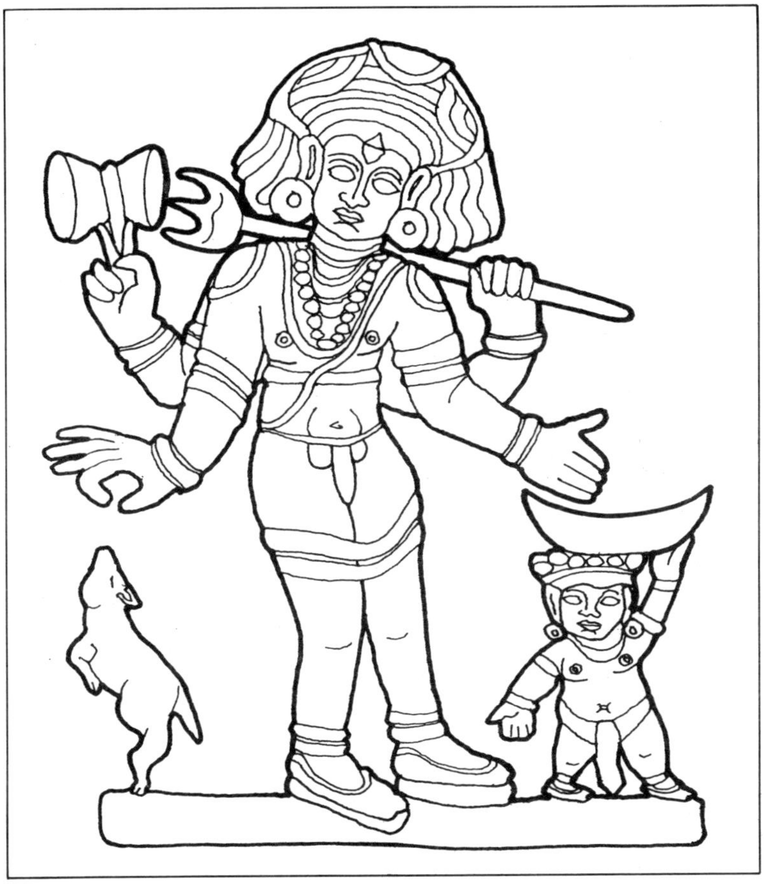

11. Bhikshatanamurti.

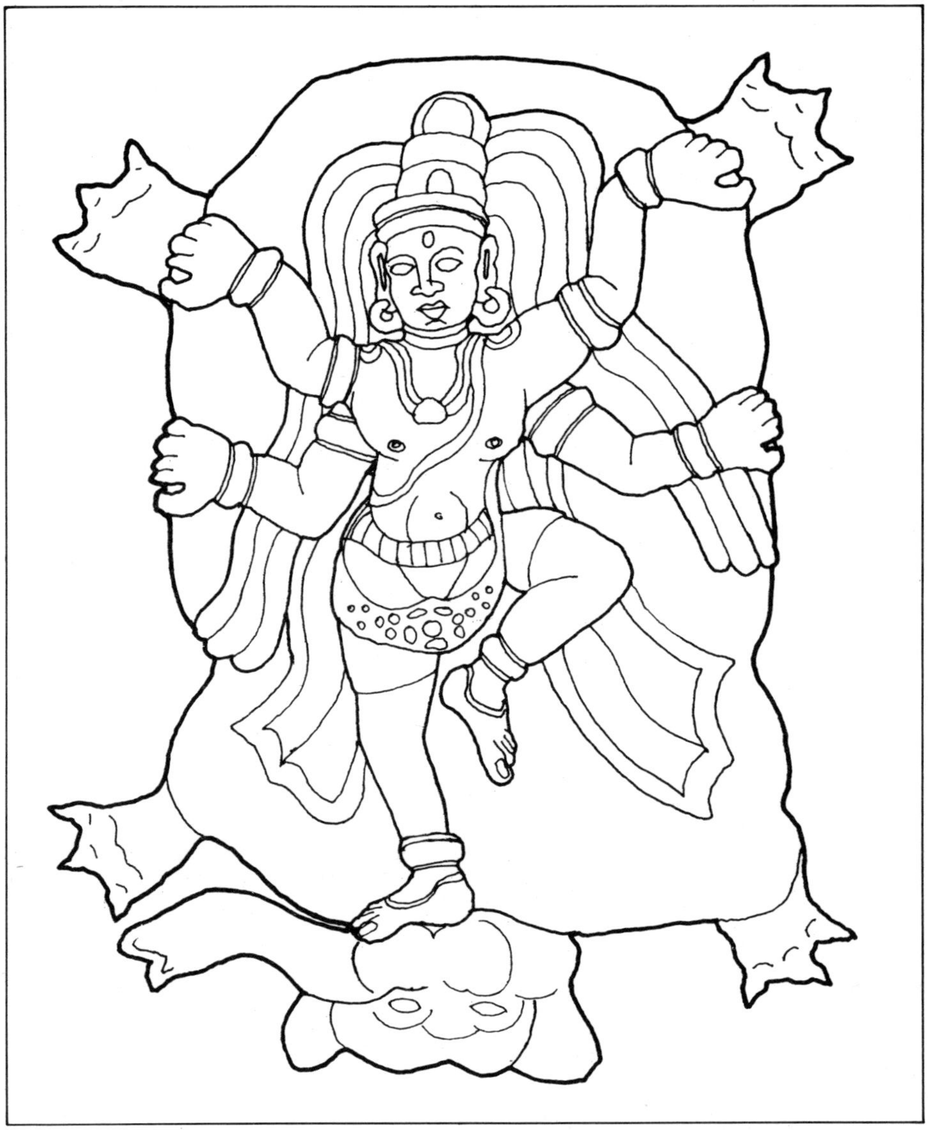

12. Gajantakamurti.

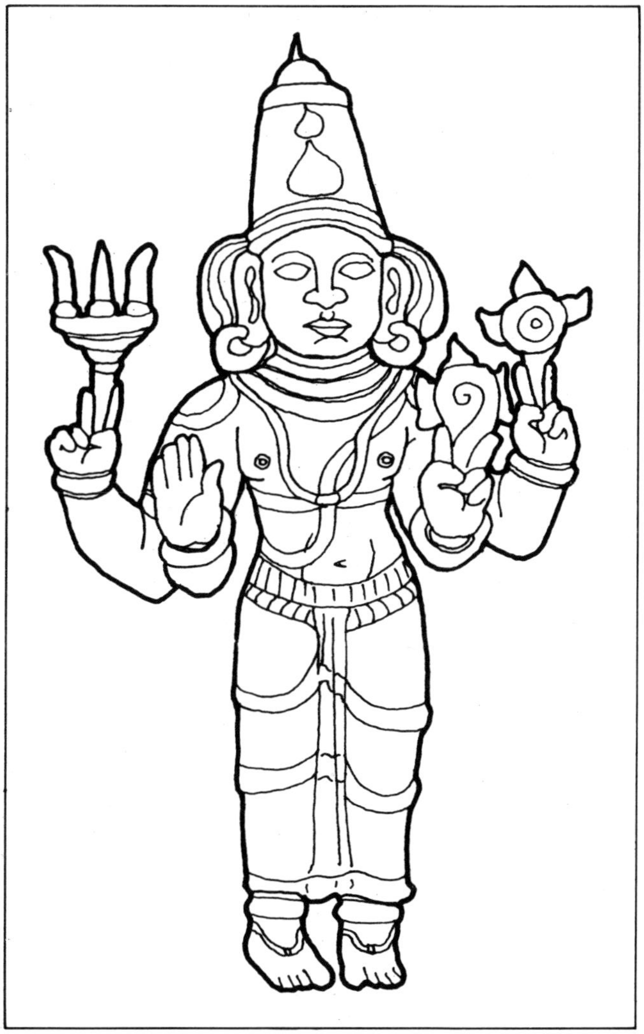

13. Harihara.

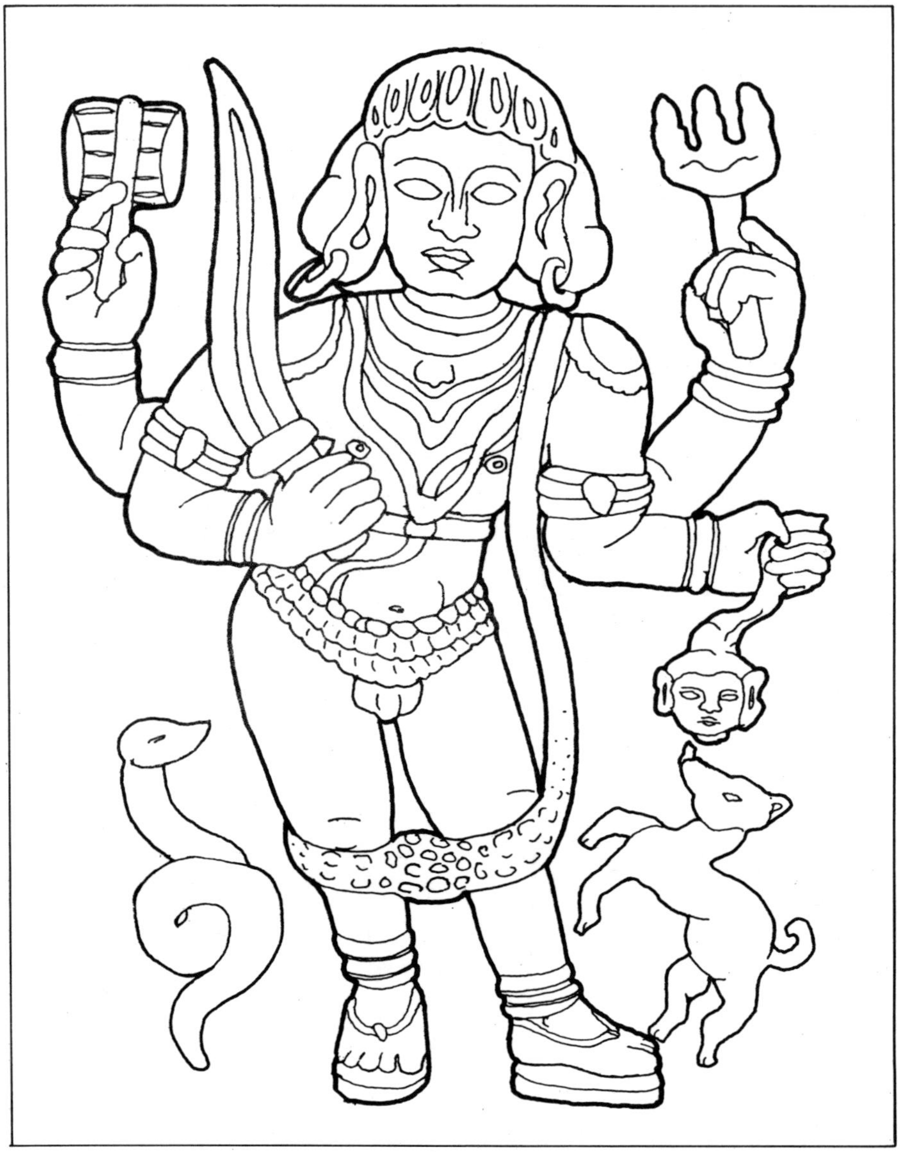

14. Standing Bhairava.

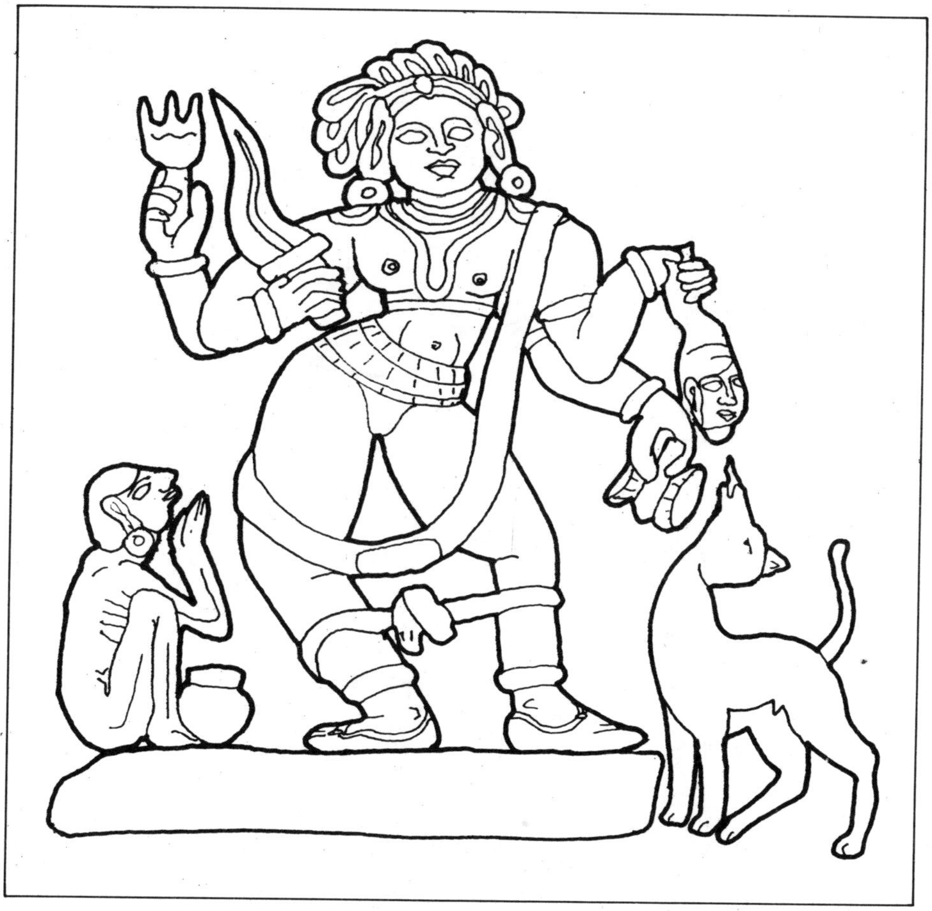

15. Standing Bhairava.

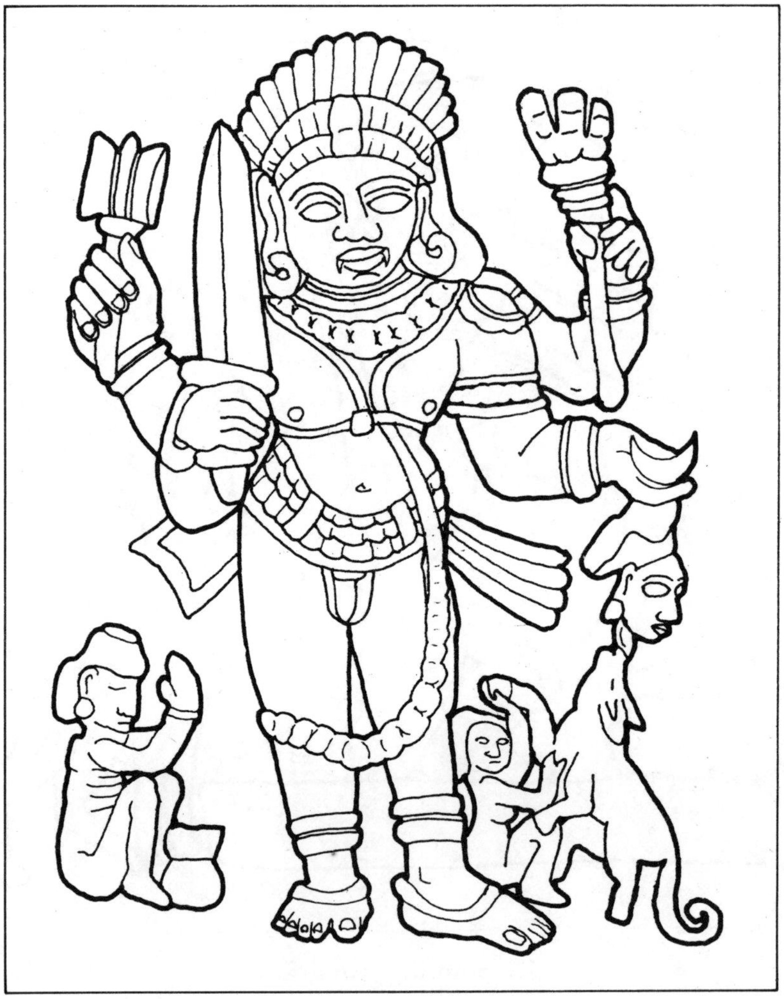

16. Standing Bhairava.

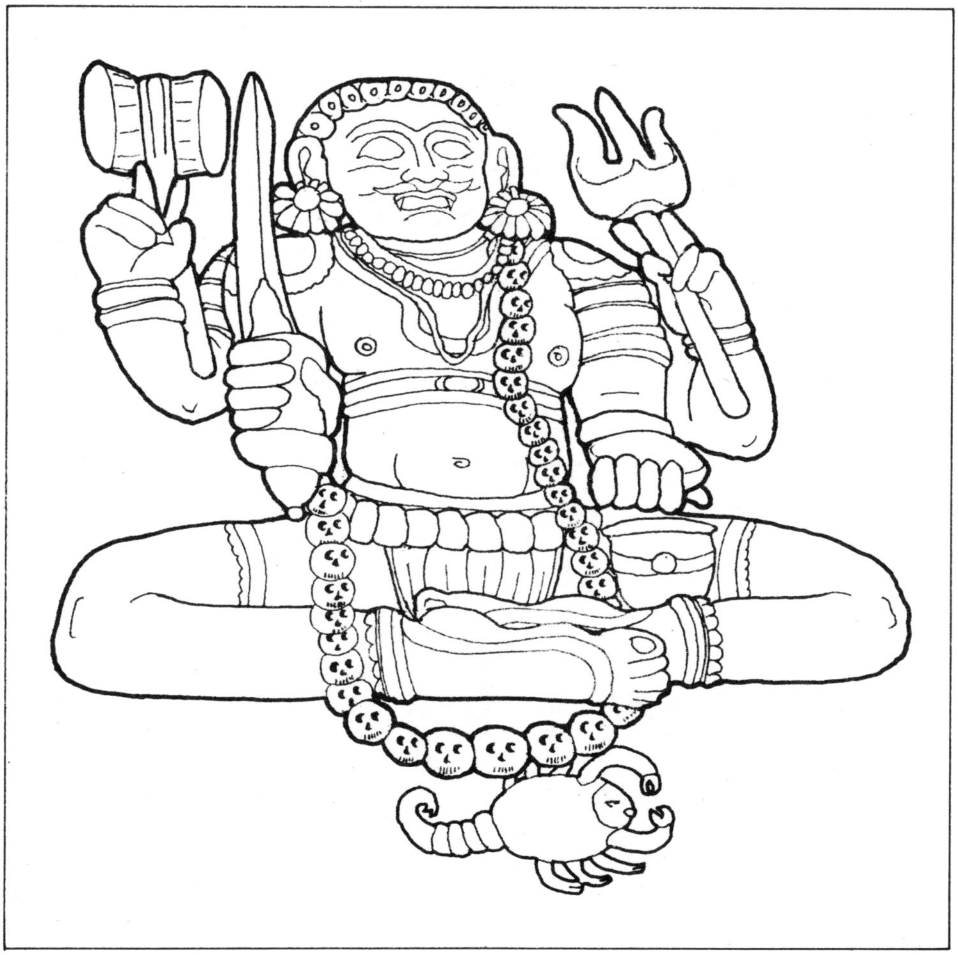

17. Seated Bhairava.

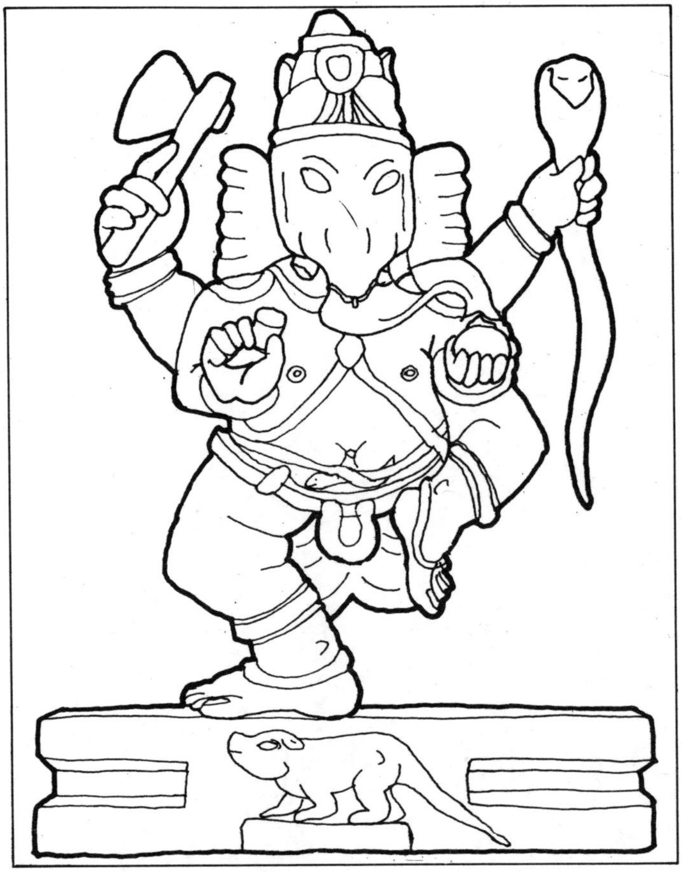

18. Dancing Ganesha.

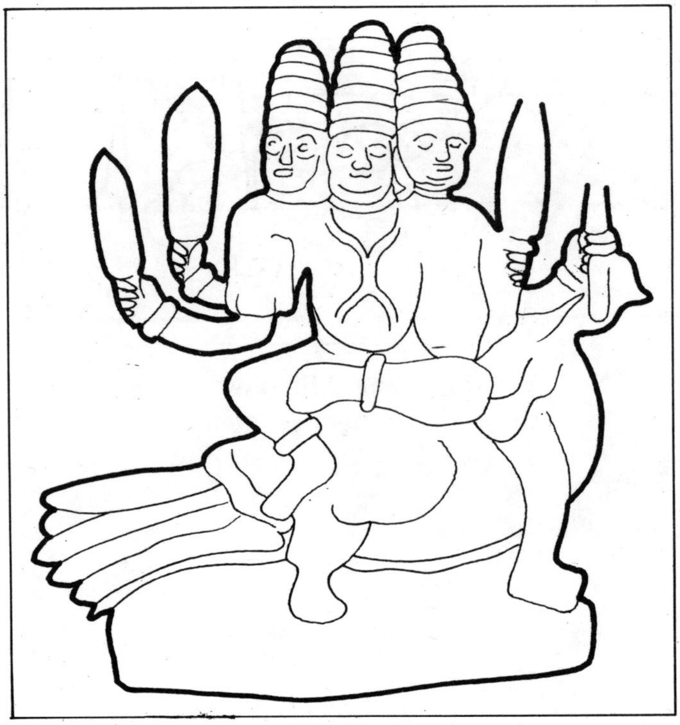

19. Karttikeya.

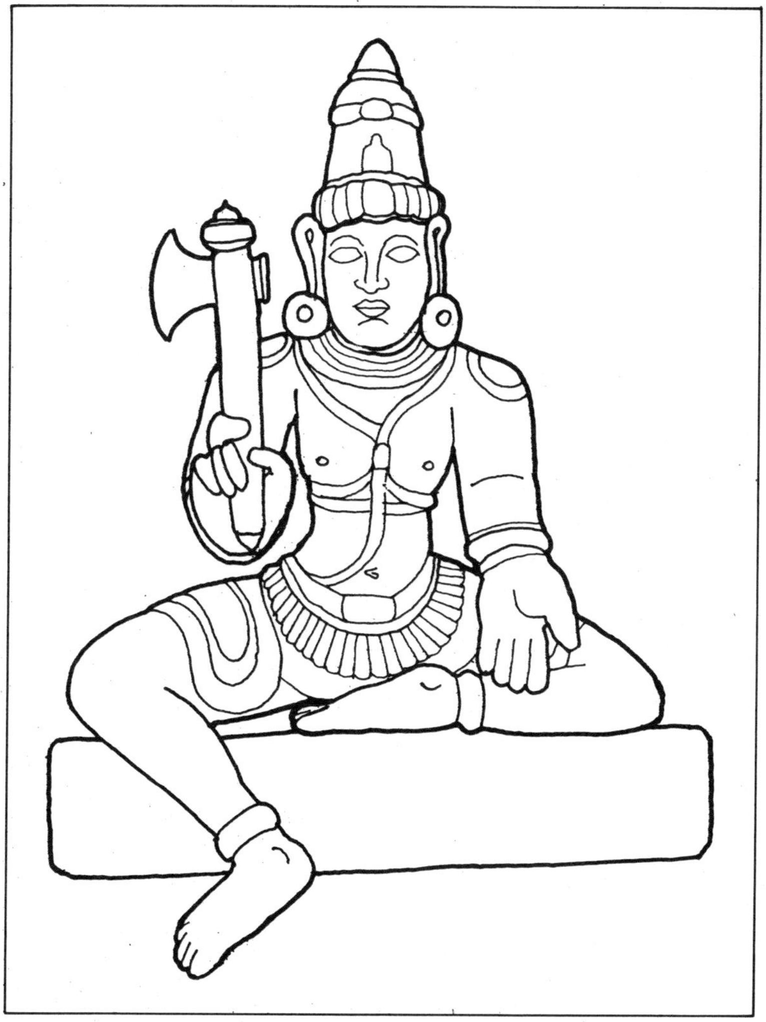

20. Chandikeshvara.

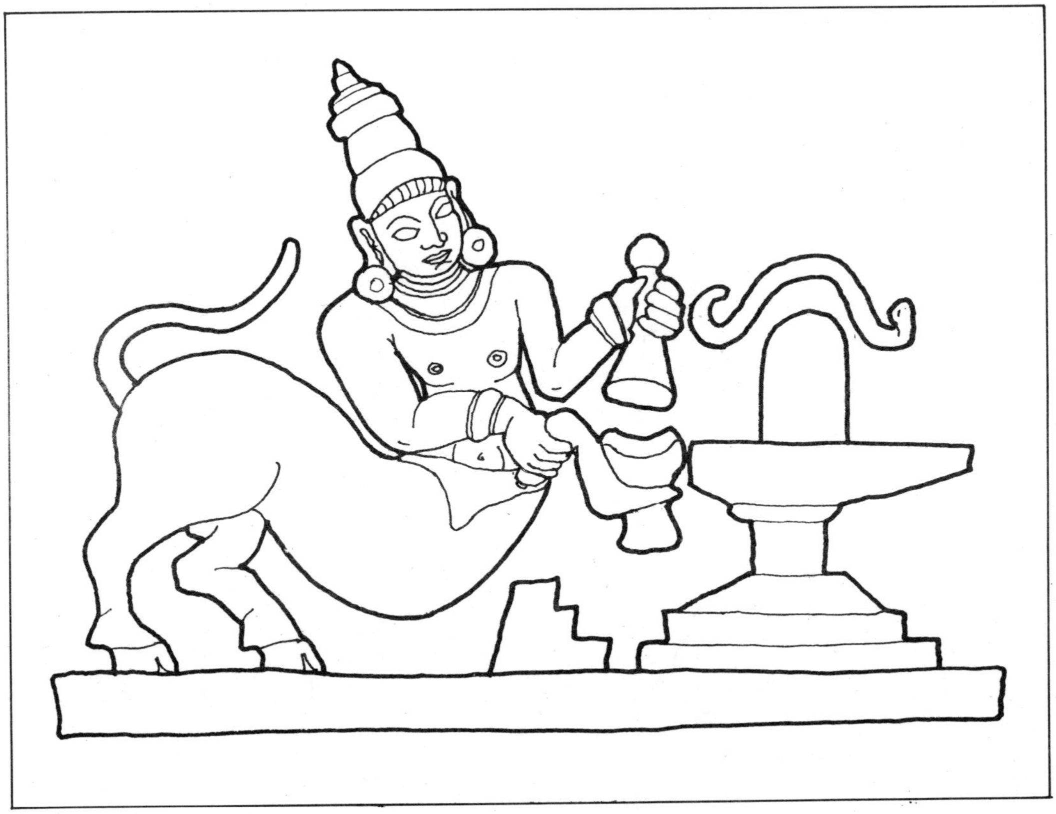

21. Vyaghrapada.

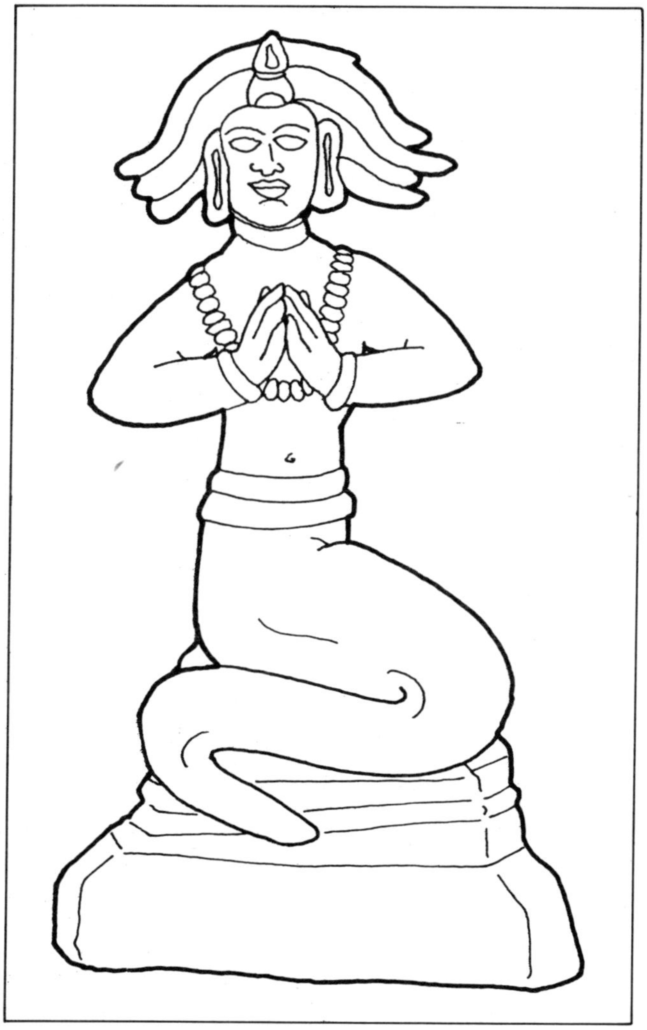

22. Patanjali.

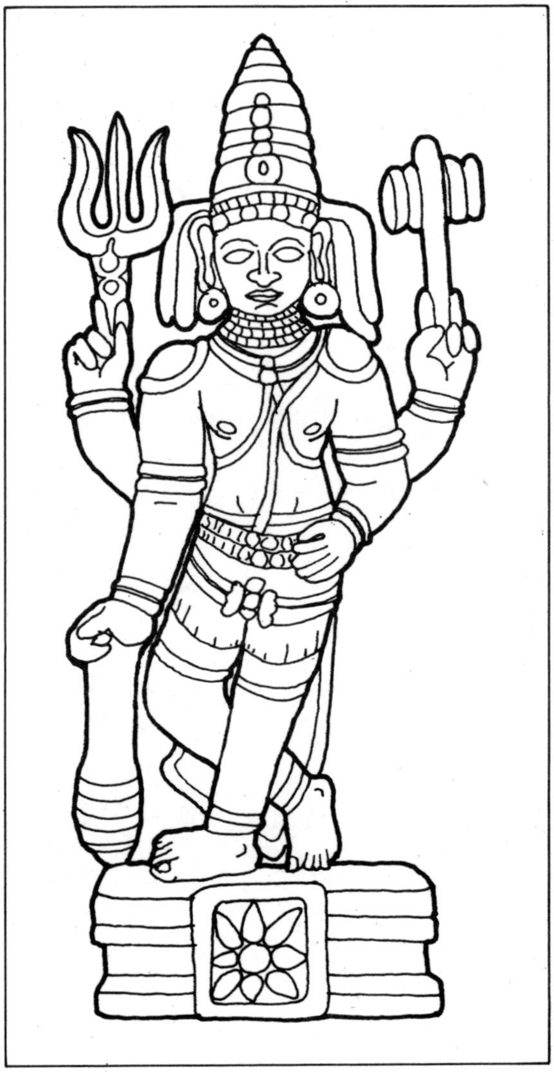

23. Shaiva dvarapala.

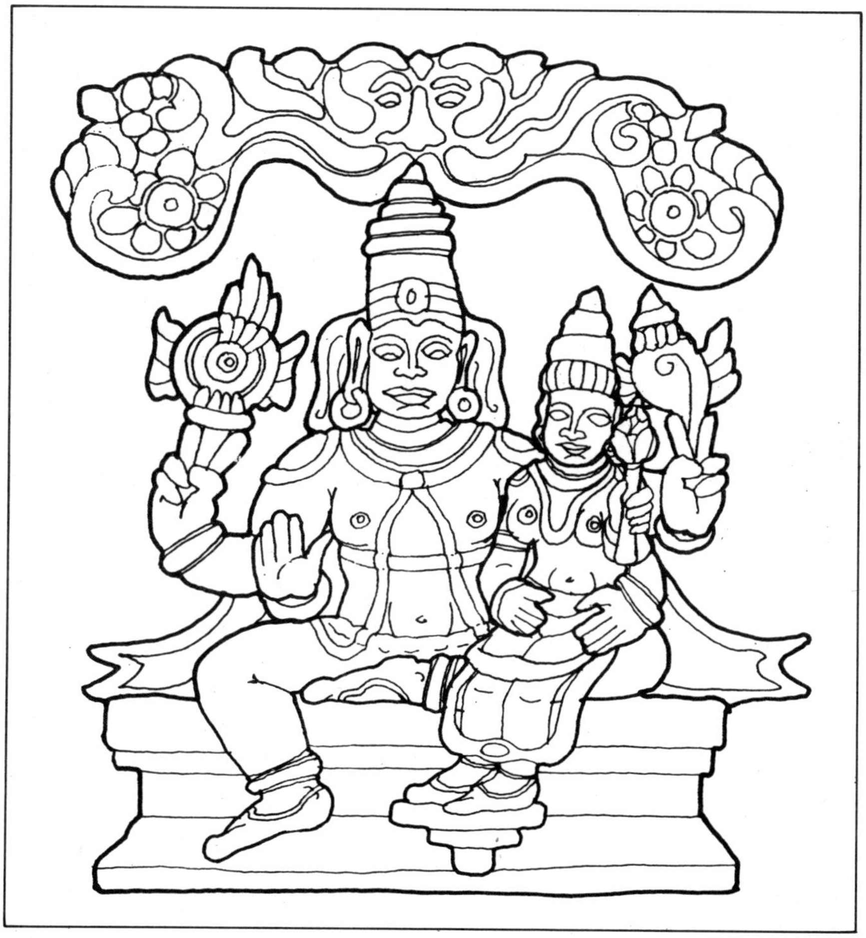

24. Lakshmi-Narasimha.

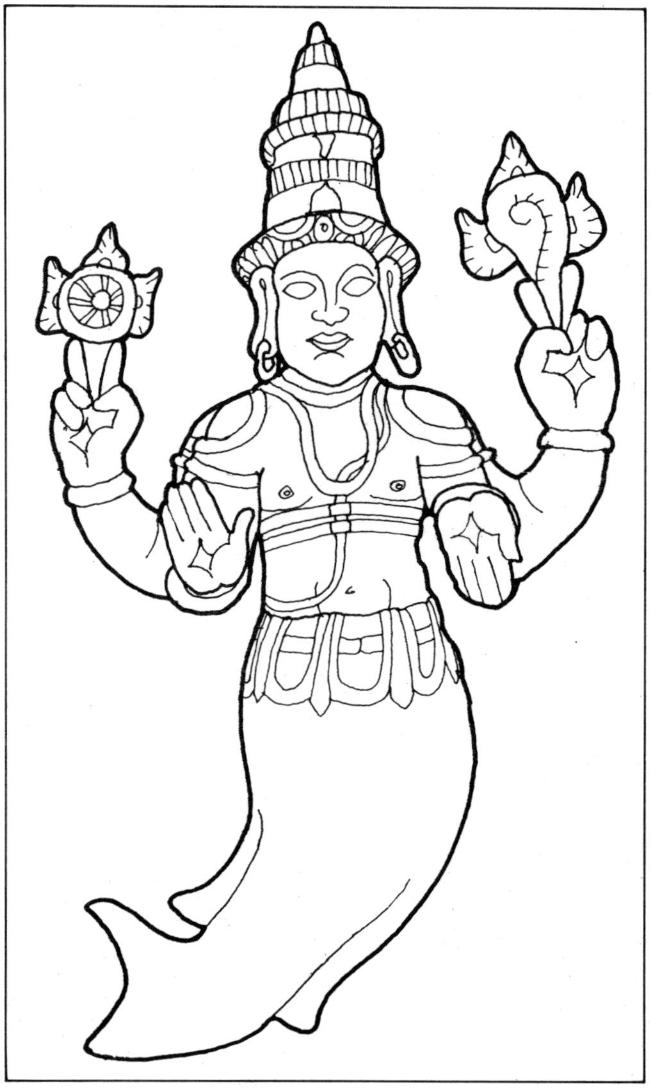

25. Matsya.

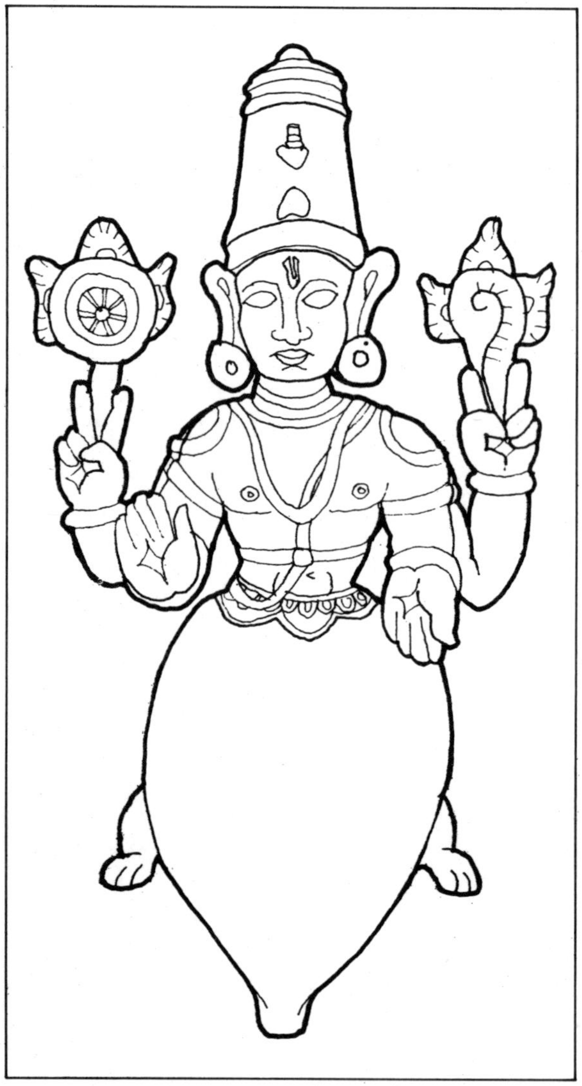

26. Kurma.

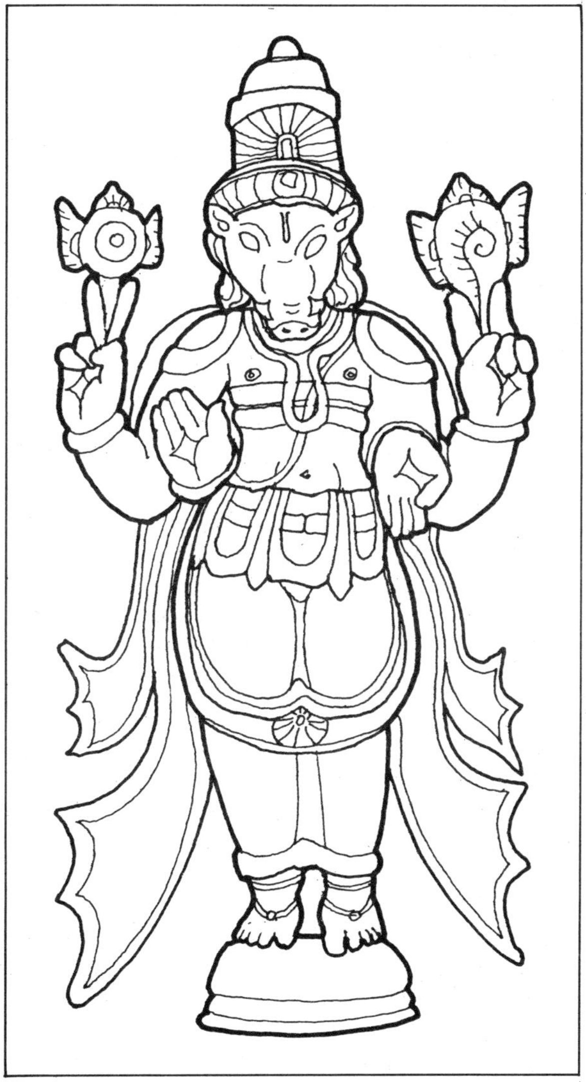

27. Varaha.

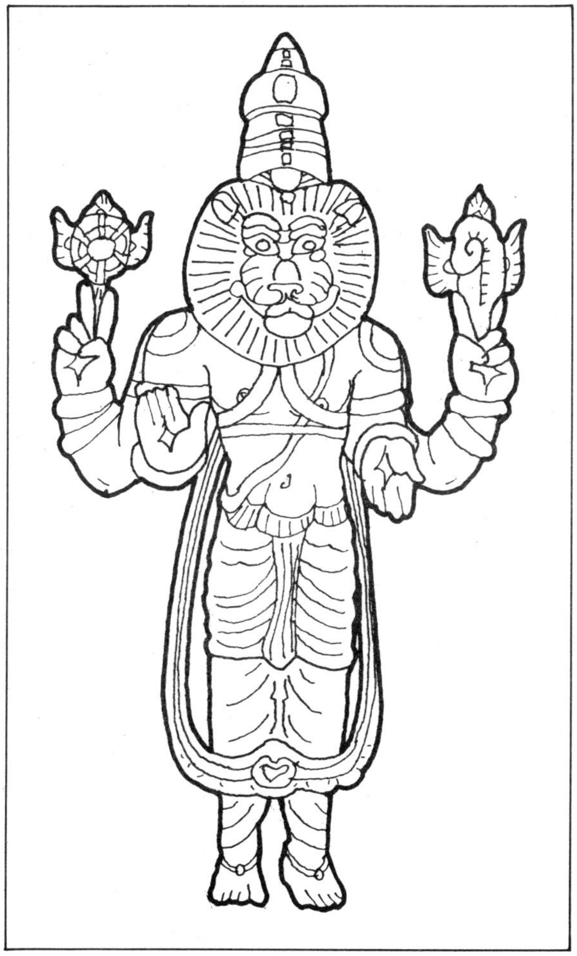

28. Narasimha.

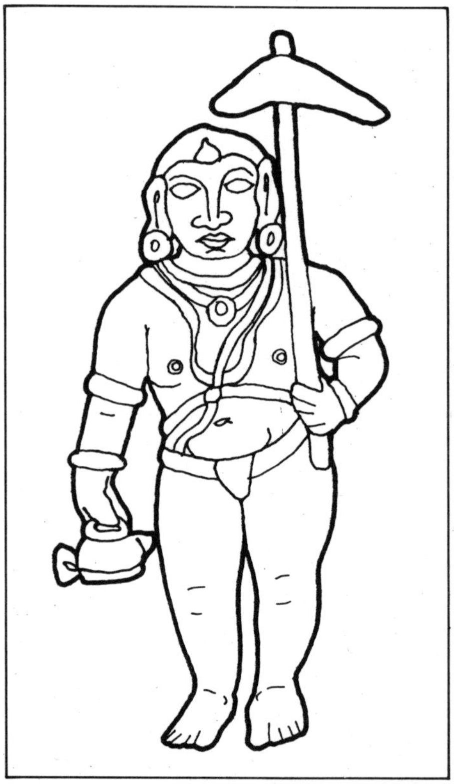

29. Vamana.

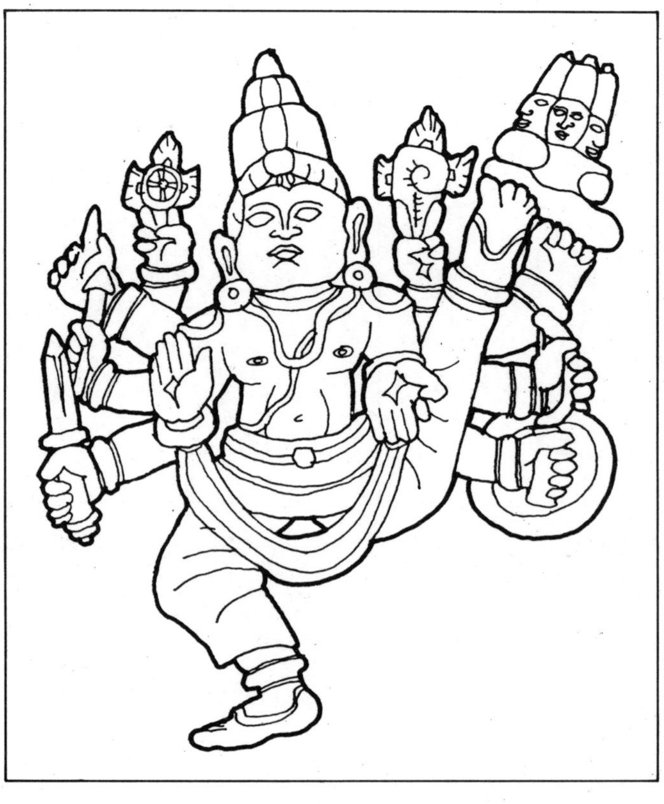

30. Trivikrama.

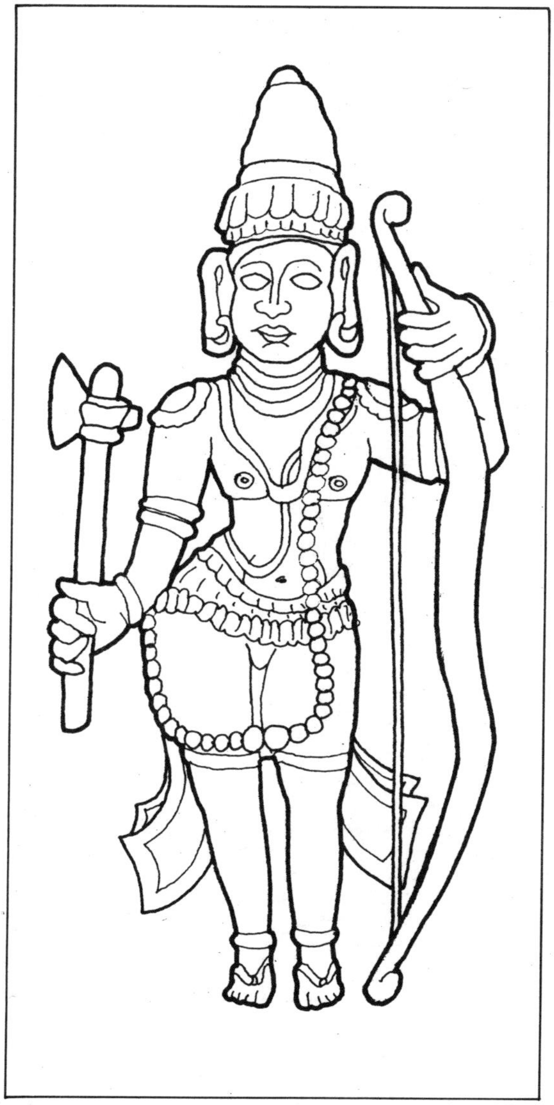

31. Parashurama.

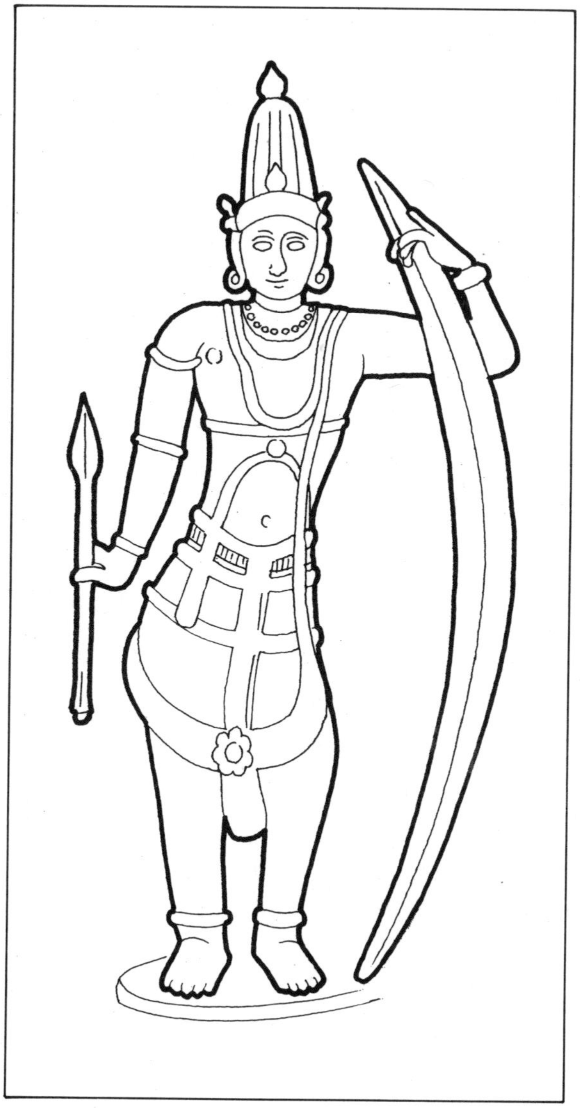

32. Ramachandra.

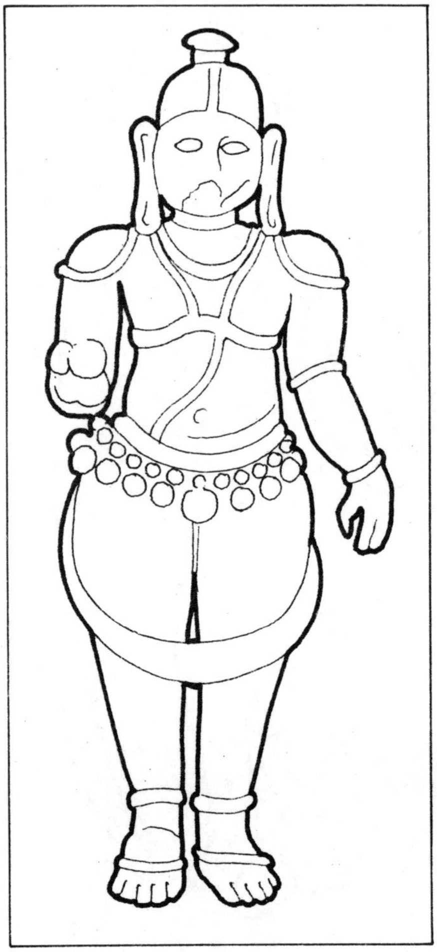

33. Krishna.

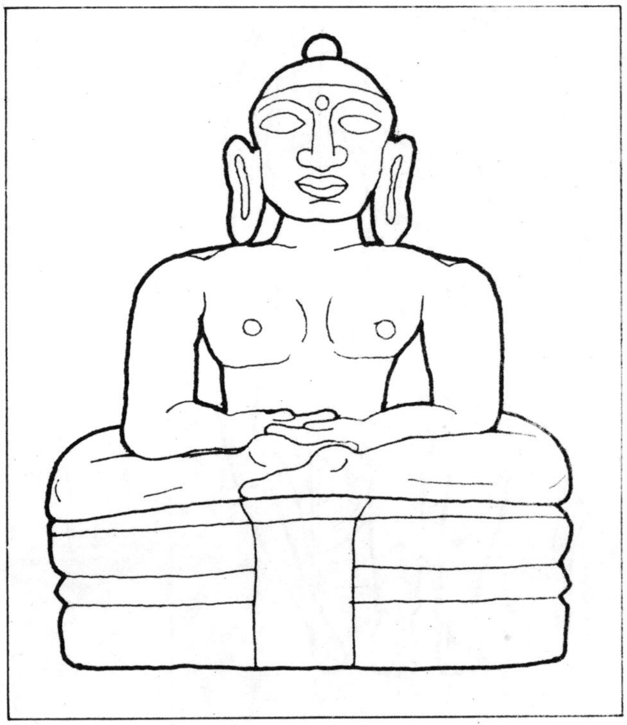

34. Buddha.

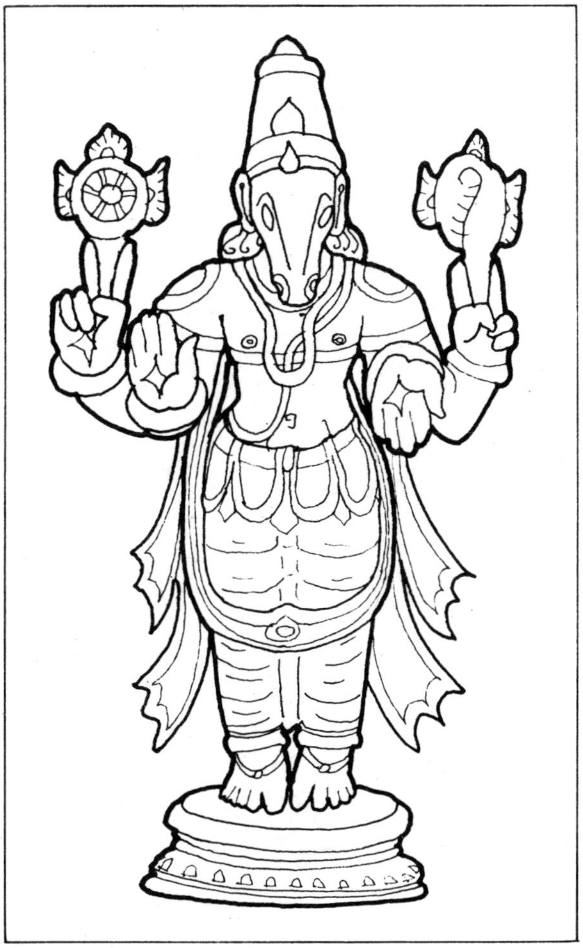

35. Kalki.

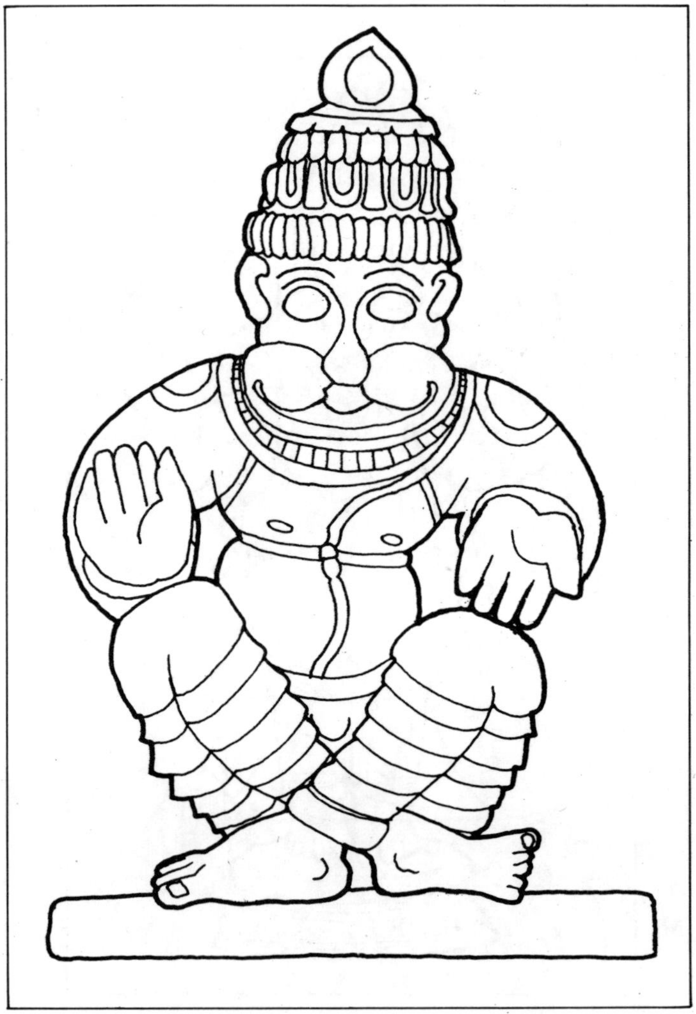

36. Two-armed Yoga-Narasimha.

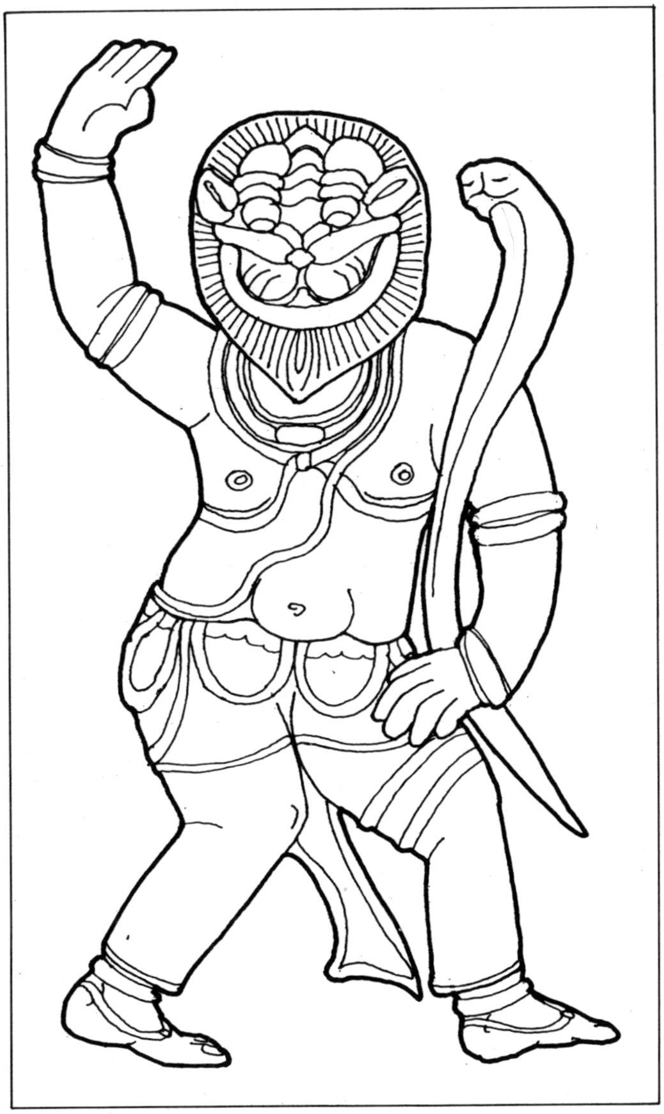

37. Narasimha holding a snake.

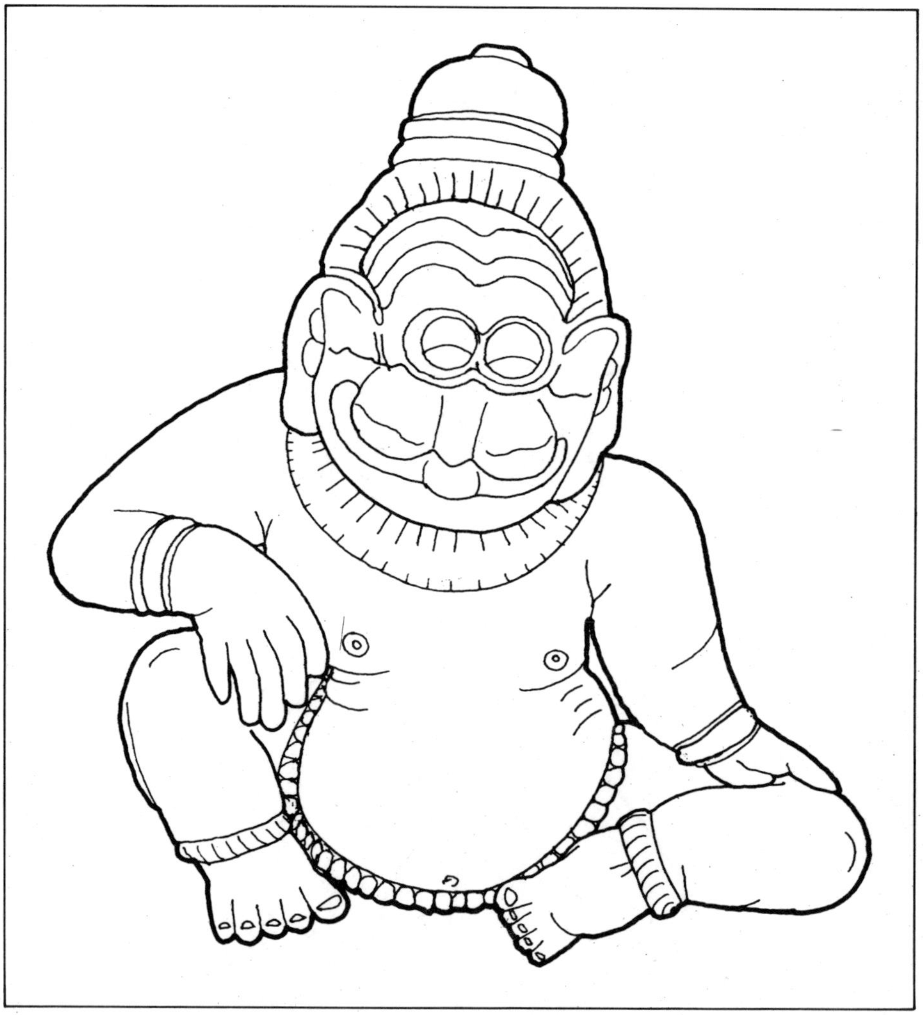

38. Seated Narasimha.

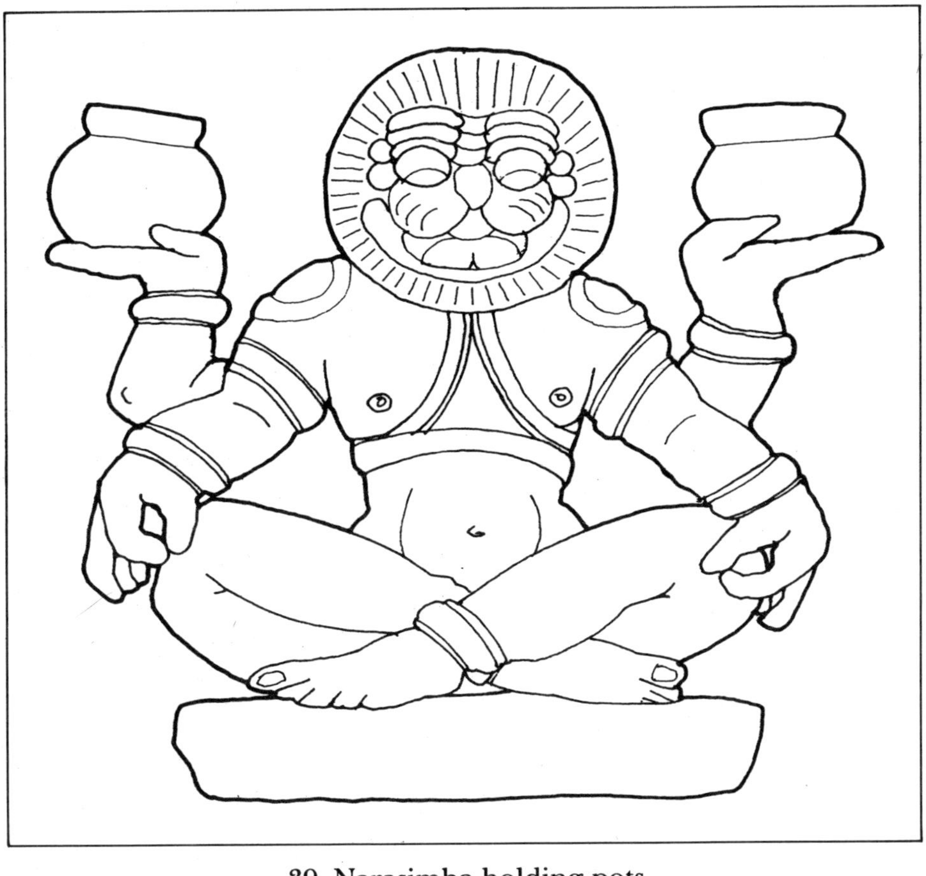

39. Narasimha holding pots.

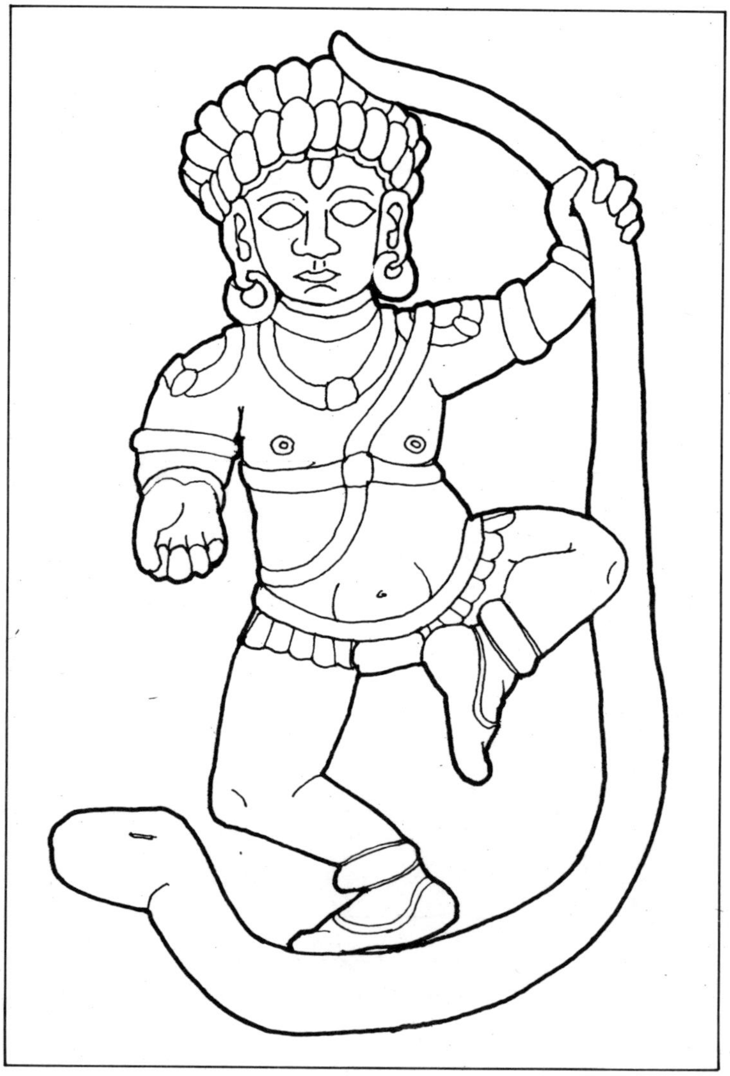

40. Kaliya-mardana Krishna.

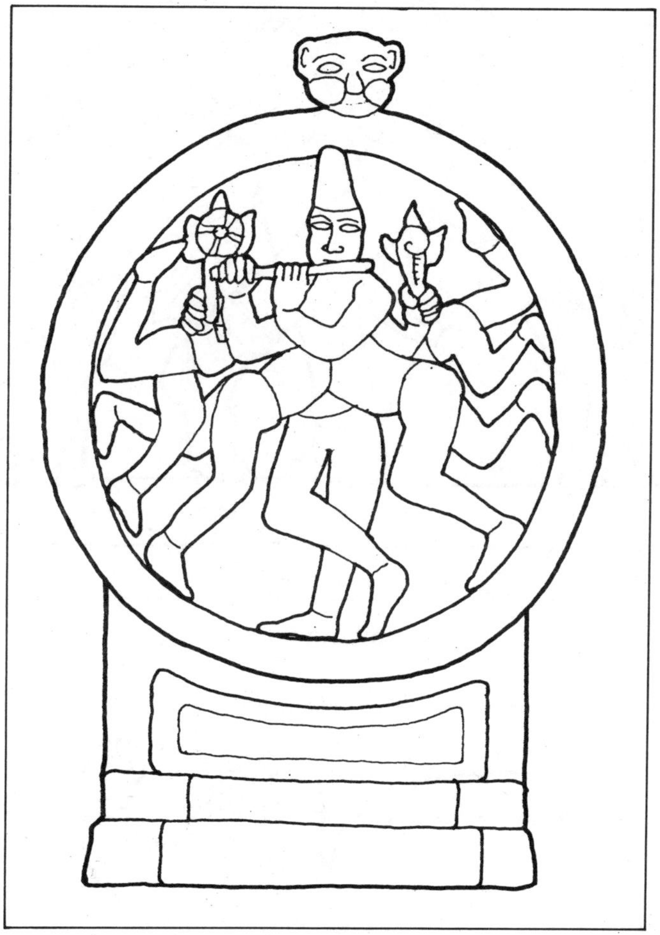

41. Multi-legged Venugopala.

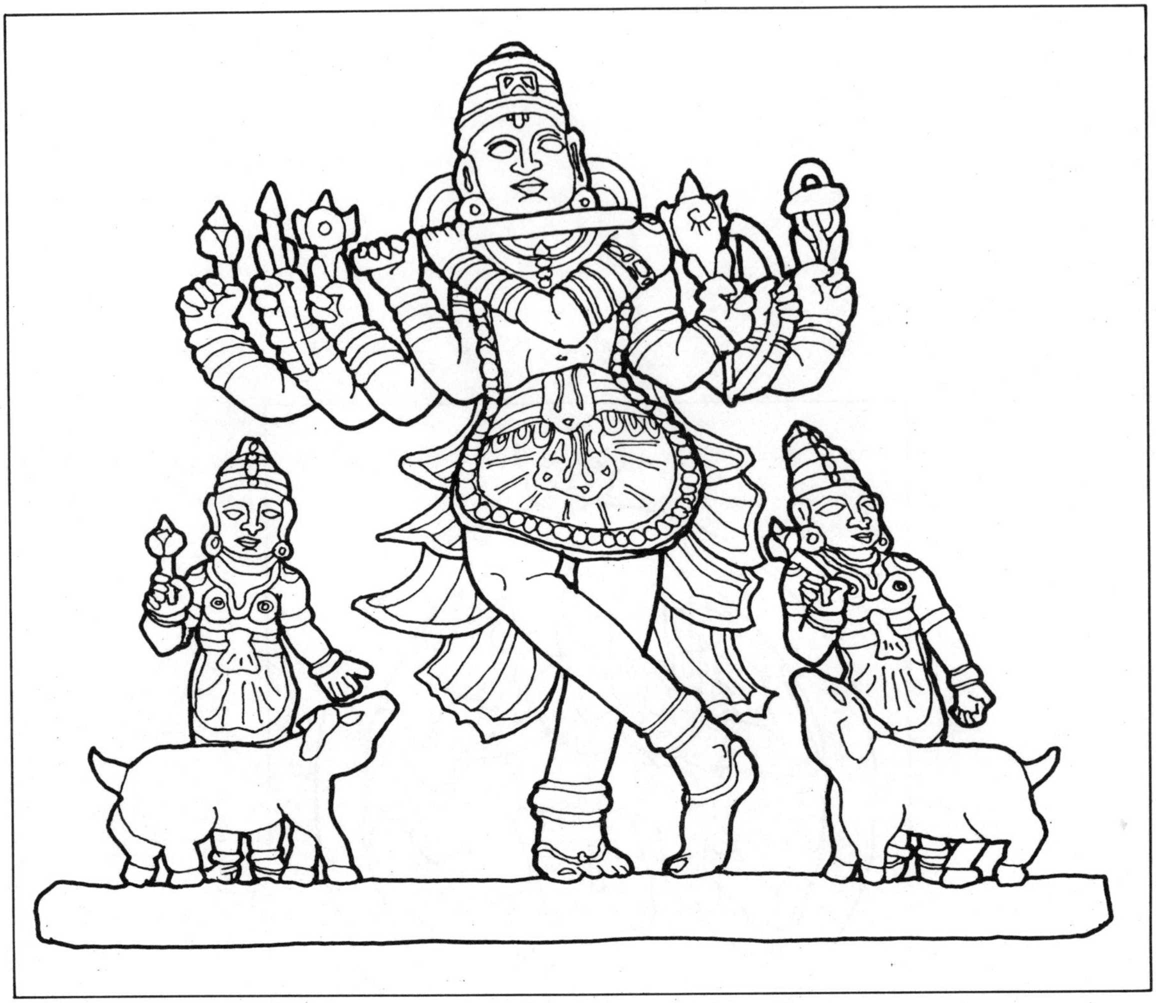

42. Madana-gopala.

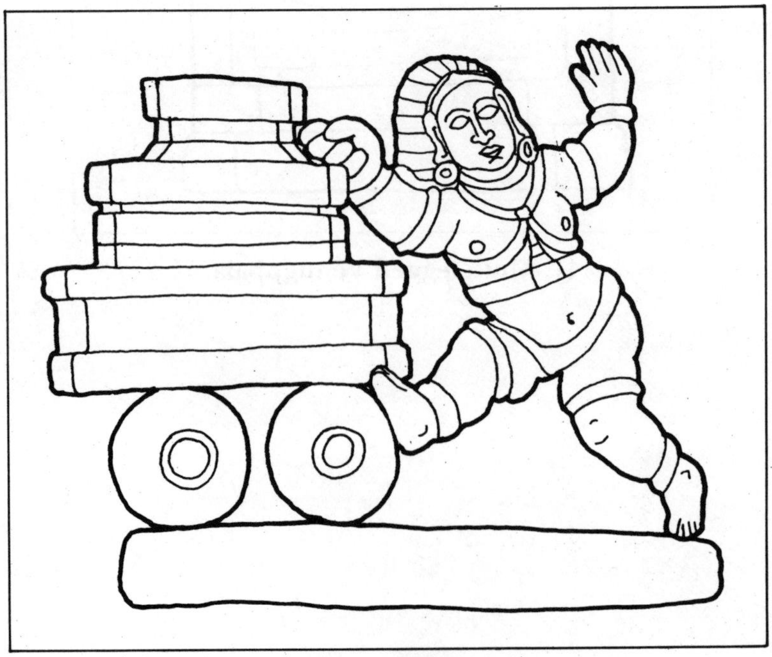

43. Shakata-bhanga.

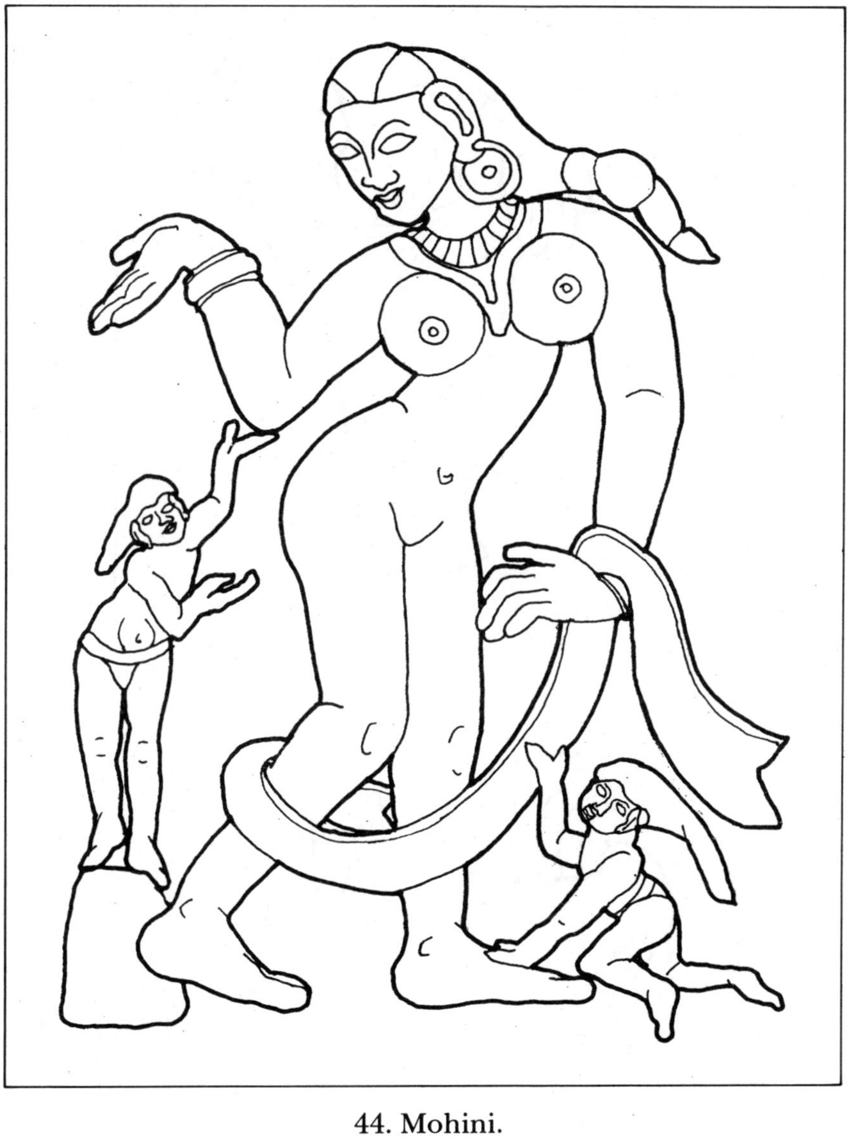

44. Mohini.

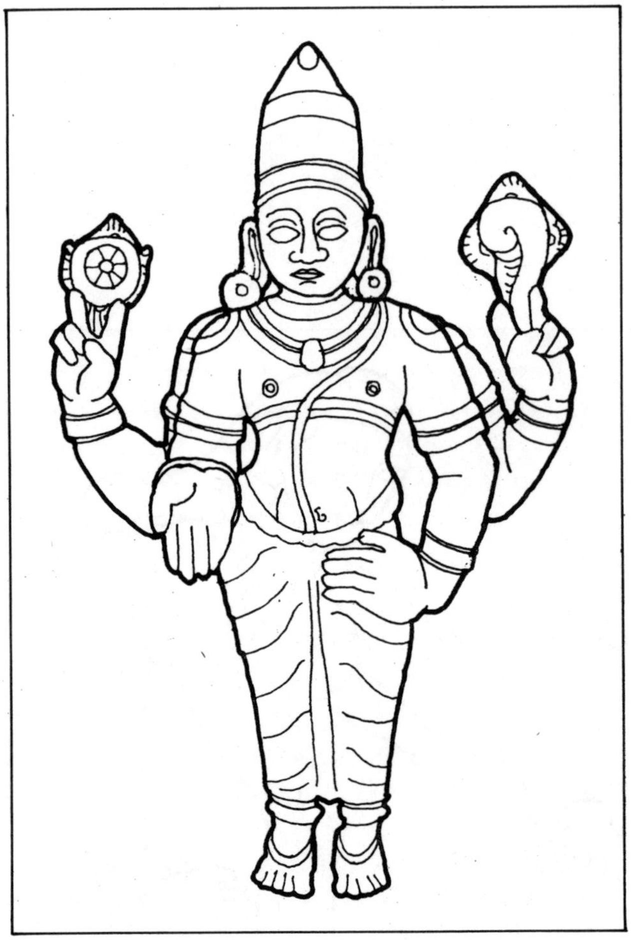

45. Venkateshvara.

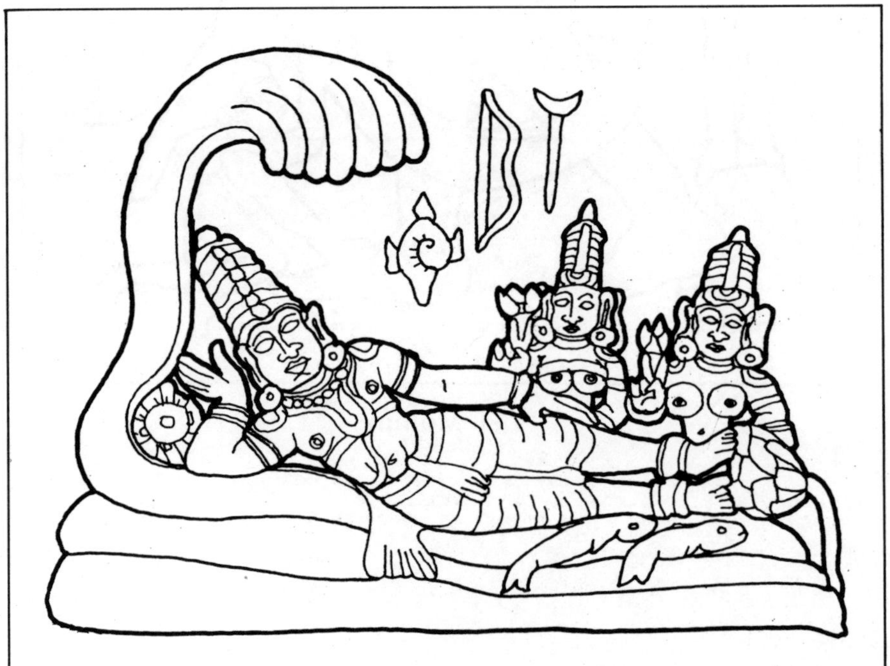

46. Ranganatha.

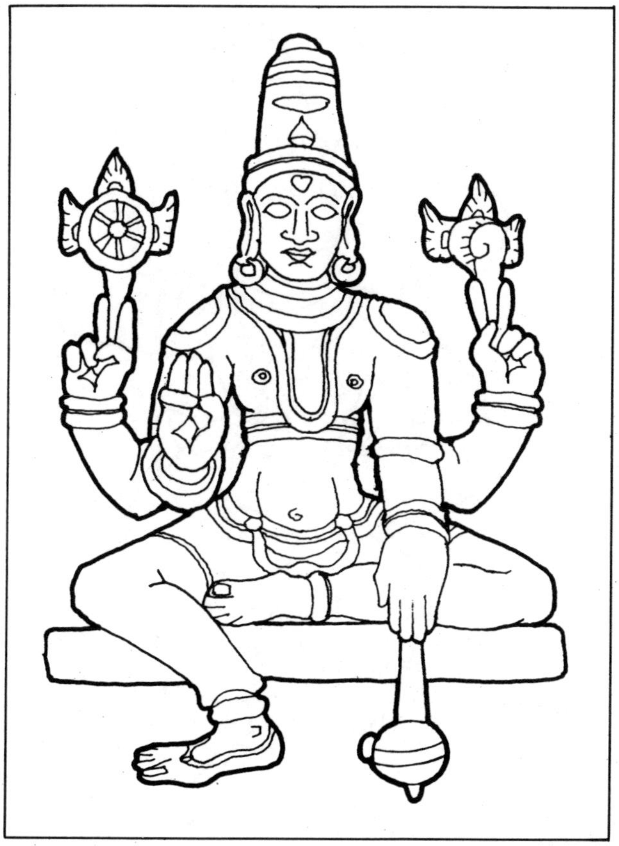

47. Vishvaksena.

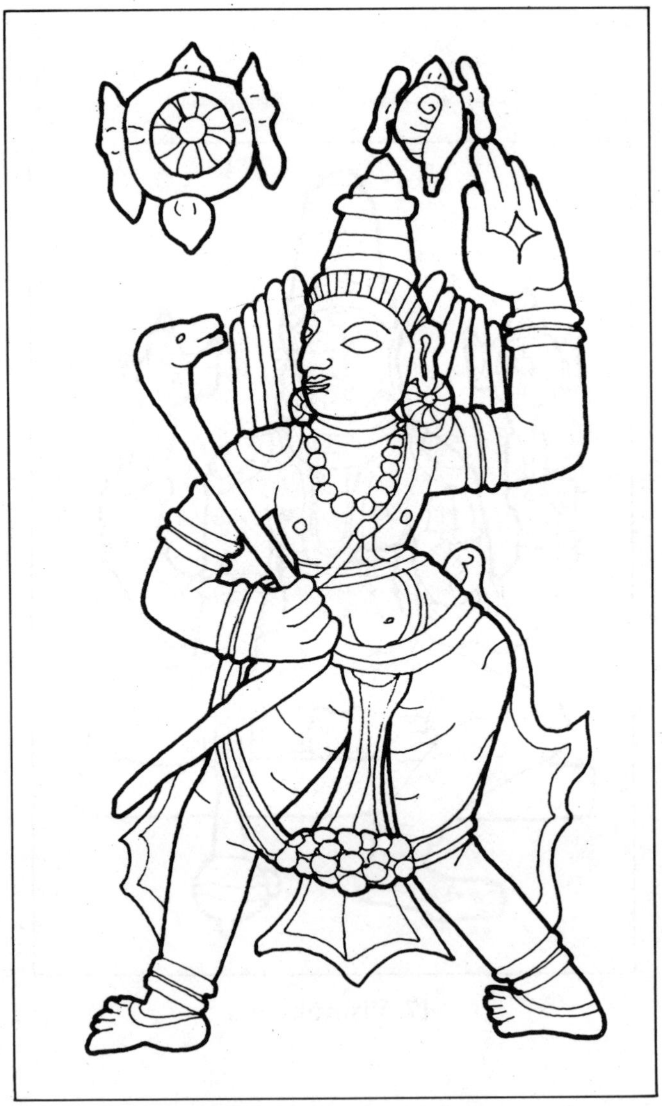

48. Garuda holding a snake.

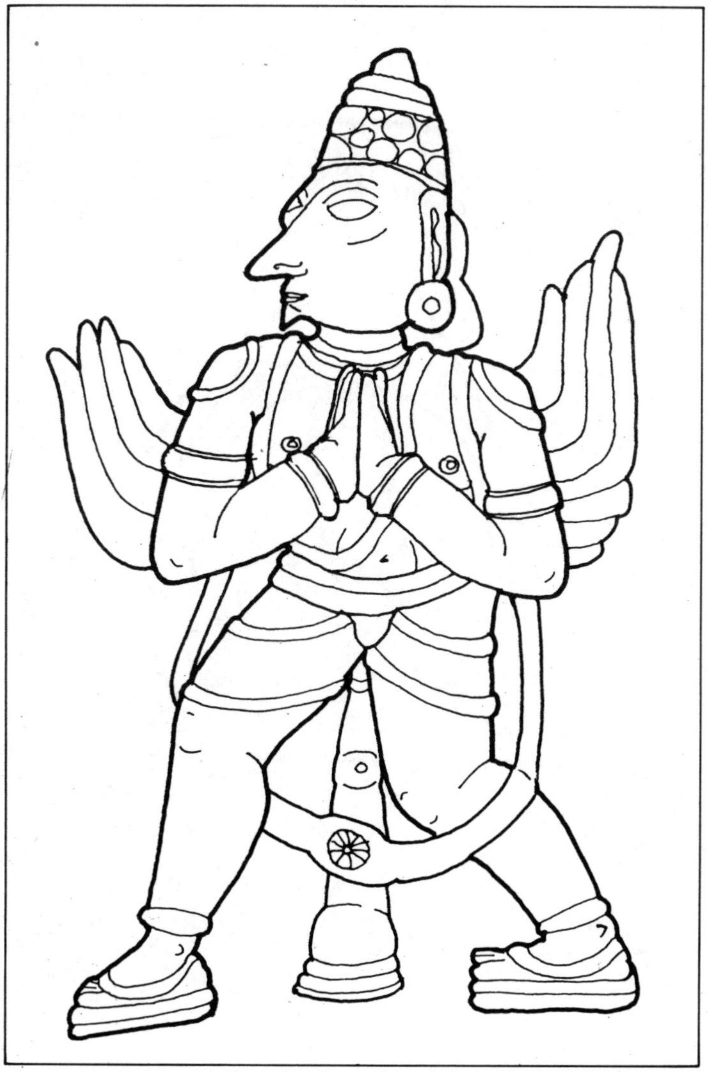

49. Garuda with hands in anjali (Bhakta Garuda).

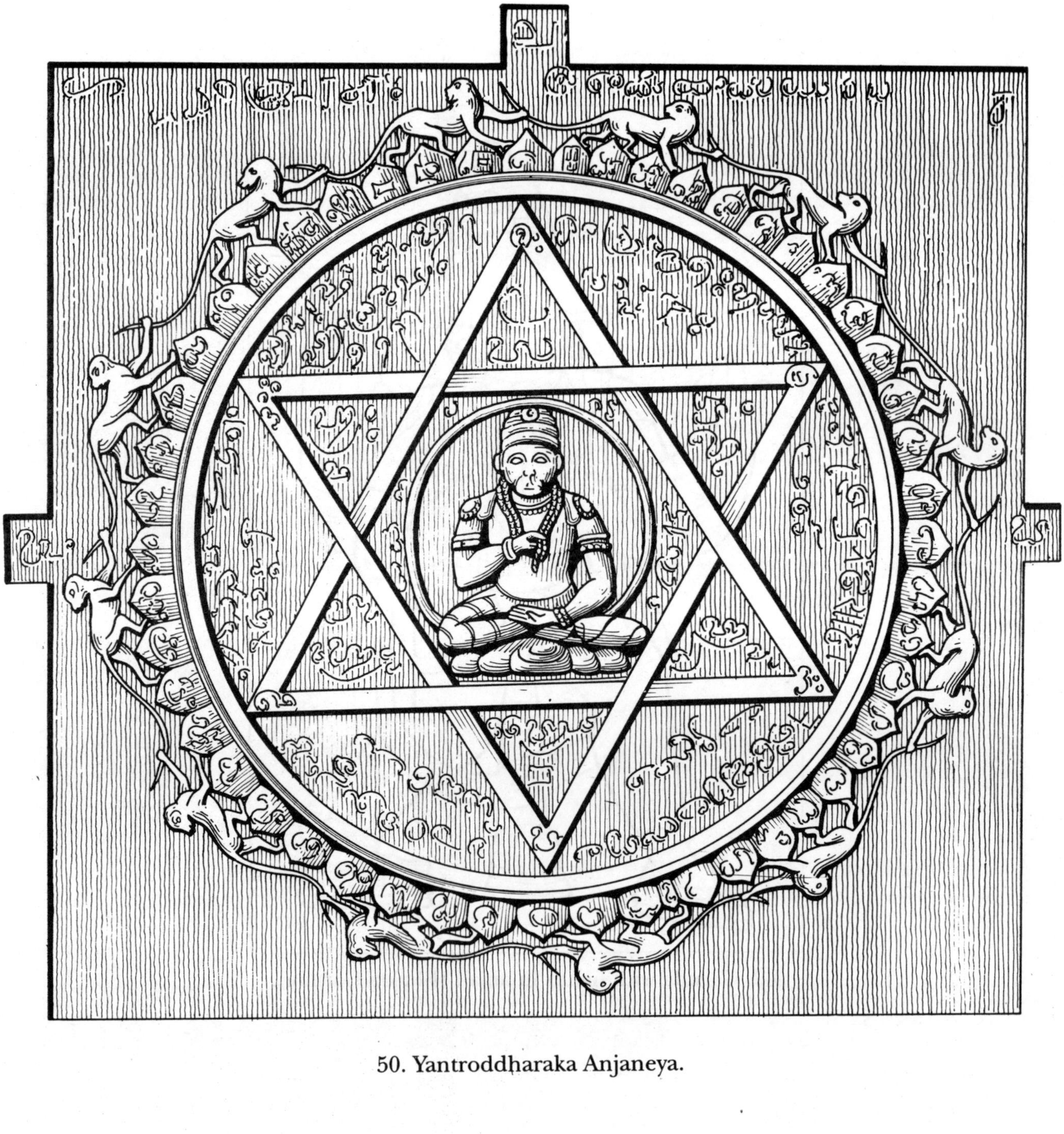

50. Yantroddharaka Anjaneya.

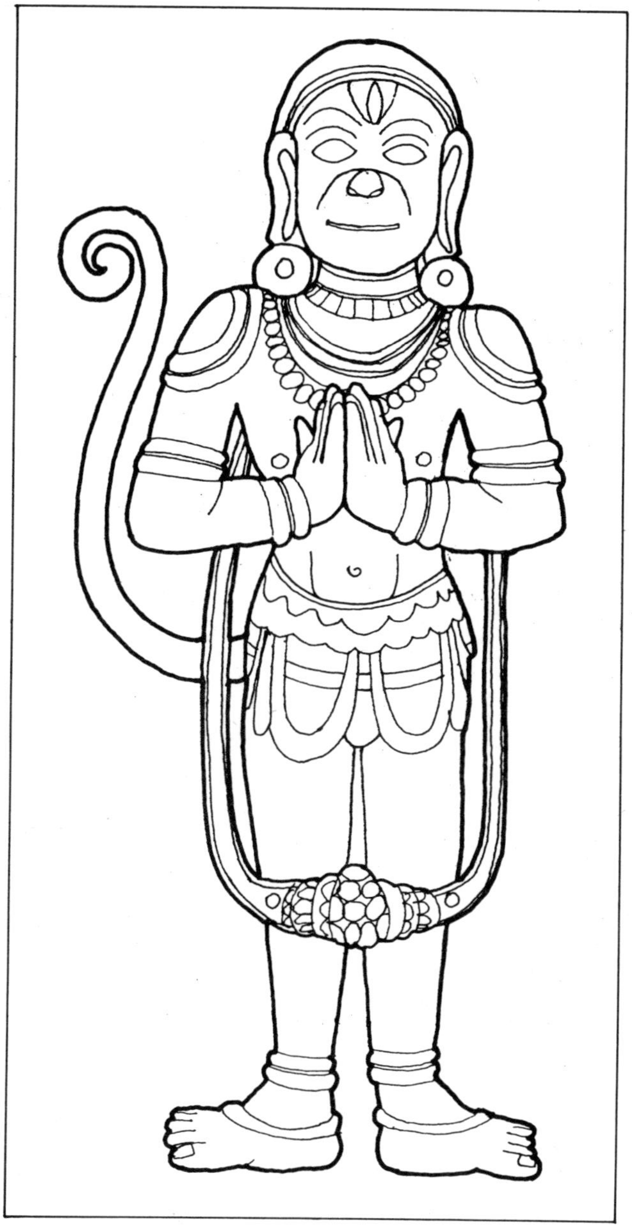

51. Bhakta Anjaneya.

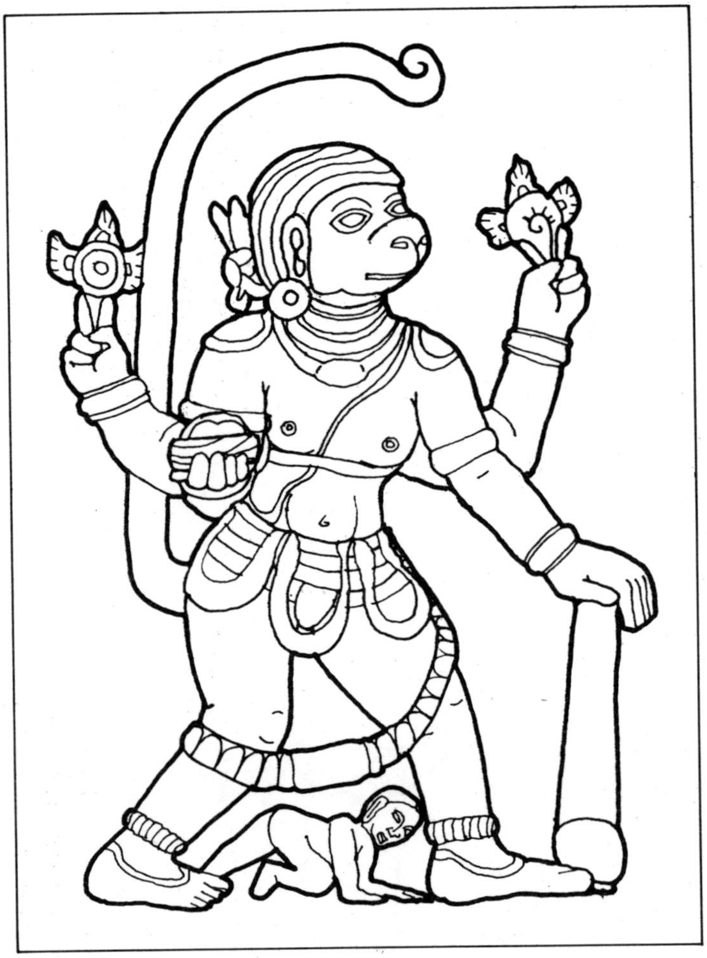

52. Chaturbhuja Hanuman.

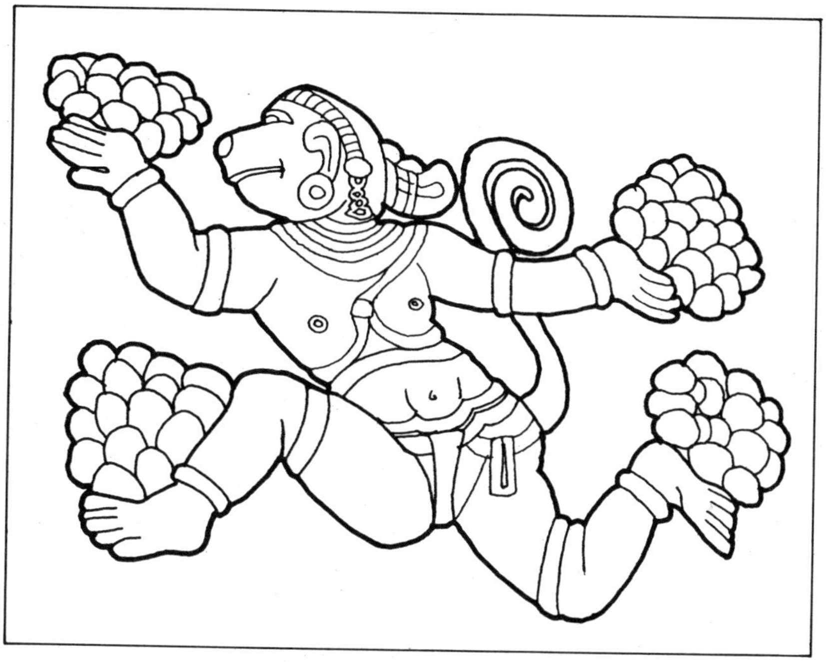

53. Hanuman carrying rocks.

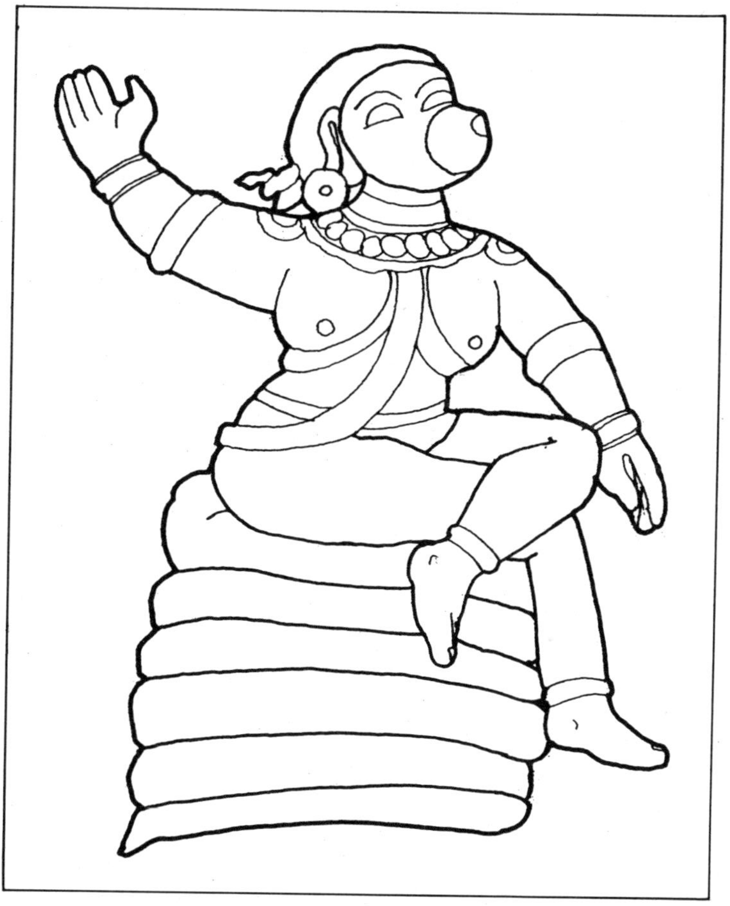

54. Hanuman seated on his coiled tail.

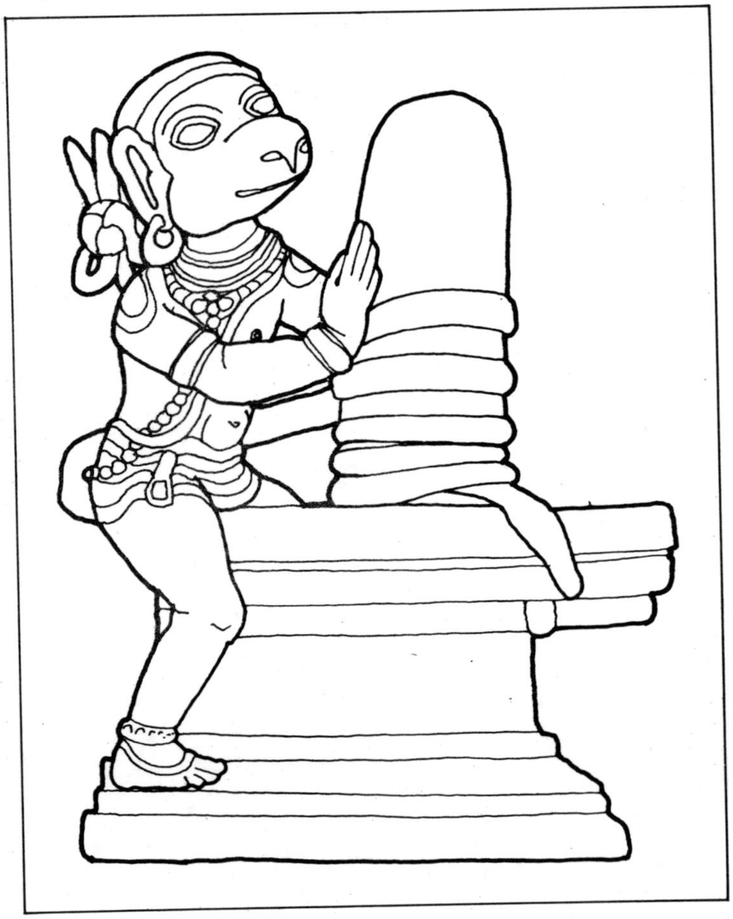

55. Hanuman with his tail coiled around the linga.

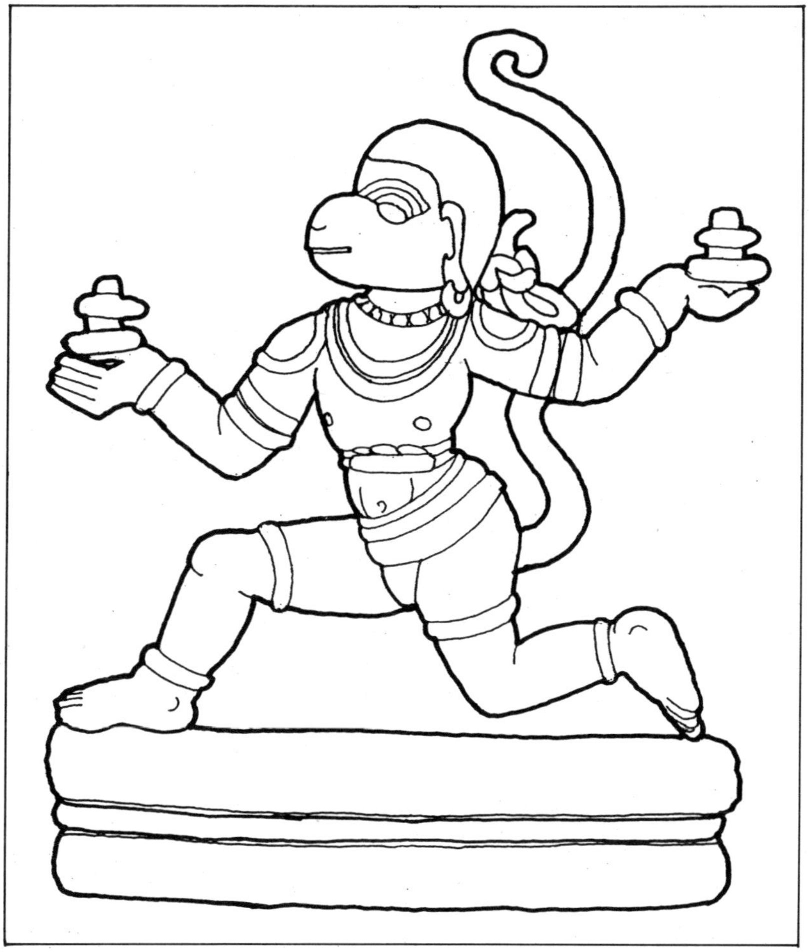

56. Hanuman carrying a linga in each hand.

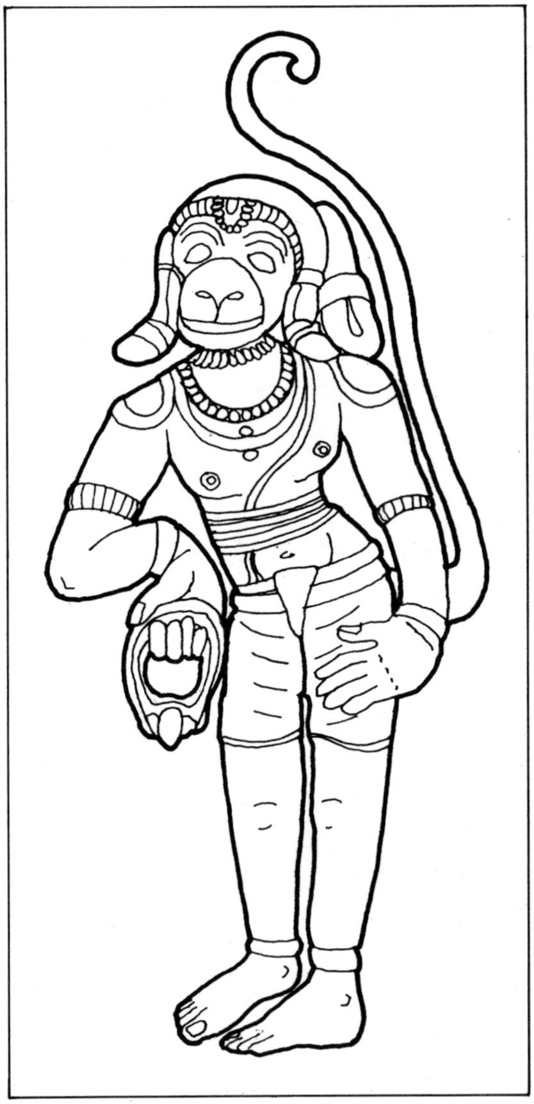

57. Hanuman holding a ring.

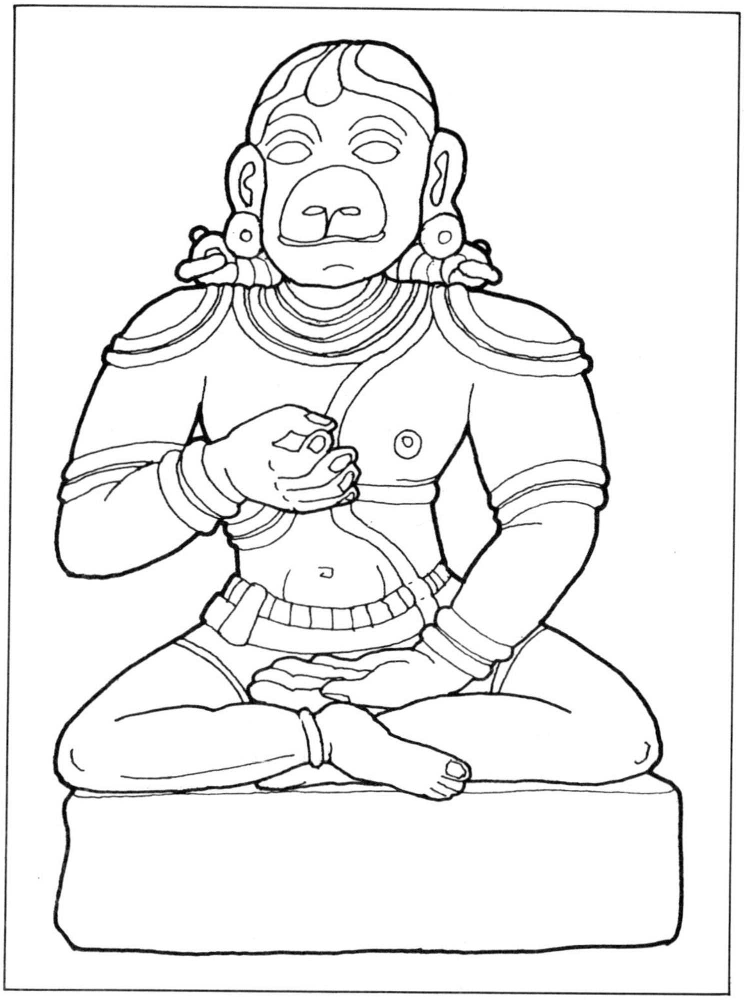

58. Hanuman in meditation.

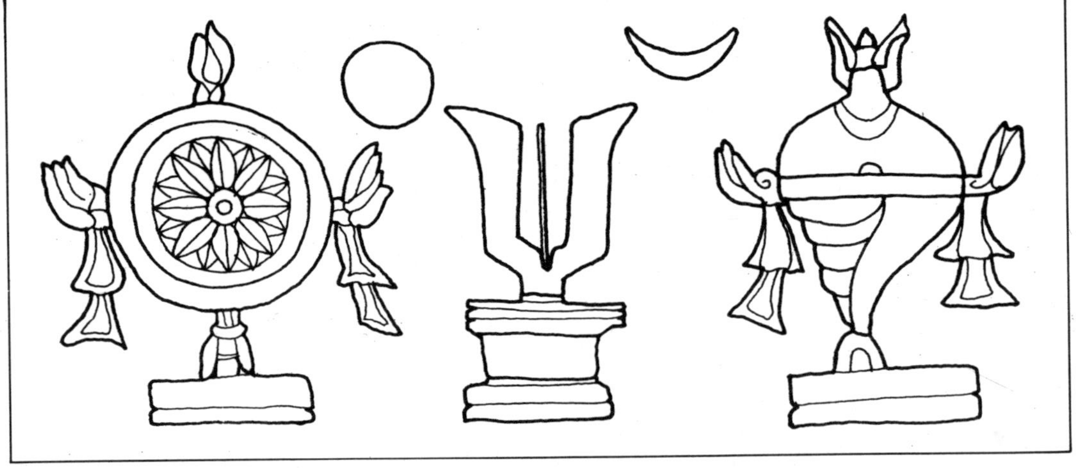

59. Vaishnava emblems.

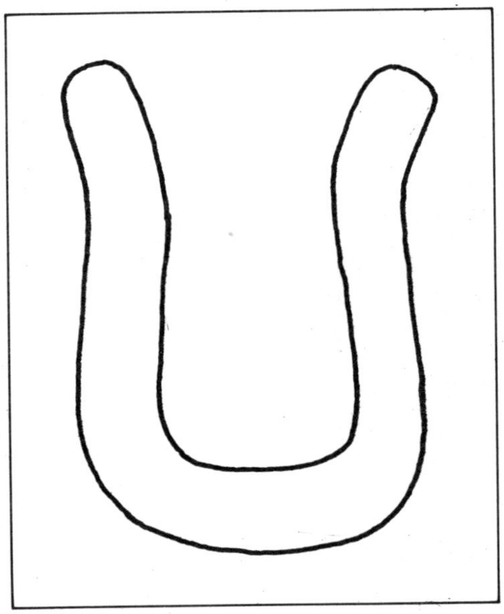

60. Vadagalai namam.

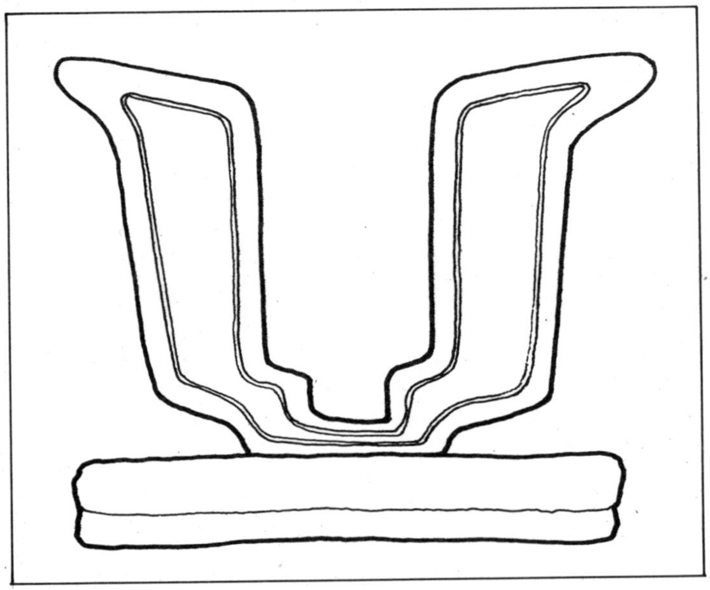

61. Tengalai namam.

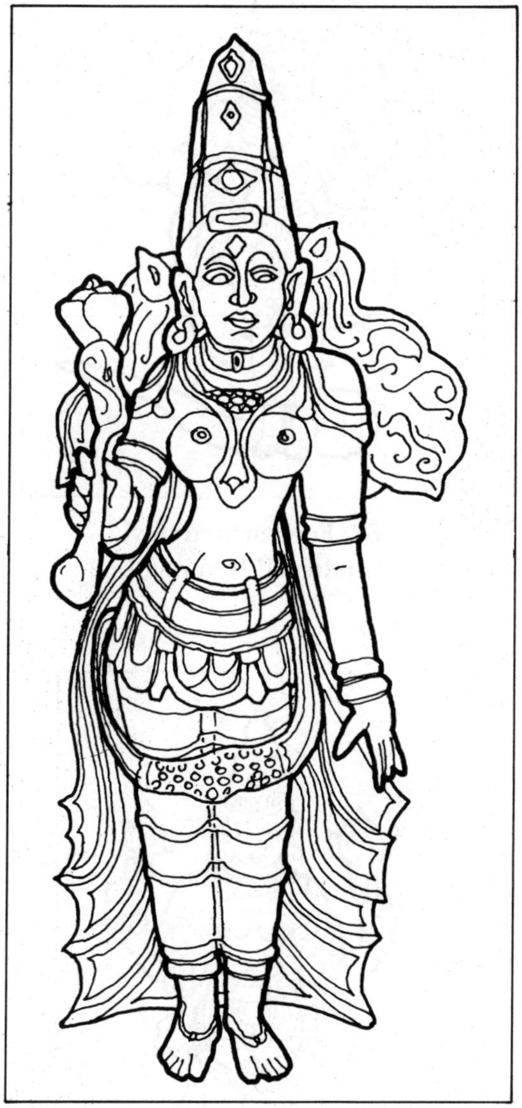

62. Parvati.

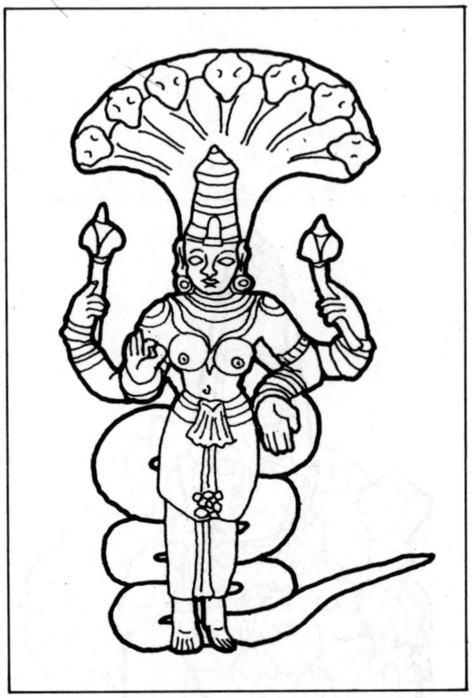

63. Four-armed devi sheltered by a naga.

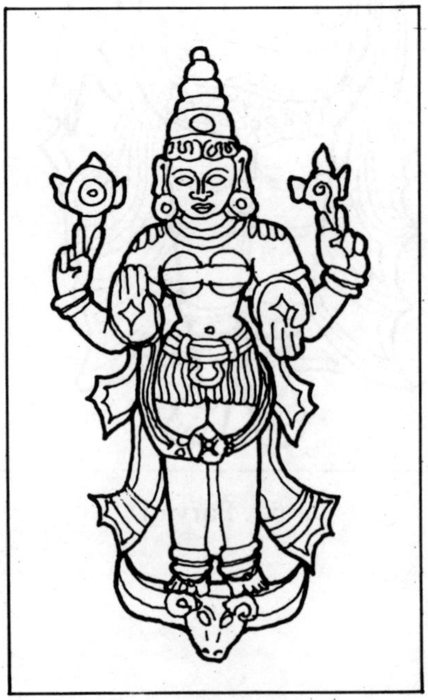

64. Durga.

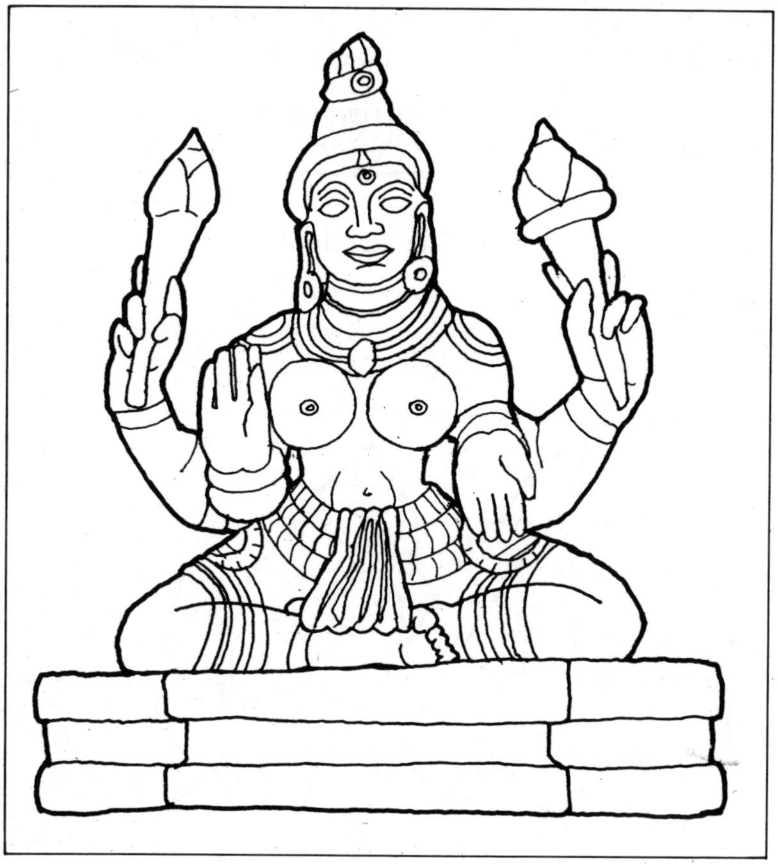

65. Lakshmi.

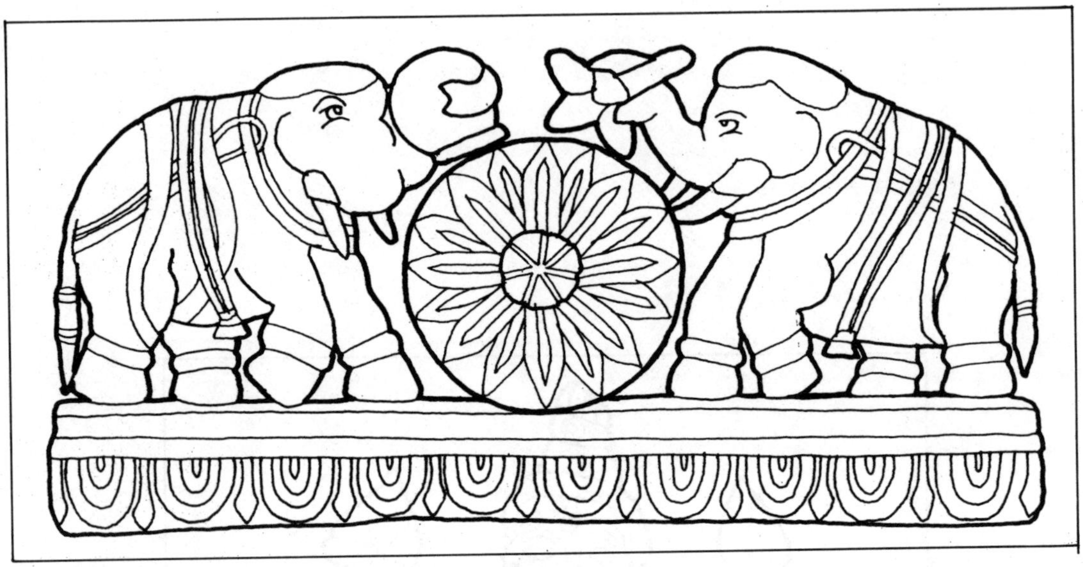

66. Gaja Lakshmi.

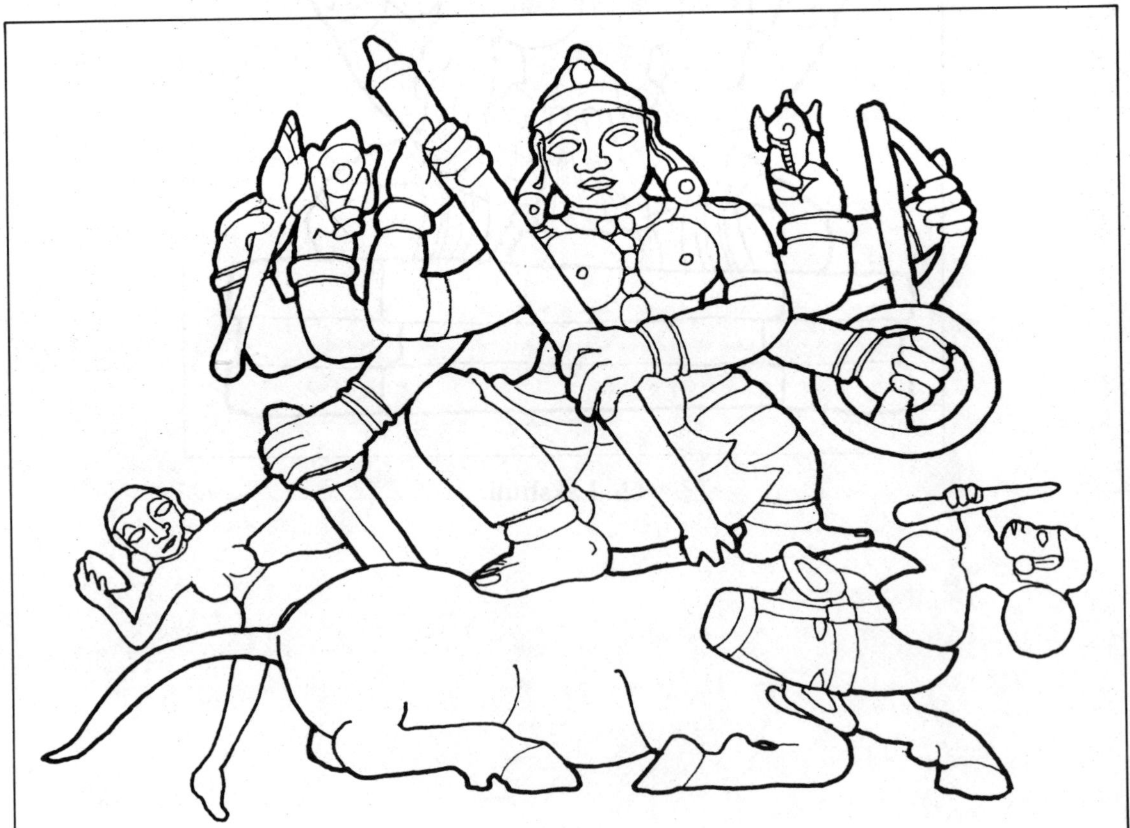

67. Mahishasuramardini.

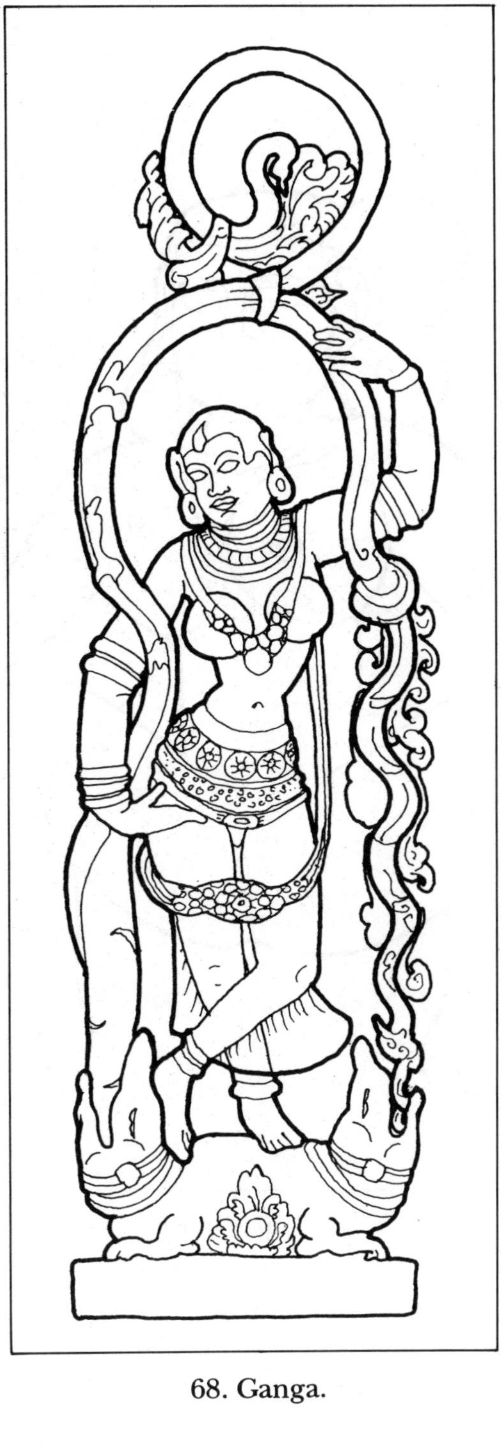

68. Ganga.

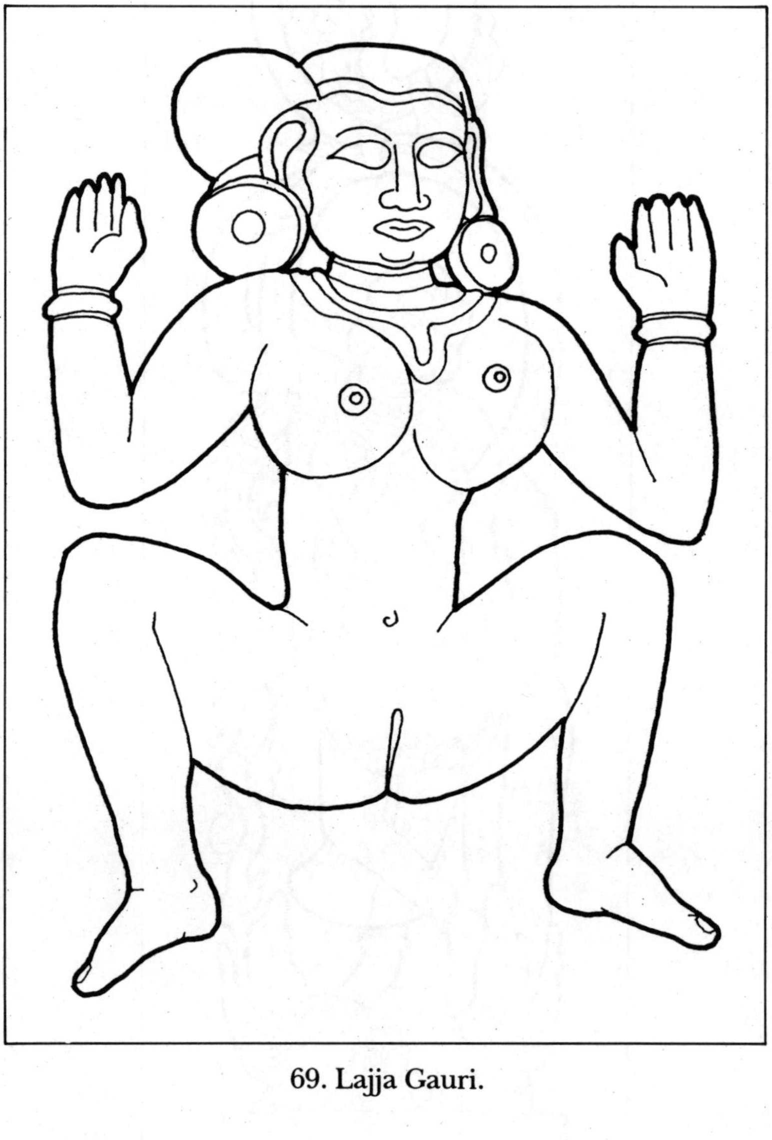

69. Lajja Gauri.

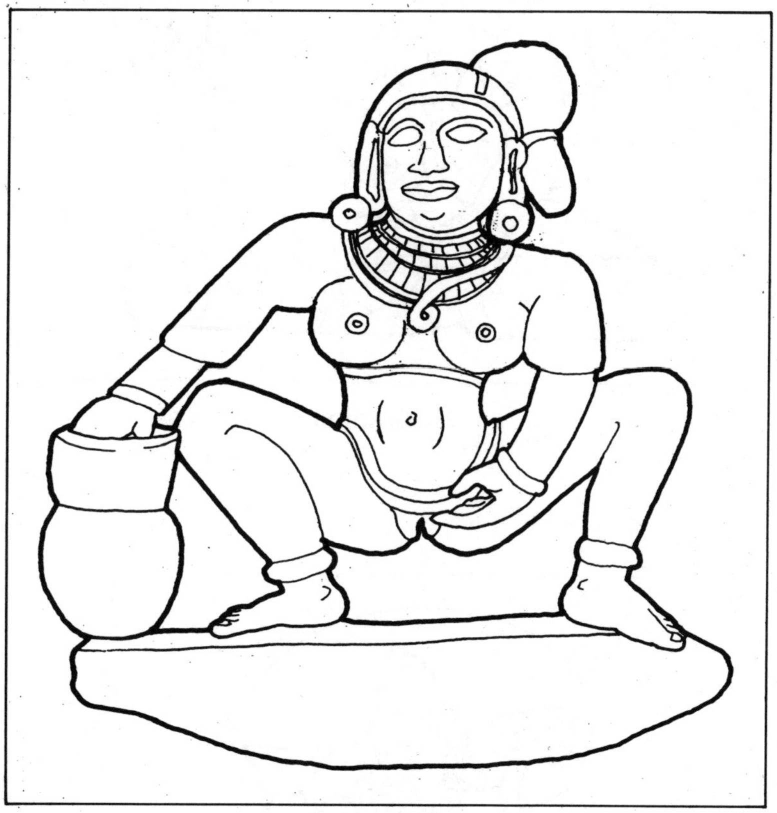

70. Lajja Gauri.

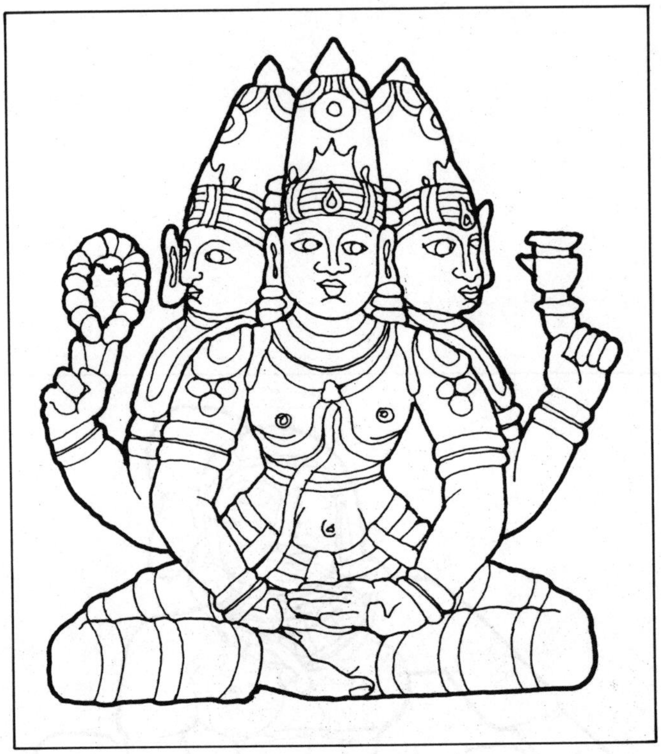

71. Brahma.

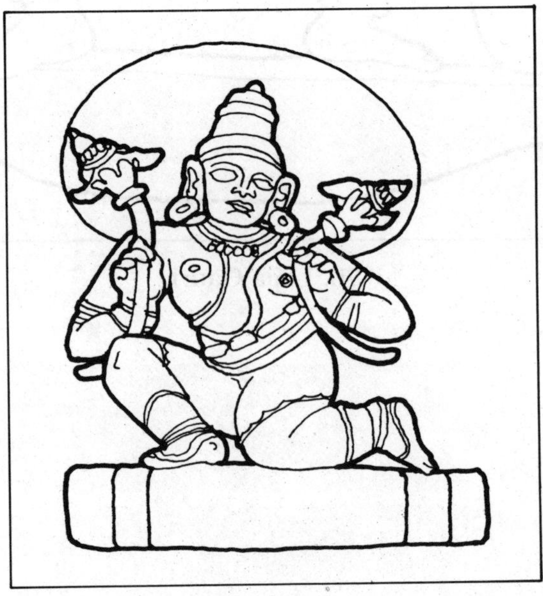

72. Surya.

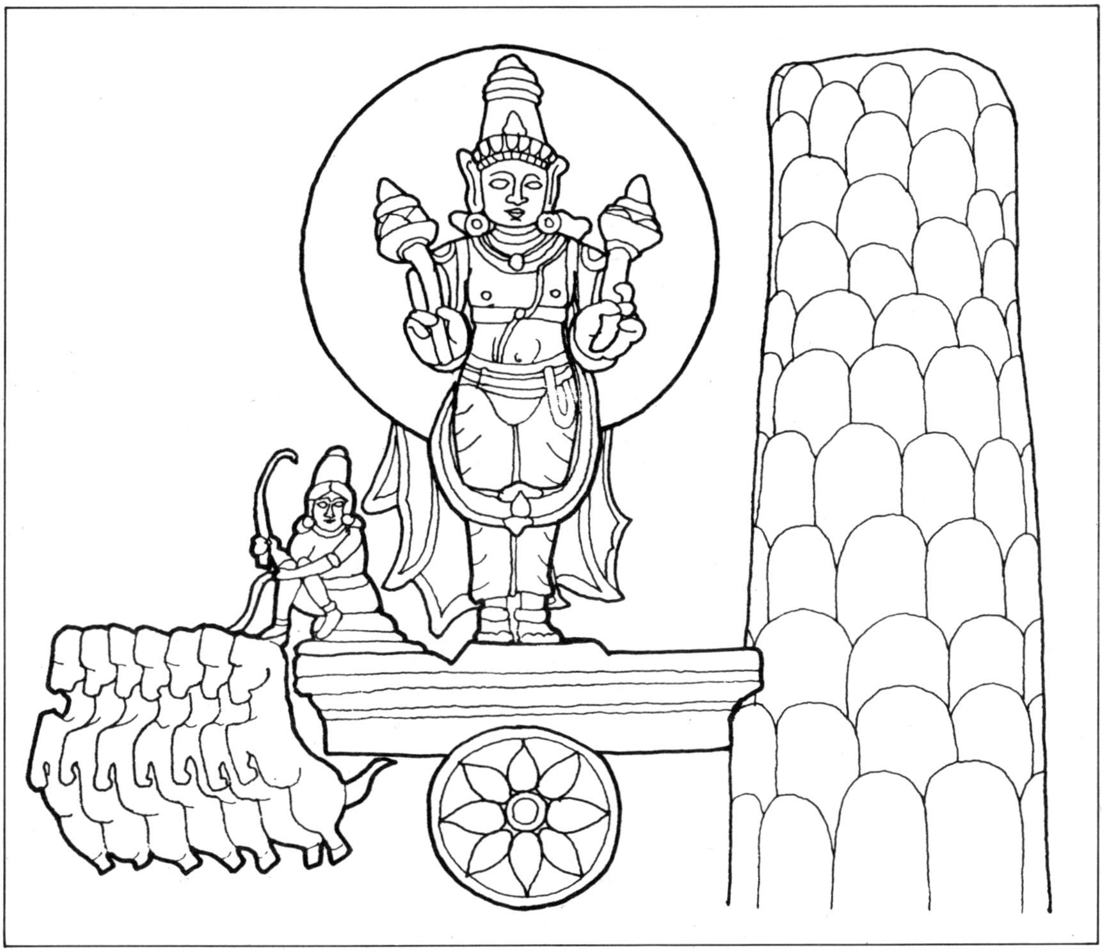

73. Surya on chariot driving around Mount Meru.

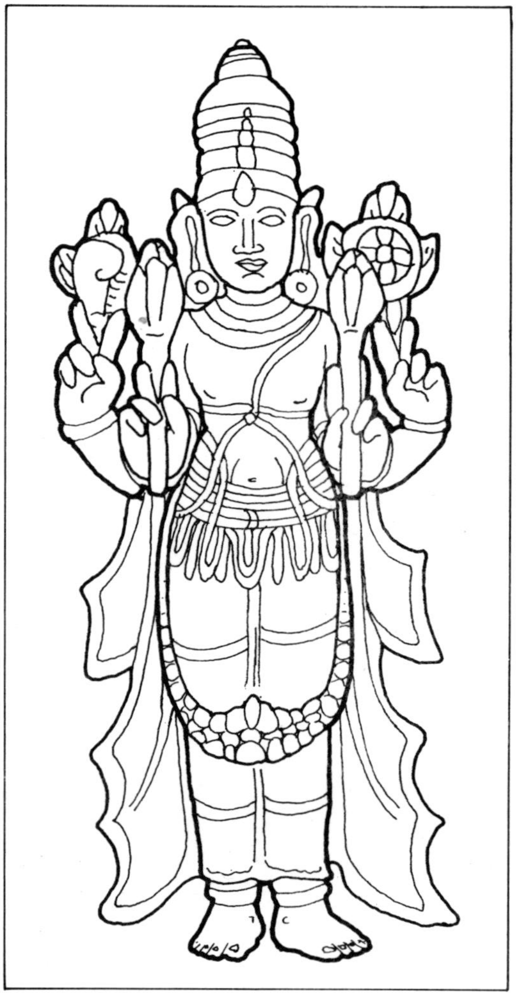

74. Surya-Narayana.

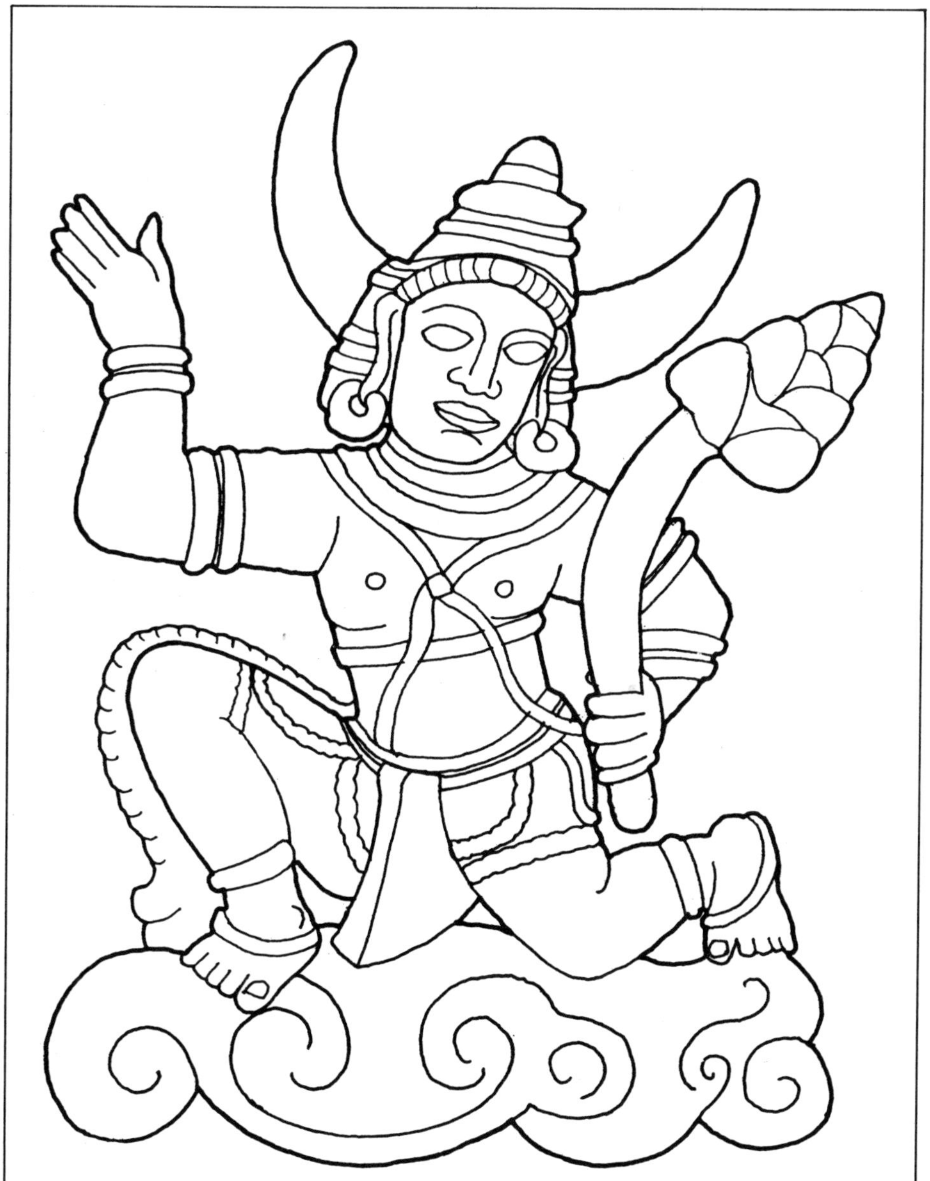

75. Chandra.

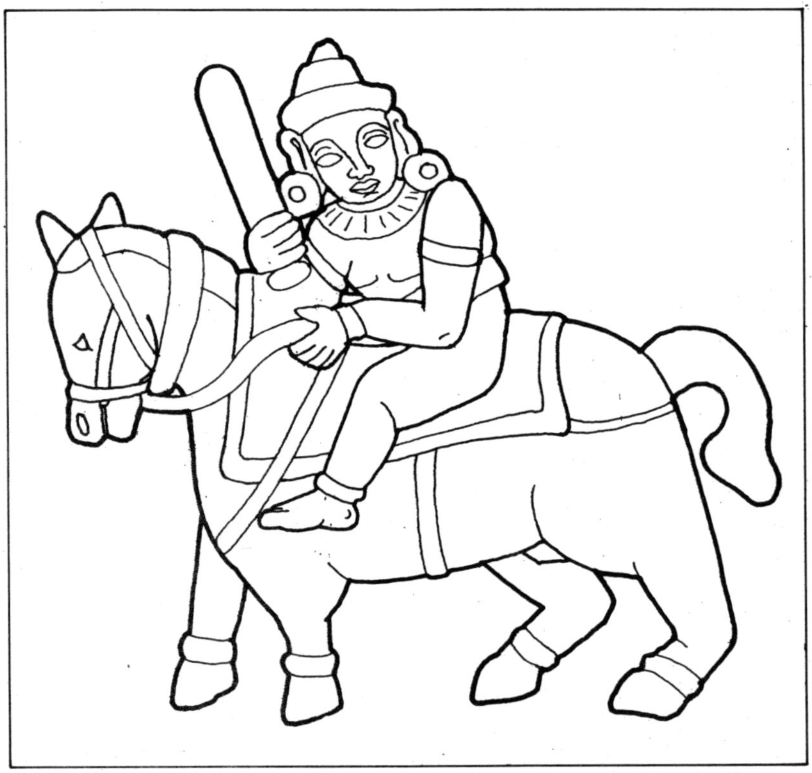

76. Kubera.

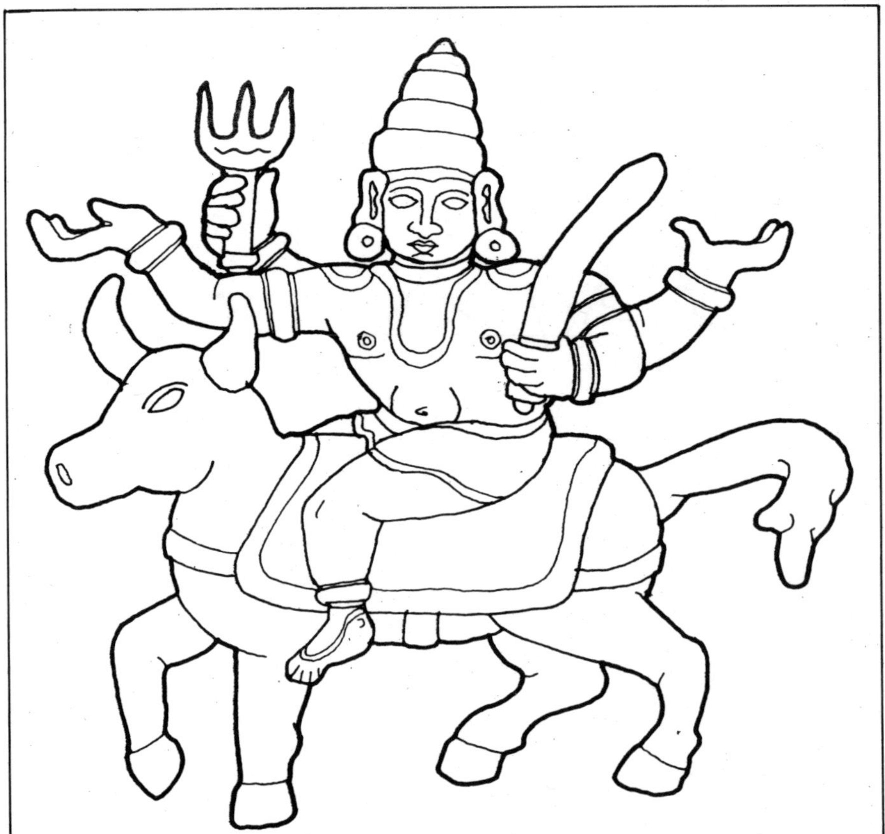

77. Ishana.

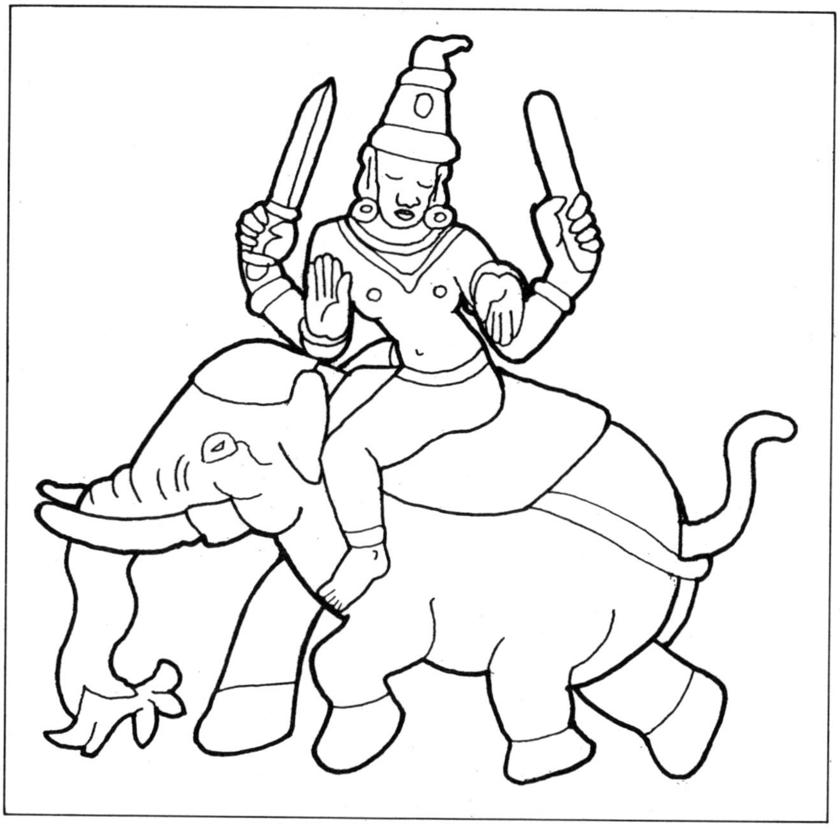

78. Indra.

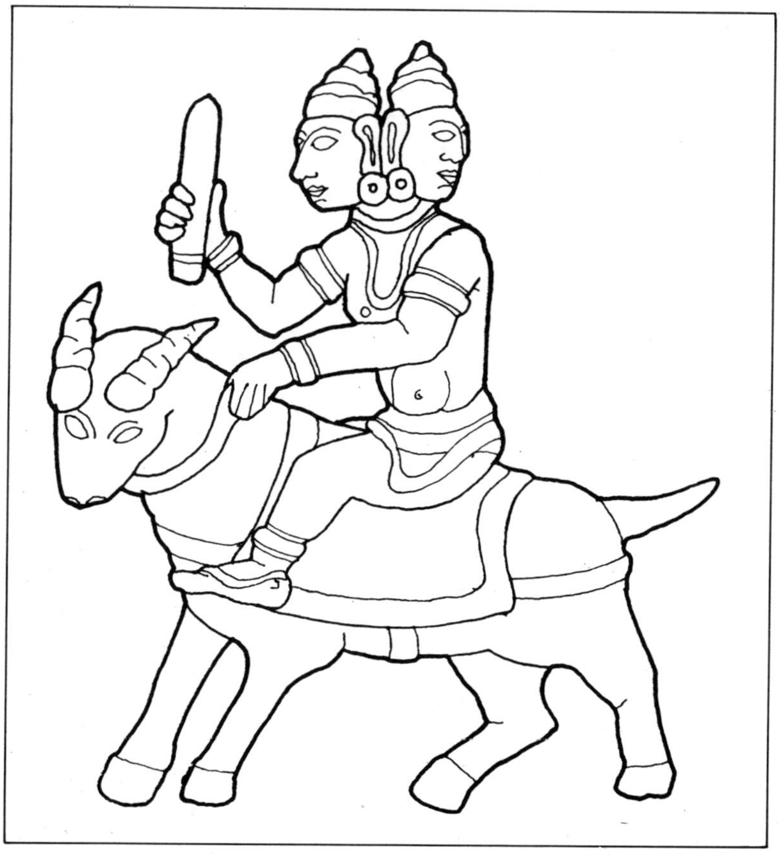

79. Agni.

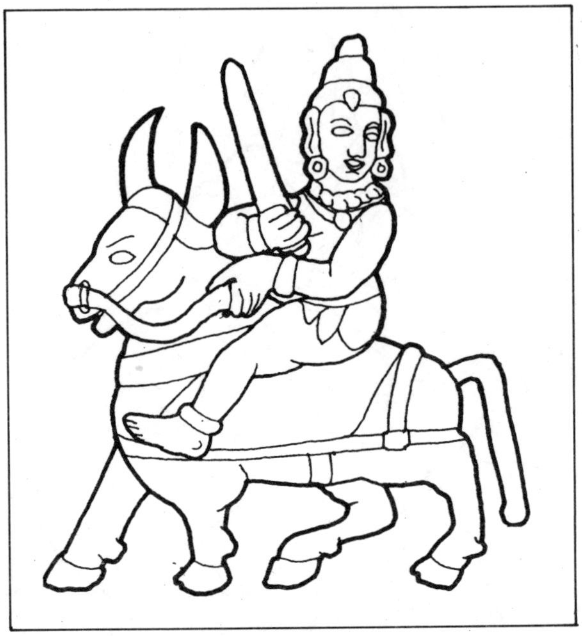

80. Yama.

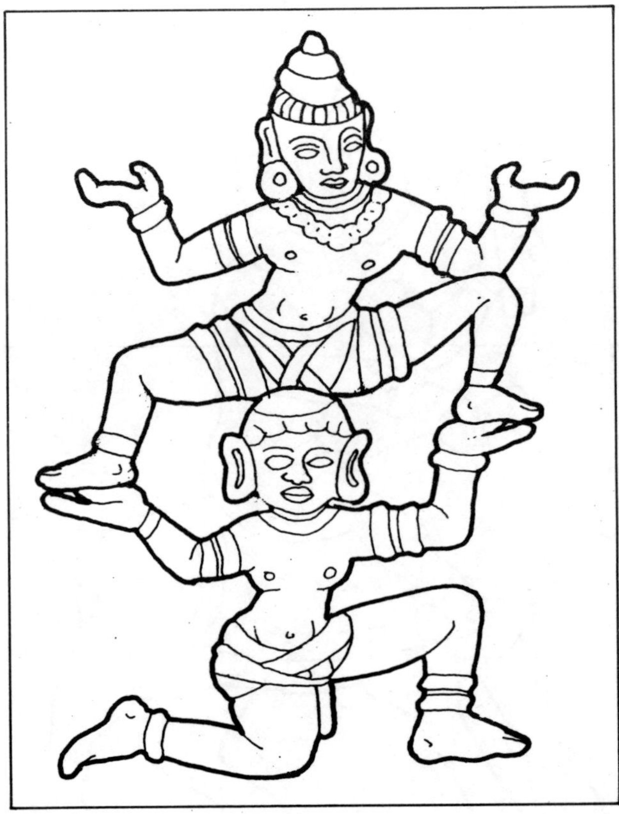

81. Nirruti.

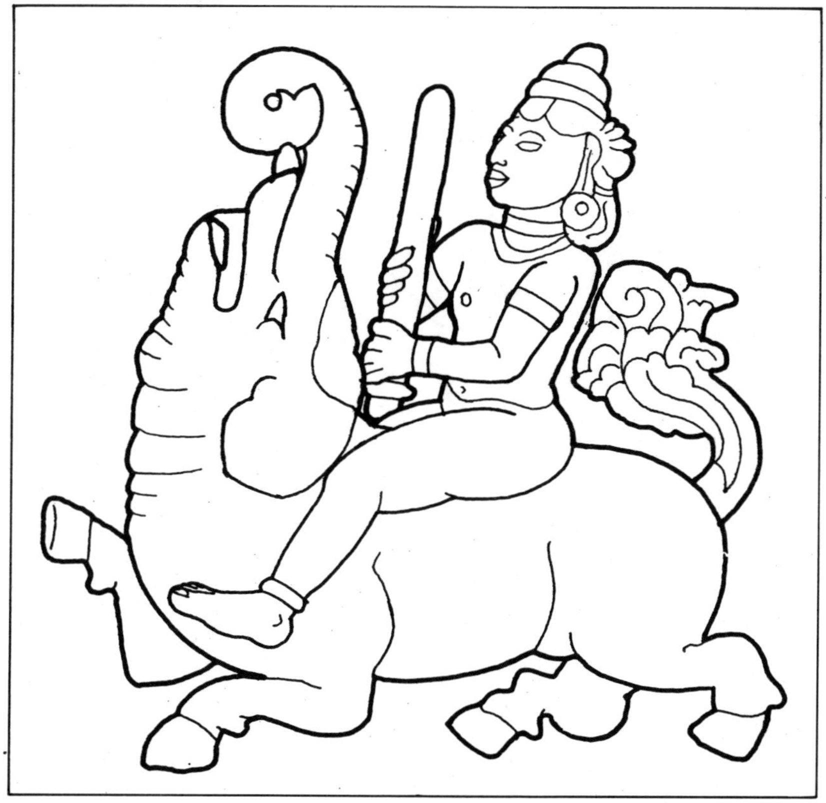

82. Varuna.

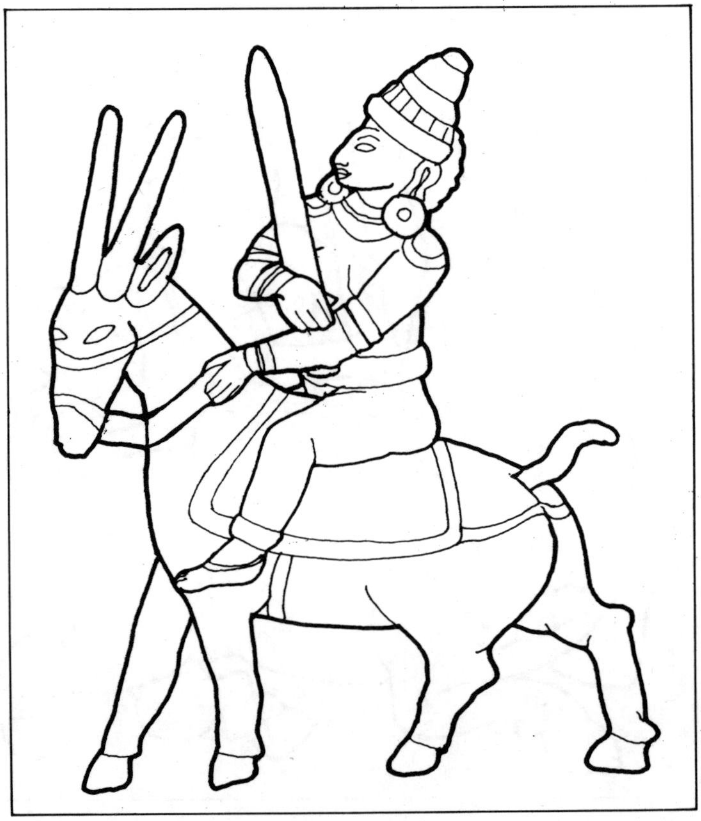

83. Vayu.

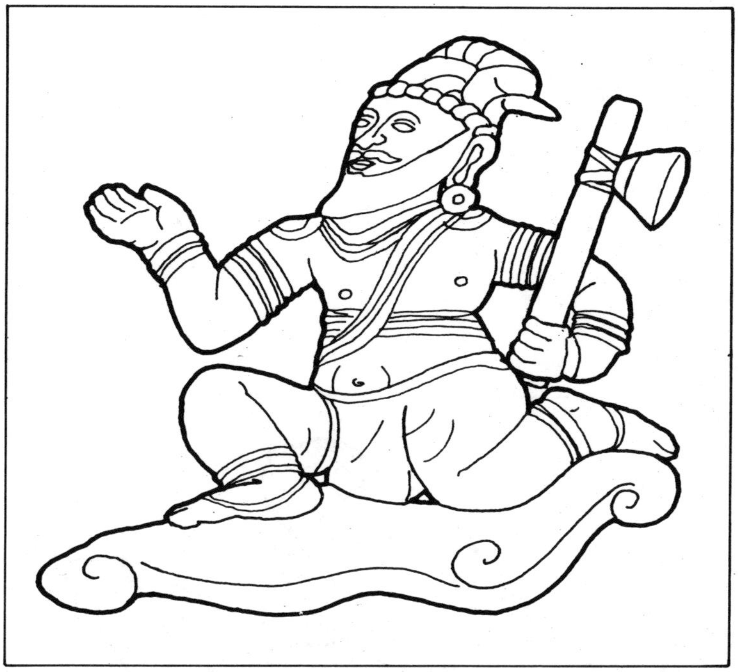

84. Narada.

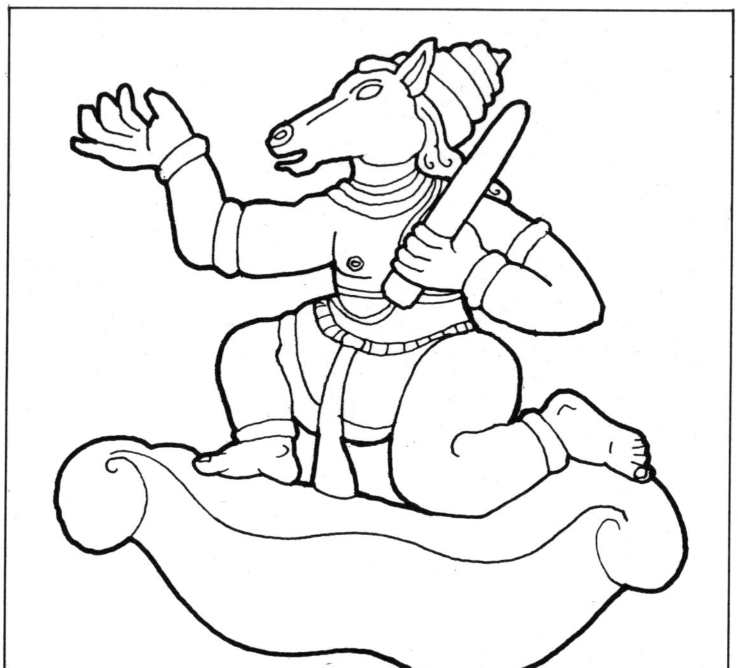

85. Tumburu.

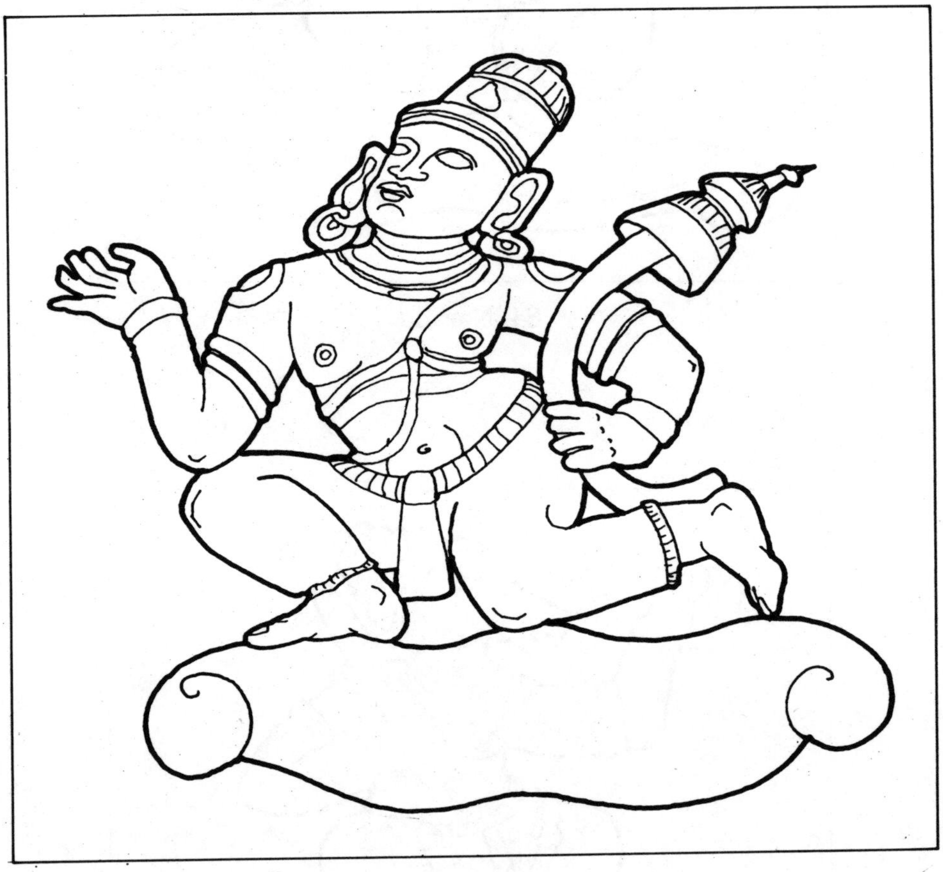

86. Gandharva.

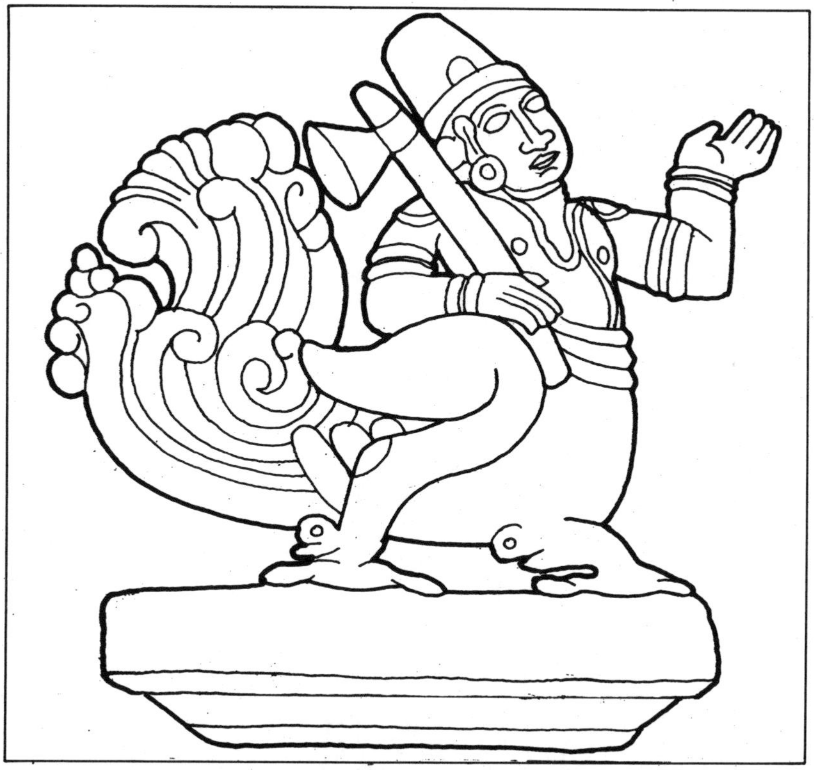

87. Kinnara.

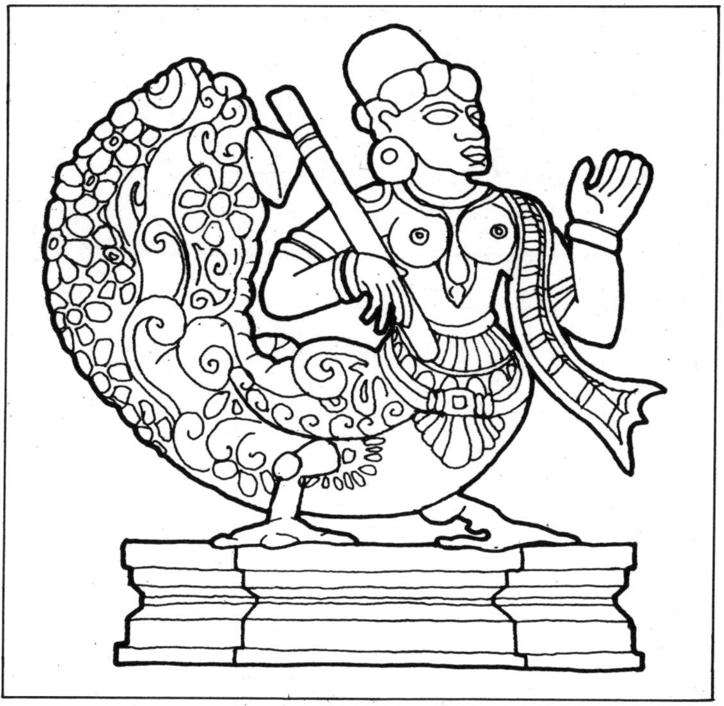

88. Kinnari.

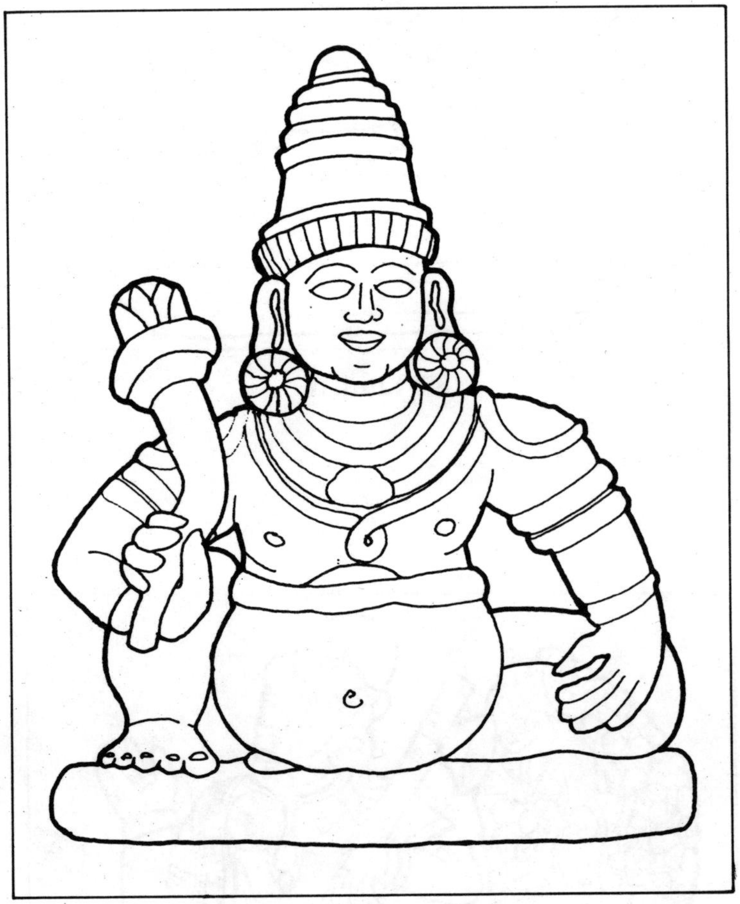

89. Padmanidhi.

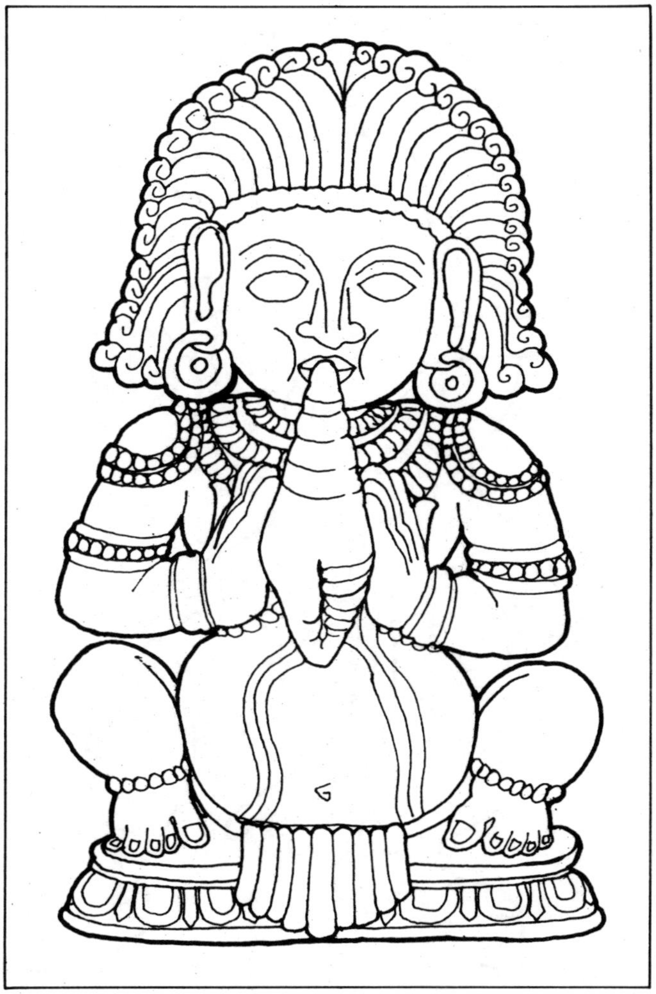

90. Shankhanidhi.

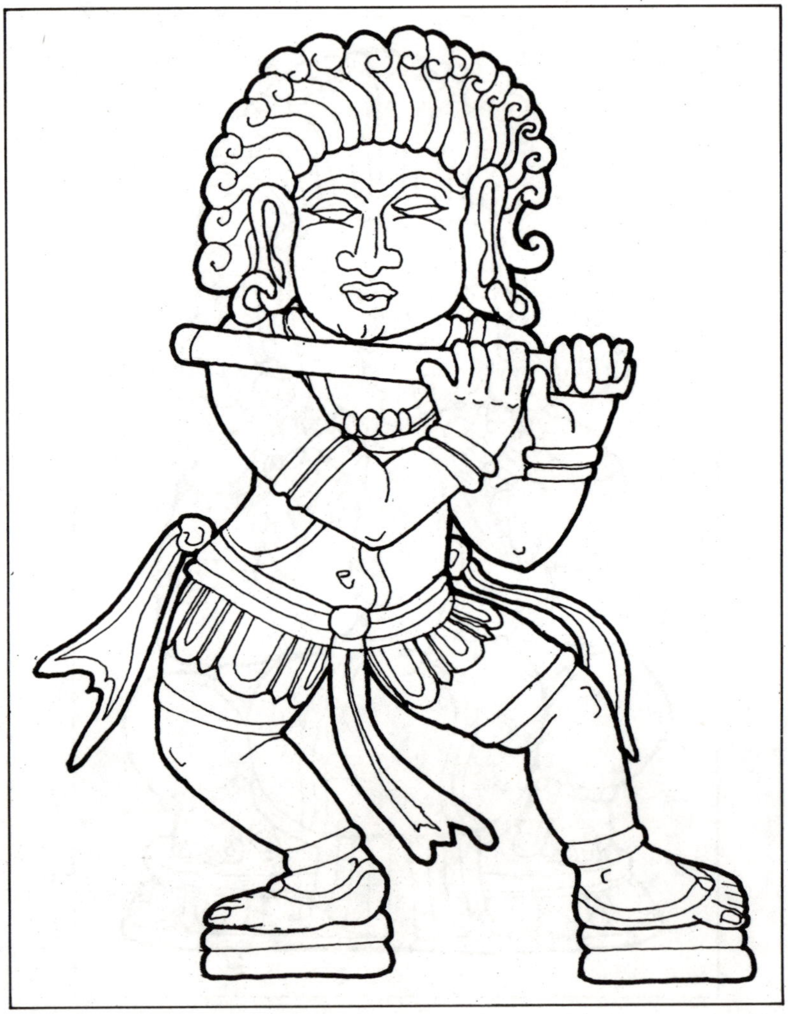

91. Gana.

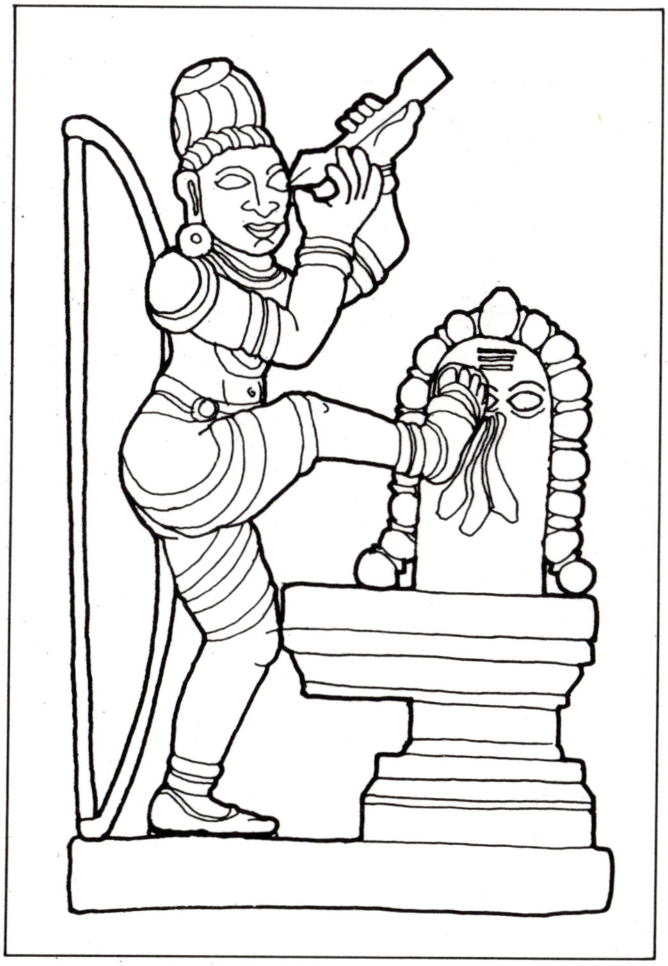

92. Kannappa nayanmar.

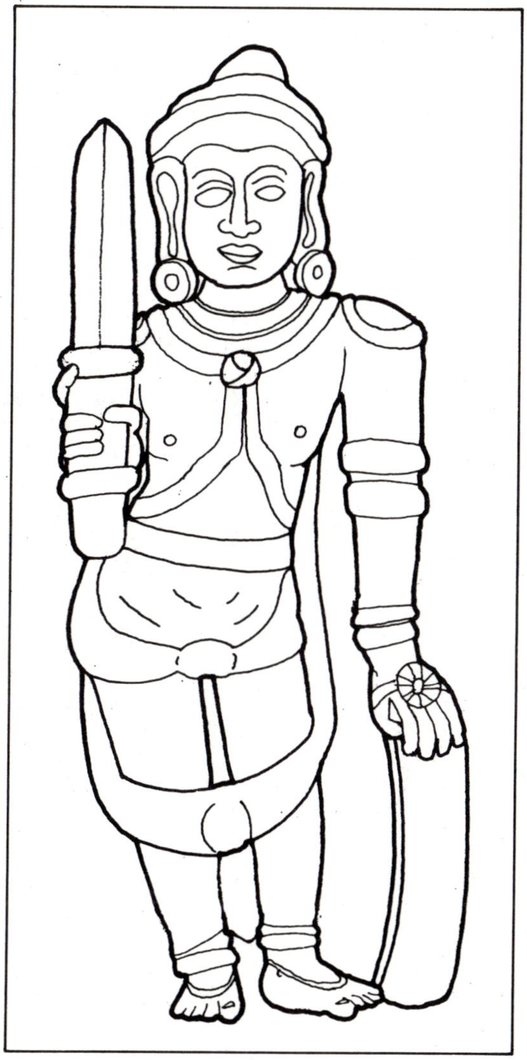

93. Tirumangai alvar.

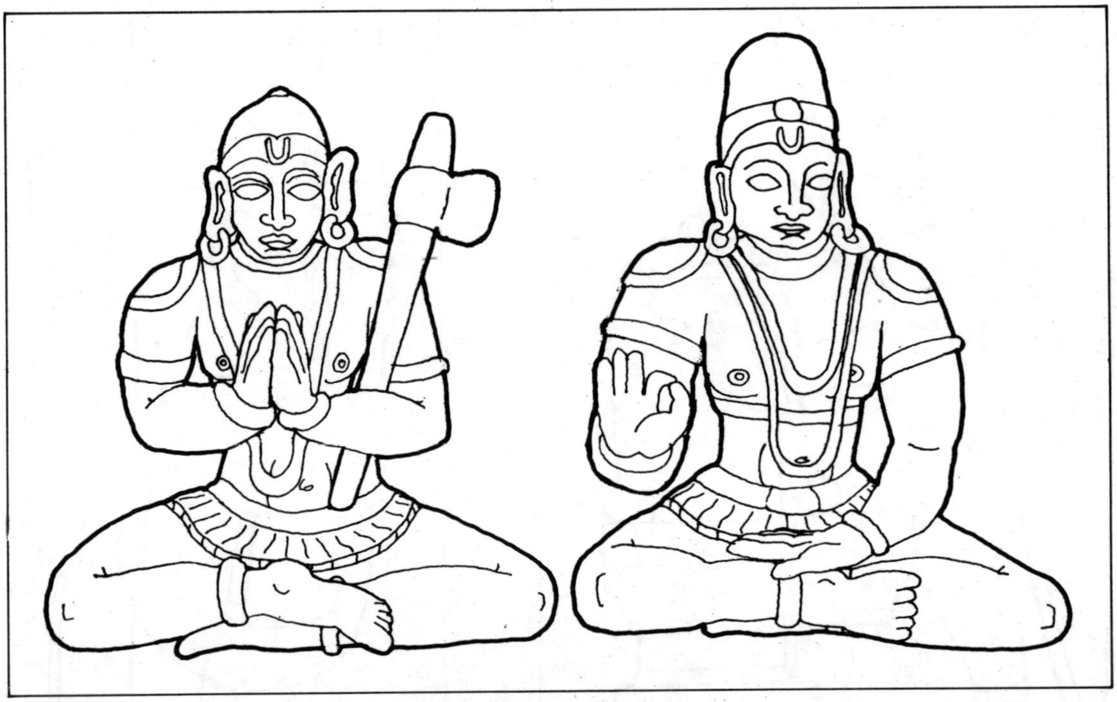

94. Ramanuja and Nammalvar.

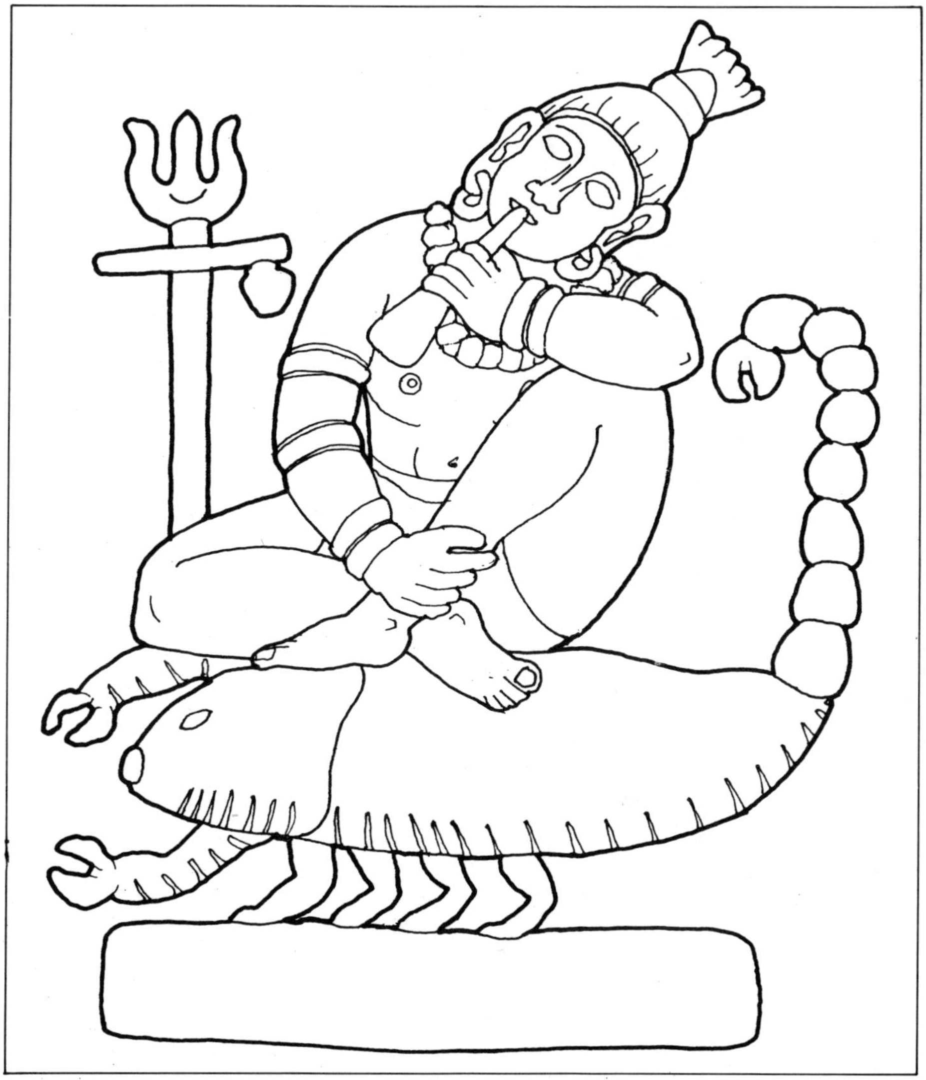

95. Natha seated on a scorpion.

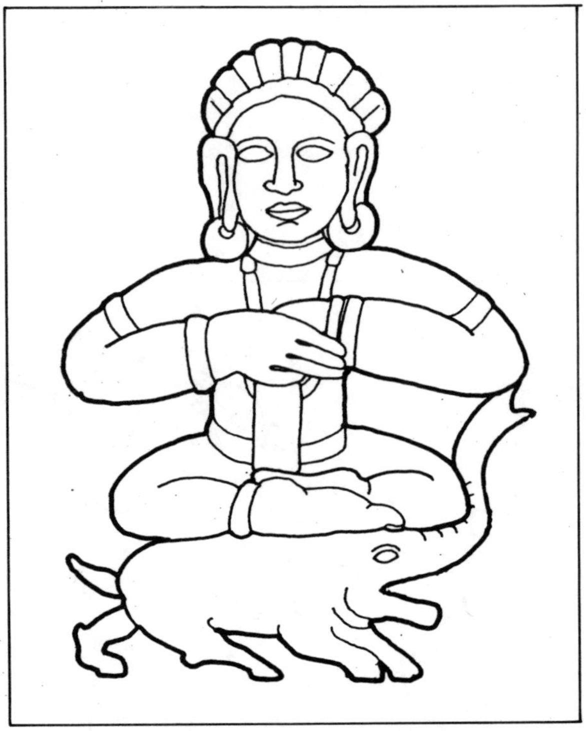

96. Natha seated on a fabulous animal.

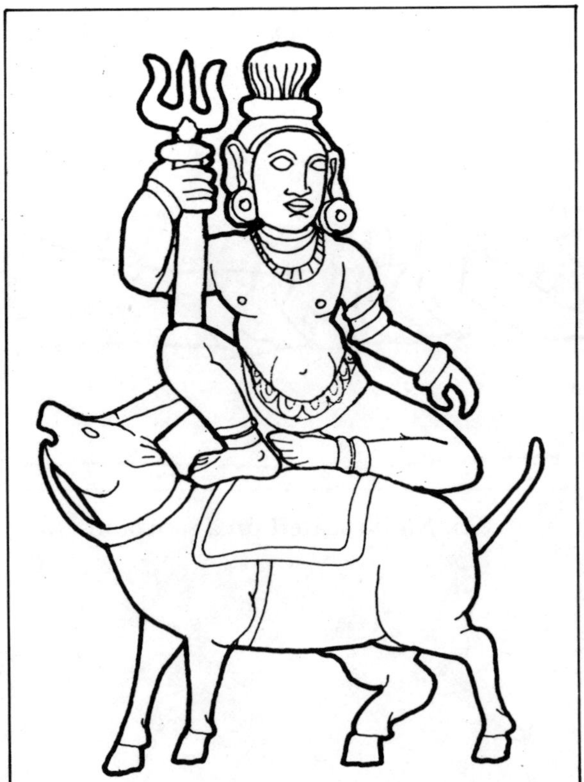

97. Natha seated on a bull.

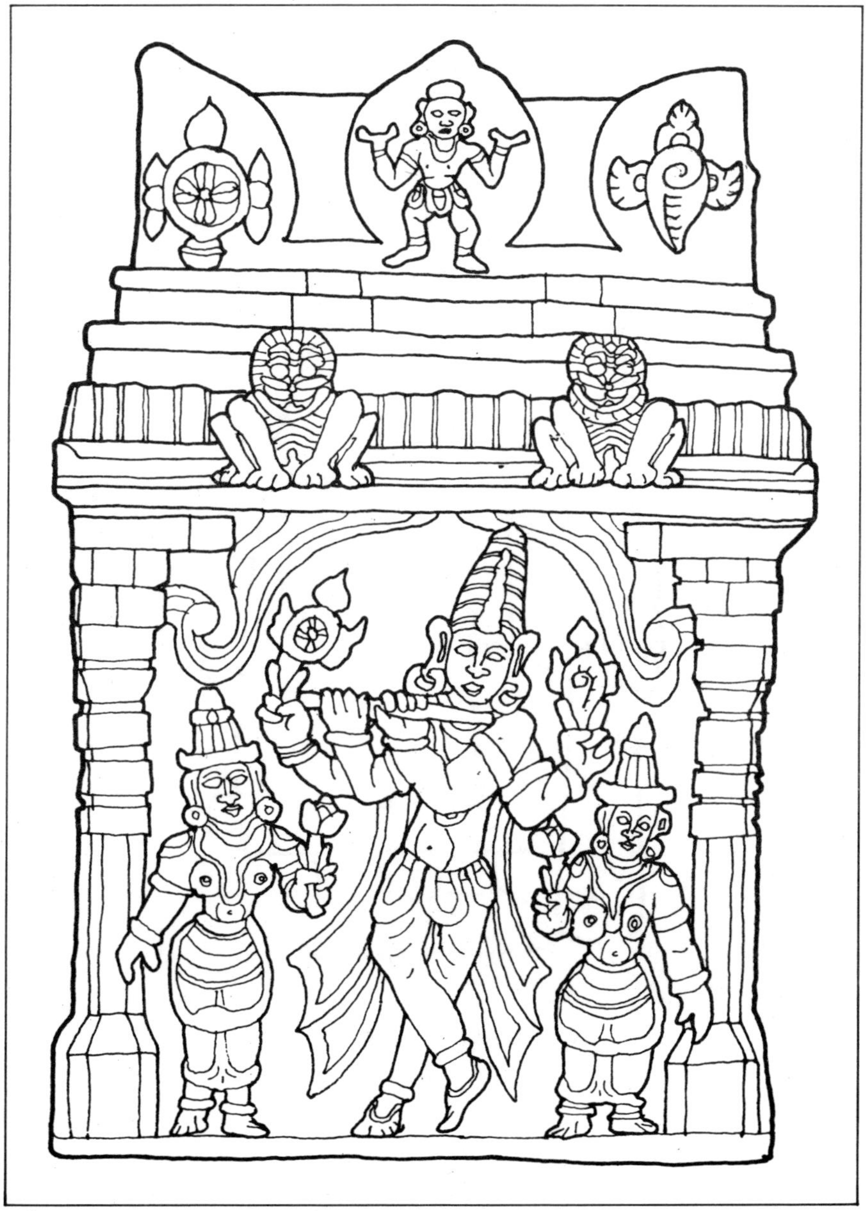

98. Brindavana.

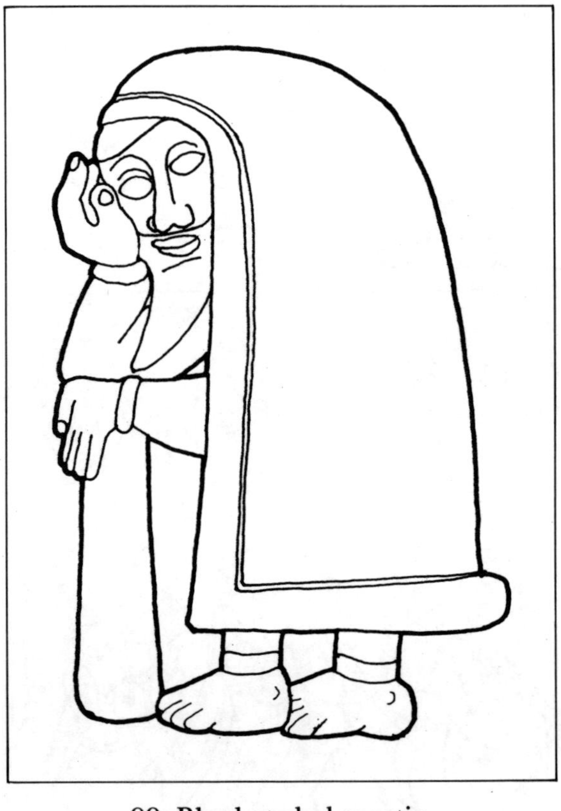

99. Blanket-clad ascetic.

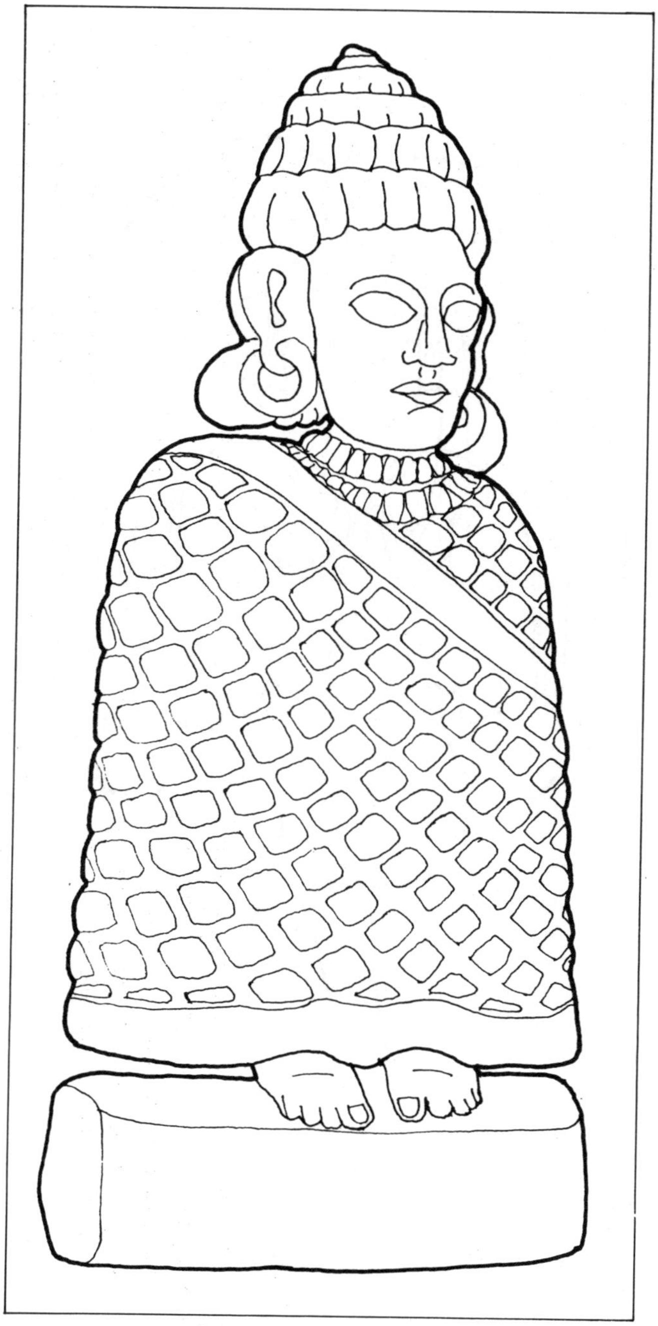

100. Ascetic in patchwork cloak.

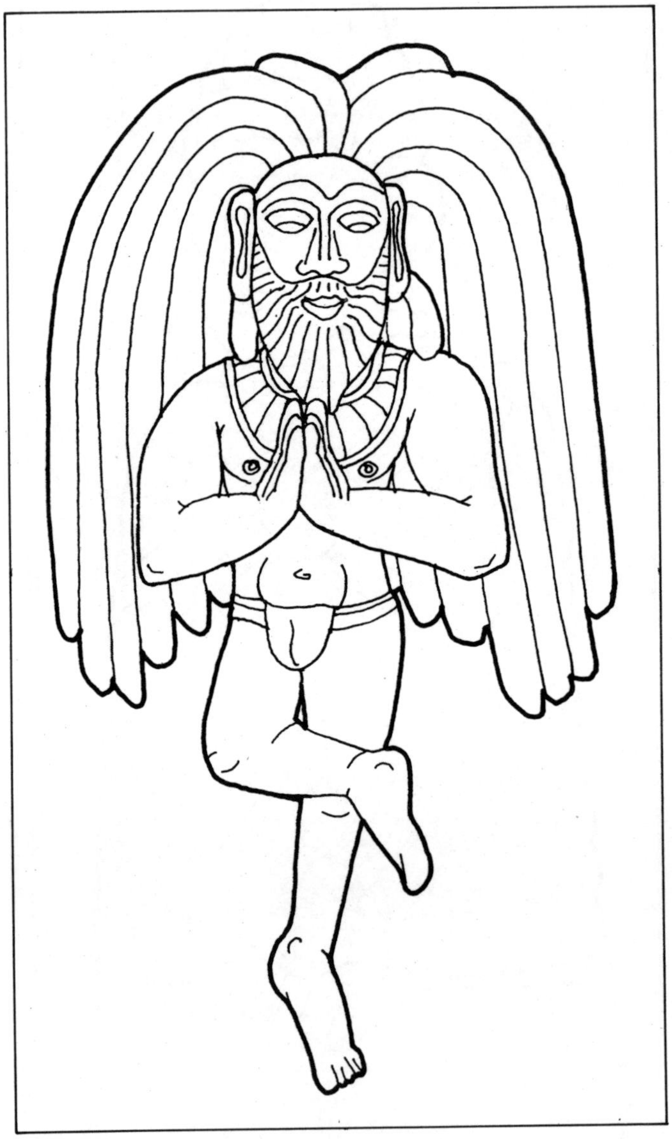

101. Ascetic in yogic pose.

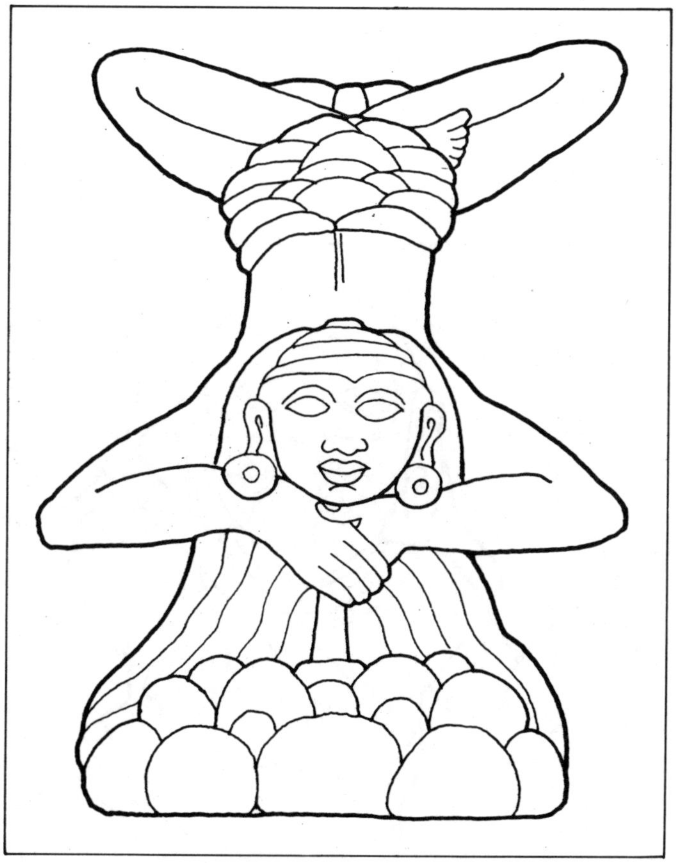

102. Ascetic in yogic pose.

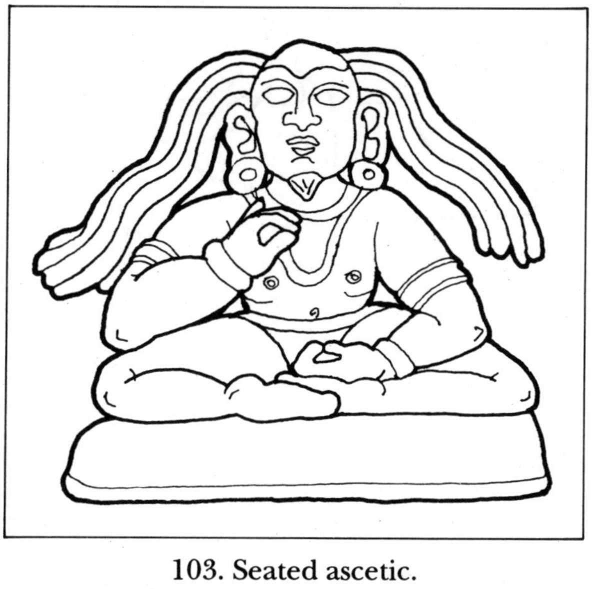

103. Seated ascetic.

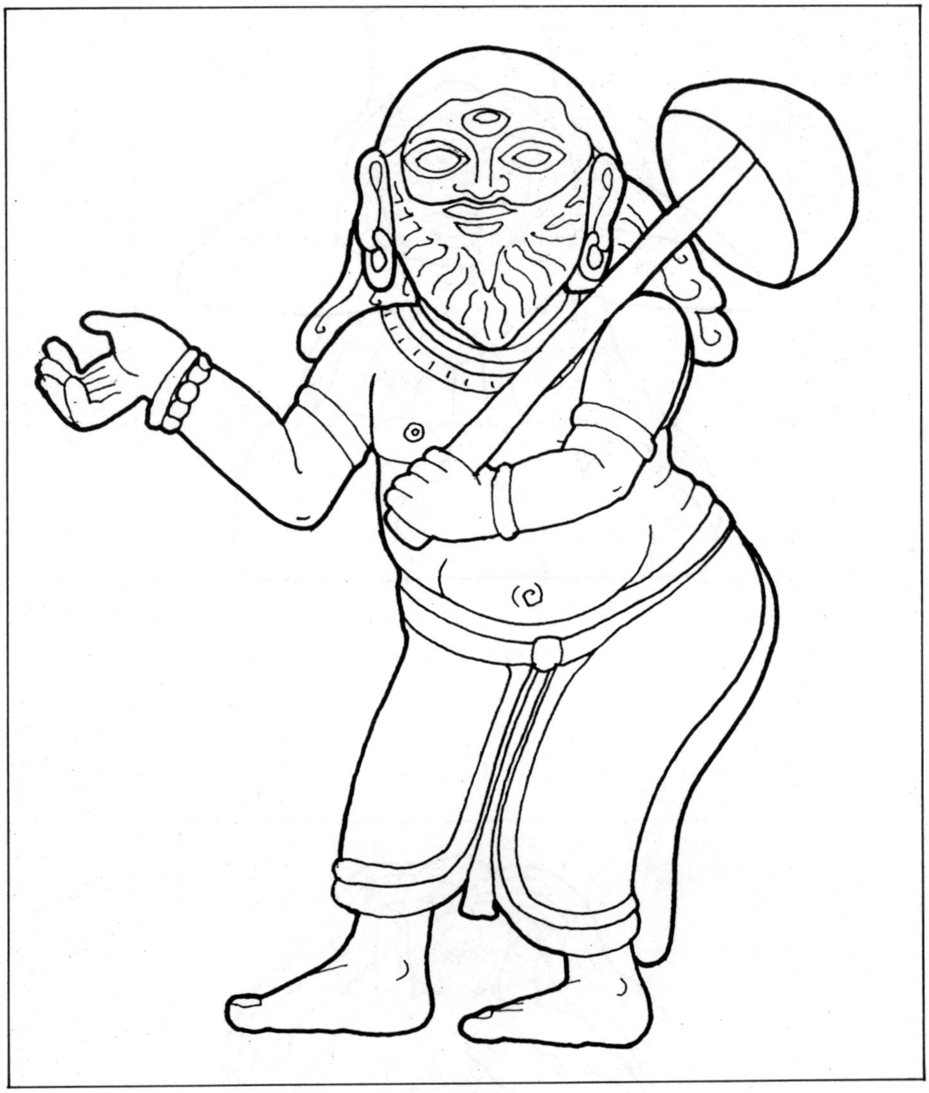

104. Ascetic with umbrella.

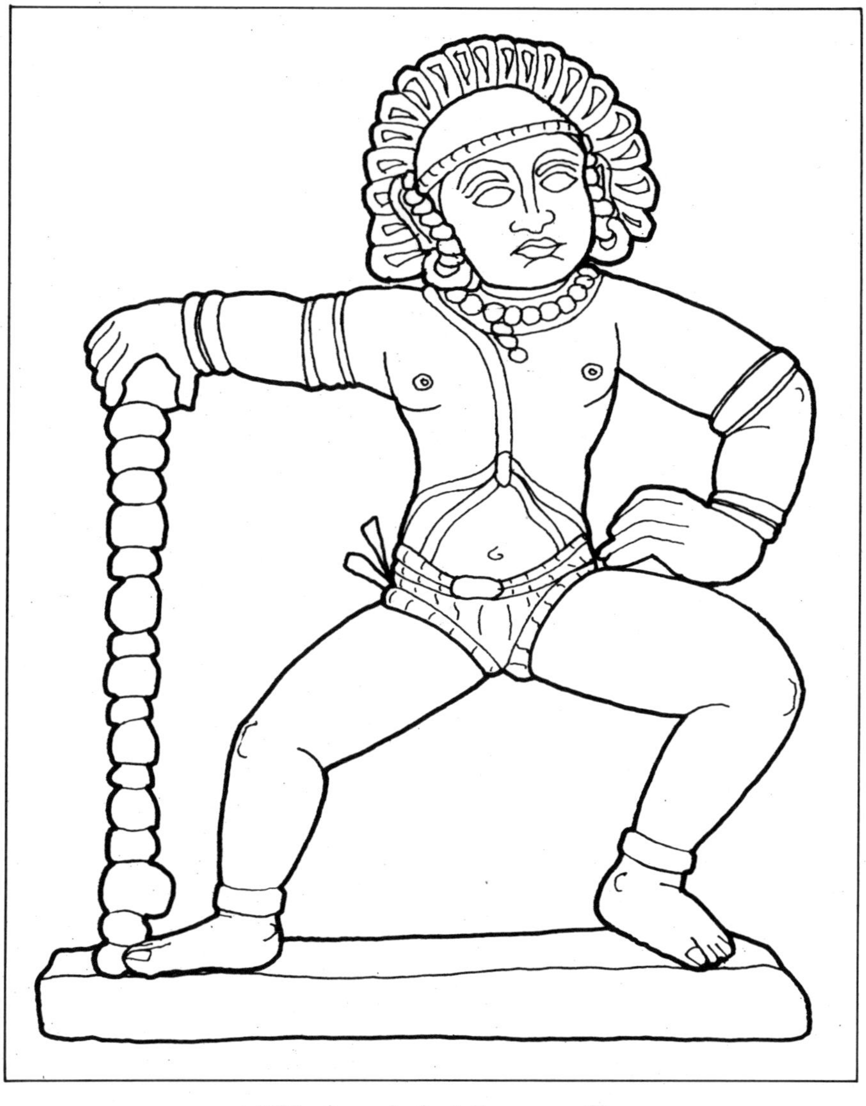

105. Ascetic holding a staff.

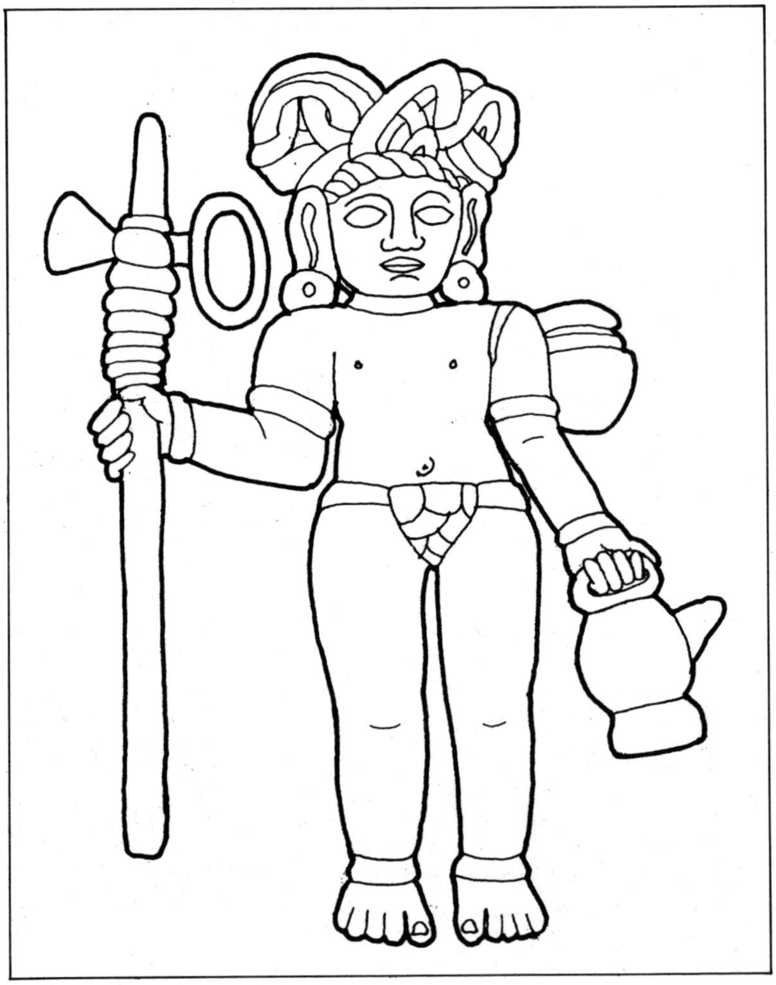

106. Ascetic with staff and kamandalu.

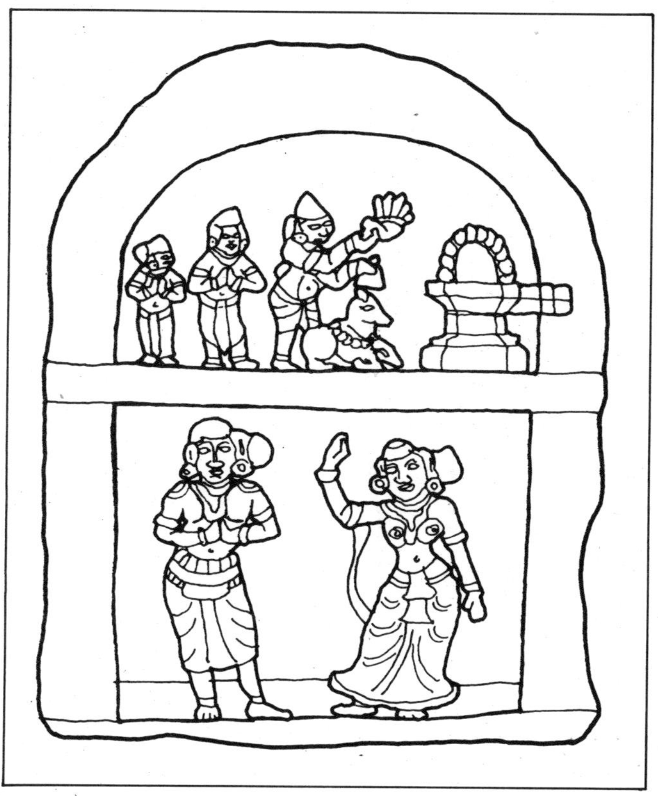

107. Sati-stone.

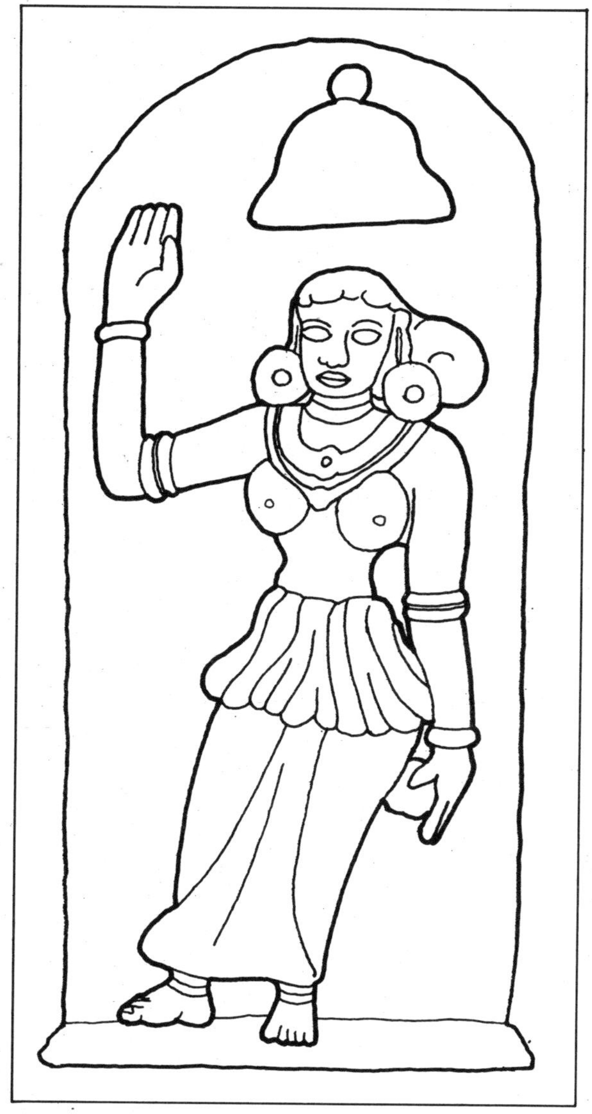

108. Sati-stone.

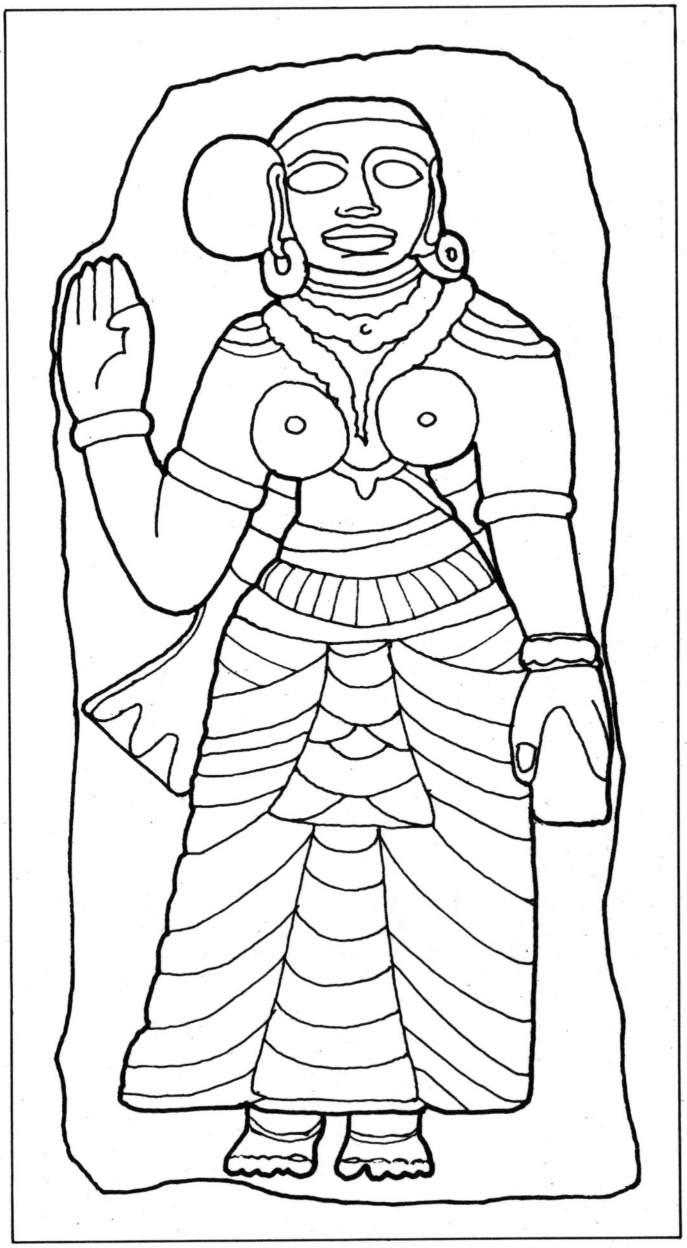

109. Sati-stone.

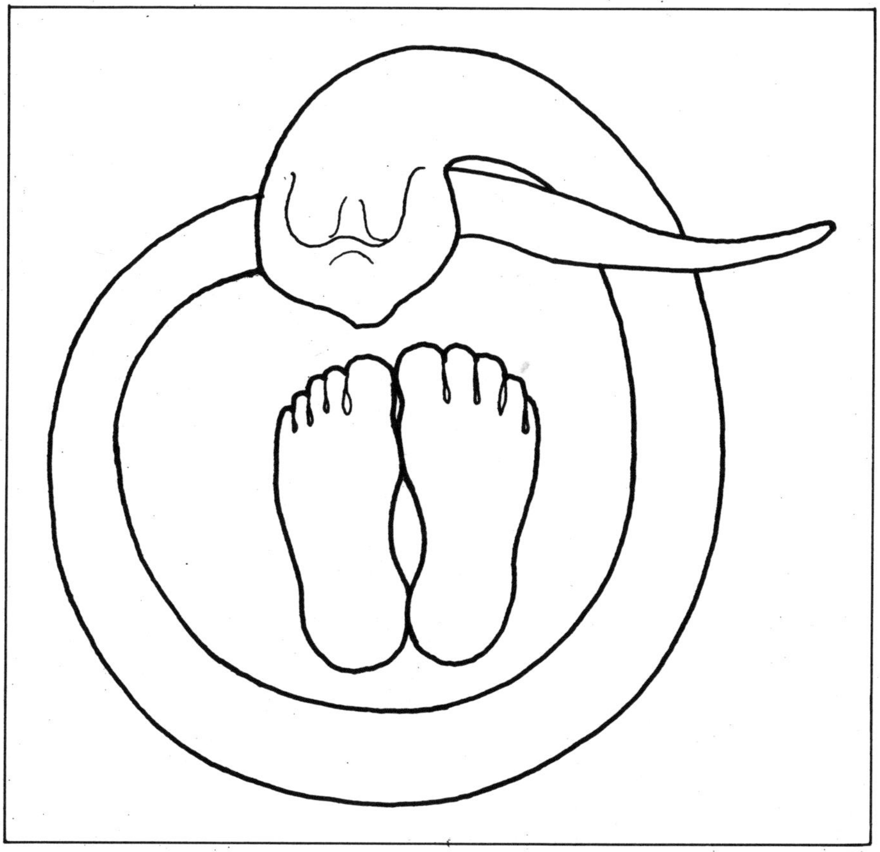

110. Feet encircled by a serpent.

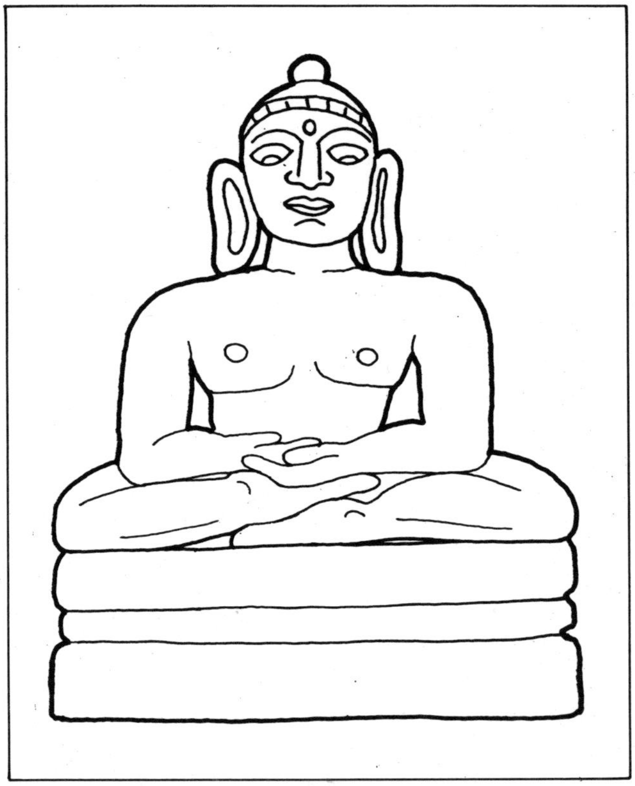

111. Seated Tirthankara.

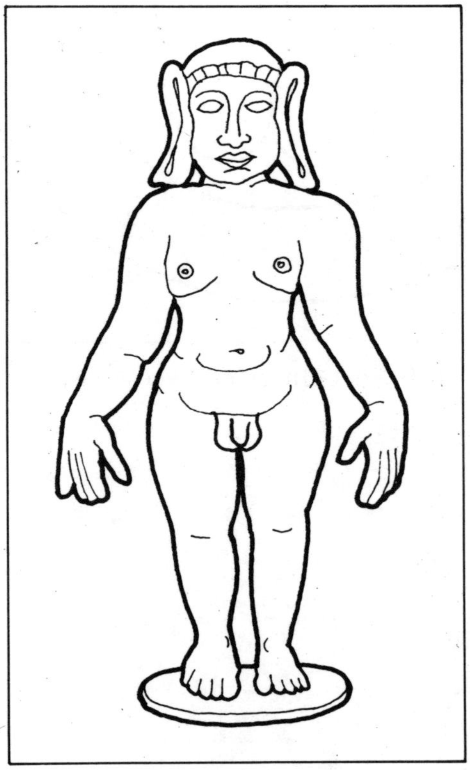

112. Standing Jina.

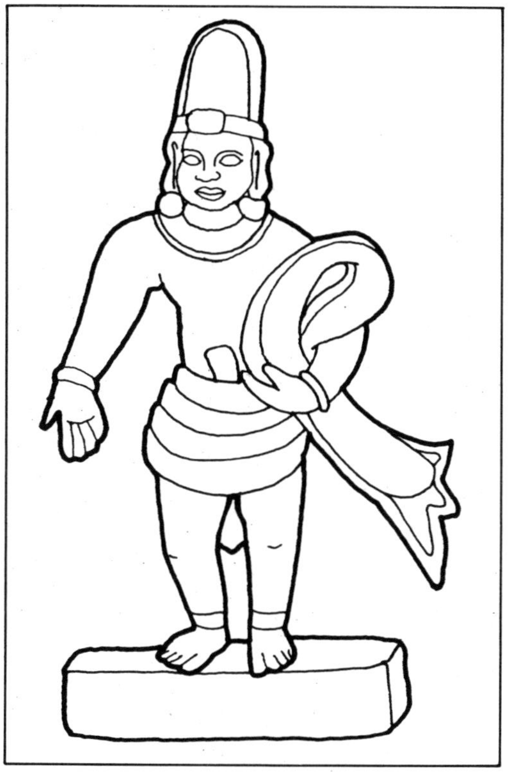

113. King Mallikarjuna.

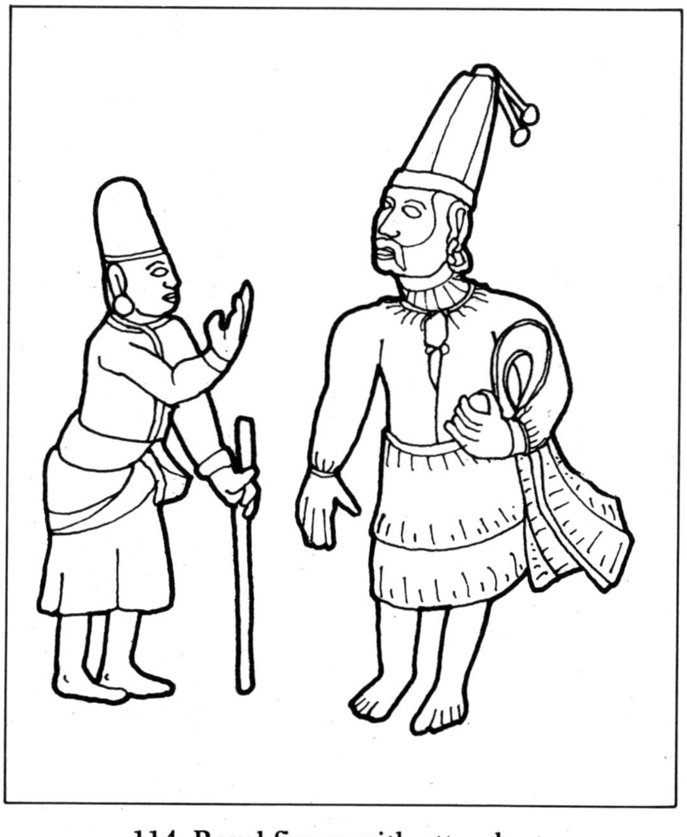

114. Royal figure with attendant.

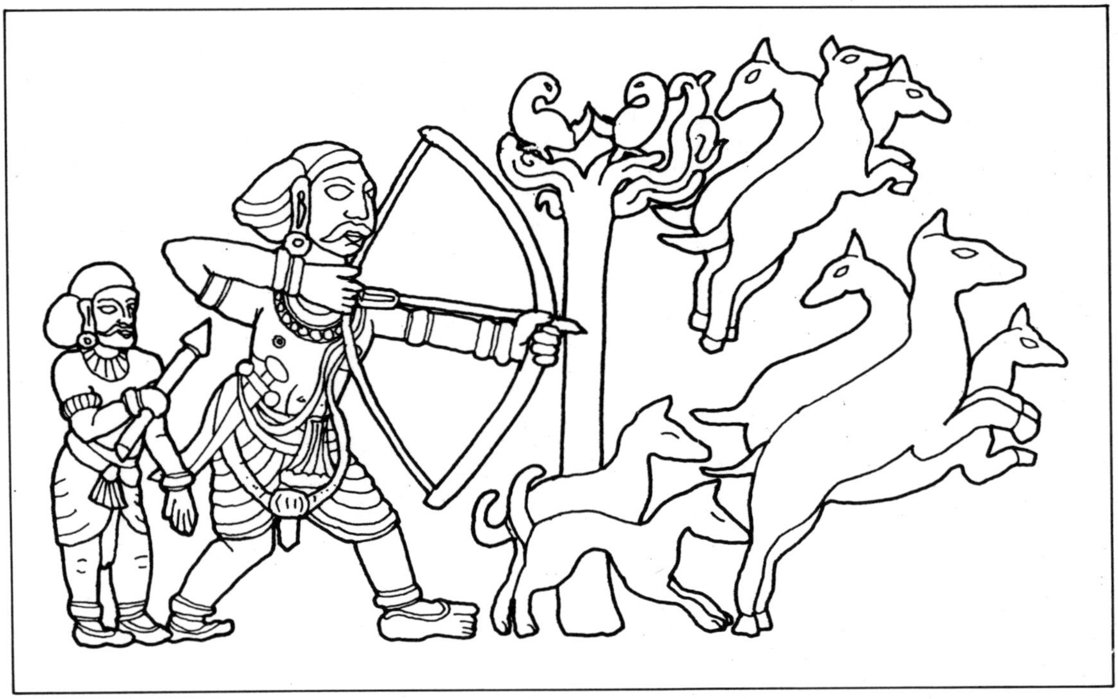

115. Royal hunter.

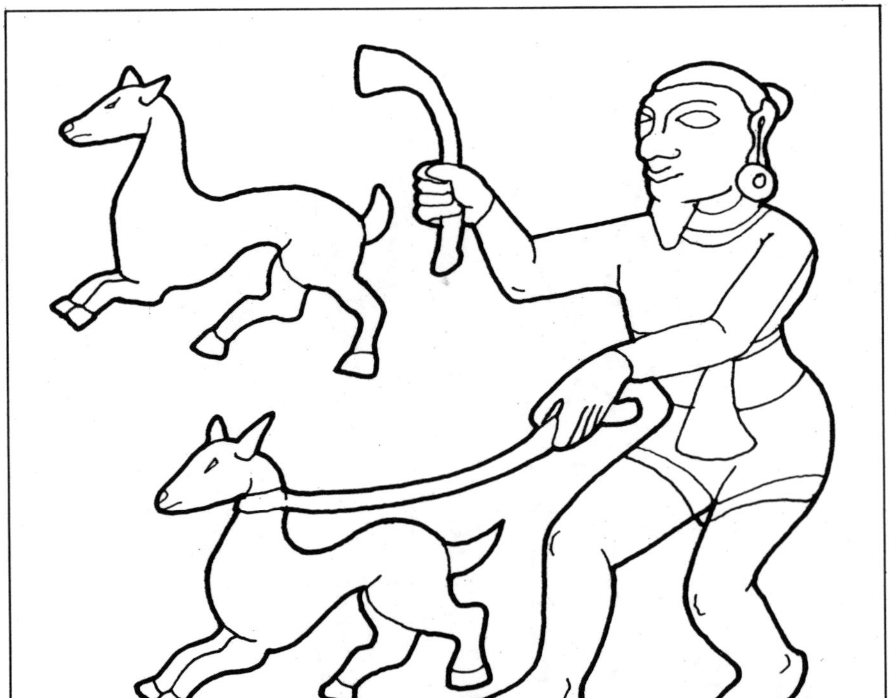

116. Hunter.

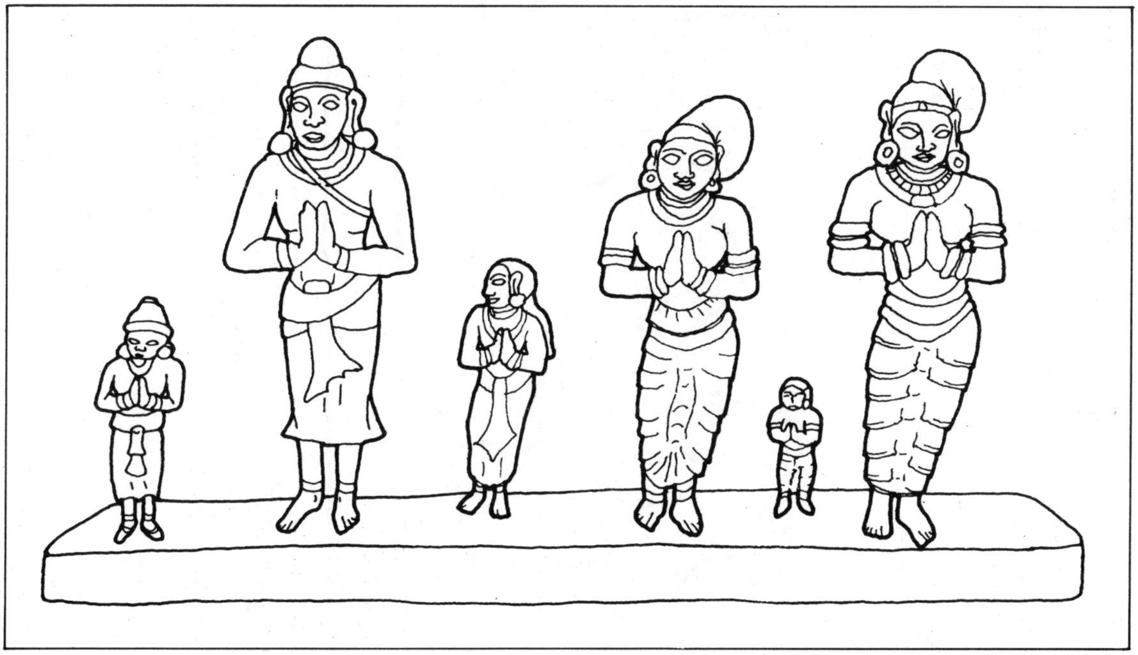

117. Devotees.

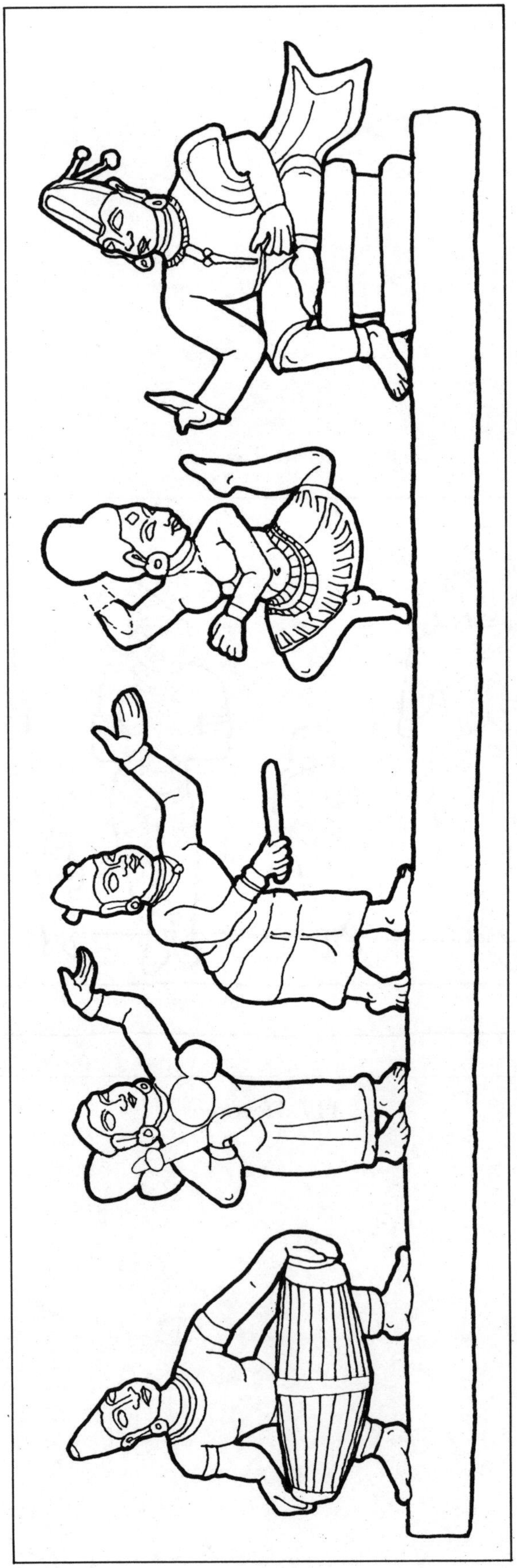

118. Dancers and musicians performing before a royal figure.

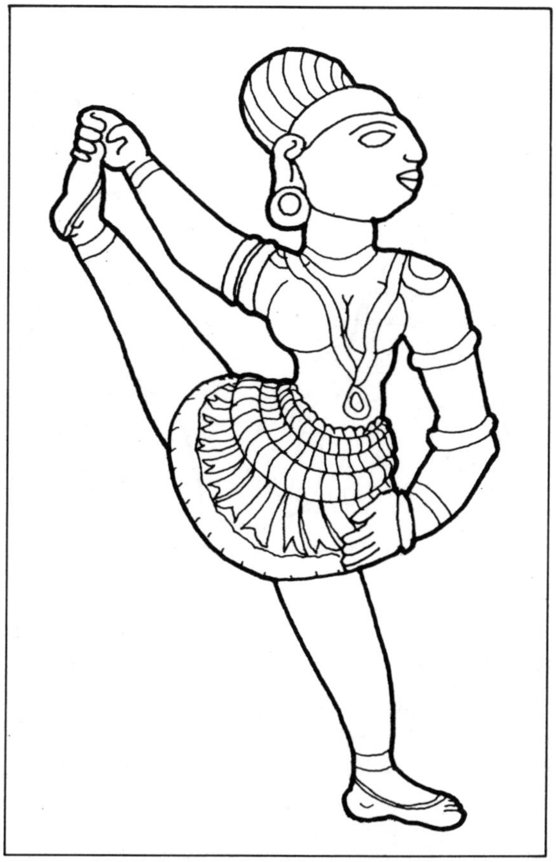

119. Classical dancer.

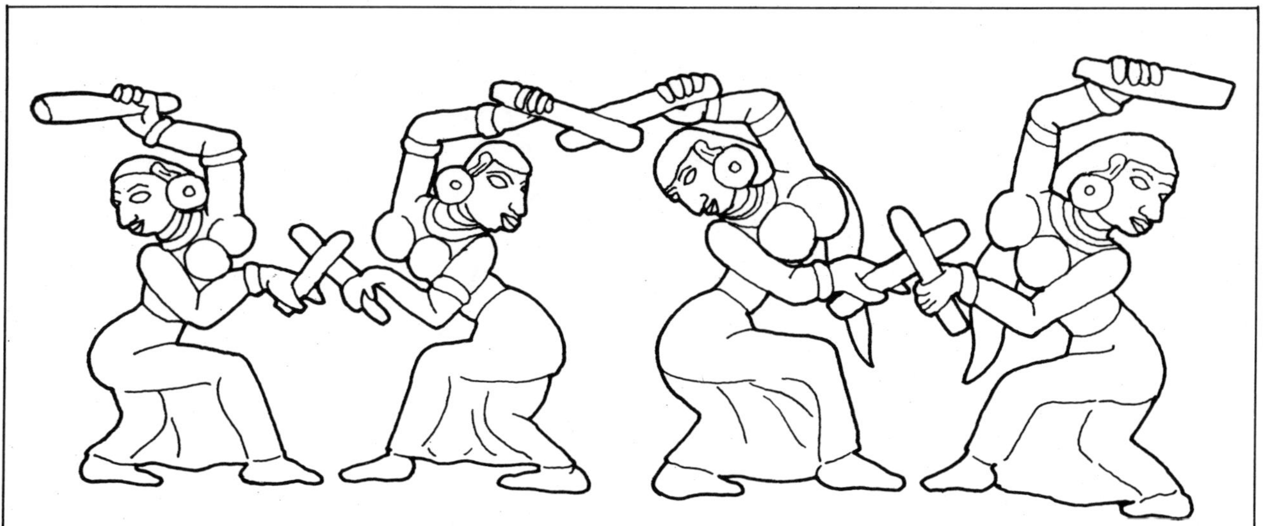

120. Kolata dancers.

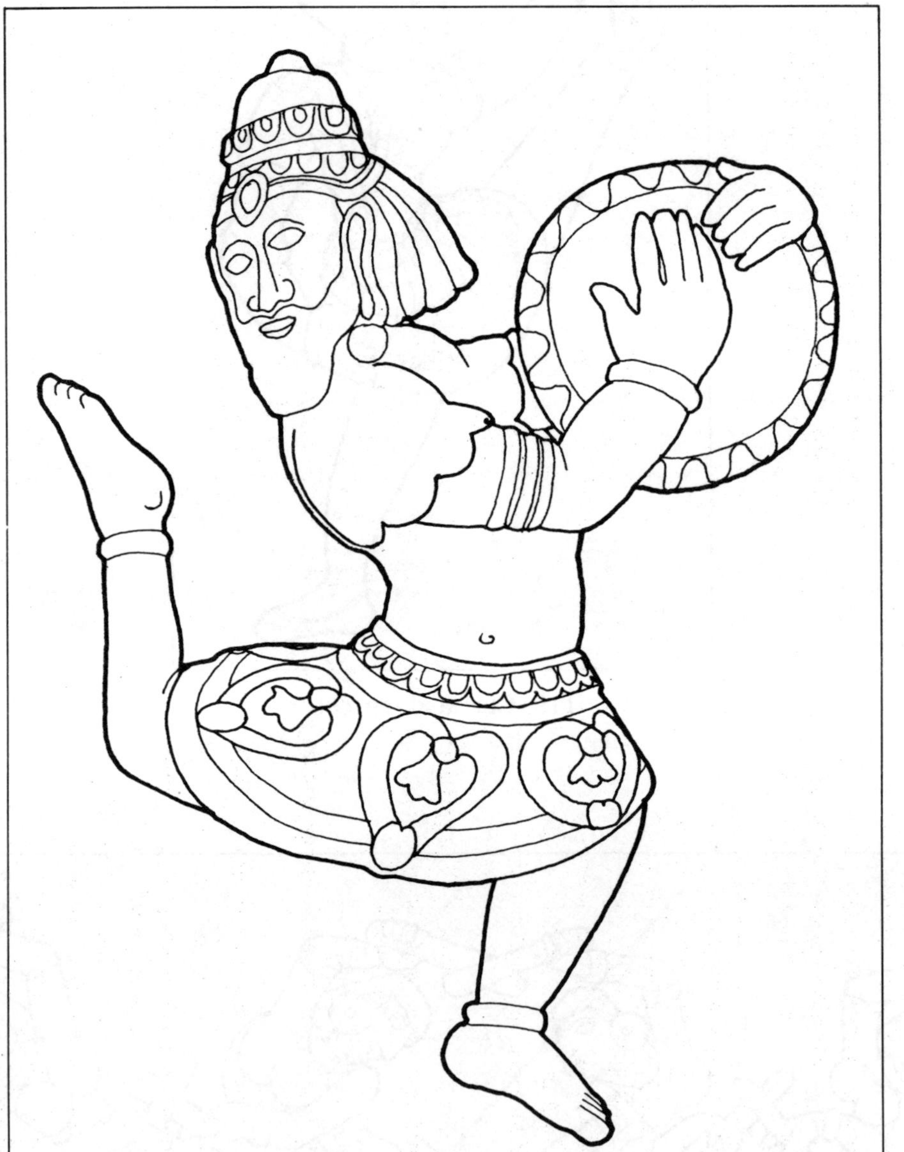

121. Male 'folk' dancer.

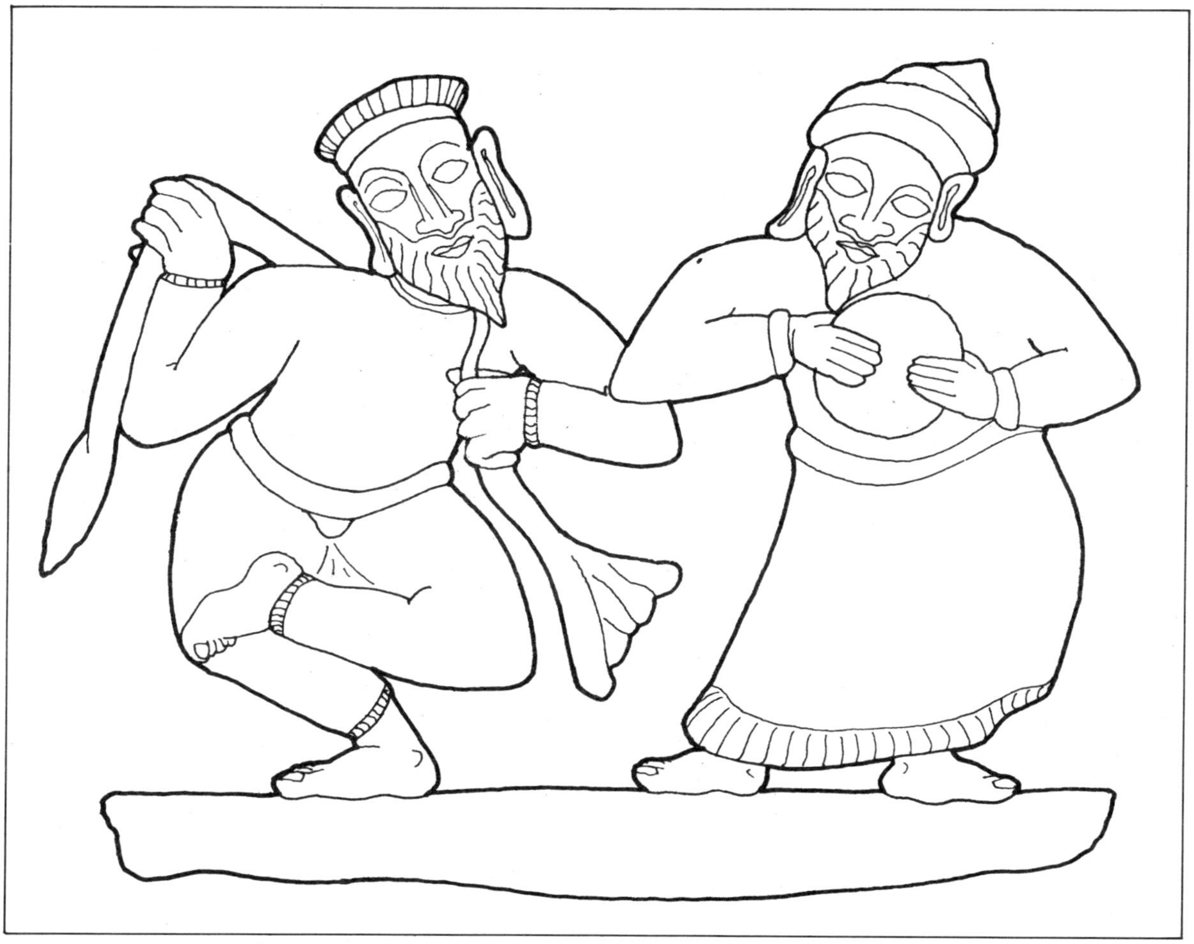

122. Foreign male dancers.

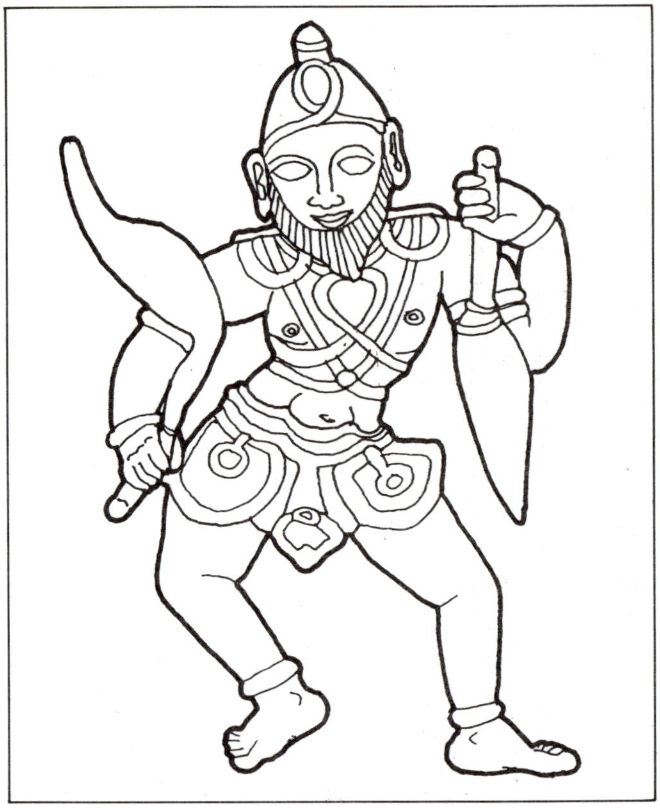

123. Male 'folk' dancers with chauris.

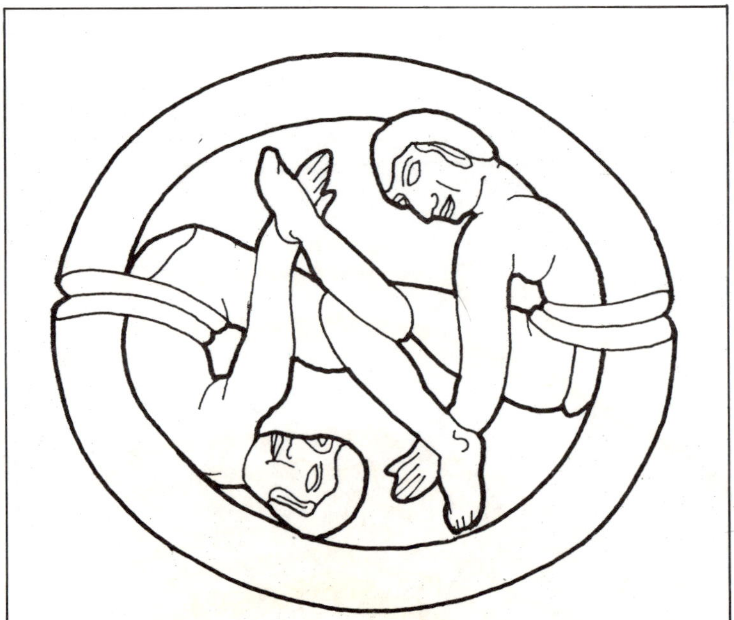

124. Acrobats.

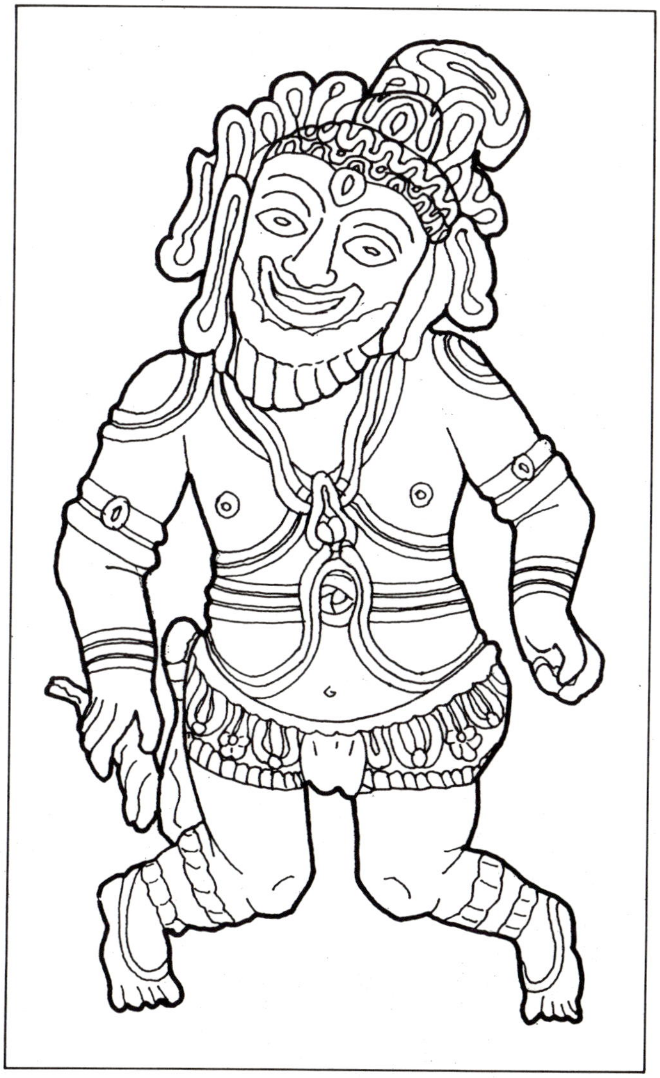

125. Knock-kneed clown.

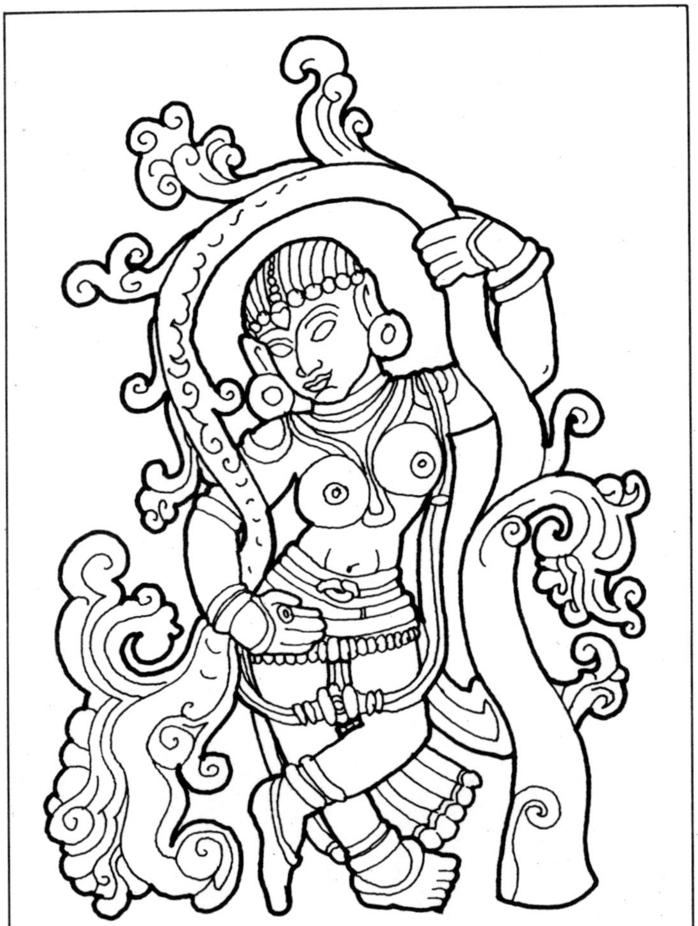

126. Latasundari.

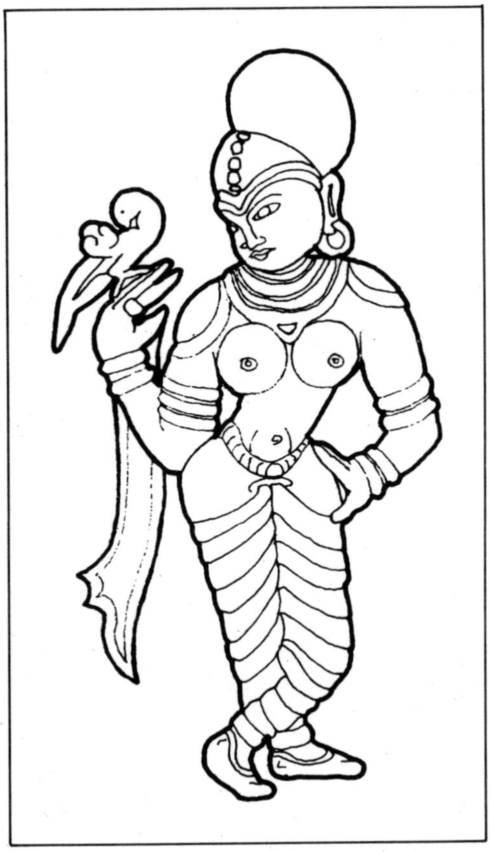

127. Woman with parrot.

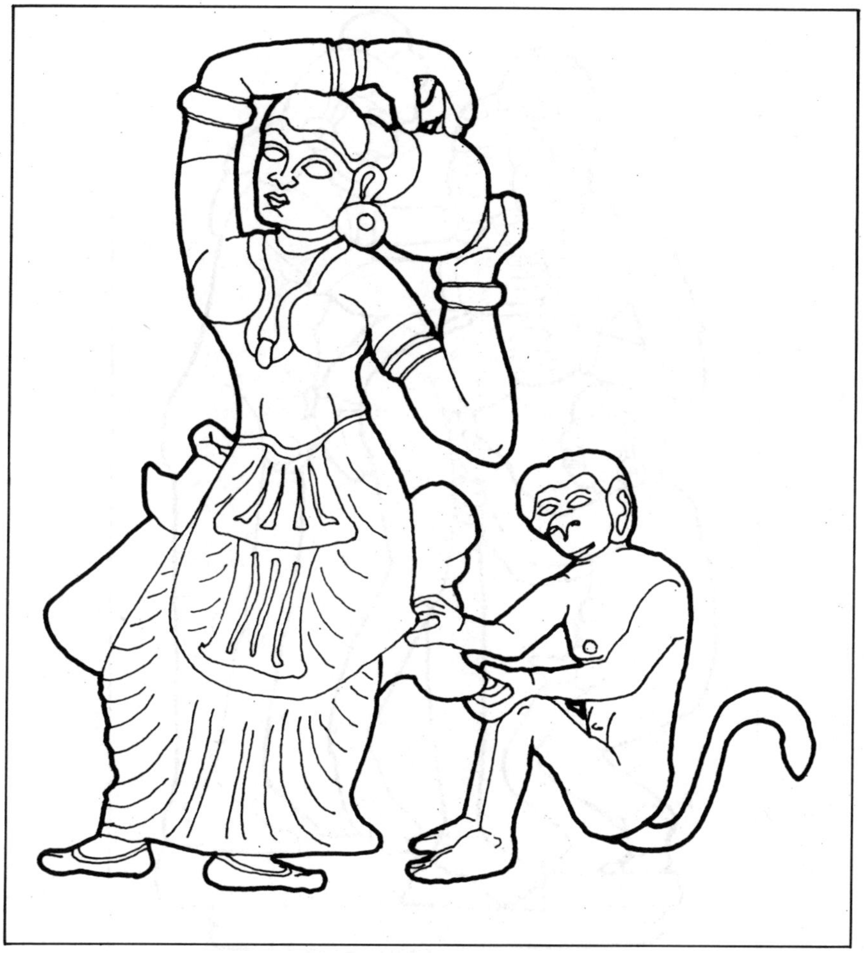

128. Woman with monkey.

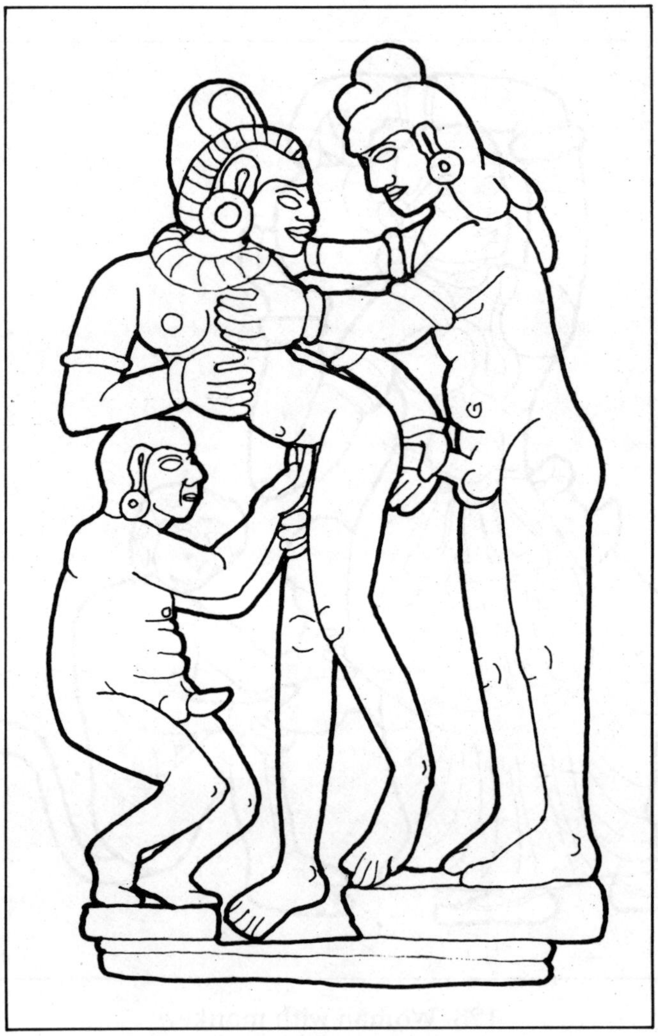

129. Erotic sculpture.

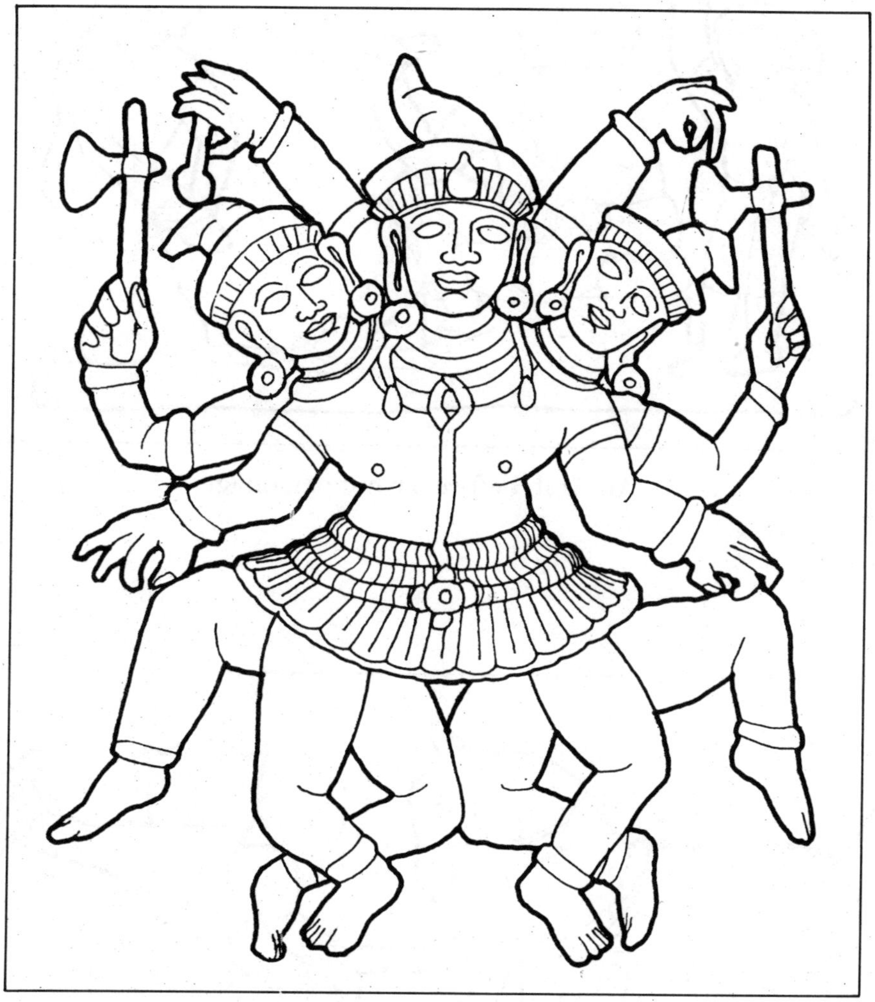

130. Composite figure.

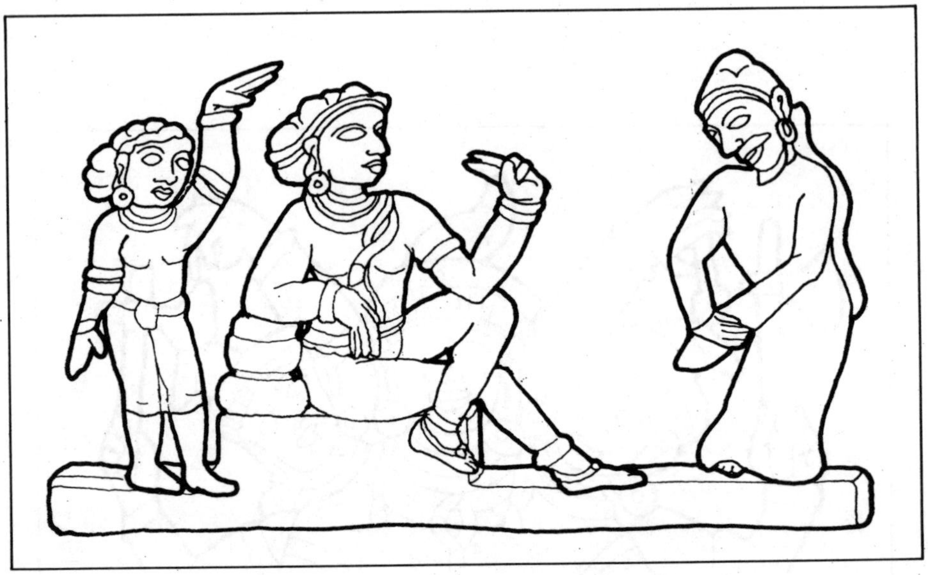

131. An Arab before a royal personage.

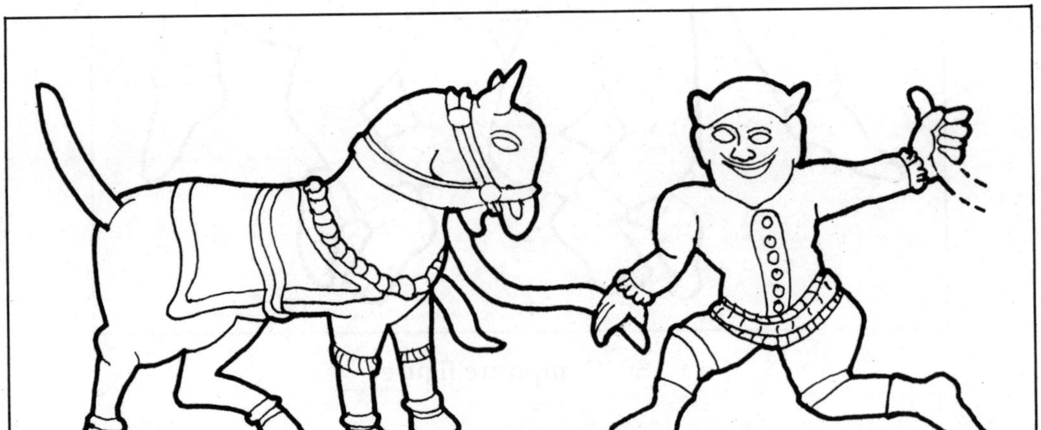

132. Portuguese horse-trader.

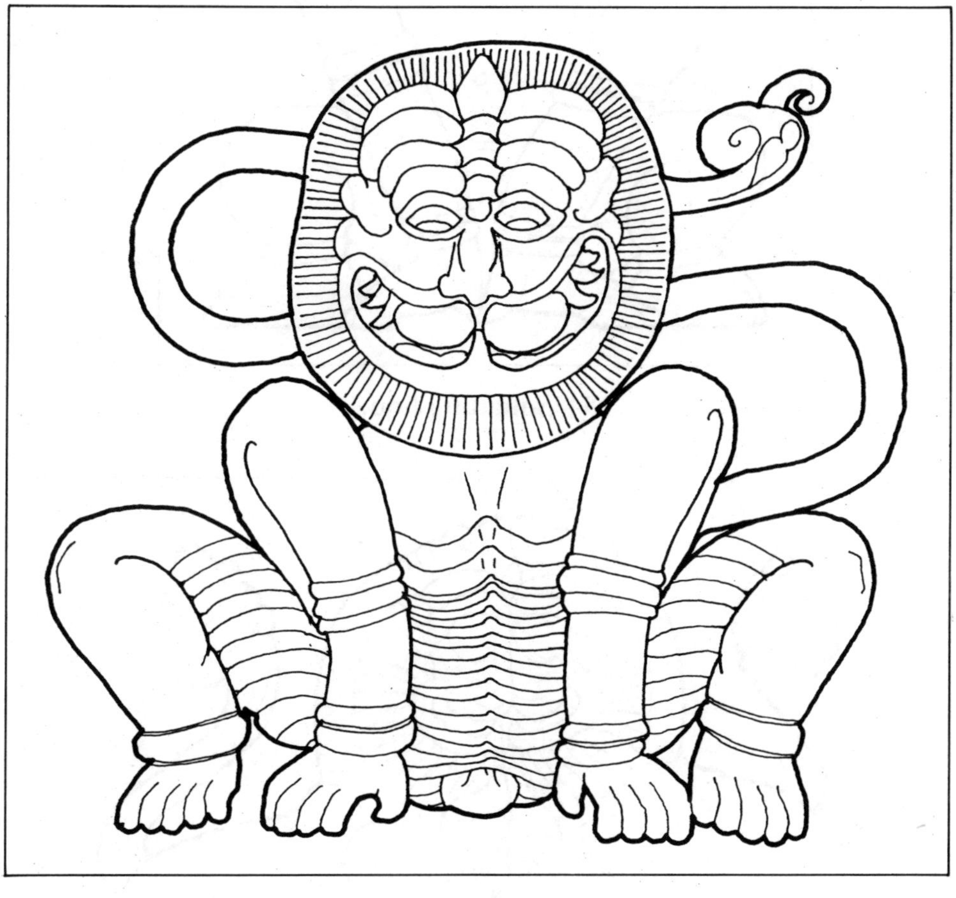

133. Squatting lion.

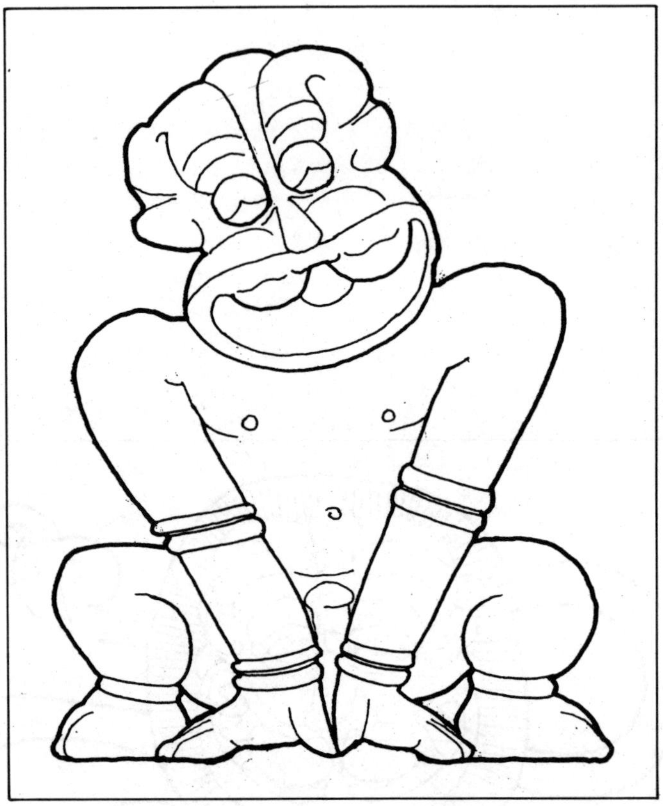

134. Squatting lion.

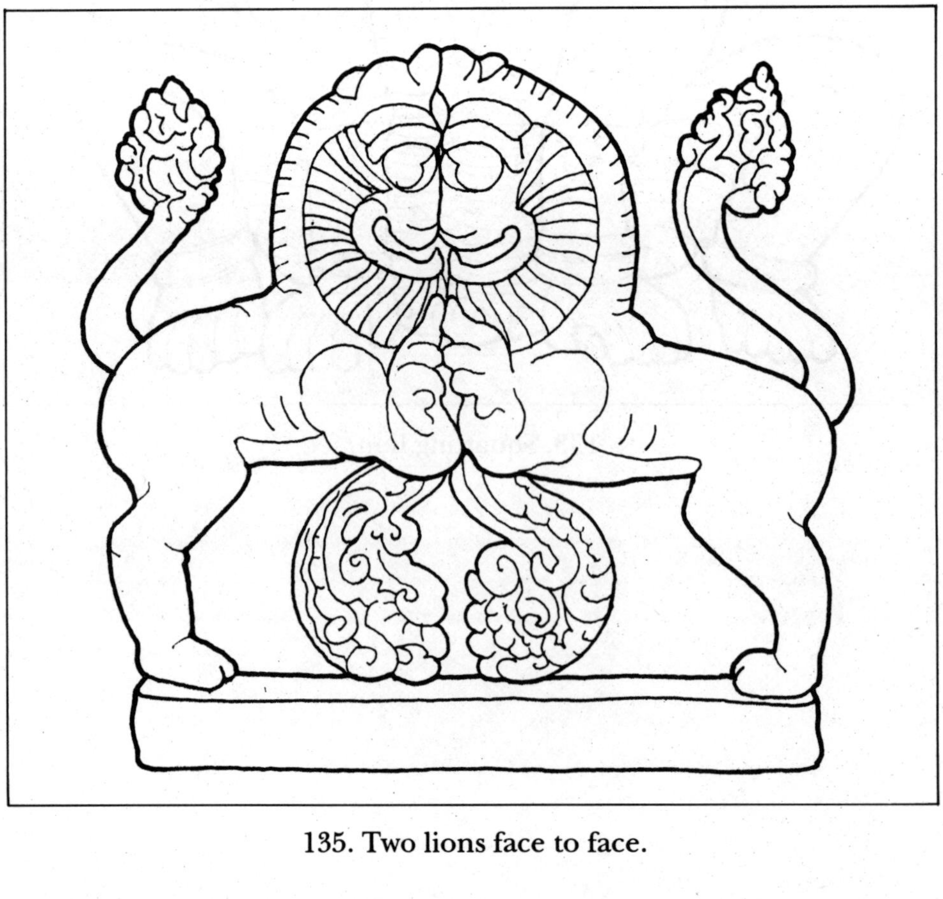

135. Two lions face to face.

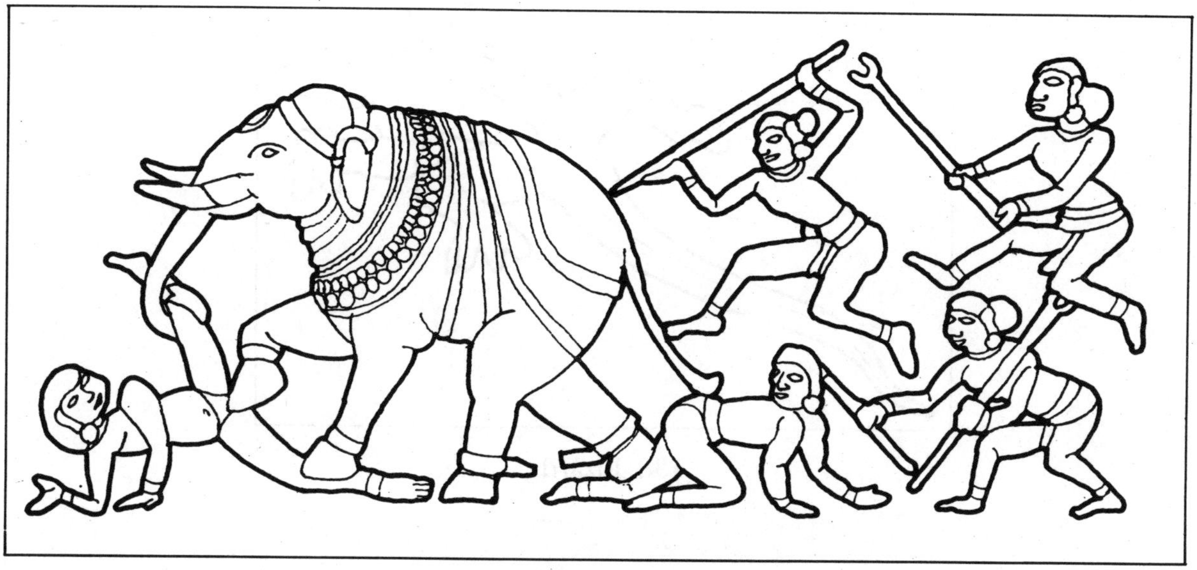

136. Enraged elephant.

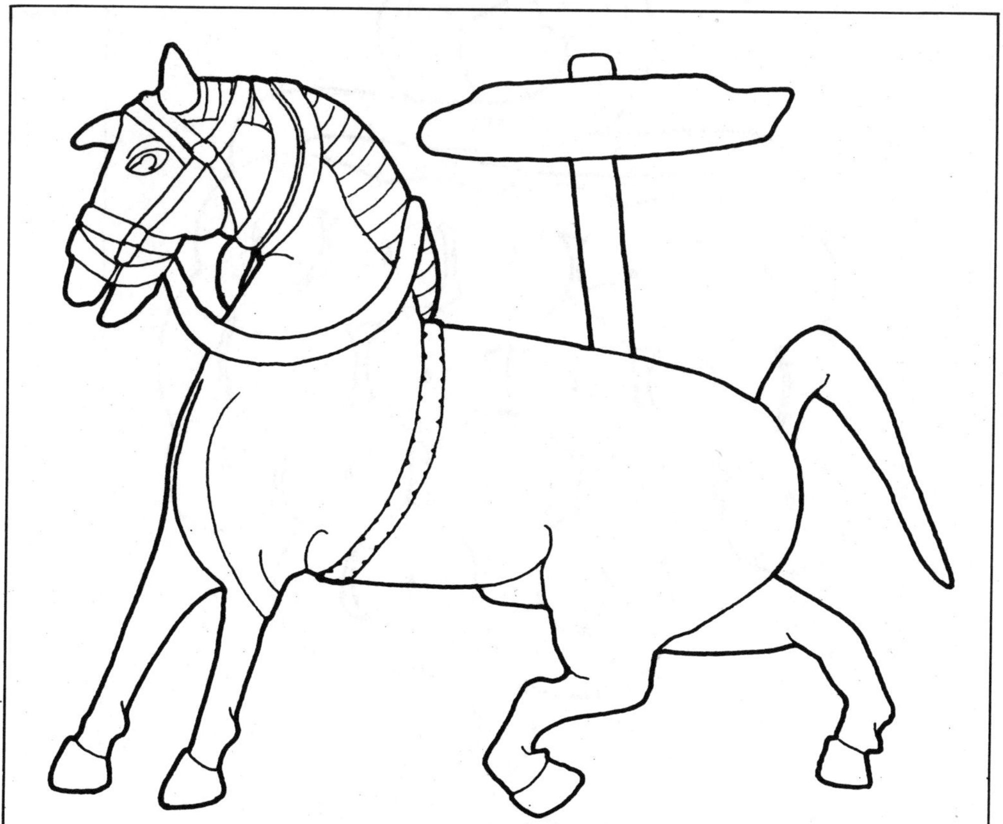

137. Royal horse.

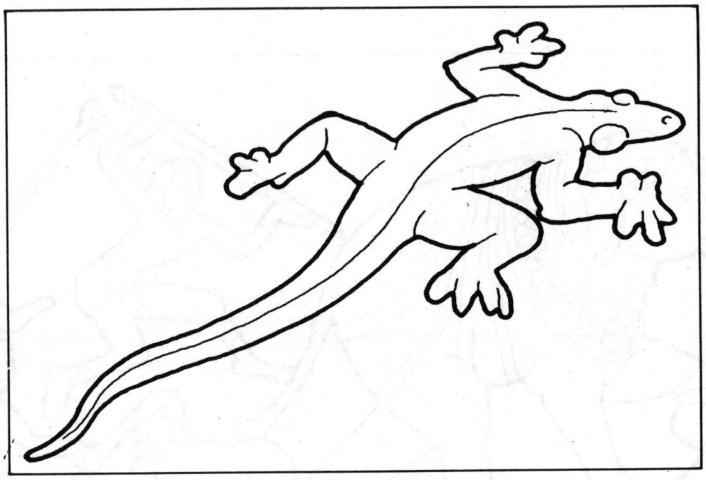

138. Lizard.

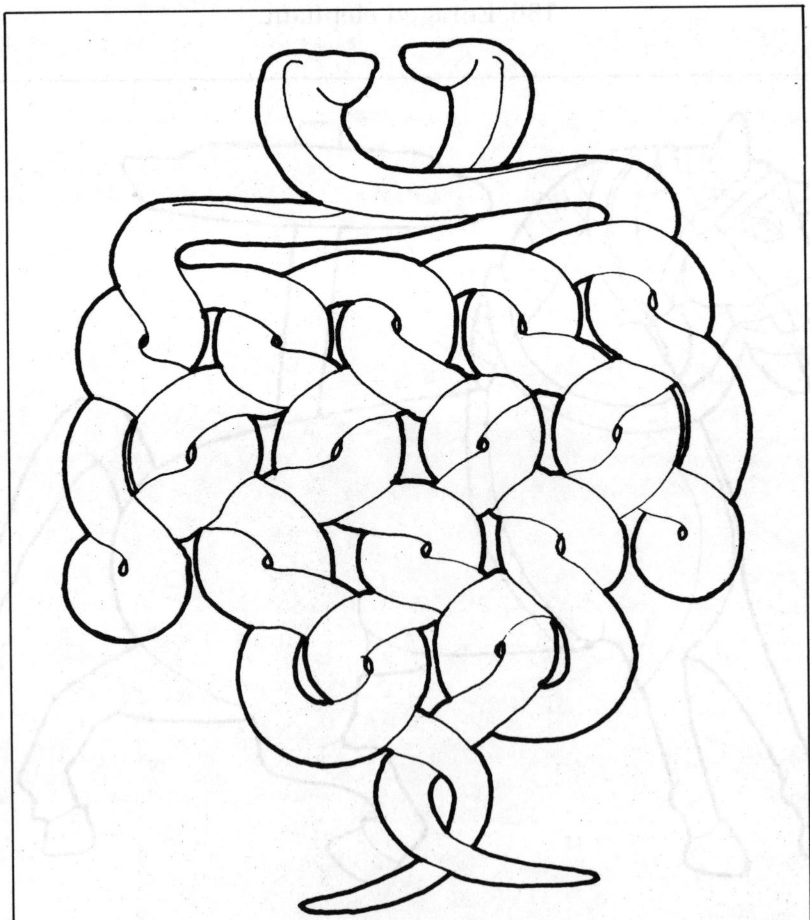

139. Naga-pasha.

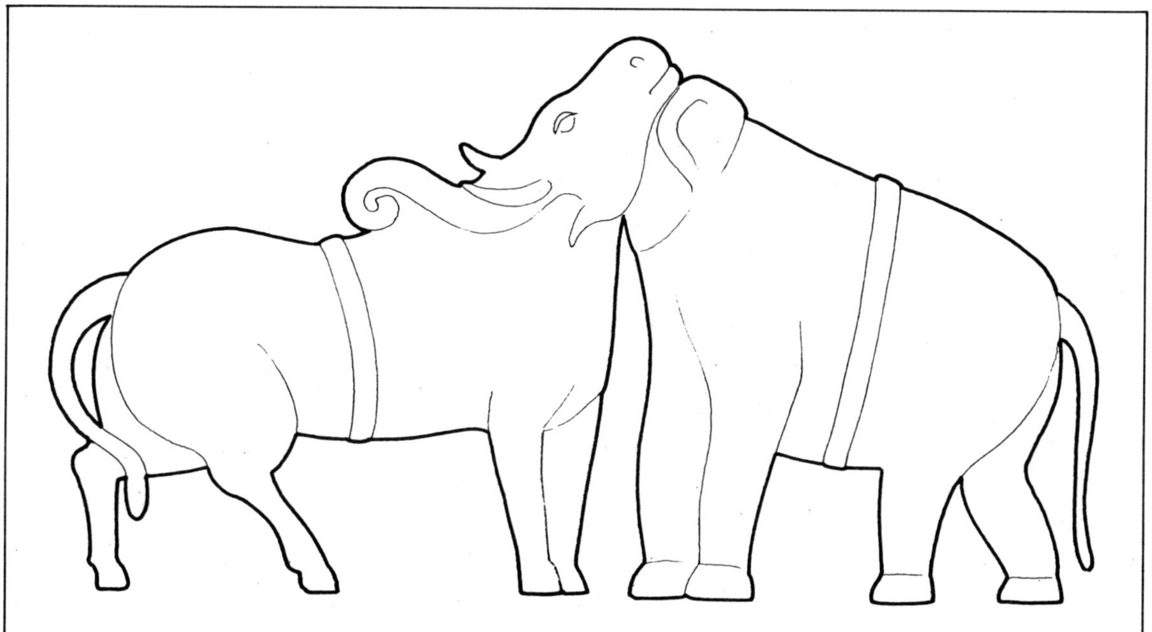

140. Gaja-vrishabha.

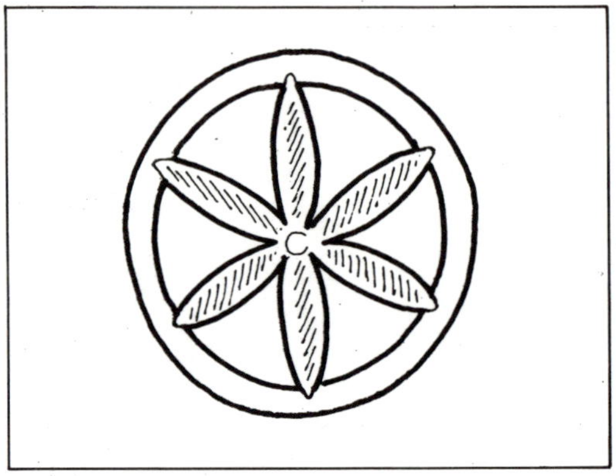

141. Lotus medallion.

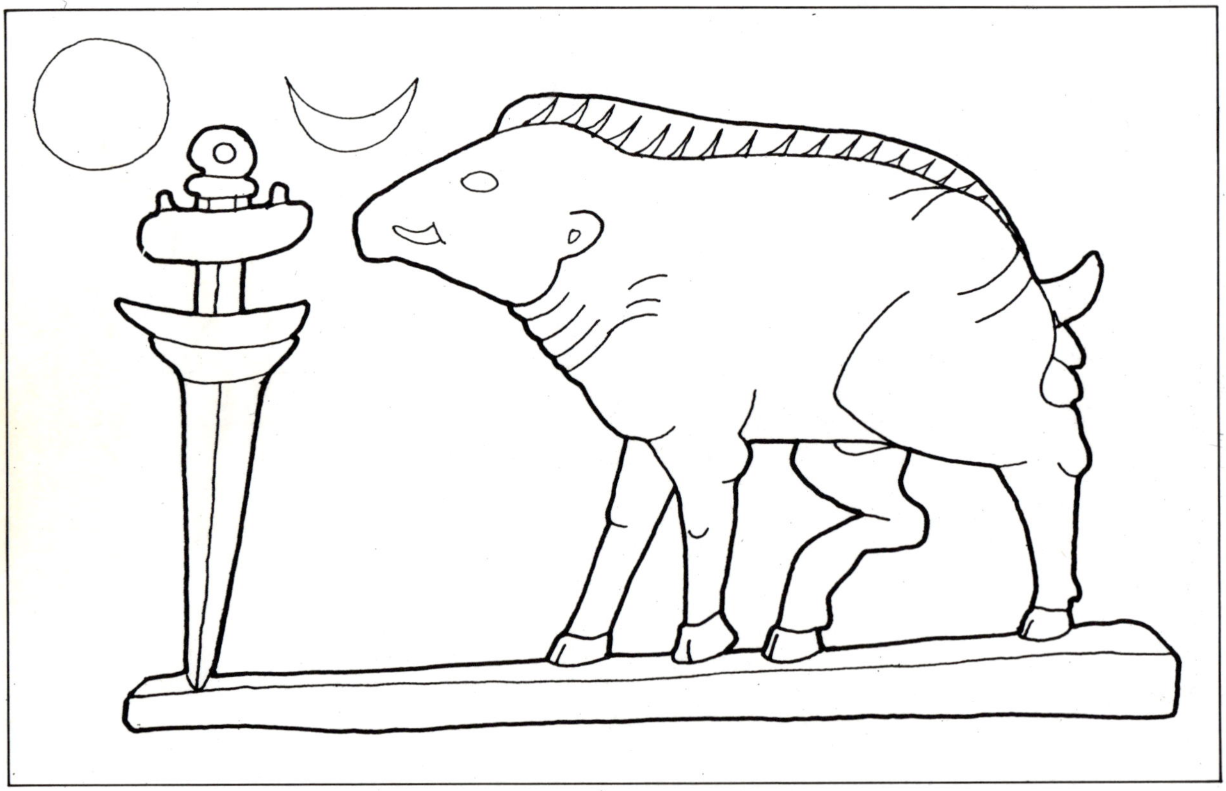

142. Vijayanagara emblem.

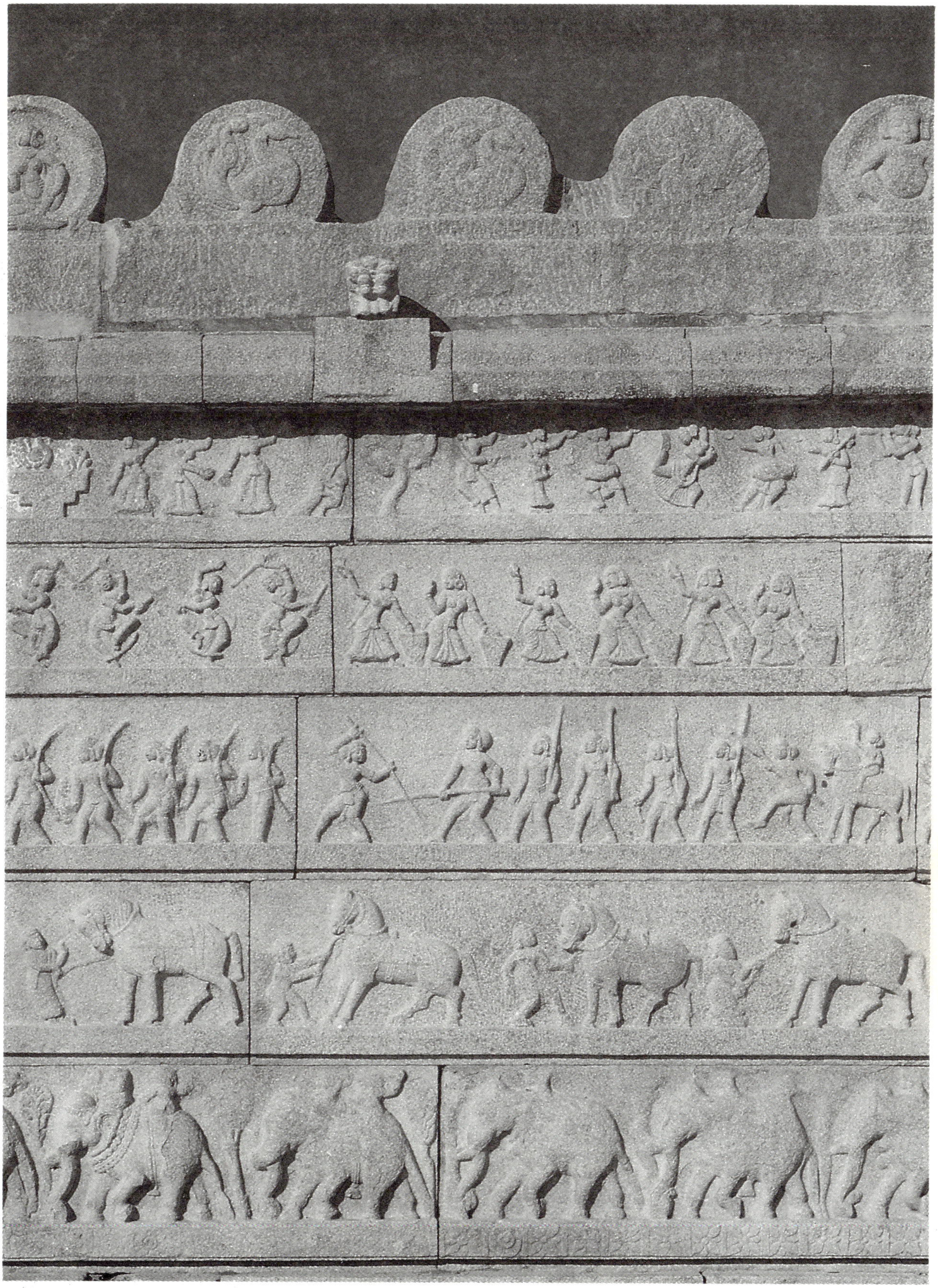

1. Friezes, Ramachandra temple, outer face of the enclosure wall, east side.

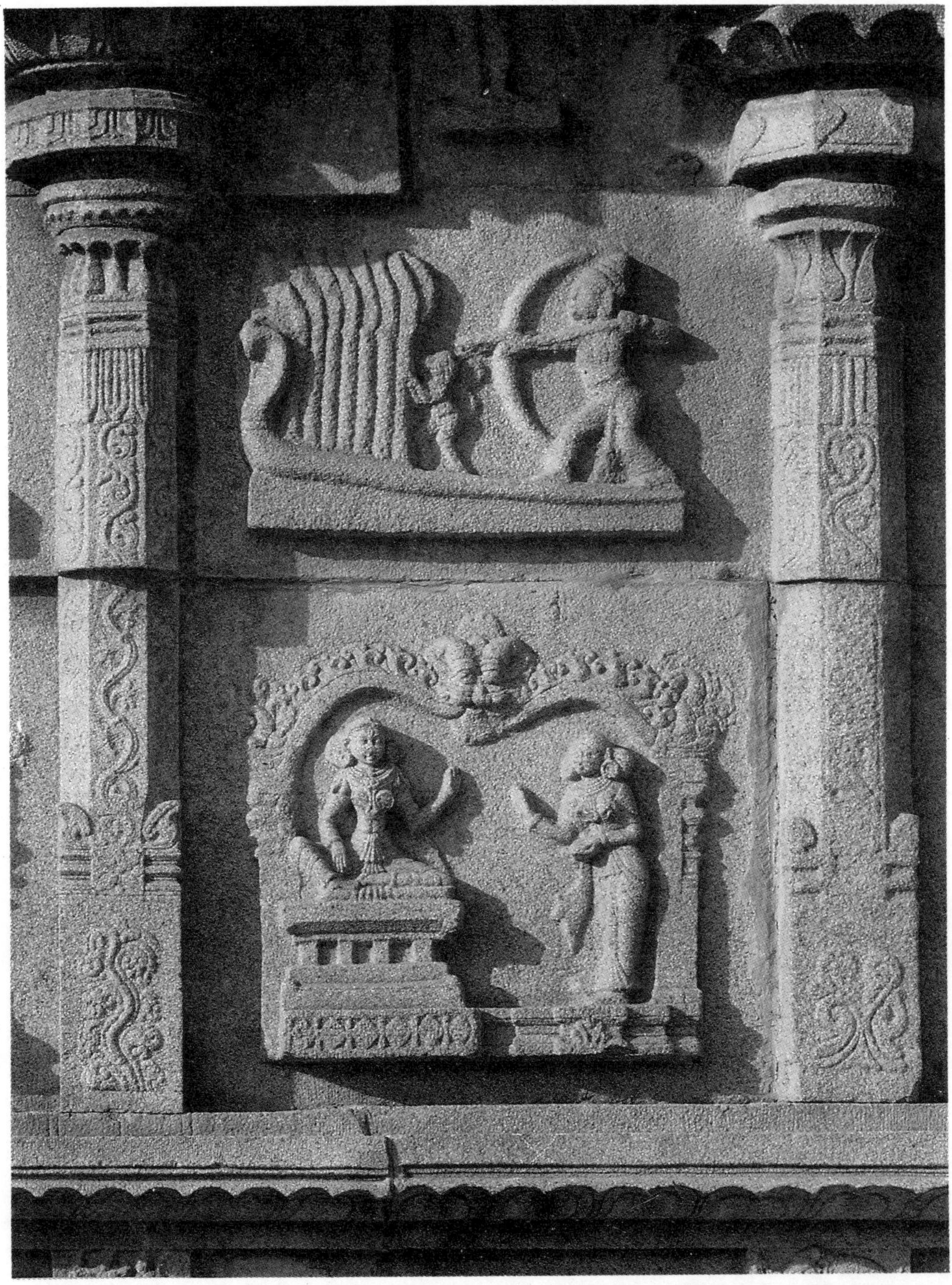

2. Ramayana scenes, Ramachandra temple, principal shrine, south wall.

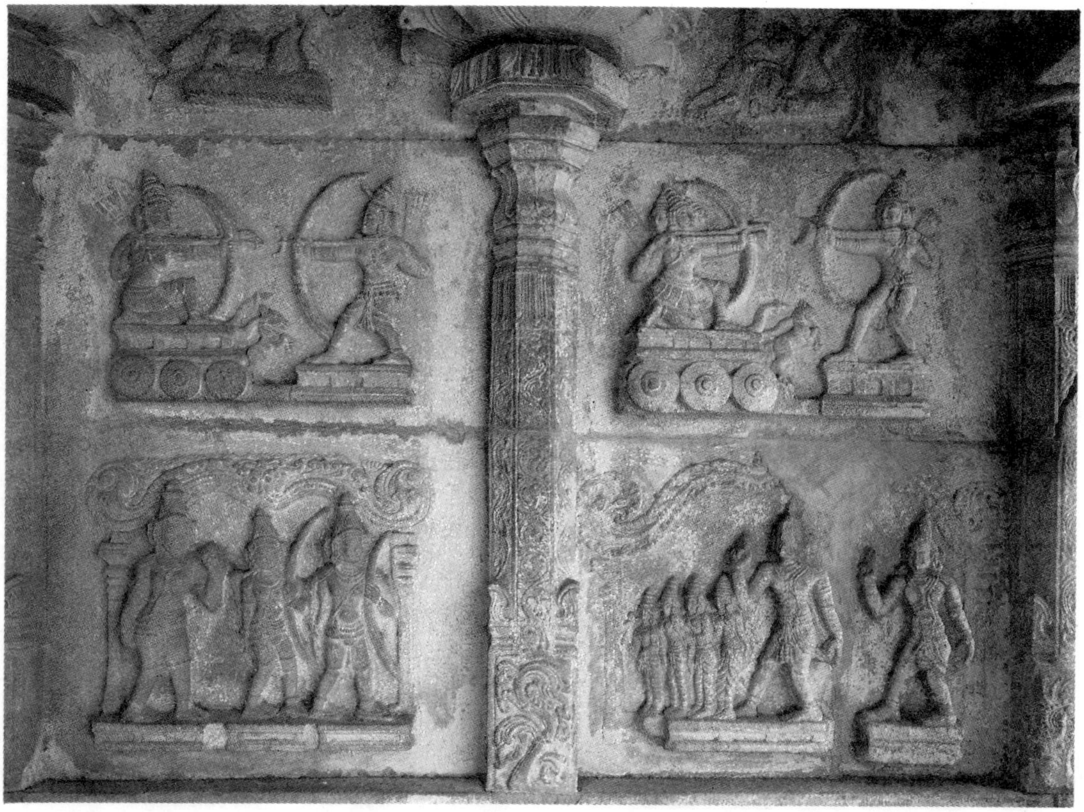

3. Ramayana scenes, Ramachandra temple, principal shrine, east wall.

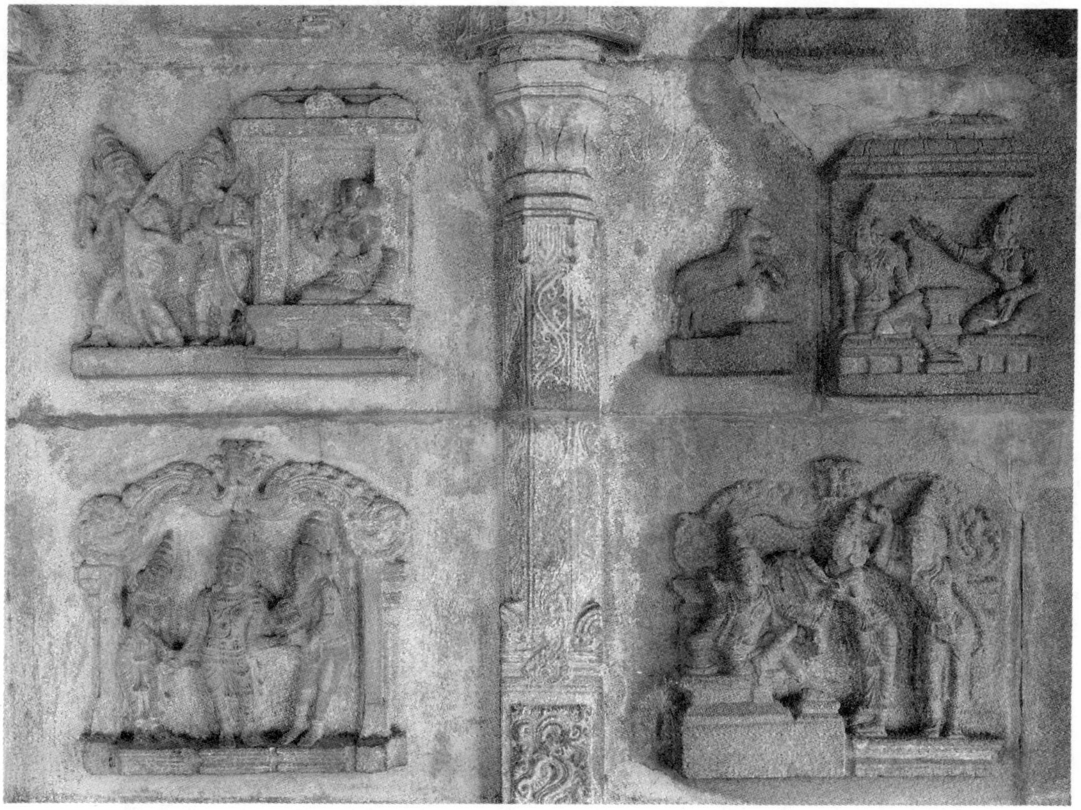

4. Ramayana scenes, Ramachandra temple, principal shrine, east wall.

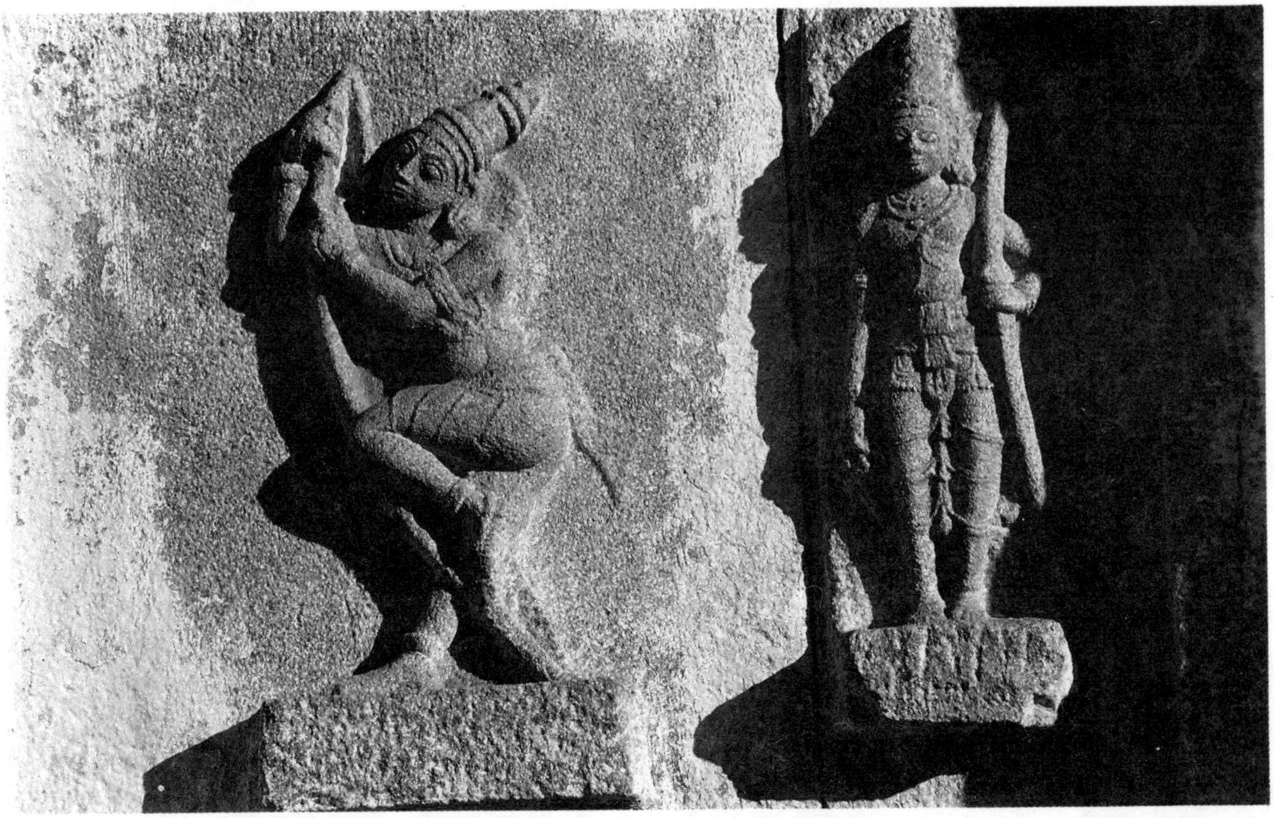

5. Rama strings Parashurama's bow, Ramachandra temple, principal shrine, south wall.

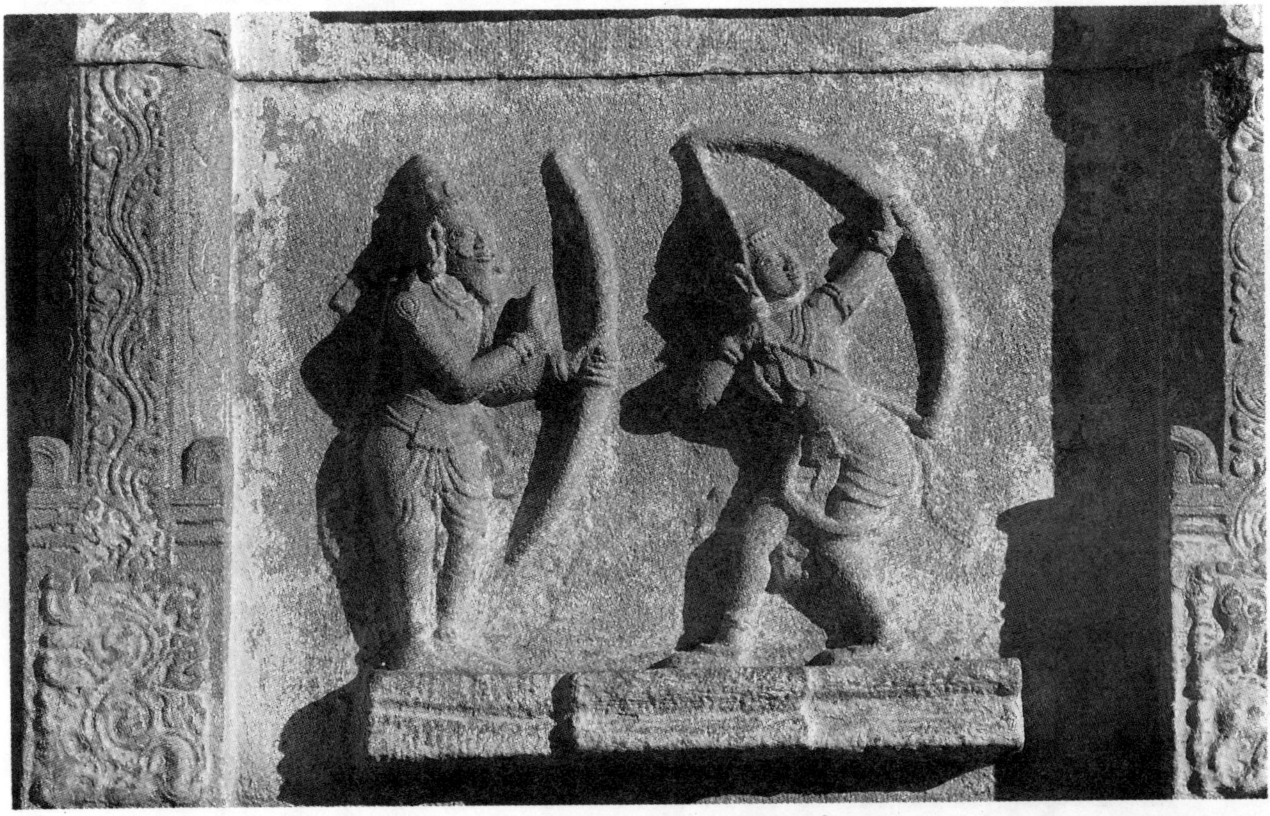

6. Rama bends Parashurama's bow, Ramachandra temple, principal shrine, south wall.

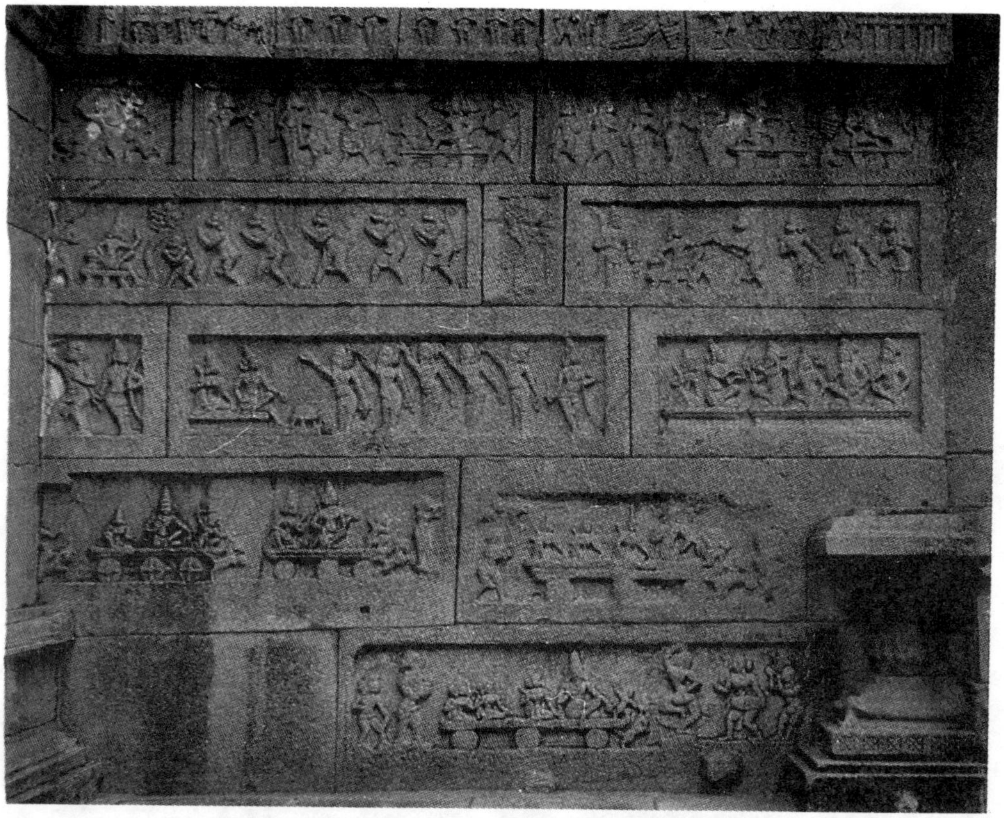

7. Ramayana scenes, Ramachandra temple, inner face of outer enclosure wall, east side.

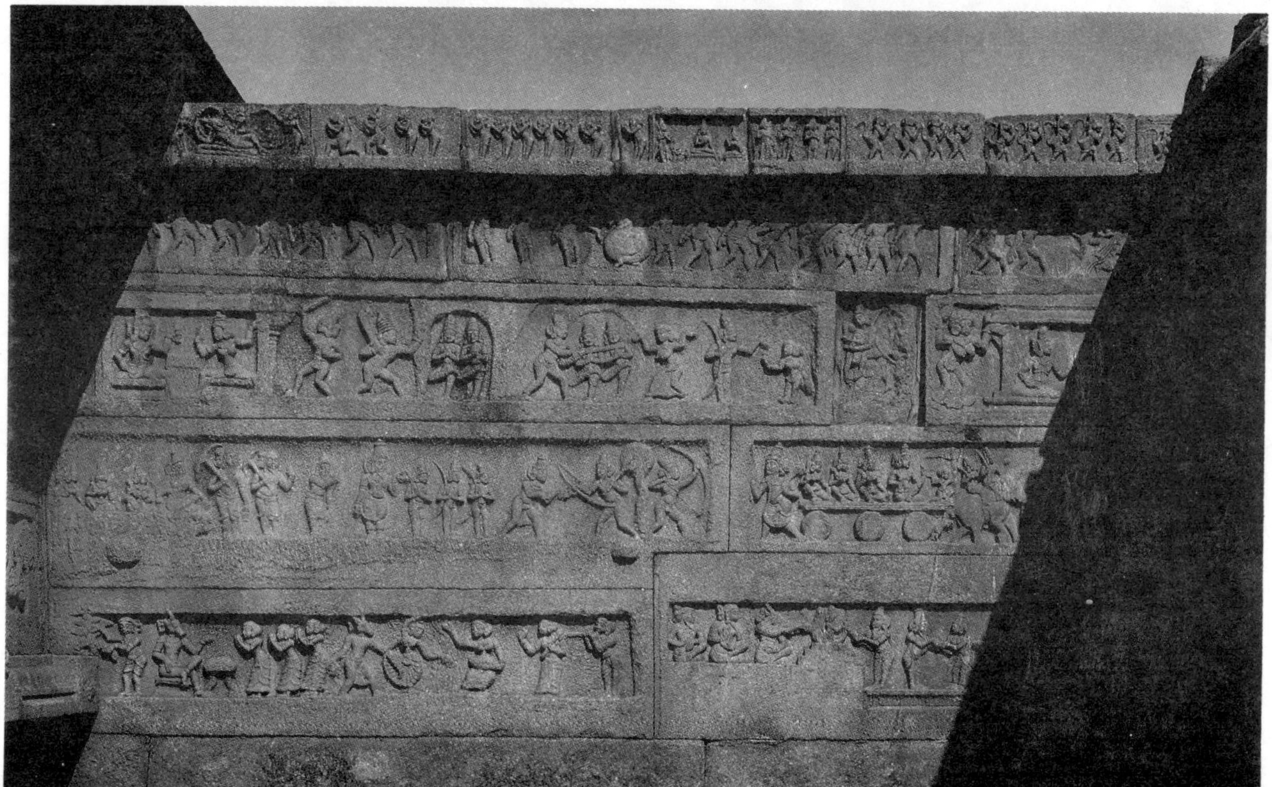

8. Ramayana scenes, Ramachandra temple, inner face of outer enclosure wall, north side.

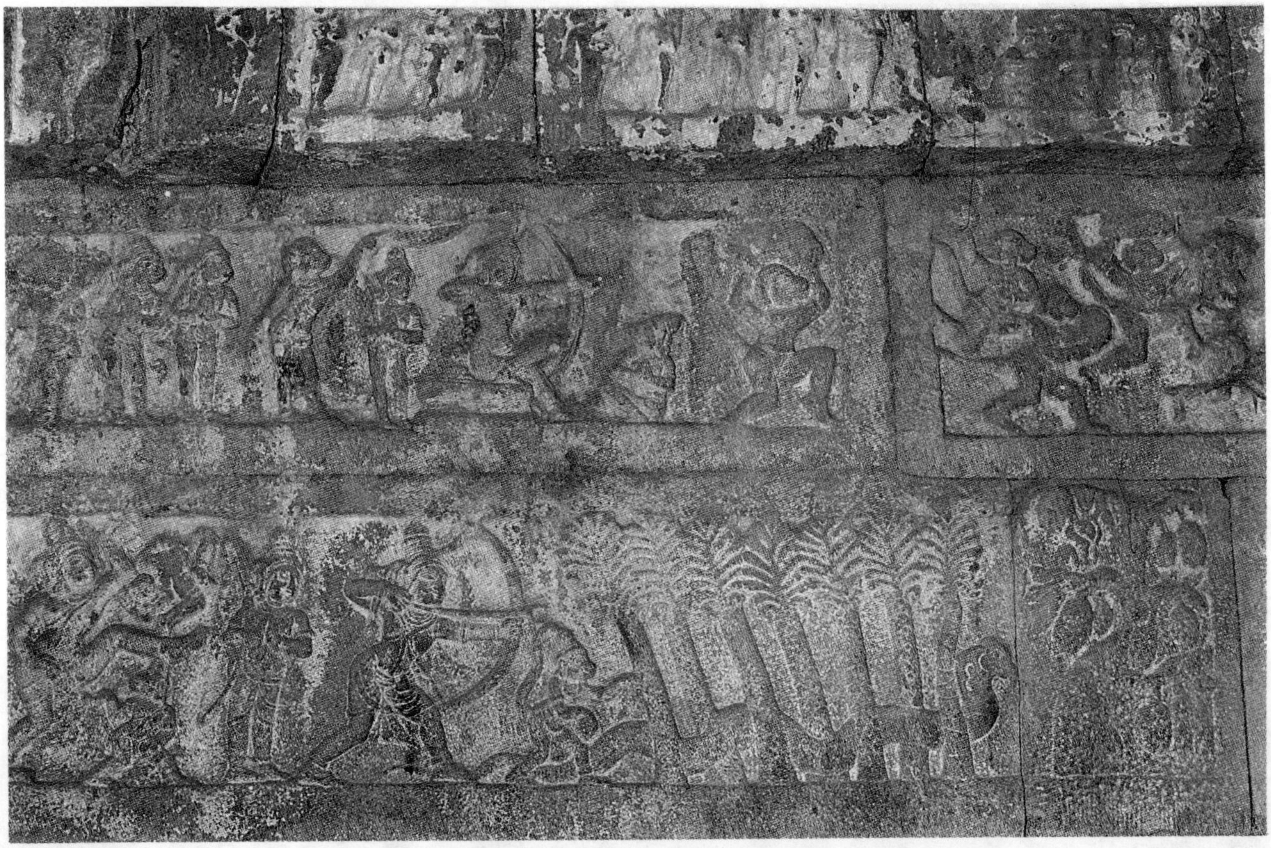

9. Ramayana scenes, Ramachandra temple, inner face of outer enclosure wall, east side.

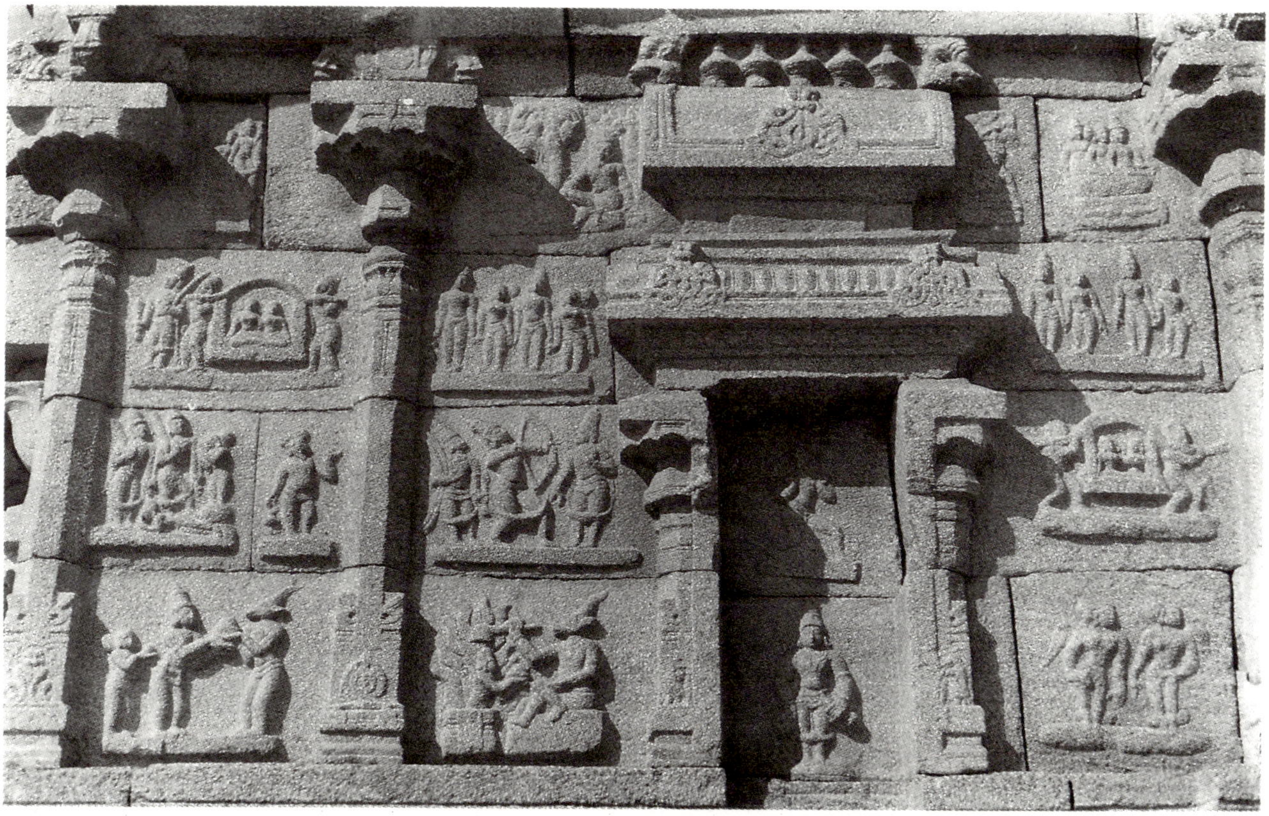

10. Ramayana scenes, Ramanuja temple, east side of gopura, outside the prakara wall.

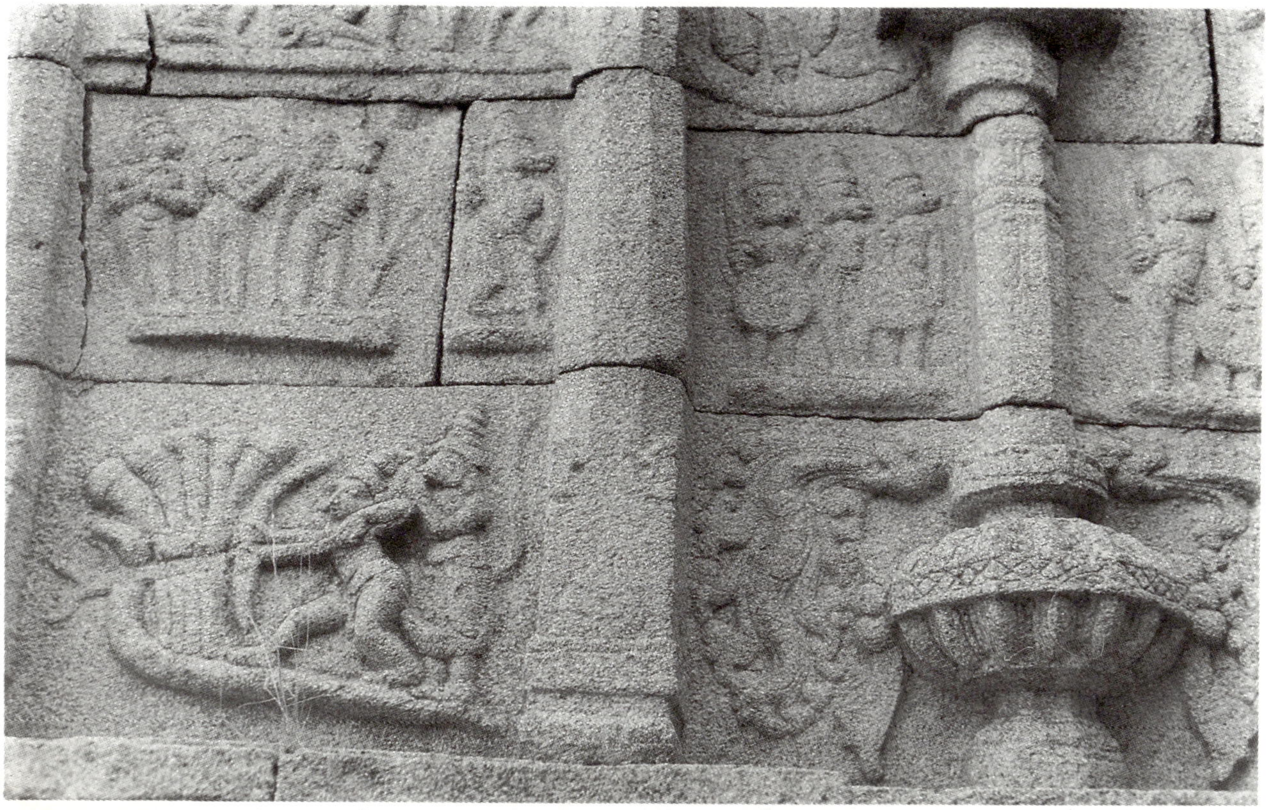

11. Ramayana scenes, Ramanuja temple, west side of the gopura, outside the prakara wall.

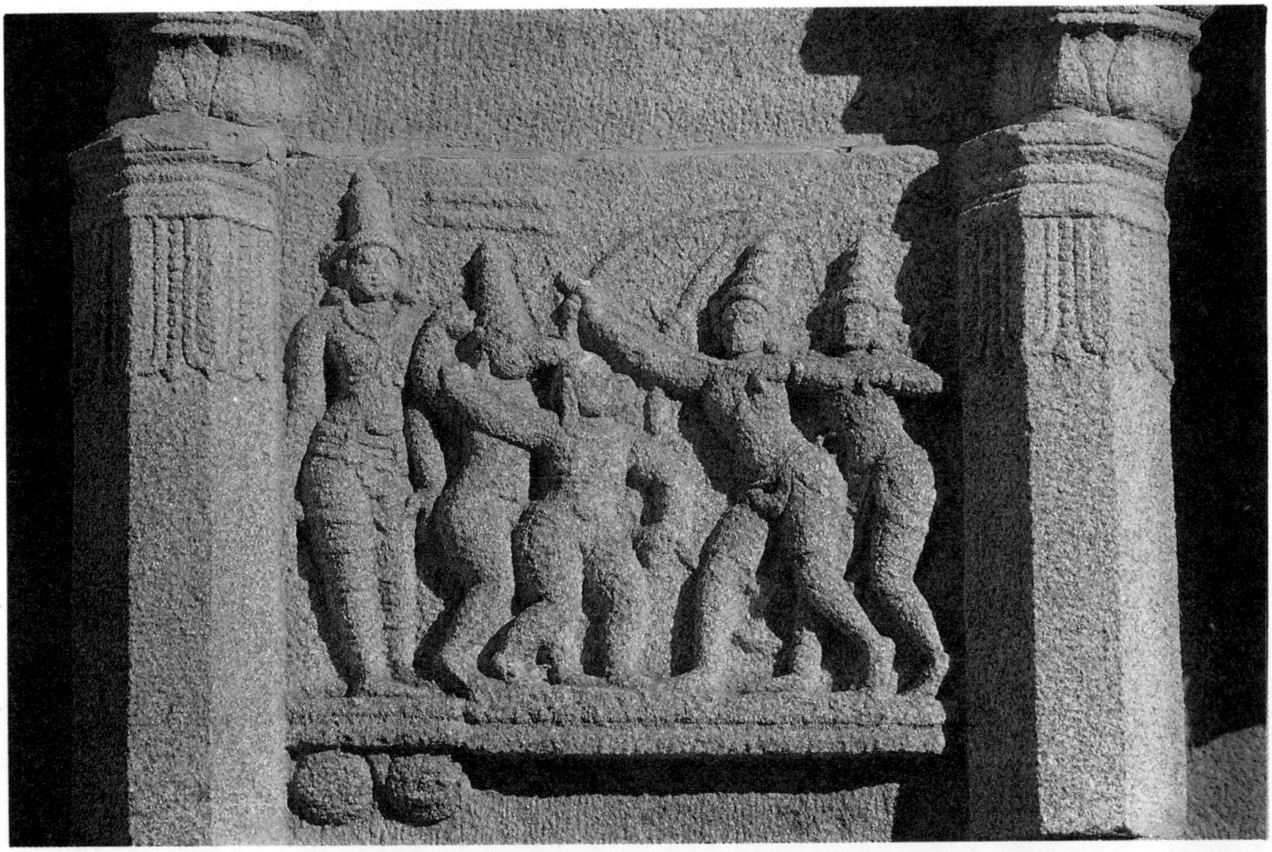

12. Kusha and Lava fight against Rama, Lakshmana and Hanuman, Ramachandra temple, minor shrine, south wall.

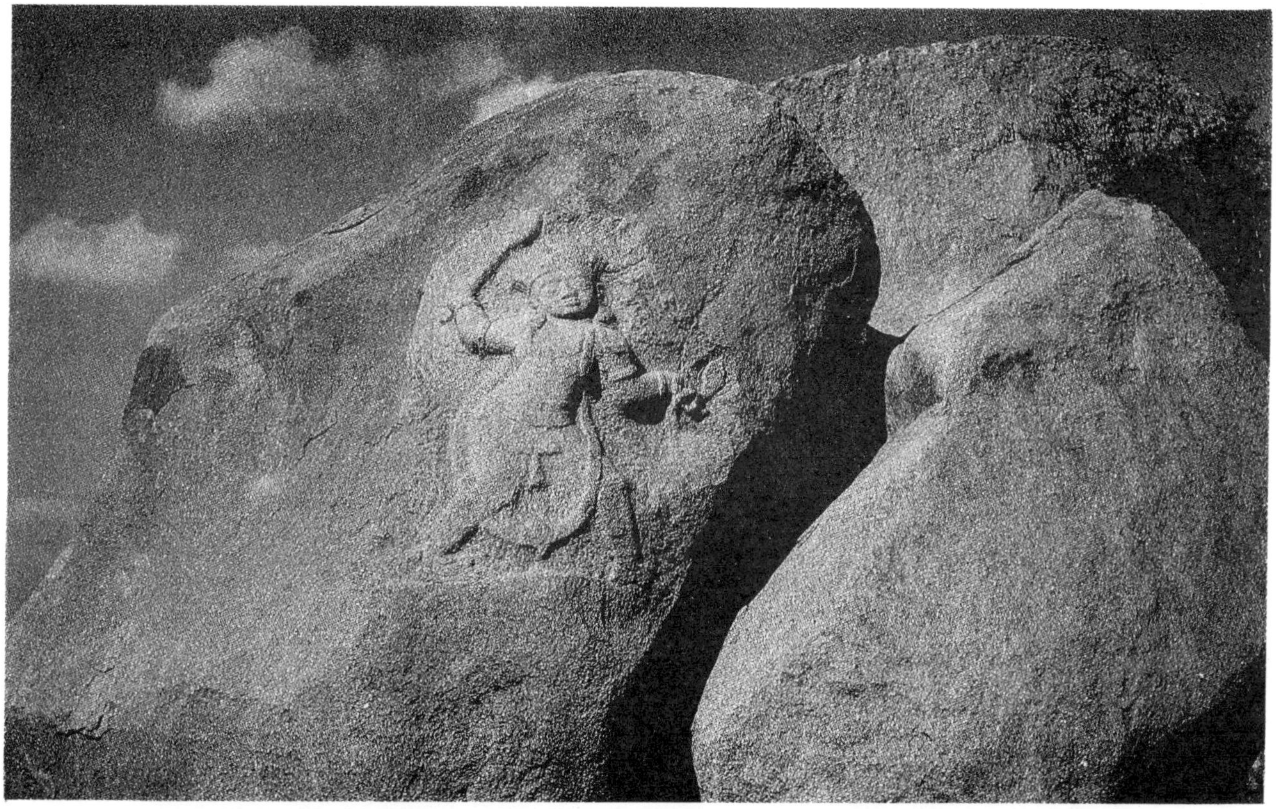

13. Bhima in pratyalidha pose. Carving on a boulder near Kudrekallu Gate.

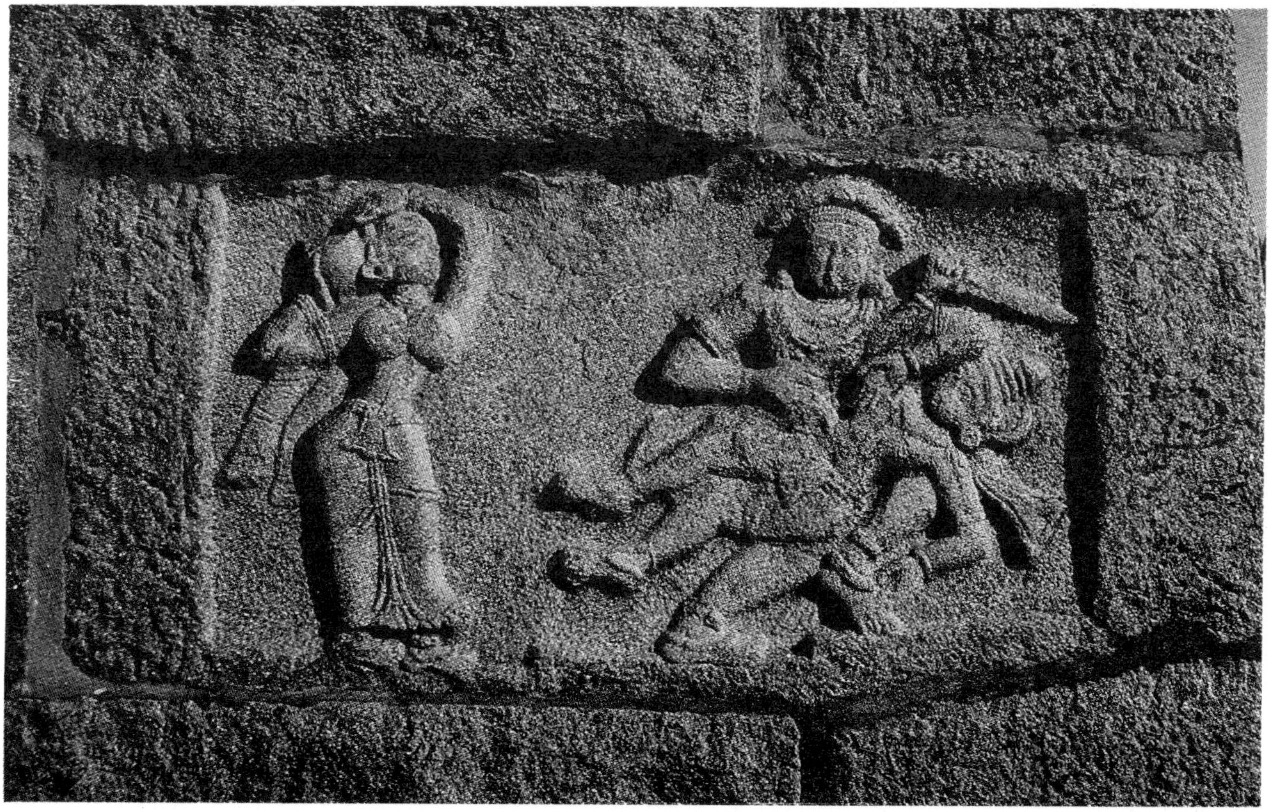

14. Bhima killing Duhshasana and Draupadi tying her hair, carving on Bhima's Gate.

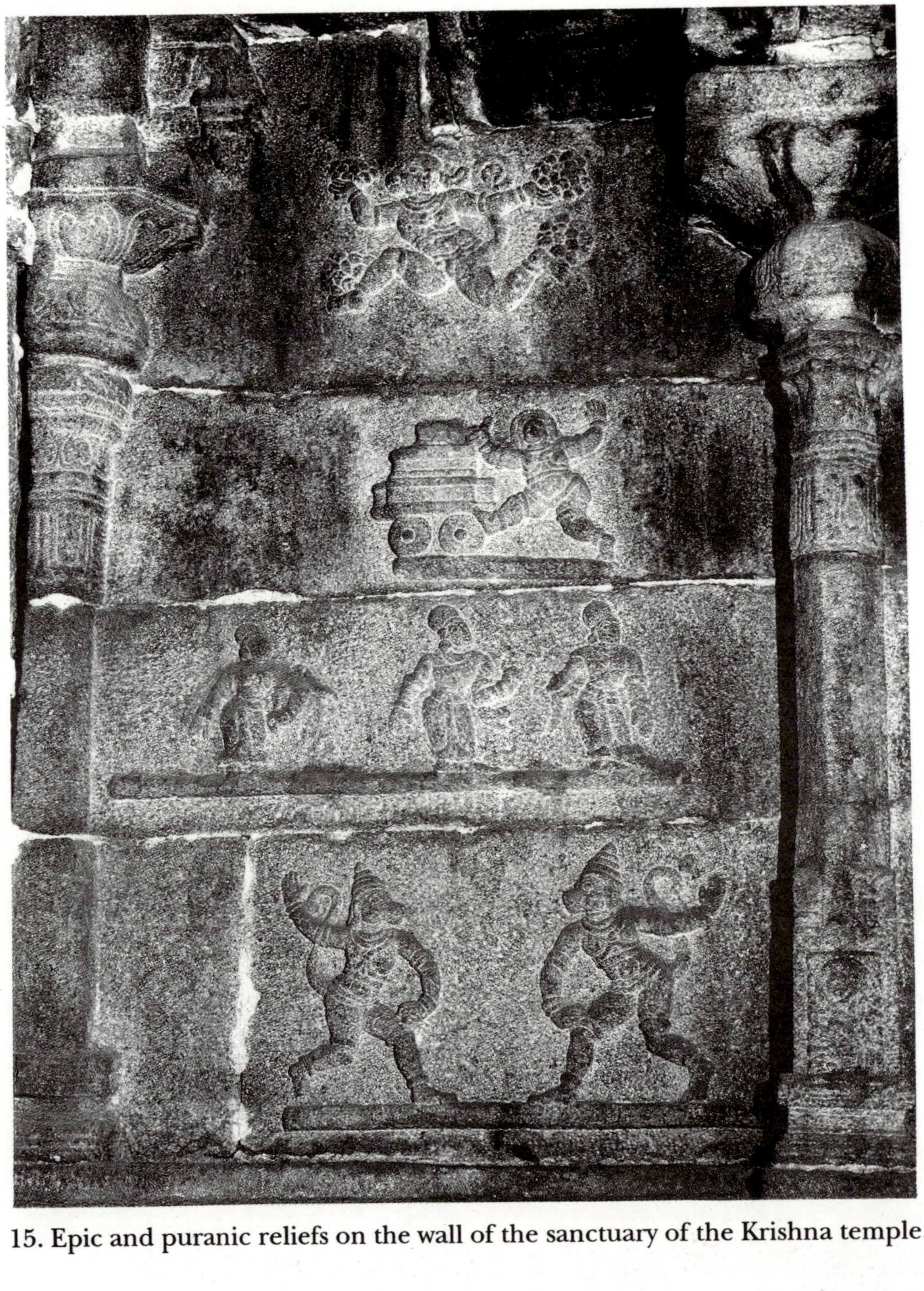

15. Epic and puranic reliefs on the wall of the sanctuary of the Krishna temple.

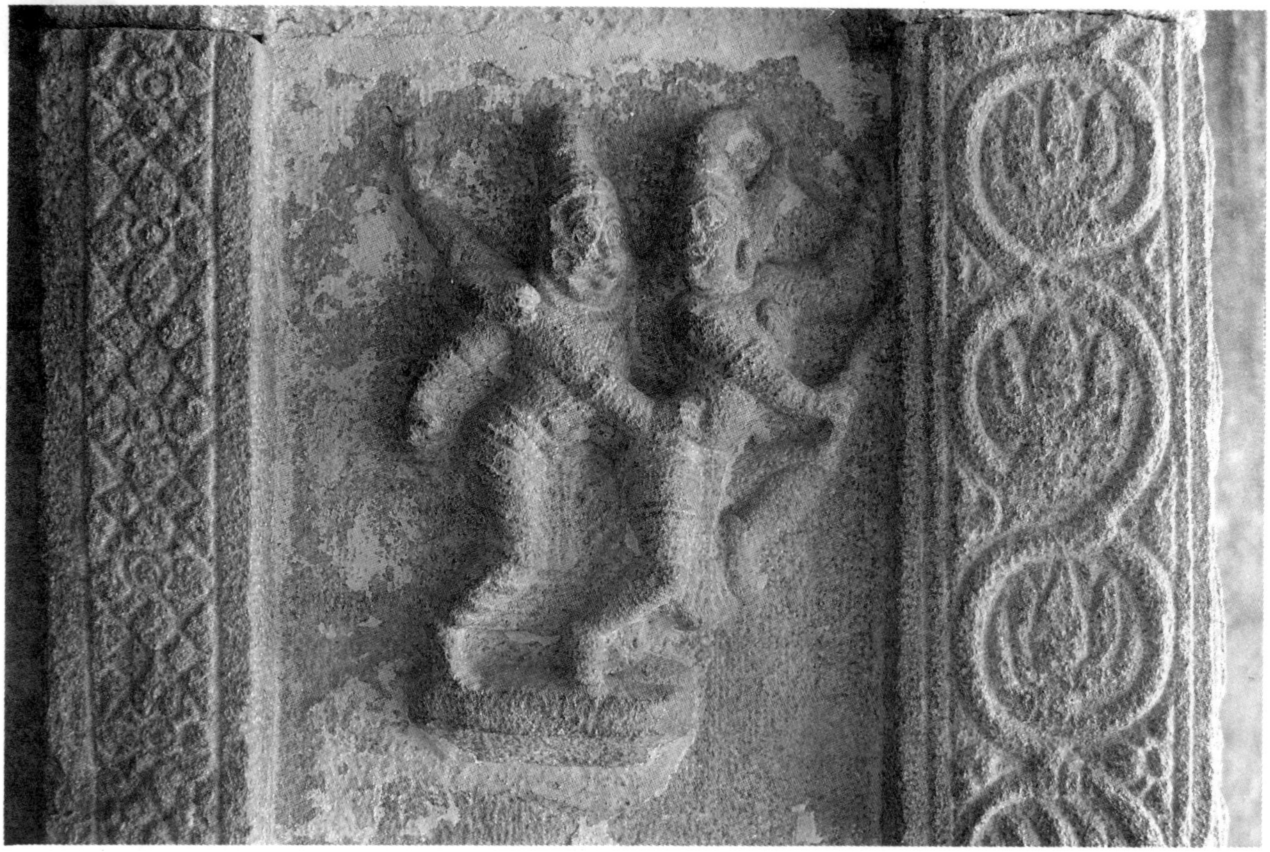

16. Narasimha grabs Hiranyakashipu, Ramachandra temple, minor shrine.

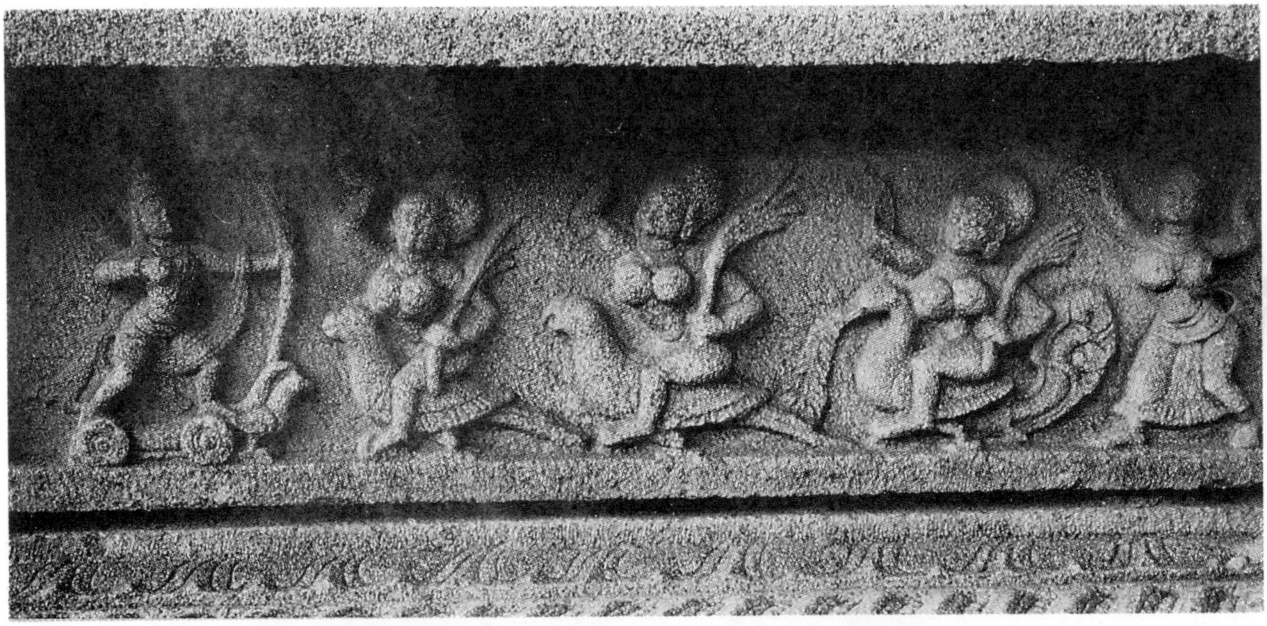

17. Rati, Kama, and retinue celebrating the Vasantotsava, Vithala temple complex, plinth of the north-east pavilion.

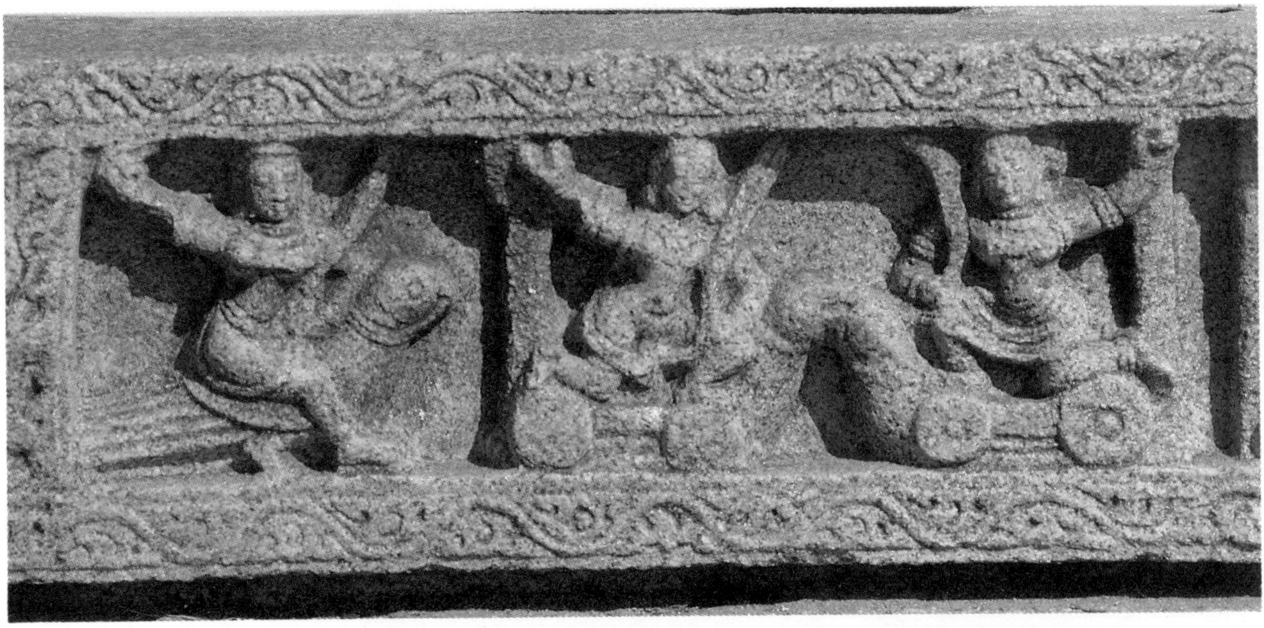

18. Vasantotsava celebrations, Vithala temple complex, base of stone chariot.

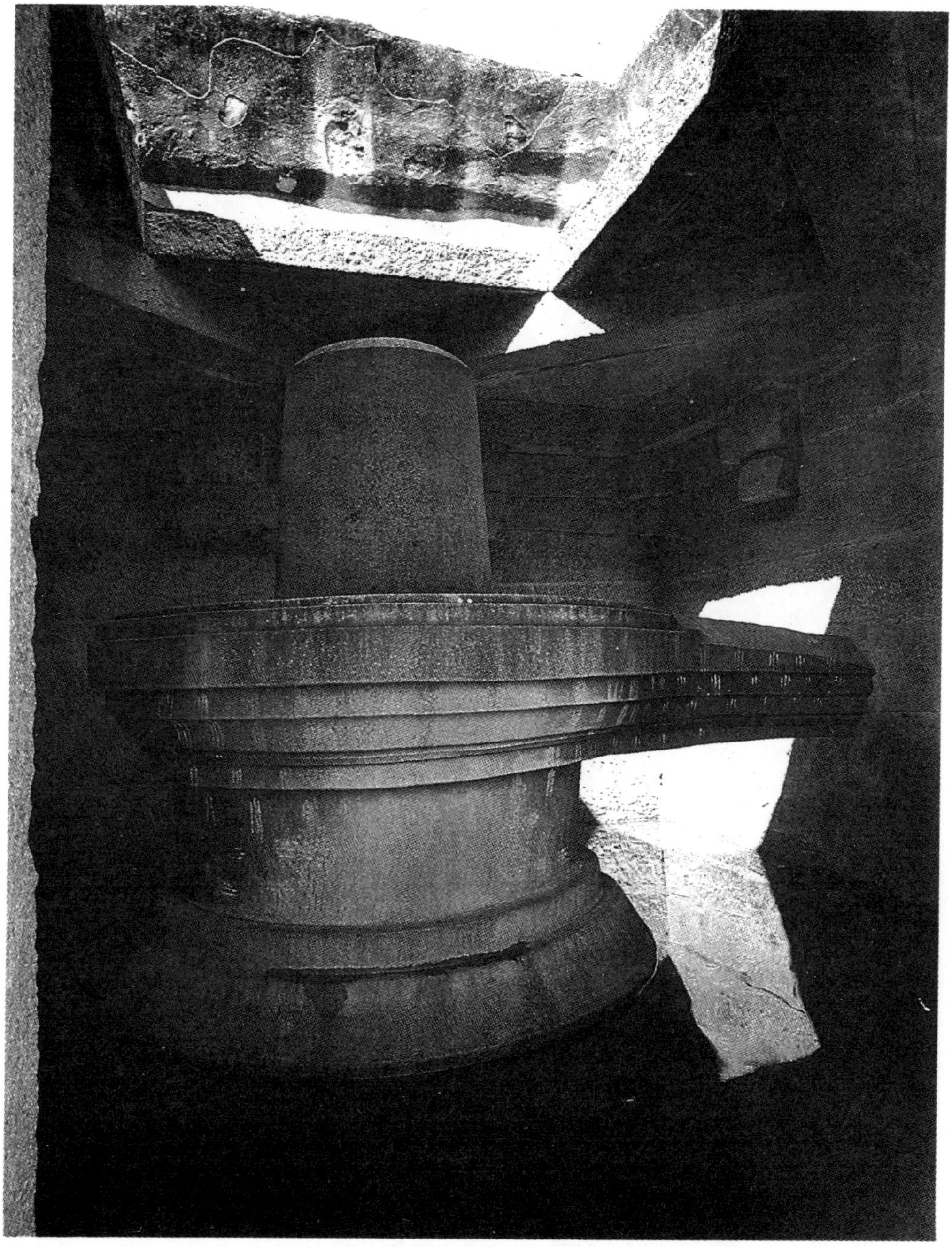

19. Giant linga in a shrine next to the Lakshmi-Narasimha monolith.

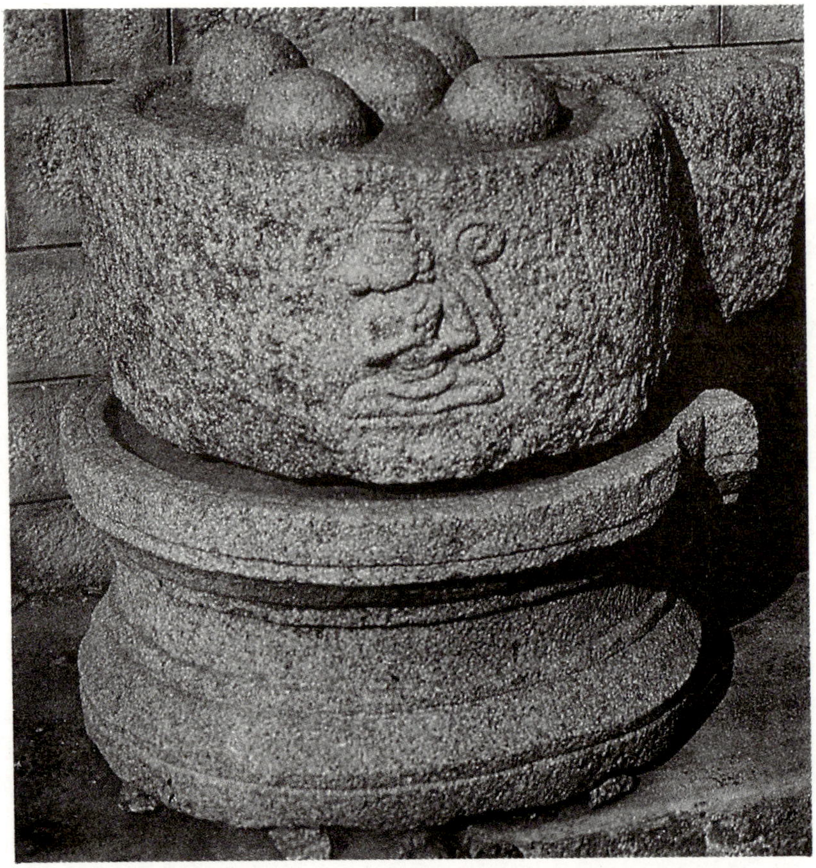

20. Hanuman and pancha-linga, Kamalapuram Museum.

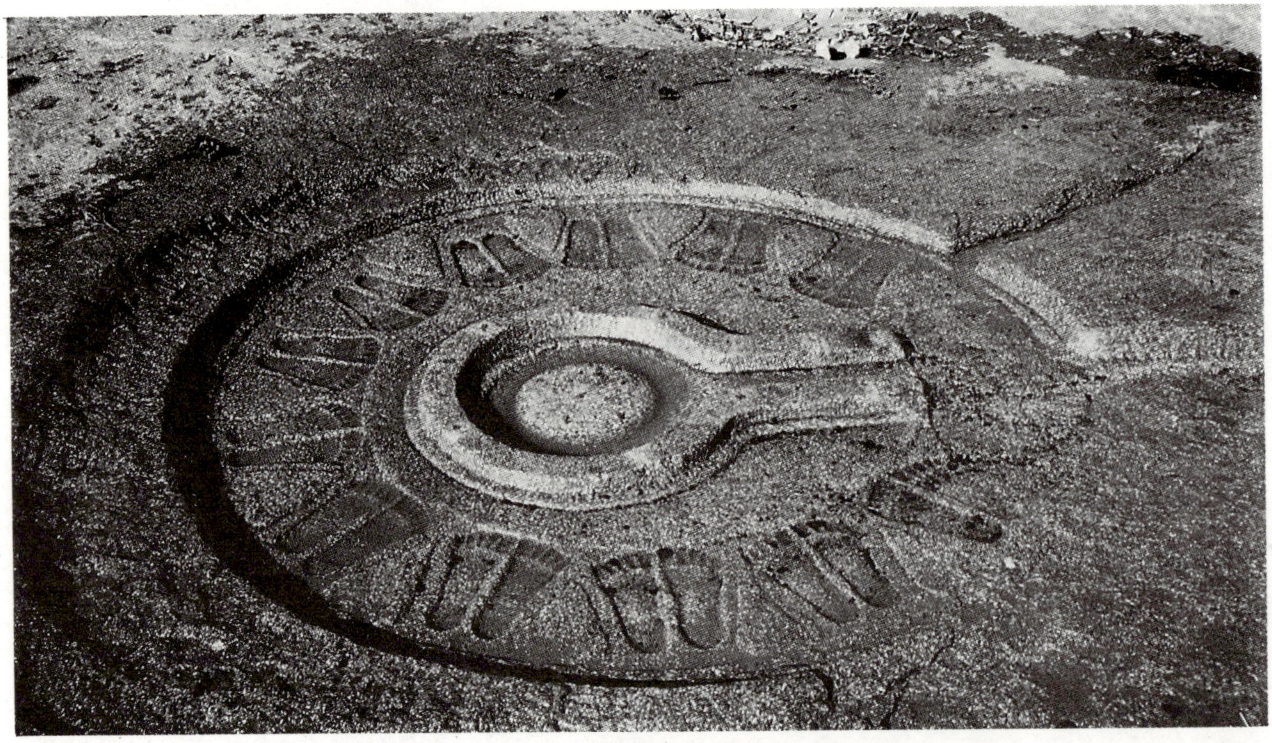

21. Linga encircled by twelve pairs of feet at Chakratirtha.

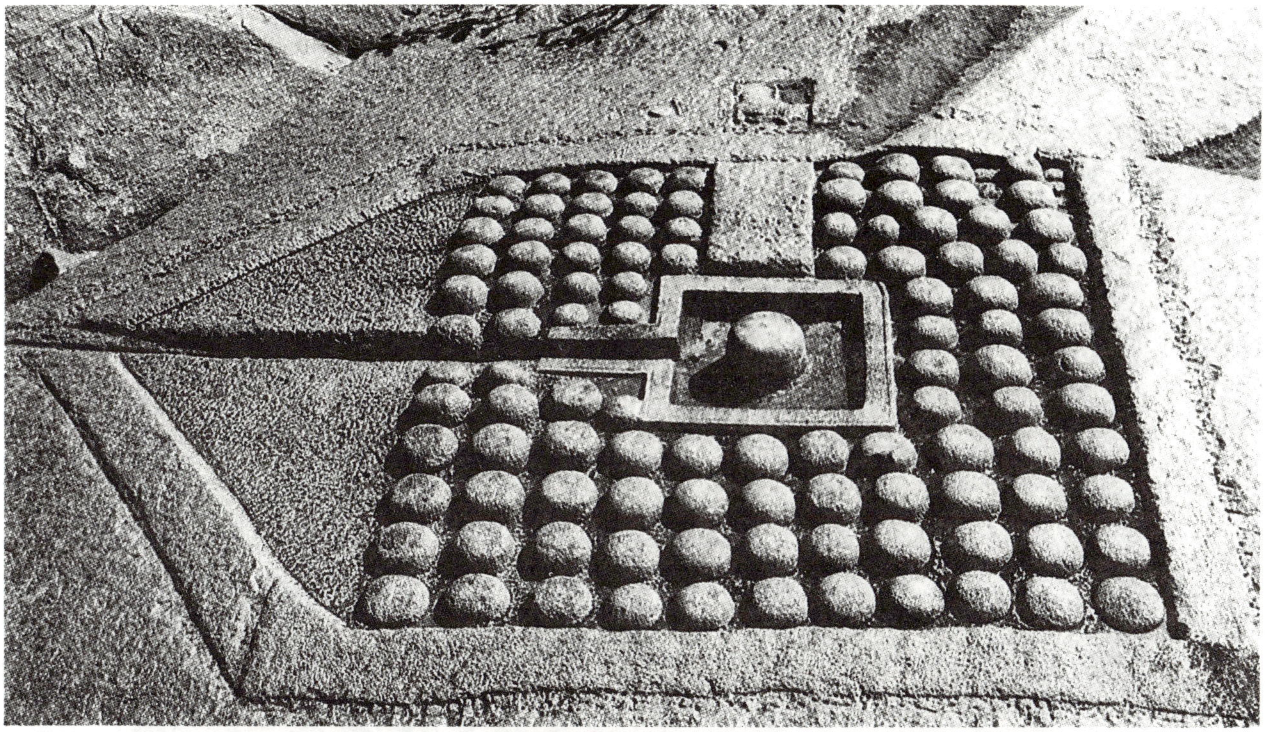

22. Group of lingas at Koti-tirtha.

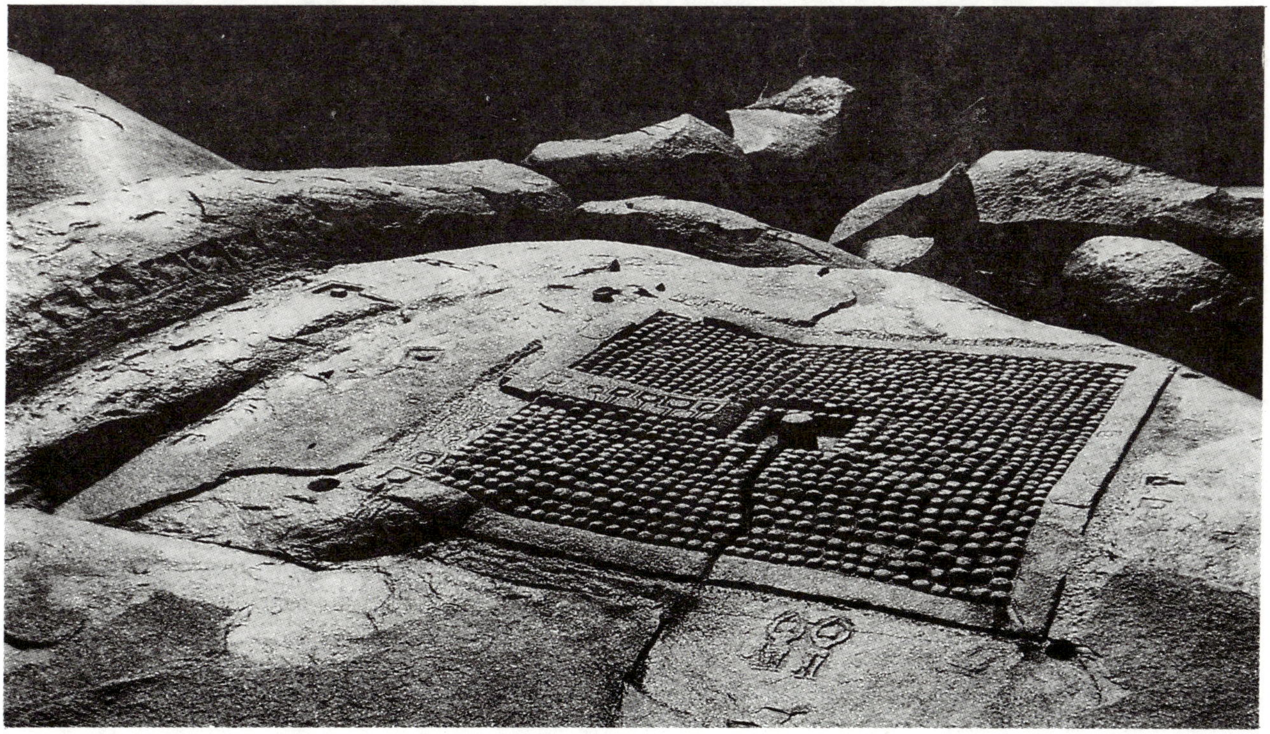

23. Big group of lingas at Koti-tirtha.

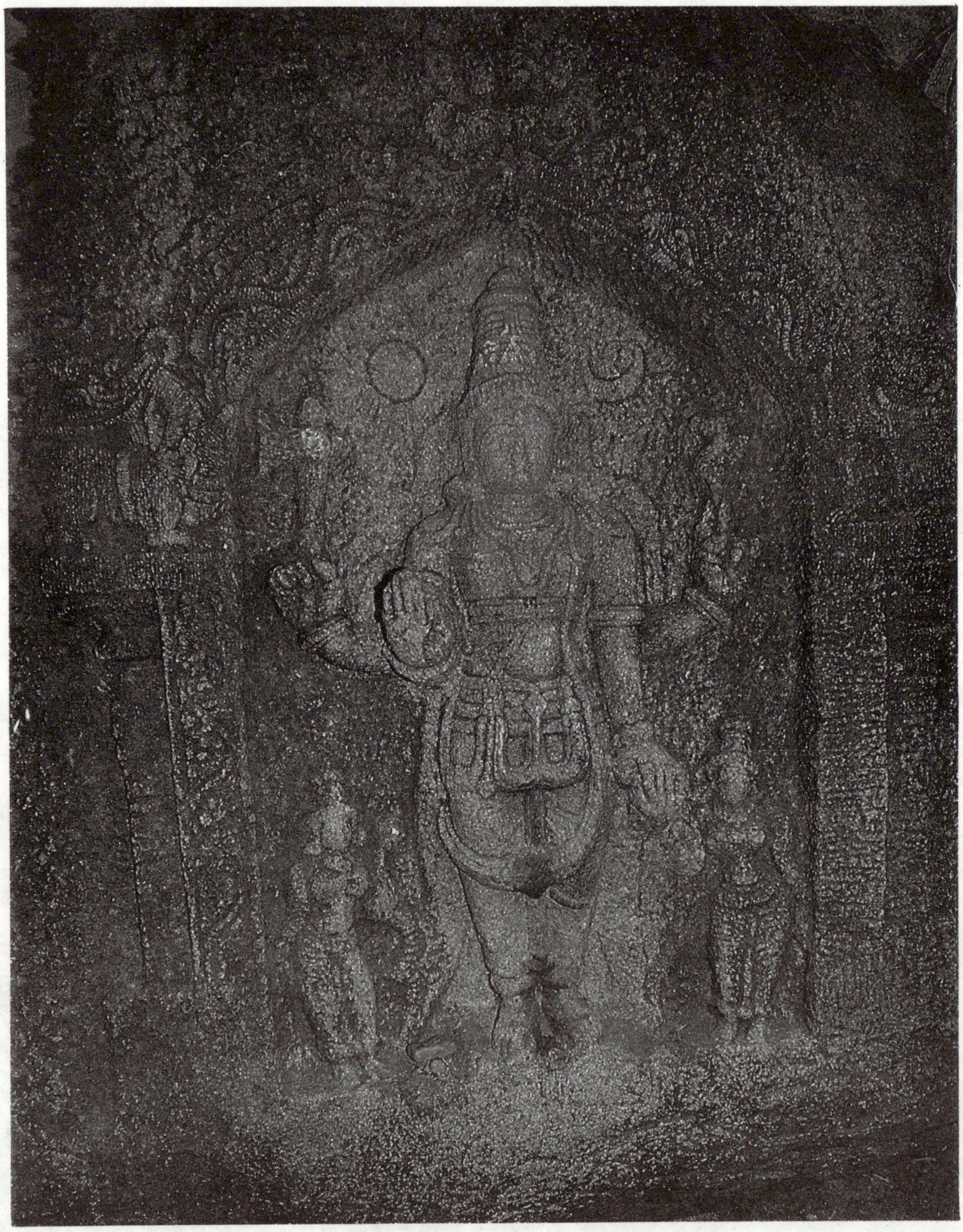

24. Chandrashekhara, larger shrine at Koti-tirtha.

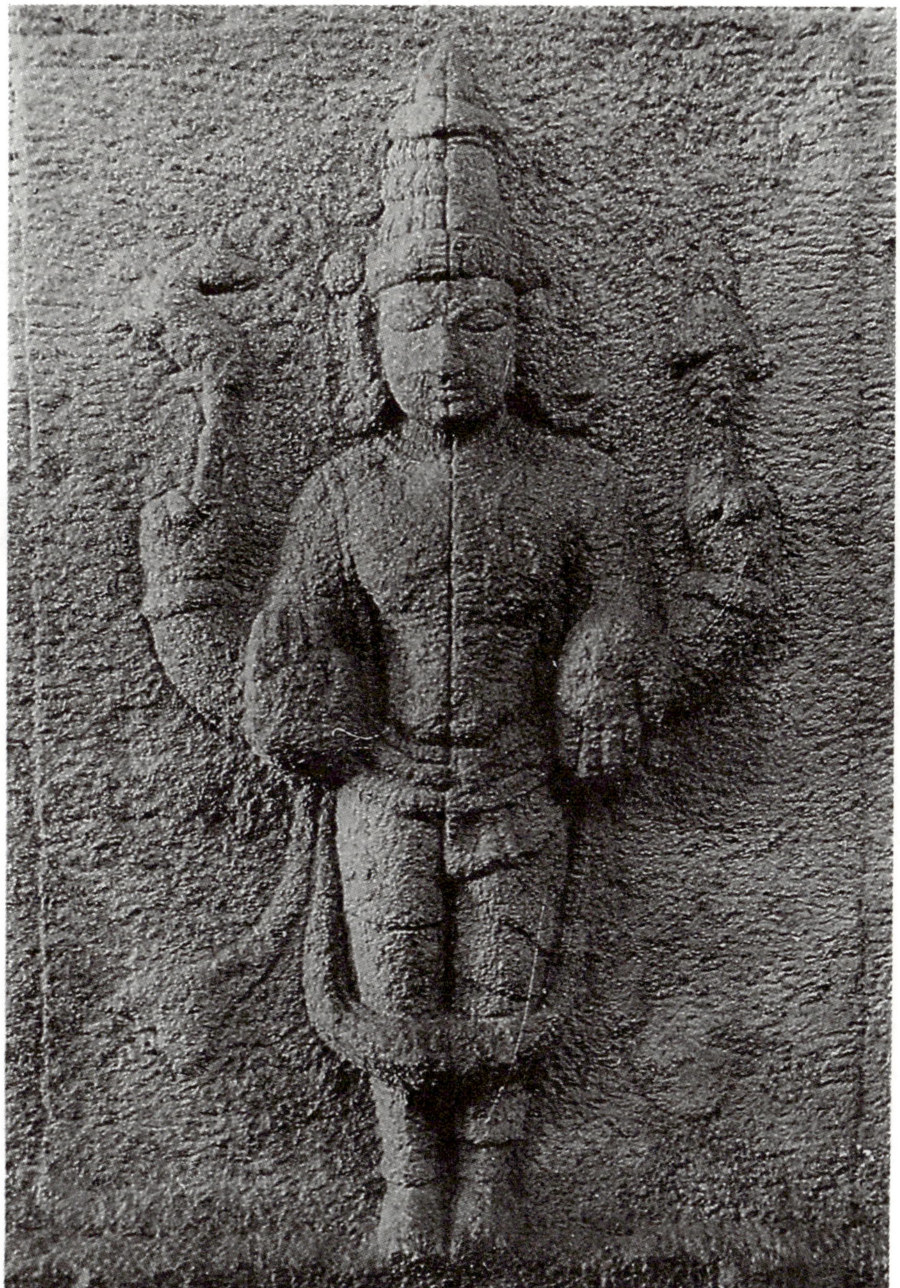

25. Harihara, Tiruvengalanatha temple, pillar relief in the hundred-pillar hall.

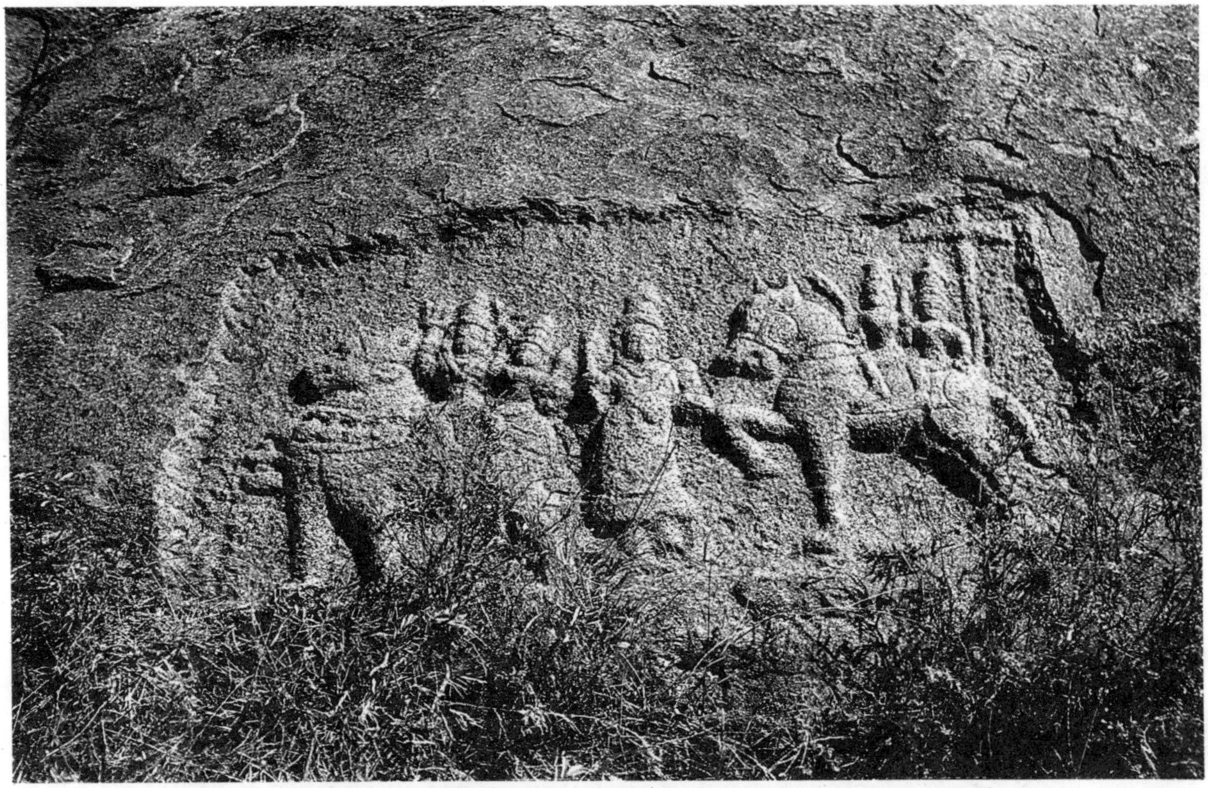

26. Shiva and Parvati on Nandi, male figure, and Mailara and Mhalsa on a horse, relief on a rock near temple NNx/5.

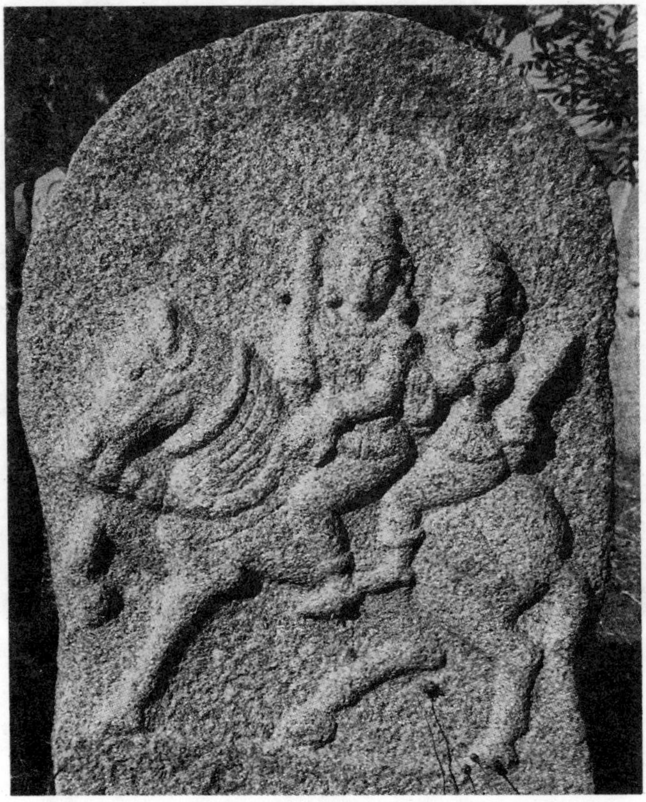

27. Mailara and Mhalsa on horseback, Kamalapuram Museum.

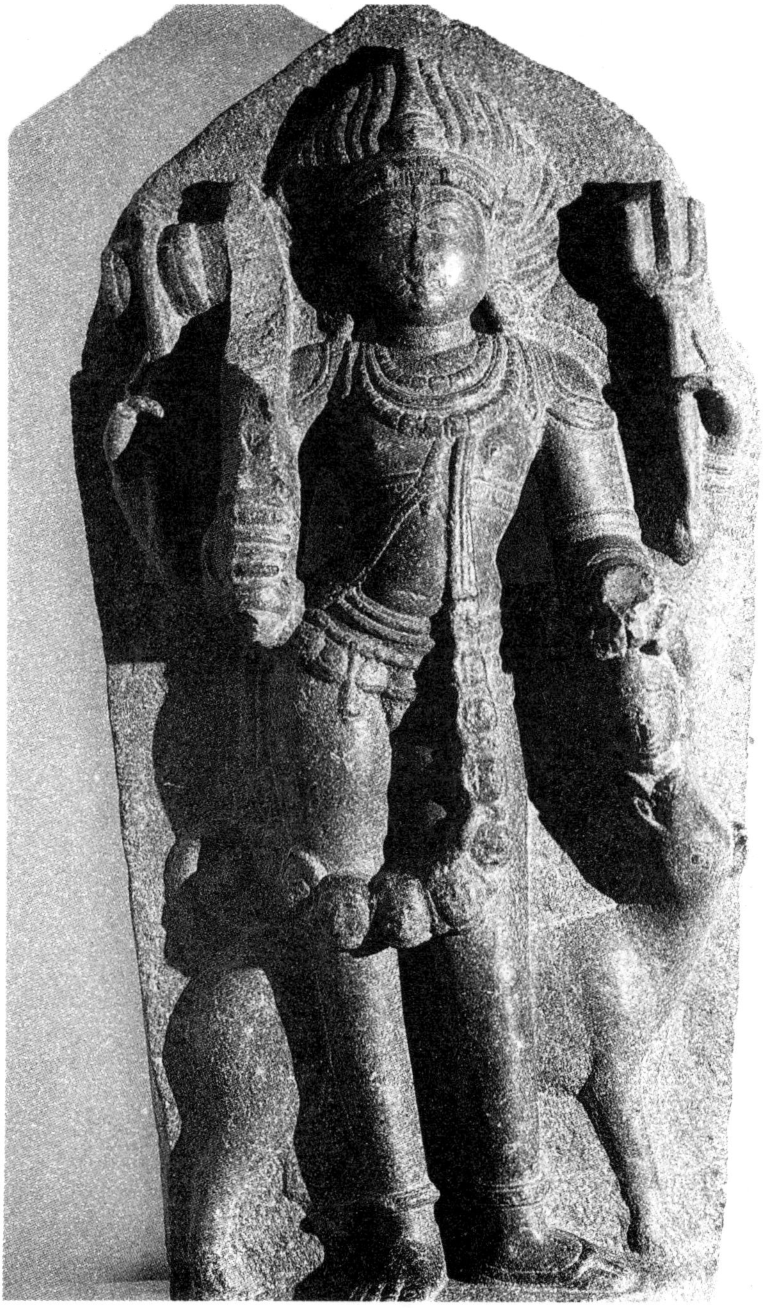

28. Four-armed Bhairava and dog, Kamalapuram Museum.

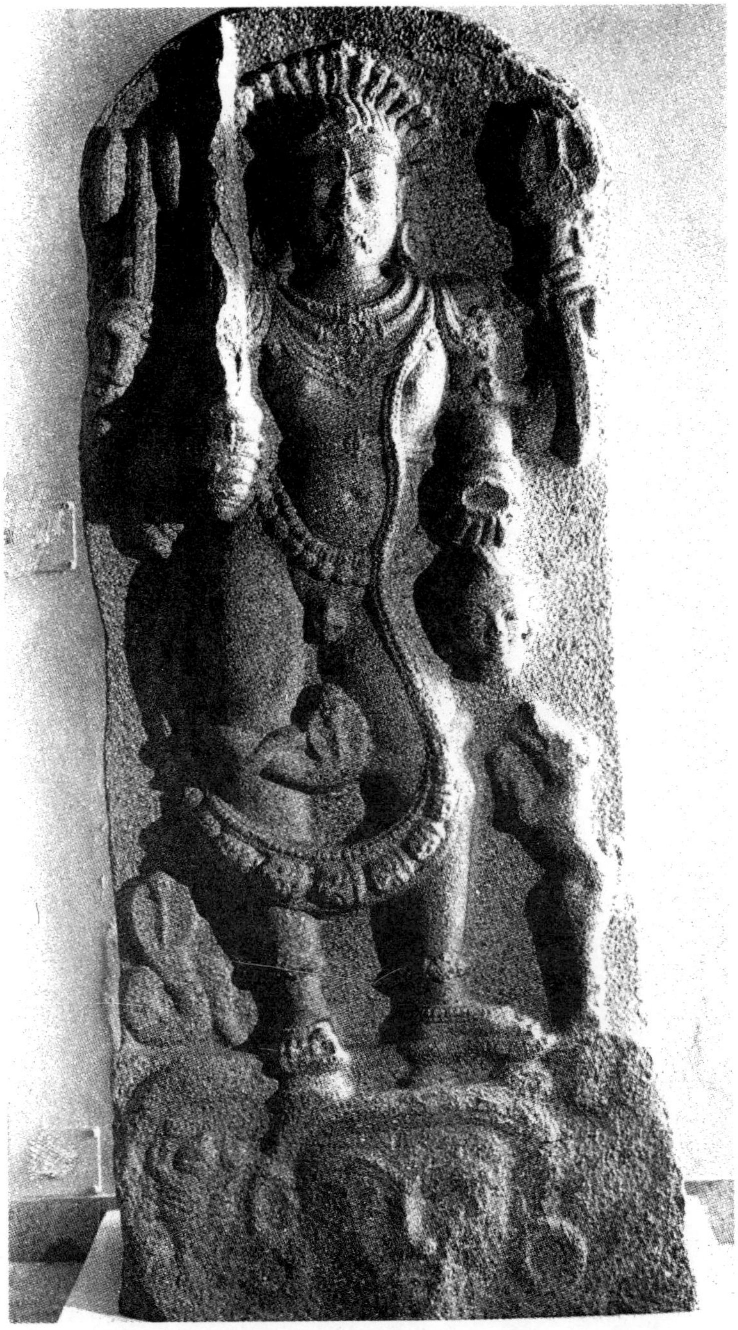

29. Four-armed Bhairava flanked by a dog and a snake, Kamalapuram Museum.

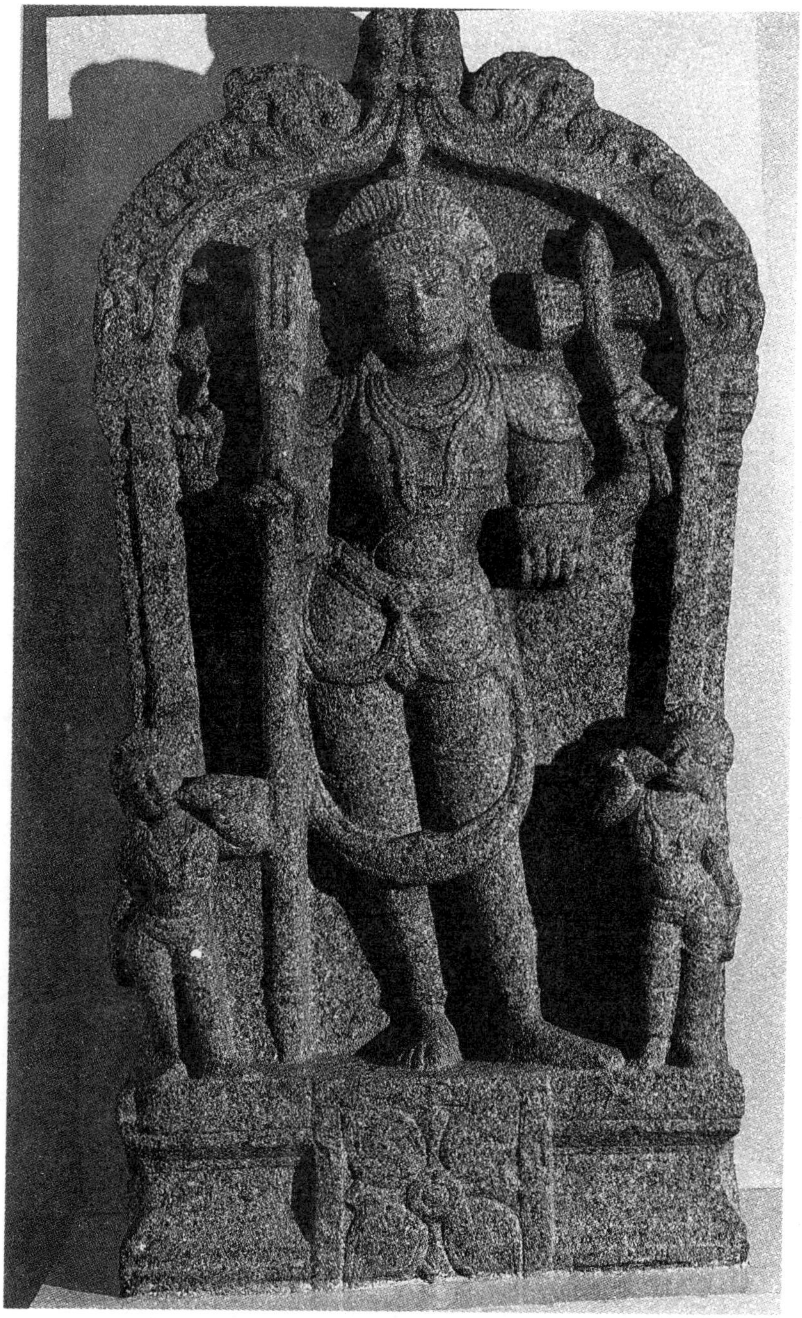

30. Four-armed Bhairava flanked by attendants, Kamalapuram Museum.

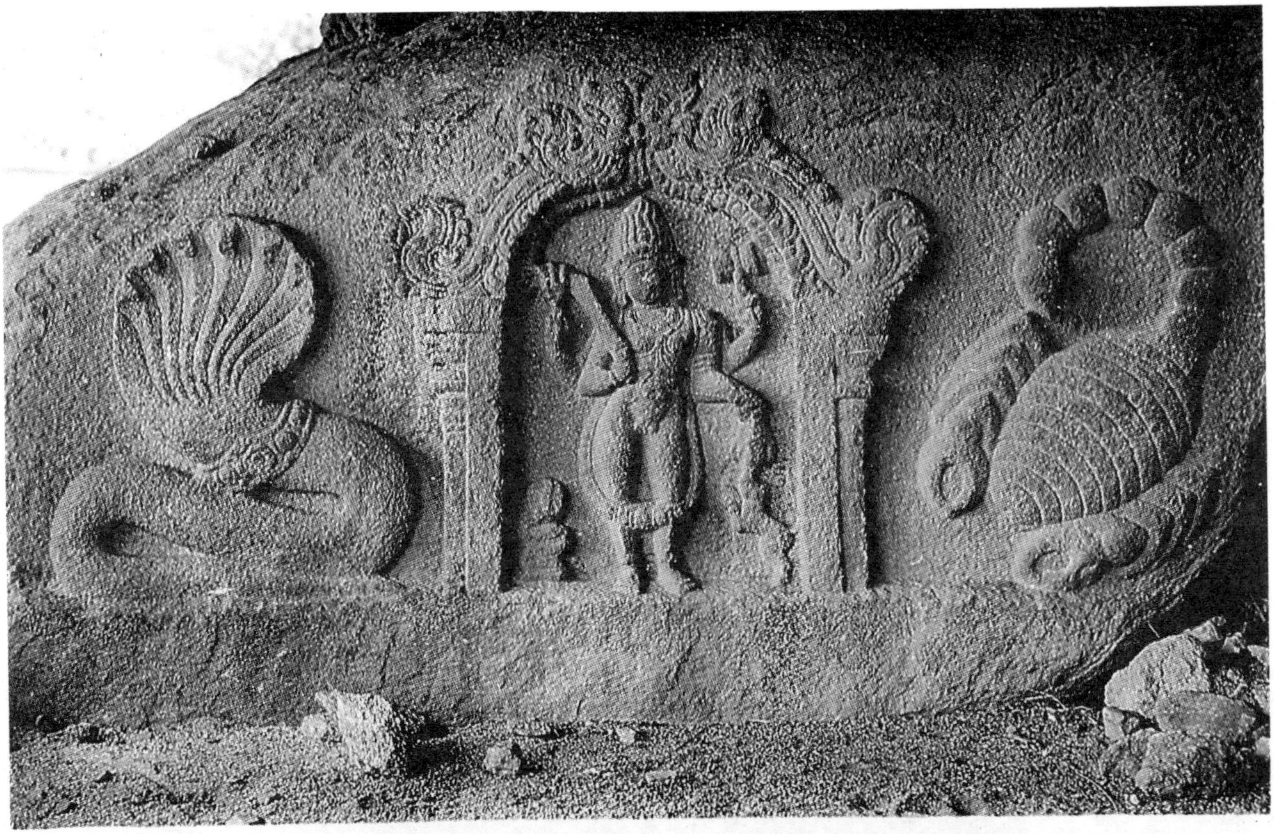

31. Four-armed Bhairva flanked by a snake and a scorpion, relief on a rock (NMz/2).

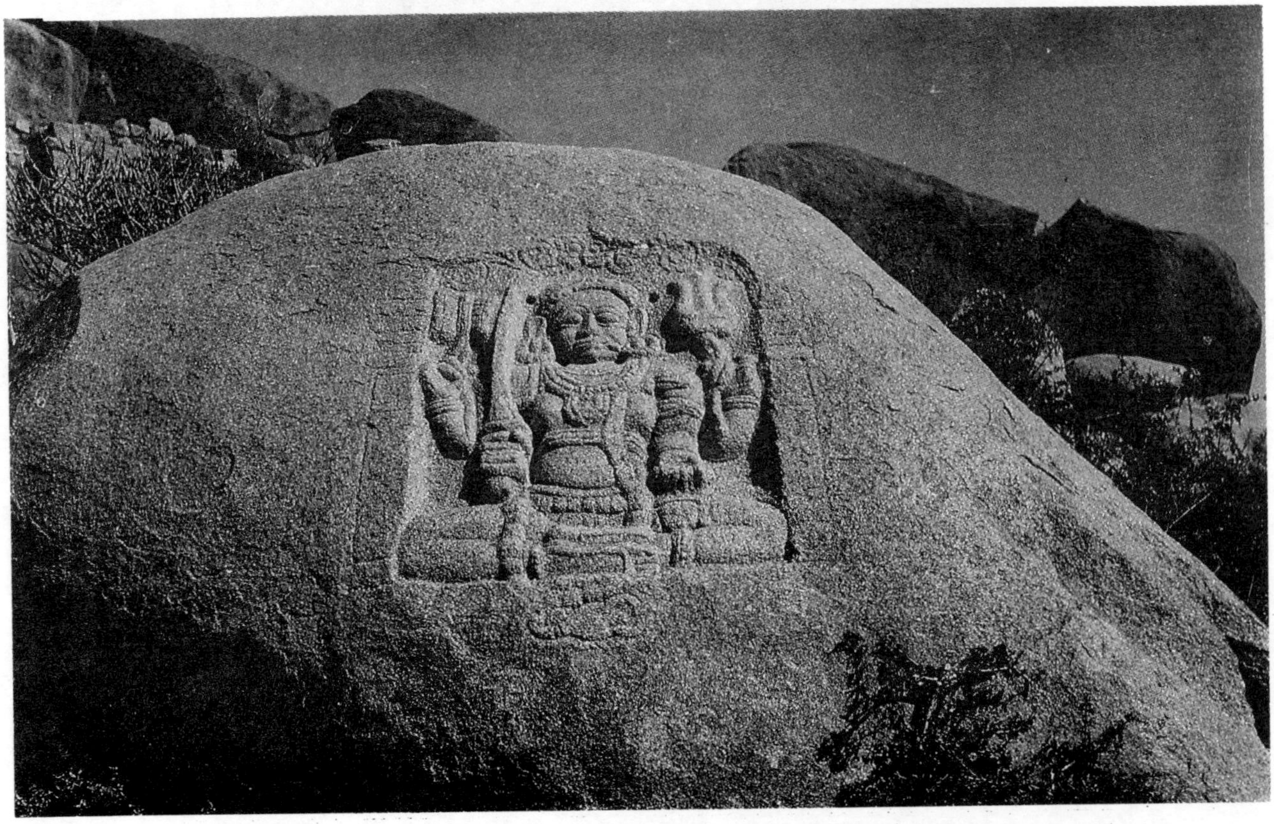

32. Seated Bhairava carved on a boulder near Malyavanta hill (NUf/6).

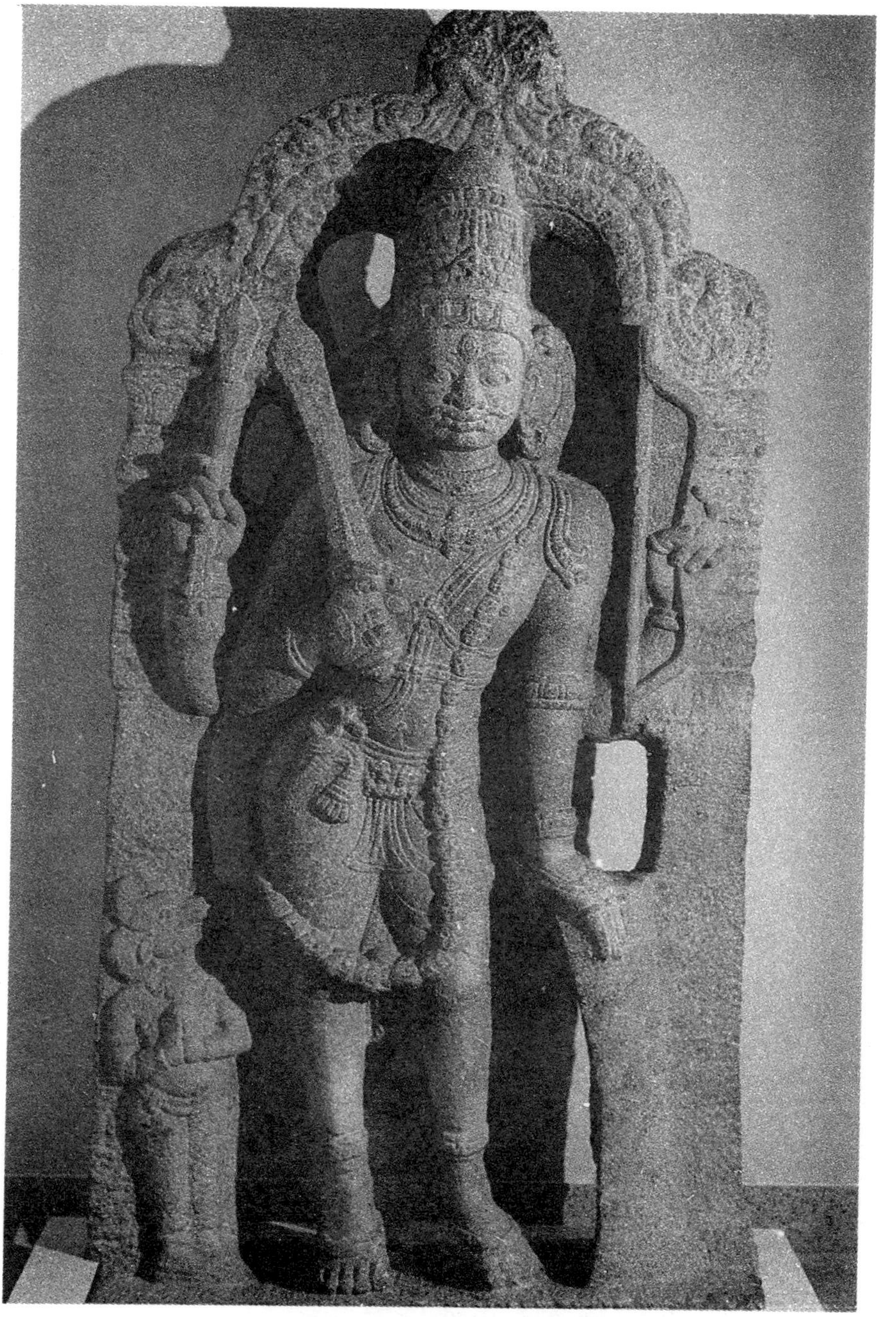

33. Virabhadra, Kamalapuram Museum.

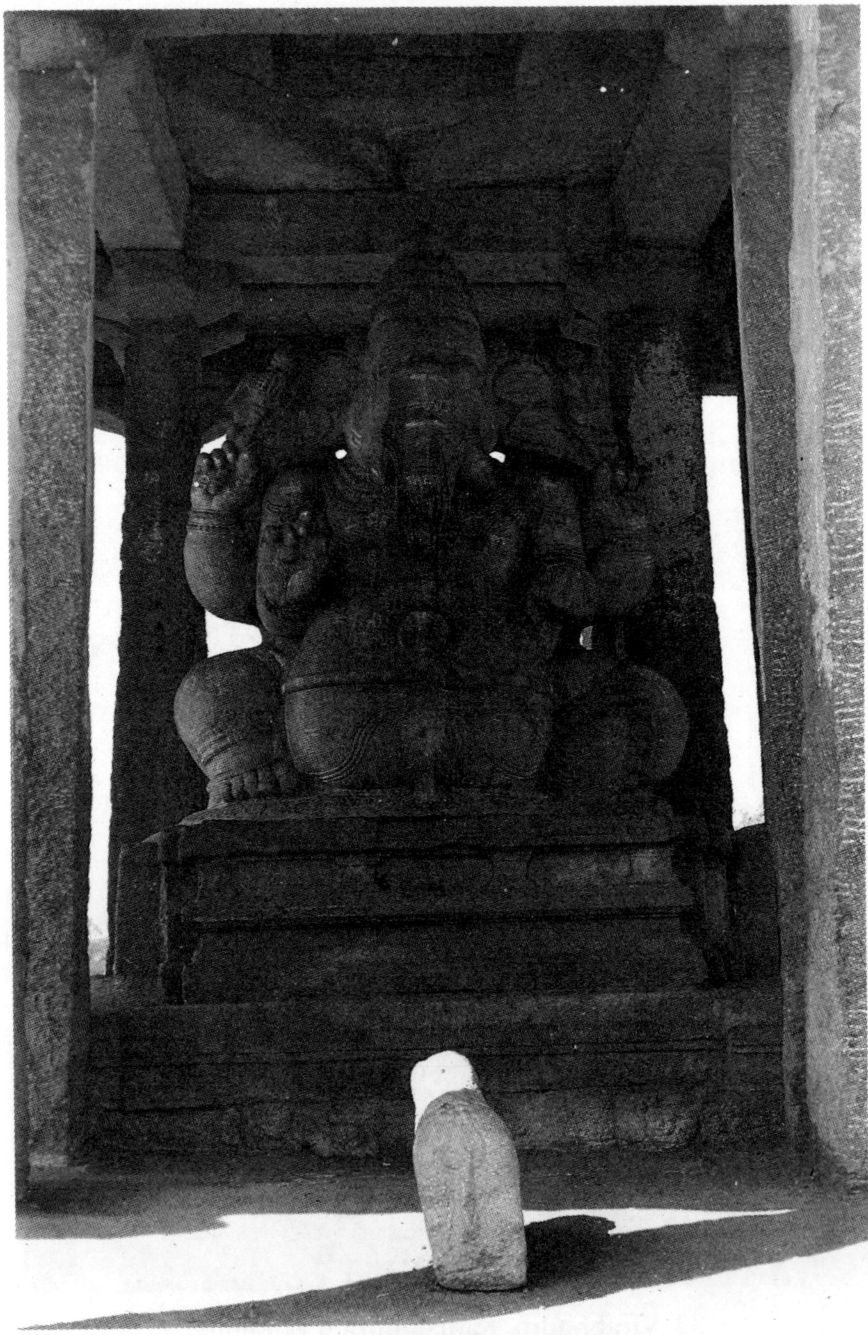

34. Sasivekalu Ganesha (NLg/2) on Hemakuta hill.

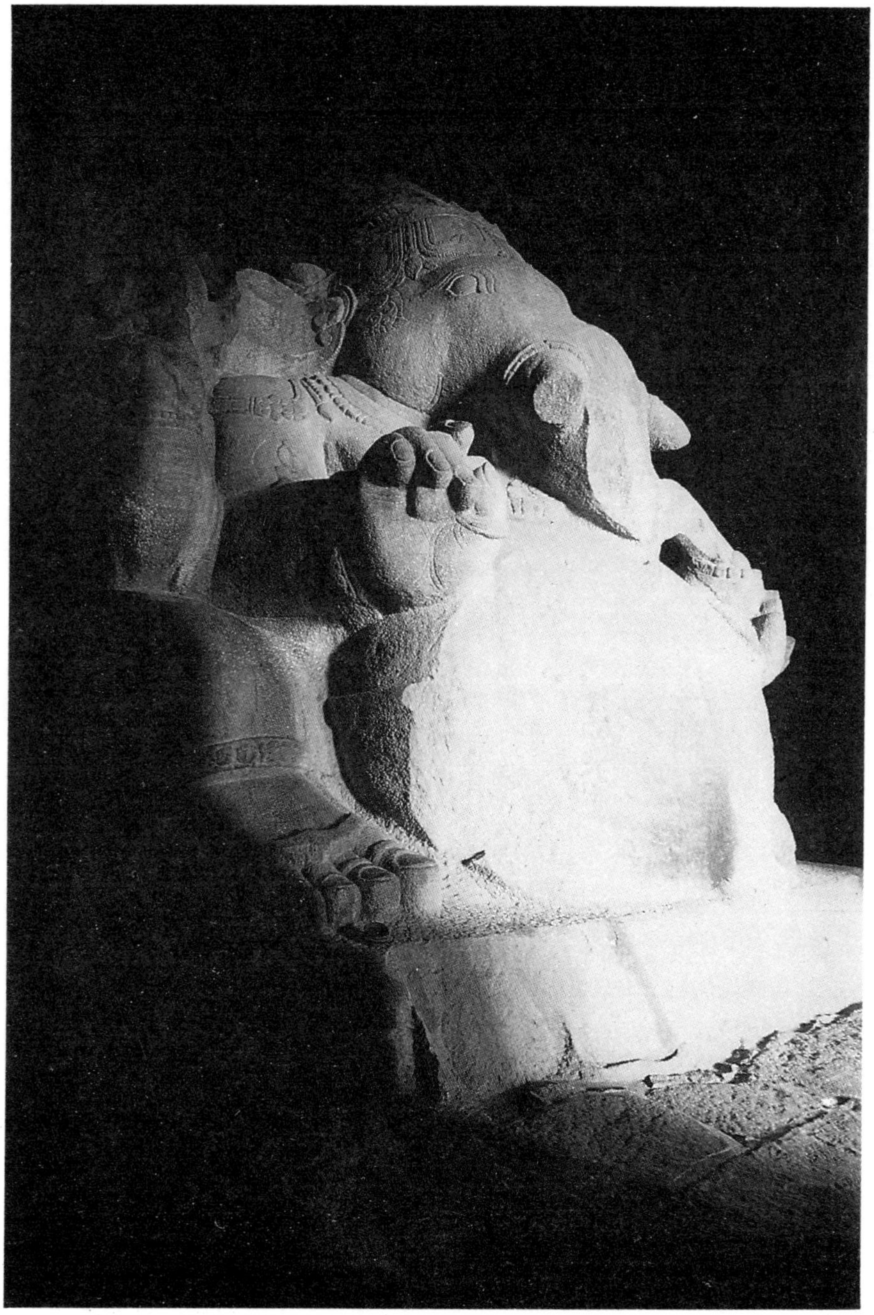

35. Kadalekalu Ganesha (NLc/2) on Hemakuta hill.

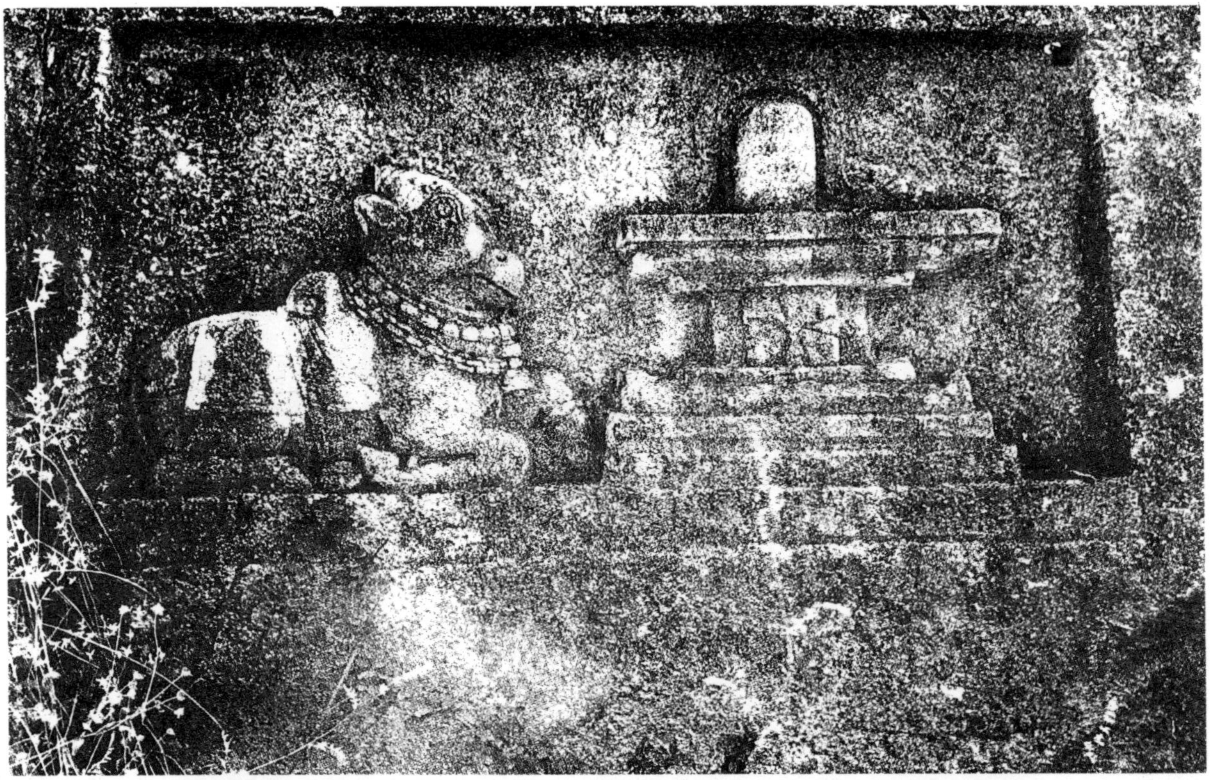

36. Nandi and linga, carving on the side of the cistern in NSa/3.

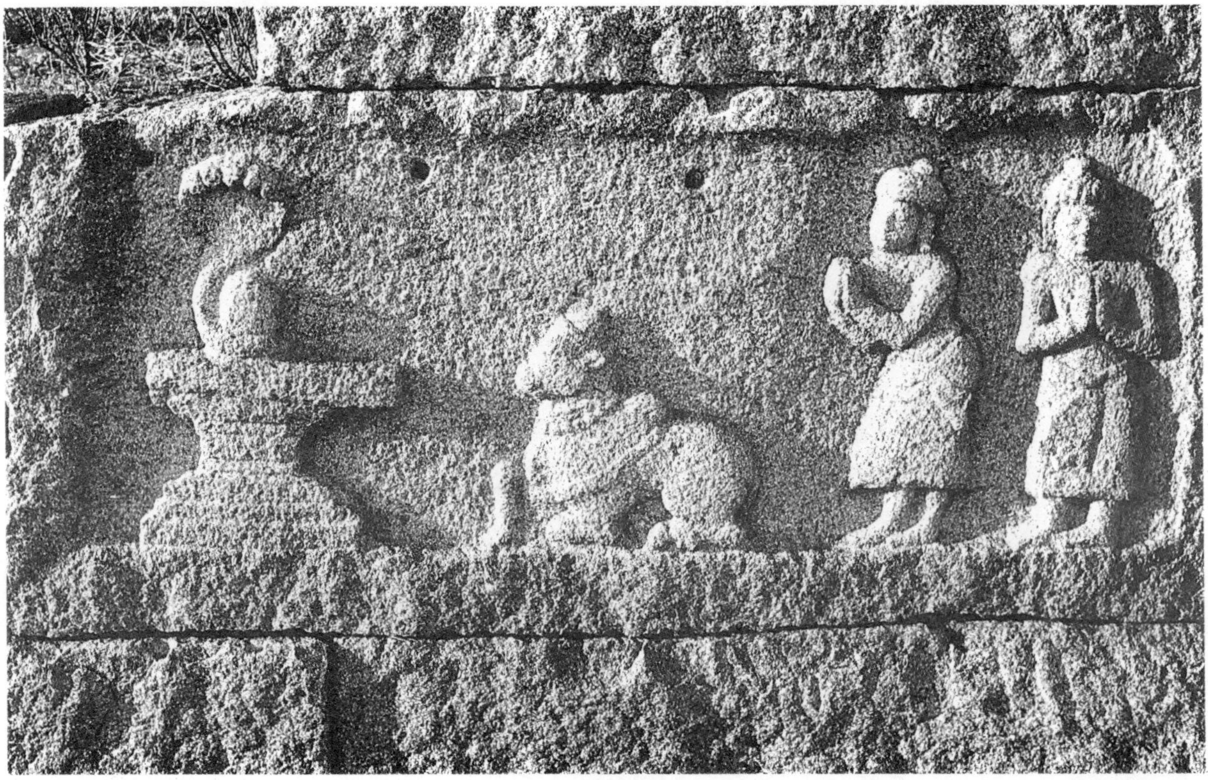

37. Nandi, linga sheltered by a a snake, and devotees, carving on a slab in a dilapidated shrine in the immediate proximity of the Ramachandra temple.

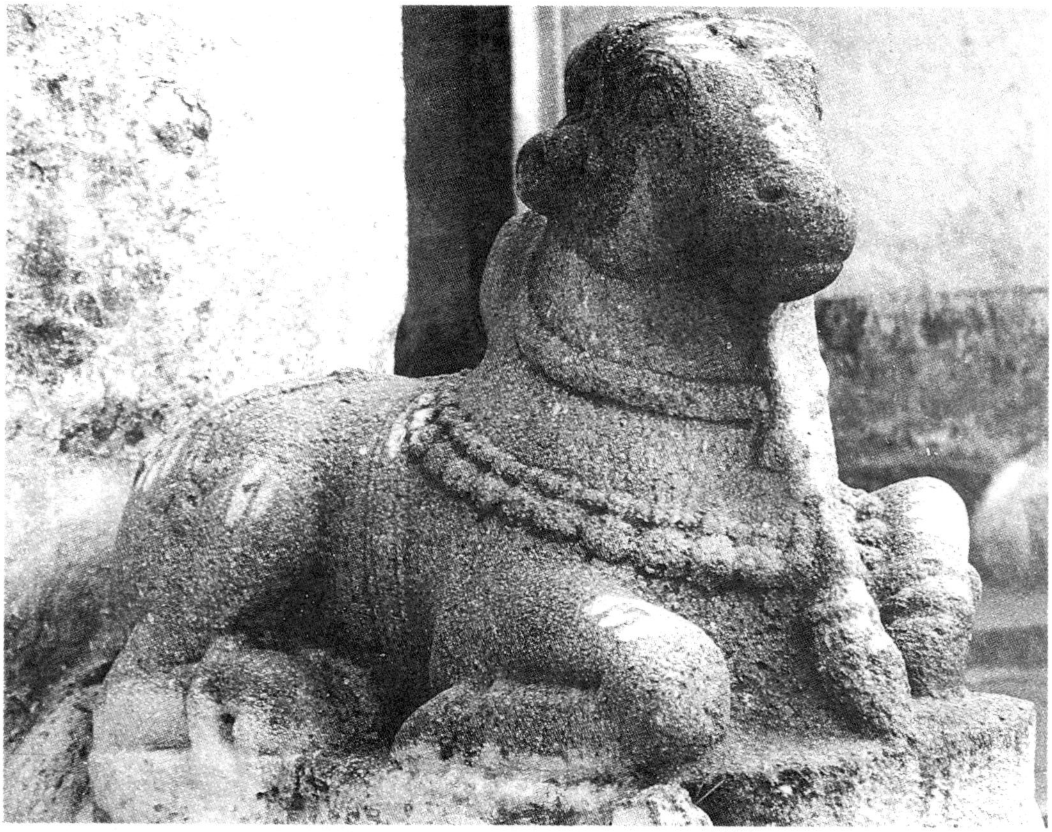

38. Nandi, Virupaksha temple, outer prakara near the east gopura.

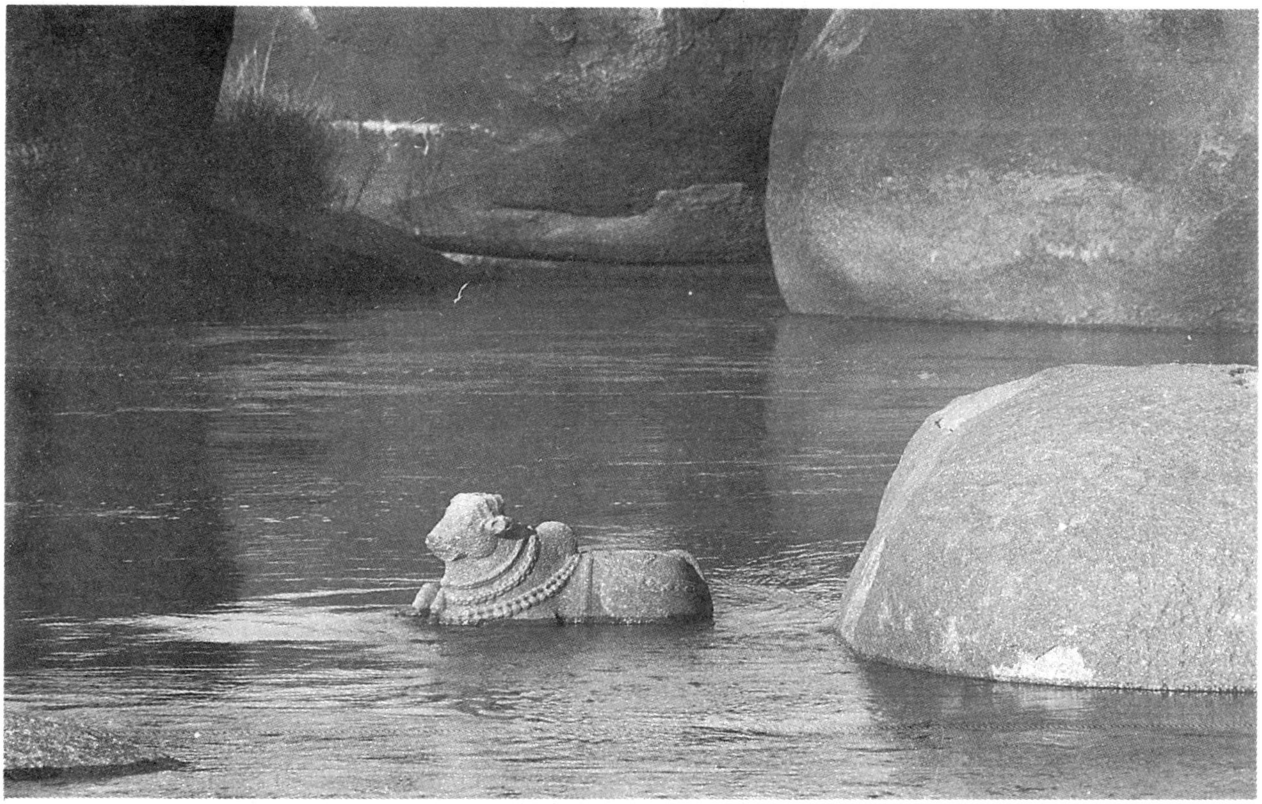

39. Nandi, sculpture on a rock in the Tungabhadra.

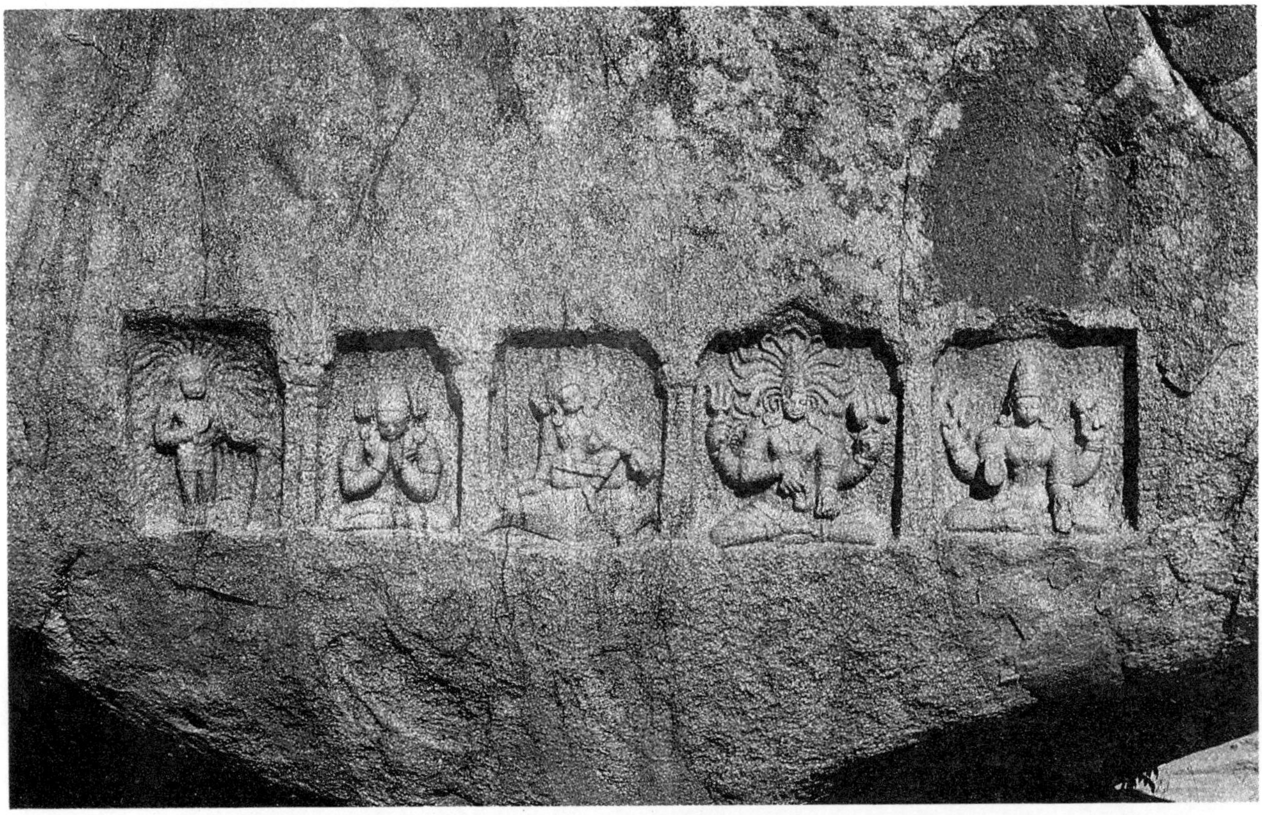

40. Standing ascetic, seated ascetic, Matsyendranath, seated Shiva and seated Vishnu, group of seated figures in NMx/2.

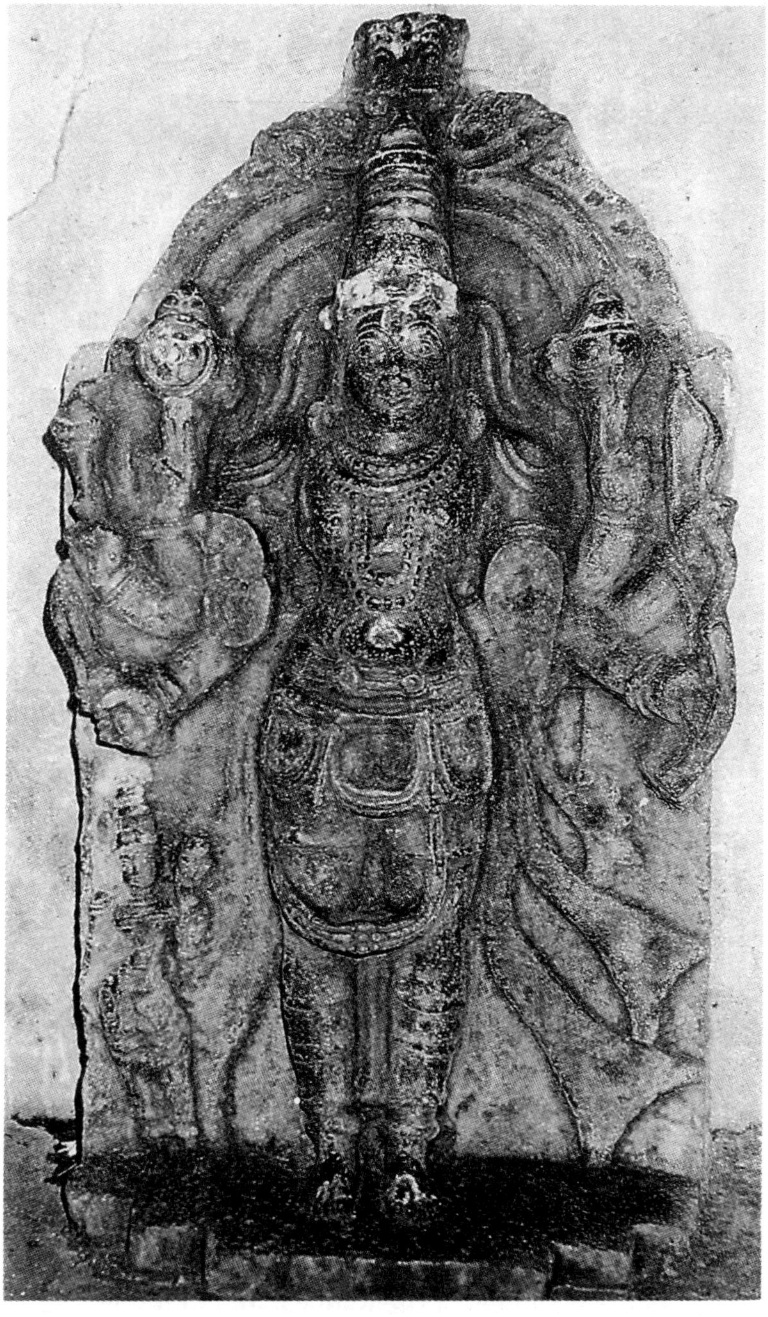

41. Vishvarupa of Vishnu, Lokapavana tank complex (NFv/1), west-facing shrine.

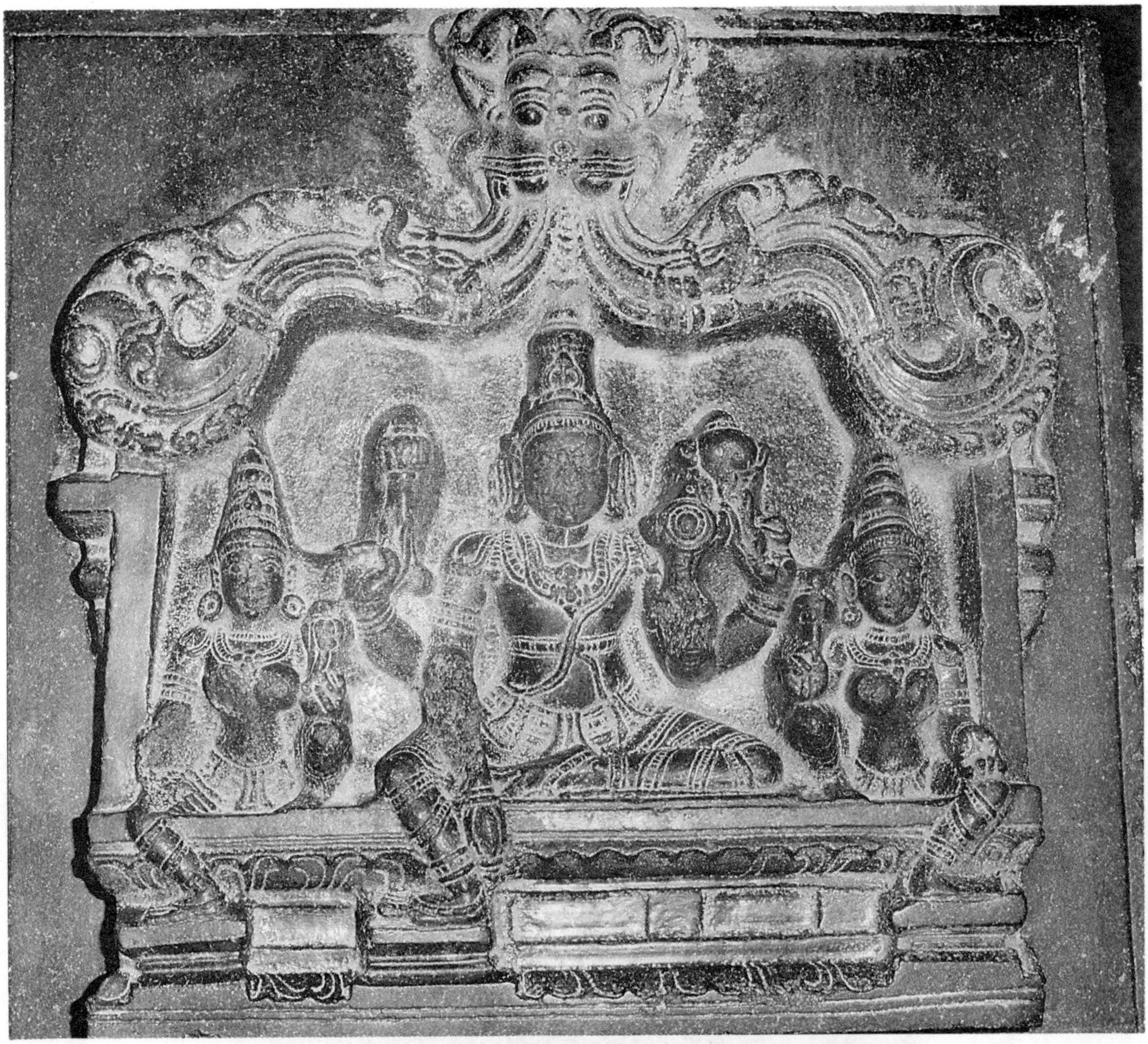

42. One of the Chaturvimshatimurtis, detail of a pillar in the mandapa of the Ramachandra temple.

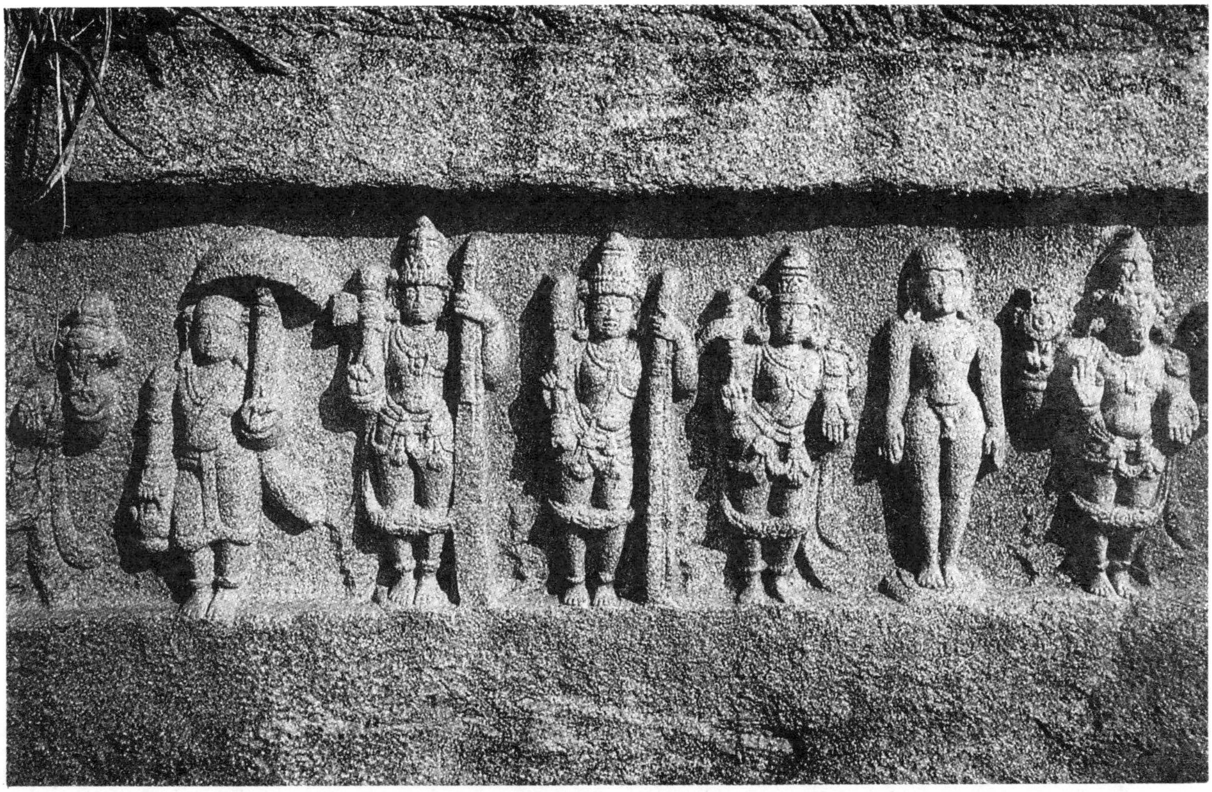

43. Dashavatara group in NSa/1: Narasimha, Vamana, Parashurama, Ramachandra, Balarama, Jina and Kalki.

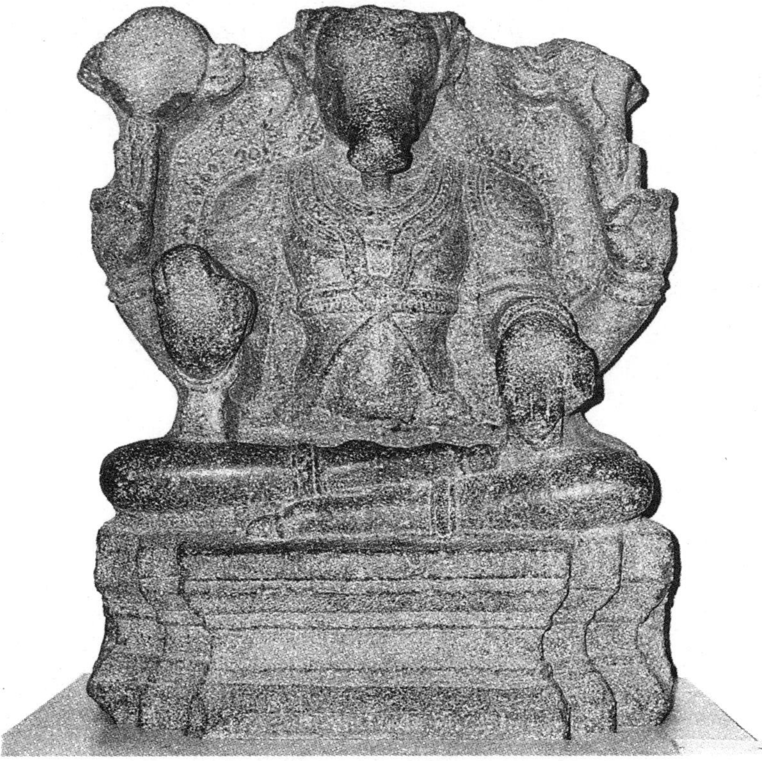

44. Seated Varaha, Kamalapuram Museum.

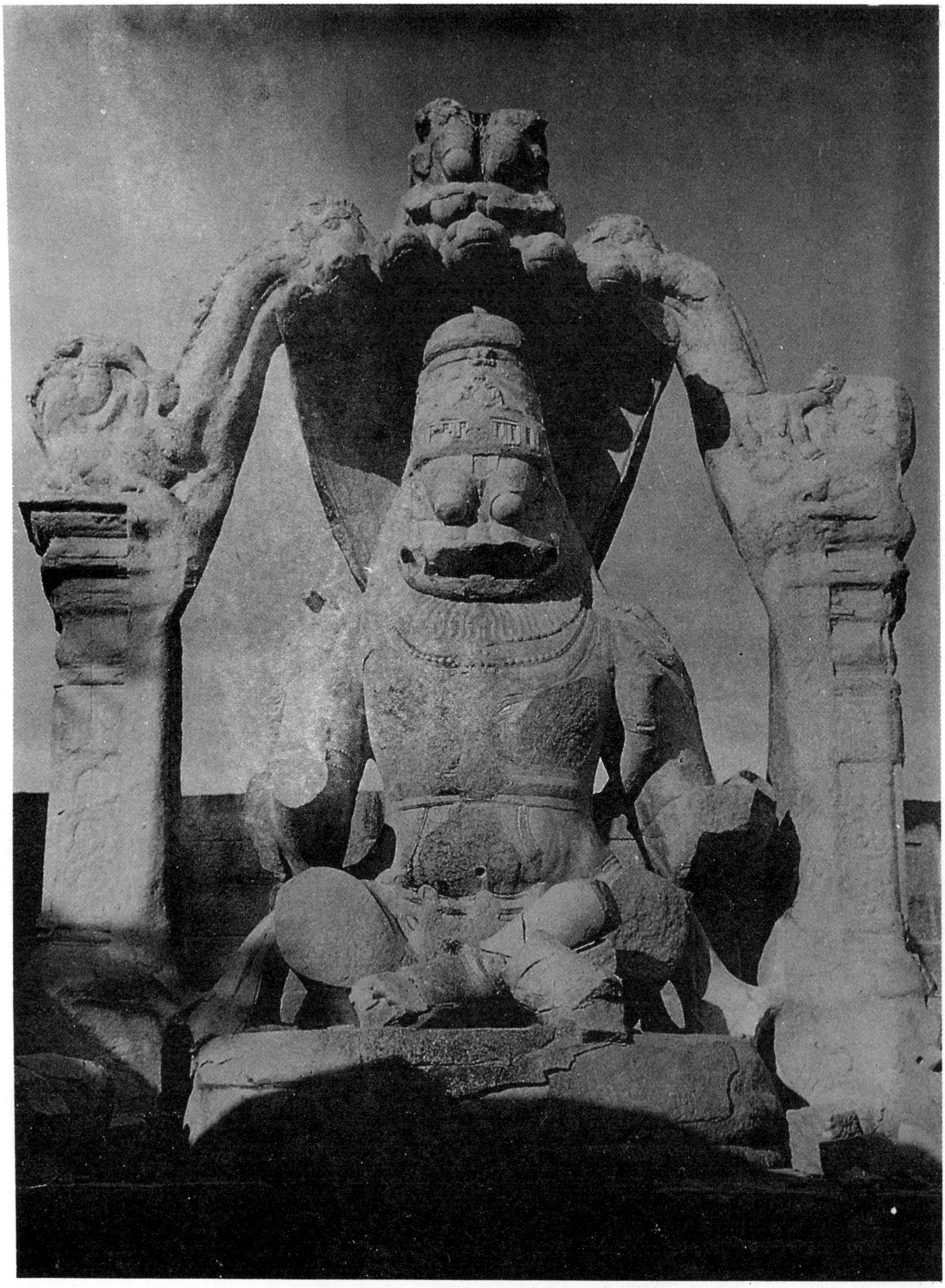

45. Lakshmi-Narasimha monolith (NLm/1).

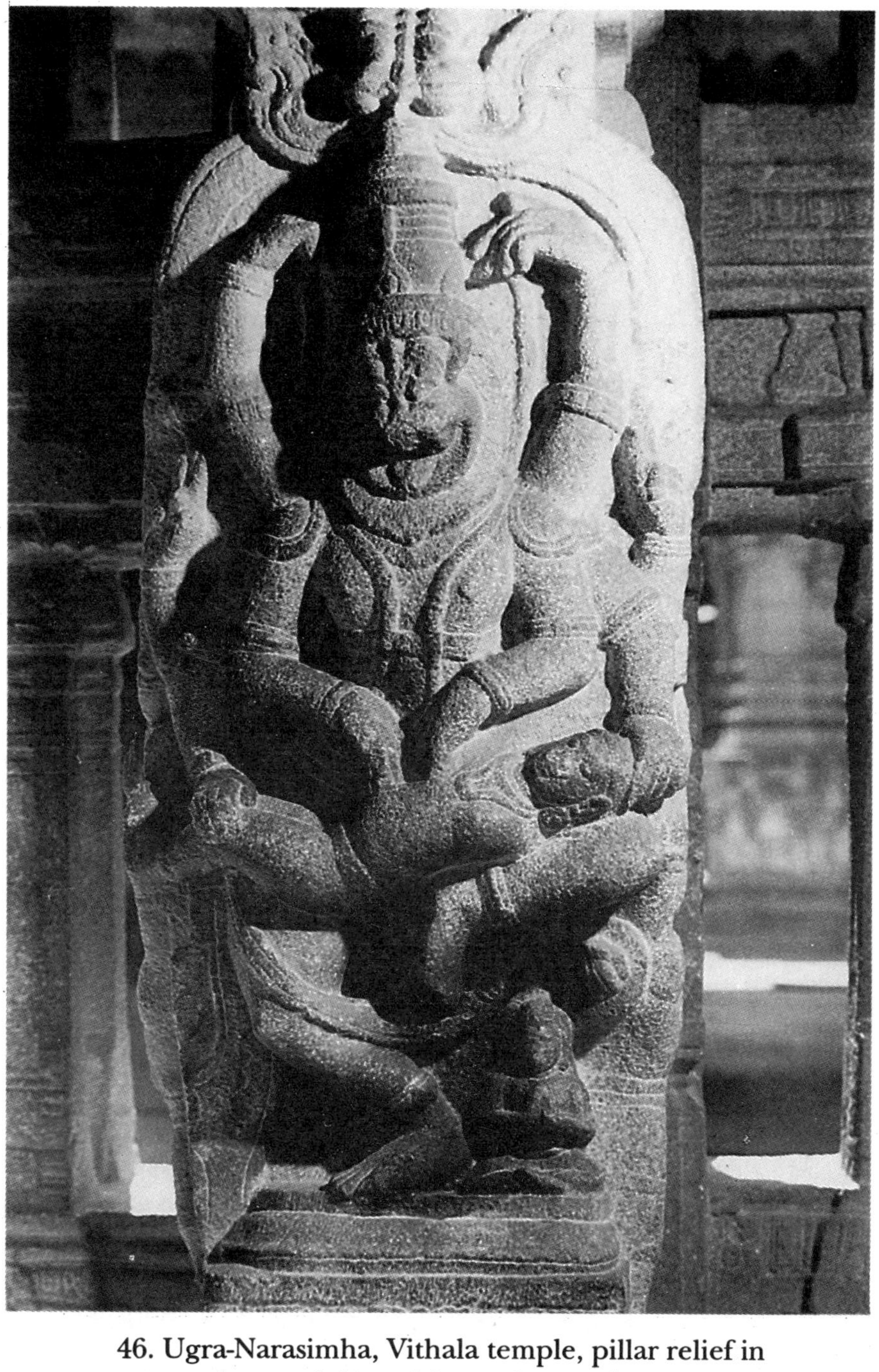

46. Ugra-Narasimha, Vithala temple, pillar relief in the north bay of the mahamandapa.

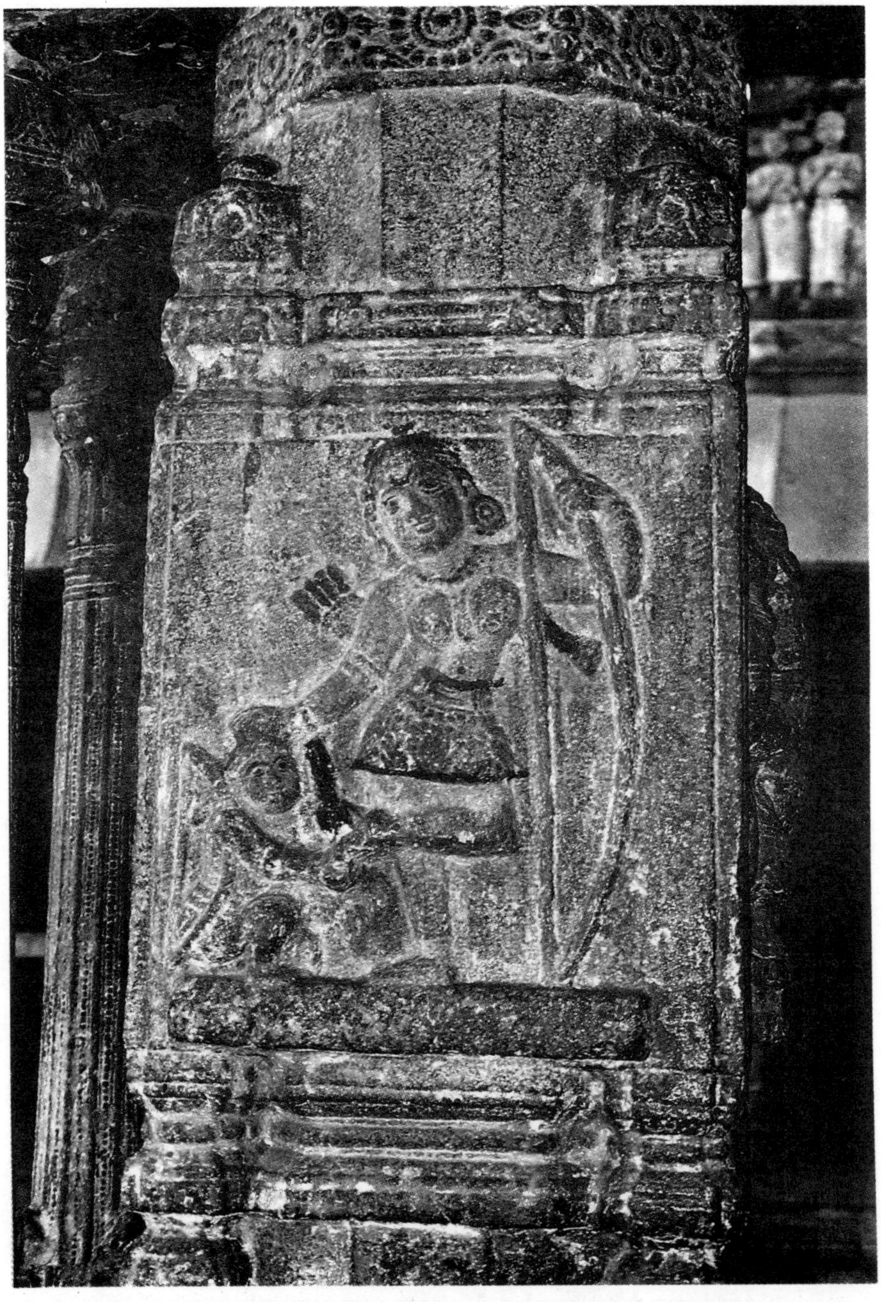

47. Narasimha extracting a thorn from Chenchu-Lakshmi's foot, Virupaksha temple, pillar relief in the maharangamandapa.

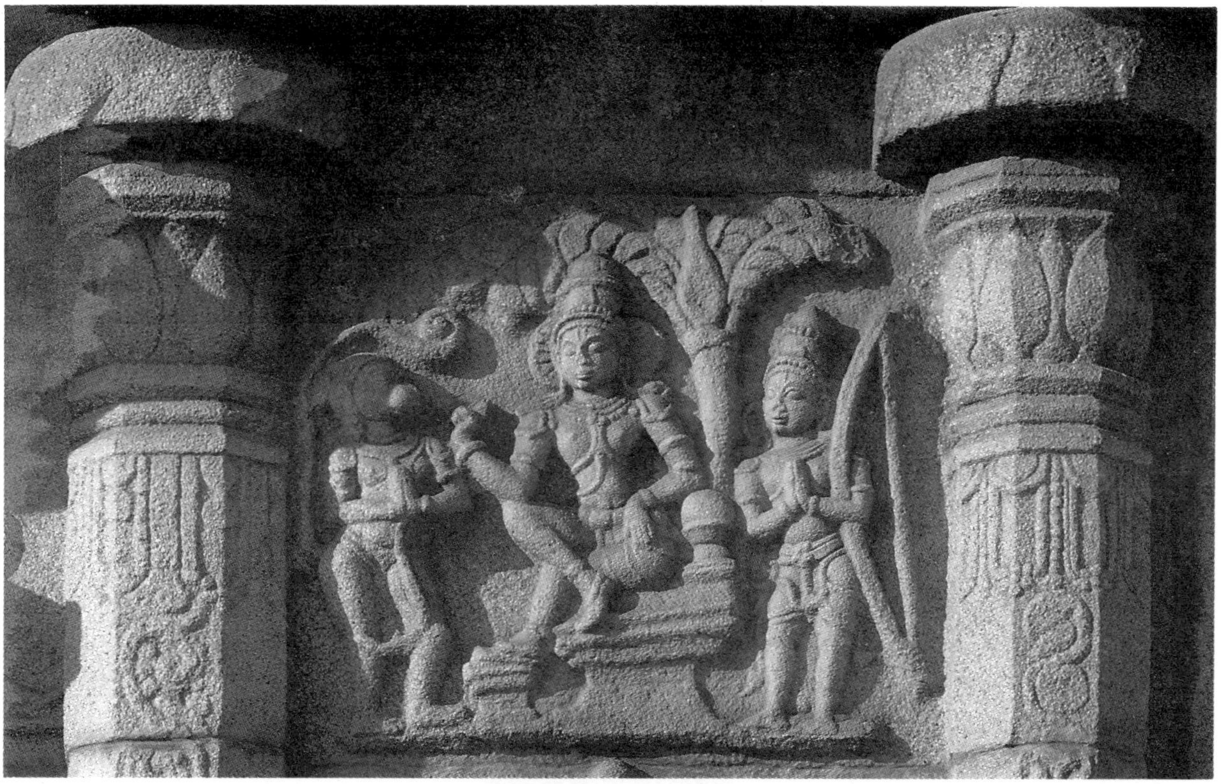

48. Rama seated, Lakshmana and Hanuman in attendance, Ramachandra temple, principal shrine, relief on the south wall of the vimana.

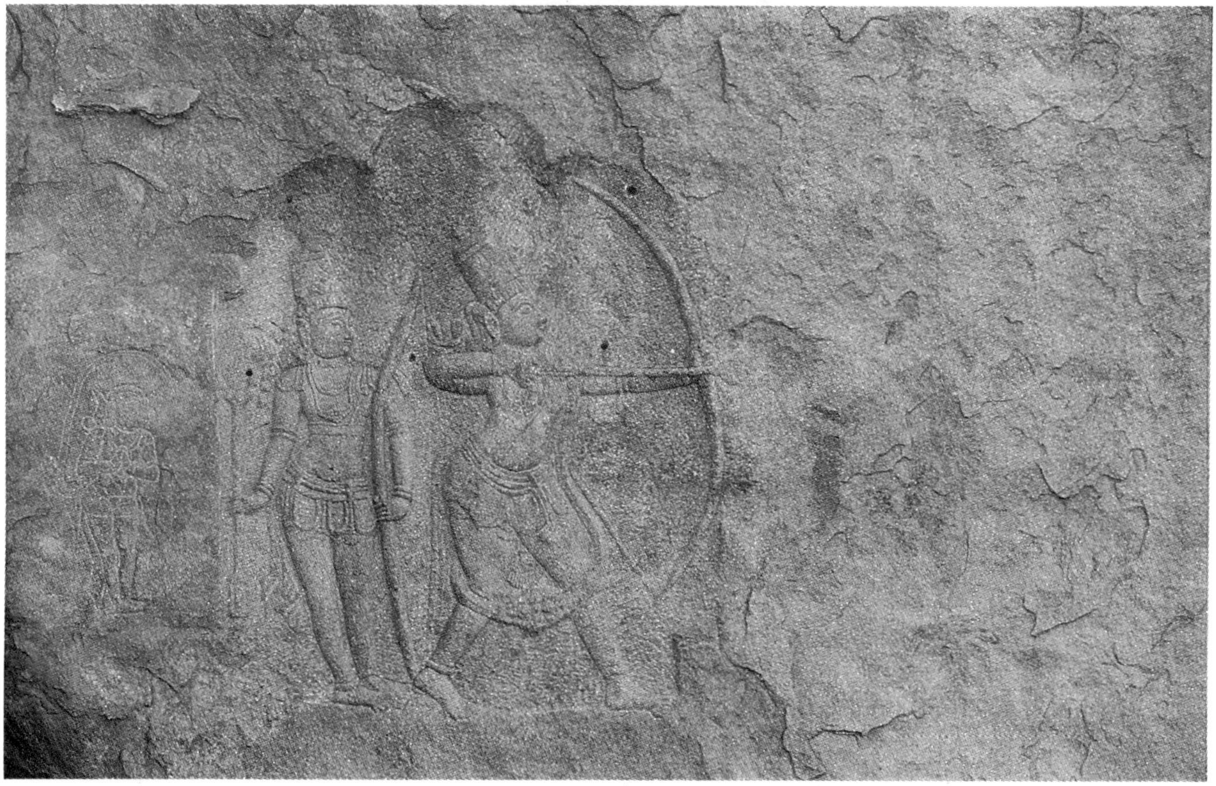

49. Rama aiming an arrow, Lakshmana stands in attendance, rock carving (NMe/1) near a dilapidated temple on the east side of the Tiruvengalanatha chariot street.

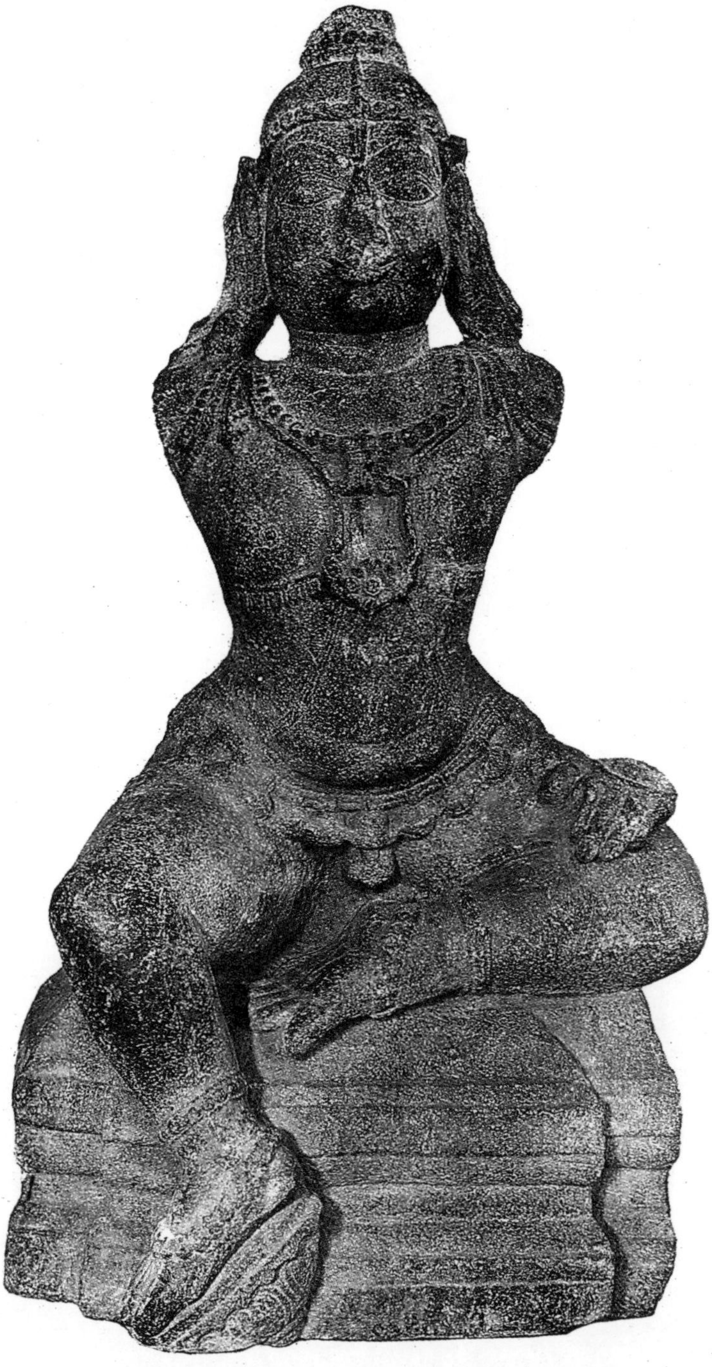

50. Balakrishna, statue from the Krishna temple complex, Government Museum, Madras.

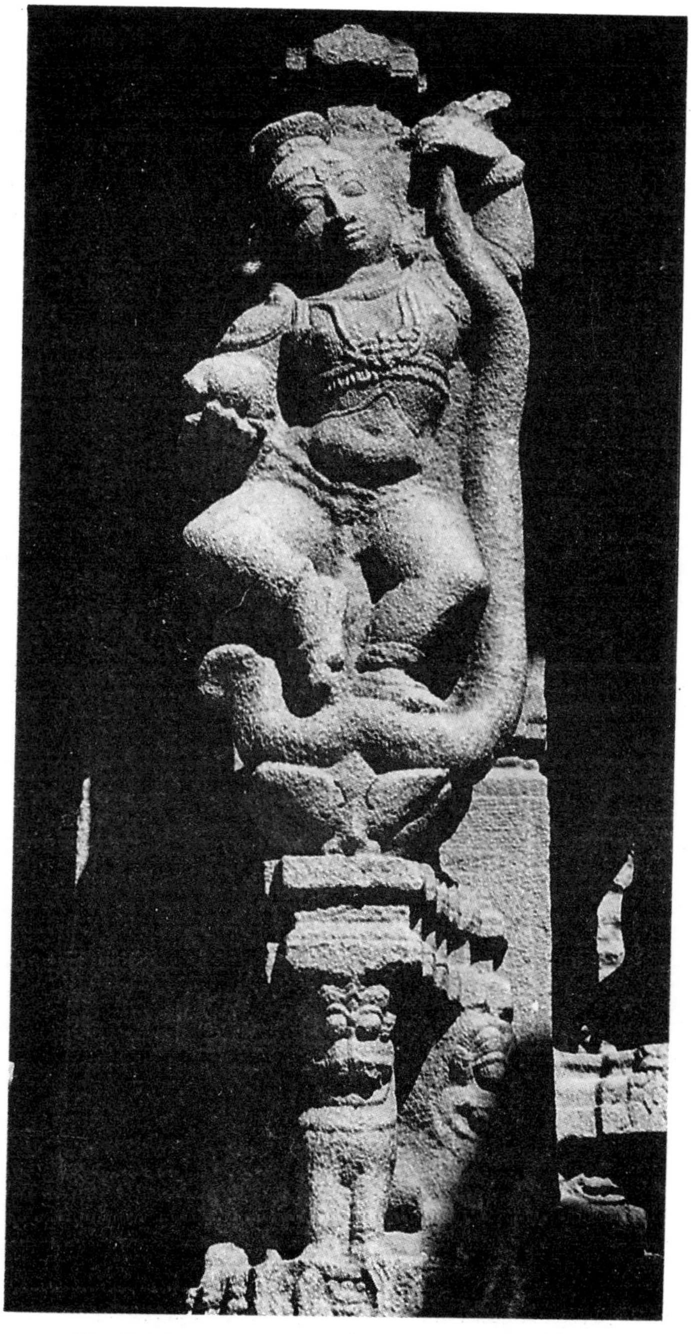

51. Krishna dancing on the serpent Kaliya,
Vithala temple, mahamandapa.

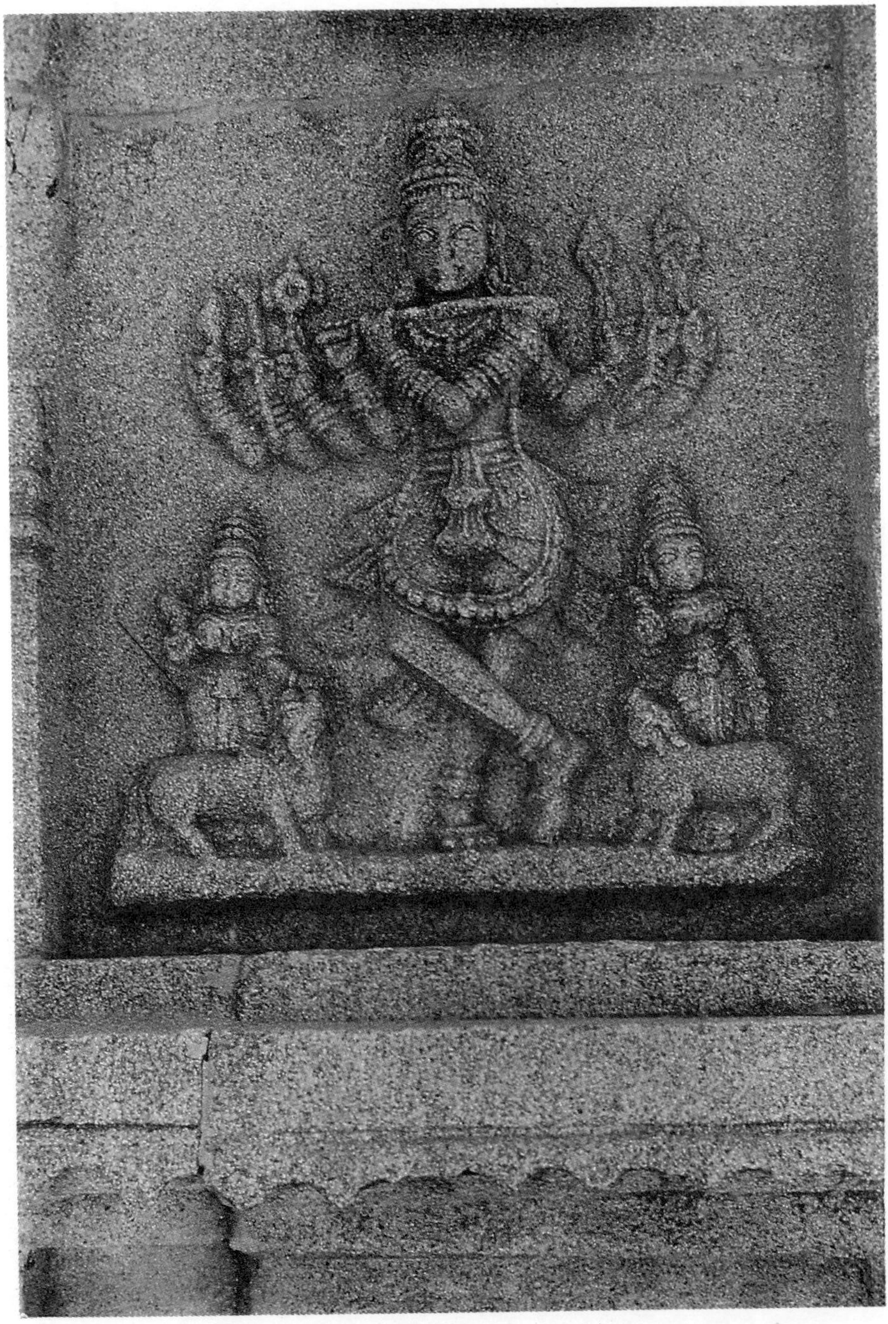

52. Madanagopala, Ramachandra temple, principal shrine, relief on the west wall of the vimana.

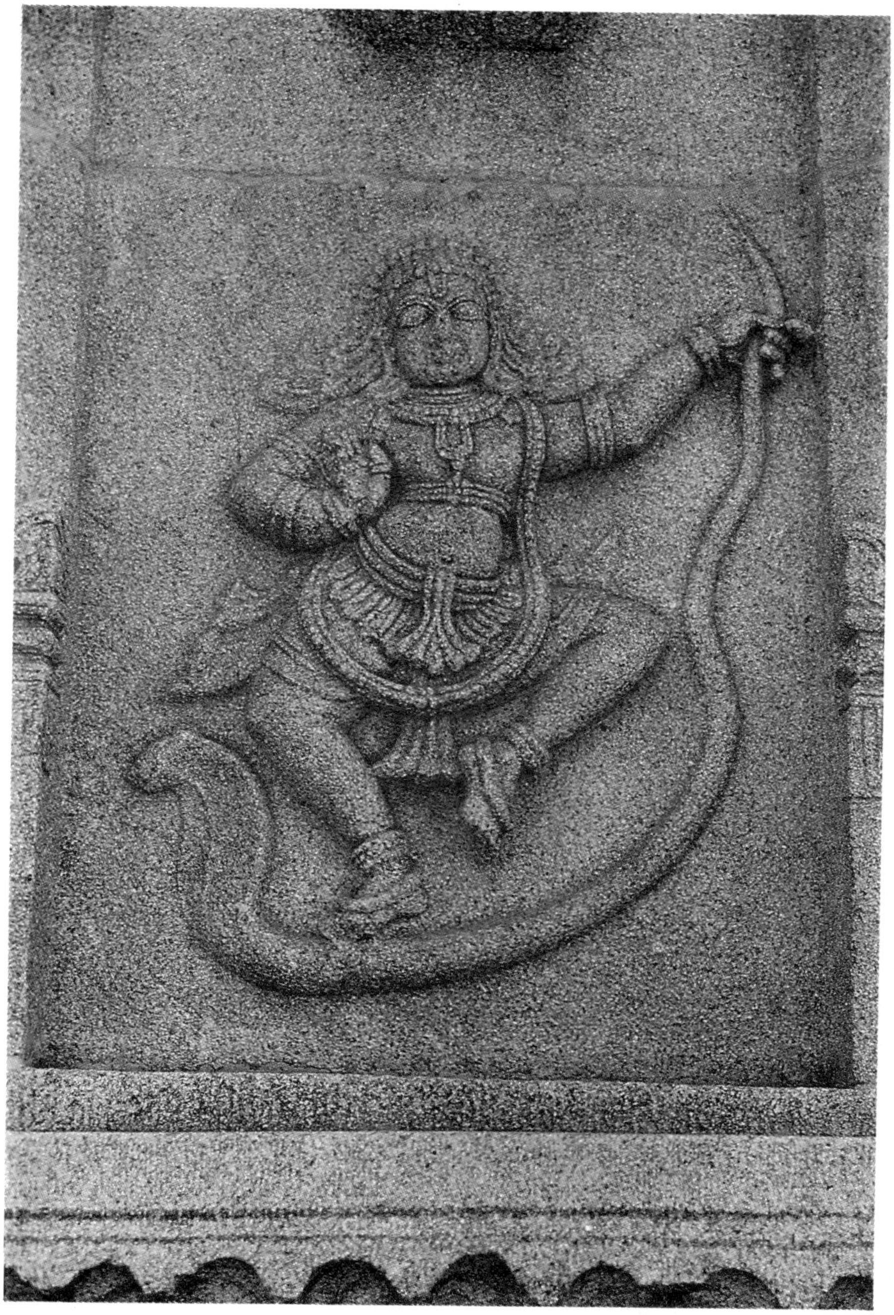

53. Krishna dancing on the serpent Kaliya, Ramachandra temple, principal shrine, relief on the west wall of the vimana.

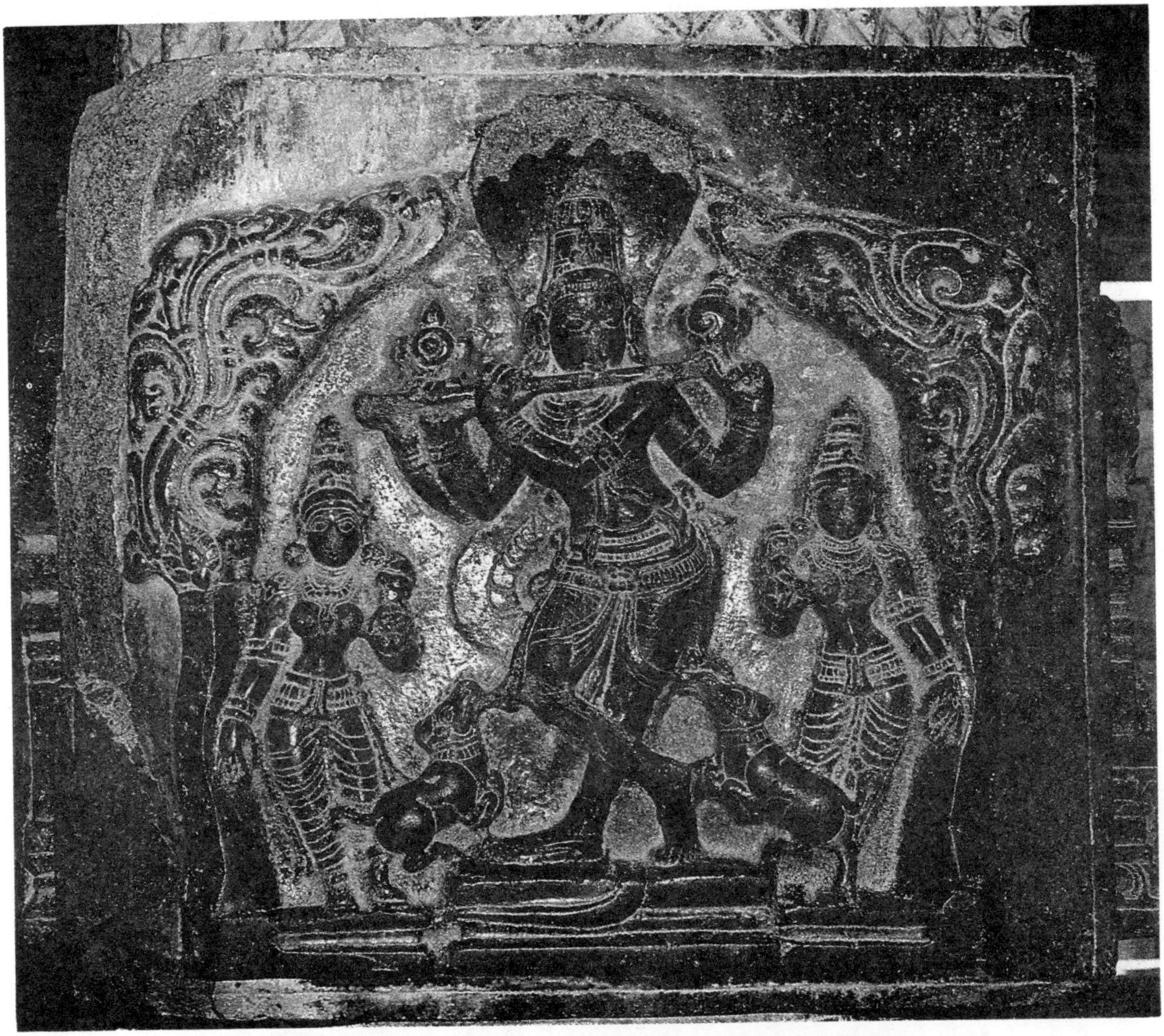

54. Venugopala, Ramachandra temple, principal shrine, detail of a pillar in the closed mandapa.

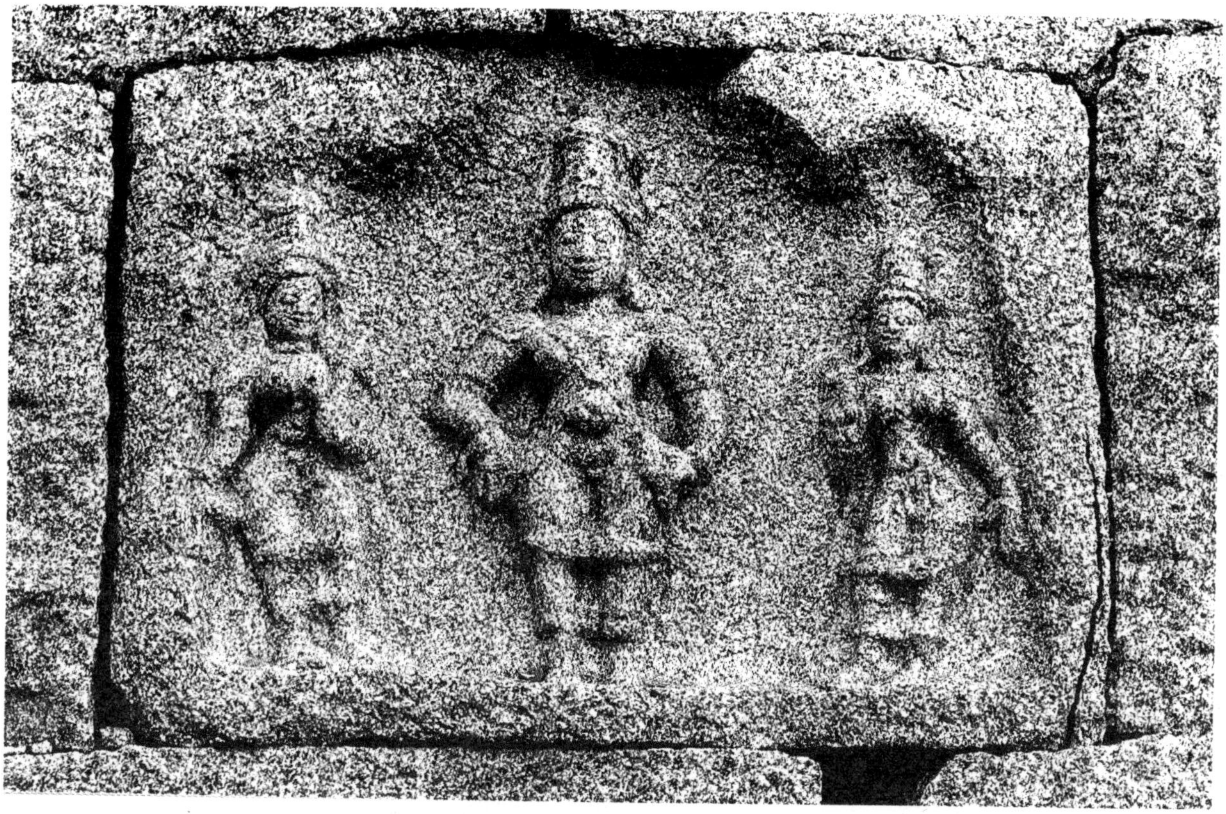

55. Vithala with Shri Devi and Bhu Devi, carving on the wall of the so-called 'Mint Enclosure' near palace base NWb/1.

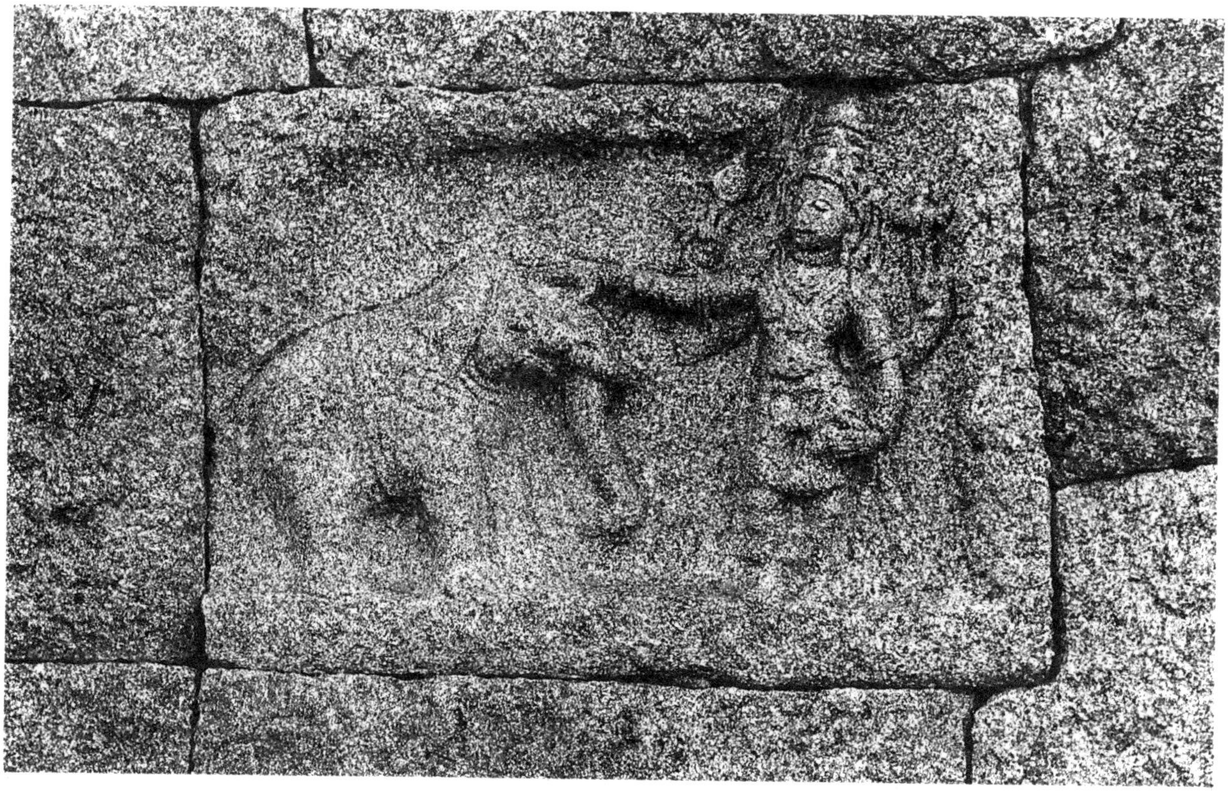

56. Kari-Varada Vishnu, carving on the wall of the so-called 'Mint Enclosure' near palace NWb/1.

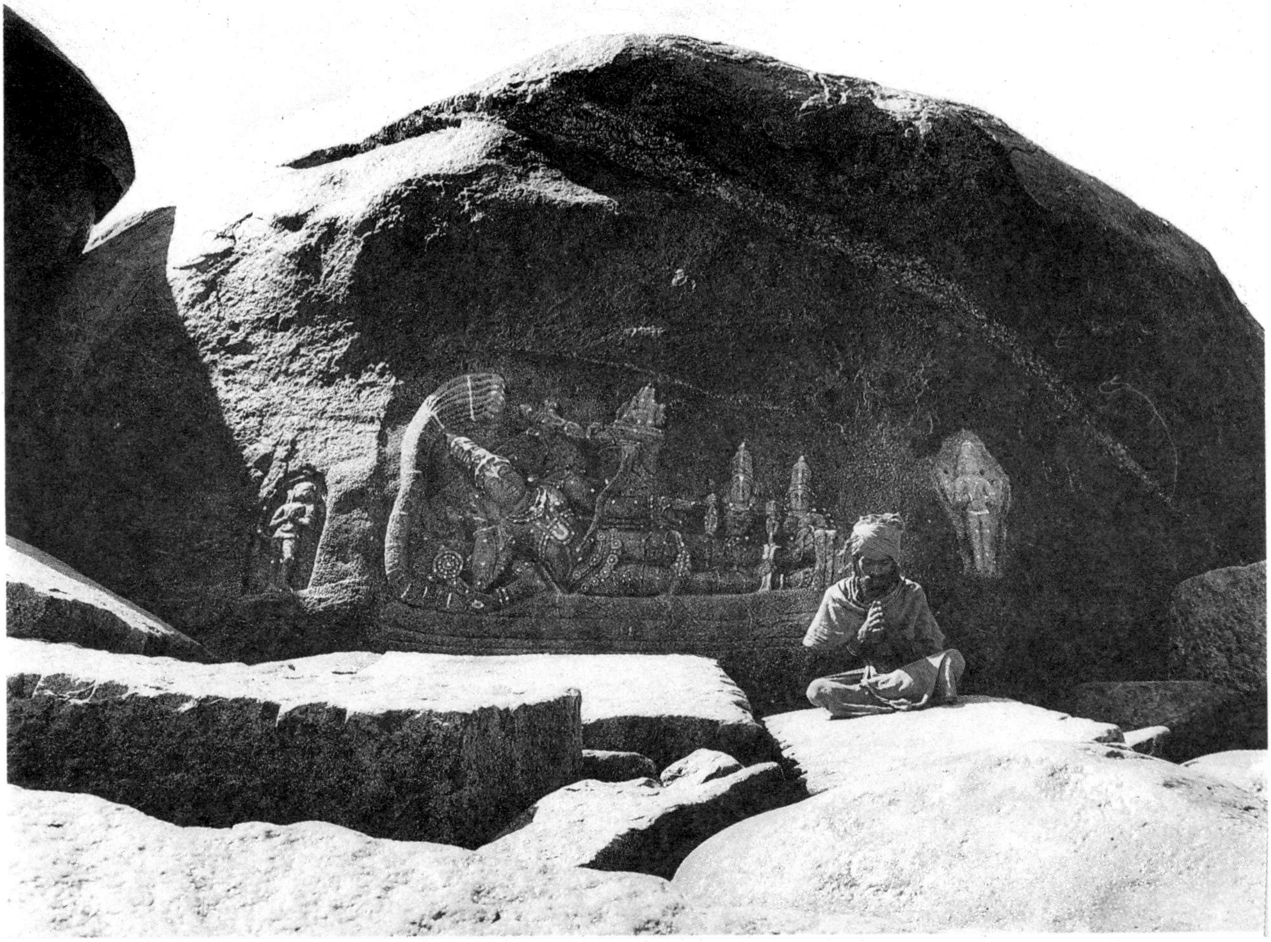

57. Ranganatha, carving on a boulder at Koti-tirtha near temple NGm/1.

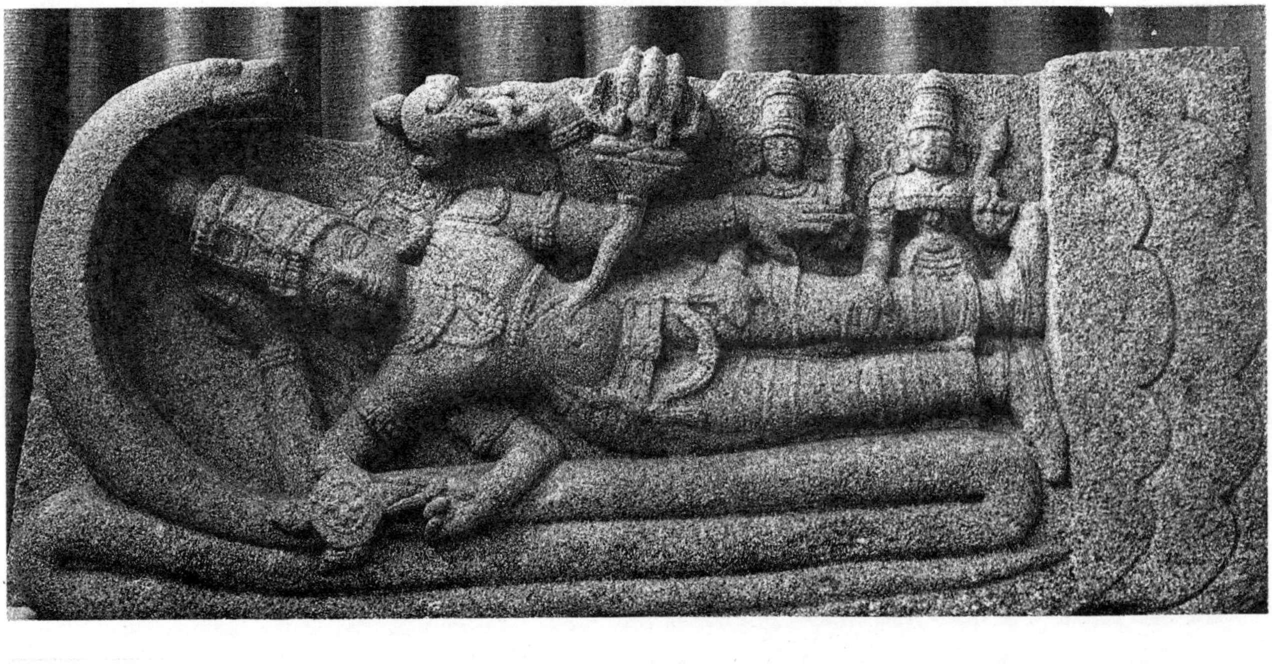

58. Ranganatha, Kamalapuram Museum.

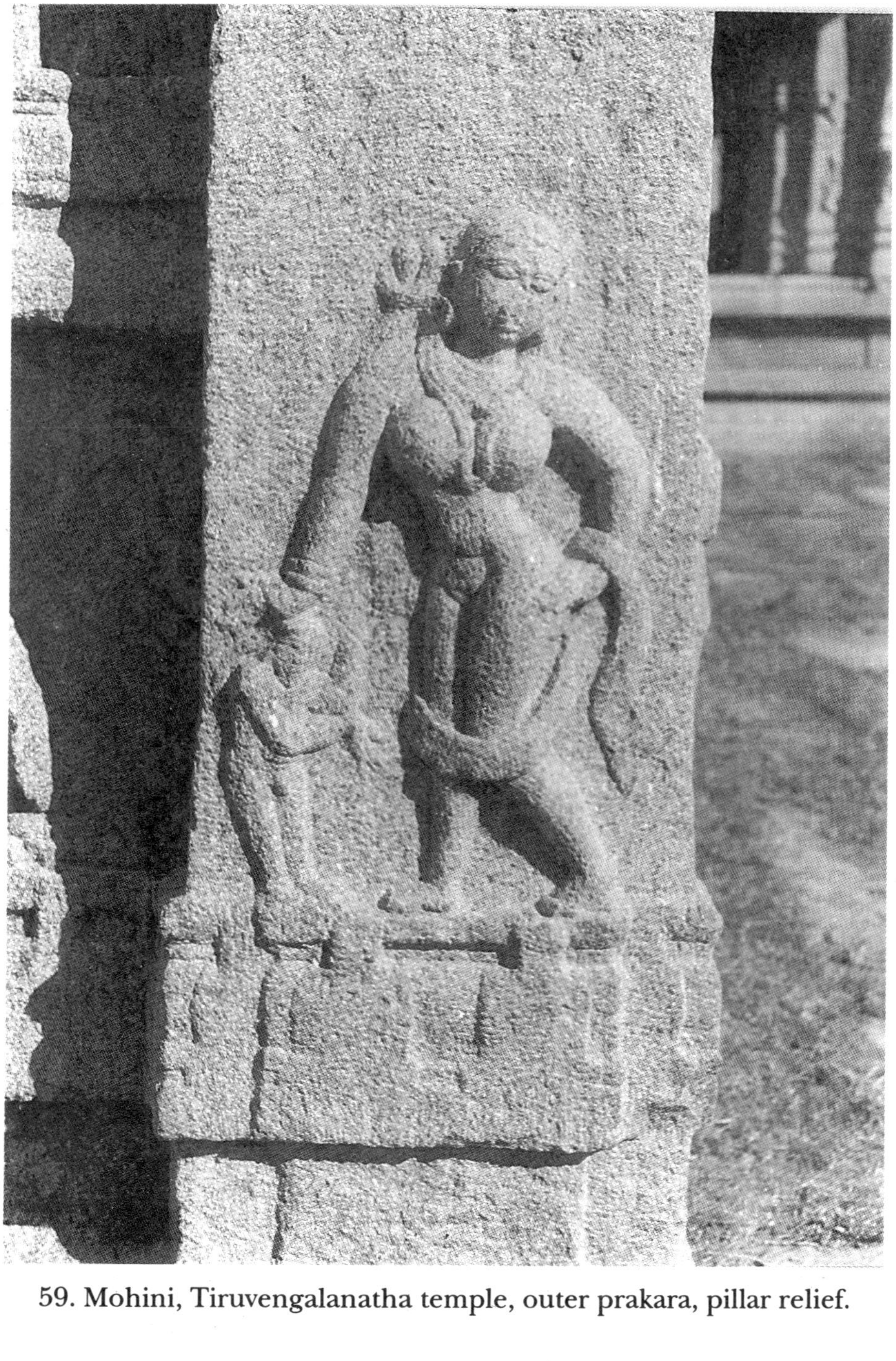

59. Mohini, Tiruvengalanatha temple, outer prakara, pillar relief.

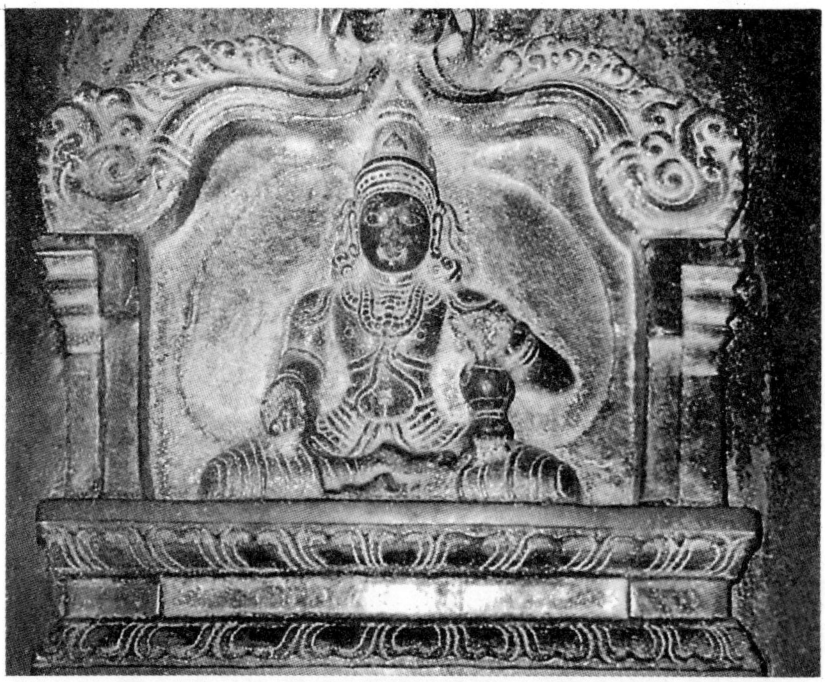

60. Annamurti or Dhanvantari, Ramachandra temple, principal shrine, closed mandapa, detail of pillar.

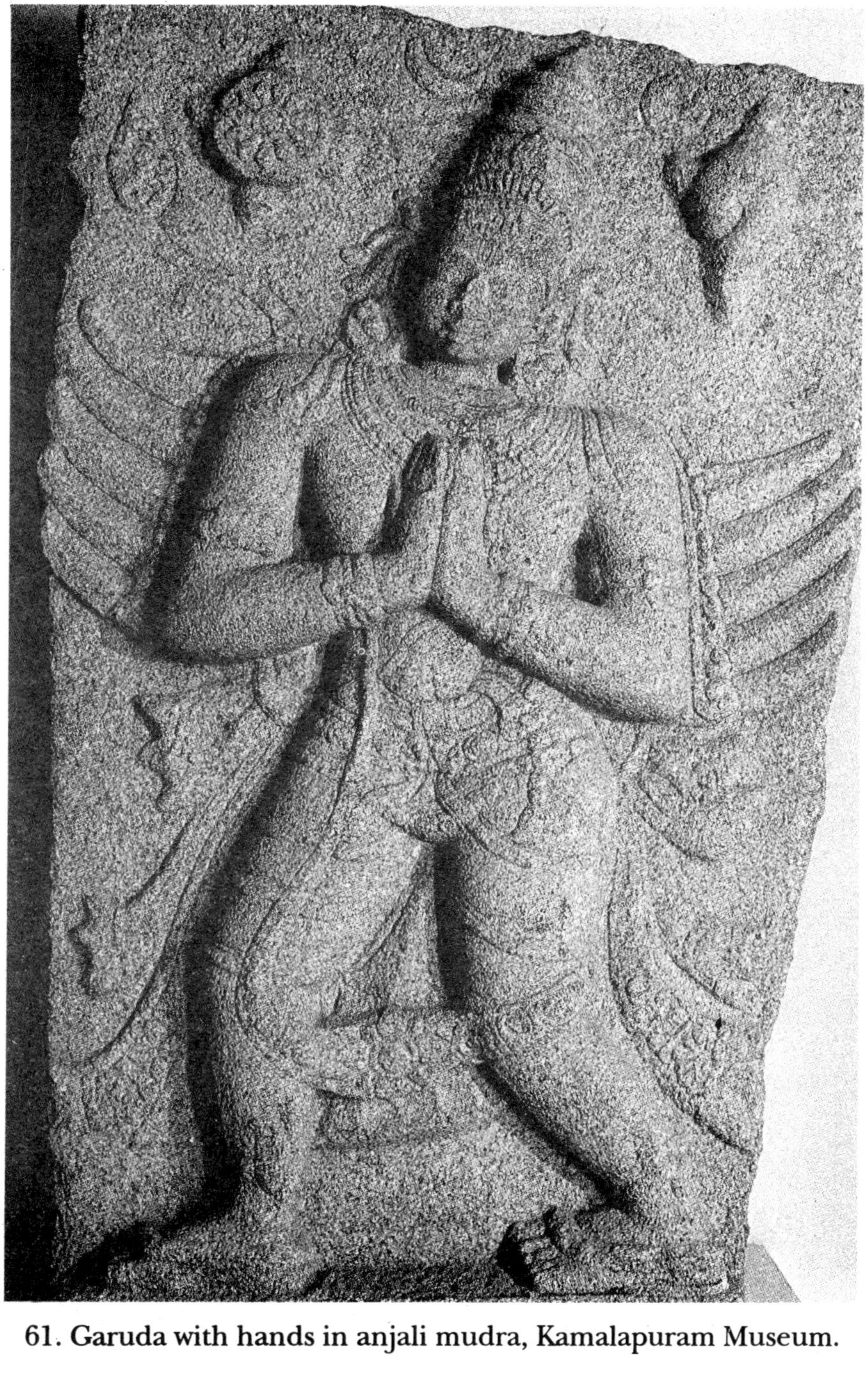

61. Garuda with hands in anjali mudra, Kamalapuram Museum.

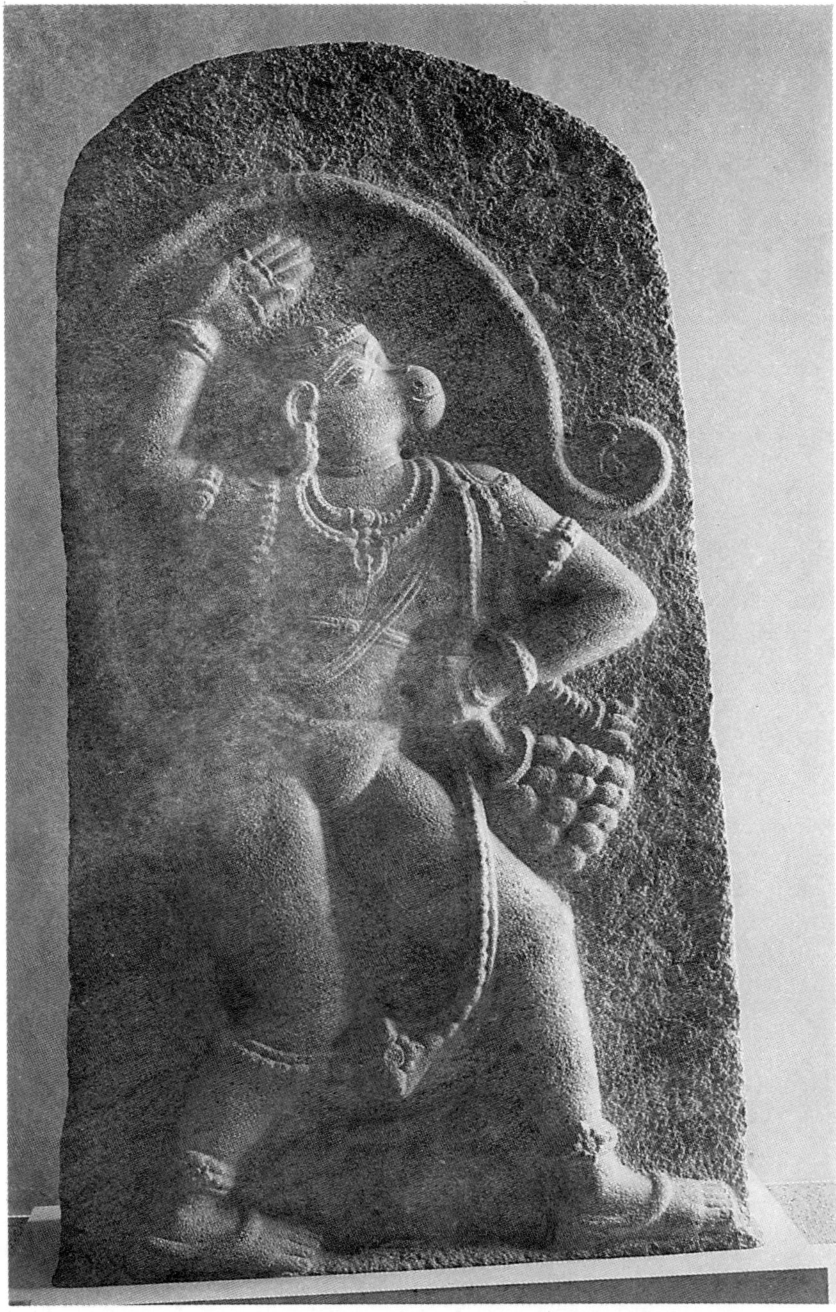

62. Vira Anjaneya, Kamalapuram Museum.

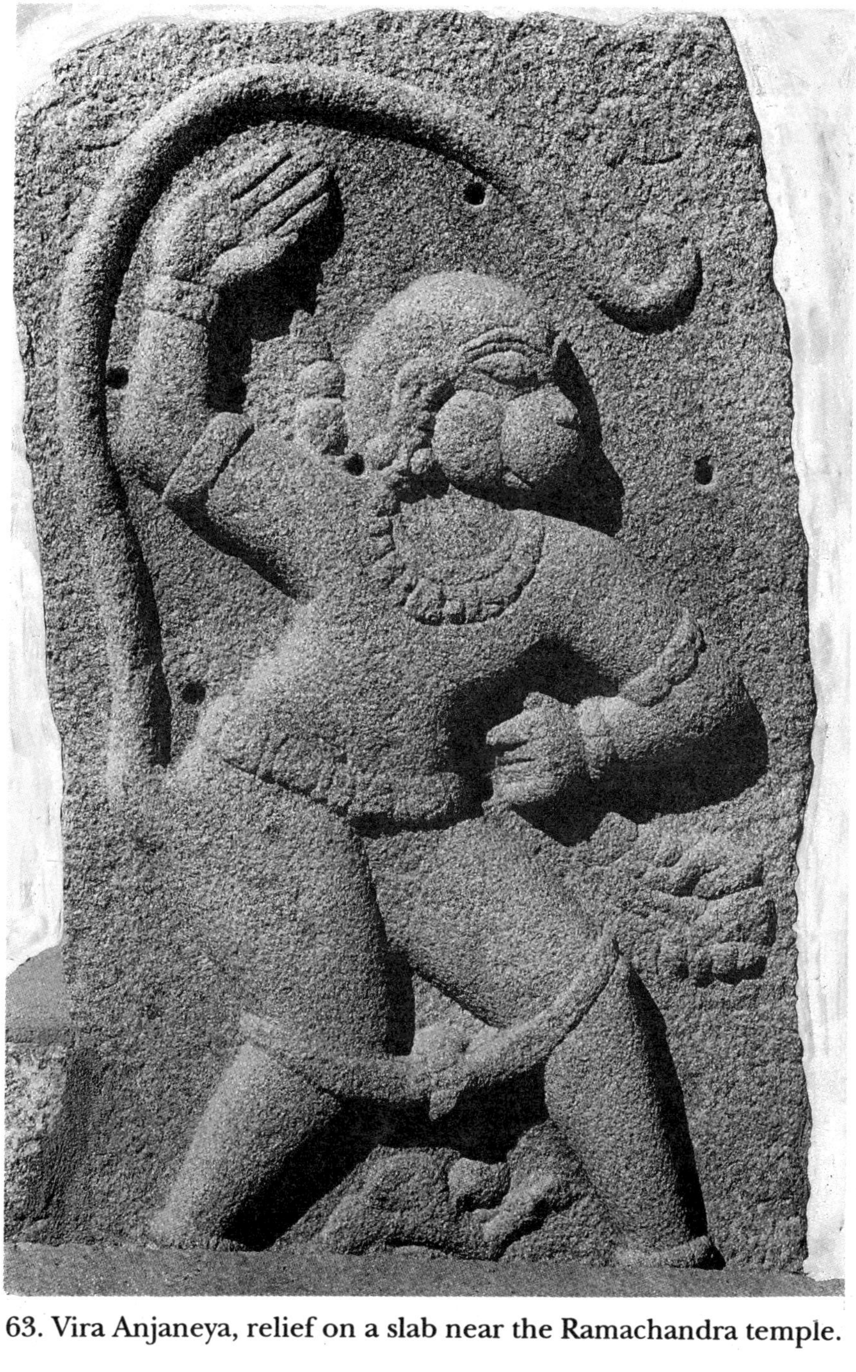

63. Vira Anjaneya, relief on a slab near the Ramachandra temple.

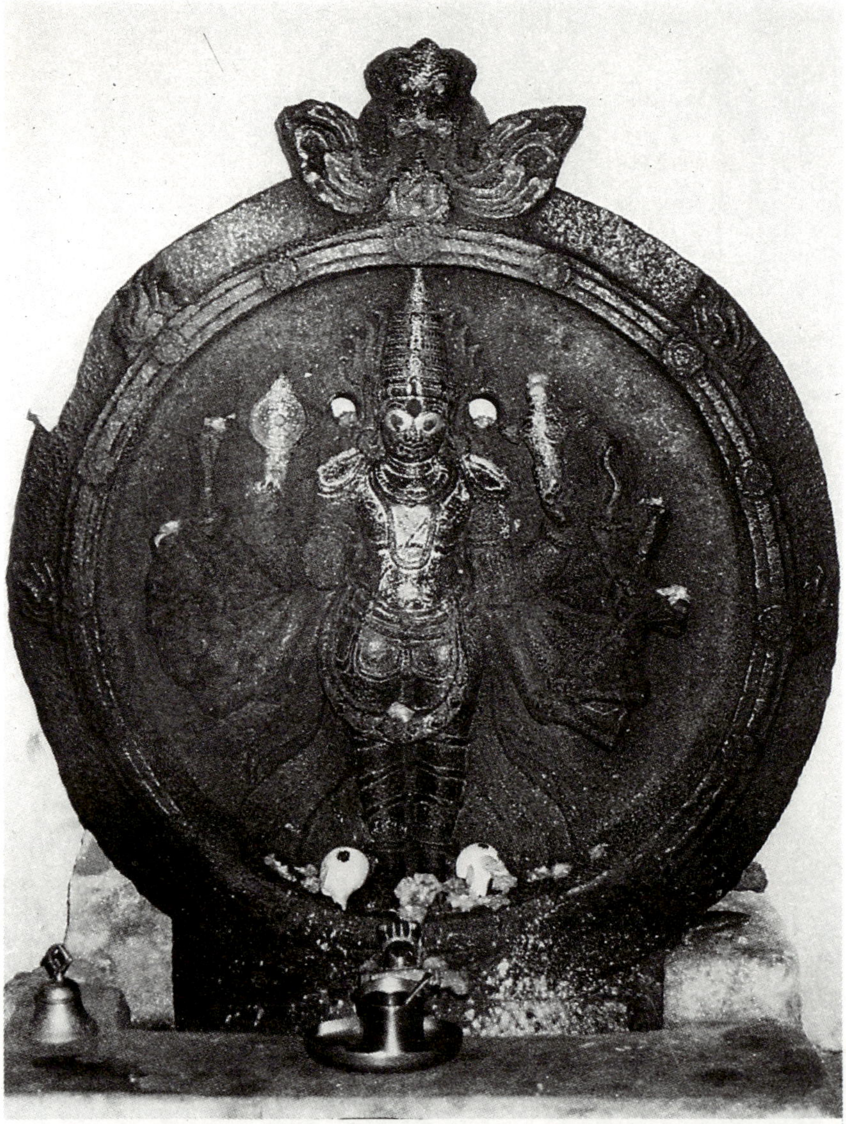

64. Sudarshana chakra, Suryanarayana temple at Chakratirtha.

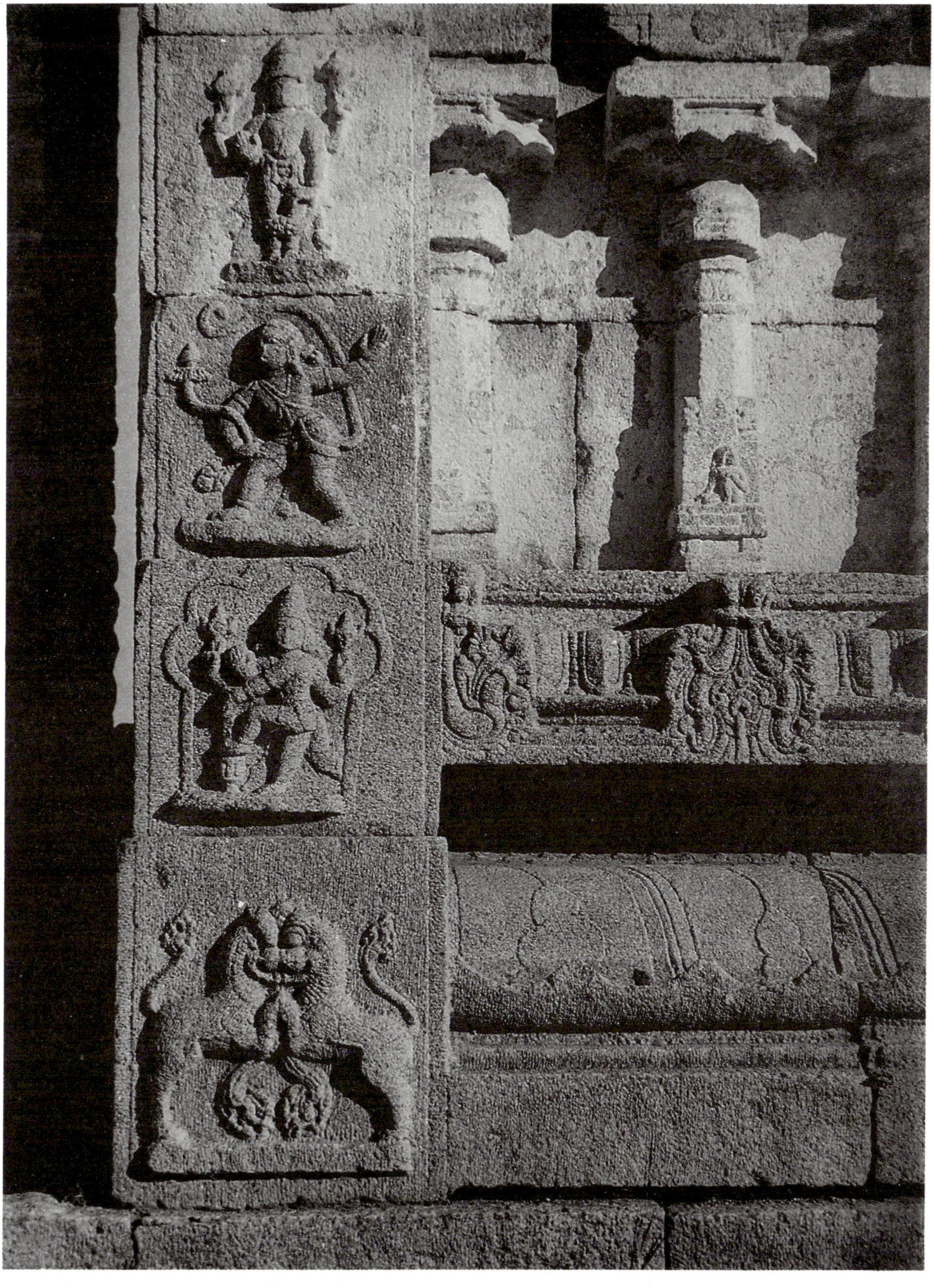

65. Tiruvengalanatha temple, Vaishnava motifs on the door-frame.

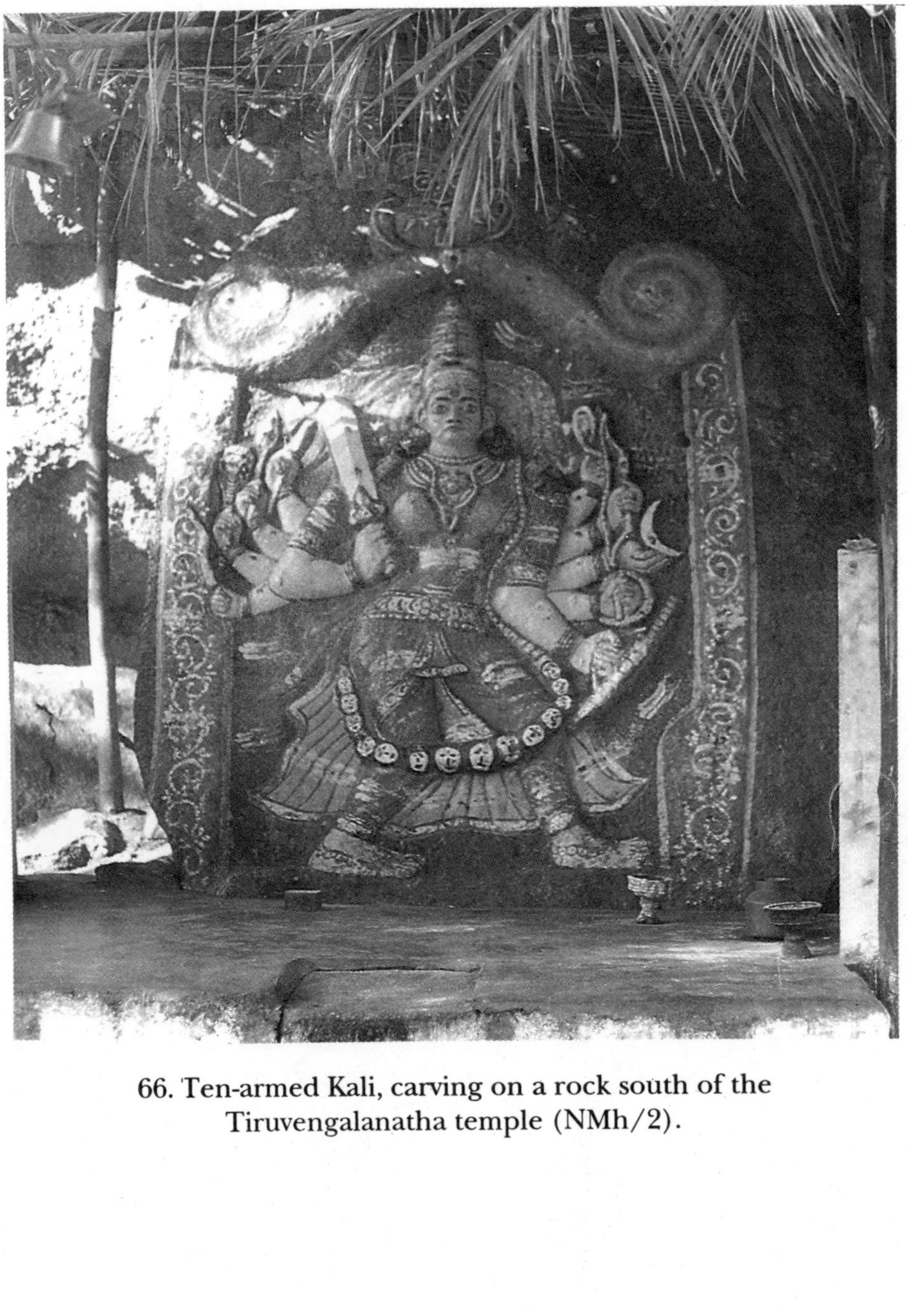

66. Ten-armed Kali, carving on a rock south of the Tiruvengalanatha temple (NMh/2).

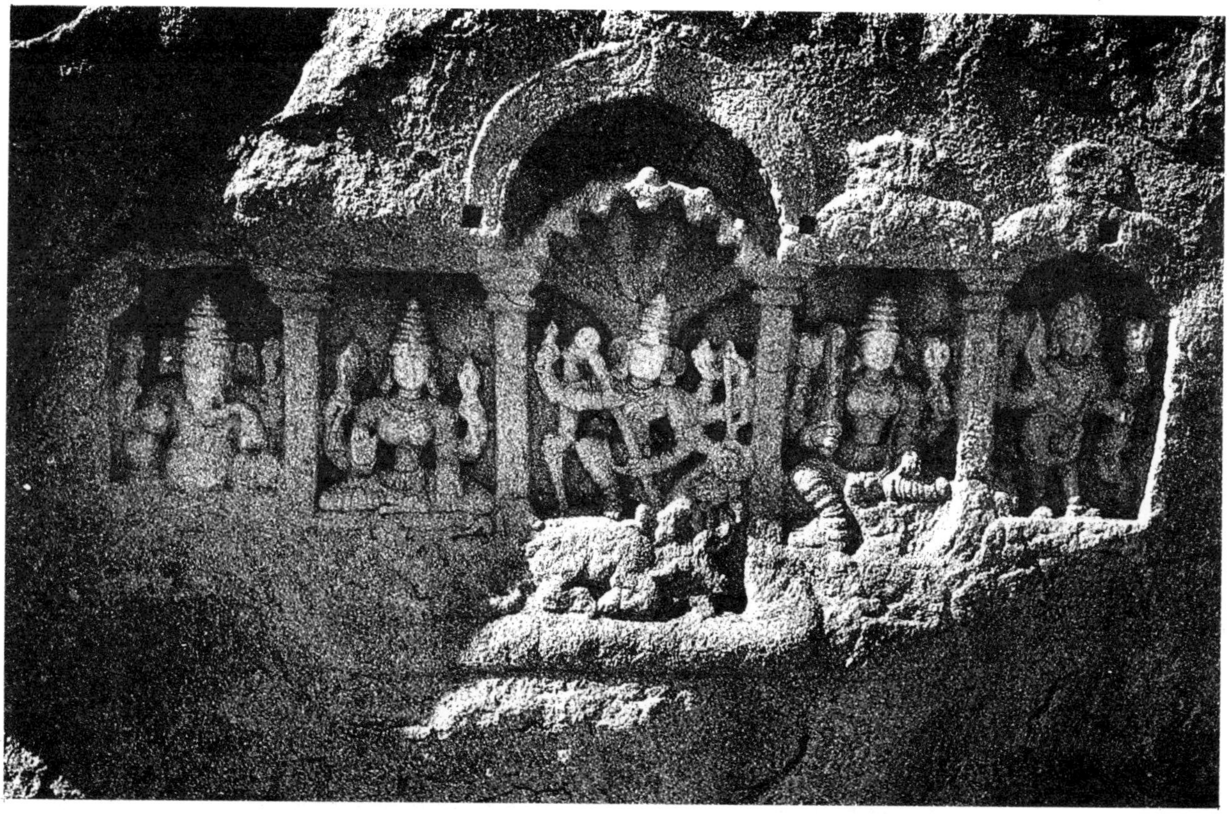

67. Ganesha, Lakshmi, Mahishasuramardini, Bhairavi and Bhairava, carving on the boulders in NMx/2.

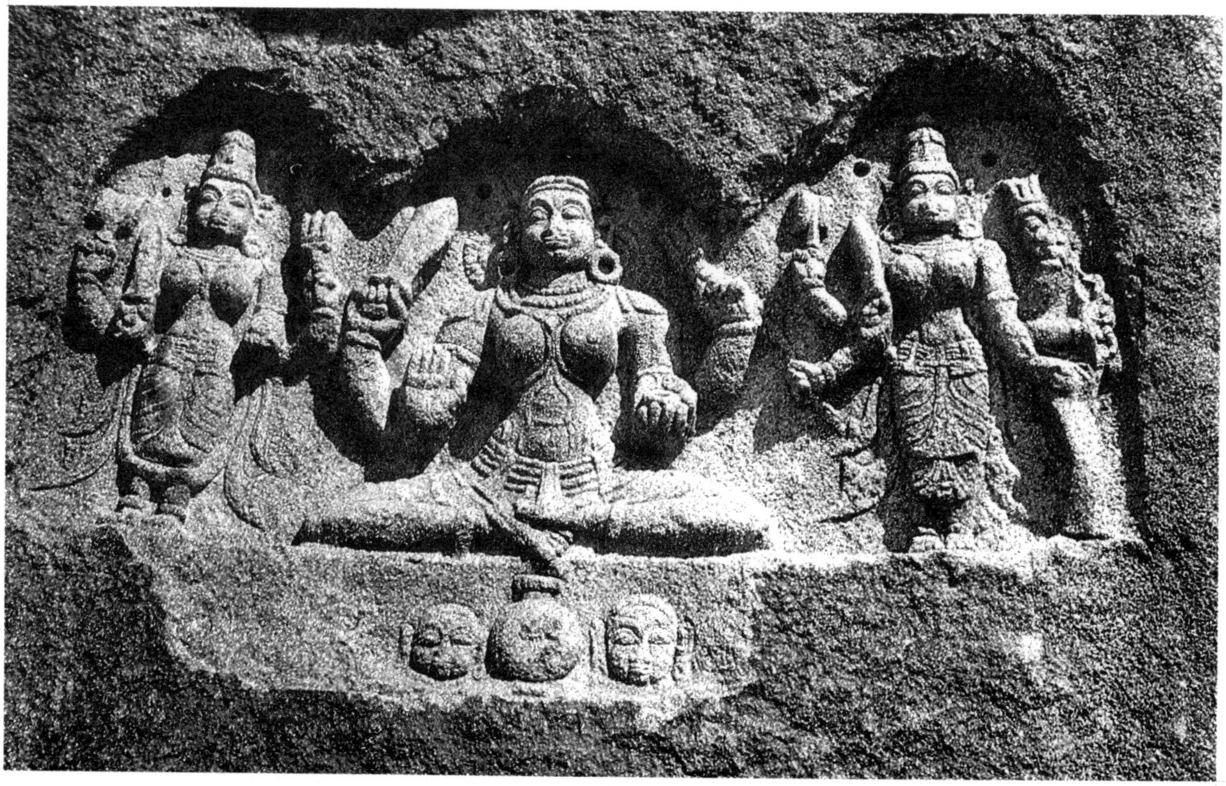

68. Seated Kali, flanked by Bhairavi and Bhadrakali, carving on the boulders in NMx/2.

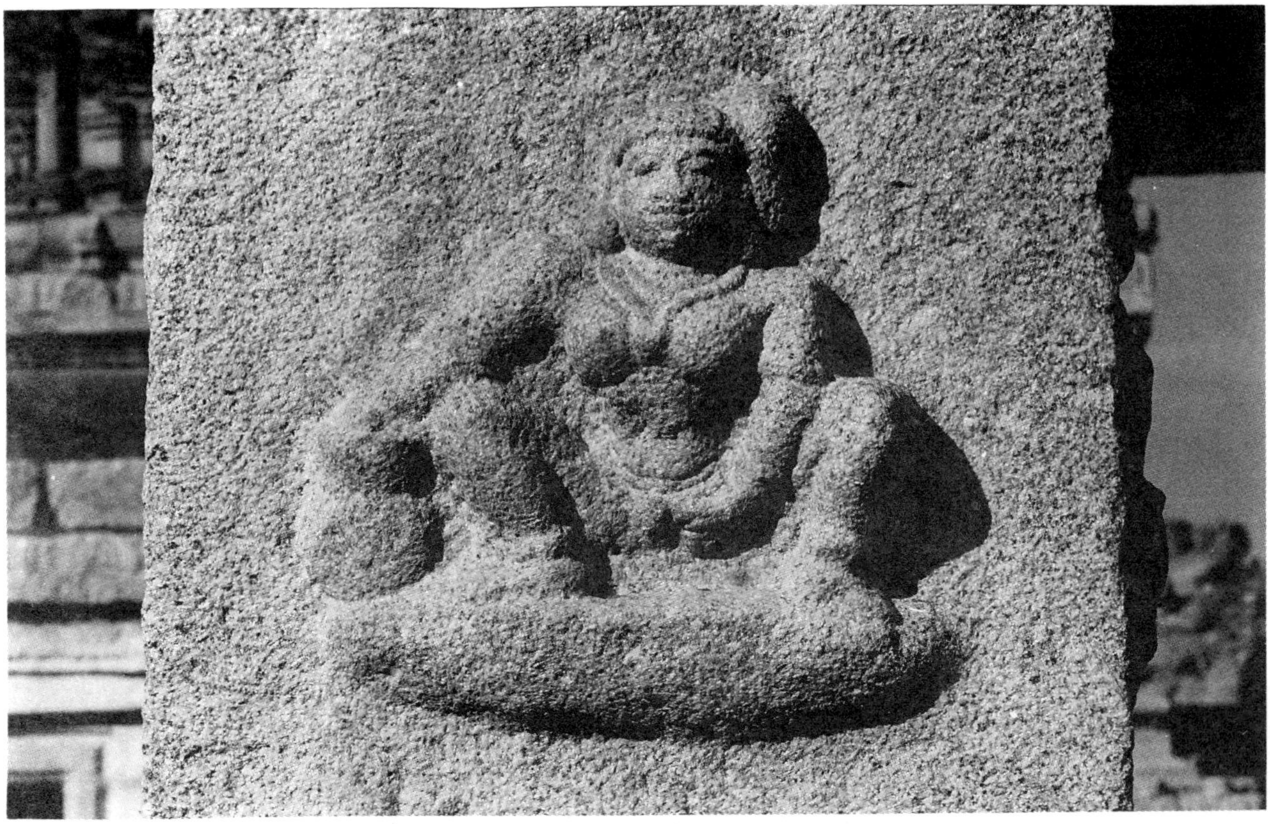

69. Lajja-Gauri with pot, Tiruvengalanatha temple, pillar relief in the open mandapa.

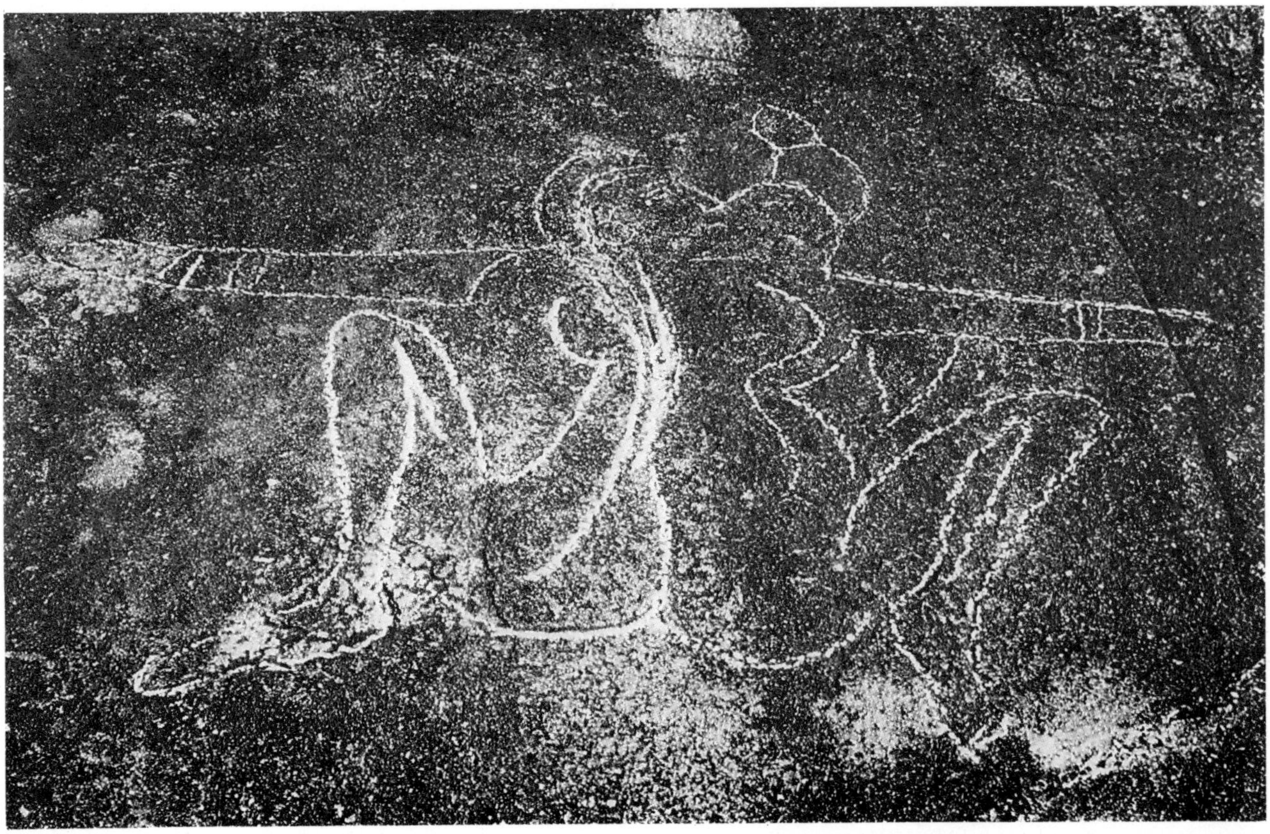

70. Lajja-Gauri, etched image on the sheet rock in NSz/4.

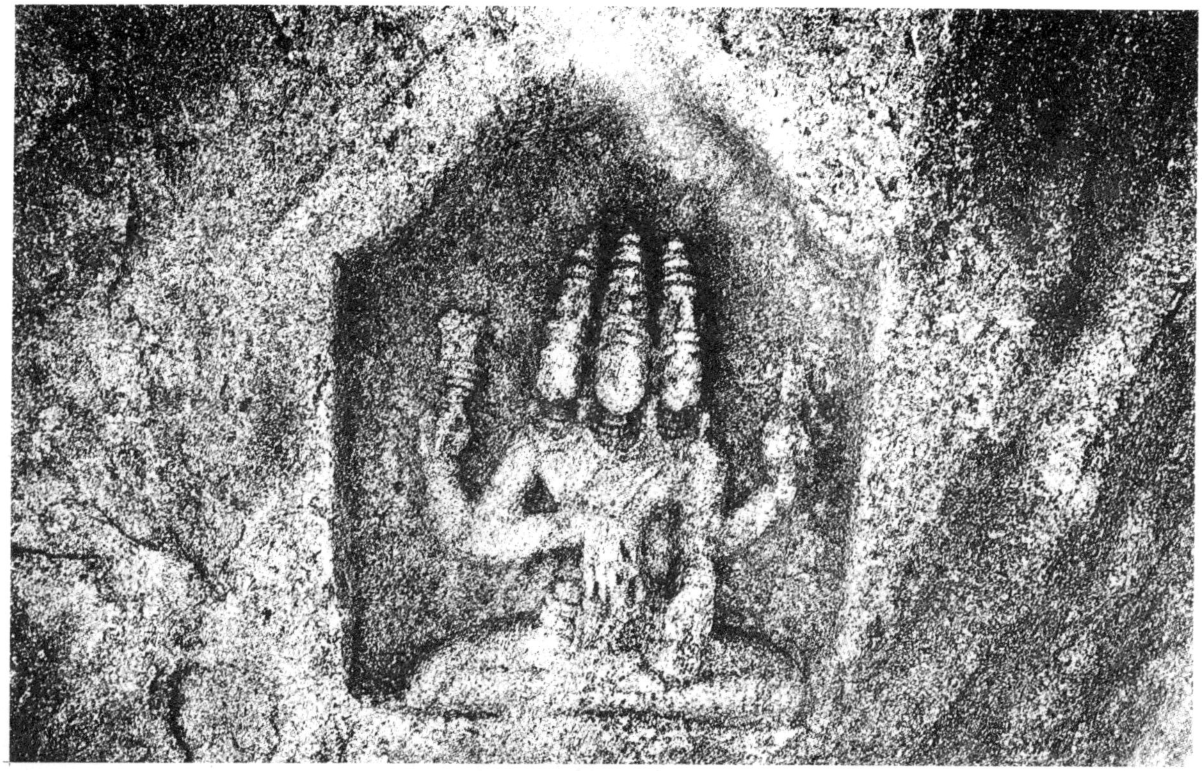

71. Brahma, carving in NMx/2.

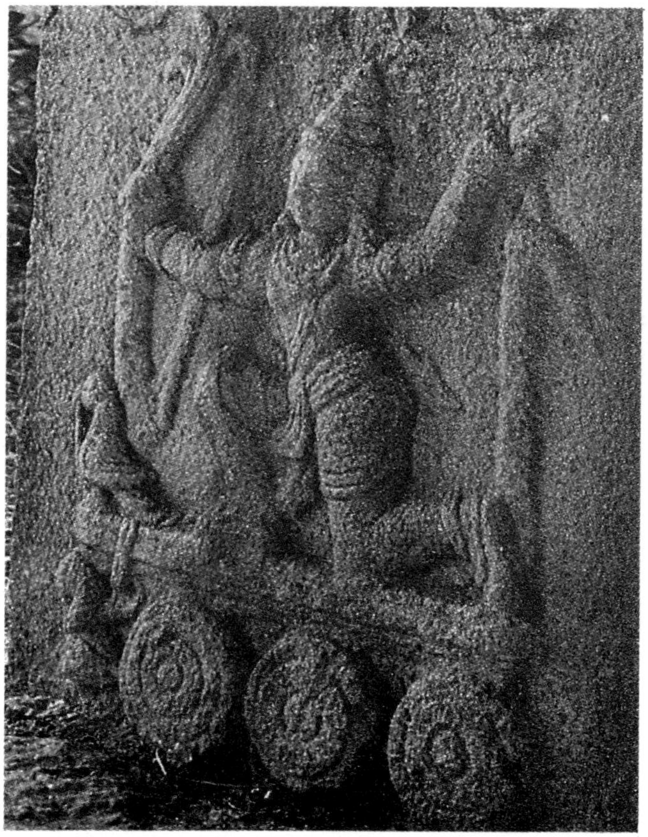

72. Kama on a parrot-drawn chariot, pillar relief in the Shiva temple (NGt/3) on the south bank.

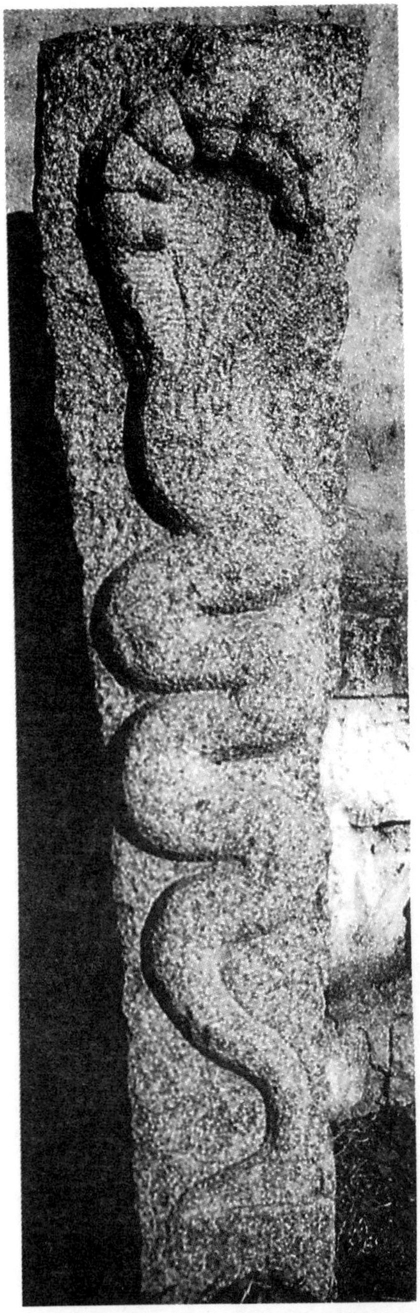

73. Seven-hooded naga, Kamalapuram Museum.

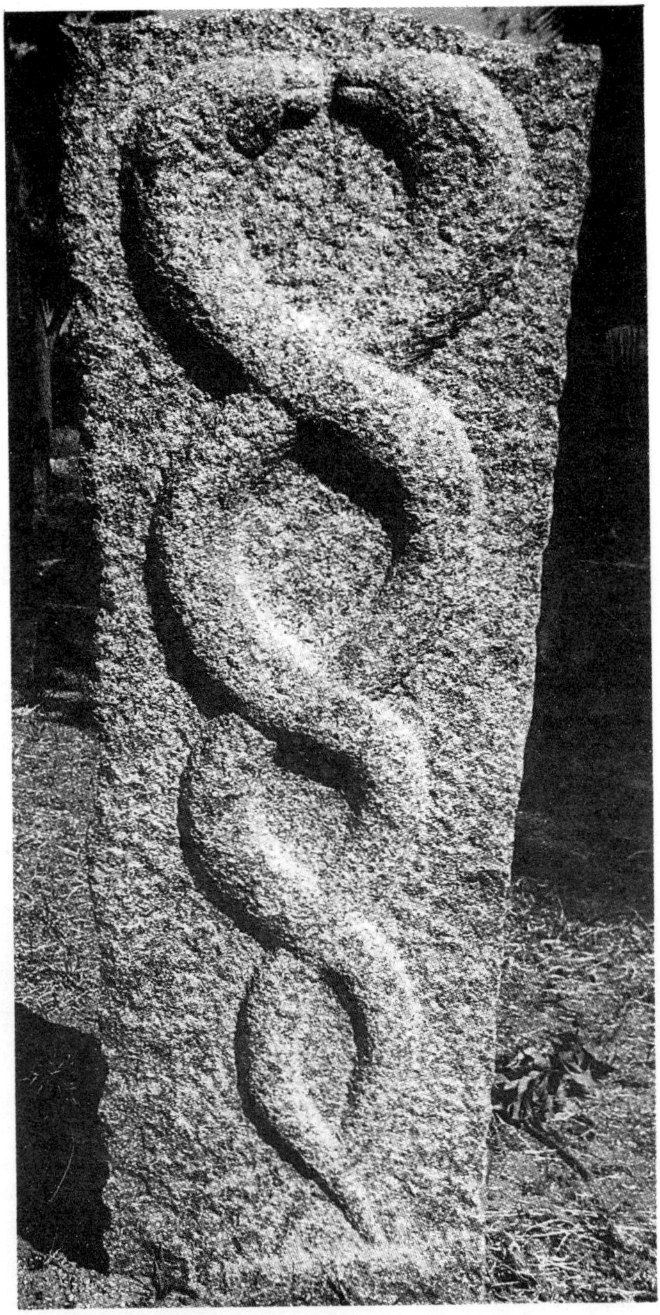

74. Intertwined nagas, Kamalapuram Museum.

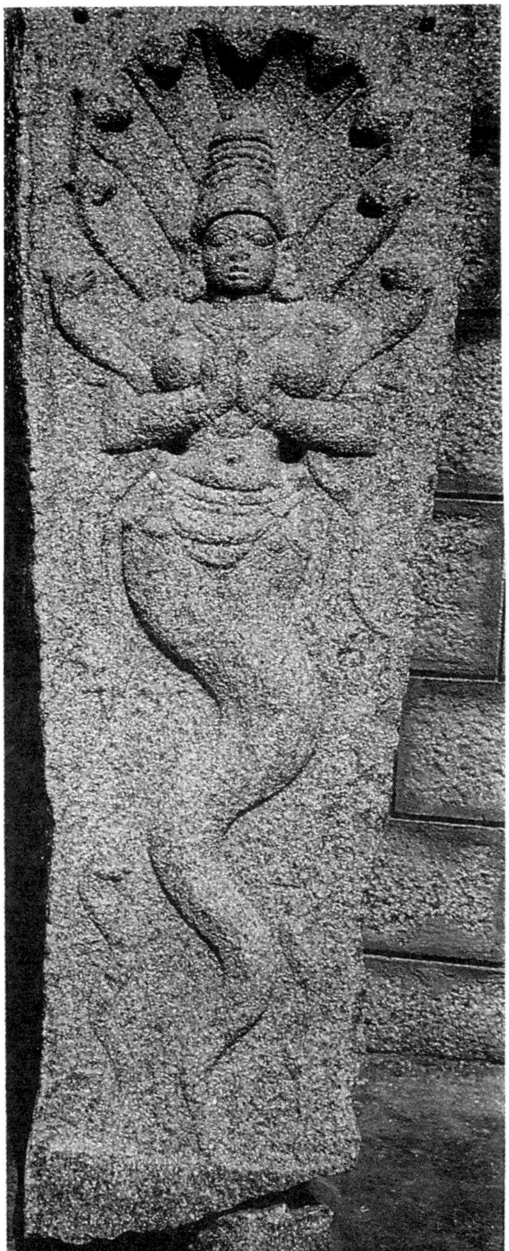

75. Nagini Mudama, Kamalapuram Museum.

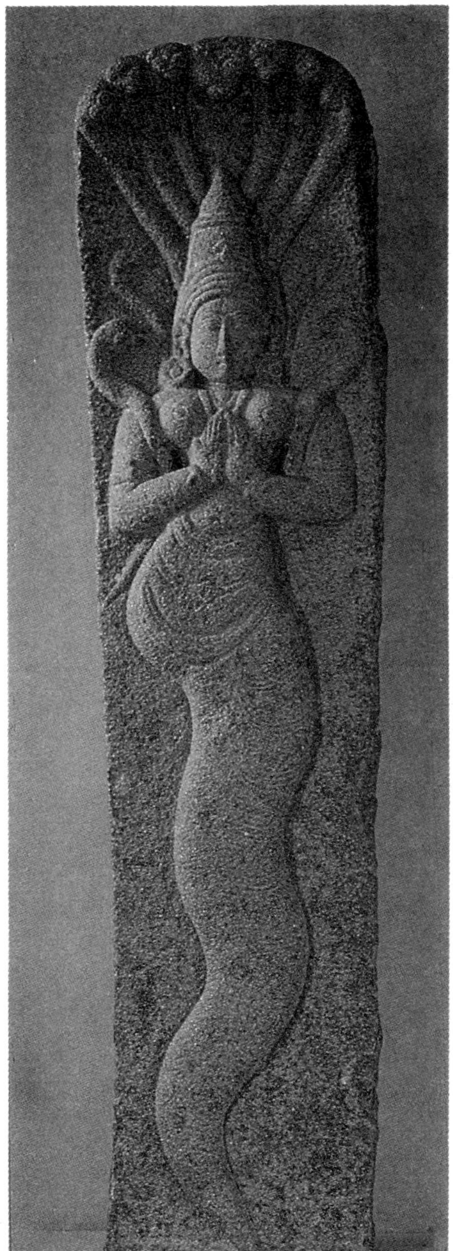

76. Nagini Mudama, Kamalapuram Museum.

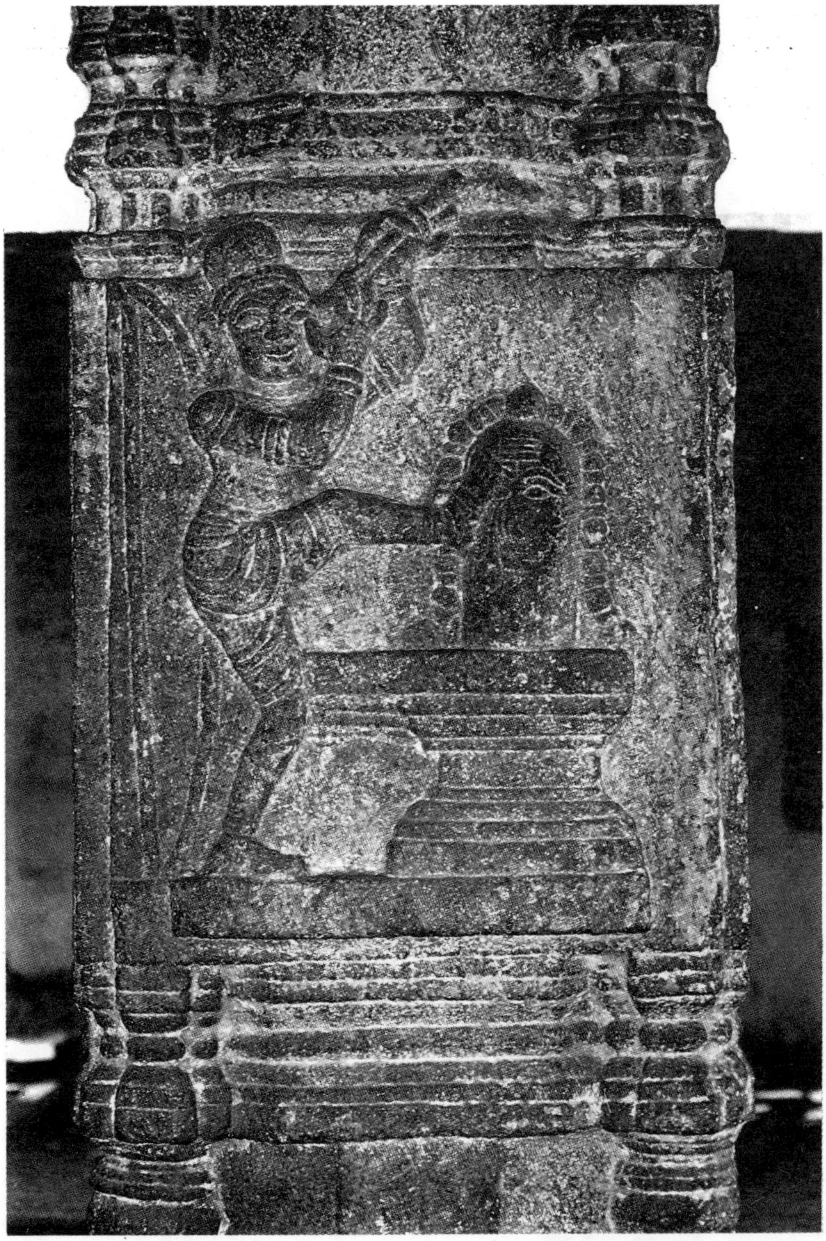

77. Kannappa Nayanmar, Virupaksha temple pillar relief in the maharangamandapa.

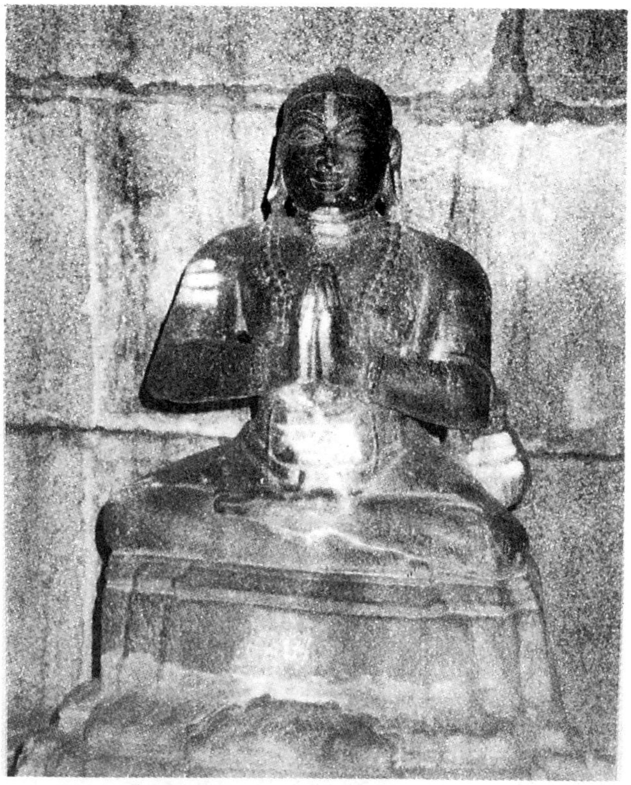

78. Tondaradippodi alvar, statue in the 'Nammalvar' temple.

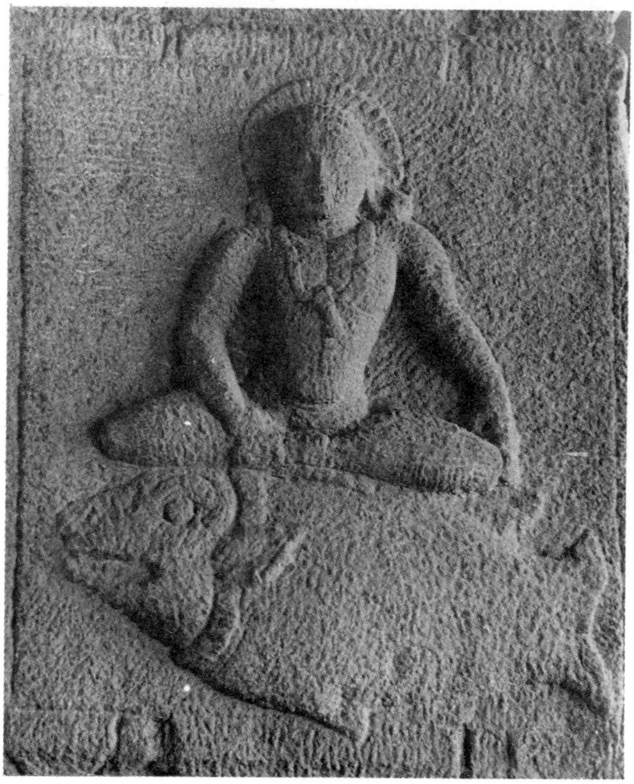

79. Matsyendranatha, pillar relief in the open mandapa of the Pattabhirama temple.

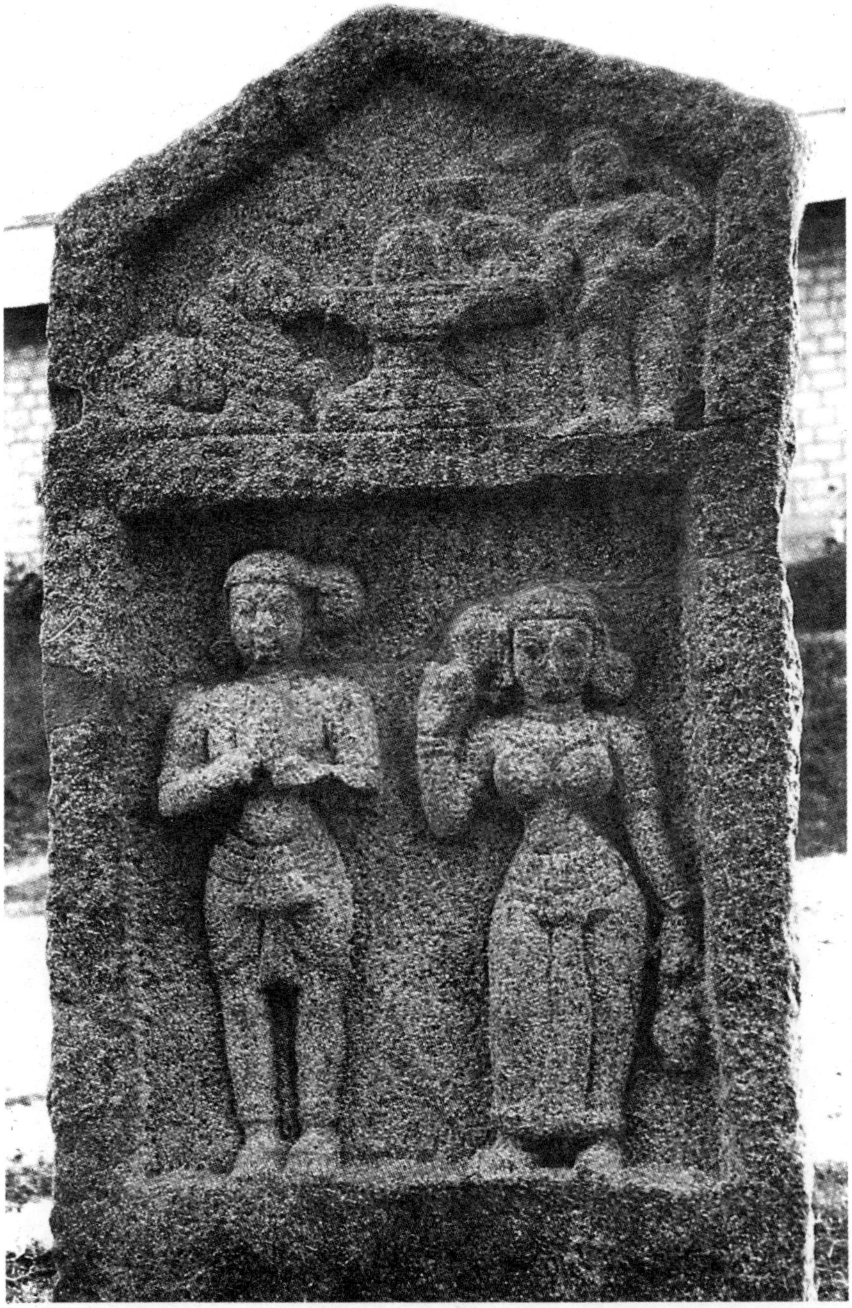

80. Sati-stone, sati with pot, Kamalapuram Museum.

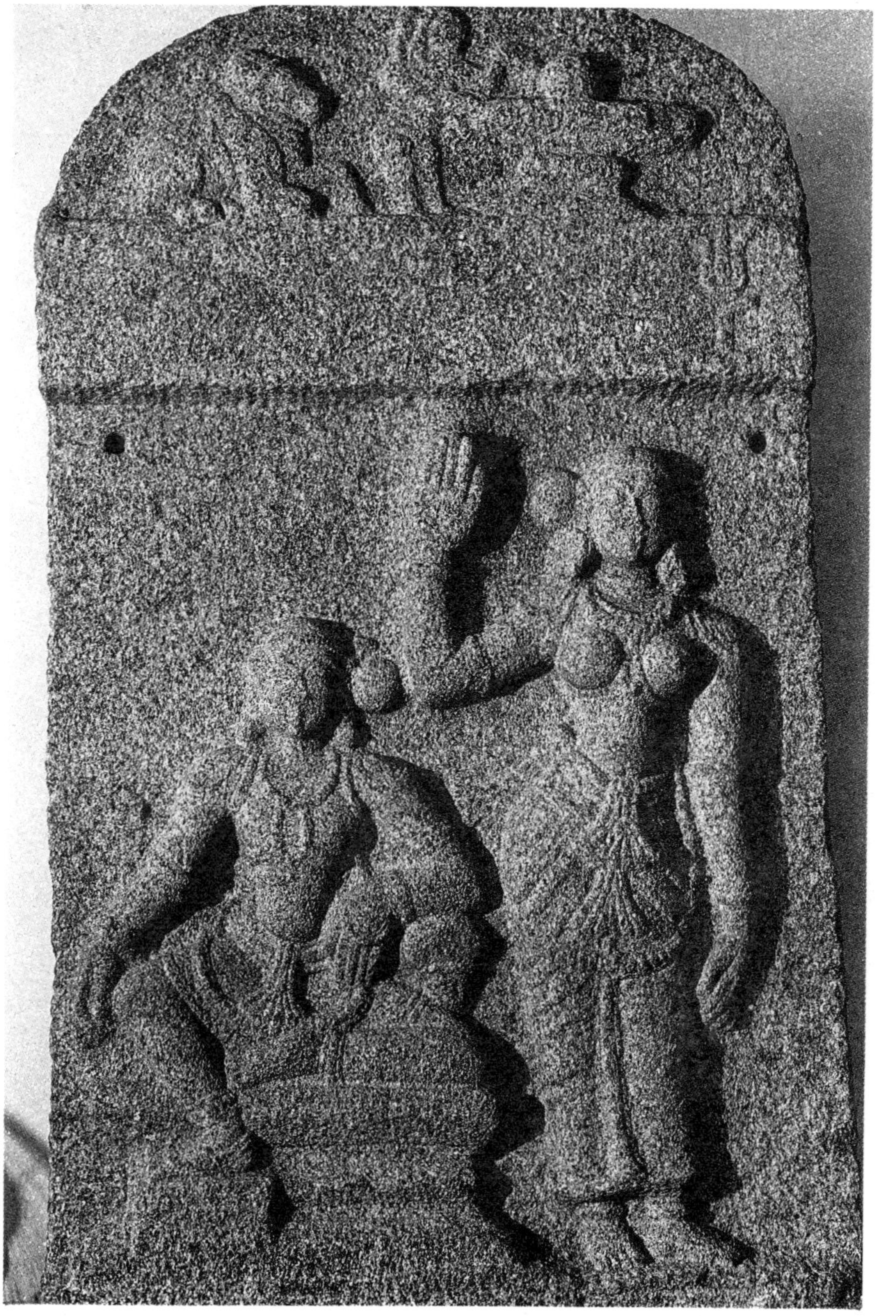

81. Sati-stone, Kamalapuram Museum.

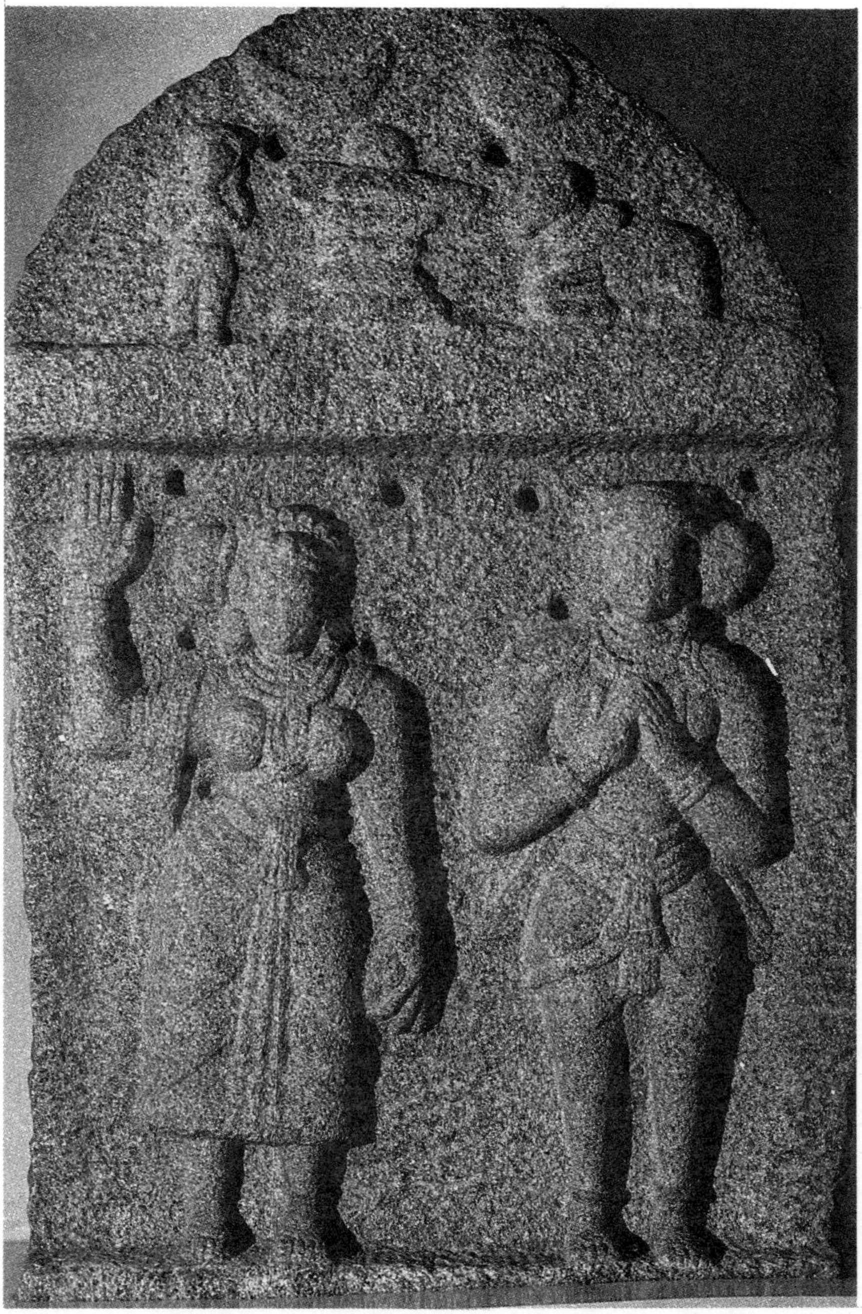

82. Sati-stone, Kamalapuram Museum.

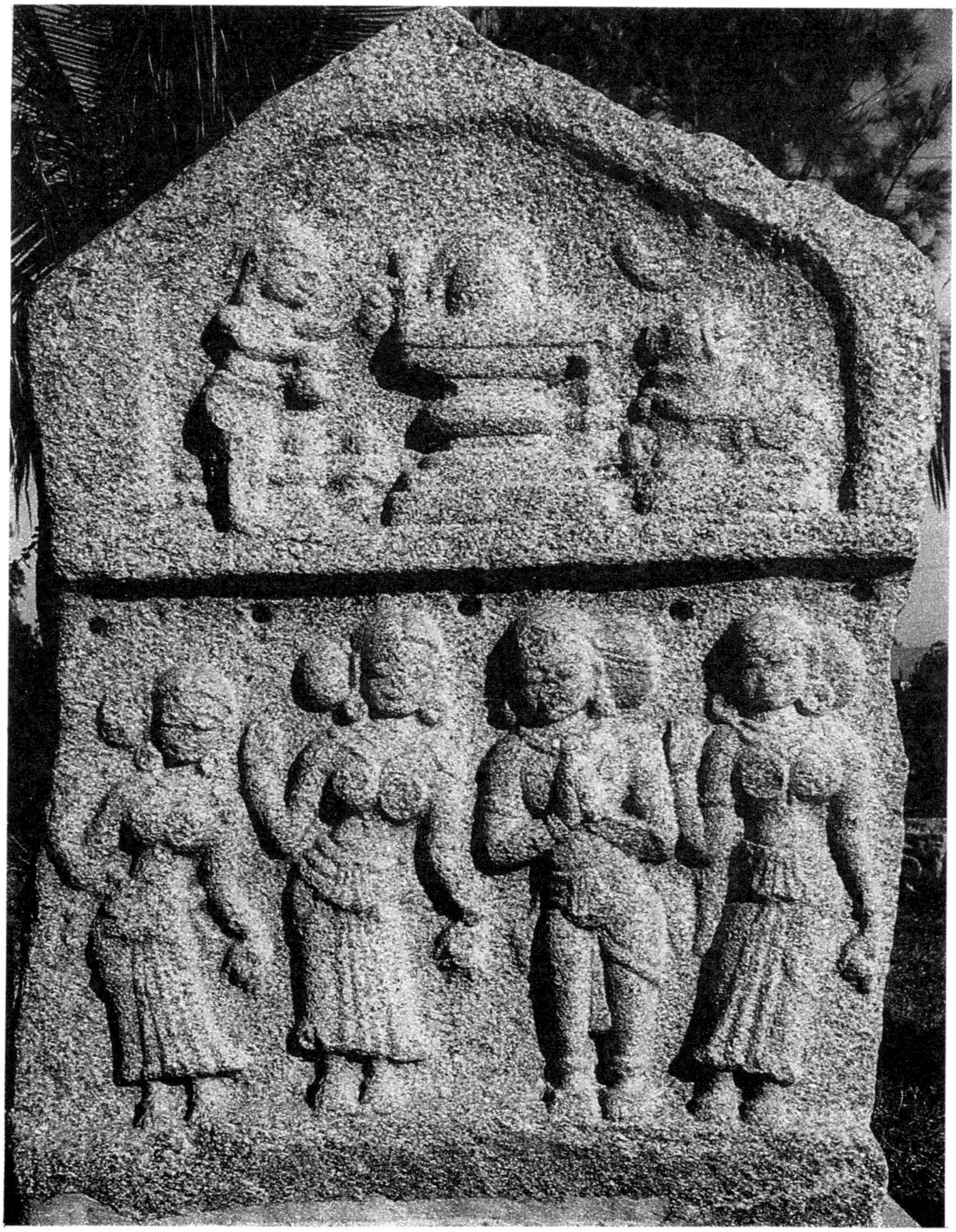

83. Sati-stone, satis with lemons, Kamalapuram Museum.

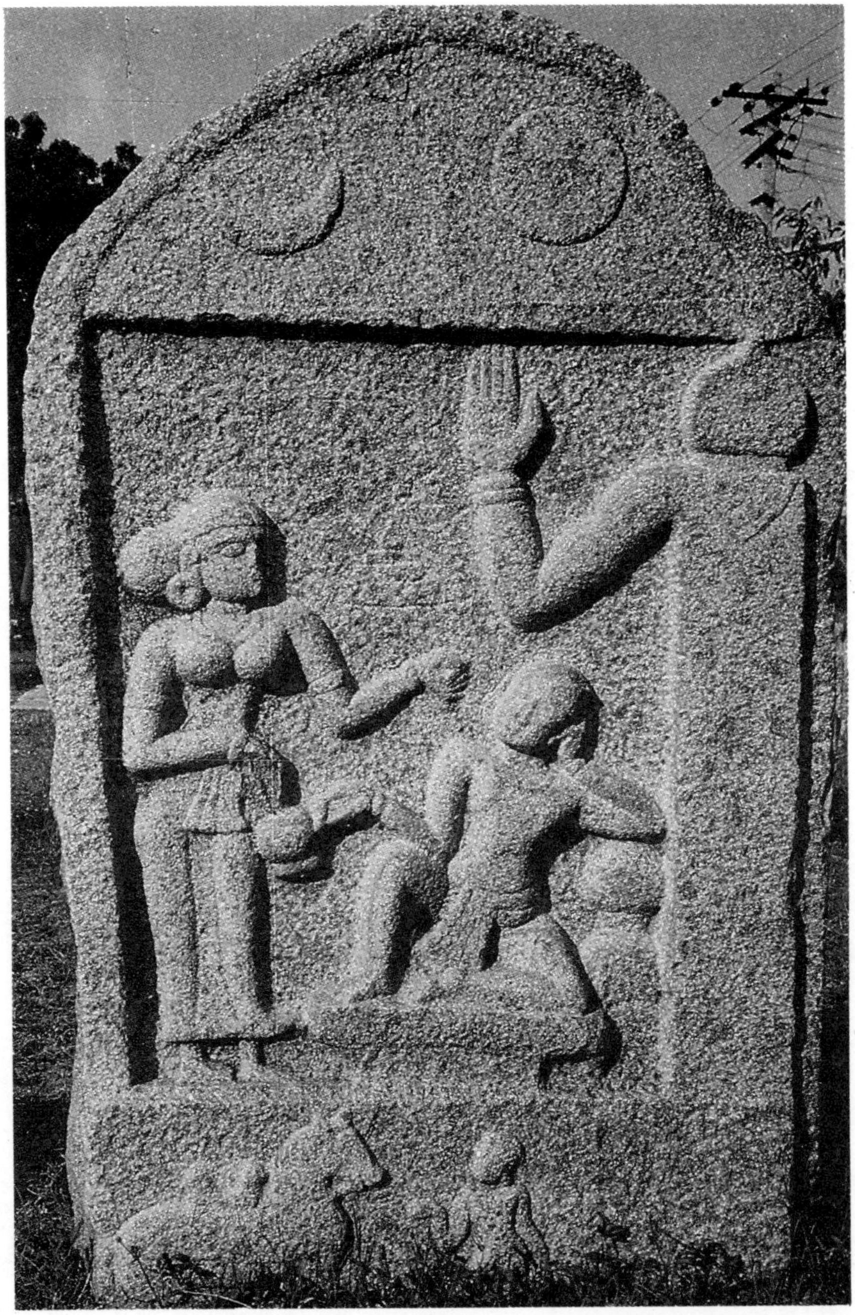

84. Sati-stone, Kamalapuram Museum.

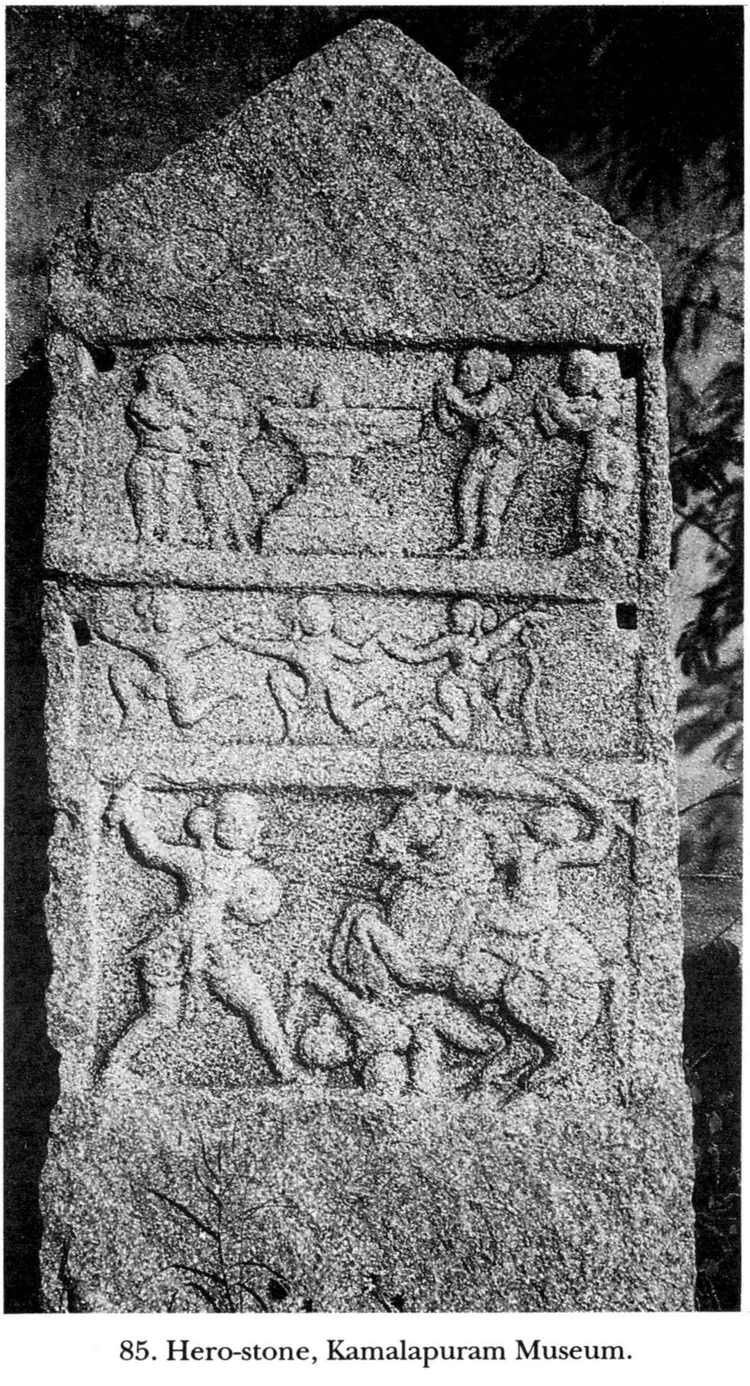

85. Hero-stone, Kamalapuram Museum.

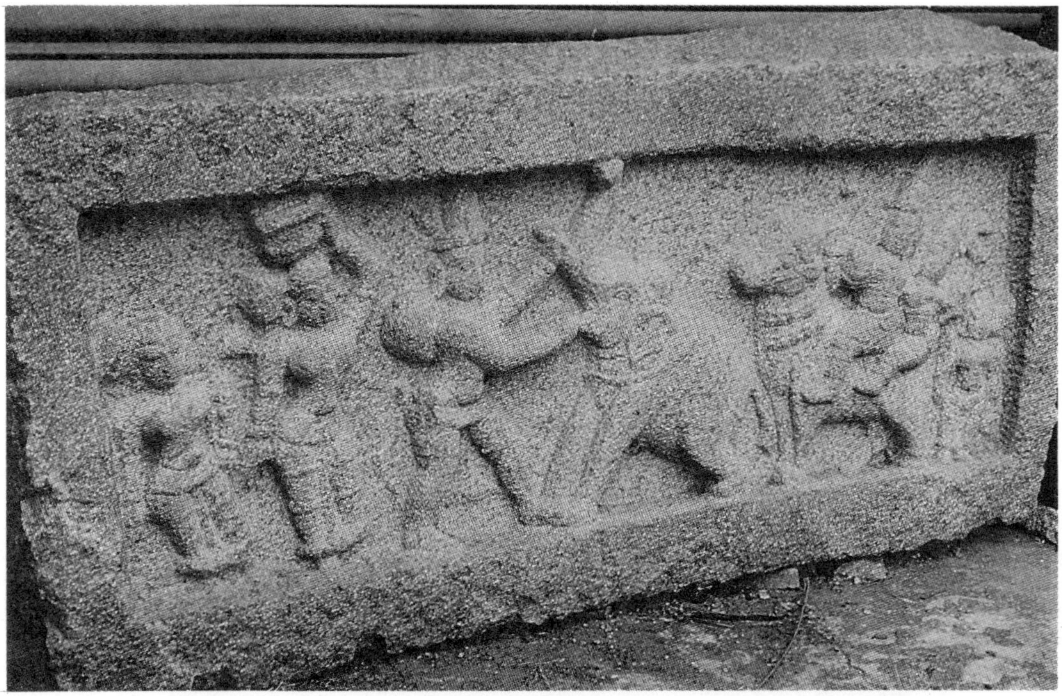

86. Hero killing an elephant, Shiva and Parvati on Nandi, Kamalapuram Museum.

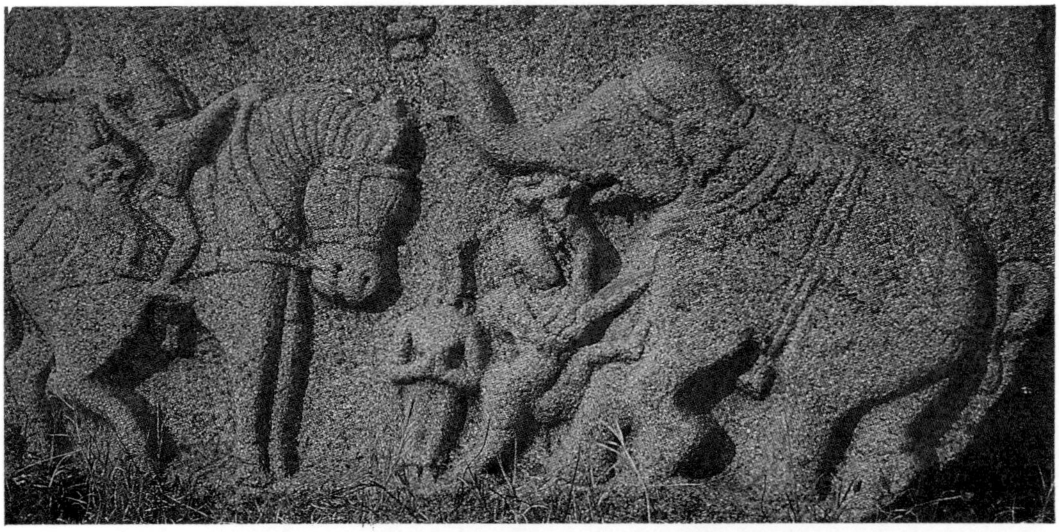

87. Hero killing an elephant, Mailara and Mhalsa on horseback, Kamalapuram Museum.

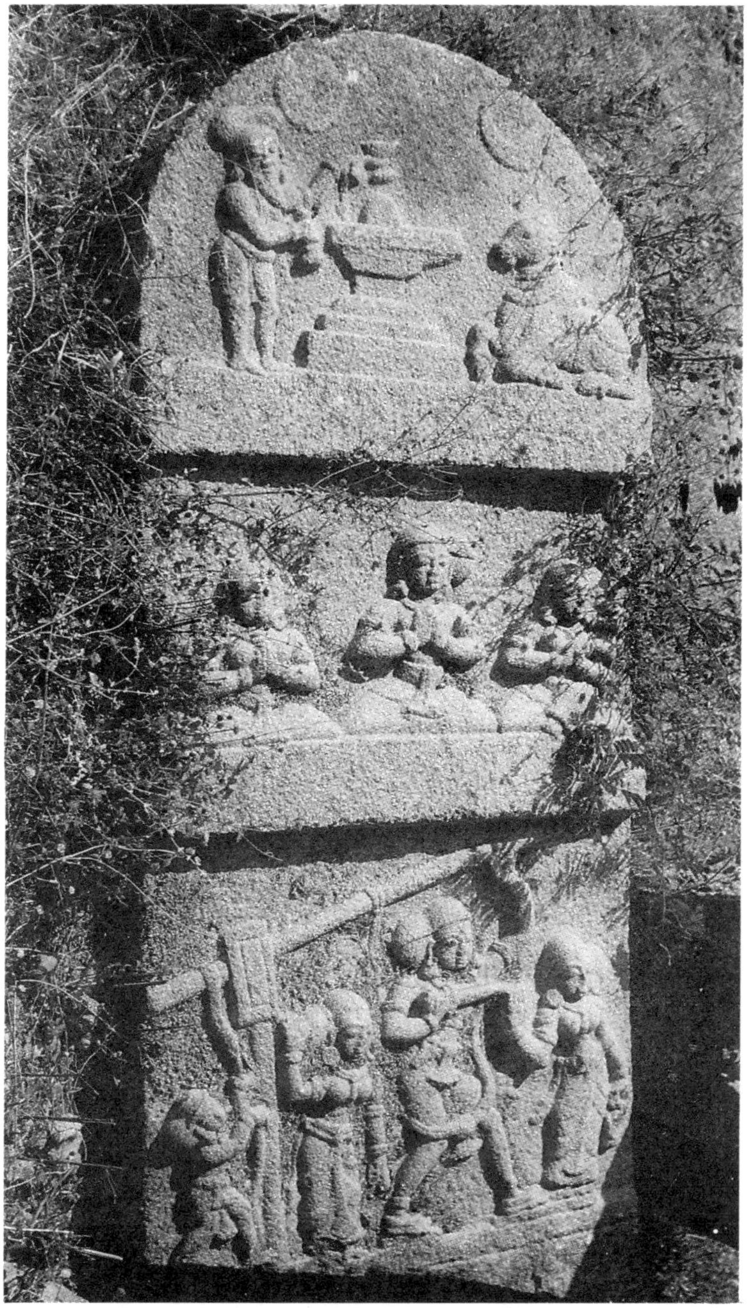

88. Slab depicting self-immolation,
Kamalapuram Museum.

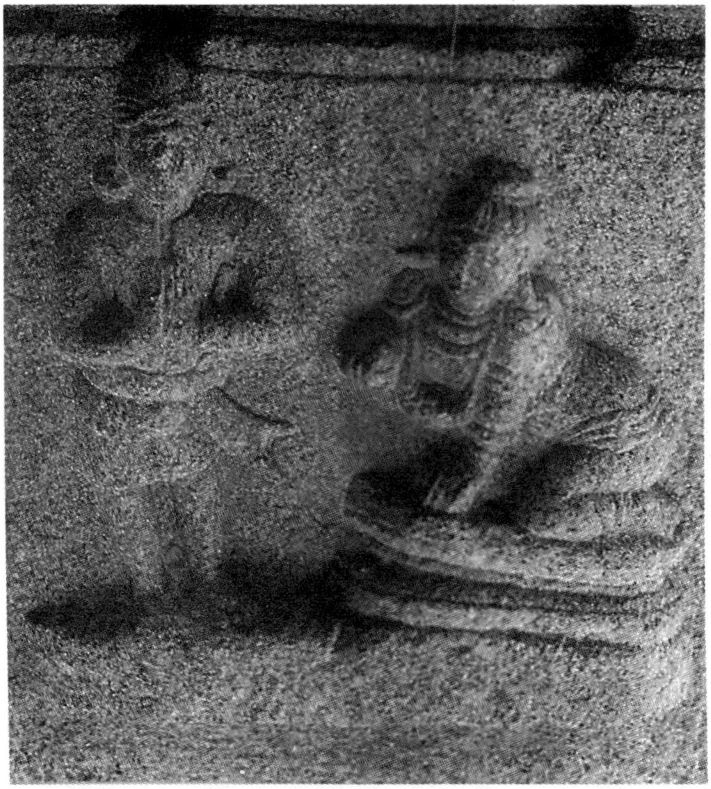

89. Royal devotee worshipping Balakrishna, Krishna temple, pillar relief in the mahamandapa.

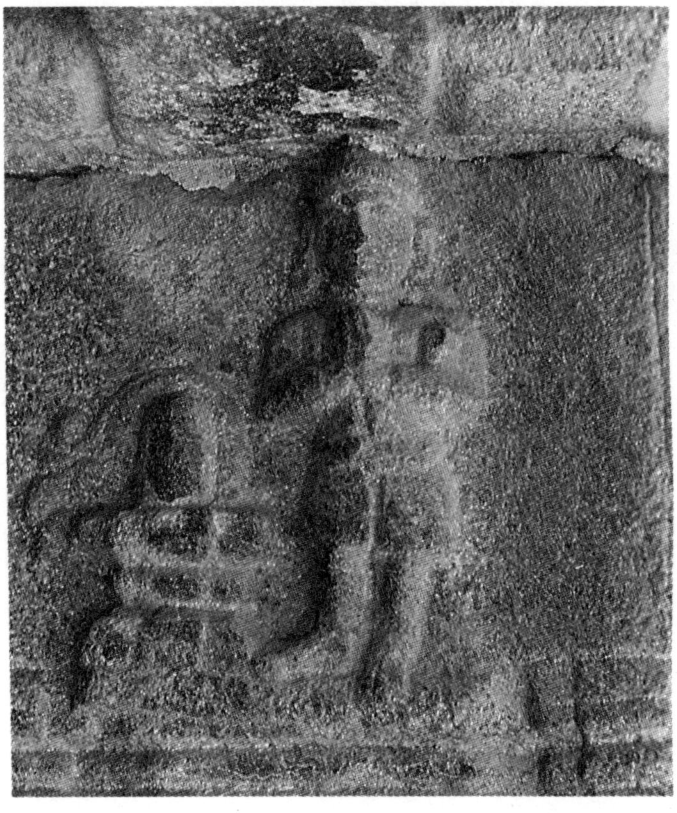

90. Royal devotee worshipping the linga, Krishna temple, pillar relief in the mahamandapa.

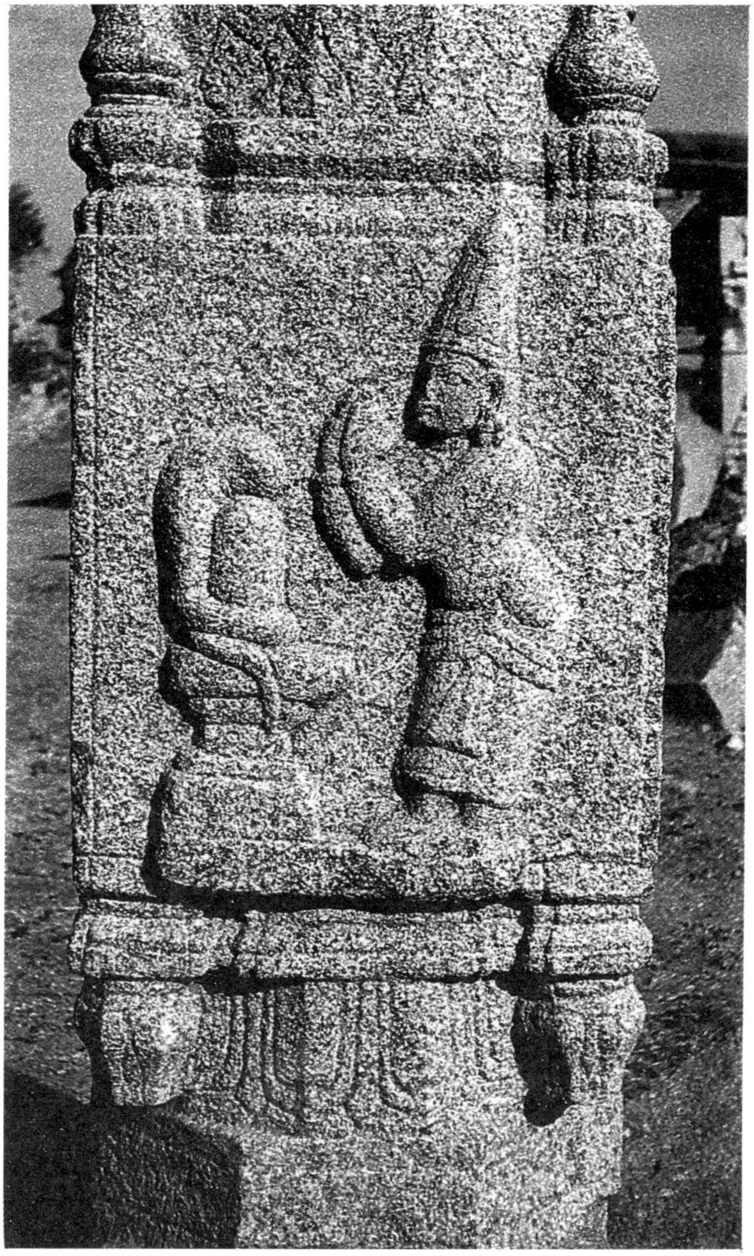

91. Royal devotee worshipping the linga,
Ranga temple, pillar relief.

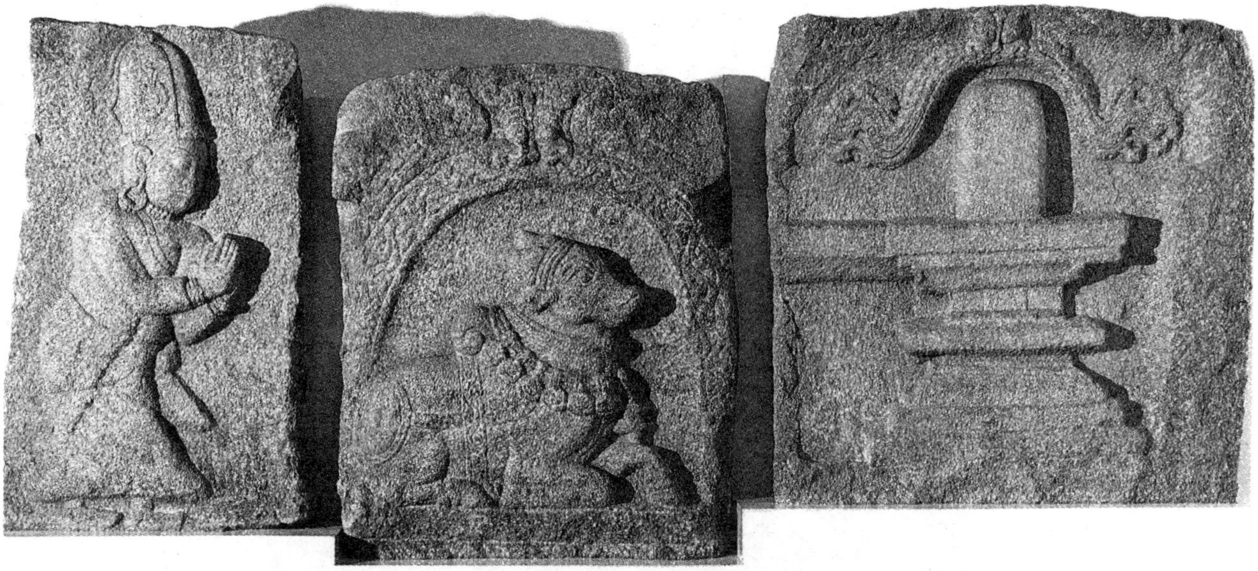

92. Royal devotee, Nandi and linga, Kamalapuram Museum.

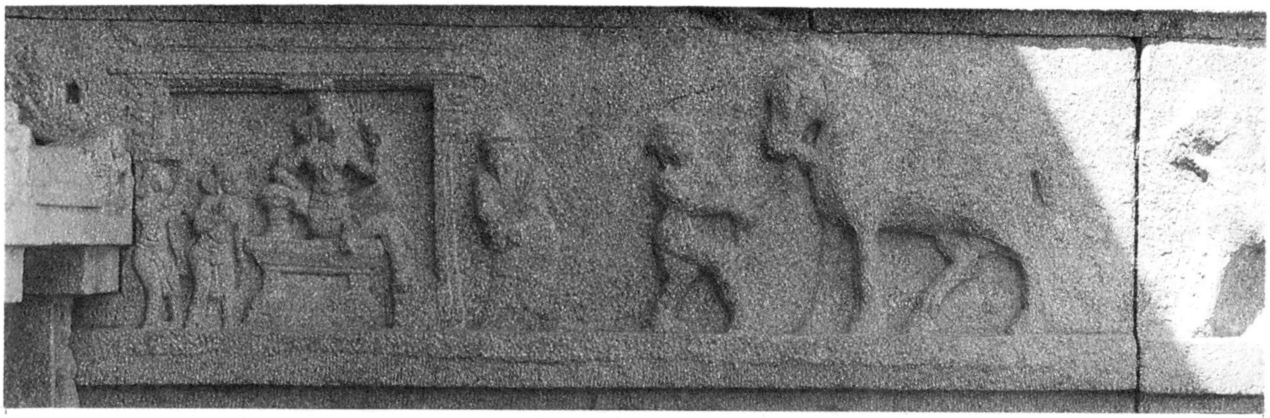

93. Royal figure in a pavilion, Ramachandra temple, outer face of enclosure, east side.

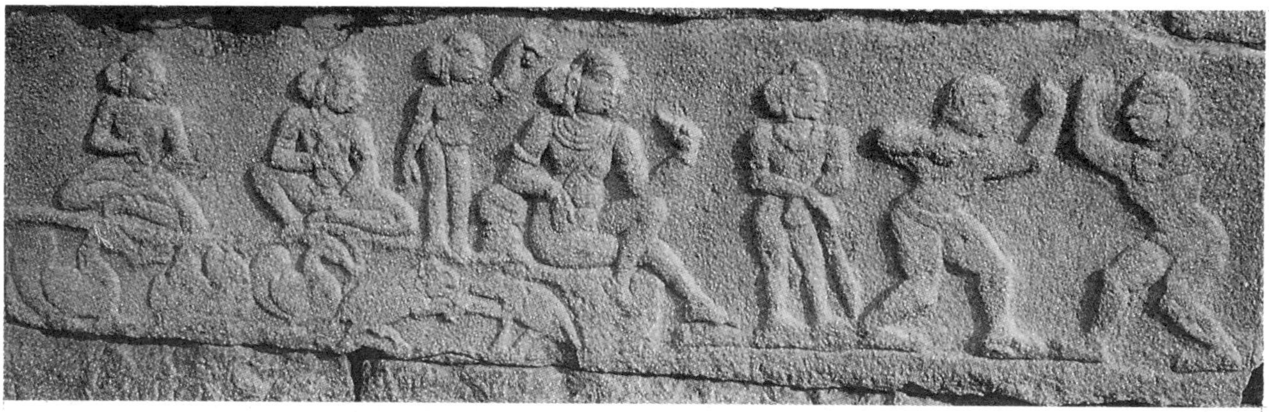

94. Royal figure watching a boxing match, relief from the Mahanavami platform, south face.

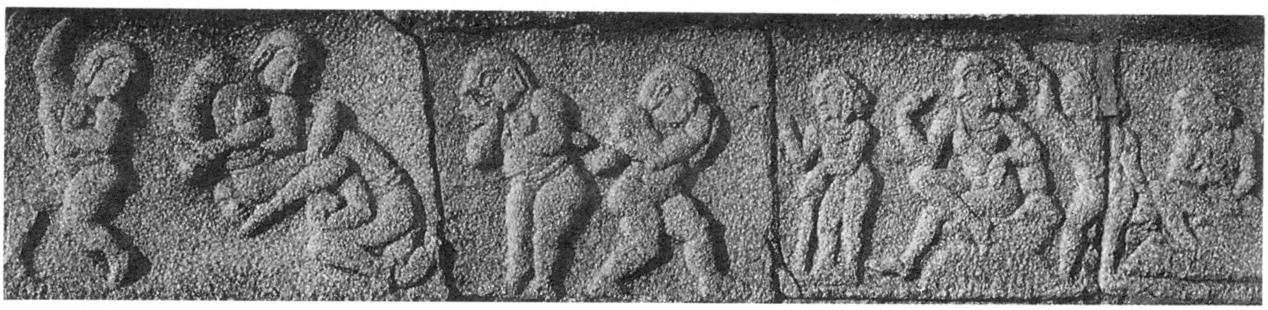

95. Royal figure watching a wrestling match, relief from the Mahanavami platform, south face.

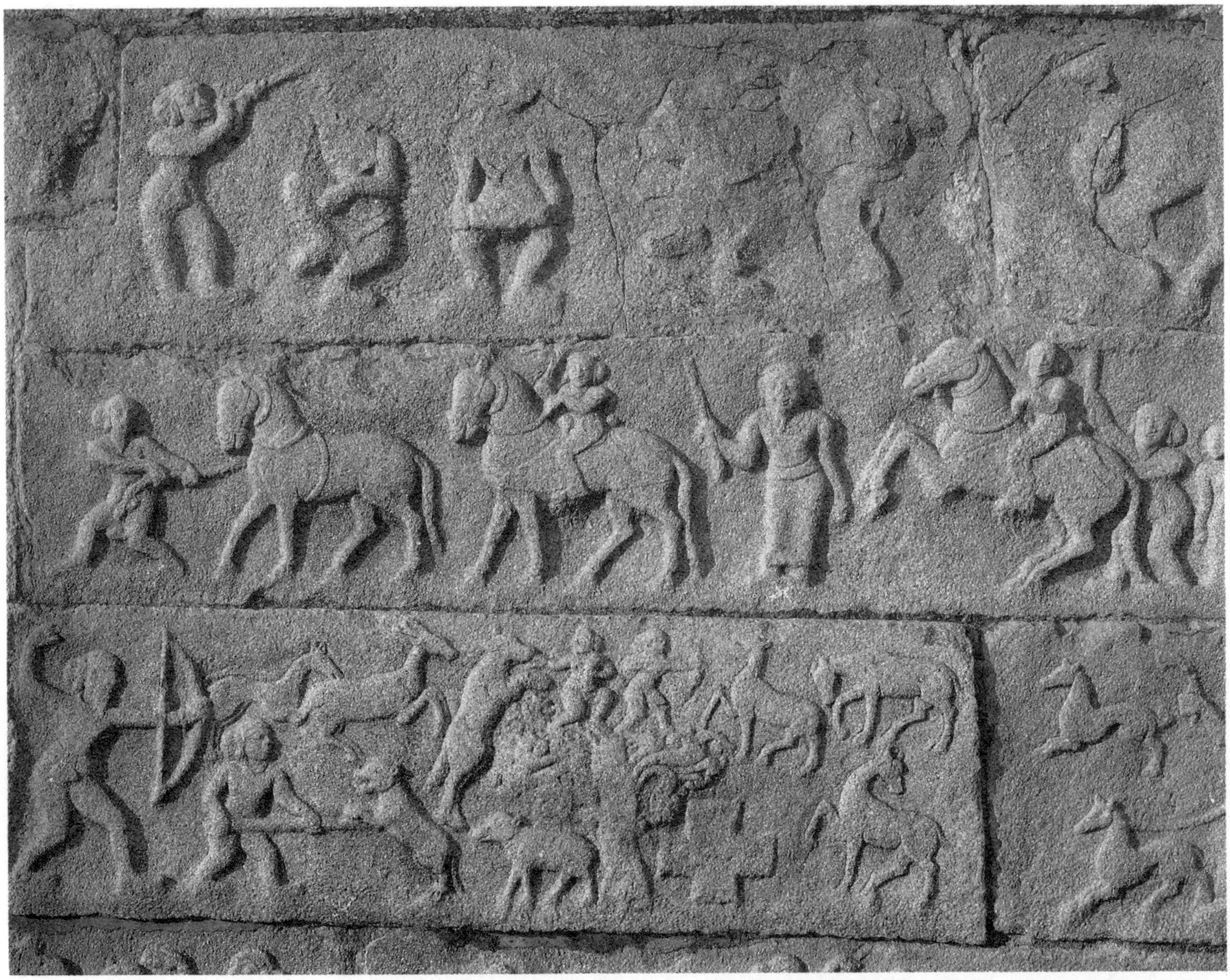

96. Hunting scenes, parading horses, music and dance, Mahanavami platform, south face.

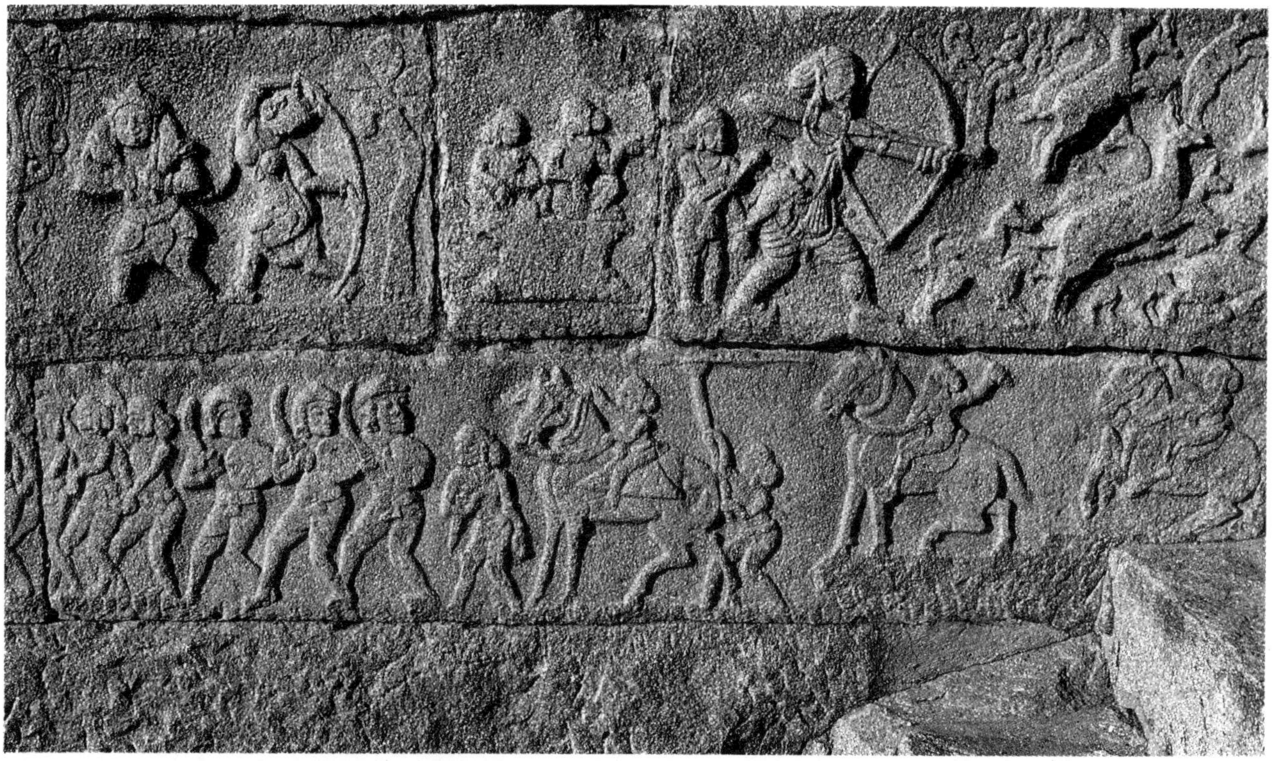

97. Parading horses and nobleman hunting, relief from the Mahanavami platform, south face.

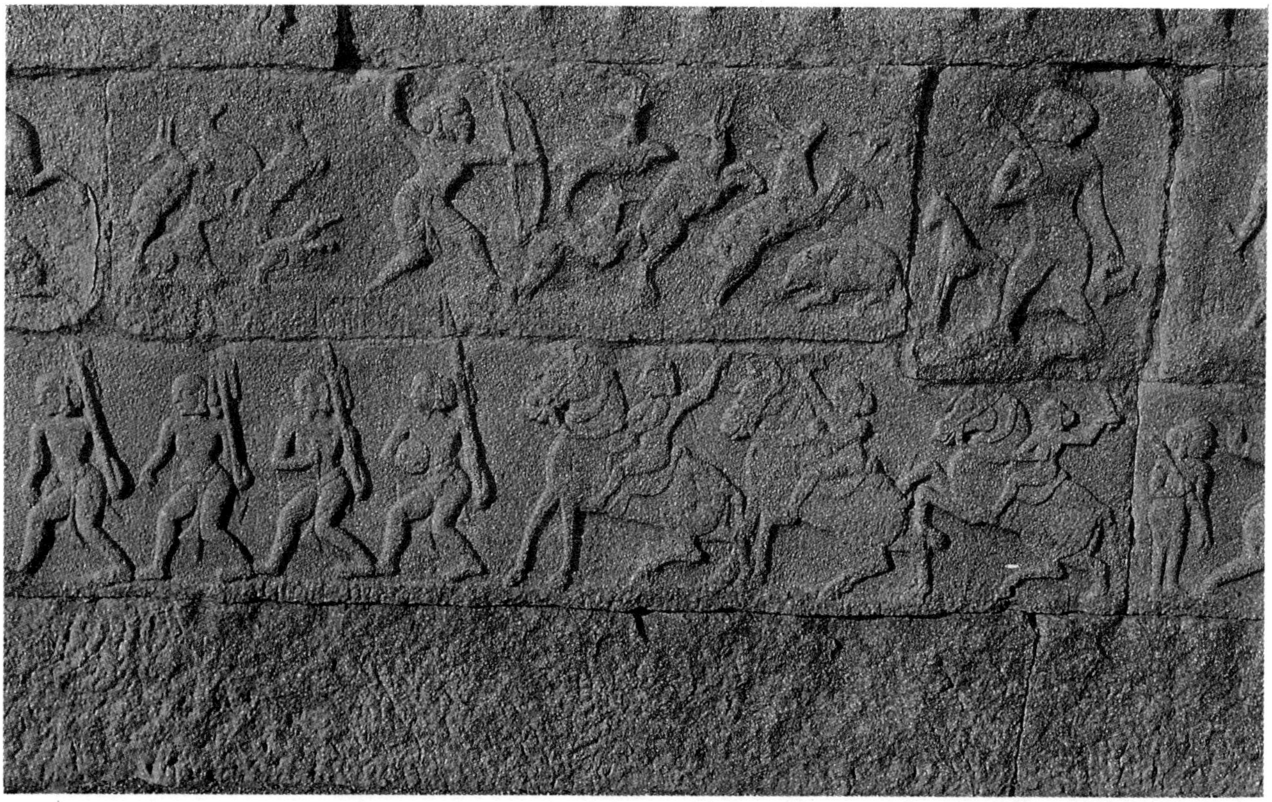

98. Parading horses and hunting scenes, relief from the Mahanavami platform, south face.

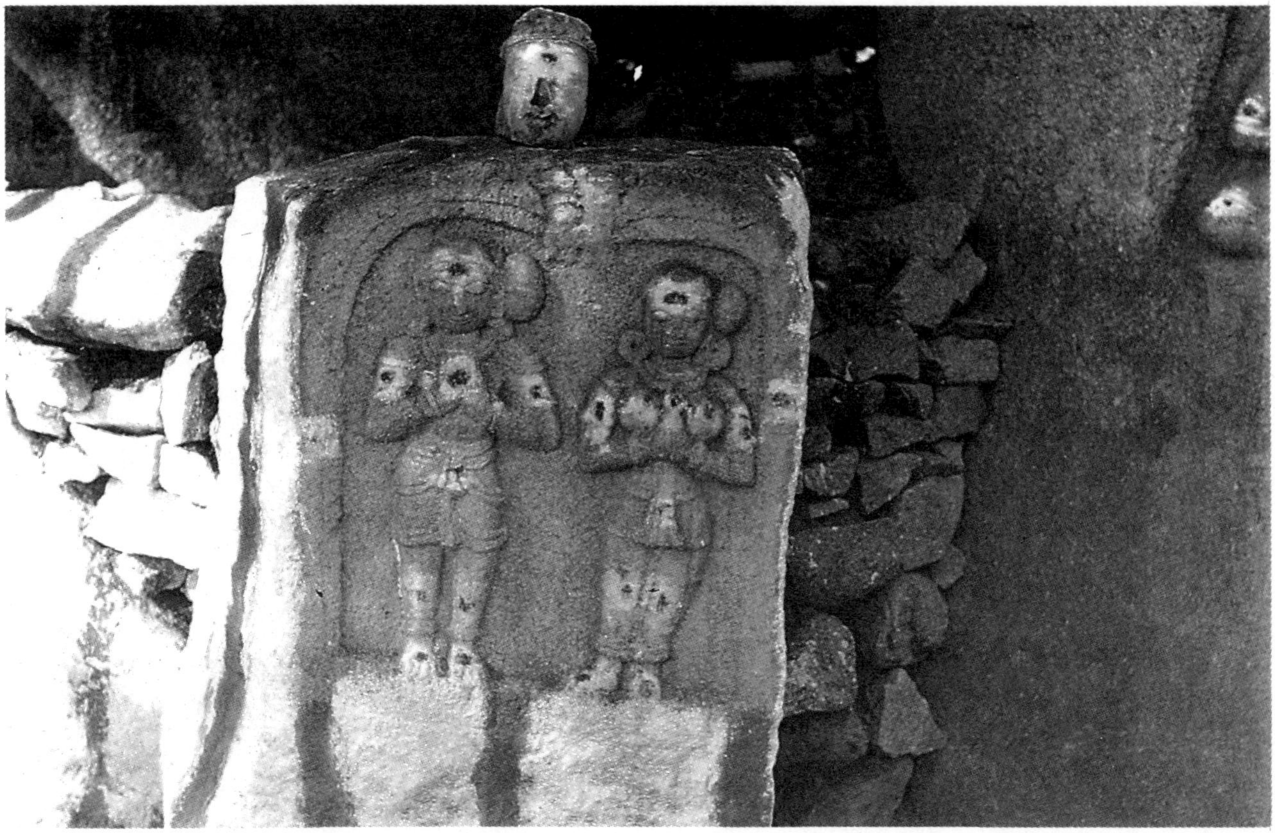

99. Donor couple, relief on a boulder near the ten-armed Kali (NMh/2).

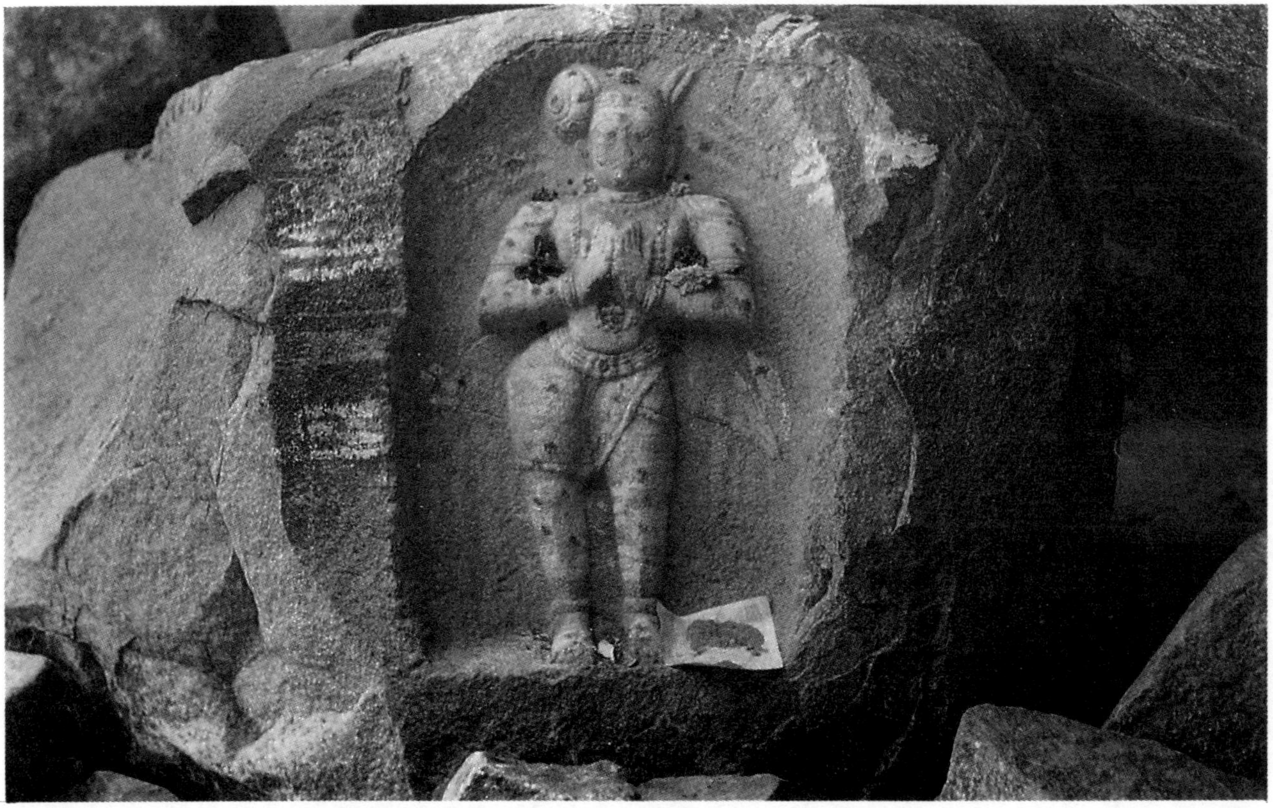

100. Devotee, carving on a boulder near Chakratirtha.

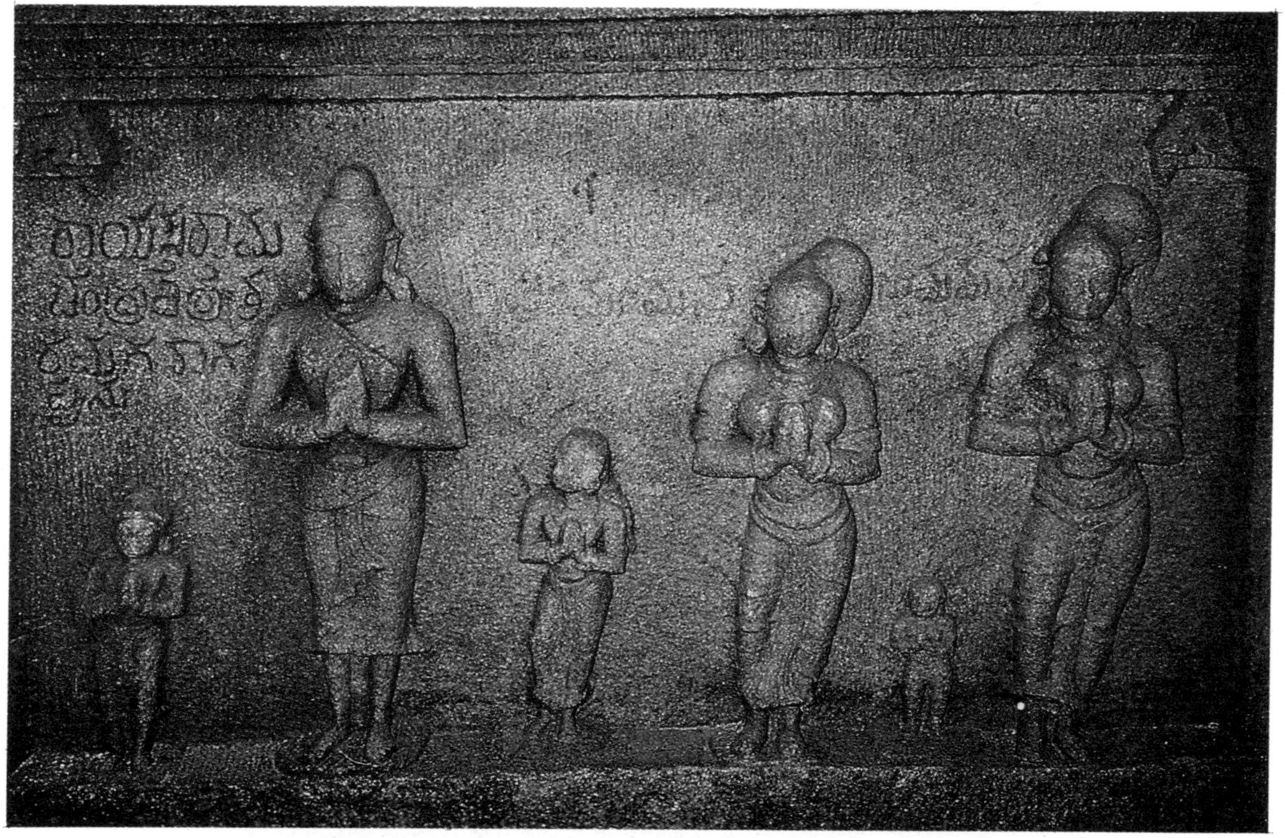

101. Rayasta Ramachandra Dikshita and family, carving in the big shrine at Koti-tirtha (NGm/2).

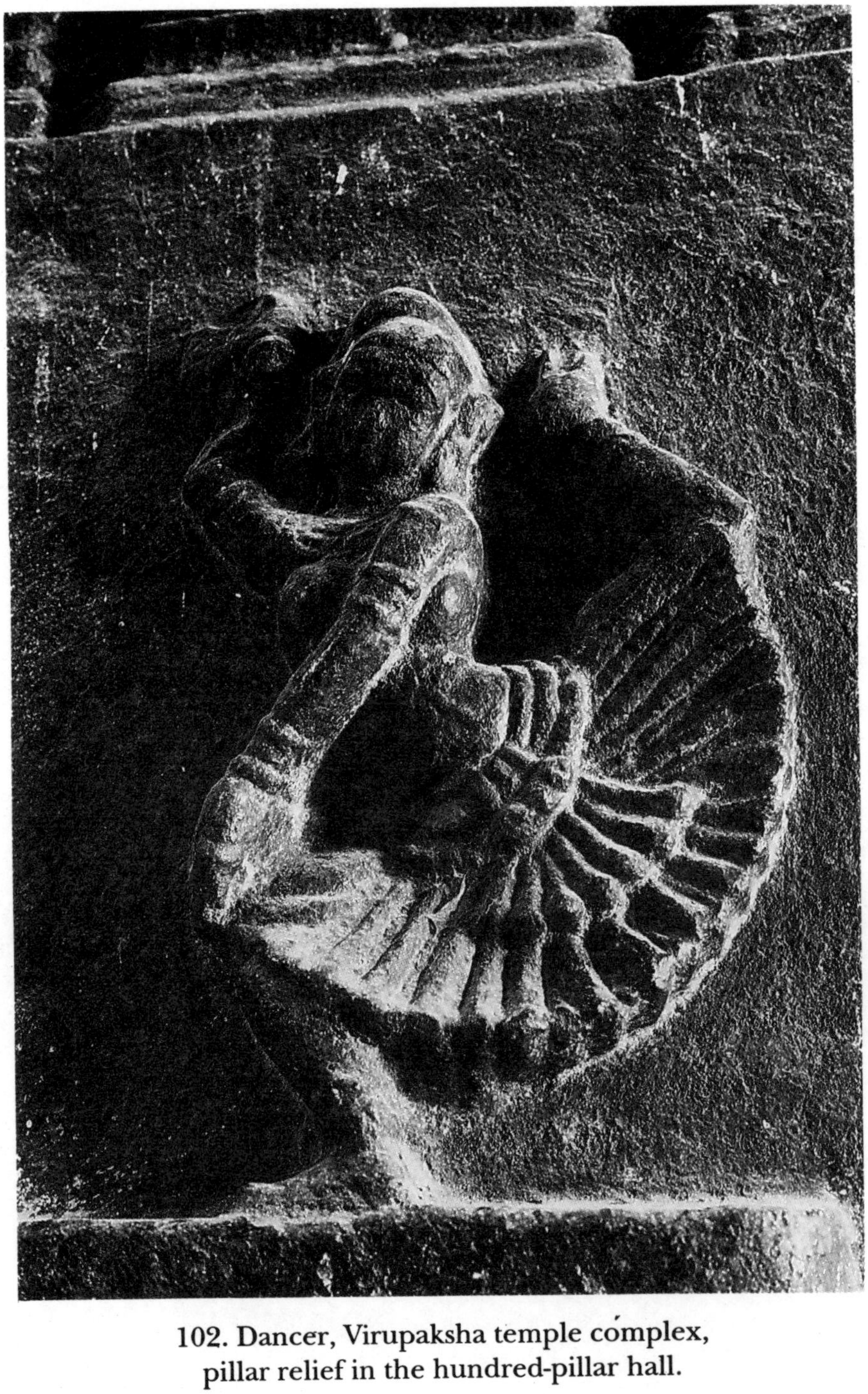

102. Dancer, Virupaksha temple complex,
pillar relief in the hundred-pillar hall.

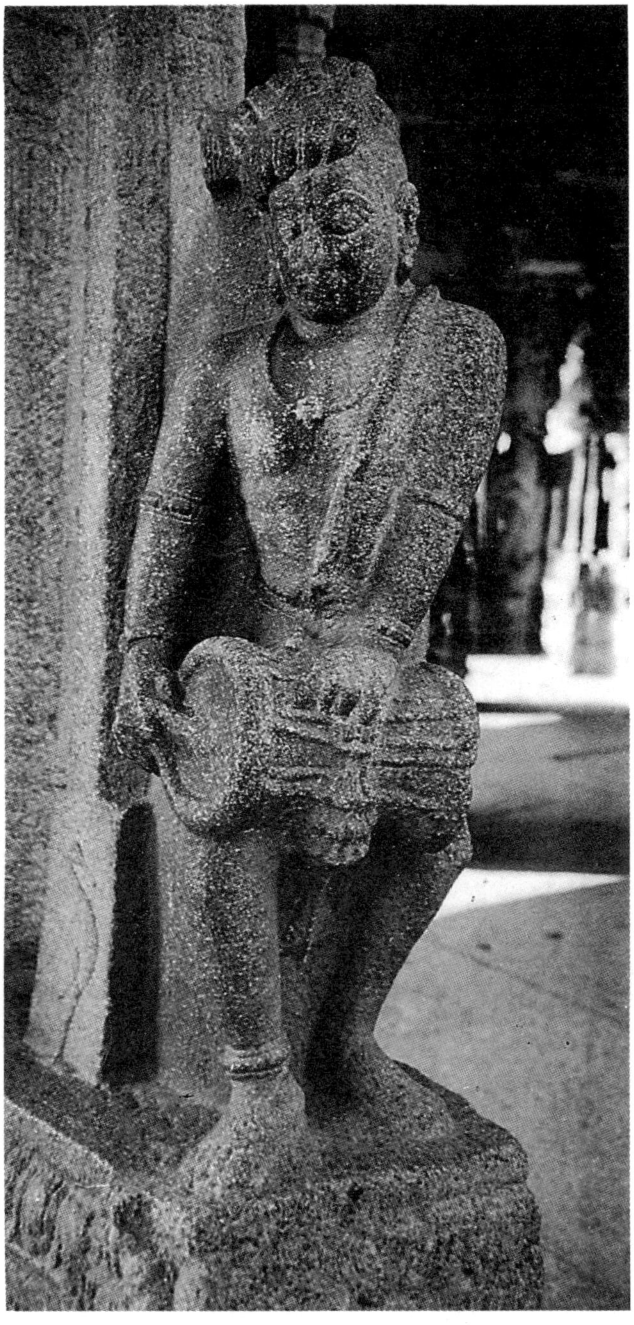

103. Musician with dholak, Vithala temple, pillar in the mahamandapa.

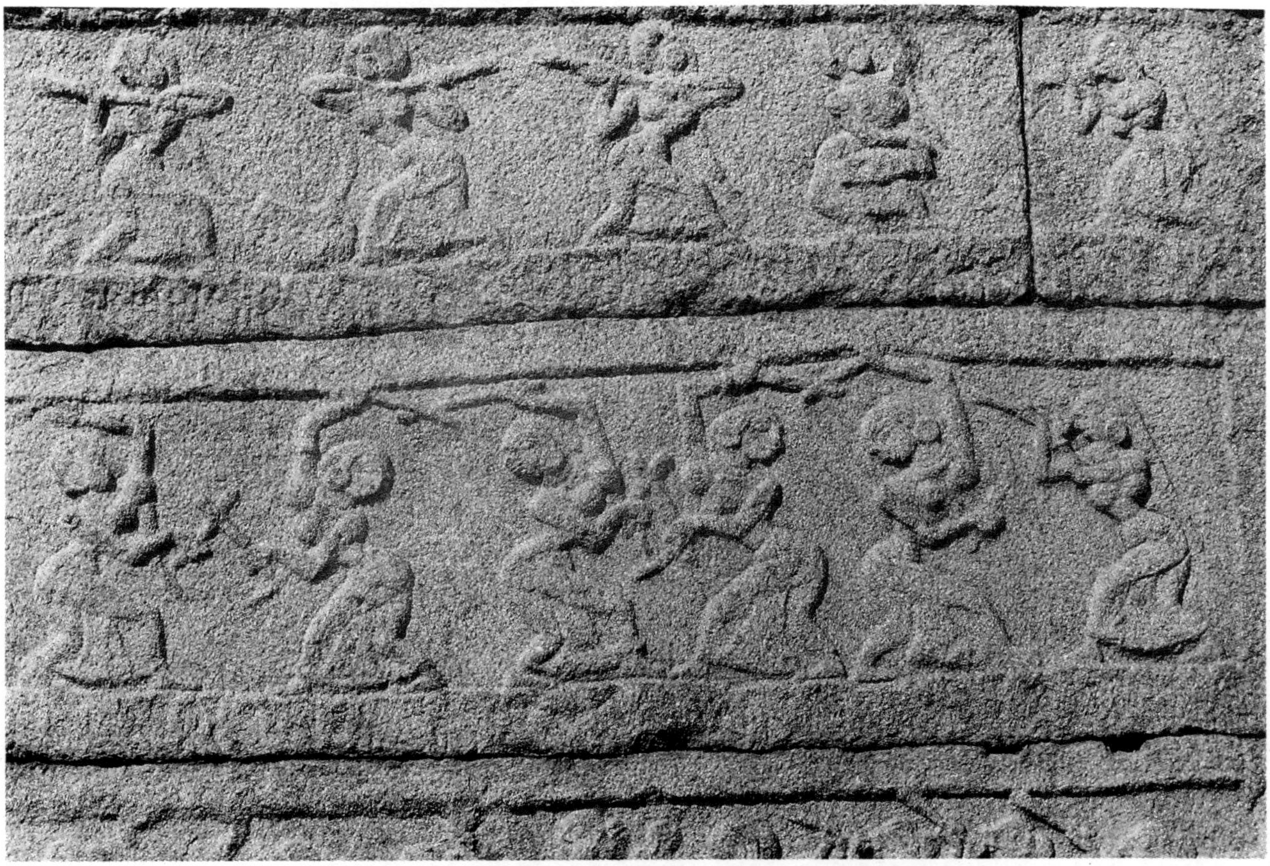

104. Friezes with kolata dancers, Mahanavami platform, south face.

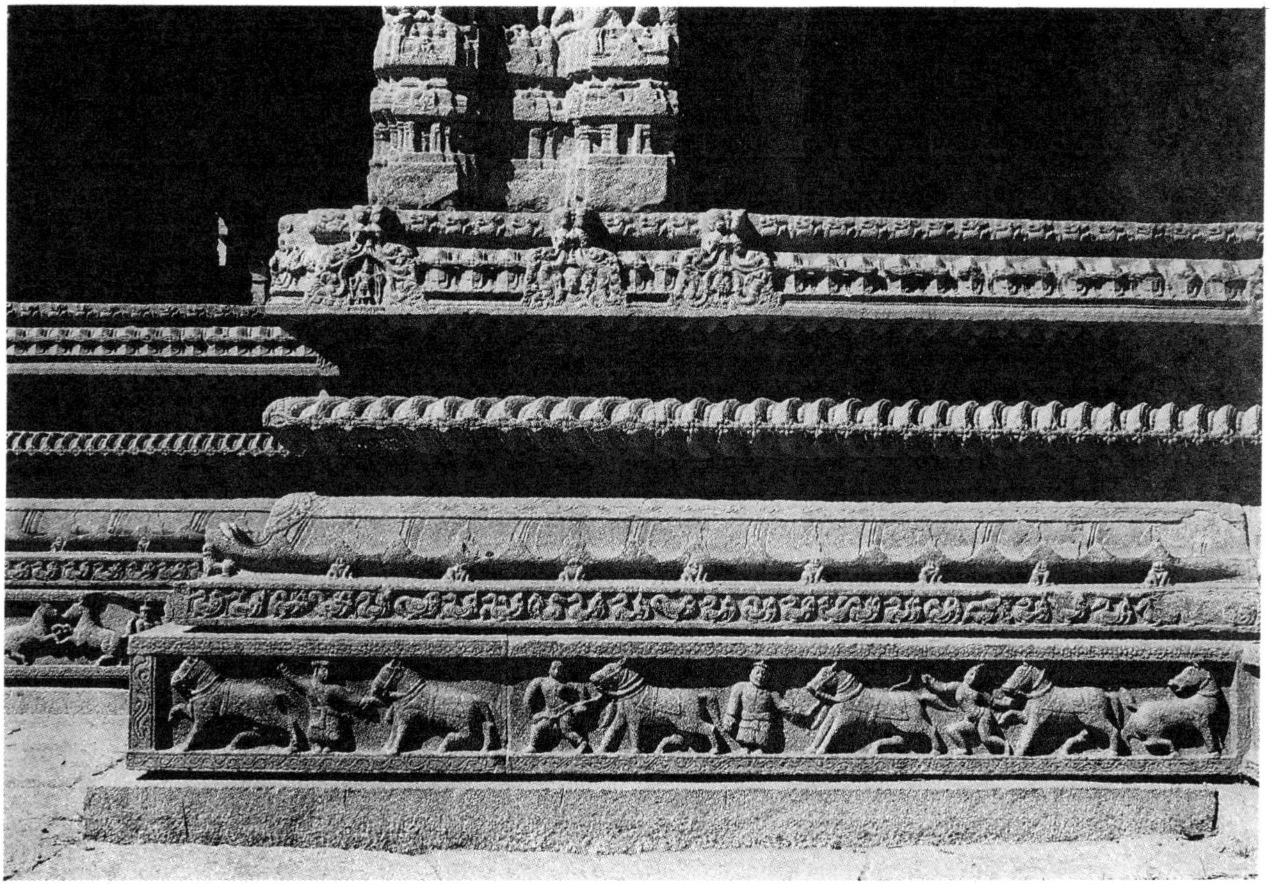

105. Portuguese traders and horses, Vithala temple, basement of the mahamandapa.

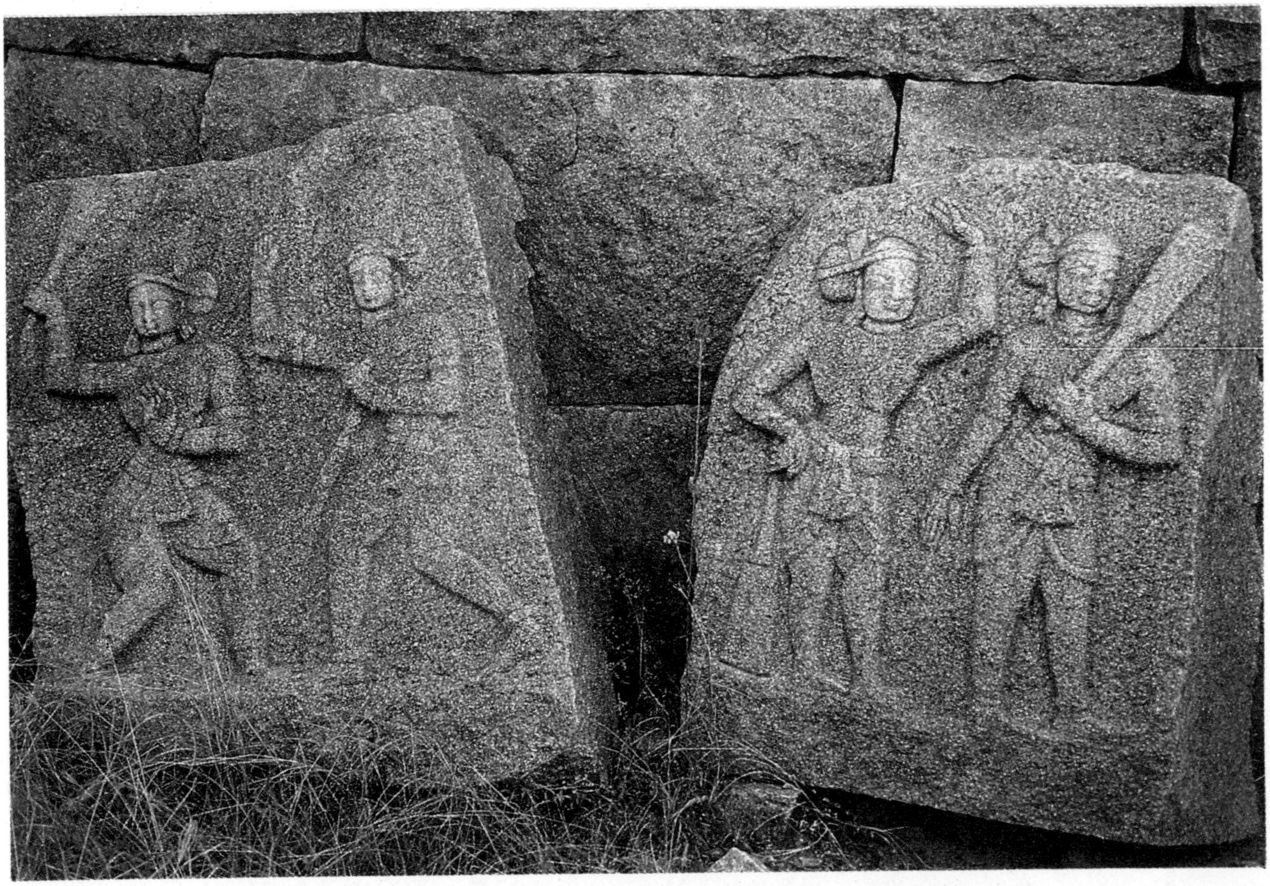

106. Boatmen, slabs near the gate on the river at Anegondi.

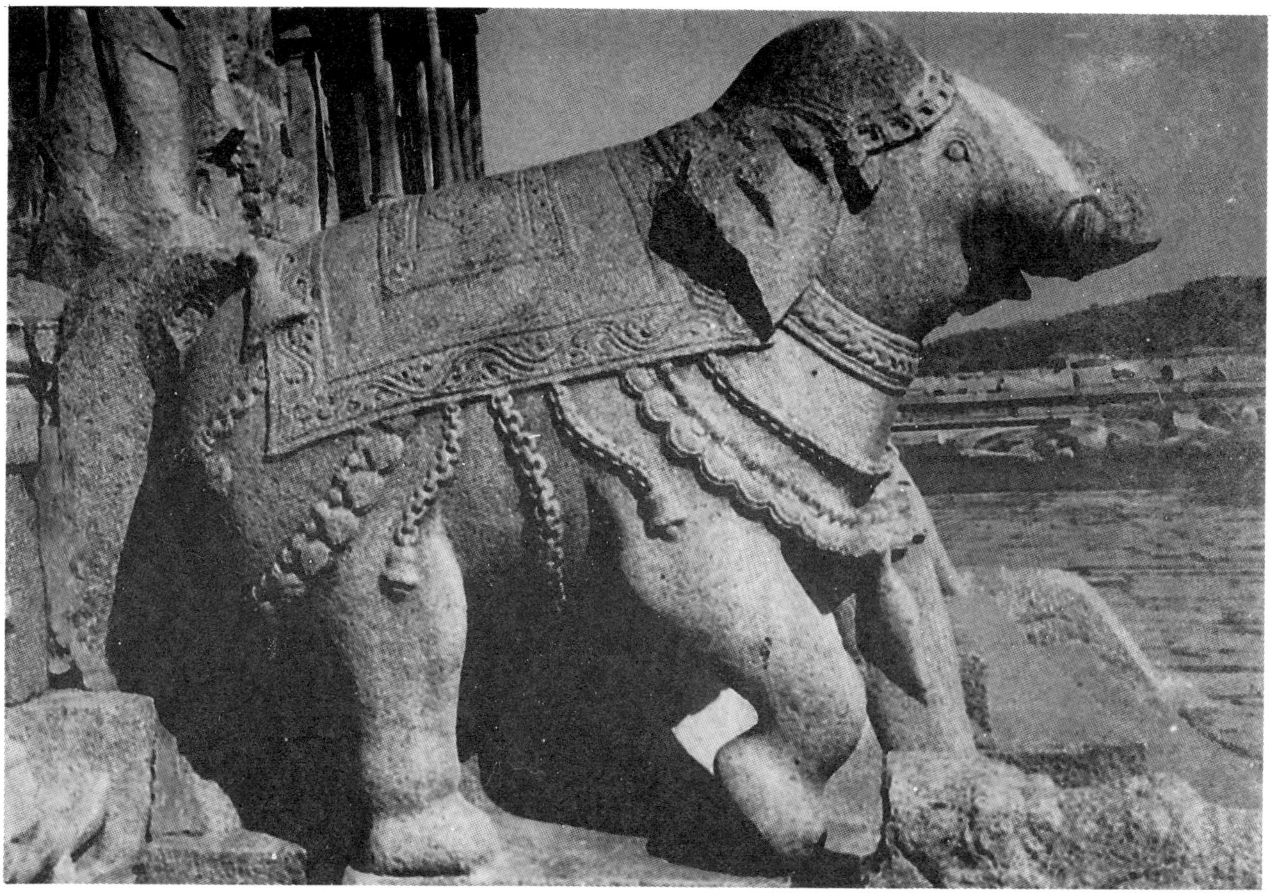

107. Elephant balustrade, Vithala temple, mahamandapa, east side.

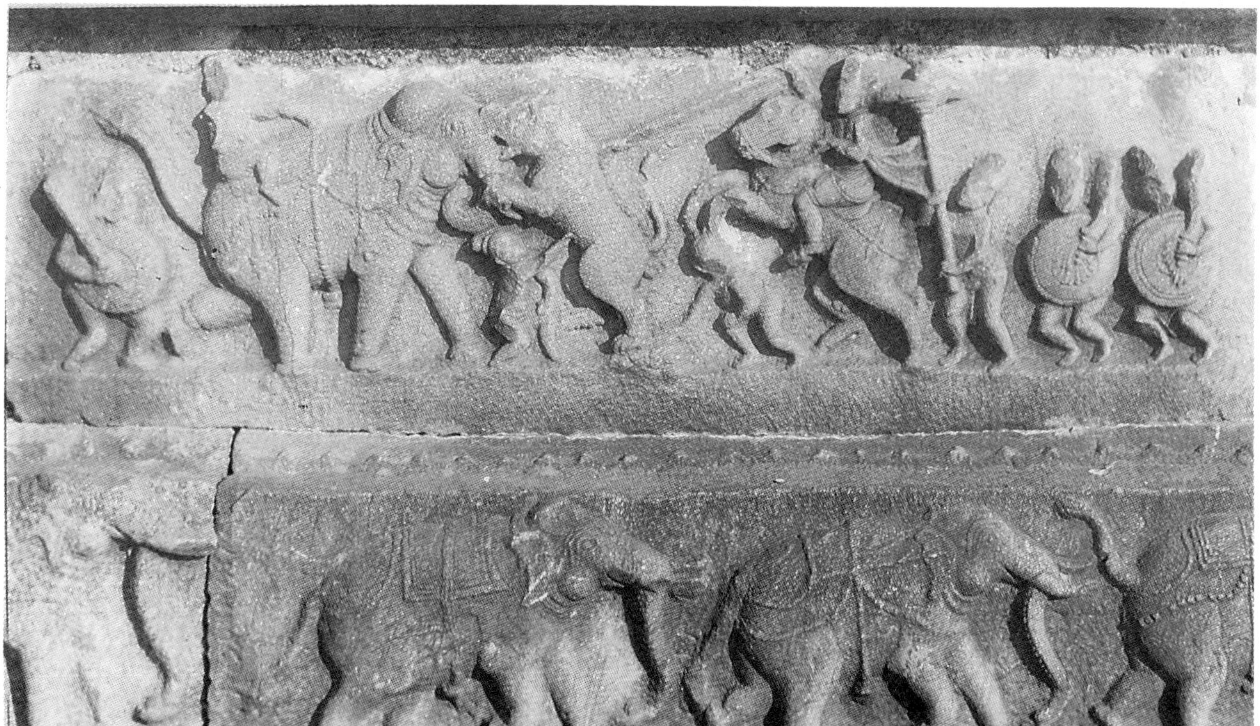

108. Tiger attacking an elephant and royal figure on horse, Mahanavami platform, west face.

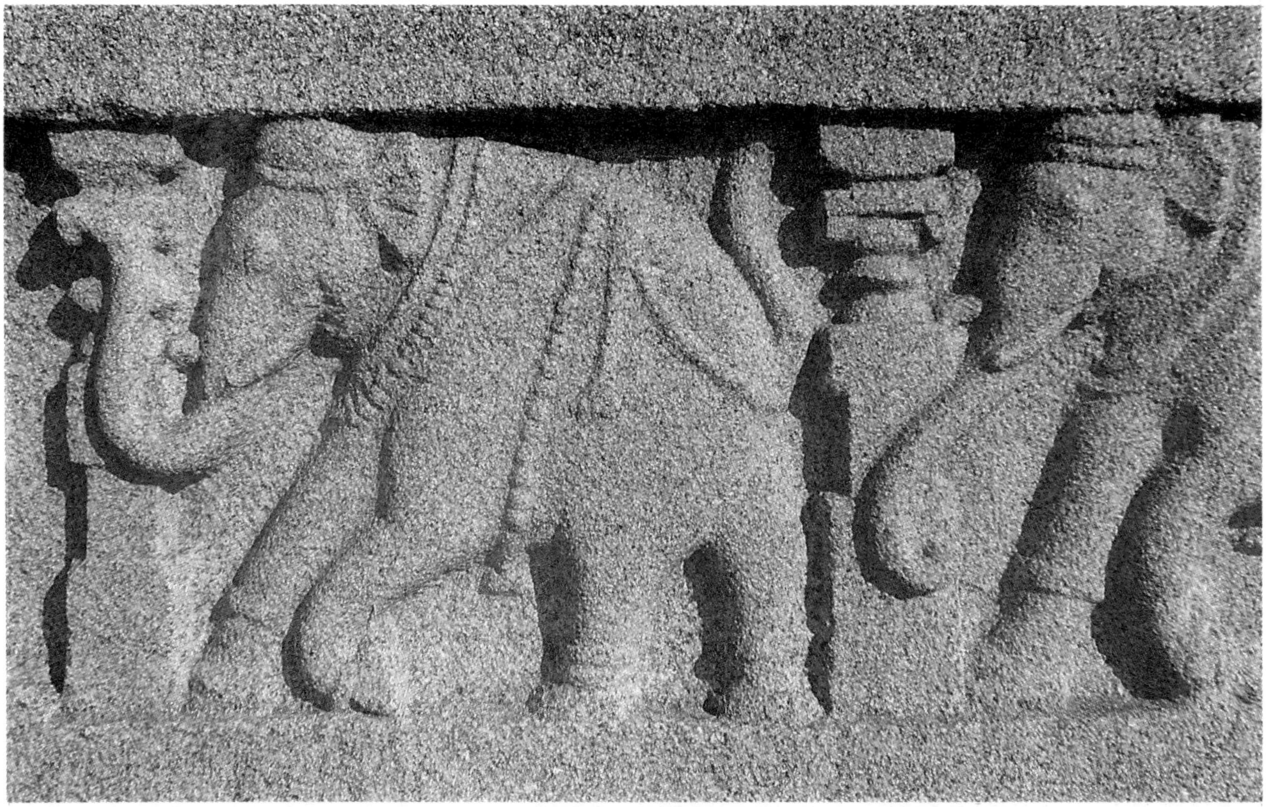

109. Elephant, Mahanavami platform, south face.

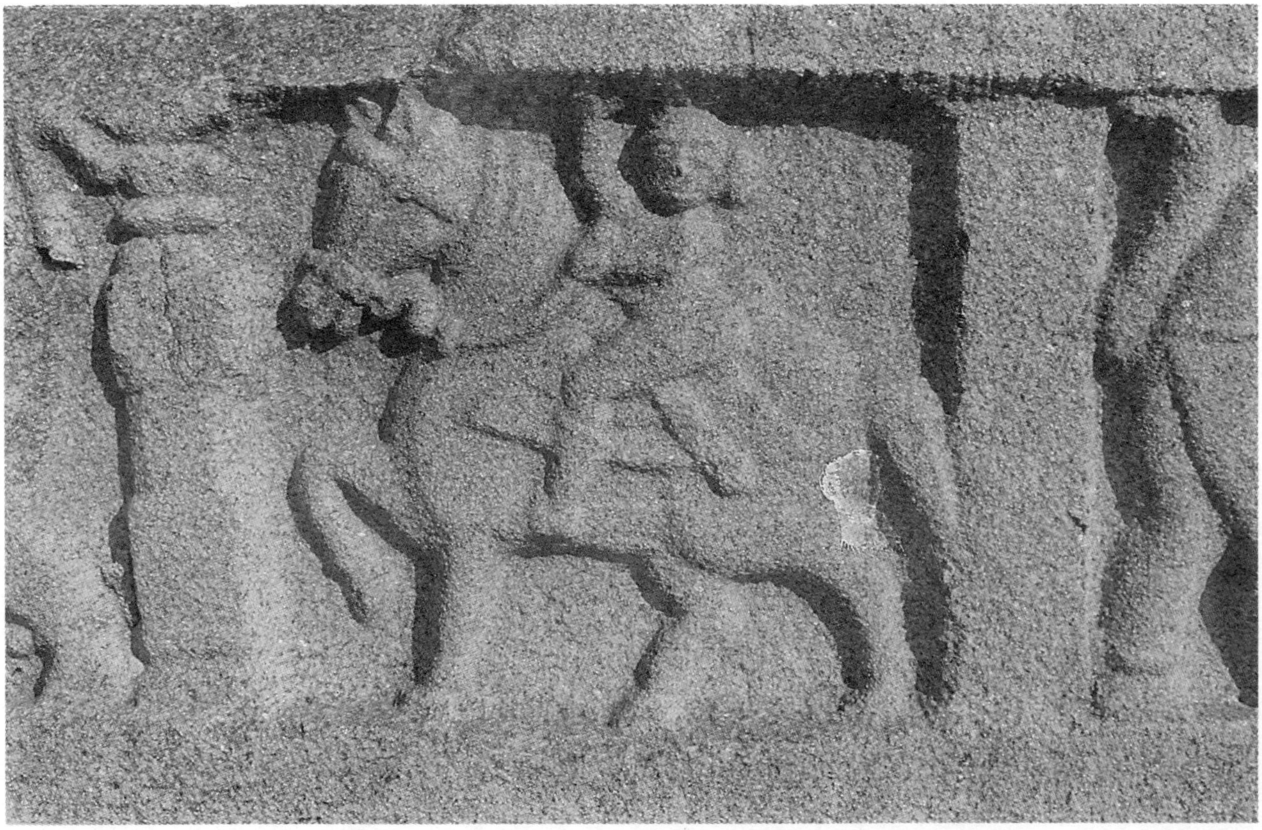

110. Horse, Mahanavami platform, south face.

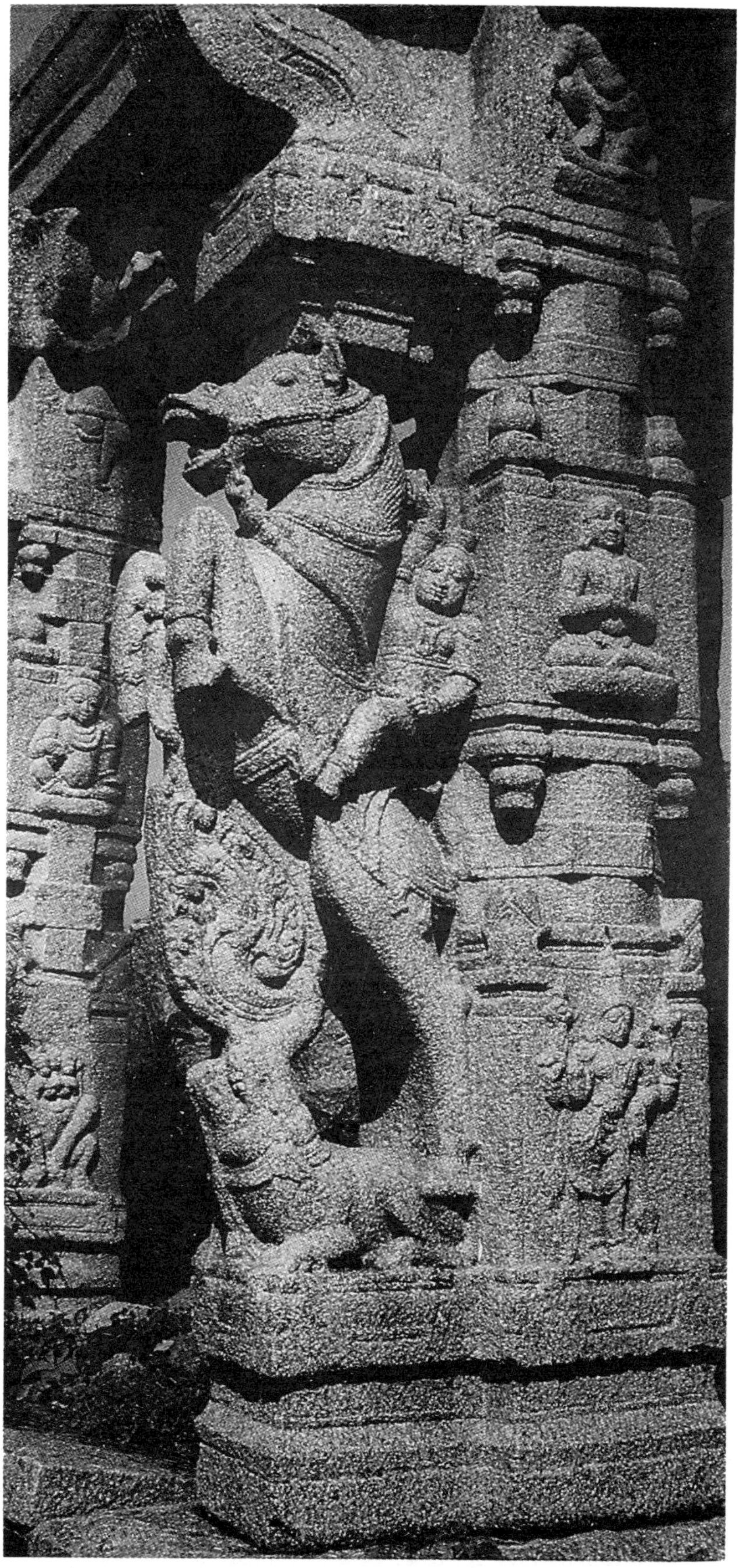

111. Rearing horse, entryway to the Vithala temple tank.

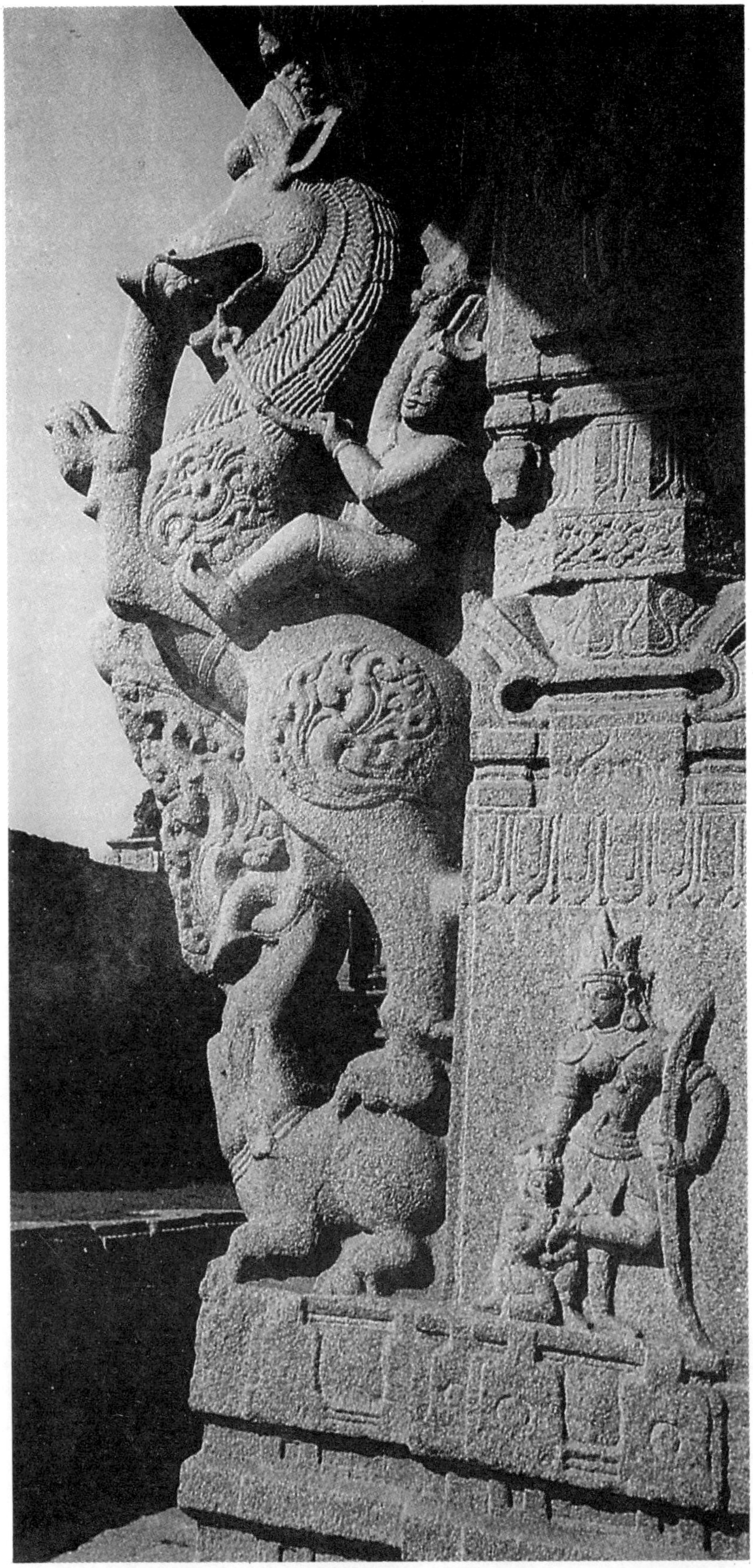

112. Yali, Vithala temple complex, south-east pavilion, south side steps.

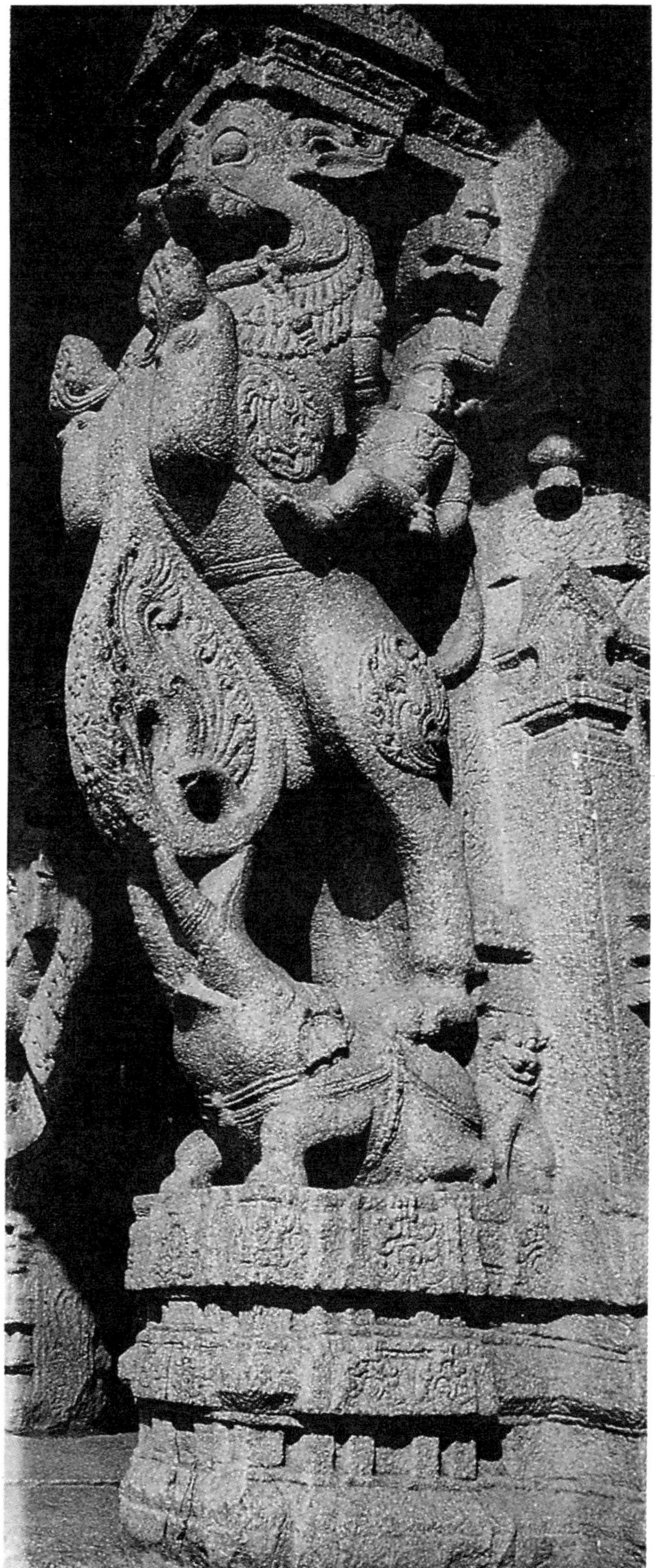

113. Yali, Vithala mahamandapa, south side steps.

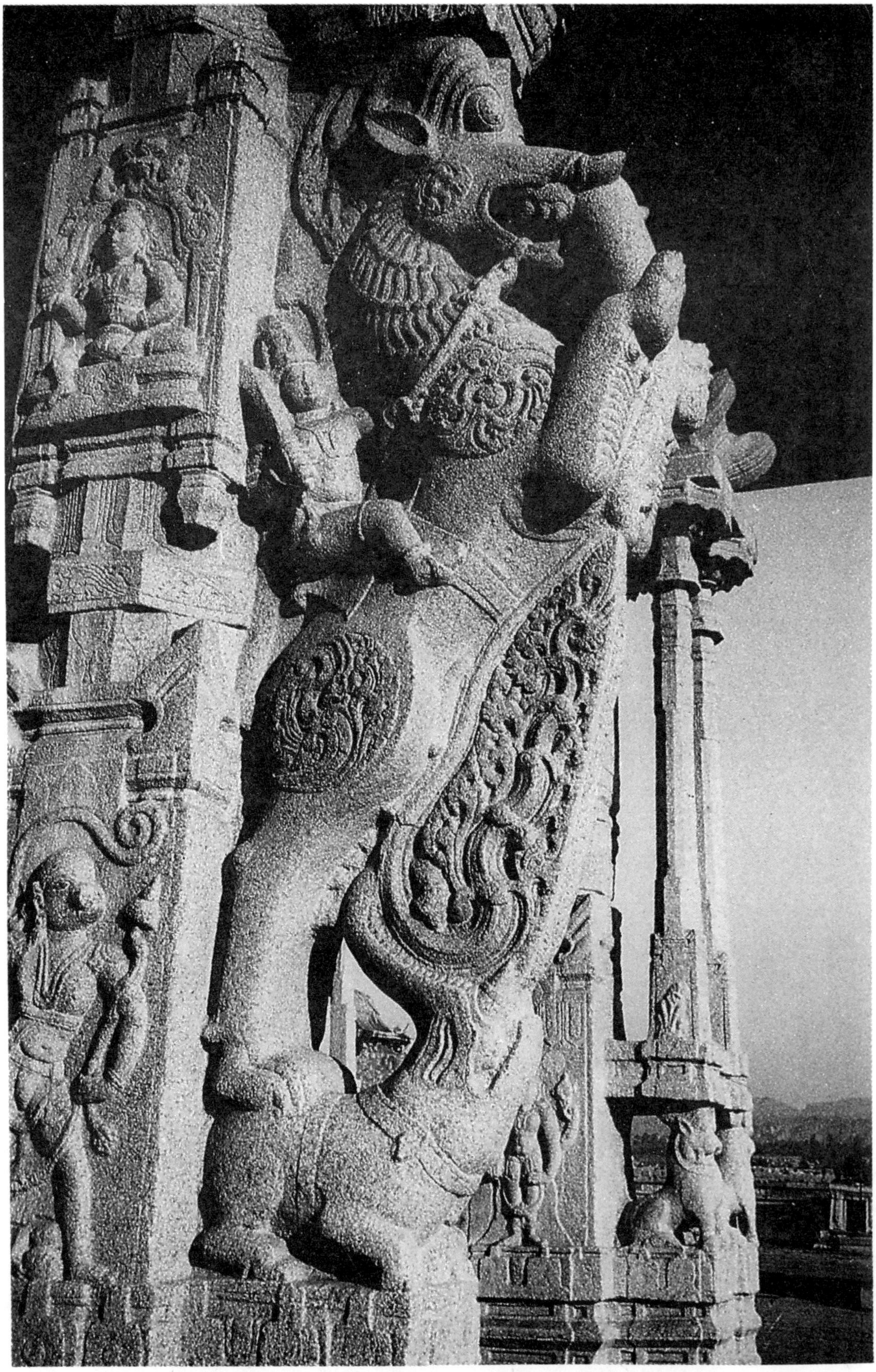

114. Gaja-yali, Vithala temple complex, south-east pavilion, east side steps.

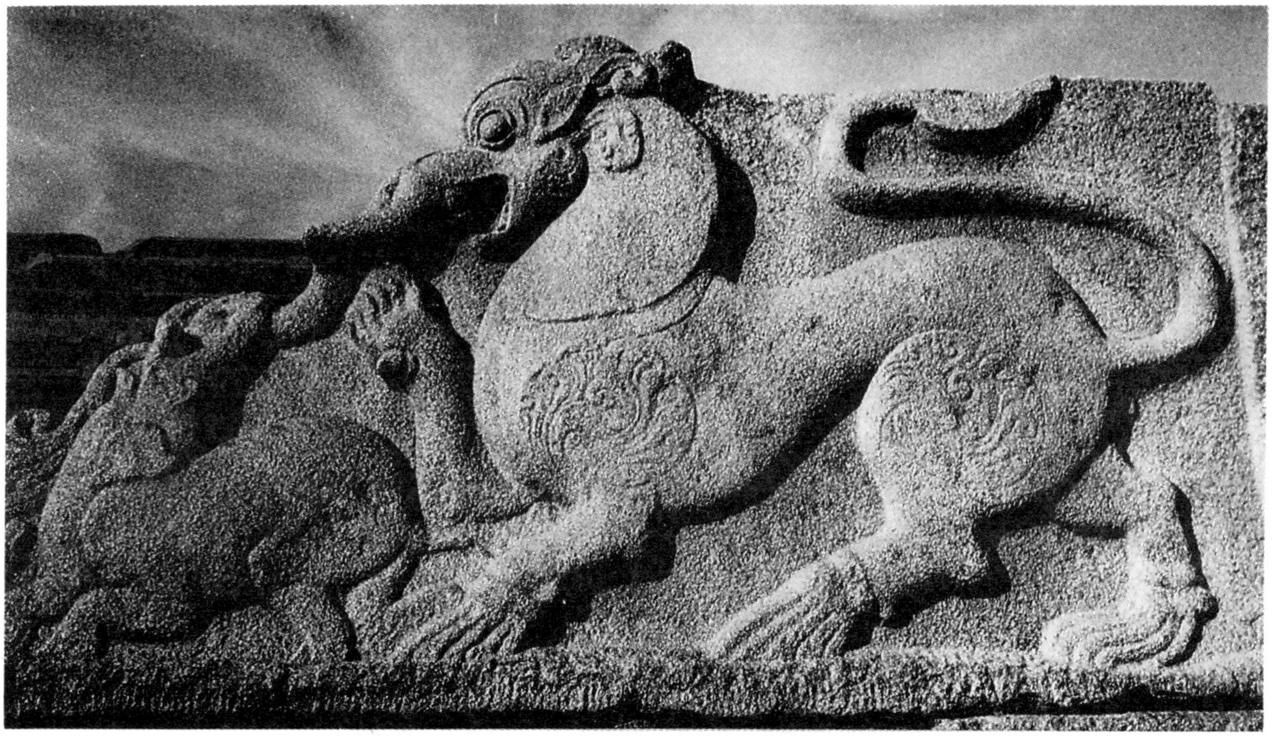

115. Yali and elephant, Mahanavami platform, south staircase.

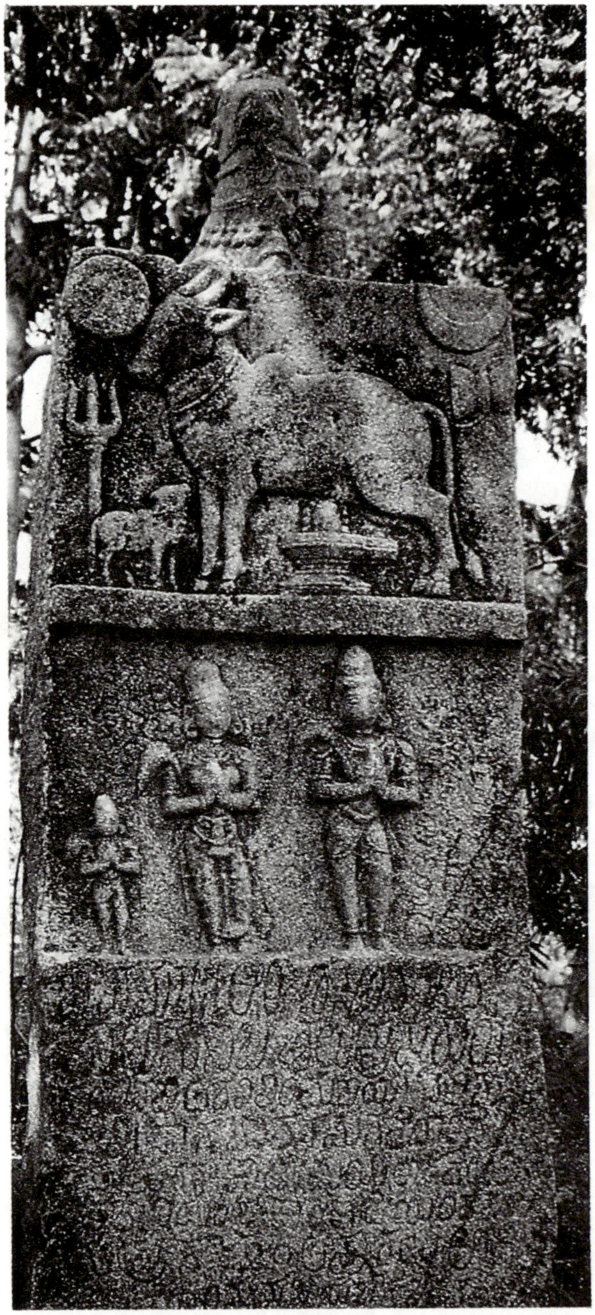

116. Cow and calf on inscribed slab near Talarighat.

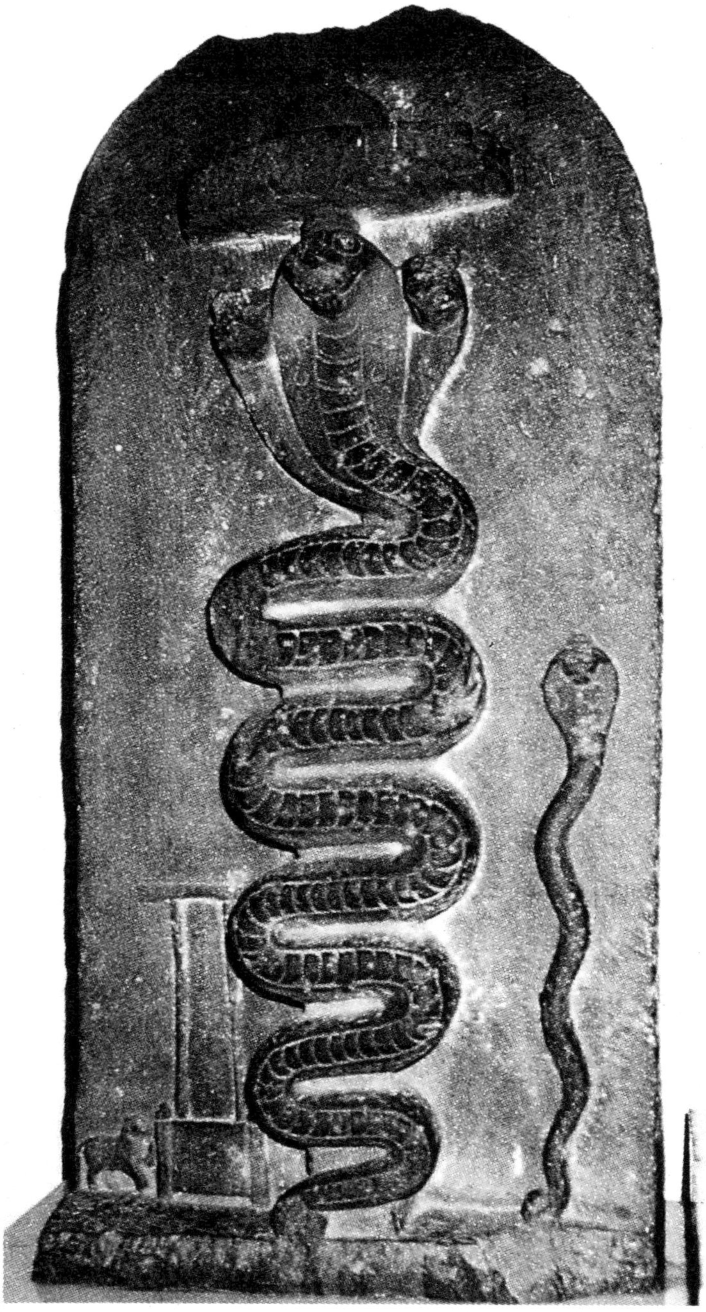

117. Cat, cradle and nagas, Kamalapuram Museum.

Map of Vijayanagara City (opposite)

Important Monuments

1. Virupaksha temple complex (NFw/1)
2. Vithala temple complex (NHa/1)
3. Tiruvengalanatha temple complex (NMh/1)
4. Krishna temple complex (NLm/4)
5. Mudu Viranna temple (NLw/3)
6. Prasanna Virupaksha temple (NQy/1)
7. Ramachandra temple (NRw/1)
8. Temple of Parshvanatha (NSq/1)
9. Pattabhirama temple complex
10. Temple of Kunthu Jinanatha (NXn/11)
11. Malyavanta Raghunatha complex (NTd/1)
12. Ramanuja temple (NCw/3)
13. Tirumangai-alvar temple (NCv/3)
14. Narasimha temple (NGt/4)
15. Shiva temple of AD 1386 (NGt/3)
16. Kodandarama temple (NGw/1)
17. 'Kadalekalu Ganesha' temple (NLc/2)
18. Harihara temple (NLc/3)
19. Lakshmi-Narasimha monolith (NLm/1)
20. Three boulders with sculptures on the north ridge (NMx/2)
21. Mahanavami platform (NWd/1)
22. 'Lotus Mahal' (NRt/3)
23. Elephant stables (NRp/3)

Landmarks, quarters, tirthas

A. Matanga hill
B. Hemakuta hill
C. Malyavanta hill
D. Vithalapura
E. Krishnapura
F. Achyutarayapura
G. Koti-tirtha
H. Chakra-tirtha

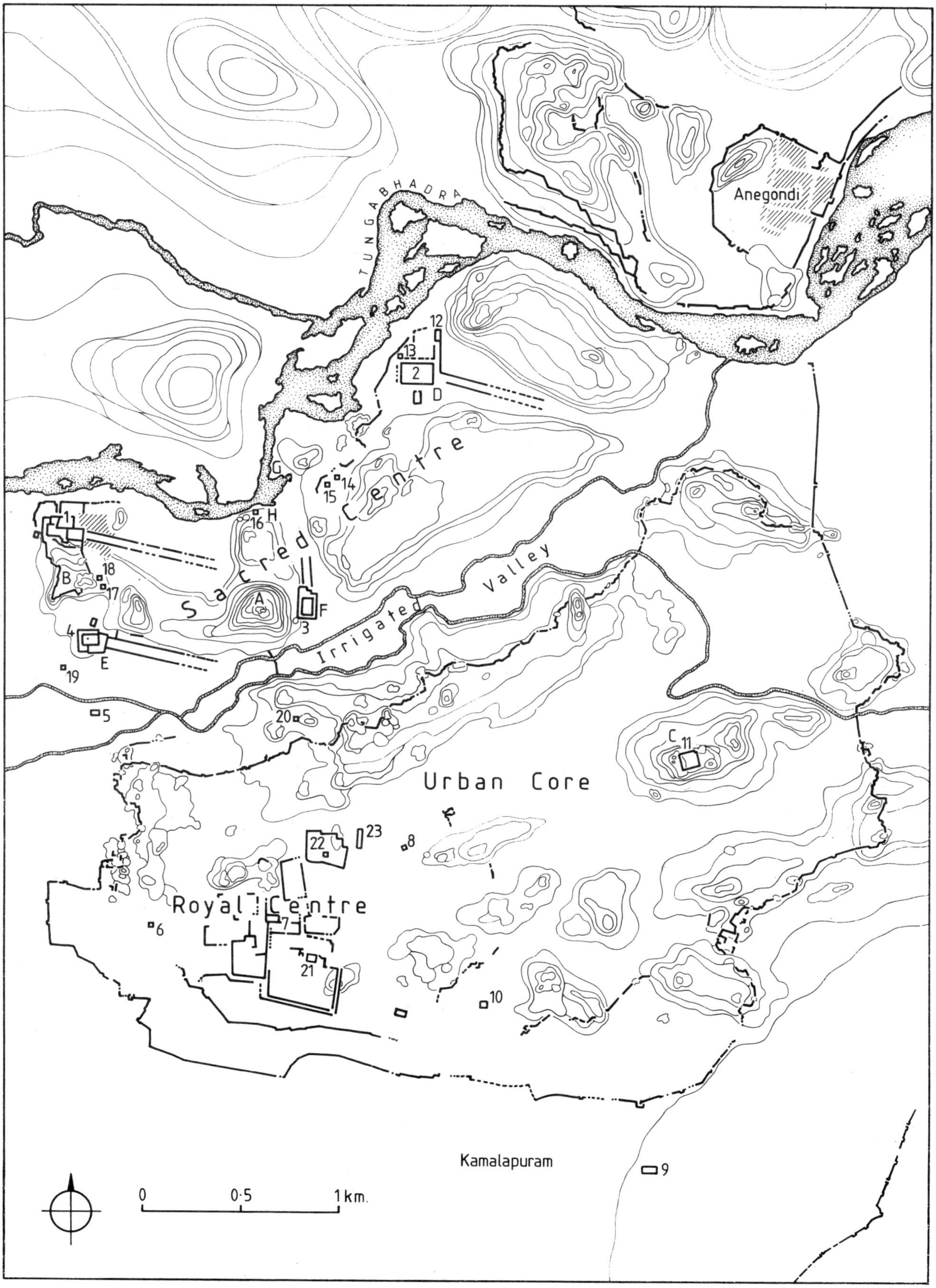
TUNGABHADRA
Anegondi
Sacred Centre
Irrigated Valley
Urban Core
Royal Centre
Kamalapuram
A
B
C
D
E
F
G
H
1
2
3
4
5
6
7
8
9
10
11
12
13
14
15
16
17
18
19
20
21
22
23
0
0·5
1 km.

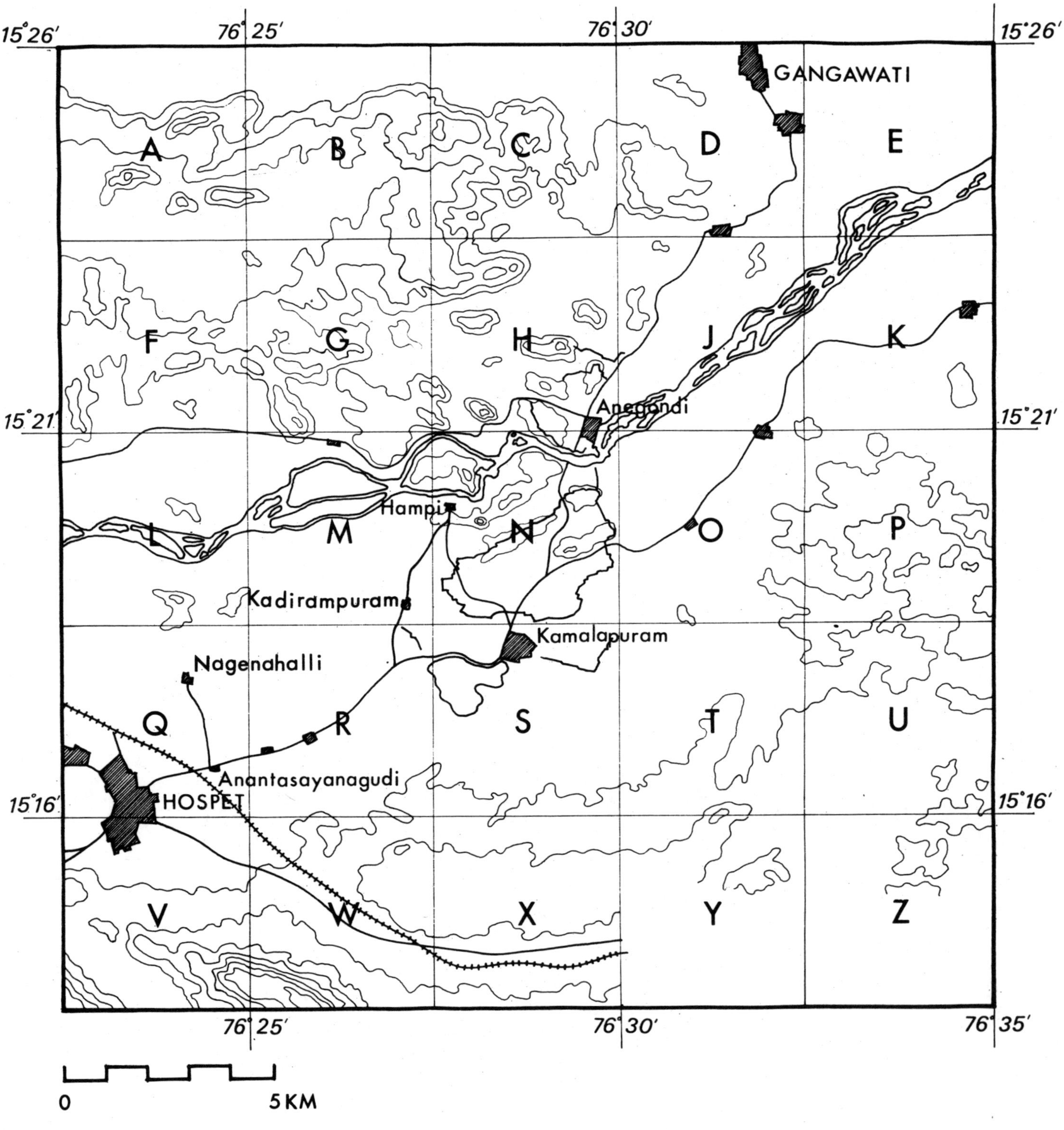
15°26′
76°25′
76°30′
15°26′
GANGAWATI
A
B
C
D
E
F
G
H
J
K
15°21′
Anegondi
15°21′
Hampi
L
M
N
O
P
Kadirampuram
Kamalapuram
Nagenahalli
Q
R
S
T
U
Anantasayanagudi
15°16′
HOSPET
15°16′
V
W
X
Y
Z
76°25′
76°30′
76°35′
0
5 KM

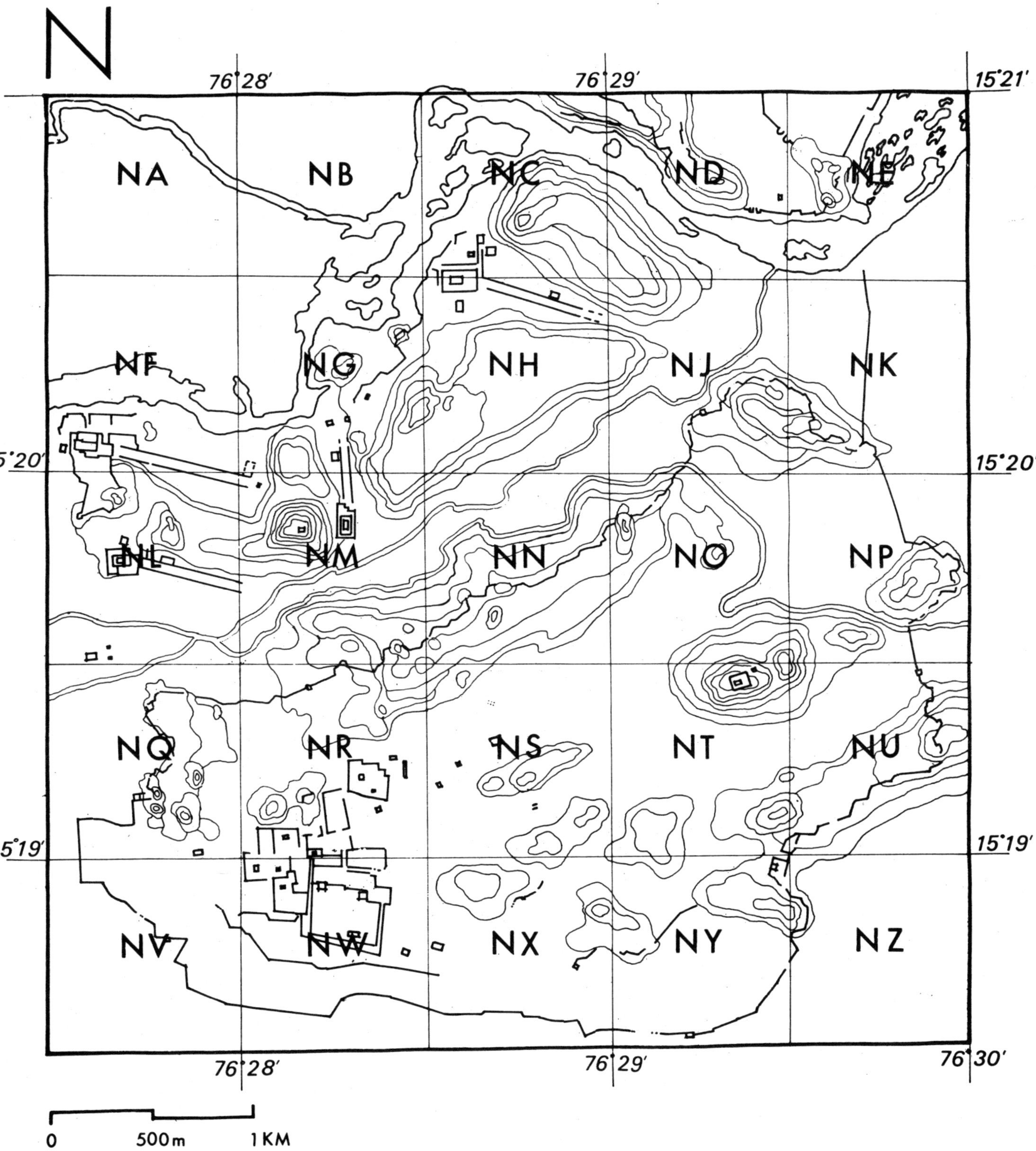
N
76°28′
76°29′
15°21′
NA
NB
NC
ND
NE
NF
NG
NH
NJ
NK
15°20′
15°20′
NL
NM
NN
NO
NP
NQ
NR
NS
NT
NU
15°19′
15°19′
NV
NW
NX
NY
NZ
76°28′
76°29′
76°30′
0
500m
1KM

NC

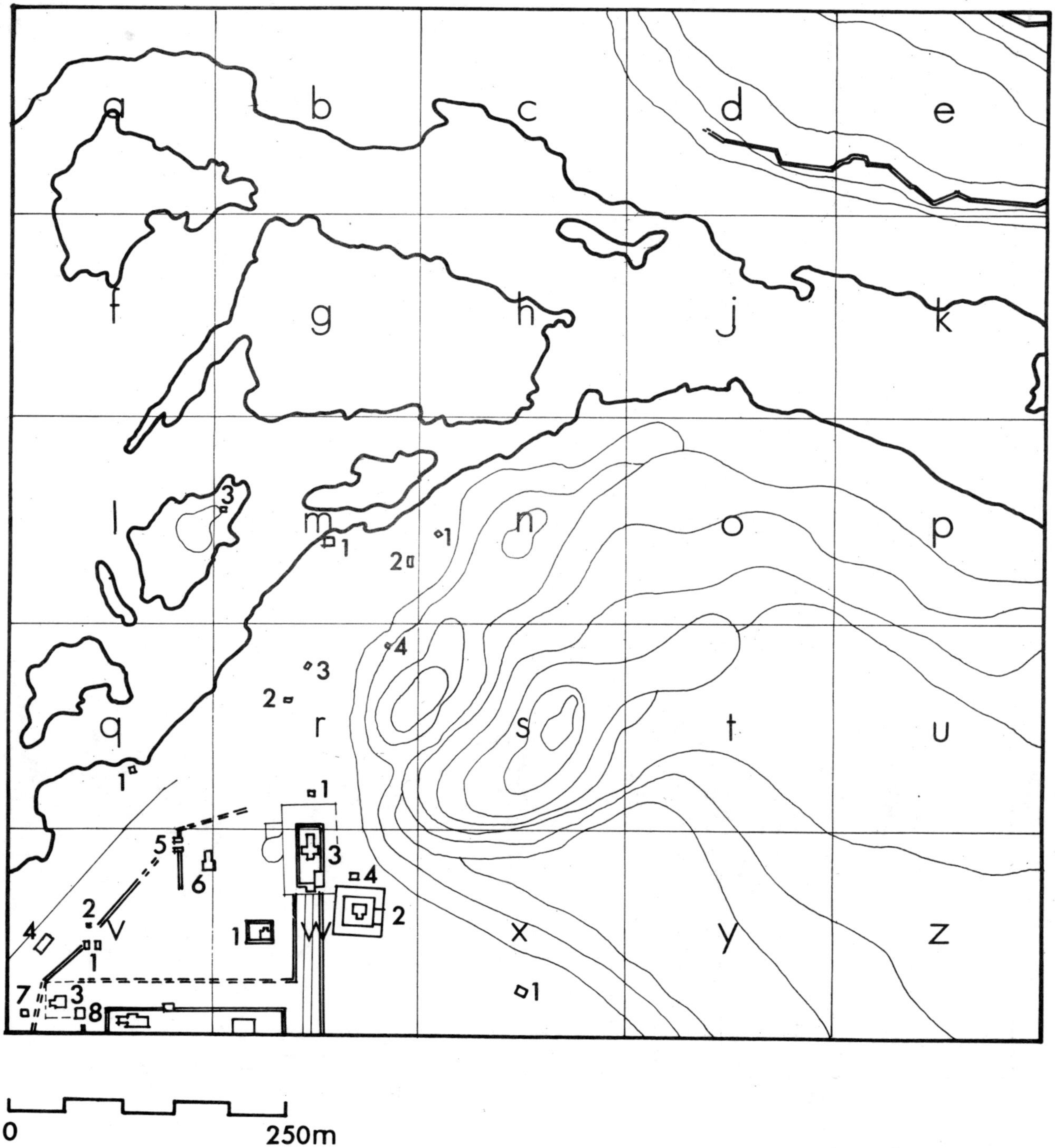

ND

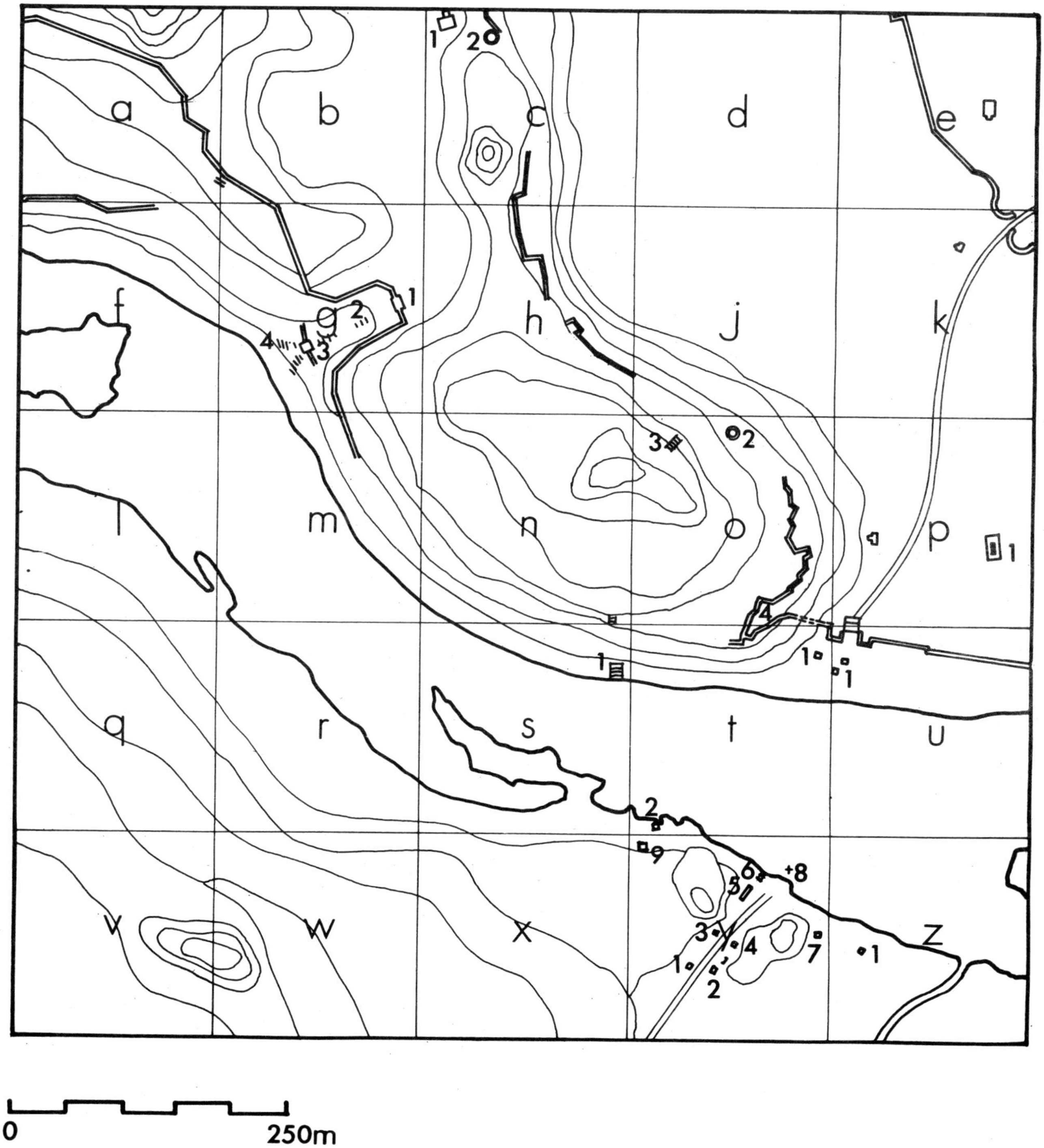

NE

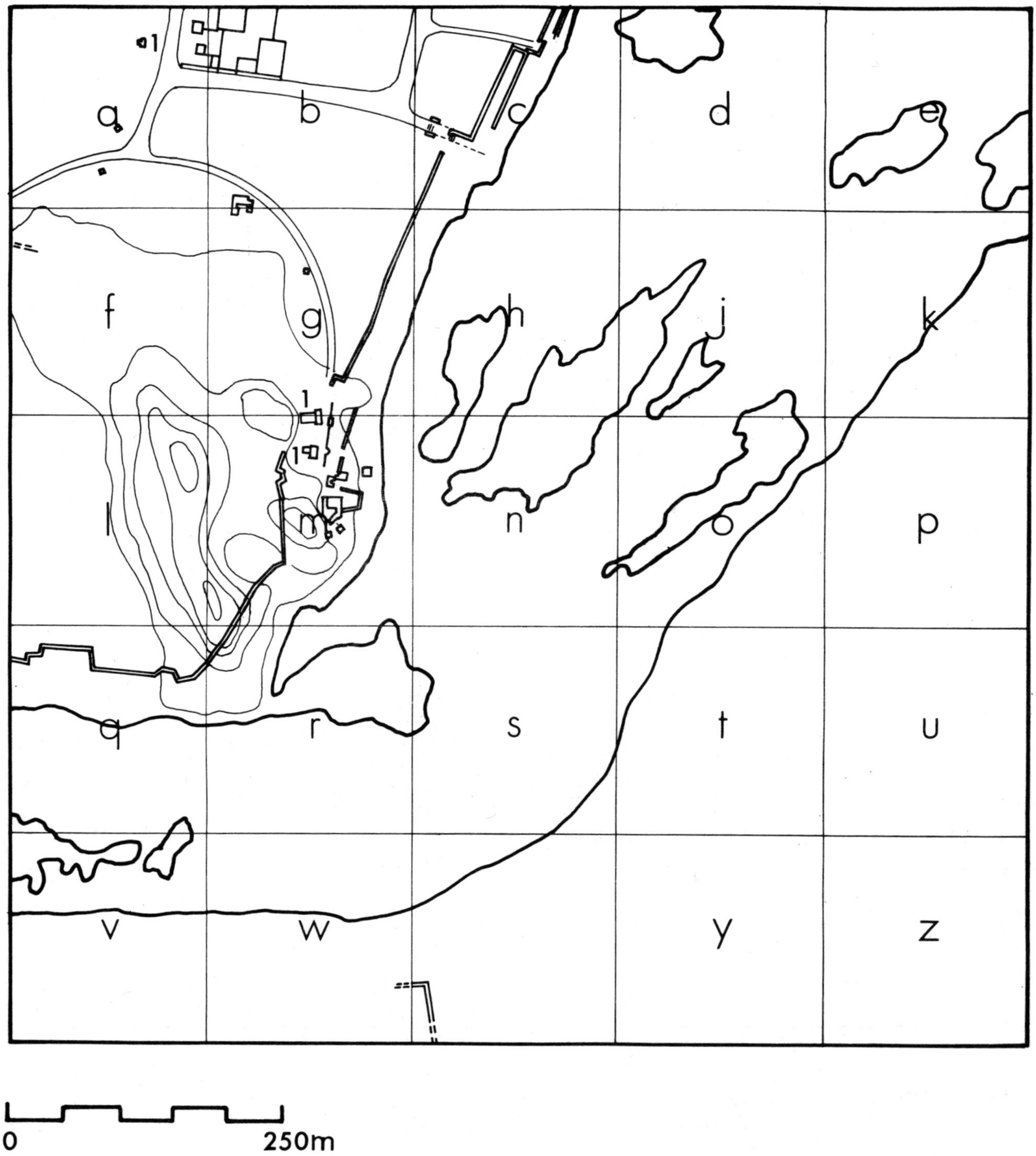

NF

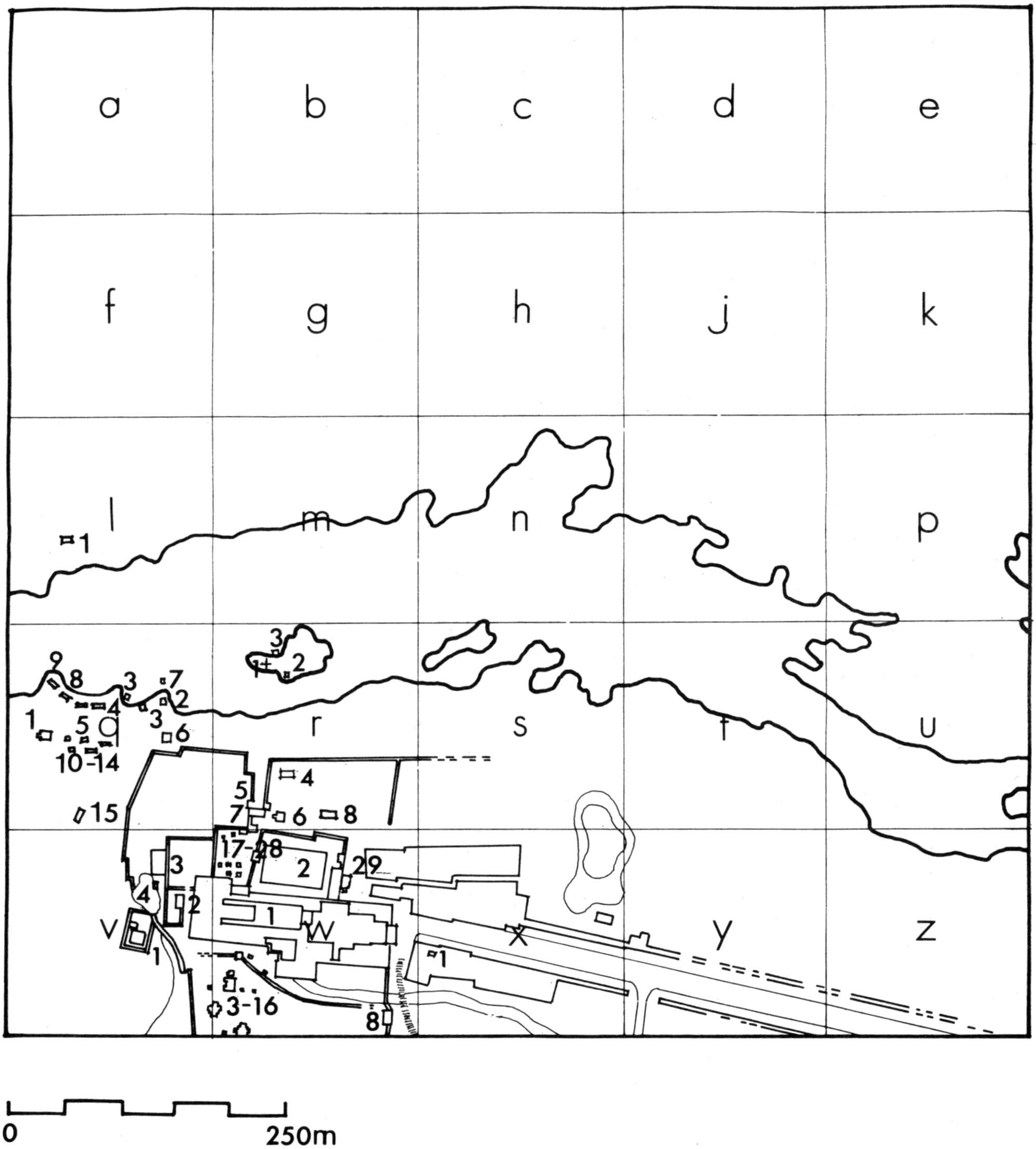

NG

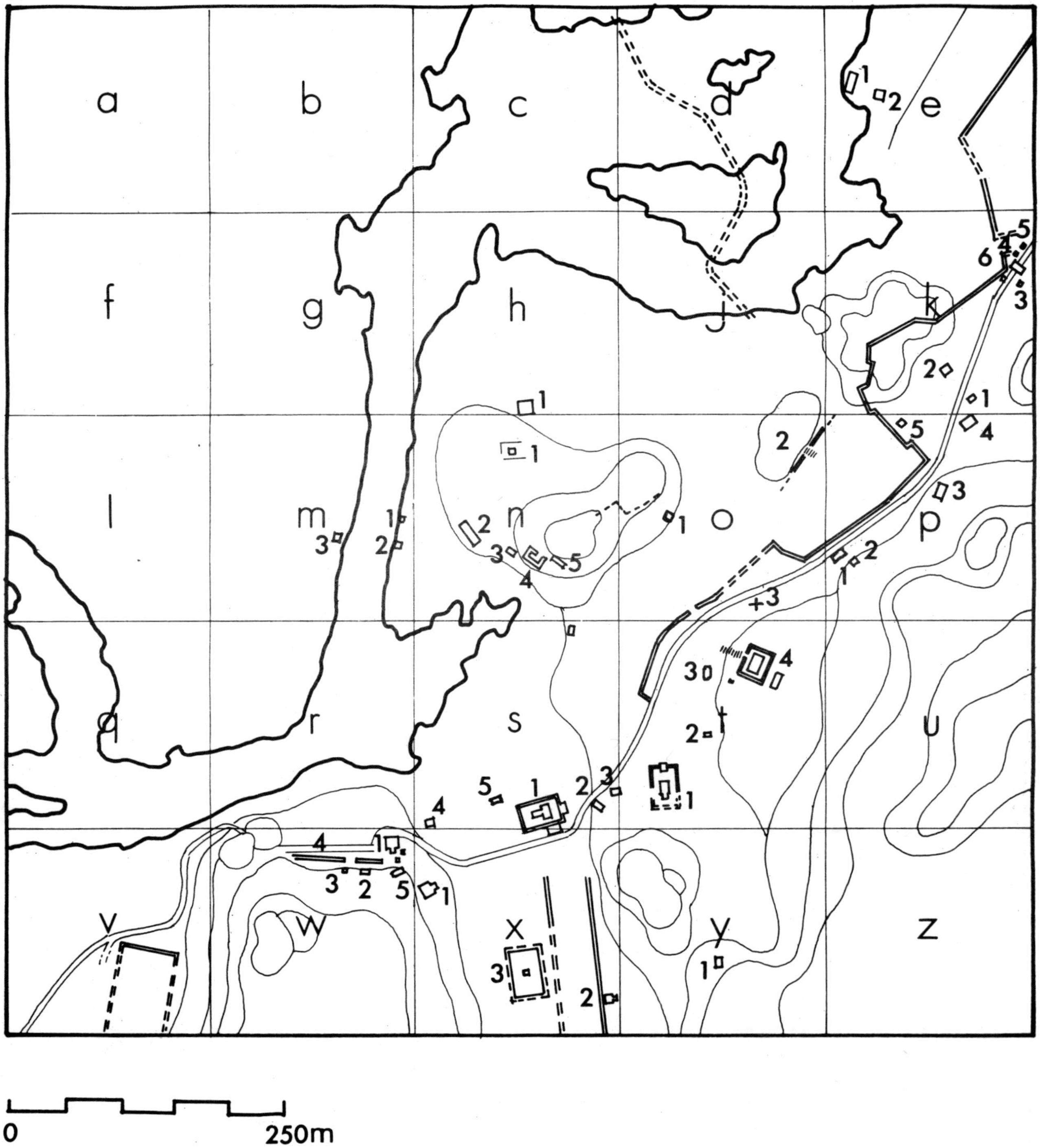

NH

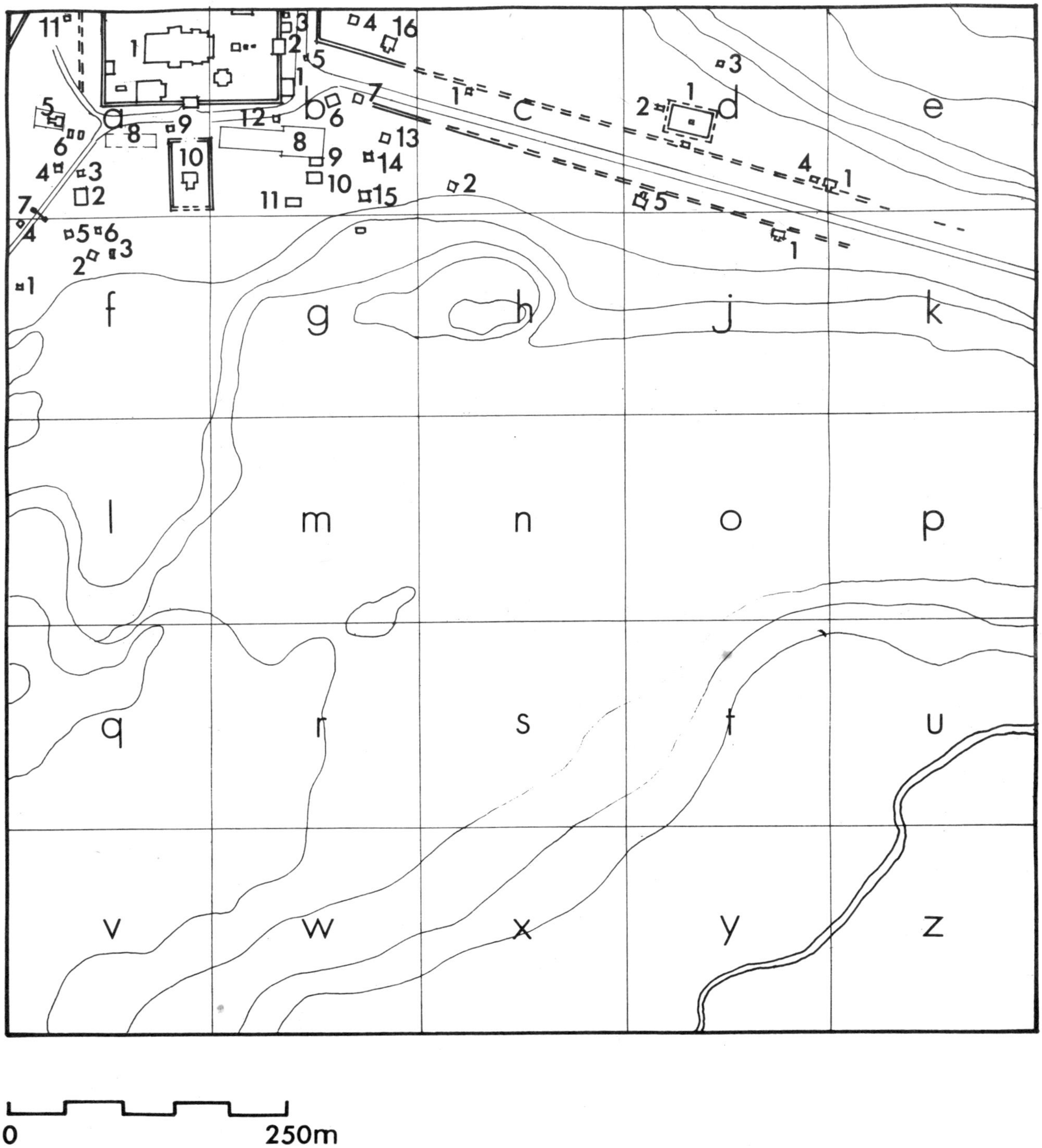

NJ

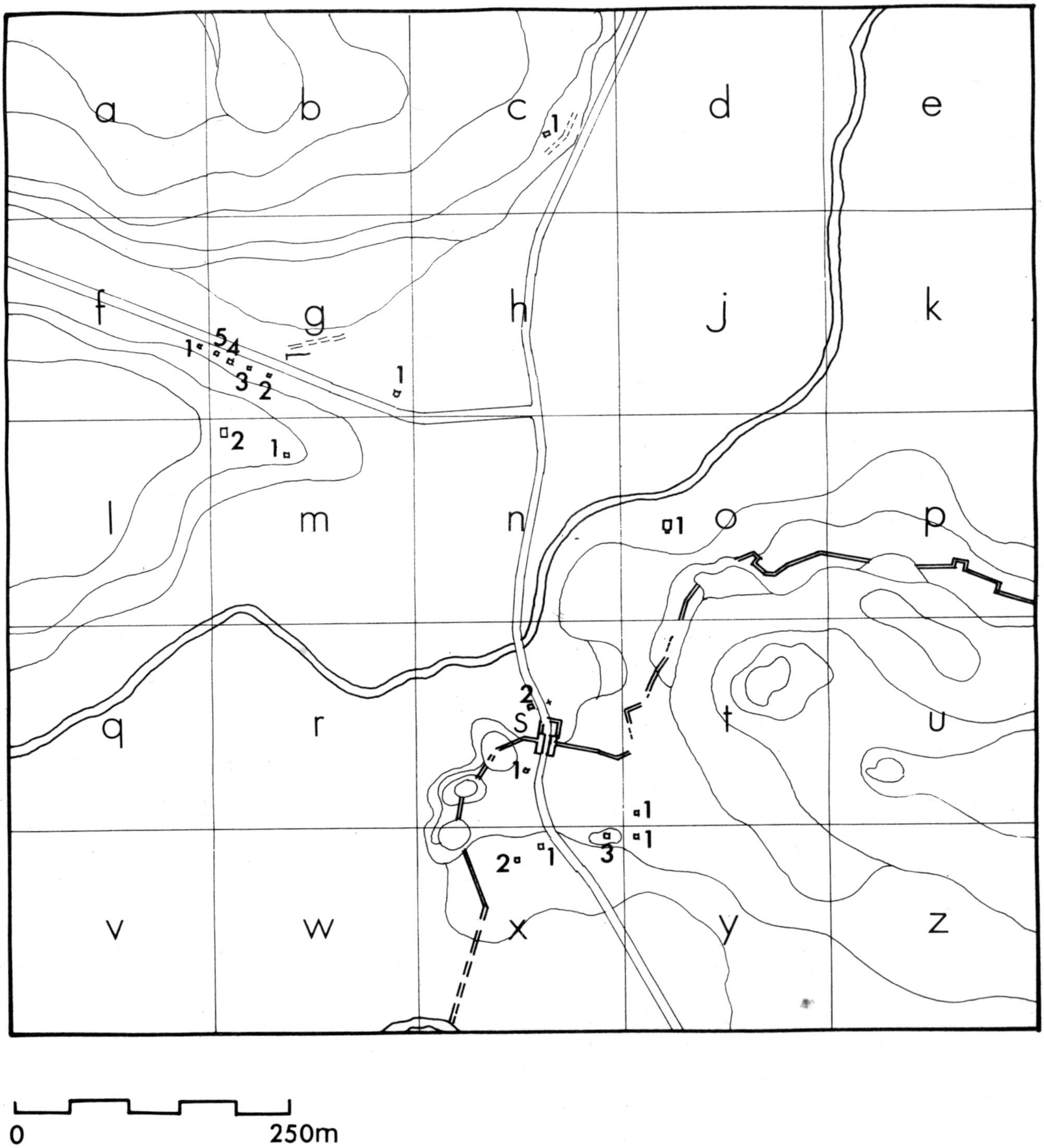

NK

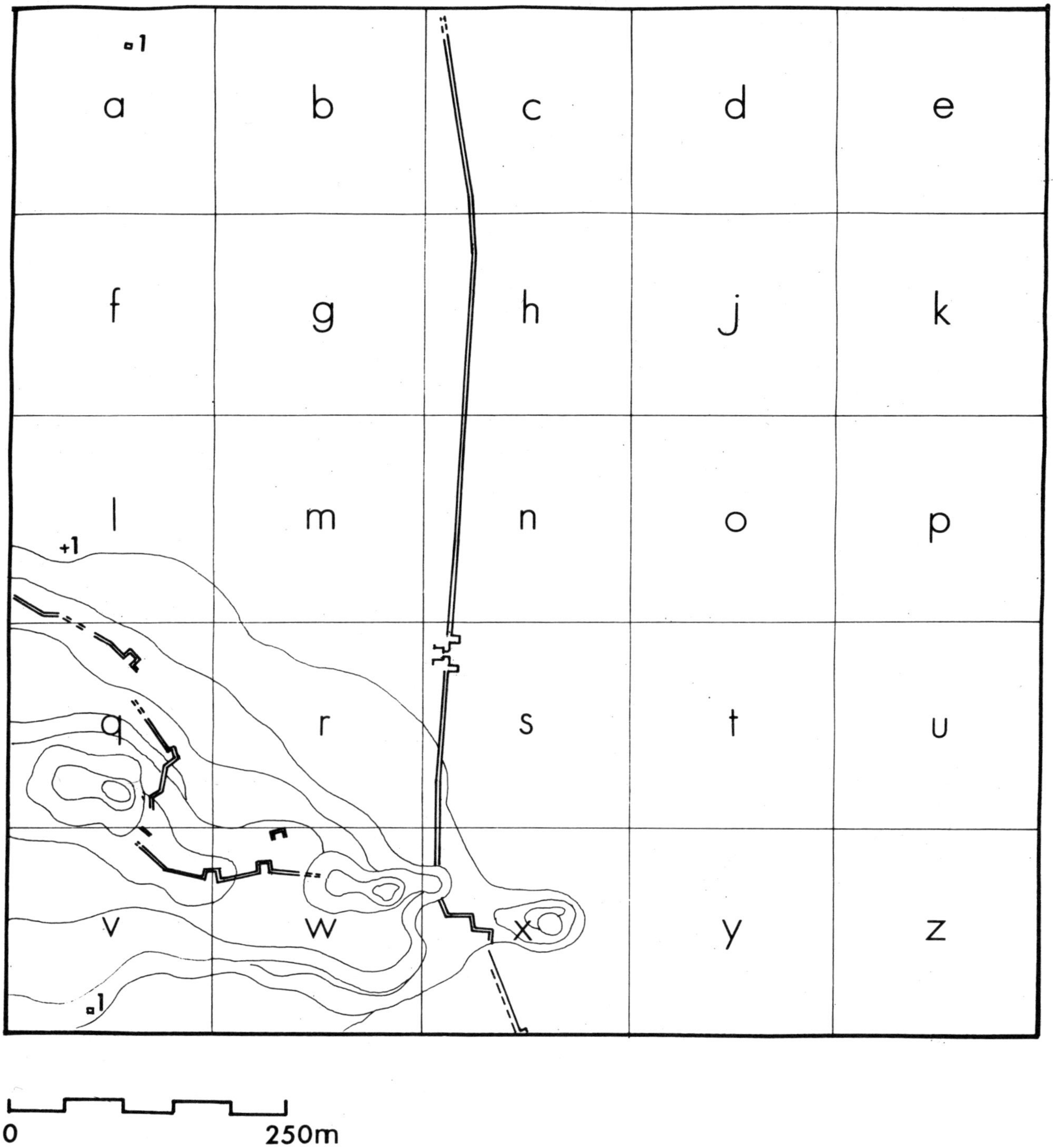

NL

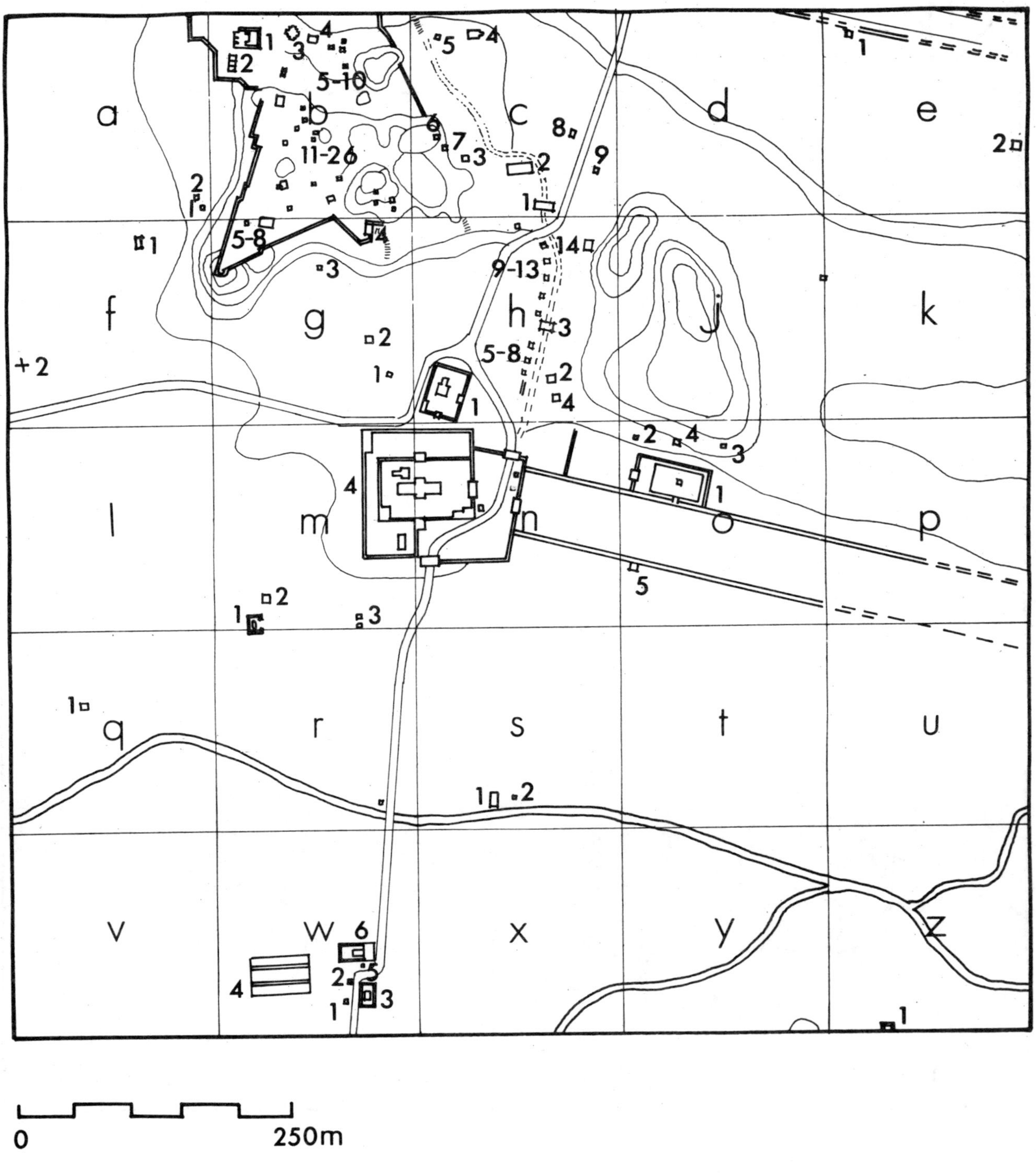

NM

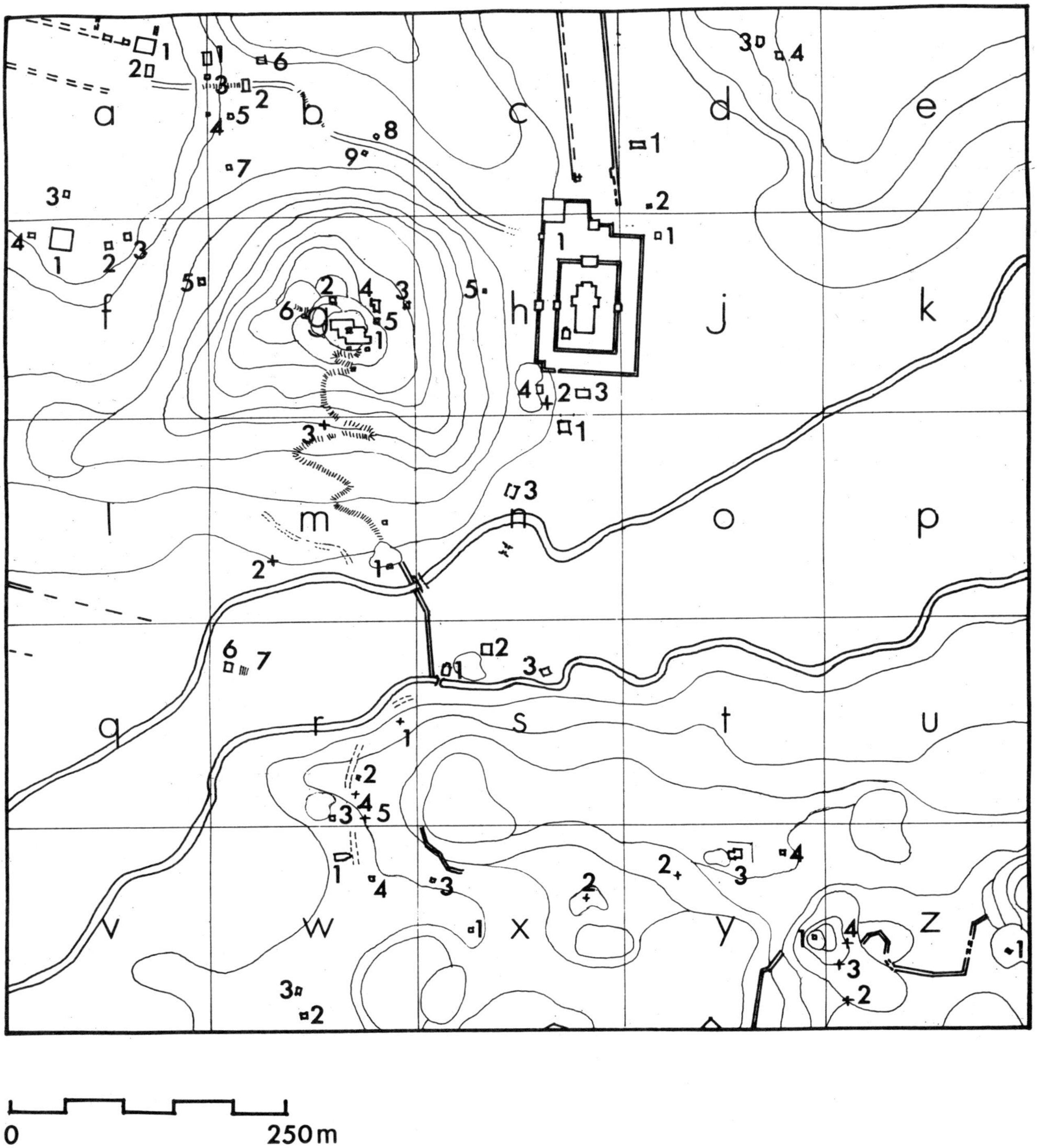

NN

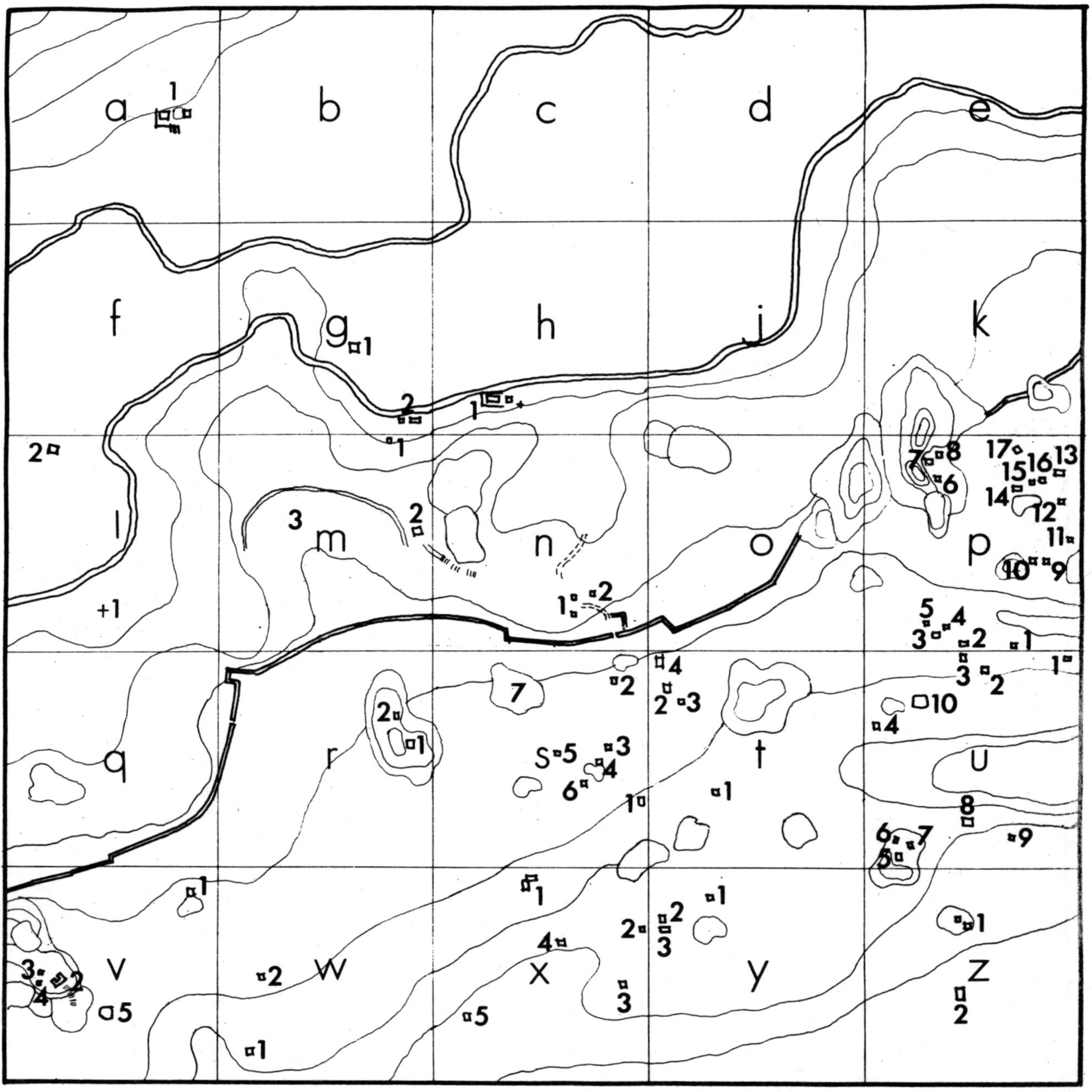

NO

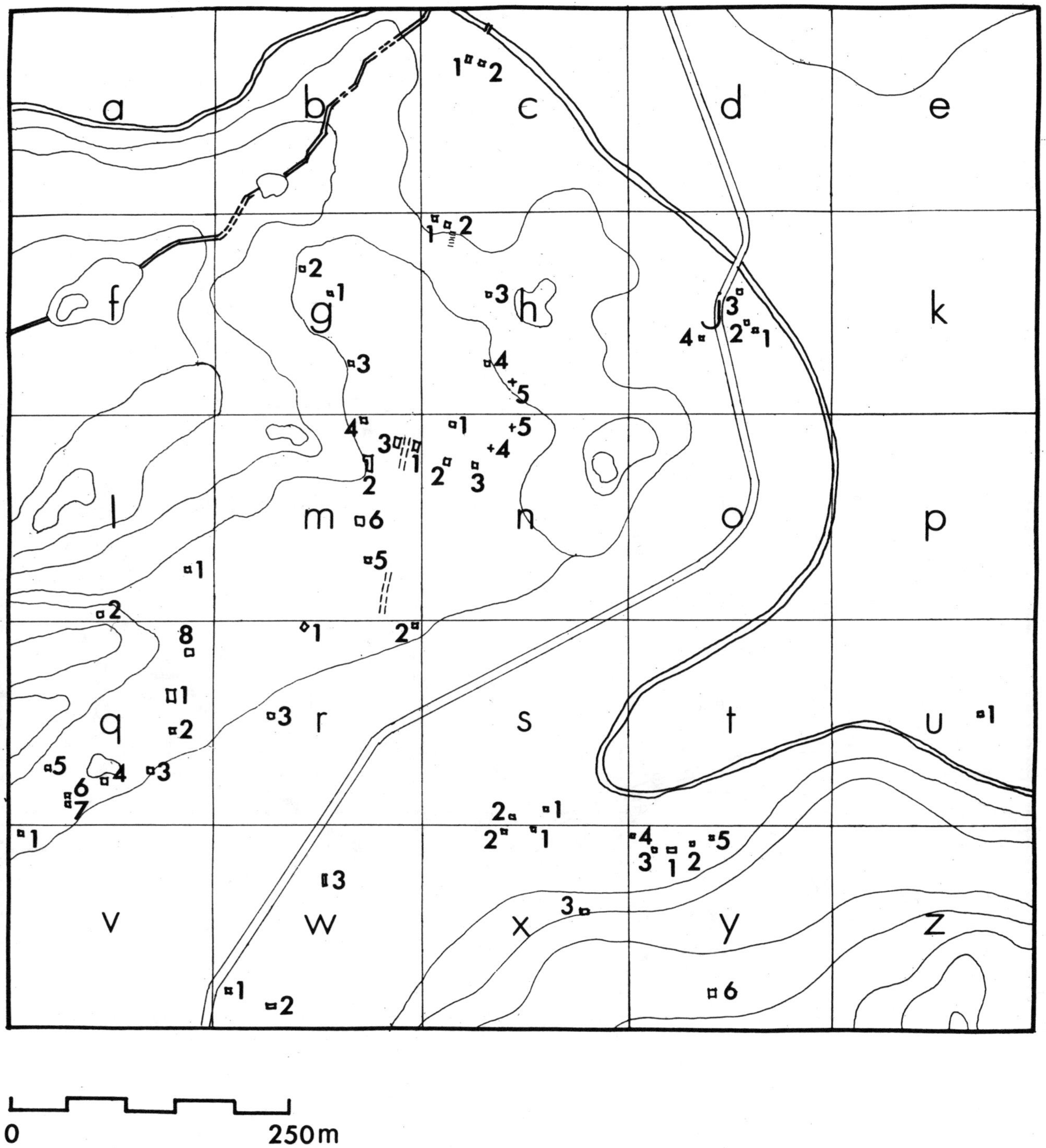

NP

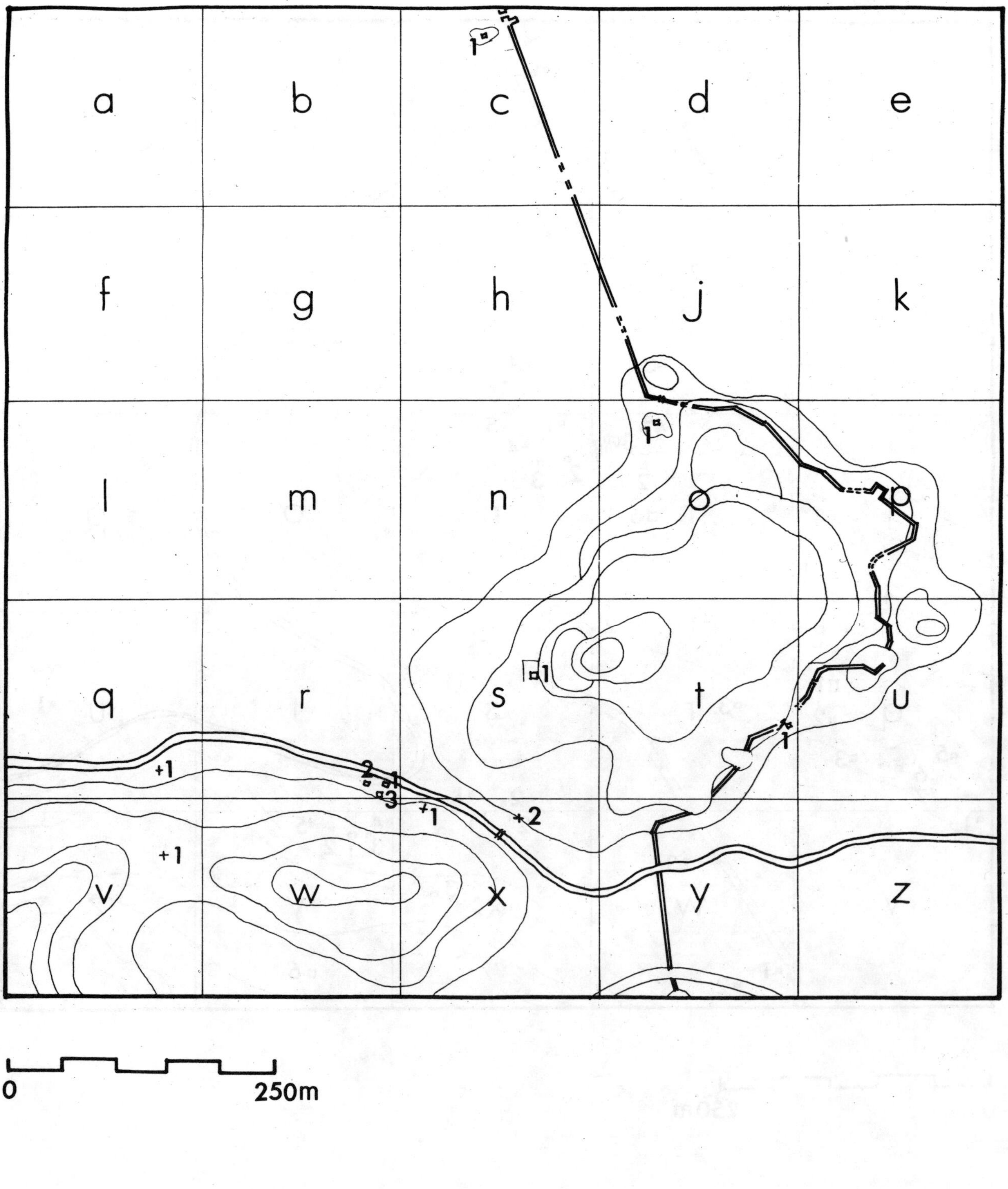

NQ

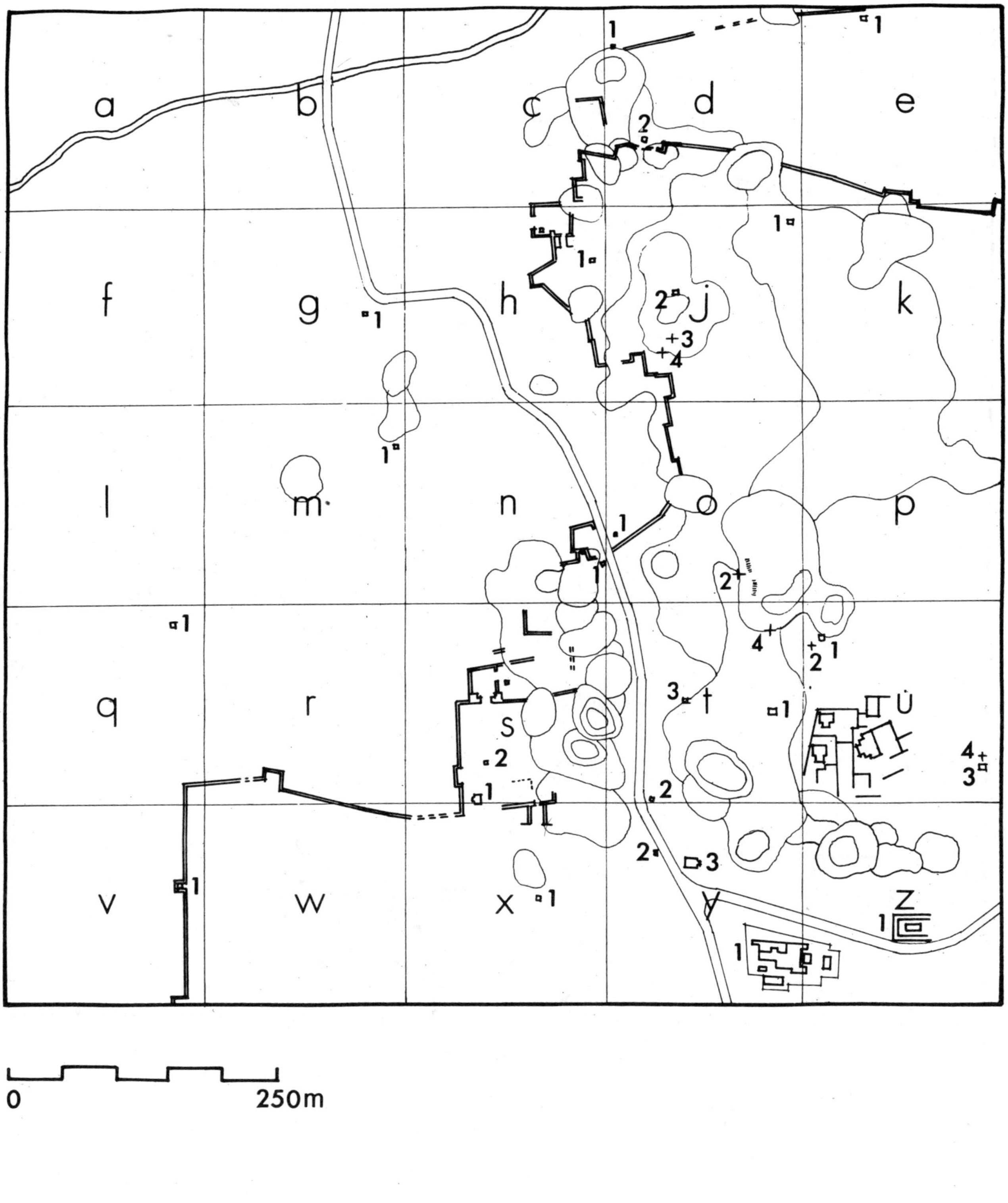

NR

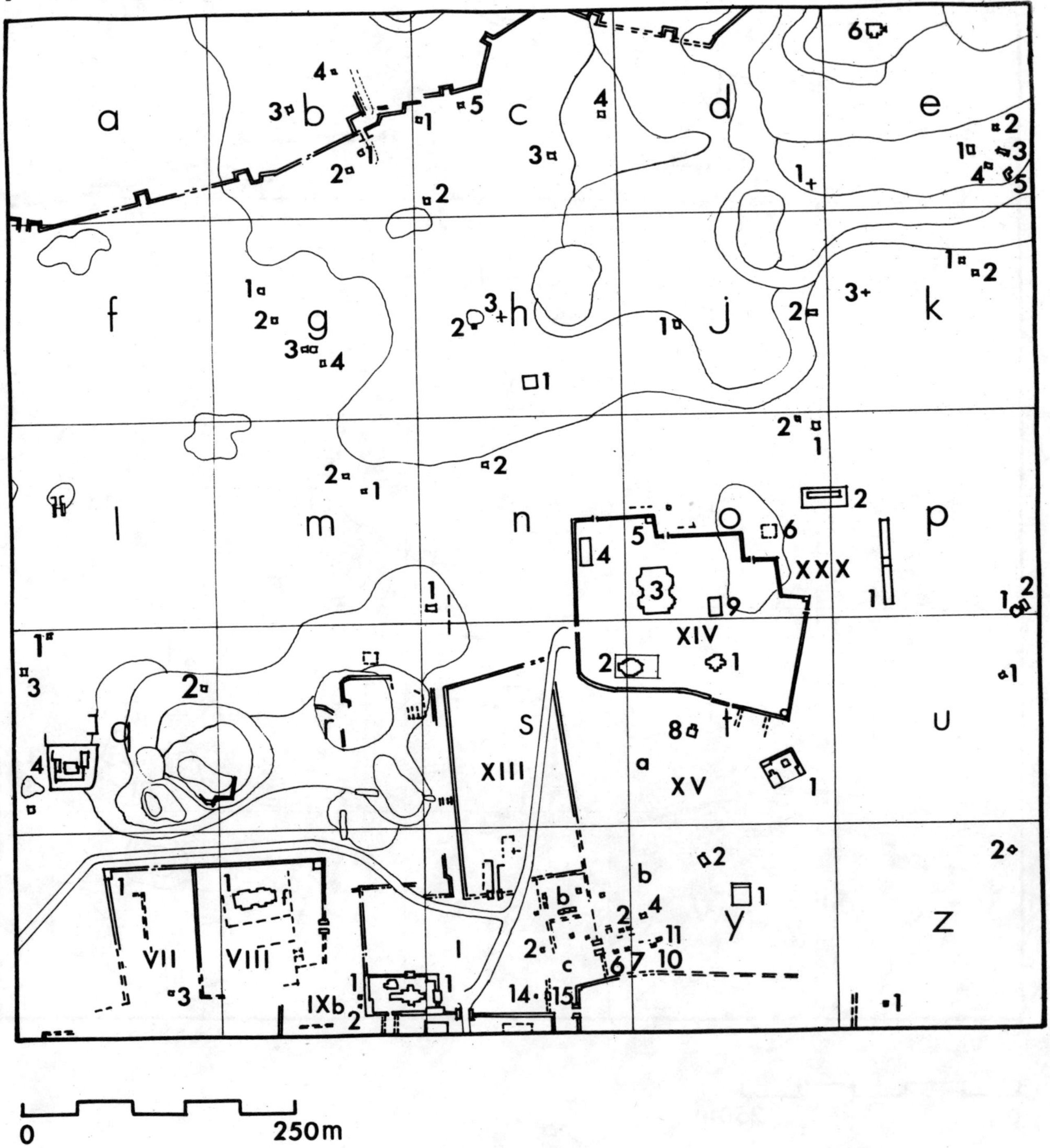

NS

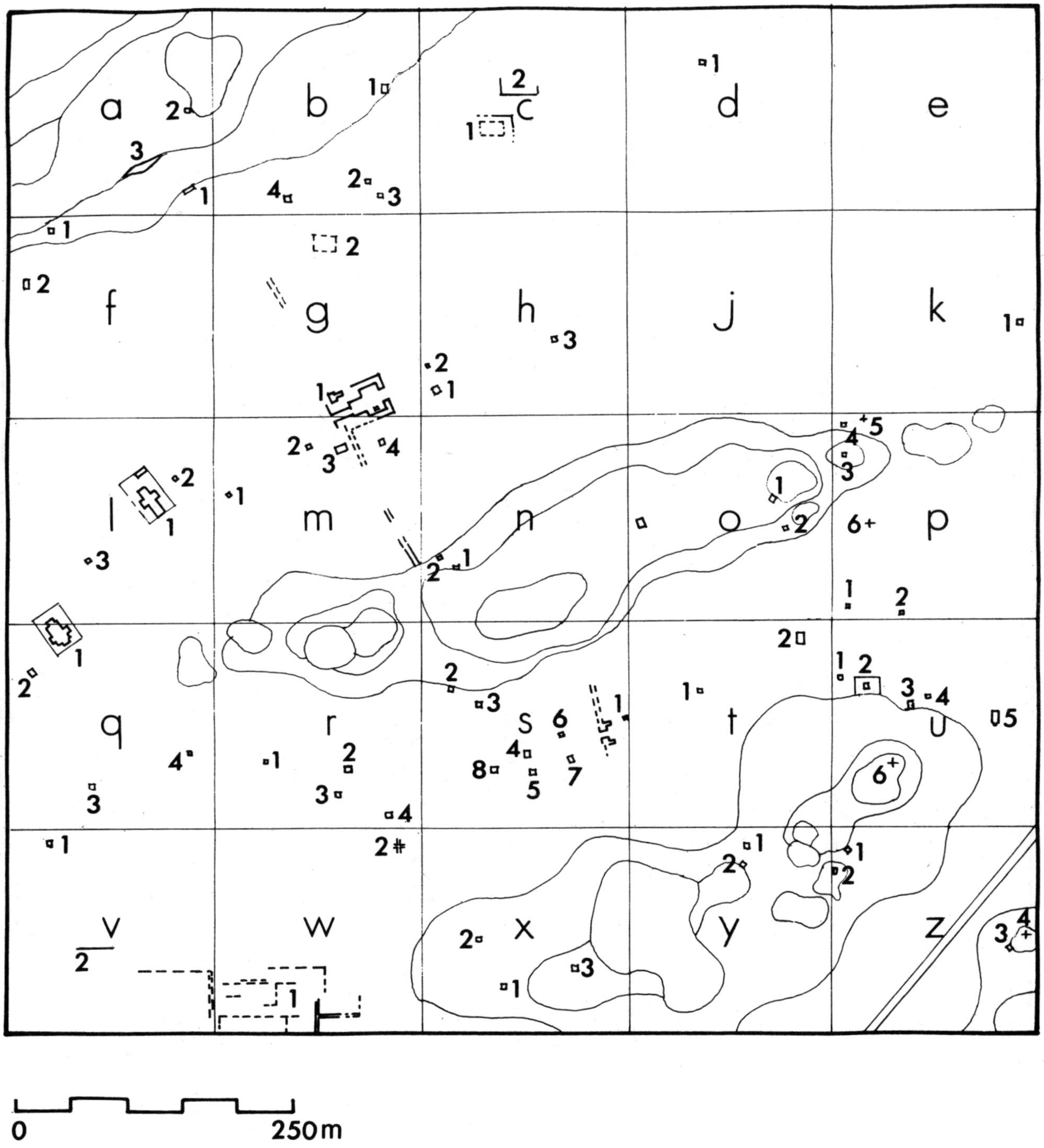

NT

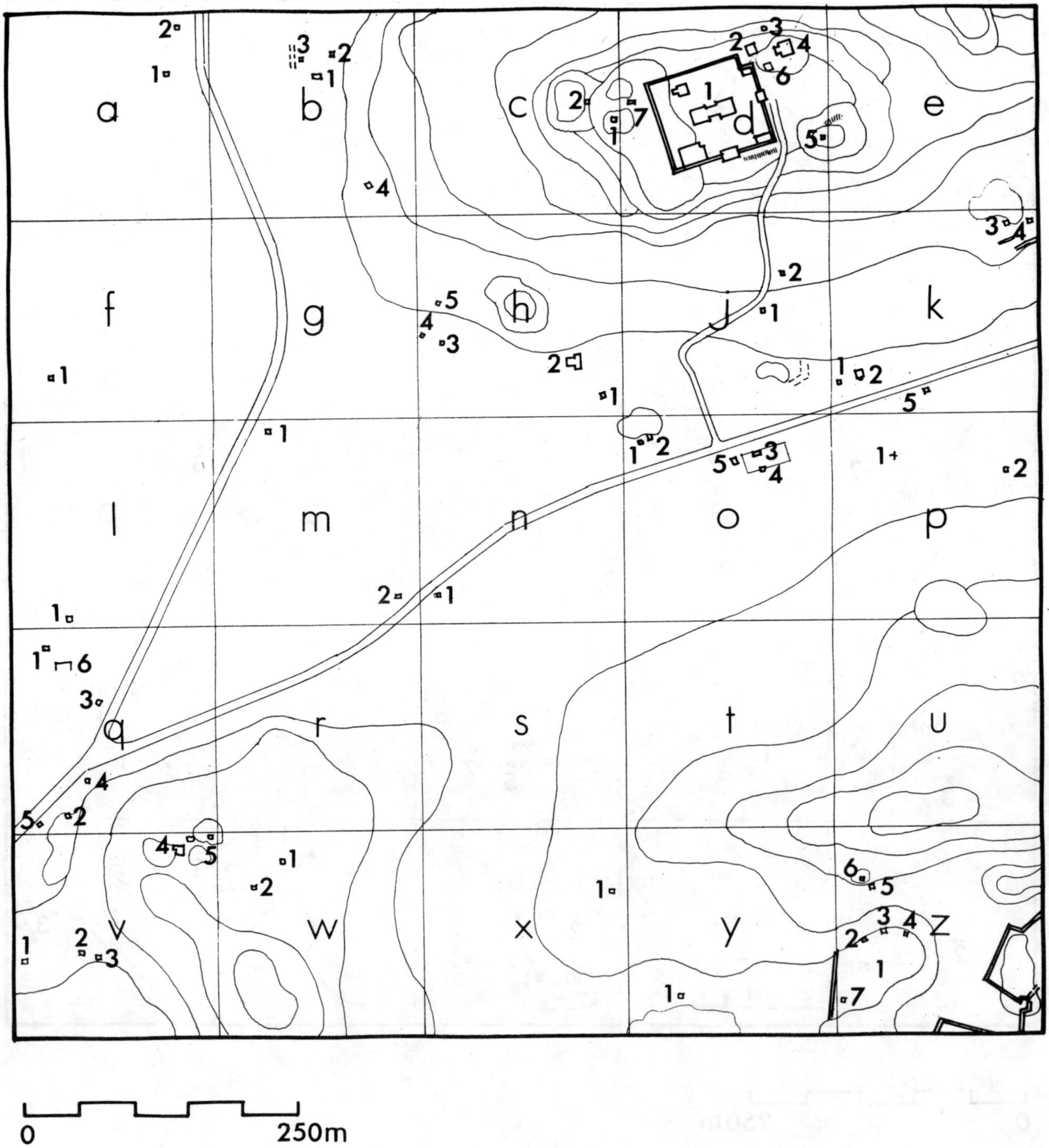

NU

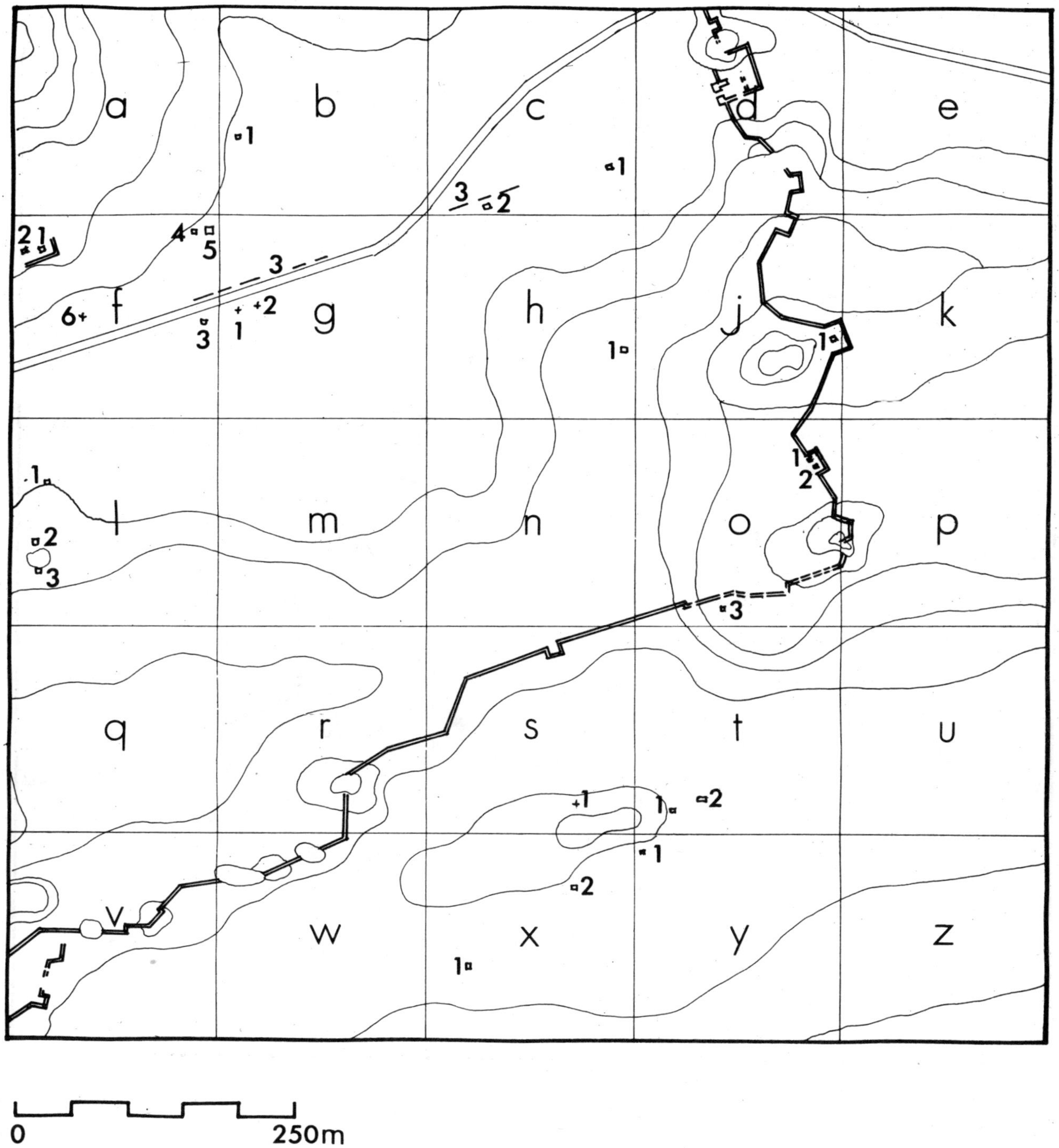

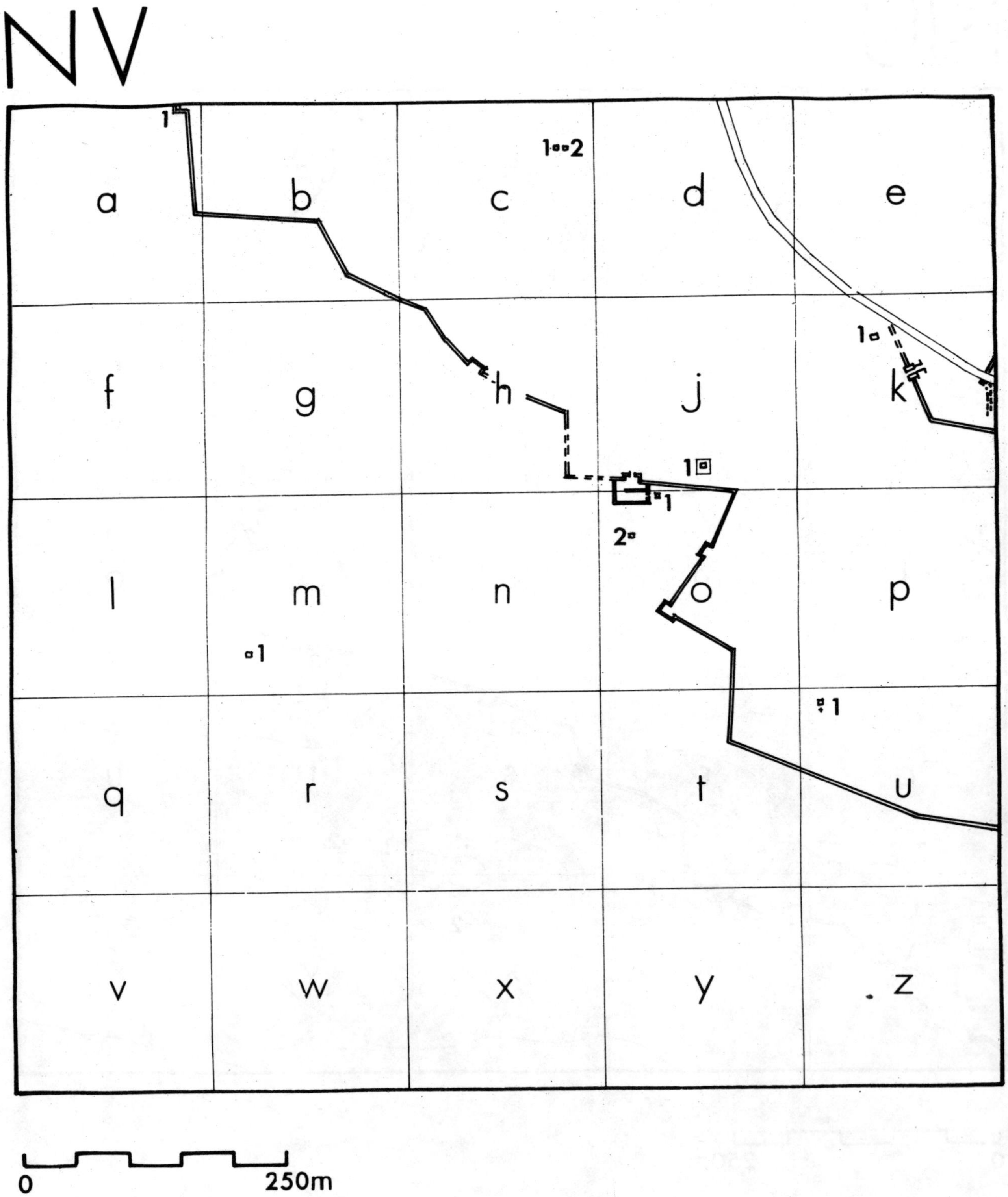
NV
a
b
c
d
e
f
g
h
j
k
l
m
n
o
p
q
r
s
t
u
v
w
x
y
z
1
1 2
1
1
1
2
1
1
0
250m

NW

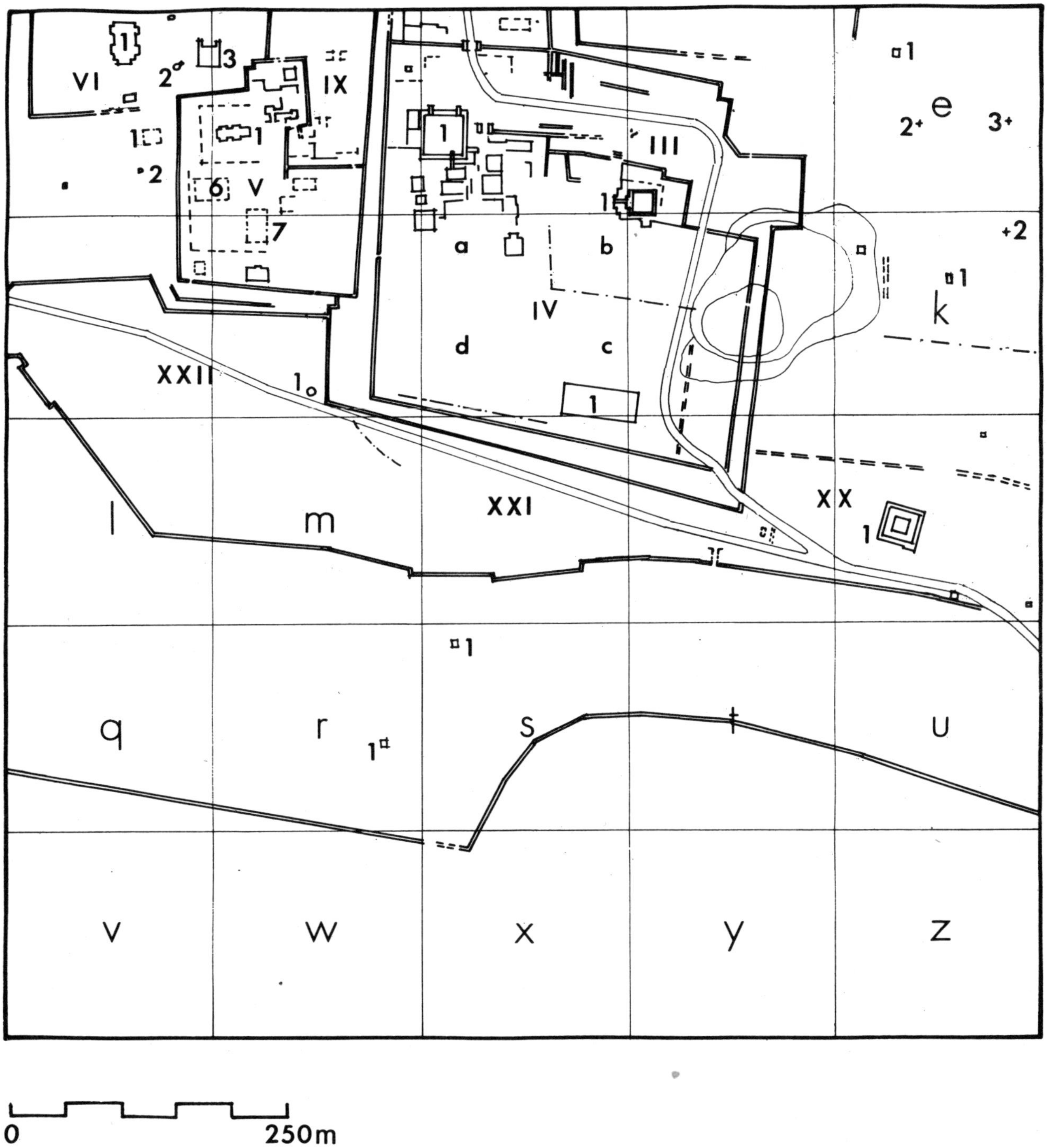

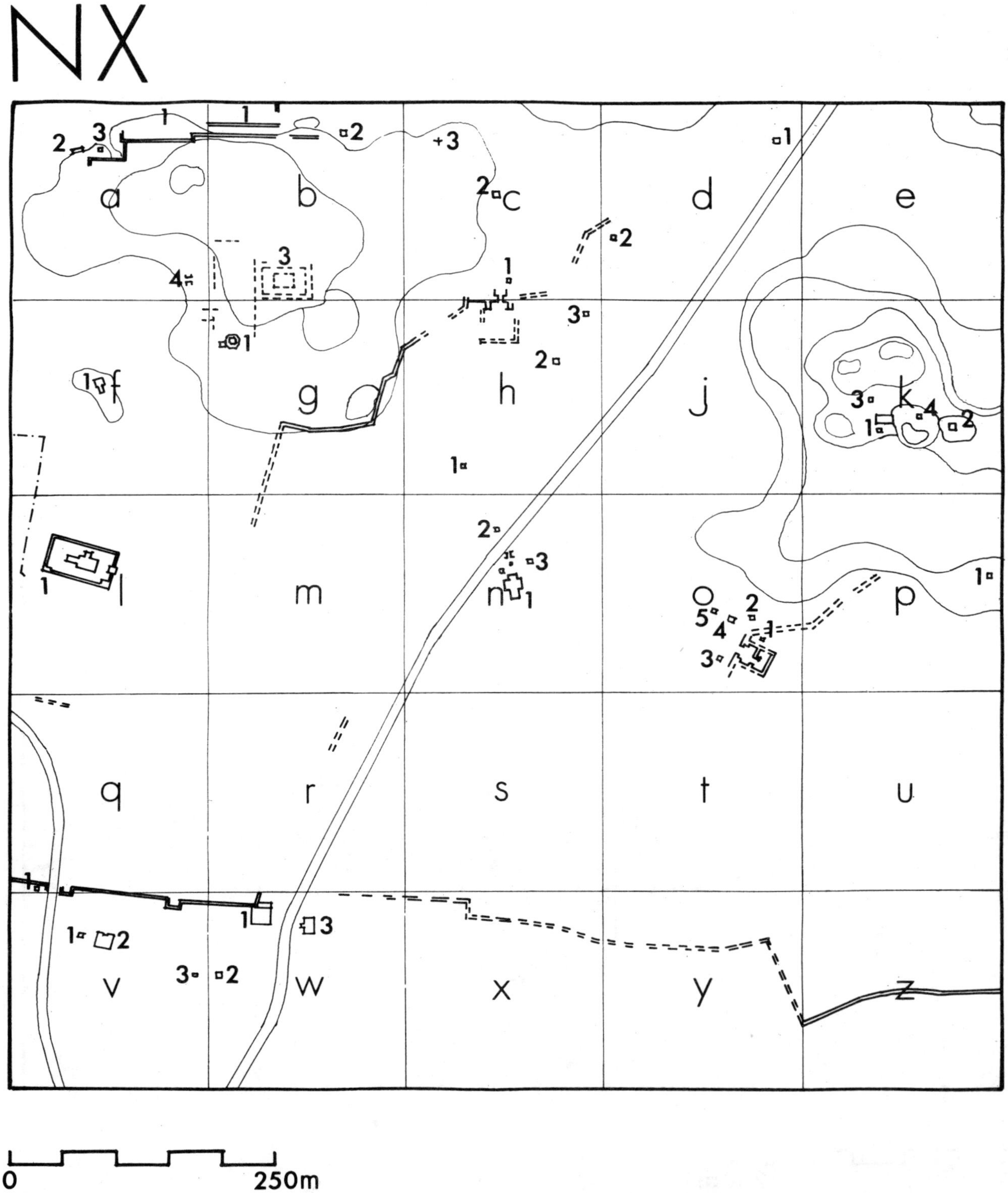
NX
a
b
c
d
e
f
g
h
j
k
l
m
n
o
p
q
r
s
t
u
v
w
x
y
z
0
250m

NY

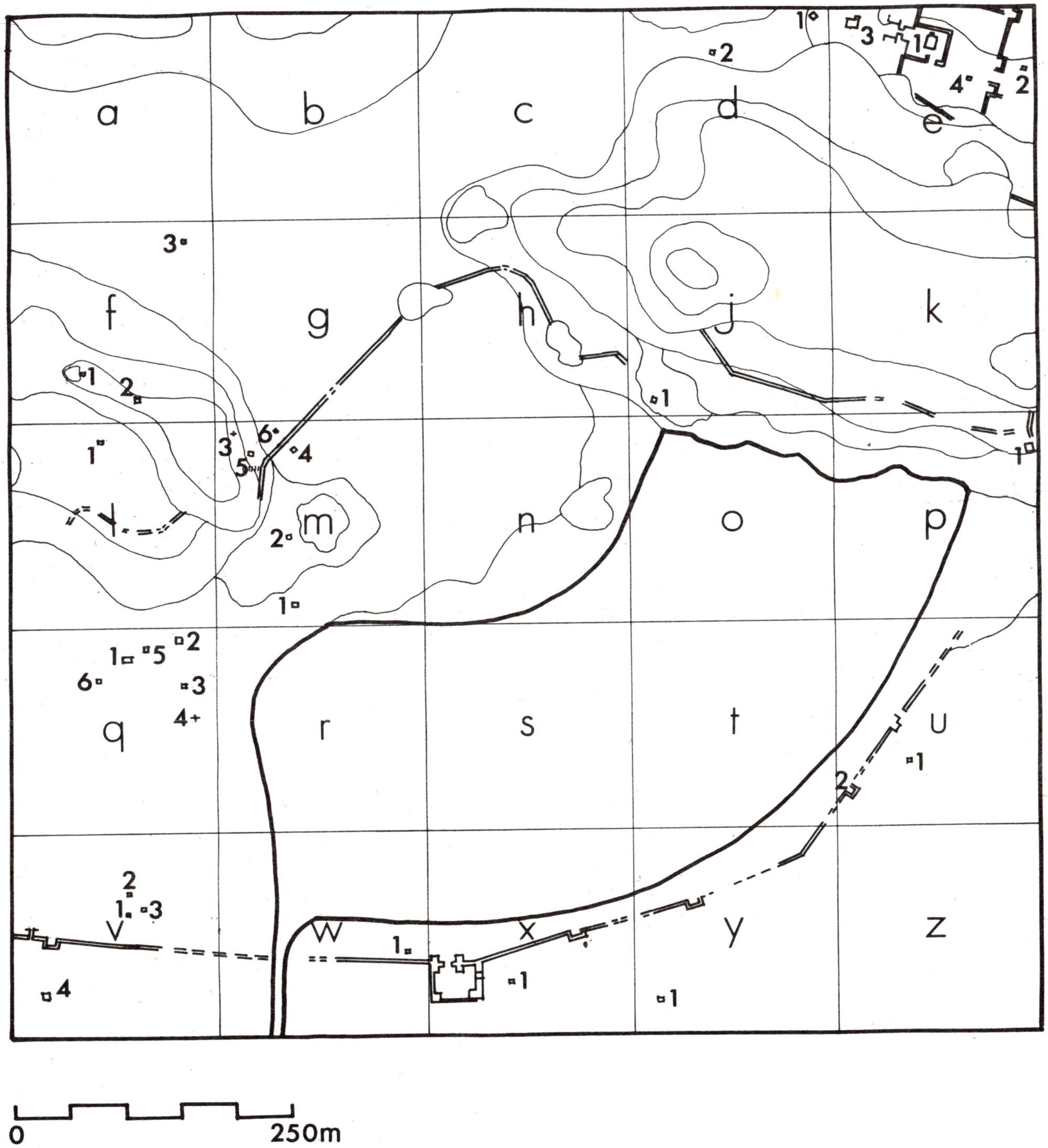

NZ

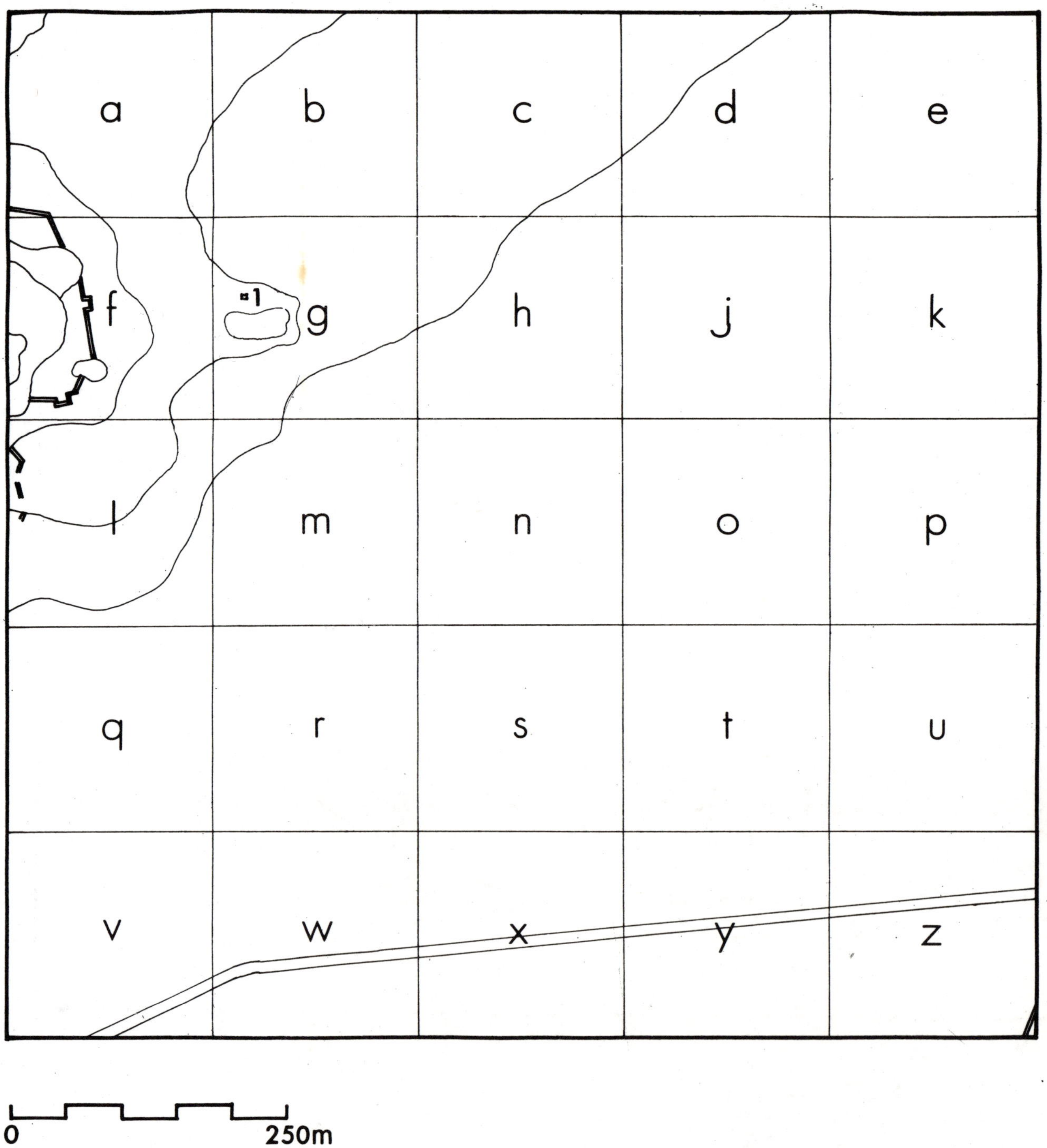